Lecture Notes in Computer Science 3544

Commenced Publication in 1973
Founding and Former Series Editors:
Gerhard Goos, Juris Hartmanis, and Jan van Leeuwen

Teruo Higashino (Ed.)

Principles of Distributed Systems

8th International Conference, OPODIS 2004
Grenoble, France, December 15-17, 2004
Revised Selected Papers

 Springer

Volume Editor

Teruo Higashino
Osaka University
Graduate School of Information Science and Technology
1-5 Yamadaoka, Suita, Osaka 565-0871, Japan
E-mail: opodis@ist.osaka-u.ac.jp

Library of Congress Control Number: 2005928959

CR Subject Classification (1998): C.2.4, D.1.3, D.2.7, D.2.12, D.4.7, C.3

ISSN   0302-9743
ISBN-10   3-540-27324-7 Springer Berlin Heidelberg New York
ISBN-13   978-3-540-27324-0 Springer Berlin Heidelberg New York

Springer is a part of Springer Science+Business Media

springeronline.com

© Springer-Verlag Berlin Heidelberg 2005
Printed in Germany

Typesetting: Camera-ready by author, data conversion by Scientific Publishing Services, Chennai, India
Printed on acid-free paper   SPIN: 11516798   06/3142   5 4 3 2 1 0

Preface

The 8th International Conference on Principles of Distributed Systems (OPODIS 2004) was held during December 15–17, 2004 at Grenoble, France. It continued a tradition of successful conferences with friendly and pleasant atmospheres. The earlier organizations of OPODIS were held in Luzarches (1997), Amiens (1998), Hanoi (1999), Paris (2000), Mexico (2001), Reims (2002) and La Martinique (2003).

OPODIS is an open forum for exchange of state-of-the-art knowledge on distributed computing and systems among researchers from around the world. Following the tradition of the previous organizations, the 2004 program was composed of high-quality contributed and invited papers by experts of international caliber in this scientific area. The topics of interest were the theory, specification, design and implementation of distributed systems, which include:

- peer-to-peer systems, cluster and grid-based computing
- fault tolerance and self-stabilizing systems
- real-time and embedded systems
- coordination and consistency protocols
- distributed and multiprocessor algorithms
- communication and synchronization protocols
- self-stabilization, reliability and fault tolerance
- performance analysis of distributed algorithms and systems
- specification and verification of distributed systems
- security issues in distributed computing and systems
- distributed collaborative environments
- location- and context-aware systems
- overlay network architectures

In response to the call for papers for OPODIS 2004, in total 102 papers in the above areas were submitted from 28 countries from over the world. Each paper was reviewed by three reviewers, and judged according to scientific and presentation quality, originality and relevance to the conference topics. Then the Program Committee selected 30 papers. The acceptance ratio was less than 30%.

Besides the technical contributed papers, the program included two exciting invited talks: Prof. David Lee (Ohio State University, USA) and Dr. Joseph Sifakis (Verimag, France). We really appreciate that these two distinguished experts accepted our invitation to share with us their views of various aspects of the field.

It is impossible to organize a successful program without the help of many individuals. We would like to express our appreciation to the authors of the submitted papers, Program Committee members and external referees. Furthermore, we would also like to thank the OPODIS Steering Committee members, who supervise and support the continuation of the event. We owe special thanks to the Organizing Committee chair, Prof. Van-Dat Cung (ENSGI-INP Grenoble), the publicity chair, Prof. Yi Zhang (Univ. of Birmingham, UK), and Mr. Akira Uchiyama (Osaka Univ., Japan) for his assistance with the electronic submission and reviewing system. We also thank Prof. Marc Bui (Univ. Paris 8/EPHE, France) for his support in the preparation of the conference proceedings. Finally, we express one more special thanks to all the other Organizing Committee members for their precious efforts that contributed to making OPODIS 2004 a successful conference.

December 2004   Teruo Higashino

Sponsors

Organization

With the support of

    Laboratory of ENS Génie Industriel and INPGrenoble,
                         France

    Laboratory of CNRS, IMAG, INPGrenoble, INRIA and
                         UJF, France

    University of Osaka, Japan

Organization

Executive Committee

Program Chair   Teruo Higashino (Osaka Univ., Japan)
Organizing Chair   Van-Dat Cung (ENSGI-INP Grenoble)
Publicity Chair   Yi Zhang (Univ. of Birmingham, UK)
Steering Committee   Philippas Tsigas (Univ. of Chalmers, Sweden)
                             Alain Bui (Univ. Reims, France)
                             Marc Bui (Univ. Paris 8/EPHE, France)
                             Hacene Fouchal (Univ. Reims, France)
                             Roberto Gomez (CEM-ITESM, Mexico)
                             Nicola Santoro (Carleton Univ., Canada)

Program Committee

Joffroy Beauquier	Univ. Paris 11, France
Azer Bestavros	Boston Univ., USA
Alain Bui	Univ. Reims, France
Marc Bui	Univ. Paris 8, France
Osvaldo Carvalho	Univ. Fed. Minas Gerais, Brazil
Van-Dat Cung	ENSGI-INP, Grenoble, France
Yves Denneulin	IMAG, France
Hacene Fouchal	Univ. Reims, France
Roberto Gomez-Cardenas	CEM-ITESM, Mexico
Hans Hansson	Malardalen Univ., Sweden
Ted Herman	Univ. of Iowa, USA
Teruo Higashino	Osaka Univ., Japan, PC Chair
Philippe Hunel	Univ. of Antilles-Guyane, France
Adriana Iamnitchi	Duke Univ., USA
Colette Johnen	Univ. Paris-Sud, France
Christian Lavault	Univ. Paris 13, France
Baochun Li	Univ. of Toronto, Canada
Toshimitsu Masuzawa	Osaka Univ., Japan
Tadanori Mizuno	Shizuoka Univ., Japan
Marina Papatriantafilou	Chalmers Univ., Sweden
Luis Rodrigues	Univ. of Lisbon, Portugal
Nicola Santoro	Carleton Univ., Canada
Alex A. Shvartsman	Univ. of Connecticut, USA
Jean-Bernard Stefani	INRIA, France
Philippas Tsigas	Univ. of Chalmers, Sweden
Hirozumi Yamaguchi	Osaka Univ., Japan
Yi Zhang	Univ. of Birmingham, UK

Referees

Filipe Araújo
Jallel Benothman
Roberto Beraldi
Nicolas Bernard
Thibault Bernard
Mats Björkman
Cristian Borcea
Abdelmadjid Bouabdallah
Emma Buneci
Franck Butelle
Emmanuel Cecchet
Jorge Cobb
Johanne Cohen
Pierpaolo Degano
Sylvie Delaët
Emmanuel Desgrippes
Stefan Dobrev
Shlomi Dolev
Jean-Christophe Dubacq
Tomoya Enokido
Andreas Ermedahl
Abdol-Hossein Esfahanian
Hugues Fauconnier
Stephen Fitzpatrick
Olivier Flauzac
Pierre Fraigniaud
Eduardo García
Anders Gidenstam
Maria Gradinariu
Vincent Gramoli
Adolfo Grego
Harry Gros-Desormeaux
Jan Gustafsson
Phuong Hoai Ha
Sammy Haddad
Tim L. Harris
Jean-Michel Hélary
Thomas Hérault
Akihito Hiromori
Jaap-Henk Hoepman

Fumihiko Ino
Michiko Inoue
Damir Isovic
Taisuke Izumi
Hirotsugu Kakugawa
Yoshiaki Katayama
Boris Koldehofe
Kishori Konwar
Michael Krajecki
Evangelos Kranakis
Danny Krizanc
Tanguy Krotoff
Shay Kutten
Cyril Labbé
Vito Latora
Pierre-Alain Laur
Ramon Lawrence
Doug Lea
Pierre Lemarinier
Jukka Mäki-Turja
Rolando Menchaca
Hugo Miranda
Mark Moir
Raul Monroy
Patrice Moreaux
Takanori Mori
Rémy Morin
Piotr Musial
Yoshihiro Nakaminami
Akio Nakata
Jonas Neander
Nicolas Nicolau
Mikael Nolin
Florent Nolot
Thomas Nolte
Kiyohiko Okayama
Fukuhito Ooshita
David Peleg
Sriram V. Pemmaraju
Adriano Peron

Ha Phuong
Laurence Pilard
Giuseppe Prencipe
Bruno Raffin
Rajmohan Rajaraman
Xavier Rebeuf
Olivier Richard
George F. Riley
Matei Ripeanu
Antoine Rollet
Claudia Roncancio
Erika Sanchez
Pierre Sens
Piyush Shivam
Michiel Smid
Devan Sohier
Gideon Stupp
Håkan Sundell
Hideharu Suzuki
Abbas Tarhini
Andréa Iabrudi Tavares
Sébastien Tixeuil
Luis Trejo
Tatsuhiro Tsuchiya
Alper Üngör
Thierry Val
Olivier Valentin
Jeroen van de Graaf
Jesus Vazquez
Nicolas Vidot
Maria Del Pilar Villamil
Jean-Marc Vincent
Anders Wall
Mirjam Wattenhofer
Ramana Yerneni
Aydan Yumerefendi
Dmitrii Zagorodnov
Xuehai Zhang
Yong Zhao

Table of Contents

Invited Session II

Session IV (Security)

Session V (Distributed Algorithms)

Session VI (Self-stabilization)

Session VII (Design of Distributed Systems II)

Session VIII (Sensor Networks)

Session IX (Task/Resource Allocation)

Protocol System Integration, Interface and Interoperability

David Lee[1], Christine Liu[2], and Mihalis Yannakakis[3]

[1] Department of Computer Sciences and Engineering, Ohio State University
[2] Bell Labs Research China, Lucent Technologies
[3] Department of Computer Science, Columbia University

Abstract. Heterogeneous network protocol systems are integrated together to fulfill complex tasks and their interoperability is a major hurdle for the network reliability and quality of services. We identify a new equivalence relation of states that preserves the integrated system interface behaviors. Based on this state equivalence we study the minimization of the system components with respect to their interfaces and design an efficient polynomial time minimization algorithm. We apply our technique to GMPLS protocols and obtain a significant state space reduction. We discuss integrated protocol system verification and interoperability testing with the minimized state system without resorting to the global state space information.

1 Introduction

With the rapid growth of Internet, new protocols are being developed and integrated into the existing network systems, such as GMPLS (Generalized Multi-Protocol Label Switching, an IETF Standards for all optical network management and interface with Internet, ATM network, and other user networks), OUNI (an OIF Standard for Optical User Network Interface), and VoIP (Voice over IP). Heterogeneity is a prominent feature of integrated network systems, and interoperability is ubiquitous and has become a major hurdle for system reliability and quality of services. When two or more system components are integrated to interface with each other to perform a required task the capability to operate as desired is called interoperability, which is an essential aspect of the correctness of integrated protocol systems. Interoperability testing is to check the interfaces and interoperations among integrated system implementations, and verification is to analyze the system design for integration and interfaces. The focus of both analyses is the interface among the integrated system components.

However, the number of states of integrated systems is often too large for a formal analysis due to the well-known state explosion problem. For our application, we want to reduce the state space by hiding the internal behaviors of the components as much as possible, while preserving completely the system interfaces. More formally, given a component or a subsystem, some of whose transitions are *interface transitions* while the rest are *internal* transitions, we want to obtain a reduced system that: (1) Has the

T. Higashino (Ed.): OPODIS 2004, LNCS 3544, pp. 1–19, 2005.
© Springer-Verlag Berlin Heidelberg 2005

same interface transitions, and (2) Has the same sequences of interface transitions, as the original system. Although this may appear to call for minimization of a nondeterministic system (because of the internal transitions, the interface behavior of the system may be in general nondeterministic), a problem that is known to be computationally hard, we show that this is not the case here. After an elimination of internal states of the system without affecting its interface behaviors, we define an appropriate state equivalence relation and present an efficient algorithm to compute it. Based on this state equivalence we can reduce the overall state space while preserving exactly the integrated system interfaces. This state space reduction facilitates formal verification and interoperability testing of integrated systems. We design and implement a polynomial time algorithm for the state space reduction, discuss its applications to integrated system verification and interoperability testing, and report the experimental results on GMPLS protocols.

In Section 2 we give some background on the model for integrated protocol systems, define interface graphs and state formally the problem. In Section 3 we study interface graphs, define state interface equivalence, and analyze its properties. In Section 4 we present a polynomial time algorithm for state equivalence and minimization of interface graphs, and its extension to minimization of integrated systems. The algorithm is applied to LMP of GMPLS for state space reduction and the experimental results are reported in Section 5. The properties of the minimized interface graphs are further studied in Section 6 for the applications to the verification and interoperability testing of integrated systems.

2   A Formal Model

A protocol system consists of a set of communicating components. Each component is represented by a finite state transition system or a finite state machine, i.e., it consists of a set of states, one of which is designated as the initial state, and a set of transitions labeled by actions, or by inputs and outputs. Some of the transitions involve interaction with other components (eg. sending or receiving messages) and are called *interface transitions*, while others represent internal local actions of the components and are called *internal transitions*. For the purposes of the problems studied in this paper, it does not matter whether transition systems or finite state systems are used as the underlying model; the issues and the algorithms are the same in both cases.

Example 1. The Link Connectivity Verification (LCVA) module of the active node of the Link Management Protocol (LMP) of GMPLS is shown in Fig. 1. It contains 5 states; the initial state is *Down*. Each transition is labeled by a pair *a/b* where *a* is the event (input) and conditions that cause the transition to occur, and *b* is the effect of the transition (output or actions that take place as a result of the transition). For example, the transition from state Test1 to state Test2 causes the sending of a message *Testmsg*, as indicated by the label *!Testmsg*. The label on the arrow from Test2 to Down is a shorthand for two transitions: one transition takes place if a message *TestStatusFailure* is received, and the other transition takes place if the *Timerexpiry* event occurs, a local internal event of the component. This component has 3 interface transitions: the abovementioned two transitions and the transition from Test2 to Up/Free. The other transitions are all internal transitions.   □

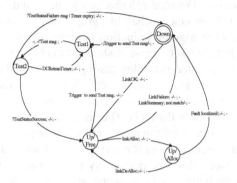

Fig. 1. A module from LMP of GMPLS

The components of a protocol system are integrated together to fulfill required tasks. The joint behaviors of the system are represented by the composition of the different components formed by taking their Cartesian product in the usual way [6,7]. The set of states is the Cartesian product of the components' state sets; the initial state is the tuple of the initial states. A transition of the composed system corresponds either to a local (internal) transition of a component (i.e. all local states remain the same in this case except for that of the component that makes the local transition), or to the simultaneous execution of matching interface transitions of different components, eg corresponding to the sending and receiving of a message. (A model may include separate components for the channels or other communication media, to separate the occurrence of the sending of a message with the reception at the other end.) We are interested only in the portion of the system that is reachable from the initial state.

The Cartesian product often leads to the familiar state explosion problem; the number of states of the product is too large. To cope with this problem various techniques have been developed in the areas of system verification, validation and testing. One can use heuristics to *prune* search state space and *random walks* for efficient exploration yet without recording the searched states. *Symbolic representation* of the state transition graphs and efficient algorithms for their manipulation avoid explicit construction of the state graph of the concurrent system. Concurrent software tends to be less structured and asynchronous, and *partial order reduction* reduces the number of interleaving sequences for analysis. *Compositional reasoning* exploits the modular structure of complex systems and conducts analysis on the components separately of a decomposed system with an assume-guarantee reasoning. *Abstraction* deals with data portion of systems to reduce the complexity of model checking. *On-line minimization* reduces transition system state space on-the-fly without constructing the whole state space [1,12] and *compositional minimization* performs stepwise bisimulation reduction steps [4]. Protocol systems often contain replicated components, and this system *symmetry* is exploited to reduce the state explosion. *Induction* analyzes families of parameterized protocol systems by providing an invariant process that represents a large number of systems with different parameter values. Detailed references can be found in [2,7]. For program testing, [11] uses an incremental reachability graph for test sequence generation for concurrent programs. Then a graph reduction is applied with path preservation (for test generation), which includes: collapse, τ-state elimination, and prune.

For the verification and interoperability testing of integrated systems, the focus is on the interface transition sequences, which characterize the system interfaces. Observing that often many of the transitions are internal transitions, we investigate state space minimization such that: (1) The interface transition sequences remain unchanged; (2) State and path information can be either preserved or retrieved (yet without blowing up the search space) for verification of integrated system properties and for constructing executable interoperability testing sequences. We can perform such minimization to the individual components at the outset before composing them, and then continue minimizing partial products iteratively as they are being computed.

2.1   System Integration and Interface Graphs

Consider a graph G of a transition system that may be an individual component or a product of several components. A subset of the transitions is specified as *interface transitions* while the rest as *internal* transitions. Let Σ be the set of interface transitions. The behaviors of the system can be represented by all the possible executable sequences (scenarios) t from the initial state v_{init} of the system graph G. Practical experiences show that integrated system interoperability problems manifest themselves when components are interfacing with each other, that is, while interface transitions are executed. Change internal transitions to τ-moves ("silent" or "invisible" transitions). Such a graph is called an *interface graph*. In terms of revealing interoperability problems, two scenarios with an identical interface transition sequence (with different τ-moves in between) provide the same information and, therefore, we do not care about τ-moves in a scenario. Specifically, let $t = t_1, t_2, ..., t_r$ be a scenario of G. Its *projection* $\pi(t)$ is obtained by removing all the τ-moves, and is a sequence of interface transitions only, i.e. a string over Σ. Two scenarios r and t are equivalent if and only if $\pi(r) = \pi(t)$. Therefore, all the integrated system behaviors are represented by the set of distinct sequences of interface transitions: $S(G) = \{ \pi(t) : t \in t \}$ where t is the set of all the scenarios from G and can be infinite. Thus, $S(G)$ is a language over the alphabet Σ consisting of all the interface transitions of G. To reduce the system complexity while maintaining the system interface behaviors, we want to obtain a reduced interface graph G^* that has the same set of interface transitions and is *interface equivalent* to the original interface graph G, i.e., $S(G^*) = S(G)$. This is the trace equivalence [14] or language equivalence [8] with respect to the alphabet Σ of interface transitions.

Note that different interface transitions of the system may have the same action (or Input/Output) label. However, we treat them as distinct because they represent execution of the action in distinct contexts, and these may have quite different implications for the integrated system interoperability testing and verification. For example, in testing of a component, we may want to generate tests that exercise all the interface transitions of the component. If we were to reduce the component while preserving only equivalence with respect to action (or I/O) labels of the transitions, then we would lose useful paths and may even eliminate some of the interface transitions, hence the reduced graph would not be sufficient for the task. Consequently, in our minimization we want to preserve the set $S(G)$ of all interface transition sequences.

In summary, we have an interface graph with τ-edges and distinct interface transitions, and we want to minimize it with respect to trace (language) equivalence. G can be viewed as an automaton whose transitions are labeled by elements of the alphabet Σ or τ, and all states are regarded as accepting. It is a nondeterministic automaton because of the τ transitions. Recall that nondeterministic automata do not have a unique minimum automaton in general, and moreover, minimization is PSPACE-complete [8]. We will show however that in this case we can do this efficiently.

3   Minimization of Interface Graphs

We propose a reduction by merging states while preserving the interface transition sequences and also the needed state and path information. We present a polynomial time algorithm for the reduction.

We use the standard procedure of merging two nodes: they are merged into one node that inherits all the incoming and outgoing edges of the two merged nodes.

We first derive necessary and sufficient conditions for a pair of nodes u and v to be merged while preserving interface equivalence. Recall that all the nodes in an interface graph are reachable from the initial node v_{init}. A node v is τ-reachable from node u if there is a path of τ-move edges from u to v. Given a node u, its *successor* nodes, denoted by succ(u), are all the τ-reachable nodes from u, and its *predecessor* nodes, denoted by pred(u), are all the nodes from which u is τ-reachable. Let S be the set of all the start nodes of interface transitions and let E be the set of all the end nodes of interface transitions and also the initial state v_{init}; in effect, we regard v_{init} as the end state of an artificial interface transition that starts the system. Define   Ssucc(u)=succ(u) $\cap$ S, and Epred(u)=pred(u)$\cap$E. Ssucc(u) is the set of all the successors of u, which are the start nodes of an interface transition. Epred(u) is the set of all the predecessors of u, which are either the initial node or an end node of an interface transition.

Proposition 1. *(Node Merging Condition)* Given an interface graph G, merging two nodes u and v yields an interface equivalent graph if and only if: every node in Ssucc(u) is τ-reachable from every node in Epred(v) and every node in Ssucc(v) is τ-reachable from every node in Epred(u).

Sketch of Proof. Obviously node merging can only produce additional interface transition sequences. Thus, we only need to verify that a merging of nodes does not introduce any new interface transition sequences. It does introduce a new interface transition sequence if and only if the merging connects two disconnected interface transition subsequences: one from the initial node to v (u) and the other starting from u (v). This is the case if and only if there is $y \in$ Epred(v) (or Epred(u)) and $x \in$ Ssucc(u) (or Ssucc(v)) but x is not τ-reachable from y.   □

Corollary 1. For a strongly connected component (SCC) of τ-moves in an interface graph, all the nodes in the SCC can be merged into one node to obtain an interface equivalent graph.   □

The condition of Proposition 1 is symmetric but not transitive: it may be the case that pairs (u,v) and (v,w) satisfy the condition, but the pair (u,w) does not. Furthermore, node merging is not independent, i.e., merging a pair of nodes may affect the validity of merging other pairs of nodes. Specifically, suppose that two pairs of nodes, u and v, u' and v', satisfy the Node Merging Condition in Proposition 1. However, merging u and v may change the topology of the graph G so that u' and v' do not satisfy the same condition anymore.

Example 2. In Fig 2, one can easily check that merging nodes w and u (u and v) is valid. However, merging both pairs is invalid; it would introduce a new interface transition sequence ab. Obviously, merging w and u would disable the Node Merging Condition of u and v.   □

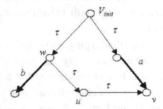

Fig. 2. An Example

Consequently, we cannot first identify all the pairs of nodes, which satisfy the Node Merging Condition, and then merge all of them. Instead, after merging a pair of nodes, we would have to find another pair of nodes that can be merged, and repeat the process iteratively.

The following is obvious from Proposition 1:

Corollary 2. Suppose that node pair u and v is invalid for merging, i.e., it does not satisfy the Node Merging Condition in Proposition 1. Then it remains invalid for merging after merging other valid node pairs.   □

However, from Example 2, a pair of nodes may lose its validity for merging after merging other valid pairs. We will show that a simple preprocessing procedure that eliminates internal nodes allows valid pairs to be merged independently.

3.1 Ubiquitous Interface Graph and Church-Rosser Property of Node Merging

Consider a node u, which is only incident to τ-moves. If all the incident τ-moves are incoming edges, then u is a sink node of τ-moves. We can remove u along with all the incident τ-moves, resulting in an interface equivalent graph. Similarly, we can remove source nodes (except for the initial node), which are only incident to outgoing τ-moves. The resulting graph contains two types of nodes: (1) Incident to at least one interface transition; or (2) incident to only τ-moves yet neither sink nor source node. We can remove type (2) node u as follows. For each pair of incoming τ-move $p \rightarrow u$ and outgoing τ-move $u \rightarrow q$, add a τ-move $p \rightarrow q$ if it is not there, and remove u along with all its incident τ-moves. Obviously, the resulting graph is interface equivalent to the original one. Since each operation reduces the number of nodes, we can repeat the process until all the nodes are incident to at least one interface transition. Note that the number of τ-moves may increase in the worst case. Yet our main concern in dealing with state explosion is the number of nodes.

In summary, given an interface graph, we can conduct a simple preprocessing to reduce it to an interface equivalent graph where each node is incident to at least one interface transition. We call such an interface graph *ubiquitous* (interface occurs with every node – everywhere). From now on we assume that all the interface graphs are ubiquitous.

Lemma 1. In a ubiquitous interface graph, the Node Merging Condition is: (1) Invariant with respect to merging of valid node pairs, and (2) Transitive.

Proof. We show (1); claim (2) follows from (1) and Corollary 3. Let the given interface graph be G and the resulting interface graph be G' after merging a valid node pair u and v. From Corollary 2, a pair of nodes u' and v' remains invalid for merging in G' if it was *not* in G. We now show that if they were valid for merging in G, then they remain valid in G'. Assume on the contrary that u' and v' become invalid for merging in G'. Then from Proposition 1 there exist $y \in \text{Epred}(v')$ and $x \in \text{Ssucc}(u')$ in G' such that x is not τ-reachable from y (the symmetric condition can be handled by the same argument). Since u' and v' were valid for merging in G, from Proposition 1, either $y \notin \text{Epred}(v')$ or $x \notin \text{Ssucc}(u')$ in G; otherwise, since x was τ-reachable from y, it also is in G', a contradiction. There are three cases.

Case 1. $y \notin \text{Epred}(v')$ and $x \in \text{Ssucc}(u')$ in G. Since $y \notin \text{Epred}(v')$ in G and $y \in \text{Epred}(v')$ in G' there is a path of τ-moves from y to v, and a path of τ-moves from u to v', and merging nodes u and v makes v' τ-reachable from y. Since G and G' are ubiquitous, there is an interface transition incident to v', and there are two cases: (A) $v' \in E$; and (B) $v' \in S$. Case (A) Since $v' \in \text{Epred}(v')$, $x \in \text{Ssucc}(u')$, and node pair u' and v' was valid to be merged in G, x is τ-reachable from v' in G and hence in G'. Since v' is also τ-reachable from y in G', x is τ-reachable from y in G', a contradiction. Case (B) Since $y \in \text{Epred}(v)$, $v' \in \text{Ssucc}(u)$ and node pair u and v was valid to be merged in G, v' was τ-reachable from y in G, a contradiction.

Case 2. $y \in \text{Epred}(v')$ and $x \notin \text{Ssucc}(u')$ in G. Since $x \notin \text{Ssucc}(u')$ in G and $x \in \text{Ssucc}(u')$ in G', there is a path of τ-moves from u' to v and a path of τ-moves from u to x, and merging of u and v makes x τ-reachable from u'. Since G is ubiquitous, there is an interface transition incident to u'. There are two cases: (A) $u' \in S$; and (B) $u' \in E$. Case (A) Since $u' \in$ Ssucc(u'), $y \in$ Epred(v'), and node pair u' and v' could be merged in G, u' was τ-reachable from y in G and hence is also in G'. Since x is τ-reachable from u' in G', x is τ-reachable from y in G', a contradiction. Case (B) Since $u' \in$ Epred(v), $x \in$ Ssucc(u), and node pair u and v could be merged in G, x was τ-reachable from u' in G, a contradiction.

Case 3. $y \notin$ Epred(v') and $x \notin$ Ssucc(u') in G. Since merging node pair u and v makes $x \in$ Ssucc(u') and $y \in$ Epred(v') in G', in graph G there were paths of τ-moves: from y to v, from u to v', from u' to v, and from u to x. See Fig 3. Therefore, $y \in$ Epred(v) and $x \in$ Ssucc(u) in G. Since node pair u and v could be merged in G, x was τ-reachable from y in G and hence also in G', a contradiction. $\square$

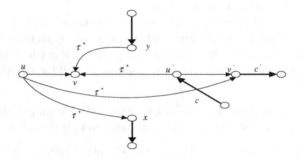

Fig. 3

Corollary 3. On a ubiquitous interface graph, the operation of merging node pairs, which satisfy the Node Merging Condition, has the Church-Rosser property, i.e., they can be merged in an arbitrary order. $\square$

Definition 1. In a ubiquitous interface graph G two nodes u and v are *interface equivalent*, denoted by $u \equiv v$, if they satisfy the Node Merging Condition; equivalently, $u \equiv v$ if merging them yields an interface-equivalent graph. $\square$

Remarks (State Equivalence Relations)

(1) By Lemma 1, node interface equivalence is indeed an equivalence relation. On the other hand, from Example 2, this is not the case if there are internal nodes, and that is why we defined it only for ubiquitous interface graphs. (2) Two interface equivalent nodes u and v may well not be trace- (or observationally) equivalent: there may be a path starting at u whose projection is a sequence of interface transitions that does not have a corresponding path from v. Thus, although reduction by trace or observational equivalence also preserves the interface language, it is a weaker reduction than that from interface equivalence and may not merge some states.

(3) There is a variety of equivalence relations defined in the literature (see [3] for a comprehensive list). As far as we know, state interface equivalence is different. One

observation is that it is common in the literature to identify states with processes; namely, a state u is identified with the process $P(u)$ that has u as its initial state, and equivalence of two states u and v (with respect to some equivalence notion) is defined as equivalence of the two processes $P(u)$ and $P(v)$. However, as we noted, even though the processes $P(u)$ and $P(v)$ may not be trace-equivalent, still we may be able to merge states u and v while preserving trace equivalence for the whole graph (starting from the initial state). □

By the Church-Rosser property of node merging according to interface equivalence, we can merge all nodes in each equivalence class. The resulting graph G^* has obviously the same interface transitions and is interface equivalent to G. The graph is unique up to the names of the nodes and the addition or deletion of transitive τ edges. We show furthermore, that G^* is *the minimum* graph with these properties.

Theorem 1. For a ubiquitous interface graph G, let G^* be the interface-equivalent graph obtained by merging interface-equivalent nodes. Let G' be any interface graph that has the same set Σ of interface edges (i.e. its interface edges are in 1-1 correspondence with those of G) and that is interface-equivalent to G. Then G' has at least as many nodes as G^*.

Sketch of Proof. Let u,v be two distinct nodes of G^*. We distinguish cases depending on whether u,v are in E or S. We will show here only the case $u \in E, v \in S$; the other cases can be argued similarly. Let a be an interface edge into u and b an interface edge out of v. Let u',v' respectively be the tail and head of the corresponding edges a,b in G'. We now argue that $u' \neq v'$.

Suppose that $u'=v'$. Since G' contains an interface sequence that contains the subsequence ab, the graph G^* must have a τ path from u to v. Since u,v are not interface equivalent (otherwise they would have been merged), there exist x in Epred(v), and y in Ssucc(u) such that there is no τ path from x to y. Let c be an interface edge into x and d an interface edge out of y, and let x',y' be the tail and head of the corresponding edges in G'. Since G^* has an interface sequence that contains the subsequence cb, the same must be true for G', hence $x' \in$ Epred(v'). Similarly since G^* has an interface sequence that contains the subsequence ad, we must have $y' \in$ Ssucc(u'). Since $u'=v'$, there is a τ path from x' to y', and therefore G' has an interface sequence that contains the subsequence cd, whereas G^* (and hence G) does not. □

We remark that it may be possible in some cases to duplicate some of the interface edges and construct thereby an equivalent graph with fewer nodes. For example, if all the incoming edges of an S node v are τ edges, then we can eliminate v and add appropriate edges from its predecessors to its successors. This however will introduce multiple copies of an interface edge, which may impact the use of the graph for testing and verification: Consider for example the problem of generating tests to cover all interface edges – now we would have to cover more edges. We defer further discussion to the full paper.

4 Minimization Algorithm

Given an interface graph, we first conduct a preprocessing to remove all the nodes, which are incident to τ-moves only, obtaining an interface equivalent ubiquitous graph. We then shrink SCCs of τ-moves, obtaining a Directed Acyclic Graph (DAG) with respect to τ-moves. We can then check interface equivalence of every pair of nodes and merge the equivalent ones. This naïve algorithm costs $O(n^4)$ where n is the number of nodes of the interface graph. We now present an efficient algorithm with a cost of O(mn) where m is the number of edges of the interface graph. Recall that S is the set of start nodes of interface transitions and E consists of the set of end nodes of interface transition and the initial node; since the graph is ubiquitous, every node belongs to S or E or both.

Lemma 2. Two nodes u and v are interface equivalent, i.e., $u \equiv v$, if and only if:

Case 1. $u,v \in$ S: Epred(u)=Epred(v);
Case 2, $u,v \in$ E: Ssucc(u) = Ssucc(v);
Case 3, $u \in$ E, $v\in$ S: v is τ-reachable from u, and
every node in Ssucc(u) is τ-reachable from every node in Epred(v).

Sketch of Proof.

Case 1. If Epred(u)=Epred(v), then each node in Ssucc(u) is τ-reachable from those in Epred(u) and hence in Epred(v), and the Node Merging Condition is satisfied. Conversely, assume that Epred(u) $\neq$ Epred(v) and, without loss of generality, assume that there is a node $y\in$ Epred(v) but $y\notin$ Epred(u). Since $u\in$ S, $u\in$ Ssucc(u), and it is not reachable from $y\in$ Epred(v). From Proposition 1, u and v are not interface equivalent.

Case 2 can be proved similarly.

Case 3. From Proposition 1, the conditions are obviously sufficient. Conversely, if v is not τ-reachable from u, then merging u and v will introduce a new interface transition sequence that contains an interface transition going to u (u in E) and an interface transition out of v (v in S).   □

A direct checking of conditions in Case 3 for each pair of nodes is costly. For a node u, let

PS(u)= $\hbar_{y\in Epred(u)} Ssucc(y)$ and

SP(u)= $\hbar_{x\in Ssucc(u)} Epred(x)$.

Proposition 2. Two nodes $u \in$ E, $v\in$ S satisfy the Node Merging Condition if and only if Ssucc(u) = PS(v) if and only if Epred(v)=SP(u).   □

From Proposition 2, Case 3 conditions in Lemma 2 can be checked with PS($\cdot$) instead (or equivalently with SP($\cdot$)) and if done properly, this reduces the overall cost to O(mn) as follows. Denote the interface equivalent minimization of a graph G by $MIN(G)$:

Algorithm 1. (Interface Graph Minimization)

```
Input: An interface graph G, which is a τ-move DAG
Output: A minimized interface equivalent graph MIN(G)
1. compute topological order of  nodes: v₁,...,vₙ
2. for i=n down to 1
3.      if  vᵢ∈ S then Ssucc(vᵢ):= {vᵢ}
4.                     else Ssucc(vᵢ):=∅ ;
5.     for each τ-edge (vᵢ,vⱼ), out of  vᵢ
6.         Ssucc(vᵢ):= Ssucc(vᵢ)∪Ssucc(vⱼ);
7. for i=1 up to n
8.      if vᵢ∈ E then
9.          Epred(vᵢ):= {vᵢ}, PS(vᵢ):=Ssucc(vᵢ);
10.                    else Epred(vᵢ):=∅ , PS(vᵢ):=V;
11.         for each τ-edge (vⱼ,vᵢ), into  vᵢ
12.             Epred(vᵢ):= Epred(vᵢ)∪Epred(vⱼ);
13.             PS(vᵢ): = PS(vᵢ)∩PS(vⱼ);
14. radix sort and order the set Ssucc(u) for u in E,
            and order the sets Epred(v) and PS(v) for v in
S;
15. for each pair of nodes u and v
16.     if  (u,v ∈ S ∧ Epred(u)=Epred(v)) ∨
17.     (u,v ∈ E ∧ Ssucc(u) = Ssucc(v)) ∨
18.     ((u ∈ E ∧ v ∈ S) ∧ (Ssucc(u) = PS(v)))
19.         merge nodes u and v;
20.  return minimized interface graph MIN(G)
```

Fig. 4. Algorithm 1: Interface Graph Minimization

Line 2-6 and 7-13 compute Ssucc($\cdot$) (Epred($\cdot$) and PS($\cdot$)) in a reverse (normal) topological order in time O(mn). We can represent each set as a list of nodes or as a characteristic vector, and use radix sorting to sort all the sets and order them lexicographically in time $O(n^2)$; at the end we can assign each set an integer (between 1 and 3n) so that equal sets receive the same integer. Checking identical sets for the three Cases of Lemma 2 in Line 16-19 takes a constant time for each pair of nodes. Since there are on the order of n^2 pairs of nodes to be checked, the total cost is $O(n^2)$.

An alternative (and generally more efficient) method for computing the equivalent nodes is the following. Scan the sorted list of the sets Ssucc($\cdot$), Epred($\cdot$) and PS($\cdot$), and partition the list into segments of equal sets (note that all equal sets are consecutive). For each segment, merge all E nodes u whose set Ssucc(u) is in the segment, merge with them any nodes v in S whose PS(v) set is in the segment; merge together all S nodes v whose Epred(v) set is in the segment. We have:

Theorem 2. Given an interface graph G, Algorithm 1 takes time $O(mn)$ to construct a minimal interface equivalent graph where m and n are the number of edges and nodes in G, respectively. □

4.1 Minimal Interface Graph of Integrated Systems

For an analysis of integrated systems we want to construct a minimal interface graph $MIN(G)$ of the Cartesian product G of all the components. Often we cannot afford to construct G due to state explosion. Indeed, there is no need to obtain G first. We can minimize each component first, take the Cartesian product of two components, minimize it and continue in this manner to obtain the minimal interface graph. Note that before minimization of an interface graph we first make it an interface equivalent ubiquitous graph using the procedure in Section 3.1. However, we need to justify first that if two nodes $u \equiv v$ in a component then they (all their duplicates) remain equivalent in the Cartesian product:

Theorem 3. If $u \equiv v$ in a component A (or B) then all their duplicates remain interface equivalent in the Cartesian product $A \otimes B$.

We need the following lemma, whose proof we omit:

Lemma 3. For a τ--path from node P to Q in $A \otimes B$, there is a τ-path of τ-moves in A (or B) only, from P to some node W, and a τ-path of τ-moves in B (or A) only, from W to Q. □

We are ready to prove the theorem.

Sketch of Proof. Assume $u \equiv v$ in A. In $A \otimes B$ node u (v) is duplicated to $(u, s_i), i = 1,...,n$ ($(v, s_i), i = 1,...,n$) where n is the number of nodes in B. To prove $(u, s_i) \equiv (v, s_i), i = 1,...,n$, we only need to show that any node $(x, s_j) \in \text{Ssucc}(u, s_i)$ is τ-reachable from any node $(y, s_k) \in \text{Epred}(v, s_i)$ and that any node $(x, s_j) \in \text{Ssucc}(v, s_i)$ is τ-reachable from any node $(y, s_k) \in \text{Epred}(u, s_i)$.

From lemma 3, there exist a node (v, s_k) so that there is a path of τ-moves (only in A) from (y, s_k) to (v, s_k) and a path of τ-moves (only in B) from (v, s_k) to (v, s_i). Hence $y \in \text{Epred}(v)$ in A and s_i is τ-reachable from s_k in B.

Similarly, there exist a node (x, s_i) so that there is a path of τ-moves (only in A) from (u, s_i) to (x, s_i) and a path of τ-moves (only in B) from (x, s_i) to (x, s_j). Hence $x \in \text{Ssucc}(u)$ in A, and s_j is τ-reachable from s_i in B.

Since $y \in \text{Epred}(v)$, $x \in \text{Ssucc}(u)$, and $u \equiv v$ in A, from Proposition 1, x is τ-reachable from y in A and, hence, there is a path of τ-moves from (y, s_k) to (x, s_k). Since s_i is τ-reachable from s_k and s_j is τ-reachable from s_i in B, s_j is τ-reachable from s_k in B and, therefore, there is a path of τ moves from (x, s_k) to (x, s_j). Hence, there is a path of τ moves from (y, s_k) to (x, s_k) and then to (x, s_j), and (x, s_j) is τ-reachable from (y, s_k).

Similarly, we can show that any node $(x, s_j) \in \text{Ssucc}(v, s_i)$ is τ-reachable from any node $(y, s_k) \in \text{Epred}(u, s_i)$. □

From Theorem 3, we can do the interface equivalence minimization either before or after taking the Cartesian product. Denote this operation by *MIN*, we have:

Proposition 3. For the interface equivalent minimization, we have:

(1) $MIN[MIN(A) \otimes MIN(B)] \equiv MIN[A \otimes MIN(B)] \equiv MIN[(MIN(A) \otimes B] \equiv MIN(A \otimes B)$;

(2) $MIN(A \otimes B) \equiv MIN(B \otimes A)$; and

(3) $MIN[A \otimes (B \otimes C)] \equiv MIN[(A \otimes B) \otimes C]$. □

From the above proposition, we have:

Corollary 4. Given an interface graph of an integrated system, which is a Cartesian product of more than one component, the interface minimization can be performed on individual components or Cartesian products of all or a subset of the components, and the resulting graphs are interface equivalent. □

5 Experiments on LMP of GMPLS

We report experimental results of the minimization algorithm on the Link Management Protocol (LMP) of GMPLS.

The IETF Standard GMPLS is a protocol suite that uses advanced network signaling and routing mechanisms to automatically set up end-to-end connections for all types of network traffic and provides a unified control plane and the necessary linkage between the IP and optical layers, allowing interoperable and scalable networks in both IP and optical domains. GMPLS protocol stack is composed of several protocols, including LMP, CR-LDP extension, RSVP-TE extension, and OSPF-TE extension. LMP is a protocol running between neighboring nodes and is used to manage TE links and verify reachability of the control channel. LMP consists of four major features: control plane management (CPM), link property correlation (LPC), link connectivity verification (LCV), and fault management (FM). Correspondingly, there are four main modules in each of the two communicating nodes. See Fig. 5.

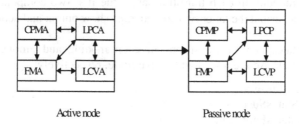

Active node   Passive node

Fig. 5. LMP Modules

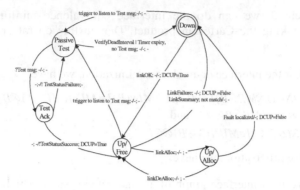

Fig. 6. LCV Passive EFSM

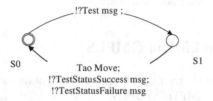

Fig. 7. *MIN(MIN*(LCV Active) ⊗ *MIN*(LCVPassive))

Each module is represented by an Extended Finite State Machine (EFSM), as is often done in protocols. An EFSM is an FSM extended with variables; transitions have besides input and output an associated *predicate* on the values of the variables, which is a condition (guard) on the occurrence of the transition, and has an *action* which is a transformation on the values of the variables. If all the variables have finite domains (eg. Boolean, finite counters) then an EFSM is simply a succinct representation of an ordinary FSM (see [7,13] for more details). As a first step we obtain from each EFSM the part of the corresponding FSM that is reachable from the initial state; this is called the *reachability graph*.

In Fig. 1 we showed the LCV module for the active node; the following figure shows the passive LCV module. In each transition label, the first two components show the input and the predicate and the latter two components show output and action.

There are 5 states and 11 transitions in each module and among them 3 are interface transitions in Active node and Passive node, respectively:

Active: -; -/!Test msg ; -
        ?TestStatusSuccess; -/-; -
        ?TestStatusFailure msg; -/-; -
Passive: ?Testmsg;-/-;-
        -;-/! TestStatusSuccess;DCUP=True
        -;-/! TestStatusFailure;-

The Cartesian product of the two reachability graphs contains 25 states and 103 transitions. Applying our minimization algorithm, we obtain $MIN(MIN(\text{LCVActive}) \otimes MIN(\text{LCVPassive}))$, which contains 2 states and 4 transitions. See Fig. 7.

We now consider the integration of the 6 modules (excluding FMA and FMP) of the two communicating LMP nodes. The Cartesian product of the reachability graphs of all the modules contains 177,000 states and 2,595,900 transitions; it is hard to handle for any available formal verification and testing techniques. Applying our minimization algorithm and taking advantage of the interface equivalence invariance of the order of minimizations on the components and products, we obtain an interface equivalent graph of 2,912 states and 24,987 transitions, which are manageable.

6 Applications

We discuss applications of our interface graph minimization technique to integrated system verification and testing. We are concerned with integrated system interoperability and want to analyze system behaviors, which are involved with interfaces among system components and ignore component local behaviors by changing them to τ-moves. We want to show that the minimized interface graph contains sufficient information for verification analysis and for constructing executable interoperability testing. We omit all the proofs.

6.1 Interface Livelock

As a simple case study, we discuss livelocks. More sophisticated properties, such as temporal properties, can be analyzed similarly.

Certain system states are specified as *progress-states* where system operation makes progress such as messages sent or received. For our study we only consider interface transitions, which are incident to progress states, i.e., integrated system makes progress before or after a system interface. We call such interface transition as *progress interface transition*. We are not concerned with system progress from components' internal behaviors. A non-progress interface cycle is a reachable cycle in the graph that contains at least one interface transition and yet does not contain any progress interface transitions. A non-progress interface cycle is called an *interface livelock*. When a communication system contains an interface livelock it can go through the cycle infinitely many times with infinitely many system interactions among the system components yet without making any progress.

We now show that to detect interface livelocks we only have to search a minimized interface graph and hence the search space is significantly reduced:

Theorem 4. Interface livelock is invariant with respect to interface equivalence minimization. □

Corollary 5. An integrated protocol system is interface livelock free if and only if its minimal interface equivalent graph is interface livelock free. □

From Corollary 5, the problem is reduced to checking interface livelocks of the minimal interface graph G^* of the integrated system. There is a variety of algorithms published on checking livelocks [2,7]. Yet they do not have interface transitions involved. We describe an algorithm that is applicable for interface livelock detection. It is a variant of algorithms for non-progress and accepting cycle detection [7].

Algorithm 2. Given an interface graph G with an initial node v_{init}, we construct an interface graph G' that is identical to G except that all the progress interface transitions are removed. Initially, all the nodes are not visited. We conduct a DFS in G from v_{init}. Whenever we visit a node v in G that is not visited we mark it *visited* and "jump" to G' to continue search from there. If we identify an SCC in G' with at least one interface transition, then we have found an interface livelock, since in the SCC we can construct a cycle with an interface transition yet there are no progress interface transitions in G'. Otherwise, we mark all the searched nodes in G' as *visited* along with the corresponding nodes in G, and return to node v in G to continue to search from there. The algorithm terminates either if it finds an interface livelock or all the nodes in G (and G') are visited without identifying any interface livelock. In the latter case, G is interface livelock free.   □

Obviously, the algorithm has a cost of DFS:

Proposition 4. Given an interface graph G, Algorithm 2 either finds an interface livelock or concludes that G is interface livelock free in time $O(m)$ where m is the number of edges in G.   □

Algorithm 2 determines whether an interface graph is interface livelock free. However, it does not identify all the possible livelocks if there are any. (Note that there may an exponential number of them.) This can be achieved by the following algorithm that is a modification of an algorithm in [5]:

Algorithm 3. Given an interface graph G, we have a tree walk from the initial node v_{init}. We continue from a current leaf node so long as no node is repeated along the tree path from v_{init}. We modify the algorithm by adding two indices at each node v, $I(v)$ and $P(v)$ where $I(v)$ records the number of interface transitions and $P(v)$ records the number of progress interface transitions from v_{init} to v along the tree path. Upon detecting a simple cycle while visiting a node v, i.e., there is an outgoing edge from v to u, which is a node on the tree path from v_{init} to v, we check whether the simple cycle from u along the tree path to v and then from v back to u is an interface livelock. It is an interface livelock if and only if there are no progress interface transitions and at least one interface transition, and this is the case if and only if: (1) $P(u)=P(v)$ and $v \to u$ is not a progress interface transition; and (2) $I(u) < I(v)$ or $I(u) = I(v)$ but $v \to u$ is a non-progress interface transition. When we complete the tree walk we have checked all the simple cycles and identified all the simple interface livelocks if there are any.   □

Proposition 5. Given an interface graph, all the simple interface livelocks can be obtained in time proportional to the size of a simple path (cycle) tree rooted at v_{init}. □

6.2 Interoperability Testing

Interoperability testing is to check the interoperations among integrated system implementations. Ideally, one might want to test on all possible interface transition sequences to reveal interoperation errors. However, the number of executable interface transition sequences could be infinite. This problem has been studied in [5,10] with different coverage criteria.

Suppose that we use a procedure for interoperability testing sequence generation and that we want to apply it to the minimized interface graph instead of the original graph, which is often impossible. In this case, the tests generated from minimized interface graph consist of interface transitions and τ-moves. We need to further process so that: (1) Each test is executable, i.e., it consists of a consecutive sequence of internal and interface transitions in the whole integrated system (the Cartesian product of all the original system components); (2) It contains the same interface transition sequence, i.e., they have the same projection to interface transition sequences; and (3) Without constructing the whole Cartesian product of all the original system components, i.e., we only need the minimized interface graph and the involved individual component information.

Suppose that we have a test sequence (path) p from a minimized interface graph G^*; it consists of interleaving interface transitions and τ-move sequences. We now discuss how to construct an executable test sequence according to the above three requirements. The basic idea is: we replace τ-move sequences between a pair of interface transitions by consecutive internal transitions, which can be obtained by examining the involved individual components only. From Lemma 3,

Proposition 6. Suppose that a τ-move sequence $\tau = \tau_1 \tau_2 \hbar \ \tau_r$ in a reachability graph of a Cartesian product is from state $(s_1,...,s_k)$ to $(t_1,...,t_k)$ where s_i and t_i are states in component $G_i, i = 1,...,k$. Then state t_i is reachable from s_i in G_i, i.e., there is a path of τ-moves ω_i and hence internal transition sequence z_i in G_i from s_i to t_i, $i=1,...,k$. Consequently, there is an internal transition sequence $z_1 z_2 \hbar \ z_k$ in the Cartesian product from state $(s_1,...,s_k)$ to $(t_1,...,t_k)$. □

Note that there is no need to construct the Cartesian product graph; we only need a minimized interface graph and a graph of each involved component. Furthermore, there is no need to construct the connecting τ-move sequences a_i; we only need to find an internal transition sequence z_i in G_i from s_i to t_i, which can be easily constructed by a BFS in G_i, i=1,...,k. We summarize:

Algorithm 4. (Interoperability Test Sequence Generation)

input: Integrated system $G = \otimes_{i=1}^{k} G_i$ with initial node v_{init} .

output: A set Γ of executable test sequences in G with a desired fault coverage

1.   construct a minimized interface graph G^* from G;
2.   construct a set **P** of paths in G^* from v_{init}
      with a desired fault coverage;
3. $\Gamma = \phi$;
4.   **for** each path **p** in **P**
5.   construct an executable test sequence
          z from v_{init} in G;
6. $\Gamma = \Gamma \cup \mathbf{z}$;
7.   **return** Γ □

As an experiment, we use the interoperability test sequence generation software tool, called *ITIS*, in [5] with Basic coverage and apply it to LMP/GMPLS: (1) Construct minimized interface graph G^*; (2) Generate Basic Coverage tests using *ITIS*; (3) Convert each test to an executable one in LMP/GMPLS.

A simple example is the communicating LCV modules, see Fig. 7. There are only two nodes and each node represents a module, LCVA (Active) and LCVP (Passive), respectively. From this minimized interface graph, 3 test sequences are generated with Basic Coverage: (1) *!Test message*, τ-move; (2) *!Test message, !TestStatusFailure*; (3) *!Test message, !TestStatusSuccess*. Using Algorithm 4, the 3 corresponding executable interoperability testing sequences are generated, involving both LCVA and LCVP:

(1) **LCVA**: I/O: Trigger to send Test msg /, I/O: *//Test message*
    LCVP: I/O: linkOK/, I/O: Trigger to listen to Test msg /, I/O: *?Test message /*
(2) **LCVA**: I/O: Trigger to send Test msg /, I/O: *//Test message*, I/O: *?TestStatusFailure/*
    LCVP: I/O: linkOK/, I/O: Trigger to listen to Test msg /, I/O: *?Test message /*, I/O: *//TestStatusFailure*
(3) **LCVA**: I/O: Trigger to send Test msg /, I/O: *//Test message*, I/O: *?TestStatusSuccess/*
    LCVP: I/O: linkOK/, I/O: Trigger to listen to Test msg /, I/O: *?Test message /*, I/O: *//TestStatusSuccess*

7 Conclusion

For a study of integrated protocol system interface and interoperability, we investigate interface graphs and their minimization, identify a new state equivalence relation suitable for this purpose, and develop and implement an efficient algorithm for it. The technique is applied to the GMPLS protocol and we also discuss how it can be used for verification and interoperability testing. A similar method can be used more generally if we want to focus on a part of the system or on a particular feature that involves a selected subset of transitions (not necessarily for interfaces); a minimum equivalent system can be computed efficiently, which contains these transitions and preserves exactly all the involved traces.

Acknowledgements

We thank Xiao-tian Yin and Hui Jian for the comments and help with part of the experiments.

References

[1] A. Bouajjani, J.-C. Fernandez, N. Halbwachs, *Minimal model generation*, Proc. CAV, 197-203, 1990.

[2] E. M. Clarke, O. Grumberg and D. A. Peled, *Model Checking*, MIT Press, 1999.

[3] R.J. van Glabbeek, *The Linear Time – Branching Time Spectrum I*, in *Handbook of Process Algebra,* Begstra, Ponse, Smolka eds., Elsevier, 3-99, 2001.

[4] S. Graf, B. Steffen, G. Luttgen, *Compositional minimization of finite state systems using interface specifications,* Formal Aspects of Computing, 1996.

[5] R. Hao, D. Lee, R. Sinha and N. Griffeth ,*Integrated System Interoperability Testing with Applications to VoIP*, IEEE/ACM Trans. on Networking, Oct. 2004. An early version appeared in FORTE/PSTV 2000.

[6] C. A. R. Hoare, *Communicating Sequential Processes*, Prentice Hall, 1985.

[7] G. J. Holzmann, *Design and Validation of Computer Protocols*, Prntice Hall, 1991.

[8] J. E. Hopcroft and J. D. Ullman, *Introduction to Automata Theory, Languages, and Computation*, Reading, MA: Addison-Wesley, 1979.

[9] P. Kanellakis and S. Smolka, *CCS Expressions, Finite State Processes and Three Problems of Equivalence*, Information and Computation, Vol. 86, 1983, pp. 43-68.

[10] S. Kang and M. Kim, *Test Sequence Generation for Adaptive Interoperability Testing*, in Proc. Protocol Testing Systems VIII, 1995, 187-200.

[11] P. V. Koppol, R. H. Carver, and K.-C. Tai, *Incremental Integration Testing of Concurrent Programs*, IEEE Trans. on Software Eng., 28(6), 607-623, 2002.

[12] D. Lee and M. Yannakakis, *Online minimization of transitions systems*, Proc. ACM STOC, 264-274, 1992.

[13] D. Lee and M. Yannakakis, *Principles and Methods of Testing Finite State Machines - A Survey,* Proceedings of IEEE, Vol. 84, No. 8, 1090-1123, 1996.

[14] R. Milner, *Communication and Concurrency*, Prentice Hall, 1989.

DART: Distributed Automated Regression Testing
for Large-Scale Network Applications

Brent N. Chun

Intel Research Berkeley, Berkeley, CA, USA

Abstract. This paper presents DART, a framework for distributed automated regression testing of large-scale network applications. DART provides programmers writing distributed applications with a set of primitives for writing distributed tests and a runtime that executes distributed tests in a fast and efficient manner over a network of nodes. It provides a programming environment, scripted execution of multi-node commands, fault injection, and performance anomaly injection. We have implemented a prototype implementation of DART that implements a useful subset of the DART architecture and is targeted at the Emulab network emulation environment. Our prototype is functional, fast, and is currently being used to test the correctness, robustness, and performance of PIER, a distributed relational query processor.

1   Introduction

Recently, we have seen the emergence of a number of novel wide-area applications and network services. Examples include distributed hash tables (DHTs) [24, 19, 21, 18, 31], wide-area storage and archive systems [11, 12, 5], distributed query processors [10, 29], content distribution networks [14, 8], robust name services [17], and routing overlays [1, 25]. These distributed applications provide diverse functionality to end users, but nevertheless have one common goal: to deliver correct behavior and high performance in the presence of high concurrency, node and network failures, and transient and persistent performance anomalies. Designing and implementing applications with these characteristics presents significant technical challenges.

With sequential (i.e., single-node) applications, unit testing [4] is an effective and widely used mechanism for building correct, robust, and maintainable software. In unit testing, users write tests that exercise and verify the functionality of specific parts of an application. Over time, users build up a collection of such tests, each covering an increasing fraction of the application's overall functionality. A testing framework automates the execution of unit tests and is applied whenever the application is modified. The end result is that code changes can be automatically verified to have not broken existing functionality (as covered by the unit tests), thereby leading to increased confidence when performing significant modifications to existing code. Building on these ideas, the motivation of this work is to develop an analogous set of automated testing mechanisms with associated benefits for large-scale network applications.

Designing appropriate mechanisms for automated testing of distributed applications presents several challenges. First, such mechanisms need to be fast and scalable to

T. Higashino (Ed.): OPODIS 2004, LNCS 3544, pp. 20–36, 2005.

enable large-scale testing and performance analysis. This, in turn, will enable programmers developing distributed applications to obtain rapid feedback on the implications of incremental design and implementation choices. Second, such mechanisms should be flexible to allow applications to be tested along multiple dimensions including correctness, robustness (e.g., in the presence of faults), and performance. Finally, these mechanisms should enable testing under a wide range of operating conditions in terms of network delays, bandwidth, and packet loss in addition to node and network faults and performance anomalies.

To address these challenges, we have designed DART, a framework for distributed automated regression testing. DART provides users with a programming environment and a set of primitives which can be used to construct a wide variety of distributed tests. Building on a set of scalable cluster tools, DART also provides a runtime that enables efficient execution of such distributed tests at scale. DART targets cluster-based network emulation environments such as Emulab [30] and ModelNet [26] to enable testing under a wide range of network operating conditions. Such environments typically provide two networks: an emulated network to emulate wide-area network delays, bandwidth, and packet loss and a separate, non-emulated control network (e.g., 100 Mbps or Gigabit Ethernet). It is the latter network that DART uses to efficiently and reliably control the execution of distributed tests.

We have implemented a prototype of DART that is targeted to the Emulab [30] network emulation environment. The system implements a core subset of our design which provides enough functionality that we have found it to be useful in practice. In particular, we have and continue to use DART to test and benchmark PIER [10], a distributed relational query processor that runs over a DHT. This paper describes the motivation, design, implementation, and performance analysis of DART and is organized as follows. In Sect. 2, we motivate the need for automated large-scale testing for distributed applications. In Sect. 3, we present DART's system architecture. In Sect. 4, we describe a prototype implementation of DART targeted for Emulab. In Sect. 5, we measure the performance of our DART implementation for core primitives, a baseline distributed application, and PIER. In Sect. 6, we present related work and in Sect. 7, we conclude the paper.

2   Large-Scale Distributed Testing

With single-node applications, unit testing frameworks provide two key components to the programmer: a set of commonly used mechanisms for writing tests and a runtime that automates test execution. Common mechanisms in unit testing frameworks include templates for setting up and tearing down unit tests, functions for verifying that actual outputs match expected outputs, and functions for communicating test outcomes back to the user. Using these mechanisms, programmers write tests that verify the functionality of specific parts of their application. Depending on the test, verification might include verifying that actual outputs match expected outputs, that bad / corner case inputs are handled correctly, that an application meets expected target performance metrics, and so forth.

A key benefit of these unit testing frameworks is that they *lower the barrier* to verifying correctness, robustness, and performance in an application's implementation. By providing a common set of mechanisms to write tests and a runtime to execute tests, unit testing frameworks make developing, maintaining, and applying unit tests less cumbersome and less error prone by factoring out a common set of machinery and by automating the test execution process. When the barrier to running tests is low, programmers employ them more often and subsequently reap the benefits of verifying that what worked before continues to work even after significant code changes.

While unit testing is pervasive in the world of single-node applications, there has been little work on providing an analogous set of mechanisms for large-scale distributed applications. We believe that providing such mechanisms will be a key enabler towards rapidly building distributed applications that are correct, robust, and deliver high performance under a wide range of operational environments. Providing such mechanisms requires factoring out and implementing commonly used mechanisms for distributed testing and implementing a runtime layer that executes these mechanisms in a fast and efficient manner. Ensuring that the testing infrastructure is itself fast and robust is key since rapid, correct feedback to the programmer usually implies that the programmer will use the system more often when developing.

3 Architecture

This section describes the DART system architecture. As mentioned, the goal of a DART system is to support automated testing of large-scale distributed applications. For a given distributed application, a user may wish to perform a variety of tests that test the application's correctness, robustness, and performance under a range of operating environments. DART supports automated execution of a suite of such distributed tests, where each test involves: (i) setting up (or reusing) a network of nodes to test the application on, (ii) setting up the test by distributing code and data to all nodes, (iii)

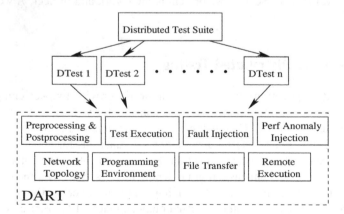

Fig. 1. DART architecture. Each distributed application has a suite of distributed tests. Each test is instantiated and executed using DART

executing and controlling the distributed test, and finally (iv) collecting the results of the test from all nodes and evaluating them. To support this automation, DART relies on a number of components (Fig. 1) which are described further in this section.

3.1   Network Topology

The first step in executing a DART test is setting up a network of nodes to test the application on. In emulated network environments, such networks are constructed using a set of cluster machines with emulated inter-node network delays, bandwidth, and packet loss. In Emulab [30], for example, users set up experiments consisting of network topologies which specify end hosts, routers, and network links with varying delay, bandwidth, and loss characteristics. Each experiment is then physically instantiated using a set of cluster nodes, a per-experiment VLAN, and wide-area network emulation using DummyNet [20]. ModelNet [26], another emulation environment, provides similar functionality. In addition, its adds per-hop delay, bandwidth, and loss emulation as well as distillation of large network topologies which enables trade-offs between scalability and emulation accuracy to be made (e.g., when using large network topologies [7]).

Given a target environment, a DART implementation provides two ways for a user to specify network topologies. First, DART provides a set of parameterizable network topologies (routers and end hosts), each of which maps down to a description in an underlying network topology language (e.g., Emulab ns-2 files). Second, DART supports raw network topologies as expressed in the target platform's network topology language. In DART, parameterizable topologies are provided mainly as a convenience. Such topologies might include topologies representative of real networks, topologies which might be easy or hard for different classes of applications, and/or topologies that reflect realistic end host heterogeneity in terms of last-hop bandwidth, latency, and host availability [22]. In many cases, we anticipate parameterizable topologies will provide a sufficiently broad range of environments to test and characterize the behavior of a distributed application before moving towards real wide-area network environments (e.g., PlanetLab [15], RON [2], etc.) where additional noise can make it difficult to ascertain whether observed problems are due to the application or due to the infrastructure and the real world.

3.2   Remote Execution and File Transfer

The second step in executing a DART test is setting up the test by distributing code and data to all nodes. Efficiently setting up and subsequently (Sect. 3.4) executing distributed tests in DART relies heavily on two key components of the DART runtime: multi-node remote execution and multi-node file transfer. In DART, there are a number of cases where multi-node remote execution is needed. For example, in testing a peer-to-peer application, multi-node remote execution might be used to start the application up on all nodes in the system and, some time later, to start a set of clients who issue requests. Before such a test can even run, code and data will also need to be distributed to all nodes, and this further requires having the ability to perform multi-node file transfers. Remote execution needs to be efficient because nodes might be controlled in various ways throughout a test (e.g., starting up servers, starting up clients, creating and controlling adversaries, etc.). File transfer needs to be efficient because code and data may be large and distributing such data to multiple nodes in a large scale test will be costly if it is read from, say, a centralized NFS file server. Consequently, a DART implementation needs to provide fast remote execution and file transfer primitives if the system aims to scale up to large system sizes.

3.3   Scripting and Programming Environment

To facilitate writing distributed tests, DART provides scripting to specify high-level details of test execution and a minimal programming environment which provides low-level details for writing actual distributed test code that runs on the system. Each test in DART has both an XML test script and test code and data. The test script specifies a unique test name, a unique topology name (to enable topology reuse), a network topology (e.g., an Emulab ns-2 file), test code and data, a test duration, a preprocessing script, a set of scripted commands, a set of scripted faults, a set of scripted performance anomalies, and a postprocessing script. Test scripts are interpreted by DART and associated actions are executed using the DART runtime. For example, a script for a distributed storage system might specify code and data for the storage system, start a set of storage servers on all nodes, start a client that writes and reads specific data, and verify consistency of the results in a postprocessing script.

DART provides a minimal programming environment to facilitate the writing of distributed test code. When executing DART tests, one node is designated as the master while all remaining nodes are designated as slaves. The DART runtime uses the master as the point of control for executing and coordinating the entire test. Similar to GLUnix [16], any scripted command executed on any node through DART is provided with the following environment variables:

- DART_TEST: unique test name.
- DART_NODES: space-delimited list of node IP addresses on the emulated network.
- DART_NUM_NODES: number of nodes in the DART test.
- DART_MY_VNN: node number from 0 to DART_NUM_NODES - 1.
- DART_MASTER: master's emulated IP address.
- DART_GEXEC_MASTER: master's control IP address.
- DART_MY_IP: this node's emulated IP address.
- DART_GPID: globally unique identifier for this particular test instance.
- DART_COMMON_DIR: directory for code and data common to all nodes.
- DART_MY_INPUT_DIR: input directory for per-node code and data.
- DART_MY_OUTPUT_DIR: output directory for per-node code and data (e.g., for writing test output, logfiles, etc).
- DART_ALL_OUTPUT_DIR: aggregated output directory of all DART_MY_OUTPUT _DIR directories. This directory is populated during a collect phase at the end of a test.

Using these environment variables facilitates writing distributed tests using DART. For example, consider testing the correctness of query evaluation in PIER. Such a test needs to instantiate a PIER process on every node and it needs to instantiate clients on a subset of nodes, each of which will issue queries to the system and save the results for verification. Starting PIER up on a node minimally requires at least one piece of information: the IP address of a landmark node to bootstrap all nodes into the DHT. Using the above environment, one obvious possibility for this is to simply use the DART master (DART_MASTER). Each PIER process will also want to save relevant output for potential debugging (e.g., stderr in case an exception occurs) and PIER clients will need to save query results for postprocessing to verify query evaluation correctness. Using the above environment, capturing program output would be done by simply writing files to DART_MY_OUTPUT_DIR. When the test completes, DART collects output from all DART_MY_OUTPUT_DIR directories on all nodes and places them in DART_ALL_OUTPUT_DIR on the master where the results of the test are then computed (e.g., checking actual output against known, correct output).

3.4   Preprocessing, Execution, and Postprocessing

The third and fourth steps of executing a DART test are executing and controlling the distributed test and, lastly, collecting the results of the test from all nodes and evaluating them. Each distributed test in DART goes through preprocessing, execution, and post-processing phases to compute the results of the test. Each of these phases is scripted by the user using the primitives provided by DART. Given a network of nodes (e.g., an experiment on Emulab) and code and data that has been distributed to those nodes, preprocessing is the first stage and entails executing whatever commands that are necessary before actually running the test. For example, if software packages (e.g., RPMs or tarfiles) were distributed as part of the code and data distribution phase, then preprocessing would be the place where one-time installations of this software would take place. We separate preprocessing from the actual execution of the test since, for a given application, we expect it will be frequently be the case that an application performs the same preprocessing in each of a series of tests (e.g., installing the same set of RPMs, such as the Java JDK in PIER's case).

Once preprocessing is complete, DART then proceeds to the execution phase where execution and control of the distributed test is performed to completion. This phase primarily entails scheduling and executing user-specified, scripted commands on specific subsets of nodes at specific points in time (e.g., starting a set of servers up, starting a set of clients, etc.). Further, depending on the test, it might also involve injecting faults and performance anomalies in certain parts of the system at certain points in time. A churn test for a peer-to-peer application, for example, might involve first starting the application on all nodes in the system, letting the system stabilize for several minutes, then injecting a sequence of node join (scheduled command) and leave (scheduled process or node fault) events into the system and measuring the system's behavior over time (e.g., the success or failure of routing requests in the case of structured peer-to-peer overlays).

Finally, once the distributed test has finished executing, a postprocessing stage is performed to collect all the output from all the nodes and to apply a user-specified post-processing test to process the test's output and verify its goodness. The definition of goodness will be specific to the application and the type of test being performed. For example, a correctness test might verify that actual replies to client requests match the correct, expected values (which would be computed offline a priori). A robustness test might verify that after killing some subset of nodes that the system continues to function as expected (e.g., suppose it was designed to be k-fault tolerant). Finally, a performance test might compute the overall performance numbers from all nodes and verify that these performance numbers lie within some expected bounds. Each test produces output, which may optionally be sent back to the user's machine (e.g., performance numbers) and returns a 1 or a 0 depending on whether the test succeeded or failed (as defined by the user).

3.5   Fault Injection

To understand how a distributed application behaves in the presence of node and network faults, DART also provides fault injection primitives which may be specified by the programmer when scripting a distributed test. Which primitives are supported in a particular implementation will depend on the capabilities of the underlying platform. In the best case, node, process, and network failures are all supported and can be scripted to execute at specific times on specific parts of the system (e.g., a specific subset of nodes):

- **Node failures:** specifies hard failures of specific subsets of nodes over specific periods in time. In Emulab, such failures can be scripted using underlying support from Emulab's event system.
- **Process failures:** specifies the hard failure of specific processes (e.g., by name, by uid, etc.) on a given node. In contrast to node failures, the node continues to operate properly.
- **Network failures:** specifies the failure of specific parts of the network at specific points in time. As with node failures, network failures can also be scripted through support from Emulab's event system (e.g., to turn a network link off at a specific time).

3.6   Performance Anomaly Injection

In addition to hard node and network faults, another important class of failures of interest are performance failures [3]. For example, consider the case where a 1.5 Mbps network link does not fail completely but its effective bandwidth drops to 0.001 Mbps. While technically the link has not failed in the sense that it fails to route packets, the performance impact of such a performance degradation is likely to have significant implications for application performance. Understanding how applications behave in the presence of such performance faults is an important step towards building robust distributed applications. Towards this end, DART provides a set of primitives to introduce performance anomalies into the system. Similar to hard failures, the types of scripted performance anomalies supported by DART include:

- **Node and process performance anomalies:** decreased or varying CPU, memory, network, and I/O performance. Such anomalies might be introduced by using sufficient powerful schedulers [28, 9, 6, 23] in combination with support from the underlying emulation environment.

– **Link performance anomalies:** increased delay, decreased bandwidth, and increased packet loss in specific parts in the network. Such anomalies might be introduced using support provided by the underlying target platform (e.g., using Emulab's event system to dynamically change link delays, bandwidth, and packet loss).

4 Implementation

We have implemented a DART prototype targeted to the Emulab network emulation environment. Our prototype is implemented using a combination of C and Python and supports a subset of the architecture described in Sect. 3. Parameterizable network topologies, efficient multi-node remote execution and file transfer, a scripting and programming environment, and preprocessing, execution, and postprocessing of arbitrary scripted commands at specific times on subsets of nodes are all supported. Our prototype is functional, efficient, and is currently being used on a routine basis for testing, debugging, and benchmarking PIER.

4.1 GEXEC and PCP

As mentioned, multi-node remote execution and file transfer are key primitives that are used heavily throughout DART and hence need to be fast and efficient. To address this need, we have designed and implemented GEXEC, a fast multi-node remote execution system, and PCP, a fast, multi-node file transfer utility. Both systems rely on a hierarchical design based on a k-ary tree of TCP sockets over a specific set of nodes (e.g, nodes specified using the GEXEC_SVRS environment variable for GEXEC). Such trees are built on every invocation of either the gexec or pcp command using a $O(log_k(n))$ tree building step which involves routing tree create messages down to leaf nodes and routing tree create acknowledgments back to the root. We use a tree-based approach primarily for parallelism and to utilize aggregate resources across all nodes.

GEXEC provides multi-node remote execution of arbitrary commands by routing commands down the tree to all nodes. For all commands, GEXEC supports transparent forwarding of Unix signals, stdin, stdout, and stderr to allow control of remote processes and also obtain remote output. Control and data are all transferred over the tree, down in the case of signals and stdin and up in case of stdout and stderr. Two remote execution models are supported: default and detached. In default mode, the failure model is that if any node fails during the execution, GEXEC aborts on all nodes. In contrast, in detached mode, GEXEC simply builds the tree, starts the command on all nodes, and exits. Both modes are used in DART (e.g., default mode for executing bootstrapping commands, detached mode for running the application being tested, which might crash).

PCP provides fast multi-node file transfer by routing files down the tree in an incremental fashion in 32 KB chunks. Starting with the root, chunks are sent to each node's children. As each chunk is received, each node writes the chunk to local disk, then forwards the chunk off to each of its children. Because files are transferred using a k-ary tree and transferred in chunks (which incur small store-and-forward delays as compared to sending the entire file at once), PCP provides both parallelism and pipelined execution that leads to very high aggregate bandwidth usage. Generally, the optimal choices for tree fanout and message size will depend on node network bandwidth, the network's configuration, and disk write bandwidth. As we show in the next section, using a fanout of 1 and 32 KB messages delivers high performance on Emulab and thereby makes multi-node file transfer a highly efficient primitive in our DART prototype.

4.2   Master and Slaves

Our DART prototype targets the Emulab network emulation environment and uses GEXEC and PCP as the basis for fast distributed test execution (Fig. 2). In our implementation, tests are remotely instantiated and controlled using two machines: users.emulab.net and a master node arbitrarily chosen from the set of nodes in the test's network topology. We use users.emulab.net to manage network topologies for DART (e.g., creating and destroying experiments). Each node in an Emulab experiment is assigned one or more emulated IP addresses and one control IP address. We use users.emulab.net to obtain information about the network configuration of each Emulab experiment. This information is subsequently used to control distributed test execution by running GEXEC and PCP over the fast, control network.

Each Emulab experiment created using DART is bootstrapped with a few common features that are required for DART to operate properly. First, each node is bootstrapped with a small set of core software including GEXEC, PCP, and authd, an authentication service used by both GEXEC and PCP. Second, each node is configured to boot the RedHat 7.3 Linux distribution which uses the Linux 2.4.18 kernel. The common software set is required since this software forms of the basis of the DART runtime. The use of Linux on the nodes is needed primarily because the versions of GEXEC and PCP currently used in DART do not run on FreeBSD, the other node operating system available on Emulab.

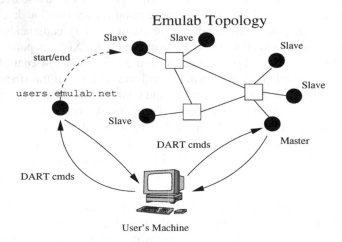

Fig. 2. DART implementation on Emulab

Once an Emulab topology is instantiated, all subsequent control is done through the master which essentially serves as a proxy for executing distributed tests in DART. Among the master's tasks are: distributing code and data to all nodes, providing the programming environment for distributed tests, and performing preprocessing, execution, and postprocessing of tests across all nodes. In our current implementation, we use ssh to securely execute commands on the master and use GEXEC to execute commands and PCP to transfer code and data to other nodes in the system. For example, to reset an experiment such that it can be reused, we use ssh to send a reset command to the master and use GEXEC, invoked from the master, to quickly reset all nodes in the network by remotely removing old files and killing old processes from the previous test.

5   Evaluation

In this section, we analyze the performance of our DART implementation. We begin by measuring the performance of two key primitives: multi-node remote execution and multi-node file transfer. As described in Sect. 4, these primitives are implemented by GEXEC and PCP, respectively, and are used extensively in our DART prototype. Next, we analyze the overall performance of performing DART tests for both a baseline distributed application and PIER, a distributed relational query processor. All experiments were performed on Emulab. The first set of experiments were performed on 64 Pentium III nodes: 18 of which were 600 MHz nodes with 256 MB of memory, 46 of which were 850 MHz nodes with 512 MB of memory. The second set of experiments were performed on 32 Pentium III nodes: 10 of which were 600 MHz nodes and 22 of which were of the 850 MHz variety. All nodes in both cases ran the Linux 2.4.18 kernel and were connected via 100 Mbps Ethernet.

5.1   Performance of DART Primitives

The first set of measurements characterizes the performance of multi-node remote execution and multi-node file transfer using GEXEC and PCP. Figure 3 depicts remote execution performance on multiple nodes using GEXEC. Each curve corresponds to GEXEC's performance using a different tree fanout. Recall that GEXEC performs multi-node remote execution by first building a k-ary tree where k is the fanout at each non-leaf node and using this tree to control remote execution. Each point on each curve represents the remote execution time (milliseconds) to execute a simple command (/bin/date) on n nodes ($n = 1, 2, 4, \ldots, 64$). Each point on each curve is the average of 30 different runs on a subset of Emulab nodes. Overall, we observe that remote execution using GEXEC is fast (typically about 100 ms) and that remote execution times do not appreciate much as we scale the system size up. This, in turn, implies fast and efficient control of distributed tests in DART using GEXEC.

Next, we perform a similar experiment to measure the performance of multi-node file transfer using PCP. Similar to GEXEC, PCP also builds a k-ary tree and uses this tree to perform parallelized, pipelined file transfer. Figure 4 shows the aggregate bandwidth delivered when distributing a 34.7 MB file (the Java 1.4.2_03 JDK RPM) to n nodes ($n = 1, 2, 4, \ldots, 64$) using PCP and using 32 KB messages. Each curve cor-

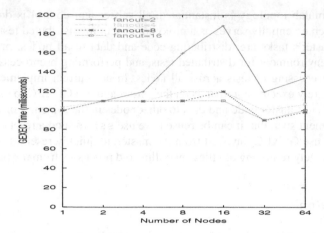

Fig. 3. GEXEC performance on Emulab. Each curve corresponds to a different tree fanout, while each point represents the remote execution time (milliseconds) to execute a simple command (/bin/date) on n nodes ($n = 1, 2, 4, \ldots, 64$)

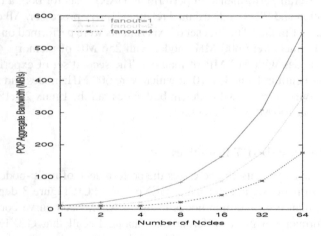

Fig. 4. PCP performance on Emulab. Each curve corresponds to a different tree fanout, while each point represents the aggregate bandwidth delivered when distributing a 34.7 MB file (the Java 1.4.2_03 JDK RPM) to n nodes ($n = 1, 2, 4, \ldots, 64$) using PCP

responds to a different tree fanout and each point on each curve is the average of 20 different runs. Using a tree fanout of 1 (i.e., a chain), we observe that PCP is able to deliver an average of 548 MB/s of aggregate bandwidth when distributing a 34.7 MB file to 64 nodes. Larger tree fanouts do not help in the case of Emulab since each node is connected by 100 Mbps Ethernet (i.e., 12.5 MB/s of peak bandwidth) and each node can write to disk at least that fast. Hence, our DART prototype uses PCP's default fanout of 1 which, as shown, delivers high performance and enables data to be moved around efficiently when conducting large-scale DART tests.

5.2   Overall DART Performance

The second set of measurements quantify the overall performance of performing DART tests for both a baseline distributed application and a real distributed application (PIER). The baseline distributed application is the null distributed application. It's an application that runs on 32 nodes but does not perform any computation. The test returns immediately and thus the times associated with this test are, in the current implementation, a lower bound on the total time to execute a distributed test in DART. PIER, as mentioned, is a distributed relational query processor that runs over a DHT. We use DART to routinely perform a number of tests on PIER. In this instance, we present performance results when testing the correctness of a distributed selection query on 32 nodes using different query plans (e.g., different packet sizes). (The test queries static per-node data and hence we know what the correct query result ought to be.) The time to perform this particular test once the test has been set up on all nodes is 700 seconds. The goal of these measurements is to show that the overhead of performing DART tests is small relative to distributed test times, which we anticipate will involve running a test for at least several minutes (e.g., as in the PIER selection query test) in most cases.

Each test involves four potential components. First, there is the time to set up the network topology for the test (*esetup*). This involves the time to securely transfer an Emulab network topology file to users.emulab.net and to instantiate the Emulab experiment. Second, there is the time to set up a particular distributed test (*dsetup*). The main cost here is transferring code and data to the master node in the Emulab experiment and distributing code and data to the slaves. Third, there is the time to perform preprocessing, execute and control the distributed test, collect the results on the master, and perform postprocessing (*drun*). Fourth, there is the cost of reseting the test environment on all nodes (*dreset*)). This involves clearing out results from the previous test and killing all processes associated with the previous test. Note that a test may reuse a network topology from a previous experiment if that test uses the same topology (e.g., the same 32-node topology in our measurements). When running a test for the first time on a network topology, no *dreset* cost is incurred since the system is clean, whereas when reusing a topology for a different test, the *dreset* cost must be paid.

Table 1 shows the overall times (seconds) to run distributed tests on 32 Emulab nodes using DART for a baseline null application and a 700 second correctness test in PIER for a distributed selection query. For both the baseline and for PIER, we present

Table 1. Breakdown of overall times (seconds) to run distributed tests on 32 Emulab nodes using DART for a baseline null application and a 700 second correctness test in PIER for a distributed selection query

	Base	Base reuse	PIER	PIER reuse
esetup	202.3	–	206.3	–
dsetup	16.2	16.0	52.6	46.2
drun	28.8	29.2	758.7	735.7
dreset	–	4.2	–	4.0
Total	247.3	49.4	1017.6	785.9

results when a new Emulab experiment is instantiated and when an existing Emulab experiment is reused (the reuse columns), the latter case requiring an additional reset component to prepare for a new test.

We observe the largest baseline cost to be *esetup*, the time to instantiate a new 32-node Emulab experiment. Measurements on Emulab revealed this time to be, on average, 204.3 seconds which is consistent with previous measurements [30]. The relatively high cost of creating a new Emulab experiment suggests reusing existing Emulab experiments when conducting tests on the same network topology. As mentioned, reusing a topology requires an additional phase to clear old files and kill old processes. Our measurements indicate that these costs are, on average, 4.1 seconds which is relatively low. Still, this number is relatively high compared to GEXEC remote execution times. (We use GEXEC to clear old files and kill old processes from the master.) This is largely due to our use of a new ssh connection each time we communicate with either users.emulab.net or the master. This overhead is also a significant component in the other baseline costs as well, namely *dsetup* and drun which on average were 16.1 seconds and 29.0 seconds respectively. When reusing the network topology, the total baseline cost to execute a null distributed test on 32 nodes was 49.4 seconds.

Turning to PIER, the key numbers of interest are the *dsetup* and *drun* times. We measured the average *dsetup* time for PIER to be 49.4 seconds, while for the baseline, the average *dsetup* cost was 16.1 seconds. The main difference between the two is the additional cost associated with transferring code and data to the master and from the master to all slaves. In the PIER case, code and data transferred from the user's desktop to the master was 3.32 MB in size (four different directories), while code and data transferred from Emulab's NFS fileserver to the master totaled 37.0 MB, the size of the Java 1.4.2_03 JDK and the static data being queried. As shown in Fig. 4, transferring data from the master to all slaves using PCP is efficient. However, as with the baseline, liberal use of new ssh connections again incur significant overhead. In the current implementation, each directory being transferred causes a new ssh connection to be created to the master, each of which usually takes approximately 2-3 seconds. We intend to optimize this by establishing a single secure connection with the master and reusing it in the future. This should reduce the gap between the baseline and PIER by approximately 12-18 seconds.

Despite the overhead of multiple ssh connections to the master, we see that the overhead of using DART to perform distributed tests of PIER is still quite reasonable relative to the typical time to perform a meaningful test. In this case, the selection query correctness test needs to run for 700 seconds. This includes a 120 second delay to allow the DHT to stabilize and for PIER to build up a multicast tree to perform query dissemination to all nodes. It also includes the time to perform a selection query in four different ways, in each case allowing the query to run for 120 seconds and leaving 10 seconds in between each query to avoid query interference. Finally, a minute is alloted before finally shutting down the test, which leads to a test time of 700 seconds. Relative to the total time, the DART overhead in this case is 11.3% (i.e., 85.9 seconds out of 785.9 seconds) which we believe is quite reasonable given the ssh performance improvements we intend to make and the fact that distributed testing using DART is entirely automated and does not require any human intervention.

6   Related Work

There have been relatively few efforts aimed at building frameworks for large-scale testing of distributed applications. In this relatively small space, the closest related project is TestZilla [27]. Like DART, TestZilla provides a framework for testing distributed applications and leverages a set of scalable cluster-based tools in its implementation. In TestZilla, distributed tests are executed through a centralized coordinator and the system provides mechanisms for network topology specification (in a non-emulated cluster setting), file system and process operations, barrier synchronization, and logging and collection of output files. Architecturally, DART and TestZilla share many of the same characteristics although both aim to provide slightly differing feature sets. Unlike DART, which focuses on wide-area distributed applications in an emulated network environment, TestZilla is focused primarily on cluster-based applications in a Windows environment. As a consequence of this, TestZilla relies heavily on Windows-specific features in its implementation. In terms of scalability, both systems rely on scalable cluster-based tools for test control. Unfortunately, given that no published numbers on TestZilla's performance were available, a direct performance comparison could not be made.

ACME [13] provides a framework for automatically applying workloads, injecting perturbations, and measuring the performance and robustness of distributed services based on user specifications written in XML. It targets both emulated network environments such as Emulab and ModelNet as well as real wide-area testbeds such as PlanetLab. In ACME, control, measurement, and injection of perturbations is done through per-node sensors and actuators which, in turn, are controlled through a distributed query processor. Like DART and TestZilla, control in an ACME experiment is done using a centralized experiment control node. Using the query processor, measurements are taken by issuing queries which read desired sensors on multiple nodes in the system. Similarly, actions (e.g., rebooting a node, modifying a link's bandwidth) are invoked by issuing queries that invoke appropriate actuators. Early experience using ACME to evaluate the robustness of three key-based routing routing layers (Chord, Tapestry, and FreePastry) showed that ACME was able to uncover a number of interesting properties and bugs under various workloads and perturbations. Compared to DART, ACME shares many of the same goals. Architecturally, however, ACME differs quite a bit owing to its use of a distributed query processor and the sensor/actuator abstraction as the basis of its implementation.

7   Conclusion

We have developed DART, a framework for distributed automated regression testing of large-scale network applications. We presented the DART system architecture and described the mechanisms DART provides, including scripted execution of multi-node commands, fault and performance anomaly injection, and the runtime layer that supports these mechanisms. We have implemented a DART prototype that implements a useful subset of the architecture and are using this prototype in ongoing testing and benchmarking of PIER, a distributed relational query processor. Our prototype is built on fast and efficient multi-node remote execution and file transfer primitives and incurs reasonable overheads (e.g., 11.3% overhead for a PIER selection query correctness test) for typical distributed tests of interest. Future work on DART includes implementation of additional test mechanisms (e.g., fault injection using Emulab's event system), additional performance optimizations, and further work on gaining experience using DART to test PIER and other wide-area distributed applications. We believe that distributed testing frameworks will be a key enabler towards rapidly building distributed applications that are fast, robust, and deliver high performance across the wide-area.

Acknowledgements

We would like to thank the Emulab team for providing access to the Utah Emulab cluster and for being highly responsive to numerous questions and various feature requests.

References

1. ANDERSEN, D., BALAKRISHNAN, H., KAASHOEK, F., AND MORRIS, R. Resilient Overlay Networks. In *Proceedings of the 18th ACM Symposium on Operating Systems Principles* (October 2001).
2. ANDERSEN, D. G., BALAKRISHNAN, H., KAASHOEK, M. F., AND MORRIS, R. Experience with an Evolving Overlay Network Testbed. *ACM Computer Communications Review 33*, 3 (2003), 13–19.
3. ARPACI-DUSSEAU, R. H. *Performance Availability for Networks of Workstations*. PhD thesis, University of California, Berkeley, 1999.
4. BECK, K. *Extreme Programming Explained: Embrace Change*. Addison-Wesley Professional, October 1999.
5. DABEK, F., KAASHOEK, M. F., KARGER, D., MORRIS, R., AND STOICA, I. Wide-area cooperative storage with CFS. In *Proceedings of the 18th ACM Symposium on Operating Systems Principles* (October 2001).
6. DEMERS, A., KESHAV, S., AND SHENKER, S. Anaylsis and Simulation of a Fair Queueing Algorithm. In *Proceedings of the 35th IEEE Computer Society International Conference (COMPCON)* (March 1990), pp. 380–386.
7. ELLEN W. ZEGURA, K. C., AND BHATTACHARJEE, S. How to Model an Internetwork. In *Proceedings of IEEE Infocom '96* (March 1996).
8. FREEDMAN, M., FREUDENTHAL, E., AND MAZIÈRES, D. Democratizing Content Publication with Coral. In *Proceedings of the 1st Symposium on Networked Systems Design and Implementation* (March 2004).
9. HAND, S. Self-Paging in the Nemesis Operating System. In *Proceedings of the 3rd USENIX Symposium on Operating Systems Design and Implementation* (February 1999).
10. HUEBSCH, R., HELLERSTEIN, J. M., LANHAM, N., LOO, B. T., SHENKER, S., AND STOICA, I. Querying the Internet with PIER. In *Proceedings of the 29th International Conference on Very Large Data Bases* (September 2003).
11. KUBIATOWICZ, J., BINDEL, D., CHEN, Y., CZERWINSKI, S., EATON, P., GEELS, D., GUMMADI, R., RHEA, S., WEATHERSPOON, H., WEIMER, W., WELLS, C., AND ZHAO, B. OceanStore: An Architecture for Global-Scale Persistent Storage. In *Proceedings of the Ninth international Conference on Architectural Support for Programming Languages and Operating Systems* (November 2002).

12. MUTHITACHAROEN, A., MORRIS, R., GIL, T., AND CHEN, B. Ivy: A Read/Write Peer-to-peer File System. In *Proceedings of the 5th USENIX Symposium on Operating Systems Design and Implementation* (December 2002).

13. OPPENHEIMER, D., VATKOVSKIY, V., AND PATTERSON, D. A. Towards a Framework for Automated Robustness Evaluation of Distributed Services. In *Proceedings of the 2nd Bertinoro Workshop on Future Directions in Distributed Computing (FuDiCo II): Survivability: Obstacles and Solutions* (June 2004).

14. PAI, V. S., WANG, L., PARK, K., PANG, R., AND PETERSON, L. The Dark Side of the Web: An Open Proxy's View. In *Proceedings of the 2nd Workshop on Hot Topics in Networks* (November 2003).

15. PETERSON, L., CULLER, D., ANDERSON, T., AND ROSCOE, T. A Blueprint for Introducing Disruptive Technology into the Internet. In *Proceedings of HotNets-I* (October 2002).

16. PETROU, D., RODRIGUES, S. H., VAHDAT, A., AND ANDERSON, T. E. GLUnix: A Global Layer Unix for a Network of Workstations. *Software - Practice and Experience 28* (1998), 929–961.

17. RAMASUBRAMANIAN, V., AND SIRER, E. G. The Design and Implementation of a Next Generation Name Service for the Internet. In *Proceedings of the ACM SIGCOMM '04 Conference on Communications Architectures and Protocols* (August 2004).

18. RATNASAMY, S., FRANCIS, P., HANDLEY, M., KARP, R., AND SHENKER, S. A Scalable Content-Addressable Network. In *Proceedings of the ACM SIGCOMM '01 Conference on Communications Architectures and Protocols* (August 2001).

19. RHEA, S., GEELS, D., ROSCOE, T., AND KUBIATOWICZ, J. Handling Churn in a DHT. In *Proceedings of the USENIX 2004 Annual Technical Conference* (June 2004).

20. RIZZO, L. Dummynet and Forward Error Correction. In *Proceedings of the USENIX 1998 Annual Technical Conference (FREENIX Track)* (June 1998).

21. ROWSTRON, A., AND DRUSCHEL, P. Pastry: Scalable, Distributed Object Location and Routing for Large-scale Peer-to-peer Systems. In *Proceedings of the 18th IFIP/ACM International Conference on Distributed Systems Platforms* (November 2001).

22. SAROIU, S., GUMMADI, K. P., AND GRIBBLE, S. D. Measuring and Analyzing the Characteristics of Napster and Gnutella Hosts. *Multimedia Systems 9* (2003), 170–184.

23. SHENOY, P., AND VIN, H. M. Cello: A Disk Scheduling Framework for Next Generation Operating Systems. In *Proceedings of the 1998 ACM SIGMETRICS Conference* (June 1998), pp. 44–55.

24. STOICA, I., MORRIS, R., KARGER, D., KAASHOEK, M. F., AND BALAKRISHNAN, H. Chord: A scalable peer-to-peer lookup service for internet applications. In *Proceedings of the ACM SIGCOMM '01 Conference on Communications Architectures and Protocols* (September 2001).

25. SUBRAMANIAN, L., STOICA, I., BALAKRISHNAN, H., AND KATZ, R. OverQoS: An Overlay Based Architecture for Enhancing Internet QoS. In *Proceedings of the 1st Symposium on Networked Systems Design and Implementation* (March 2004).

26. VAHDAT, A., YOCUM, K., WALSH, K., MAHADEVAN, P., KOSTIC, D., CHASE, J., AND BECKER, D. Scalability and Accuracy in a Large-Scale Network Emulator. In *Proceedings of the 5th USENIX Symposium on Operating Systems Design and Implementation* (December 2002).

27. VOGELS, W. TestZilla: a Framework for the Testing of Large-Scale Distributed Systems. Available from: http://www.cs.cornell.edu/vogels/TestZilla/default.htm.

28. WALDSPURGER, C. A., AND WEIHL, W. E. Lottery Scheduling: Flexible Proportional-Share Resource Management. In *Proceedings of the 1st USENIX Symposium on Operating Systems Design and Implementation* (1994), pp. 1–11.

29. WAWRZONIAK, M., PETERSON, L., AND ROSCOE, T. Sophia: An Information Plane for Networked Systems. In *Proceedings of the 2nd Workshop on Hot Topics in Networks* (November 2003).

30. WHITE, B., LEPREAU, J., STOLLER, L., RICCI, R., GURUPRASAD, S., NEWBOLD, M., HIBLER, M., BARB, C., AND JOGLEKAR, A. An Integrated Experimental Environment for Distributed Systems and Networks. In *Proceedings of the 5th USENIX Symposium on Operating Systems Design and Implementation* (December 2002).

31. ZHAO, B. Y., KUBIATOWICZ, J. D., AND JOSEPH, A. D. Tapestry: An Infrastructure for Fault-tolerant Wide-area Location and Routing. Tech. Rep. CSD-01-1141, University of California, Berkeley, Computer Science Division, 2001.

Testing Mobile and Distributed Systems: Method and Experimentation

Patrice Laurençot and Sébastien Salva

LIMOS, Université de Clermont-Ferrand,
Campus des Cézeaux, BP 10125 Aubière, France
laurenco@isima.fr, sebastien.salva@iut.u-clermont1.fr

Abstract. Mobile and distributed systems are generally composed of components which interact together with input/output events by using a least a mobile network (GSM, wireless lan), and eventually others heterogeneous ones. Such systems are generally complex so they need to be tested in order to check their reliability. However, no distributed testing tool is proposed. In this paper, we propose a complete method to test such systems and an experimentation which aims to test a WAP application. From a formal specification, the testing method generates test cases and deploys them on a test architecture. This one is composed of several testers which must be synchronized for testing. For the experimentation, we have implemented: a distributed test architecture composed of several testers, a WAP architecture and a WAP application. The experimentation results show that the testing method can be used in practice.

1   Introduction

Since recent years, major progresses have been completed in the mobile network area, particularly concerning Internet and mobile networks. Nowadays, it is possible to access to various services with a mobile phone and to send, receive or search information located on different servers. All these functionalities are obtained with the development of new protocols and applications for mobile telecommunications. Such systems are becoming more and more complex to be implemented and the risk of malfunctioning is more and more important on account of the distributed algorithms used and of the deployment of components on several heterogeneous networks. Validation technics, inherited from the protocol engineering area, are solutions to ensure that a final system has no error by testing it. Different categories of tests can be found in literature. These ones are grouped into two categories:

- the verification technics, which handle a specification and try to prove its correctness (in this case the system can be seen as a white box),
- the testing technics [3, 6, 8, 18], which check various aspects: performance testing, robustness testing, and conformance testing which will be dealed with in this paper. A formal specification is generally needed as well to extract or automatically generate a set of scenario sequences (called *'test*

T. Higashino (Ed.): OPODIS 2004, LNCS 3544, pp. 37–51, 2005.
© Springer-Verlag Berlin Heidelberg 2005

cases'). By executing these test cases on the implementation under test with
a tester, these methods can detect incorrectness and compare the specification behavior to the implementation one. Such methods have been widely
developed in the communication protocol area.

In conformance testing, implementations are generally seen as "black boxes",
where internal structures are unknown and which are accessible only through one
or several interfaces. This is the case for a lot of protocols (for example, ABR
for ATM, WAP,...). Therefore, test cases are executed on the implementation by
using a test architecture which can access to the implementation interfaces. With
systems composed of several mobile components, the classical test architecture
cannot be used [17] since these interoperable components must be tested in the
same time with a distributed architecture of testers. Some test architectures of
distributed systems have been proposed [4, 19, 20, 14] but none of them have
been experimented and no tool is proposed.

This paper presents a practical testing method of mobile systems composed of
components distributed on heterogeneous networks. This method has been completely implemented and used to test a WAP (Wireless Application Protocol) application. The main goal of this paper is to detail the method implementation and
this experimentation. In a first part, we present two test architectures composed
of several testers : the first one is composed of two networks, one for the mobile
components and one dedicated to the testers for testing. With specific systems,
it may be difficult to deploy it, so we describe a second architecture, composed
of an unique mobile network on which are connected the testers and the mobile
components together. In a second part, we show how we generate, from a formal
specification, test cases which check only functional properties of the specification
and which can be used with the previous test architectures. The main problem
is to split a test case into several ones which can be deployed on a distributed
test architecture. Then, we use the second one, which has been implemented in
our laboratory, to test a WAP (Wireless Application Protocol [9]) application.
This well-known protocol allows to access to Internet sites and data bases for
embedded systems like PDA (Personal Digital Equipment) or mobile phone.
We detail the components used to test the WAP protocol (servers, PDA), their
accessible interfaces and the tools developed to perform the experimentation.

The paper is structured as follows. Section 2 provides an overview of the
testing process. Section 3 introduces the different test architectures which can
be used for testing mobile and distributed applications. Section 4 presents the
method developed to generate test cases which can be executed with distributed
test architectures. The implementation of the second test architecture and the
experimentation on a WAP application are described in Section 5. Finally, we
conclude in Section 6.

2   Protocol Conformance Testing

Testing consists in checking whether the implementation is consistent with the
specification by stimulating the implementation and observing its behavior.

Sequences of events, called test cases, are constructed by hands or generated automatically by testing methods from formal specifications, modelled by automata, petri nets or by specific languages such as LOTOS or LDS. Usually, test cases are composed of two kinds of interactions:

- the **outputs**, which model the observation and the sending of a message from the system
- the **inputs**, which model the sending of a message to the system.

In literature, testing methods can be gathered together in two categories:

a) **the exhaustive testing methods**, which involve generation of test cases on the complete specification, execution of the test cases on the implementation and analysis of the test results. To describe the confidence degree between the specification and the implementation, a conformance relation is first defined, then test cases are given or generated from the specification to check if the relation is satisfied or not. Two categories of exhaustive methods can be found :
   - Canonical tester based methods: in this approach, the conformance relations, called implementation relation, are defined with some algebraic properties. Some conformance relations can be found in [16]. An automaton called *tester* is computed on the global specification so that it can detect any violation of the implementation relation.
   - FSM based approaches: historically, finite state machine (FSM) have been widely used in the networks and telecommunications area to specify communicating softwares such as telecommunication protocols. An FSM transition is fired, in a deterministic way, when an input event is received from the environment. The execution of the transition may produce a possible output event toward the environment. The major work on test generation from this model consists of:
     - the specification of a system by an FSM SPEC
     - the assumption that the implementation of the system can also be described as an FSM IMP
     - the identification of the structure of SPEC on the structure of the IMP.
b) **the non exhaustive testing methods**, which test local parts of implementations [2, 5, 10]. This concept, formalized in [12], aims to check if a set of properties, called a test purpose, is satisfied on an implementation during the testing process. Checking the satisfaction of test purposes on implementation describes a conformance relation. Test purpose based approaches are oriented methods: designers or experts who have a good knowledge of the system, describe the requirements to test, which are generally the important or critical parts of the system. Sometimes protocol standards give guidelines for test selection based on test criteria. In [5], the authors propose an automatic test purpose construction. Then, either test cases are constructed manually or are generated on these requirements and on specification parts, reducing the specification exploration in comparison with exhaustive methods (reducing in the same time the test costs).

Afterwards, test cases are executed on the implementation by mean of a test architecture. This one describes the configuration in which the implementation will be experimented which includes at least the interfaces of the implementation (called PCO, *point of control and observation*) and the tester which applies the test cases on the implementation. Test architectures can be found in [12, 17] for untimed system testing. The execution of such test cases leads the tester to emit requests to the implementation (inputs) and then to wait for answers (outputs). Depending on the observed results, the tester can deduce a final verdict for the test: *pass* which means that the implementation conforms the specification, *inconclusive* which means that we cannot conclude or *fail*.

3   Test Architectures of Distributed Systems

Test architectures, suggested by the standard[12], cannot be used since different entities cooperate in the network to provide a desired service. To test such systems, we need to observe and to analyze the transit of input and output events, received or transmitted from each component. So it's necessary to introduce different Points of Control and Observation (PCO), generally at least one for each component. These PCO are designed to access to the component interface: that is they can send events to the component (by the point of control) and observe the results (by the point of observation).

Several test architectures of distributed systems have been proposed [4, 19, 20, 14]: these ones can be centralized systems where a single tester is connected to some PCO and sends or receives events from all the component interfaces. An example of centralized architecture is given in Figure 1. Such architectures are generally easier to implement since only one tester is needed. However, the PCO involves a high traffic of data which requires a specific network and which may overload the system.

So, a second category of distributed test architectures has been proposed. These ones are composed of local testers, each of them checks one component and communicates with the others ones. These communications are necessary to synchronize the testers between them and to synchronize the execution of the system components.

The local testers also produce and send local verdicts which must be analyzed by a coordinator tester to obtain a final one. To communicate, these testers can be connected to:

- a dedicated network. In this way, each local verdict can be got back as soon as this one is produced, without interfering with the system. If one local verdict is FAIL, the coordinator tester can directly stop the test after receiving it.
- the network of the system. Local verdicts cannot be sent to the coordinator tester once they are created since the network may be used by the system components. Consequently, the local verdicts are sent to the coordinator tester once the test is terminated.

These two solutions are detailed below.

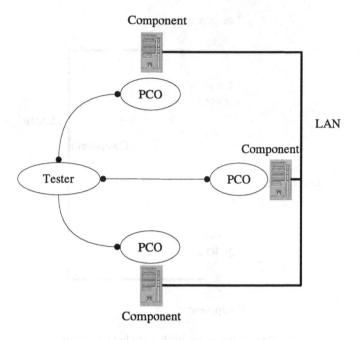

Fig. 1. A centralized test architecture

3.1   Test Architecture with a Dedicated Network

Such test architectures use a dedicated network connecting each tester with. These architectures require additional equipments, since each entity has at least two connections: one with the other components for the regular traffic, and the other connection used for the data exchanged for testing. The architecture is depicted in Figure 2.

The main advantage of this architecture is the complete independence between the regular traffic and the data exchanged between the testers. As there is no interference, we are sure that the verdict which is obtained reflects the reality. Even more, if an error occurs, the PCO which detects it, can alert the coordinator tester so the test can be stopped immediately with a FAIL verdict. However, mobile applications cannot be always tested with such architectures: a mobile terminal must have access to the two different networks simultaneously. In practice, this is not always possible or difficult to set up. For example, a mobile phone has generally only one network interface (GSM interface). A wireless equipment should have two interfaces, each one linked to a different access point. As the mobile terminal can move, we should check that the two cards stay on different networks. Therefore, this architecture is hard to implement (because of hardware constraint), but the verdict of the test can be given rapidly.

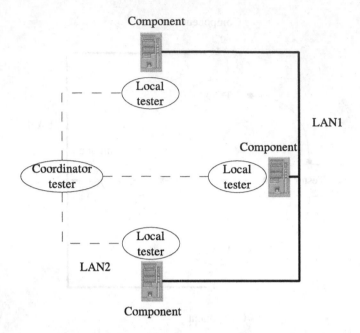

Fig. 2. Test architecture with a dedicated network

3.2   Test Architecture Using the System Network

In this case, the local testers and the coordinator one are connected directly on the system networks, as the system components. So, the regular data of the system and the specific data of the test take the same medium. To avoid collision, the local testers wait the end of the test before sending to the coordinator tester the local verdicts. This solution does not perturb the test since the results are sent after it is completed.

This architecture has the advantage to be used with most of the mobile applications, since it's the same medium which is used to transmit regular or test data. However, the test must be completely executed before obtaining a verdict even it's a FAIL one, whereas the test could be stopped immediately with the first architecture. Moreover, we must suppose that the local testers have sufficient memory to store the local verdicts.

In the next section, we introduce the method which is used to create a test case and to distribute it to the different local testers.

4   Test Methodology

Many testing methods have been proposed to generate automatically test cases from untimed specifications [7, 6, 5, 11]. To use them, specifications must be modelled with a formal language. Among the various existing ones (LOTOS, LDS,

Petri Nets, automata...), we propose to use the IOSM [1, 16] (Input Output State Machine).

Definition 1 (Input Output State Machine).
An IOSM $\mathcal{A}$ is defined as a tuple $< \Sigma_\mathcal{A}, S_A, s_A^0, E_A >$, where:

- *$\Sigma_\mathcal{A}$ is a finite non-empty alphabet, S_A is a finite set of states, s_A^0 is the initial state,*
- *$E_A \subseteq S_A \times (\{?,!\} \times \Sigma_A) \times S_A$ is the finite set of transitions.*
  An input symbol begins with "?" and an output one begins with "!".
  A tuple $< s, a, s' >$ represents a transition from state s to state s', labelled with the symbol a.

Furthermore, we consider that for a distributed system $\mathcal{A}$, the language Σ_A is the union of languages used by every components. And, for two components x and y, the two languages are disjoined, $\Sigma_x \cap \Sigma_y = \varnothing$. This property guarantees that each entity, and consequently each tester, takes into account only the messages concerning it. An example of IOSM is given in Figure 6.

We propose to use a test purpose based method [5, 8] (Section 2) which generates test cases from requirements given by designers. From these requirements, called a test purpose, this method generates the test cases which aims to check whether the test purpose is satisfied or not on the implementation. However, this generation is not sufficient: in the previous test architectures, we have considered that each component of a distributed system is connected to a local tester. This implies that the test cases must be distributed on the local testers. So, a test case will consist of several "dedicated-tests", allocated to each tester. Each one will perform its dedicated-test and will communicate with the other ones to synchronize the tests of every components.

4.1   Generation of the Dedicated Test Cases for Local Testers

The algorithm, introduced below, aims to extract from a test case ω, each local test case ω_t, intended for each local tester t. Furthermore, it adds to the local test cases, some synchronization data needed to synchronize the testers between them. Synchronizations are obtained by one or several locks, modelled by data exchanged between testers and designed by $(-sync_j^p, +sync_j^p)$:

- $+sync_j^p$ locks the current tester until a message of synchronization is received from the tester j.
- $-sync_j^p$ represents the sending of synchronization to the tester "j" with the number p. This one unlocks the tester "j" which can continue to execute its test case on the component until another lock or until the end of the test case.

To sum up the algorithm, it consists of dividing a test case into several dedicated ones by analyzing its symbols and by determining which tester must use them. When two successive interactions (symbols) are not destined to the same local tester, a synchronization is used: $+sync_j^p$ is added to lock the tester which must execute the second interaction. $-sync_j^p$ is added in the test case devoted of the tester which must execute the first interaction. An example of test case generation is given in the following Section.

Algorithm

Hypothesis: The number of testers is known and is equal to N.
Input: A test case $\omega = \gamma_1\gamma_2\gamma_3...\gamma_x$, with x the number of requests.
Output: N dedicated-test sequences, $\omega^1, \omega^2...$
BEGIN:
for k from 1 to N **do**
$\quad \omega^k \leftarrow 0$
end for
$p \leftarrow 1$
for k from 1 to x-1 **do**
$\quad$**Read** γ_k in ω, search for the tester t_i which has this alphabet
$\quad$**Read** γ_{k+1} in ω, search for the tester t_j which has this alphabet
$\quad$**If** $(t_i \neq t_j)$
$\quad$/* installing coordination */
$\qquad$**If** $(\gamma_k$ is an emission) **then**
$\qquad\qquad \omega^{t_i} \leftarrow \omega^{t_i} + \text{``}-sync_{t_j}^p\text{''} + \gamma_k$
$\qquad\qquad$**else** $\omega^{t_i} \leftarrow \omega^{t_i} + \gamma_k + \text{``}-sync_{t_j}^p\text{''}$
$\qquad$**end if**
$\qquad \omega^{t_j} \leftarrow \omega^{t_j} + \text{``}+sync_{t_i}^p\text{''}$
$\qquad p \leftarrow p+1$
$\quad$**else** $\omega^{t_i} \leftarrow \omega^{t_i} + \gamma_k$
$\quad$**end if**
end for
Read γ_x in ω, search for the tester t_i which has this alphabet
$\omega^{t_i} \leftarrow \omega^{t_i} + \gamma_x$
END

Each local tester produces a local verdict: PASS if all the traces correspond to the test case, INCONCLUSIVE if the tester cannot execute the test case, or FAIL otherwise. The global test verdict, given by the coordinator tester is given by this definition:

Definition 2 (Test verdict).
$\quad$*Let $l_1,...,l_n$ be the local verdicts of the testers $t_1,...,t_n$. The final verdict of the test T is given by:*

$$T = \begin{cases} PASS \text{ iff } \forall 1 \leq i \leq n \, , l_i = PASS \\ INCONCLUSIVE \text{ iff } \exists 1 \leq i \leq n \mid l_i = INCONCLUSIVE \\ FAIL \text{ otherwise} \end{cases}$$

5   Experimentation and Results

In this section, we present our experimentation and results of a WAP system test. This system is composed of a WAP architecture (WAP protocol, gateways, HTTP server, database,...) and of an application which aims to update or search information in a database, specialized in cattle diseases.

Before describing the test architecture and our implementations, we briefly expose the WAP and its requirements.

5.1   The WAP (Wireless Application Protocol) and Our WAP System

The WAP is a result of continuous work to promote industrywide specifications for technology useful in developing applications and services that operate over wireless communication networks. The aim of the WAP is to access to Internet with devices which have less powerful CPU, less memory, restricted power consumption and different input devices.

On the one hand, the WAP gathers several protocol layers which allow the access of HTTP servers and databases: the Wireless Application Environment (WAE) includes a micro-browser which permits to view the environment information. The Wireless Session Protocol (WSP) provides the application layer of the WAP with a consistent interface for two session services. The first one is connected-oriented and operates above the Wireless Transaction Protocol (WTP). The second one is connectionless and operates above a datagram service (UDP). All these layers are involved in the communication and their interactions have been described using formal methods by the Platonis project [15].

On the other hand, the WAP represents a programming model, similar to the WWW one. It defines a set of standard components that enable communication between mobile terminals and network servers, including standard naming model, content typing and standard content formats (wml language). This wml language, close to the html one can be used to construct pages accessible via a wml browser. To have a full working WAP service, a gateway is used to transform the data coming from wireless communication with a WAP encapsulation to data understandable by an HTTP server. For this article and our experimentation, we use the open source Kannel[13] gateway since its implementation respects the standard established by the WAP Forum.

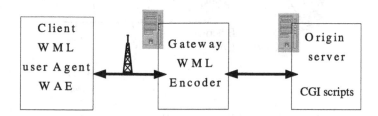

Fig. 3. WML user agent logical architecture

The WAP architecture, that we have deployed, is composed of a PDA connected to a GSM phone by an IrDA port. The PDA runs a WAP navigator, written with Embedded C++, which implements the WSP and WTP layers. With the WAP protocol, this one can access to an HTTP server via a Kannel Gateway. The HTTP server and the Kannel gateway are connected by an Ethernet network. To access to the HTTP server, the PDA must obtain an IP address, so we implement a PPP (Point to Point Protocol) server. This one is set on the same computer running the Kannel gateway in order to simplify the WAP system.

The WAP application is a "classical" Internet one: the WAP navigator proposes different wml pages which allow to request information on a database or to update it. The HTTP server contains several CGI programs which return wml pages to response at the previous requests.

5.2   Test Architecture and Testers Implementations

Since we use a GSM phone which has only one network interface, we use the second test architecture. The test architecture, devoted to our system, is illustrated in Figure 4 and described bellow.

Three testers have been implemented : two of them have the mission to detect wrong messages in the Kannel gateway and in the local network connected to the HTTP server. The third tester is a coordinator, located on the PDA. Each tester is composed of two programs: *PO_trace* for traffic inspection and *PO_analysis* for giving the local verdict. The "dedicated test cases" are loaded on each PO_analysis. During the test execution, each PO_analysis compares its local test case with the frames that are stocked by PO_trace. If no error is detected, PO_analysis sends a PASS verdict at the end, if PO_trace does not respond for any reason it sends INCONCLUSIVE, otherwise it sends a FAIL one.

The tester number 1 observes the traffic received and emitted by the WAP gateway. The open source Kannel gateway was modified for installing the trace tools. The Kannel software is structured as different layers, each one implemented by a thread which communicates with the other ones by exchanging messages. Different point of observation are inserted between each layer, and a thread is

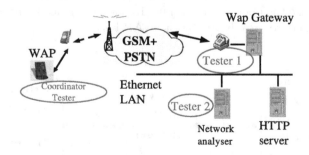

Fig. 4. Test architecture for the experimentation

added to analyze the traffic of the gateway. In fact, the modifications to install the trace tools are very small. Each time, a thread wants to send a message to another thread, the message is duplicated in a file before being emitted. The analyse thread contains a PO_trace_in which retrieves incoming traffic, a PO_trace_out which retrieves outgoing traffic and a PO_analysis which inspects the different traces and gives out the local verdict.

Since the WAP gateways are in general connected to Internet via a local network, the tester number 2 corresponds to a network analyzer, that will not perturb the network while the frame capture. For portability reasons, this analyzer was implemented in Java using *Jpcap*. Once all the test case is executed and inspected by PO_trace, the thread PO_analysis produces the local verdict and sends it to the coordinator tester.

The coordinator tester, located on the mobile system, must be able to send and receive different frames as well as the different local verdicts. A PDA running Windows CE is used, making it easier to program and establish a connection to GSM through a mobile phone equipped with an IrDA port. The WAP navigator, which implements the WSP and WTP layers with threads, provides also a graphical user interface that enables the load of the test cases. Figure 5 shows the graphical user interface of the PDA with the beginning of a test case. The thread PO_trace listens for all the messages received or sent by the WTP layer, while PO_analysis gives indications on the evolution of the test on the user interface, and produces the final verdict as well. if all the received local verdicts are PASS, the final verdict is PASS, otherwise it can be FAIL or INCONCLUSIVE. These softwares have been programmed with Embedded Visual C++.

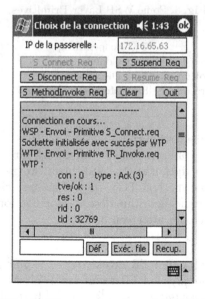

Fig. 5. The user interface of the PDA

5.3   Test Case Generation and Experimentation Results

For the experimentation, we propose to test the "get" function of the WAP which requests and receives wml pages from http servers. This function is transcribed by the service *S_MethodeInvoke.req* of the WSP layer. As we want a connected mode (which will use the WTP layer), we will have to add the S_connect.req primitive in the test purpose.

To generate test cases, we use the formal specification of the WSP layer whose a partial view is given with the IOSM of the figure 6.

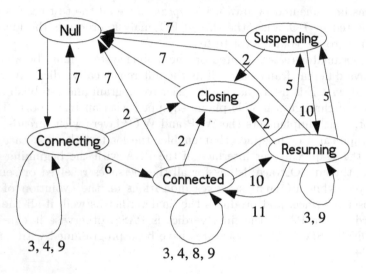

Fig. 6. Some WSP Layer Primitives

legend :

1 : ! Connect.req	5 : ! Suspend.req	9 : ? MethodAbort.ind
2 : ! Disconnect.req	6 : ? Connect.cnf	10 : ! Resume.req
3 : ! MethodeInvoke.req	7 : ? Disconnect.ind	11 : ? Resume.cnf
4 : ! MethodAbord.req	8 : ? MethodeInvoke.ind	

First, we construct the test purpose $\xrightarrow{S\_connect.req} \xrightarrow{S\_MethodeInvoke.req}$ which allows to instantiate the connected mode and to ask for a wml page. With this test purpose and our description of the WSP layer, we generate a first test case by using the test purpose method TGV ([8]). This test case is composed of 19 transitions. Then, we use the algorithm described in Section 4 to create the three "dedicated-tests". These ones are given bellow:

Coordinator Tester:

? S_connect.req + $-sync^1_{PO1}$ + ! TR_invoke.req + $+sync^2_{PO1}$ + ? TR_result.ind
+ ! S_connect.cnf + $-sync^3_{PO1}$ + ! TR_result.res + ? S_MethodInvoke.req
+ $-sync^4_{PO1}$ + ! TR_invoke.req + $+sync^{10}_{PO1}$ + ? TR_result.ind
+ ! S_MethodResult.ind $-sync^{11}_{PO1}$ + ! TR_result.res

Tester 1:

$+sync^1_{PCO}$ + ? TR_invoke.ind + ? TR_invoke.res + $-sync^2_{PCO}$ + ! TR_result.req
$+sync^3_{PCO}$ + ? TR_result.cnf $+sync^4_{PCO}$ + ? TR_invoke.ind + ? TR_invoke.res +
$-sync^5_{PO2}$ + ! TCP_connexion.req $+sync^6_{PO2}$ + ? TCP_connexion.ind + $-sync^7_{PO2}$
+ ! TCP_ack.req + $-sync^8_{PO2}$ + ! TCP_data.req $+sync^9_{PO2}$ + ? TCP_data.cnf +
$-sync^1_{PCO}0$ + ! TR_result.req $+sync^{11}_{CO}$ + ? TR_result.cnf

Tester 2:

$+sync^5_{PO1}$ + ? TCP_connexion.ind $-sync^6_{PO1}$ + ! TCP_connexion.res $+sync^7_{PO1}$
+ ? TCP_ack .req $+sync^8_{PO1}$ + ? TCP_data.ind + $-sync^9_{PO1}$ + ! TCP_data.res

During the first experimentations, we always obtained a FAIL verdict from the coordinator tester, located in the PDA. We searched in the PO_trace for some errors and we found that instead of receiving a TR_result.ind, the PDA received an Ack frame for a confirmation of the TID (Transaction IDentification). The TID, which is increased for each frame, is used to number all the frames of the WAP to easily detect a loss. At the beginning of a communication, if a client sends a frame with an unexpected TID to the server, this one asks for a confirmation (with an ACK) to update its TID. Consequently, the WAP navigator, executed by the PDA, sent frames with bad TID. This error was confirmed by the PO_traces of the tester located on the Kannel server. So, we correct this error on the WAP navigator. Afterwards, we have experimented once again and we have obtained a PASS verdict, which means that the mobile application can ask for an information and receive a response in the connected mode of the WAP protocol. Other tests have been completed to check different functionalities of the WAP application. All the tests have been created with the aim of testing a functionnality of the application, and so the test purposes were created by hand and their lengths were less than six primitives.

6   Conclusion

We have introduced in this paper different test architectures and a testing method which can test mobile and distributed applications. One test architecture has been completely implemented and used to test a WAP application. The experimentations show that the method and the test architecture can be used in practice to detect errors on components distributed in different heterogeneous networks. We have used the GSM network as a mobile one, but other trace tools (PO_trace) have been implemented to use wireless networks (802.11). The networks, we have considered for the test architecture, are LAN, however a perspective could be the use of Internet to connect the components of the application: in such as case, the deployment of the test architecture could not be done manually. An automatic deployment of test architectures could be planned and proposed, that is at least an automatic download and installation of the testers on the components (or stations connected to theses ones).

References

1. R. Alur and D. Dill. The theory of timed automata. In J.W. de Bakker, C. Huizing, W.P. de Roever, and G. Rozenberg, editors, *Proceedings REX Workshop on Real-Time: Theory in Practice,* Mook, The Netherlands, June 1991, volume 600 of *LNCS,* pages 45–73. Springer-Verlag, 1992.
2. I. Berrada, R. Castanet, and P. Felix. A formal approach for real-time test generation. *WRTES, satellite workshop of FME symposium,* pages 5–16, 2003.
3. G.v. Bochmann, G. Das, R. Dssouli, and M. Dubuc. Fault Models in Testing. In *Proceedings of the International Workshop on Testing of Communicating Systems IWTCS'91,* 1991.
4. L. Cacciari and O. Rafiq. Controllability and observability in distributed testing. *Information and Software Technology,* 1999.
5. R. Castanet, C. Chevrier, O. Kon, and B. Le Saec. An Adaptive Test Sequence Generation Method for the User Needs. In *Proceedings of IWPTS'95, Evry, France,* 1995.
6. A. Cavalli. Different approach to protocol ans service testing. *Proceedings of the Twelfth IFIP Workshop on Testing of Communicating Systems (IWTCS'99),* September 1999.
7. T.S. Chow. Testing software design modeled by finite-state machines. *IEEE Transactions on Software Engineering,* SE-4(3):178–187, 1978.
8. J. Cl. Fernandez, C. Jard, T. Jron, and C. Viho. Using on-the-fly verification techniques for the generation of test suites. In *CAV'96. LNCS 1102 Springer Verlag,* 1996.
9. WAP forum. Wap specification. http://www.wapforum.org.
10. H. Fouchal, E. Petitjean, and S. Salva. Testing Timed Systems with Timed Purposes. In *Proceedings of the 7th International Conference on Real-Time Computing Systems and Applications, RTCSA'00 (Cheju Island, South Korea),IEEE Computer Society,* pages 166–171, December 2000.
11. S. Fujiwara, G. von Bochmann, F. Khendek, M. Amalou, and A. Ghedamsi. Test selection based on finite-state models. *IEEE Transactions on Software Engineering,* 17(6):591–603, June 1991.
12. ISO. Conformance Testing Methodology and Framework. International Standard 9646, International Organization for Standardization — Information Technology — Open Systems Interconnection, Genève, 1991.
13. kannel group. Kannel, open source wap and sms gateway. http://www.kannel.org.
14. G. Luo, R. Dssouli, G. Bochman, P. Venkatraam, and A. Ghedsami. Test generation with respect to distributed interfaces. In *Computer Standards and Interfaces,* volume 16, pages 119–132, 1994.
15. A. Mederreg, F. Zaidi, P. Combes, W. Monin, R. Castanet, M. Mackaya, and P. Laurenot. Une plate-forme de validation multi-protocoles et multi-services - rsultats d'exprimentation. *Colloque Francophone de l'ingénierie des Protocoles, CFIP,* October 2003.
16. M. Phalippou. *Relation d'implantation et hypothses de test sur des automates entres et sorties.* PhD thesis, Univ. of Bordeaux, September 1994.

17. O. Rafiq, R. Castanet, and C. Chraibi. Towards an environment for testing osi protocols. *Proc of the International Workshop on Protocol Specification, testing and Verification*, 1985.
18. S. Salva and P. Laurençot. Génération de tests temporisés orientée caractérisation d'états. *Colloque Francophone de l'ingénierie des Protocoles, CFIP*, October 2003.
19. A. Ulrich and H. Knig. Architecture for testing distributed systems. In *Proc of Inter. Workshop on testing of Communicating Systems, IWTCS'99*, 1999.
20. T. Walter, I. Schieferdecker, and J. Grabowski. Test architectures for distributed systems - state of the art and beyond. In *Testing of Communicating Systems*, 1998.

A UNITY-Based Framework Towards Component Based Systems

I.S.W.B. Prasetya[1], T.E.J. Vos[2], A. Azurat[1], and S.D. Swierstra[1]

[1] Informatica Instituut, Universiteit Utrecht
wishnu@cs.uu.nl
http://www.cs.uu.nl/staff/wishnu.html
[2] Instituto Tecnológico de Informática, Universidad Politécnica de Valencia
tanja@iti.upv.es
http://www.iti.upv.es/~tanja

Abstract. Compositionality provides the foundation of software modularity, re-usability and separate verification of software components. One of the known difficulties, when separately verifying components, is producing compositional proofs for progress properties of distributed systems. This paper offers a UNITY-based framework to model distributed applications which are built with a component based approach. The framework enables components to be abstractly specified in terms of contracts. Temporal properties are expressed and proven in the UNITY style. Compositional reasoning about components' properties, including progress, is supported. The semantical model is simple and intuitive.

Keywords: component based applications, compositionality, verification.

1 Introduction

Component based models, like COM, CORBA, and JavaBeans, result in applications built from components that interact by calling each other's operations. The different components can be owned and controlled by other applications, which may run on yet different machines and locations. Consequently, component based applications are essentially distributed systems whose temporal properties have to be verified to guarantee their correctness.

Verifying a global property of a component based system is complicated because we may not have access to the source code of all its components. Instead, we have to rely on their specifications or *contracts*. However, verifying the preservation of progress properties' specifications while composing distributed components is known to be difficult [7, 5, 1, 2, 8, 9]. In order to be able to infer global temporal properties, the components will have to offer a stronger kind of contracts. Merely specifying the pre- and post-conditions of an object's operations, like for example as in OCL, is usually not sufficient.

This paper offers a UNITY-based framework to specify the components of an application and to infer temporal properties of the application from the contracts of its components.

T. Higashino (Ed.): OPODIS 2004, LNCS 3544, pp. 52–66, 2005.

2   Overview on the Model

We will take the same basic model as in CORBA: an *application* consists of *clients* and *objects*. Both are computing entities, and to keep it simple, we assume that they run continuously. These computing entities interact by performing *operations* (methods) provided by the objects[1][2]. Objects are available as *components*. Components are objects that, for various reasons, only reveal a limited amount of information about themselves. The information they reveal is laid down in a *contract*, and a component is *committed* to behave as indicated in its contract[3]. An object that is bound by a contract is also called a *contractor*.

The framework, described in this paper, offers formal notions of objects, contracts, and applications, and a set of laws that allow us to infer global properties, including progress, of an application in a compositional way from the specifications of its components. Refinement is used as a part of the component-contract relation. The refinement relation is defined in a way such that checking component-contract consistency is cheap and that a component's author gets more flexibility in hiding aspects of his component from its contract (while still offering a consistent contract).

3   Preliminaries

Predicate Confinement. Predicates specify a set of program states. A predicate p is *confined* by a set of variables V (written p **conf** V) if p does not constrain the value of any variable outside V. As a rule of thumb, if V is the set of free variables of an expression e, then e is confined by V. We write p, q **conf** V to abbreviate p **conf** V and q **conf** V.

Actions. An *action* is an atomic, terminating, and non-deterministic state transition. An action can be modelled by a function from the universe of states, denoted by State, to $\mathcal{P}(\text{State})$.

Actions can be (multiple) assignments or guarded actions. If V is a set of variables, skip V is an action that does not change the variables in V. Guarded

---

[1] This is consistent with Szyperski's definition of *object* (essentially: an object is something that has state, behavior, and encapsulation) [20], which is quite commonly accepted.

[2] We will not venture into complex features, such as inheritance and the ability to pass object reference, or to pass an entire object, through an operation call. Furthermore, our model is an abstract model: details of implementational nature, such as parameters marshaling, object deployment, and optimization of resources' utilization will not be visible in the model.

[3] This is also consistent with Szyperski's definition of *component* [20], essentially: component is a unit of composition with contractually specified interfaces and subject to composition by third parties. Our definition is stricter by saying the only knowledge we can rely on, placing ourselves as a third party, about a component is its contracts.

actions are denoted by $g \dashrightarrow a$, meaning that a will be executed if g is true, otherwise the action behaves as a skip.

If a and b are actions, $a \sqcup b$ is an action that either behaves as a or as b. So, $(a \sqcup b) \ s = a \ s \ \cup \ b \ s$. If Σ is a set of actions then $\sqcup \Sigma$ is a shorthand for $(\sqcup a : a \in \Sigma : a)$.

We write $\{var \ x; \ a\}$ to introduce a local variable x. The meaning is expressed in terms of Hoare triple as follows:

$$\{p\} \ \{var \ x; \ a\} \ \{q\} \ \overset{d}{=} \ \{p\} \ a[x'/x] \ \{q\}$$

where $a[x'/x]$ means the action obtained by replacing x in a with a fresh variable x'.

Action Refinement. We define the following notion of refinement over actions —it is a variant of the standard one, e.g. as in [3]. Let V be a set of variables, and let i be a predicate (i is intended to be an invariant). Action b *weakly refines* action a (or a is an abstraction of b) with respect to V and i, if b can either simulate whatever a can do on the variables in V, assuming i holds initially, or it skips. Formally:

$$V, i \vdash a \sqsubseteq b$$
$$\overset{d}{=}$$
$$(\forall p, q : p, q \ \mathbf{conf} \ V : \{i \wedge p\} \ a \sqcup \mathsf{skip} \ V \ \{q\} \ \Rightarrow \ \{i \wedge p\} \ b \ \{q\})$$

Notation. We will use tuples to represent composite structures, and selectors to select the various parts. For example, $Object = (\mathsf{prg} :: Program, \mathsf{ops} :: \{Operation\})$ defines a type $Object$ consisting of two-elements tuples. If $x(P, M)$ is a value of this type, then $x.\mathsf{prg} = P$ and $x.\mathsf{ops} = M$.

4   UNITY

We will use the original UNITY operators from [6] as a base for our extension. We could have used those of new-UNITY [14] since both set of operators are in principle of equal strength. Our choice, however, is a subjective one, we find the "old" operators simply more intuitive.

4.1   Programs

We will represent a UNITY program P by a tuple of this type:

$$Prog_{\mathrm{UNITY}} \ \overset{d}{=} \ (\mathsf{acts} :: \{Action\}, \mathsf{init} :: Pred, \mathsf{pub} :: \{Var\}, \mathsf{pri} :: \{Var\})$$

$P.\mathsf{init}$ is a predicate specifying P's possible initial states, $P.\mathsf{pub}$ is the set of P's public (shared) variables, and $P.\mathsf{pri}$ is the set of P's private (local) variables. We write $P.\mathsf{var}$ to refer to $P.\mathsf{pub} \cup P.\mathsf{pri}$. Implicitly, $P.\mathsf{init}$ has to be confined by $P.\mathsf{var}$; $P.\mathsf{pub}$ and $P.\mathsf{pri}$ are disjoint; and for every action $a \in P.\mathsf{acts}$, it holds that for every state s, $a \ s$ is non-empty.

An execution of a UNITY program is infinite, in each step an action is selected nondeterministically. Selection is weakly fair, every action is selected infinitely often.

We do not expect real programs to be written entirely in UNITY. Each UNITY action serves as an abstraction of a sequential program, which may be several times larger and written in another language. In Misra's words [14]: a UNITY program merely orchestrates executions of its constituent sequential programs, by specifying the conditions under which each sequential program is to be executed.

When composing *different* programs, we assume that each component is given a unique name space to name its private variables. So, when composing P and Q, we know that the names in P.pri and Q.pri do not clash with the names in, respectively, Q.var and P.var. Unique name spaces can, for example, be achieved by prefixing the names of all private variables of a program with the program's name. We will not concern ourselves here with these issues.

Composing two programs means running them in parallel. The behavior of the parallel composition of P and Q is modelled by the $P \| Q$ which is defined as follows:

Definition 4.1: PARALLEL COMPOSITION

$$P \| Q \ \overset{d}{=} \ (P.\text{acts} \cup Q.\text{acts}, \ P.\text{init} \wedge Q.\text{init}, \ P.\text{pub} \cup Q.\text{pub}, \ P.\text{pri} \cup Q.\text{pri})$$

4.2 Properties

A predicate i is a *strong invariant*[4] of P, denoted by $P \vdash \text{sinv } i$, if it holds initially, and it is maintained by every action of P. A predicate j is an *invariant* if there exists a strong invariant i implying j.

Definition 4.2: STRONG INVARIANT

$$P \vdash \text{sinv } i \ \overset{d}{=} \ P.\text{init} \Rightarrow i \ \wedge \ (\forall a : a \in P.\text{acts} : \{i\} \, a \, \{i\})$$

To specify safety and one-step progress properties we use extended UNITY operators from [15]. We repeat them below for convenience.

Definition 4.3: UNITY OPERATORS

1. $P, i \ \vdash\!\!- \ p \text{ unless } q$
   $$\overset{d}{=}$$
   $$P \vdash \text{sinv } i \ \wedge \ p, q \text{ conf } P.\text{var} \ \wedge \ (\forall a : a \in P.\text{acts} : \{i \wedge p \wedge \neg q\} \, a \, \{p \vee q\})$$

2. $P, i \ \vdash\!\!- \ p \text{ ensures } q$
   $$\overset{d}{=}$$
   $$P, i \ \vdash\!\!- \ p \text{ unless } q \ \wedge \ (\exists a : a \in P.\text{acts} : \{i \wedge p \wedge \neg q\} \, a \, \{q\})$$

---

[4] We are going to use invariants to parameterize UNITY properties, in the style of Sanders [18]. Strong invariants are however used here instead of just invariants (predicates that hold through out any execution of a given program) as in [18], because the later cause a certain technical problem [16].

4.3   Refinement

We will use the following simple notion of refinement on UNITY programs.

Definition 4.4: PROGRAM REFINEMENT AND ABSTRACTION

For a set of variables V, and a predicate i that is intended to be a strong invariant of P, we define that Q is a refinement of P (or P is an *abstraction* of Q) as follows:

1. $V, i \mathrel{\vdash\!\!-} P \sqsubseteq Q \overset{d}{=} P.\text{pub} \subseteq Q.\text{pub} \;\wedge\; P.\text{pri} \subseteq Q.\text{pri} \;\wedge\; Q.\text{init} \Rightarrow P.\text{init}$

$$\wedge$$
$$\forall b : b \in Q.\text{acts} : V, i \;\vdash\; \sqcup\, P.\text{acts} \sqsubseteq b$$

2. $i \vdash P \sqsubseteq Q \overset{d}{=} P.\text{var}, i \mathrel{\vdash\!\!-} P \sqsubseteq Q$

So, under the invariance of i, $V, i \vdash P \sqsubseteq Q$ means that every action of Q behaves, with respect to the variables in V, no worse than some action of P, or it just skips V (note the use of weak refinement at the action level).

5   Specification of Objects and Components

In order to be able to reason about the preservation of progress properties, we need contracts that specify those progress properties that can be preserved if a component P is composed with some environment B. Consider the property $P\|B, i \vdash p \mapsto q$. Suppose we know that this progress is driven solely by component P. If B is an *abstraction* of a concrete environment Q, then we can expect that the same property will be preserved in $P\|Q$. To express this kind of reasoning, we need a new set of extended UNITY operators, with which the notion of "progress is driven solely by P" can be specified.

Definition 5.1: EXTENDED UNITY OPERATORS

Let P and B be UNITY programs. We define:

1. $P_{\triangleleft}\|B,\; i \;\vdash\; p \text{ ensures } q$
$$\overset{d}{=}$$
$P\|B,\; i \;\vdash\; p \text{ unless } q \;\wedge\; (\exists a : a \in P.\text{acts} : \{i \wedge p \wedge \neg q\}\, a\, \{q\})$

2. $P_{\triangleleft}\|Q,\; i \vdash p \mapsto q$ is defined such that $(\lambda p, q.\ P_{\triangleleft}\|Q,\; i \vdash p \mapsto q)$ is the smallest transitive and disjunctive closure of $(\lambda p, q.\ P_{\triangleleft}\|Q,\; i \vdash p \text{ ensures } q)$.

Now we can state the theorem that makes it possible to specify progress properties in a contract such that their preservation can be inferred regardless of the environment its contractor is composed with. More specifically, the theorem states that every progress property from p to q made by P, when specified in terms of $P_{\triangleleft}\|B$, will be preserved when P is composed with any program Q that refines B.

Theorem 5.2: Preservation of $\mapsto$

$$\frac{P_{\triangleleft}\|B, i \vdash p \mapsto q \quad \wedge \quad j \vdash B \sqsubseteq Q \quad \wedge \quad i \Rightarrow j}{P\|Q, i \vdash p \mapsto q}$$

The rule's premise assumes that i is a strong invariant of P. However, P may not reveal i in its contract, for example because it exposes too much of its internal state. However it is sufficient if the contract exposes a weaker invariant j, since we can infer the conclusion above by showing the refinement based on the weaker j.

6   Objects and Their Operations

In our model, an *object* is a UNITY program that exposes some of its variables to its environment. This program is called the *internal* program of the object. The exposed variables are called *public* or shared variables. Access to these variables is restricted: the environment can only inspect or update them via a set of operations provided by the object. Any program can be deployed as an object by encapsulating it with the necessary interface implementing the above restriction for accessing public variables.

6.1   Semantical Model

We will semantically model an object x with a tuple of this type:

$$Object = (\mathsf{prg} :: Prog_{\mathrm{UNITY}}, \mathsf{ops} :: \{Operation\})$$

where $x.\mathsf{prg}$ models the object's internal program, $x.\mathsf{ops}$ is the set of operations offered by the object, and *Operation* denotes the universe of operations that objects can offer.

The selectors used on programs are overloaded so that they work on objects, e.g. if x is an object, $x.\mathsf{pub}$ is equal to $x.\mathsf{prg.pub}$. We also overload $\|$ and $_{\triangleleft}\|$, e.g., $x\|Q$ means $x.\mathsf{prg}\|Q$.

Two objects have an *identical interface* if they offer the same set of public variables and operations. An operation has the following structure: $mname(y, r) = $ do b, where y is a parameter used to pass input data to $mname$, r is a parameter used to hold the return value of $mname$, and b is an *action* describing the operation's body. The names of the parameters are assumed not to collide with the names of any variable of x. Parameters are passed either by value or by reference, passing aliases by reference is *not* allowed. An operation has no access to global information, other than the public variables of the object it belongs to.

If x is an object to which $mname$ belongs to, then a call to $mname$ is denoted by $x.mname(e, z)$. If b is the body of $mname$, the effect of such a call is equivalent to:

$$\mathtt{atomic}\{\mathtt{var}\ y, \mathtt{return};\ y := e;\ b;\ z := \mathtt{return}\}$$

The execution of an operation is assumed to be *atomic*. This may not be efficient, if it, for example, works on a large data structure. However, there are

ways to infer which operations can be safely executed in parallel. We will abstract
away this issue, and leave it up to the implementator to optimize the utilization
of the objects.

Object Properties. Since the environment of an object x can only interact
with it through its operations, the worst possible environment of x can be characterized by the following UNITY program:

$$x.\text{env} \overset{d}{=} (\Sigma, x.\text{init}, x.\text{pub}, \emptyset)$$

where Σ is a set of actions modelling all possible calls to the operations in $x.\text{ops}$:

$$\Sigma = \{\text{var } y, z; \ x.m_1(y, z)\} \ \| \ \ldots \ \| \ \{\text{var } y, z; \ x.m_k(y, z)\}$$

for all operations $m_1, \ldots, m_k \in x.\text{ops}$. So, any real or *proper* environment Q of
x is a refinement of $x.\text{env}$. Formally:

$$Q \text{ is a proper environment of } x \overset{d}{=} (\forall i :: x.\text{pub}, i \vdash x.\text{env} \sqsubseteq Q)$$

Any unless and $\mapsto$ properties proven with respect to $x\|x.\text{env}$ and $x_q\|x.\text{env}$ re-
spectively, will be preserved when x is composed with any proper environment.

7   Contract

A component is an object that does not release full information about itself to its
environment. Instead, is offers a *contract* that specifies what the object does. A
contract is binding, as the object is obliged to realize anything it commits in the
contract. A simple form of contract can just list the headers of the operations
offered by the object. Such a contract can be strengthened by putting more
information in it, thus enabling the users to infer more properties about the
object. Of course, strengthening a contract makes an object less reusable, and
its verification more expensive.

We will use the abstraction relation from Section 4.3 as the base of a contract.
We use an abstract object a as a contract of a concrete object x. The definition
of $\sqsubseteq$ tells us how to check if x will fulfil a. This powerful abstraction relation
gives us the advantage that we obtain a considerable level of freedom in deciding
how detailed a is (how much aspects of x we want to expose in a).

7.1   Semantical Model

Formally, we will represent a contract c with a tuple of this type:

$$Contract = (\text{smodel} :: Object, \text{inv} :: Pred, \text{progress} :: \{ProgressSpec\})$$

where $c.\text{inv}$ is a predicate specifying an invariant, and $c.\text{progress}$ is a set of specifications in form $p \mapsto q$ specifying progress made by c's contractor. We impose
that $a.\text{smodel}$ is a so-called *abstract object*, which is an object that has no private

variables[5] (so a.smodel.pri $= \emptyset$). Moreover, c.inv specifies a strong invariant of c.smodel, and of any proper environment of c.smodel. Furthermore, c.inv has to be confined by c.pub. Formally:

$$c\text{.inv }\mathbf{conf}\ c\text{.pub}\ \wedge\ c\text{.smodel}\|c\text{.env}\ \vdash\ \mathbf{sinv}\ c\text{.inv}$$

We will again overload the meaning of the selectors used on objects so that they also work on contracts. For example, if c is a contract, c.pub denotes the set of all c's public variables, which is just equal to c.smodel.pub.

If x is an object, its contract is denoted by x.contract. The relation between an object and its contract is defined below:

Definition 7.1: OBJECT-CONTRACT RELATION
Let x be an object and $c = x$.contract. The relation between x and c is as follows:

1. x and c.smodel have the same interface. So x.pub $= c$.pub and x.ops $= c$.ops.
2. There exists a predicate i such that:
   (a) i is a strong invariant of $x\|x$.env and it implies c.inv.
   (b) c.smodel is a consistent abstraction of x. More precisely: $i\ \vdash\ c\text{.smodel} \sqsubseteq x$
   (c) For every specification $p \mapsto q$ in c.progress: $x_\lhd\|x$.env, $i\ \vdash\ p \mapsto q$

The invariant i mentioned above is called the *concrete invariant* of x, and will be denoted by x.concreteInv. Note that since x and c have the same set of operations, then x.env $= c$.env. So, any proper environment of c.smodel is also a proper environment of x. Also note that c.inv is an invariant of $x\|x$.env because the object-contract relation implies the existence of a invariant i of $x\|x$.env implying c.inv. However, c.inv is not a *strong* invariant of $x\|x$.env.

7.2   Inferring Object's Properties

From the object-contract relation and from Theorem 5.2, it follows that the composition of x with any proper environment Q will maintain all progress properties specified in R:

Corollary 7.2: PROGRESS COMMITMENT
Let x be an object and $c = x$.contract. Let Q be a proper environment of x.

$$\frac{p \mapsto q \in c\text{.progress}}{x_\lhd\|Q,\ x\text{.concreteInv}\ \vdash\ p \mapsto q}$$

Any unless property proven with respect to the safety model in the contract is also a property of the actual object. More precisely:

---

[5] This is not a restriction, but more a matter of choice in defining how expressive a contract should be.

Theorem 7.3: SAFETY COMMITMENT

Let x be an object and $c = x$.contract. Let Q be a proper environment of x. Then:

$$\frac{c.\mathsf{smodel}\|c.\mathsf{env}, c.\mathsf{inv} \;\vdash\; p \text{ unless } q}{x\|Q, x.\mathsf{concretelnv} \;\vdash\; p \text{ unless } q}$$

Contract Refinement. One could define a notion of contract refinement. This can be useful when an object broker cannot find an object offering a contract c. In that case it may try to find another object whose contract refines c. We will not work out this idea further here.

8 Application

An application consists of a set of objects and a set clients. An object can be either *private* (it cannot be accessed by the application's environment) or *public*[6].

8.1 Semantical Model

We will semantically model an application $\mathcal{A}$ with a tuple of this type:

$$App \;\overset{d}{=}\; (\; \begin{aligned}
&\mathsf{pubobjs} && :: \{ObjDecl\} &&, \\
&\mathsf{priobjs} && :: \{ObjDecl\} &&, \\
&\mathsf{clients} && :: \{Prog_{\text{UNITY}}\} && \\
&\mathsf{clientsinv} && :: Pred &&)
\end{aligned}$$

where $ObjDecl$ represents object declarations. We will use the notation $\mathcal{A}.\mathsf{objs}$ to refer to the set of all (public as well as private) objects of $\mathcal{A}$. The predicate $\mathcal{A}.\mathsf{clientsinv}$ is intended to augment the invariants of $\mathcal{A}$'s objects with information about the clients' (private) variables. In addition, there are several constraints, for example concerning the well-formedness of the model; we will show them later, since we need to introduce some concepts first.

The set of all public variables of $\mathcal{A}$, denoted by $\mathcal{A}.\mathsf{pub}$, consists of the public variables of its public objects. $\mathcal{A}$'s private variables, denoted by $\mathcal{A}.\mathsf{pri}$, consists of the union of the set of private variables of its public objects, and the sets of variables of its private objects and clients. The set of all $\mathcal{A}$'s variables is denoted by $\mathcal{A}.\mathsf{var}$. The concrete program induced by an application $\mathcal{A}$ is the following:

$$\mathcal{A}.\mathsf{prg} \;\overset{d}{=}\; ([x : x \in \mathcal{A}.\mathsf{objs} : x) \;\|\; ([Q : Q \in \mathcal{A}.\mathsf{clients} : Q)$$

---

[6] In CORBA a public object may be located outside the application itself. It may belong to and be controlled by another application, which may even be owned by a foreign organization. In such a setting a so-called *object broker* is used for searching the objects needed by an application and to facilitate the communication between the application and those foreign objects. This paper will however not concern itself with brokers.

The abstract model, or contract, of the whole application, denoted by $\mathcal{A}$.smodel, is the union of the contracts of the objects, composed with the clients:

Definition 8.1: ABSTRACT MODEL OF APPLICATION

$$\mathcal{A}.\text{model} \stackrel{d}{=} (\| x : x \in \mathcal{A}.\text{objs} : x.\text{contract.smodel}) \quad \| \quad (\| Q : Q \in \mathcal{A}.\text{clients} : Q)$$

The worst environment of an application can be modelled by a program that tries all possible calls to the operations of the public objects:

Definition 8.2: APPLICATION'S ABSTRACT ENVIRONMENT

$$\mathcal{A}.\text{env} \stackrel{d}{=} (\| x, X : x :: X \in \mathcal{A}.\text{pubobjs} : x.\text{env})$$

The notation $\mathcal{A}$.inv refers to the conjunction of the invariants specified by the contracts in $\mathcal{A}$, strengthened by $\mathcal{A}$.clientsinv. Similarly, we define $\mathcal{A}$.concreteInv:

Definition 8.3: APPLICATION'S INVARIANTS

$$\mathcal{A}.\text{inv} \stackrel{d}{=} (\bigwedge x : x \in \mathcal{A}.\text{objs} : x.\text{contract.inv}) \wedge \mathcal{A}.\text{clientsinv}$$

$$\mathcal{A}.\text{concreteInv} \stackrel{d}{=} (\bigwedge x : x \in \mathcal{A}.\text{objs} : x.\text{concreteInv}) \wedge \mathcal{A}.\text{clientsinv}$$

8.2 Constraints

In order to prove the laws that enable us to infer the properties of an application, we need to impose some constraints on its semantical model. Let $\mathcal{A}$ be an application:

1. [CA1] Each object in $\mathcal{A}$ has its own unique name space. So, for any two distinct objects x and y in $\mathcal{A}$, $x.\text{var} \cap y.\text{var} = \emptyset$.
2. [CA2] A client can only interact with an object through its operations. Furthermore, a client can only do a single operation in one atomic step. In other words, with respect to every object x in $\mathcal{A}$, each client should be a proper environment of x.
3. [CA3] The only public information a client has access to is the set of all public variables of the objects in $\mathcal{A}$.
4. [CA4] $\mathcal{A}$.clientsinv is maintained by $\mathcal{A}$'s abstract model. Note that this constraint implies that $\mathcal{A}$.clientsinv can only specify the variables known to the clients.

8.3 Inferring an Application's Properties

A safety property proven with respect to the abstract model of an application will extend to the application itself, under any proper environment.

Theorem 8.4: SAFETY BY ABSTRACT MODEL

$$\frac{\mathcal{A}.\text{model}\|\mathcal{A}.\text{env}, \ \mathcal{A}.\text{inv} \ \vdash \ p \text{ unless } q}{\mathcal{A}.\text{prg}\|\mathcal{A}.\text{env}, \ \mathcal{A}.\text{concreteInv} \ \vdash \ p \text{ unless } q}$$

Any progress property committed in the contract of any object in an application, will be preserved by the application, and by its environment.

Theorem 8.5: Progress by Contract
Let x be an object in $\mathcal{A}$ and $c = x.$contract.

$$\frac{p \mapsto q \in c.\mathsf{progress}}{\mathcal{A}.\mathsf{prg}_\lhd \| \mathcal{A}.\mathsf{env}, \ \mathcal{A}.\mathsf{concreteInv} \vdash p \mapsto q}$$

The next theorem states which progress made by the clients that can be be preserved by the application and its environment.

Theorem 8.6: Client Progress

$$\frac{\mathcal{A}.\mathsf{model} \| \mathcal{A}.\mathsf{env}, \ \mathcal{A}.\mathsf{inv} \vdash p \mapsto q}{\mathcal{A}.\mathsf{prg}_\lhd \| \mathcal{A}.\mathsf{env}, \mathcal{A}.\mathsf{concreteInv} \vdash p \mapsto q}$$

Note that theorems 8.4 and 8.6 reflect what was mentioned at the beginning of section 7. The stronger we make an object's contract, i.e. the more information we put in the model of the object, the more expensive its verification gets.

9   Example

Consider the `VotingService` application in Figure 1, it has one client `superviseVoting`, an object `SimpleVotingSystem` that allows users to send

```
application votingService
  public   v :: SimpleVotingSystem ;
           d :: SimpleCalendar
  client superviseVoting
    private   closingDate :: Date = 01/01/2005 ;
              today       :: Date = 00/00/0000
    action    d.getDate(today)   []   today>=closingDate --> v.count()


  contract SimpleCalendar
    smodel
      public   current :: Date
      init     true
      action   current := current + unittime

    operation  getDate(&today::Date) = do today:=current
    inv        current>=0
    progress   !D. true |--> current>=D
```

Fig. 1. An example of a simple application to do electronic voting and a contract of a simple calendar object

votes, and a `SimpleCalendar` object to keep track of the current date. The figure also shows the contract of `SimpleCalendar`.

Although the contract of `SimpleVotingSystem` is not shown, imagine that it has two operations: `vote` and `count`. The first is used to send a vote to the object. Incoming votes are collected in the variable `votes`. The second will close the voting and count the votes. A variable `isOpen` is used to indicate whether or not the voting is still open. If this variable has been flipped to false, then `vote` will not add any new vote. Given this description, one can expect the following property. For any value v:

$$v[\![x.\text{env}, \text{ true} \quad \vdash \quad \neg v.\text{isOpen} \wedge v \notin v.\text{votes} \text{ unless false} \tag{1}$$

In other words, once the voting process is closed, no new vote will be accepted. Note that the property is an unless property over $v[\![x.\text{env}$: it will be preserved in the composition of v with any proper environment of v. Suppose we need to infer this property for the whole application, i.e. we want to verify:

$$\text{app.prg}[\![\text{app.env}, \ i \ \vdash \ \neg v.\text{isOpen} \wedge v \notin v.\text{votes} \text{ unless false} \tag{2}$$

where app = `VotingService` and $i$app.concreteInv. By Theorem 8.4 it is sufficient to show the following:

$$\text{app.model}[\![\text{app.env}, \ j \ \vdash \ \neg v.\text{isOpen} \wedge v \notin v.\text{votes} \text{ unless false} \tag{3}$$

where j = app.inv. The only action in app.model$[\![$app.env that can violate this property is the operation `vote`, because it can insert to `votes`. However, it can only do so if `isOpen` is true, which is not the case in the unless property above. Hence (2) is valid.

Now, suppose not all incoming votes are valid votes. The object `v` will internally filter the valid votes and put them in a list `validvotes`. Consider the following progress specification: if there are already more than 100 valid, then eventually the value of a variable `accept` will be set to true. This indicates that the voting results positively.

$$\text{app.prg}_\lhd[\![\text{app.env}, \ i \ \vdash \ \text{length } v.\text{validvotes} > 100 \mapsto v.\text{accept} \tag{4}$$

To show (4) it is sufficient (by transitivity of $\mapsto$) to show the following properties with respect to app.prg $_\lhd[\![$ app.env and invariant i:

$$\text{true} \ \mapsto \ d.\text{current} \geq \text{closingdate} \tag{5}$$

$$d.\text{current} \geq \text{closingdate} \ \mapsto \ \text{afterClosingDate} \tag{6}$$

$$\text{length } v.\text{validvotes} > 100 \text{ unless false} \tag{7}$$

$$\text{length } v.\text{validvotes} > 100 \ \wedge \ \text{afterClosingDate} \mapsto \ v.\text{accept} \tag{8}$$

where:

```
afterClosingDate
=
d.current ≥ closingdate ∧ today ≥ closingdate
```

Consider (5). Since this progress is realized by the `SimpleCalendar` object of `app`, we use Theorem 8.5 to reduce the application level property to an object level one. By the theorem it suffices to show that the same property is specified in the `progress`-part of the object d, which is indeed the case (see the contract in Figure 1).

Consider (6). We expect this progress to be realized by the client. Using Theorem 8.6, we need to show the same progress, but with respect to app.model$_\triangleleft$‖app.env and invariant j. This can be proven easily, since this progress is realized by the action `d.getDate(today)` of the client. Consequently, it is easy to prove the following ensures property, which implies $\mapsto$:

$$\text{app.model}_\triangleleft\|\text{app.env}, \ j \tag{9}$$
$$\vdash$$
$$\texttt{d.current} \geq \texttt{closingdate} \ \ \texttt{ensures} \ \ \texttt{afterClosingDate}$$

The approach to prove (7) is similar to that of (2), and that of (8) similar to that of (6).

10   Deploying an Application as an Object

Since an application $\mathcal{A}$ is essentially just a program, it can be deployed as an object by wrapping it. For this we need to define an interface, because an object has public and private variables, initial condition, and operations. Evidently, a wrapper can only expose all or some public objects of $\mathcal{A}$. Therefore, the actual environment of a wrapped $\mathcal{A}$ will not behave worse that $\mathcal{A}$.env. Consequently, properties infered using the theorems from Subsection 8.3, which assume $\mathcal{A}$.env, will be preserved by the wrapping.

11   Related Work

Various other frameworks exist. The one in [13] is based on Z and focuses on formalizing static relations between components, specified in terms of UML class diagrams. In [12] a framework is described that relies on Hoare triple specifications to infer behavioral properties. It is suitable to deal with components that have no internal programs of their owns, and hence cannot, on their own, enforce temporal properties. If internal programs are added, specifying temporal properties would require the use of auxiliary variables to record the objects' history. Broy's framework [4] has built in history variables as part of its logic. The framework is especially tailored for dealing with components that synchronize with channels. It may however be too detailed if the components exchange information through operation calls instead. Our framework is more suitable in the latter context.

An important part of our framework is the use of an abstract program to specify (a certain aspect of) the behavior of a concrete program or environment.

It turns out to be quite convenient. Refinement has been used by many other researches, e.g. [3, 10, 11, 21, 19, 12].

We favor the use of UNITY as the underlying theory, because of its simplicity and its axiomatic style. It yields a semantical model which is simple and intuitive. The use of UNITY as the underlying theory to support component based design has been proposed by other researchers in [10, 11, 21]. However, as far as we know, our work is the first UNITY framework offering formal notions of objects, contracts, and application. We also want to mention Seuss due to Misra [14]. It is an excellent object oriented language and logic layer on top of UNITY. Our work can be seen as a component oriented extension to Seuss.

12   Conclusion

We have offered a formal framework to support a component based approach to build distributed applications. The framework offers formal notions of objects, contracts, and applications, and a set of laws to compositionally infer temporal properties of an application.

The underlying theory is in UNITY style, which compared to for example LTL is less expressive. However, because of UNITY's axiomatic style, it yields a semantical model which is simple and intuitive.

A small experiment with a simple voting system [17] seems to show that contracts in our framework can adequately and abstractly capture the system's components' temporal properties. Using the laws provided by the framework we were able to compositionally infer interesting properties of the system.

We have chosen for a weak notion of refinement, which gives more freedom to developers to hide components' details in the contracts. It is possible to take a stronger notion of refinement, for example as in [22, 23], but in exchange checking if a component satisfies its contract will be more expensive. Our framework is suitable for dealing with systems in which components synchronize by operations calls. It is less suitable to deal with message passing systems, or with systems where components require tight synchronization as in protocols.

We believe that our framework is worth further research. Future activities include its application to real-world examples in order to check out its scalability.

References

1. M. Abadi and L. Lamport. Composing specifications. *ACM Transactions on Programming Languages and Systems*, 15(1):73–132, January 1993.
2. M. Abadi and L. Lamport. Conjoining specifications. *ACM Transactions on Programming Languages and Systems*, 17(3):507–534, May 1995.
3. R.J.R. Back and J. Von Wright. Refinement calculus, part I: Sequential non-deterministic programs. *Lecture Notes of Computer Science*, 430:42–66, 1989.
4. M. Broy. Multi-view modelling of software sytems. In Hung Dang Van and Zhiming Liu, editors, *Proceedings of the Workshop on Formal Aspects of Component Software (FACS)*, 2003. Also as UNU/IIST Report no. 284, available on-line at www.iist.unu.edu/newrh/III/1/page.html.

5. K. Chandy and M. Charpentier. An experiment in program composition and proof. *Formal Methods in System Design*, 20(1):7–21, 2002.
6. K.M. Chandy and J. Misra. *Parallel Program Design – A Foundation*. Addison-Wesley Publishing Company, Inc., 1988.
7. K.M. Chandy and B.A. Sanders. Reasoning about program composition. Technical Report 96-035, University of Florida, 1996.
8. K.M. Chandy and B.A. Sanders. Reasoning about program composition. Draft. Presently available via: www.cise.ufl.edu/~sanders/pubs, 2000.
9. M. Charpentier and K. Chandy. Theorems about composition. *Lecture Notes of Computer Science*, 1837:167–186, 2000.
10. P. Collette. Composition of assumption-commitment specifications in a UNITY style. *Science of Computer Programming*, 23:107–125, December 1994.
11. P. Collette and E. Knapp. Logical foundations for compositional verification and development of concurrent programs in UNITY. *Lecture Notes of Computer Science*, 936:353 – 367, 1995.
12. He Jifeng, Lui Zhiming, and Li Xiaoshan. A contract-oriented approach to CBP. In Hung Dang Van and Zhiming Liu, editors, *Proceedings of the Workshop on Formal Aspects of Component Software (FACS)*, 2003. Also as UNU/IIST Report no. 284, available on-line at www.iist.unu.edu/newrh/III/1/page.html.
13. Soon-Kyeong Kim and David Carrington. A formal mapping between UML models and Object-Z specifications. *Lecture Notes in Computer Science*, 1878:2–??, 2000.
14. J. Misra. *A Discipline of Multiprogramming*. Springer-Verlag, 2001.
15. I. S. W. B. Prasetya. *Mechanically Supported Design of Self-stabilizing Algorithms*. PhD thesis, Inst. of Information and Comp. Science, Utrecht Univ., 1995. Download: www.cs.uu.nl/library/docs/theses.html.
16. I.S.W.B. Prasetya. Error in the UNITY substitution rule for subscripted operators. *Formal Aspects of Computing*, 6:466–470, 1994.
17. I.S.W.B. Prasetya, T.E.J. Vos, A. Azurat, and S.D.. Swierstra. A unity-based framework towards component based systems. Technical Report UU-CS-2003-043, Inst. of Information and Comp. Science, Utrecht Univ., 2003. Download: www.cs.uu.nl/staff/wishnu.html.
18. B.A. Sanders. Eliminating the substitution axiom from UNITY logic. *Formal Aspects of Computing*, 3(2):189–205, 1991.
19. N. Shankar. Lazy compositional verification. *Lecture Notes of Computer Science*, 1536:541–564, 1999.
20. C. Szyperski. *Component Software, Beyond Object-Oriented Programming*. Addison-Wesley, 1998.
21. R.T. Udink. *Program Refinement in UNITY-like Environments*. PhD thesis, Inst. of Information and Computer Sci., Utrecht University, 1995. Downloadable from www.cs.uu.nl.
22. T.E.J. Vos. *UNITY in Diversity: A Stratified Approach to the Verification of Distributed Algorithms*. PhD thesis, Inst. of Information and Computer Sci., Utrecht University, 2000. Download: www.cs.uu.nl.
23. T.E.J. Vos, S.D. Swierstra, and I.S.W.B Prasetya. Yet another program refinement relation. In *International Workshop on Refinement of Critical Systems: Methods, Tools and Experience*, 2002.

Searching for a Black Hole in Tree Networks

Jurek Czyzowicz[1,*], Dariusz Kowalski[2,3,**],
Euripides Markou[1,***], and Andrzej Pelc[1,†]

[1] Département d'informatique, Université du Québec en Outaouais,
Hull, Québec J8X 3X7, Canada
{jurek, evripidi, pelc}@uqo.ca
[2] Max-Planck-Institut für Informatik,
Stuhlsatzenhausweg 85, 66123 Saarbrücken, Germany
darek@mpi-sb.mpg.de
[3] Instytut Informatyki, Uniwersytet Warszawski,
Banacha 2, 02-097 Warszawa, Poland

Abstract. A black hole is a highly harmful stationary process residing in a node of a network and destroying all mobile agents visiting the node, without leaving any trace. We consider the task of locating a black hole in a (partially) synchronous tree network, assuming an upper bound on the time of any edge traversal by an agent. The minimum number of agents capable to identify a black hole is two. For a given tree and given starting node we are interested in the fastest possible black hole search by two agents. For arbitrary trees we give a 5/3-approximation algorithm for this problem. We give optimal black hole search algorithms for two "extreme" classes of trees: the class of lines and the class of trees in which any internal node (including the root which is the starting node) has at least 2 children.

Keywords: algorithm, black hole, mobile agent, tree.

1 Introduction

1.1 The Background and the Problem

Security of mobile agents working in a network environment is an important issue which receives recently growing attention. Protecting agents from "host attacks", i.e., harmful items stored in nodes of the network, has become almost as urgent as protecting a host, i.e., a node of the network, from an agent's attack [8, 9]. Various methods of protecting mobile agents against malicious hosts have been discussed, e.g., in [5, 6, 7, 8, 9, 10].

---

* Research supported in part by NSERC grant.
** Research supported in part by grants from KBN (4T11C04425) and UE DELIS.
*** This work was done during this author's stay at the Research Chair in Distributed Computing of the Université du Québec en Outaouais, as a postdoctoral fellow.
† Research supported in part by NSERC grant and by the Research Chair in Distributed Computing of the Université du Québec en Outaouais.

T. Higashino (Ed.): OPODIS 2004, LNCS 3544, pp. 67–80, 2005.
© Springer-Verlag Berlin Heidelberg 2005

In this paper we consider hostile hosts of a particularly harmful nature, called *black holes* [1, 2, 3, 4]. A black hole is a stationary process residing in a node of a network and destroying all mobile agents visiting the node, without leaving any trace. Since agents cannot prevent being annihilated once they visit a black hole, the only way of protection against such processes is identifying the hostile node and avoiding further visiting it. Hence we are dealing with the issue of locating a black hole: assuming that there is at most one black hole in the network, at least one surviving agent must find the location of the black hole if it exists, or answer that there is no black hole, otherwise. The only way to locate the black hole is to visit it by at least one agent, hence, as observed in [2], at least two agents are necessary for one of them to locate the black hole and survive. Throughout the paper we assume that the number of agents is minimum possible for our task, i.e., 2, and that they start from the same node, known to be safe.

In [1, 2, 3, 4] the issue of efficient black hole search was extensively studied in many types of networks. The underlying assumption in these papers was that the network is totally asynchronous, i.e., while every edge traversal by a mobile agent takes finite time, there is no upper bound on this time. In this setting it was observed that, in order to solve the problem, the network must be 2-connected, in particular black hole search is infeasible in trees. This is because, in asynchronous networks it is impossible to distinguish a black hole from a "slow" link incident to it. Hence the only way to locate a black hole is to visit all other nodes and learn that they are safe. (In particular, it is impossible to answer the question of whether a black hole actually exists in the network, hence [1, 2, 3, 4] worked under the assumption that there is exactly one black hole and the task was to locate it.)

Totally asynchronous networks rarely occur in practice. Often a (possibly large) upper bound on the time of traversing any edge by an agent can be established. Hence it is interesting to study black hole search in such partially synchronous networks. Without loss of generality, this upper bound on edge traversal time can be normalized to 1 which yields the following definition of the time of a black hole search scheme: this is the maximum time taken by the scheme, i.e. the time under the worst-case location of the black hole (or when it does not exist in the network), assuming that all edge traversals take time 1.

Our partially synchronous scenario makes a dramatic change to the problem of searching for a black hole. Now it is possible to use the time-out mechanism to locate the black hole in any graph, with only two agents, as follows: agents proceed along edges of a spanning tree. If they are at a safe node v, one agent goes to the adjacent node and returns, while the other agent waits at v. If after time 2 the first agent has not returned, the other one survives and knows the location of the black hole. Otherwise, the adjacent node is known to be safe and both agents can move to it. This is in fact a variant of the *cautious walk* described in [2] but combining it with the time-out mechanism makes black hole search feasible in any graph. Hence the issue is now not the feasibility but the time efficiency of black hole search, and the present paper is devoted to this problem.

Since for any network, black hole search can be done using only the edges of its spanning tree, solving the problem of fast black hole search on trees seems a natural first step. Hence in this paper we restrict attention to black hole search in tree networks using two agents, and our goal is to accomplish this task in minimum time. Clearly, in many graphs, there are more efficient black hole search schemes than those operating in a spanning tree of the graph, and the generalization of our problem to arbitrary networks remains an important and interesting open issue.

The time of a black hole search scheme should be distinguished from the time complexity of the algorithm producing such a scheme. While the first was defined above for a given input consisting of a network and a starting node, and is in fact the larger of the numbers of time units spent by the two agents, the second is the time of producing such a scheme by the algorithm. In other words, the time of the scheme is the time of walking and the time complexity of the algorithm is the time of thinking.

Constructing a fastest black hole search scheme for arbitrary trees turns out to be far from trivial. In particular, the following problem remains open. Does there exist a polynomial time algorithm which, given a tree and a starting node as input, produces a black hole search scheme working in shortest possible time for this input? Nevertheless, we show fastest schemes for some classes of trees and give a 5/3-approximation algorithm for the general case.

1.2 Our Results

For arbitrary trees we give a 5/3-approximation algorithm for the black hole search problem. More precisely, given a tree and a starting node as input, our algorithm produces a black hole search scheme whose time is at most 5/3 of the shortest possible time for this input.

We give optimal black hole search algorithms for two "extreme" classes of trees: the class of lines and the class of trees in which any internal node (including the root which is the starting node) has at least 2 children. More precisely, for every input in the respective classes these algorithms produce a black hole search scheme whose time is the shortest possible for this input.

All our algorithms work in time linear in the size of the input.

2   Model and Terminology

We consider a tree T rooted at node s which is the starting node of both agents, and is assumed to be safe (s is not a black hole). Notions of child, parent, descendant and ancestor, are meant with respect to this rooted tree. Agents have distinct labels. They can communicate only when they meet (and not, e.g., by leaving messages at nodes). We assume that there is at most one black hole in the network. This is a node which destroys any agents visiting it. A black hole search scheme (*BHS-scheme*) for the input (T, s) is a pair of sequences of edge traversals (moves) of each of the two agents, with the following properties.

- Each move takes one time unit.
- Upon completion of the scheme there is at least one surviving agent, i.e., an agent that has not visited the black hole, and this agent either knows the location of the black hole or knows that there is no black hole in the tree. The surviving agents must return to s.

The time of a black hole search scheme is the number of time units until the completion of the scheme, assuming the worst-case location of the black hole (or its absence, whichever is worse). It is easy to see that the worst case for a given scheme occurs when there is no black hole in the network or when the black hole is the last unvisited node, both cases yielding the same time. A scheme is called *fastest* for a given input if its time is the shortest possible for this input.

For any edge of a tree we define the following states:

- *unknown*, if no agent has moved yet along this edge (initial state of every edge),
- *explored*, if either the remaining agents know that there is no black hole incident to this edge, or they know which end of the edge is a black hole.

Note that in between meetings, an edge may be neither unknown nor explored. This is the case when an unknown edge has been just traversed by an agent.

Any BHS-scheme must have the following property: after a finite number of steps, at least one agent stays alive and all edges are explored (there is at most one black hole, so once the black hole has been found, all edges are explored).

The *explored territory* at step t of a BHS-scheme is the set of explored edges. At the beginning of a BHS-scheme the explored territory is empty. We say that a *meeting* occurs in node v at step t when the agents meet at node v and exchange information which *strictly increases* the explored territory. Node v is called a *meeting point*.

In any step of a BHS-scheme, an agent can traverse an edge or wait in a node. Also the two agents can meet. If at step t a meeting occurs, then the explored territory at step t is defined as the explored territory *after* the meeting. The sequence of steps of a BHS-scheme between two consecutive meetings is called a *phase*.

3   Preliminary Results

Lemma 1. *In a BHS-scheme, an unexplored edge cannot be traversed by both agents.*

Hence in a BHS-scheme, an edge can be explored only in the following way: an agent traverses this edge and then a meeting is scheduled. Whether it occurs or not (in the latter case the agent vanished in the black hole) the edge becomes explored.

Lemma 2. *During a phase of a BHS-scheme an agent can traverse at most one unexplored edge.*

Therefore an unknown edge could be explored in the next phase only if it is adjacent to the explored territory. The explored territory increases only at scheduled meeting points.

Lemma 3. *At the end of each phase, the explored territory is increased by one or two edges.*

We define a *1-phase* to be a phase in which exactly one edge is explored. Similarly, we define a *2-phase* to be a phase in which exactly two edges are explored. In view of Lemma 3, every phase is either a 1-phase or a 2-phase.

Lemma 4. *Let v be a meeting point at step t in a BHS-scheme. Then at least one of the following holds: $v = s$ or v is an endpoint of an edge which was already explored at step $t - 1$.*

Hence an agent which traversed an unexplored edge must return to the explored territory in order to go to the meeting point. A corollary of Lemmas 1, 2 and 4 is that at any step of a BHS-scheme the explored territory is connected.

A node p is called a *limit* of the explored territory at step t if it is incident both to an explored and to an unexplored edge.

A way of exploring exactly one edge in a phase is the following: one of the agents walks through the explored territory to its limit p, while the other agent walks through the explored territory to p, traverses an unknown edge and returns to p. If we assume that both agents are at a limit p of the explored territory at step t and (p, u) is an unknown edge towards node v, we define the following procedure:

probe(v): one agent traverses edge (p, u) (which is towards node v) and returns to node p to meet the other agent who waits. If they do not meet at step $t + 2$ then the black hole has been found.

We also define a procedure that the two agents could follow to explore two new edges in a phase. Suppose that the two agents reside at node m at step t. Let $p_1, ..., p_i$ be the limits of the explored territory at that step. Each of the unknown edges which could be explored in the following phase has to be incident to a node from the set $\{p_1, ..., p_i\}$. Let the two selected unknown edges for exploration be (k, p_k) and (l, p_l), $p_k, p_l \in \{p_1, ..., p_i\}$ (possibly $p_k = p_l$). We assume that node m belongs to the path $< k, l >$. The definition of the procedure is the following:

split(k, l): One of the agents traverses the path from node m to node k and returns towards node p_l. The other traverses the path from node m to node l and returns towards node p_k. Let $dist(l, k)$ denote the number of edges in the path from node k to node l. If they do not meet at step $t + dist(l, k)$ then the black hole has been found.

4   Black Hole Search in a Line

In this section we construct an optimal black hole search algorithm for lines, with linear time complexity. A line is a graph $L = (V, E)$, where $V = \{0, ..., n\}$

and $E = \{[i, i+1] : i = 0, 1, ..., n-1\}$. 0 and n are called endpoints of the line. The starting node is denoted by s, while a and b denote the distances between s and the endpoints of the line, with $a \leq b$, hence $a + b = n$. We assume $b > 0$, otherwise the line consists of a single node. We call *right* the direction from s towards the closer endpoint and *left* the other direction.

Theorem 1. *The time of any BHS-scheme on the line is at least:*

- $4n - 2$, *when* $a = 0$
- $\sum_{i=1}^{a} 2i$, *when* $1 \leq a = b \leq 5$
- $4n - 6$, *when* $a = 1 < b$
- $4n - 10$, *when* $a = 2 < b$ *or* $a = 3 < b$
- $4n - 8$, *when* $a = 4 < b$ *or* $a = 5 < b$ *or* $a \geq 6$

We will now give an optimal algorithm to solve the black hole search problem for the line (i.e. an algorithm which produces a fastest BHS-scheme for any line). Suppose that both agents reside at the same node m. The algorithm uses procedures *probe*, *split* and the following ones:

- **walk(k):** both agents go 1 step towards node k.
- **walk-and-probe(v):**
  while the position of the agents is not adjacent to node v **do**
        walk(v);
        probe(v)
- **return(s):**
  repeat walk(s) **until** all remaining agents are at s

The high-level description of Algorithm Line is the following:

- **case** $a = 0$: the two agents explore the line by probing left of s and return
- **case** $1 \leq a = b \leq 5$: the two agents explore the line by repeated splits
- **case** $a = 1 < b$: the two agents first do a split and then explore the rest of the line by probing left and return
- **case** $a = 2 < b$: the two agents first do a split, then explore all edges left of s except one by probing, and finally explore the last two edges by a split
- **case** $3 \leq a < b$ **or** $a \geq 5$: the two agents first do two splits, then explore all edges left of s except one by probing. They explore the last left edge together with an edge right of s by a split and finally explore the remaining edges (if any) which are right of s by probing and return

The precise formulation of the algorithm is given as Algorithm 1. The time complexity of the algorithm is linear.

Theorem 2. *Algorithm Line produces a fastest BHS-scheme for any line.*

The proofs of the results of this section are omitted due to lack of space and will appear in the full version of the paper.

Algorithm 1. Algorithm Line

---

case $a = 0$
      probe(0);
      walk-and-probe(0);
case $1 \leq a = b \leq 5$
      for $i := 1$ **to** a
            split$(s - i, s + i)$;
case $a = 1 < b$
      split$(s - 1, s + 1)$;
      walk-and-probe(0);
case $a = 2 < b$
      split$(s - 1, s + 1)$;
      walk-and-probe(1);
      split$(0, s + 2)$;
case $a = 3 < b$
      split$(s - 1, s + 1)$;
      split$(s - 2, s + 2)$;
      walk$(s - 1)$;
      walk-and-probe(1);
      split$(0, s + 3)$;
case $4 \leq a < b$ **OR** $a \geq 6$
      split$(s - 1, s + 1)$;
      split$(s - 2, s + 2)$;
      walk$(s - 1)$;
      walk-and-probe(1);
      split$(0, s + 3)$;
      walk$(s + 2)$;
      walk-and-probe(n);
return(s)

---

5 Black Hole Search in a Tree

In this section we study the problem of black hole search in trees.

Consider a tree T rooted at the starting node s. If e is an edge, $e = (u, v)$ means that v is the child of u. Let $e = (u, v)$ be an edge of the tree. Consider the following coloring which creates a partition of the edges of the tree. This partition will be used in the analysis of our algorithms.

- assign red color to edge e if node v has at least two descendants,
- assign green color to edge e if v is a leaf and exactly one of the following holds: $u = s$ or the edge (t, u) is a red edge (where t is the parent of u),
- assign blue color to edge e if it has none of the above properties

Let $e = (u, v)$ and $e' = (v, z)$ be two blue edges such that v is the unique child of u and z is a leaf and the unique child of v. We call the set of these two edges a *branch*. The set of all branches of blue edges with upper node u is called a *block*.

Lemma 5. *In any BHS-scheme, the following holds: a green edge has to be traversed by the agents at least 2 times, a red edge has to be traversed at least 6 times and a branch of blue edges requires a total of at least 6 traversals.*

Proof. By Lemma 1 any edge has to be traversed 2 times by one agent to become explored. In particular a green edge needs 2 traversals.

Consider a red edge $e = (u, v)$. Let l be the number of descendants of node v. In view of Lemmas 1 and 2, if during any phase after exploration edge e is traversed always by only one agent then at least $2l \geq 4$ additional traversals are required (an agent has to traverse e two times for every descendant of v). If there is at least one phase after exploration of e where the edge is traversed by both agents then at least 4 additional traversals of e are required for the exploration of the edges with upper node v (both agents traverse e and return). Thus the total minimum number of traversals is 6.

A branch of 2 blue edges can be traversed in the following ways. 2 traversals are required for the exploration of the upper edge of the branch. If during any phase after exploration of the upper edge, this edge is traversed always by only one agent then at least 4 additional edge traversals on this branch are required. If there is at least one phase after exploration of the upper edge when this edge is traversed by both agents then at least 6 additional edge traversals on this branch are required (both agents traverse the upper edge, then one of them explores the lower edge and finally they return). Therefore the total minimum number of traversals on each branch is 6.

Lemma 6. *Any BHS-scheme requires at least 3, 1 and 3b time units for the traversals of a red edge, a green edge and a block of b branches of blue edges, respectively.*

5.1   An Optimal Algorithm for a Family of Trees

Consider the family $\mathcal{T}$ of rooted trees with the following property: any internal node of a tree in $\mathcal{T}$ (including the root) has at least 2 children. Trees in $\mathcal{T}$ will be called *bushy trees*.

Let T be a bushy tree with root s and let u be an internal node of T. The *heaviest child* $v = H(u)$ of u is defined as a child v of u such that the subtree $T(v)$ rooted at v (which is also a bushy tree) has a maximum height among all subtrees rooted at children of u. The *lightest* child $v' = L(u)$ of u is defined as a child v' of u such that the subtree $T(v')$ rooted at v' has a minimum height among all subtrees rooted in a child of u. Ties are broken arbitrarily. Notice that $H(u)$ and $L(u)$ can be computed for all nodes u in linear time.

The high-level description of Algorithm Bushy-Tree is the following. Let m be the meeting point of the two agents after a phase (initially $m = s$).

- Explore any pair of unknown edges (m, x), (m, y) with upper node m by executing procedure $split(x, y)$, leaving edge $(m, L(m))$ last.
- If there is one unknown edge with upper node m (which must be $(m, L(m))$) explore this edge together with another unknown edge (if any) again using

procedure *split*. If edge $(m, L(m))$ is the last unknown edge in the tree, explore it by executing procedure $probe(L(m))$.

- If all edges with upper node m are explored, explore similarly as before any unknown edges incident to the children of m and to ancestors of m. Below we give the precise formulation of the algorithm.

Algorithm. Bushy-Tree

special-explore(s)

Procedure special-explore(v)

    for every pair of unknown edges $(v, x), (v, y)$ with upper node v **do**

        split(x, y), so that edge $(v, L(v))$ is explored last

    end for

    if every edge is explored **then**

        repeat walk(s) **until** (all remaining agents are at s)

    else

        case 1: every edge incident to v has been explored

            $next :=$ relocate(v);

            special-explore($next$);

        case 2: there is an unknown edge (v, z) incident to v

        (* must be $z = L(v)$ *)

            explore-only-child($v, next$);

            special-explore($next$);

    end if

Function relocate(v) takes as input the current node v where both agents reside and returns the new location of the two agents. If there is an unknown edge incident to a child of v then the agents go to that child. Otherwise the two agents go to the parent of v.

Function relocate(v)

    case 1.1: $\exists$ an unknown edge incident to $w \in children(v)$

        walk(w);

        relocate $:= w$

    case 1.2: every edge incident to any child of v is explored

        let t be the parent of v;

        walk(t);

        relocate $:= t$

Procedure explore-only-child($v, next$) takes as input the current node v where both agents reside and returns the new meeting point after the exploration of edge $(v, L(v))$. The description of the procedure is the following:

- If there is an unknown edge incident to a child w of v, $w \neq L(v)$, then the agents explore edge $(w, H(w))$ together with edge $(v, L(v))$ by $split(H(w), L(v))$. The new meeting point is w.
- If every edge incident to any child w of v, different from $L(v)$, is explored and edge $(v, L(v))$ is not the last unknown edge in the tree, then find the deepest ancestor a of v with unknown edges whose upper node is a descendant of a; the agents explore edge $(D(a), H(D(a)))$ (where $D(a)$ is the closest descendant of a with incident unknown edges), together with edge $(v, L(v))$, by $split(H(D(a)), L(v))$; the new meeting point is $D(a)$.
- If edge $(v, L(v))$ is the last unknown edge in the tree then explore it by calling $probe(L(v))$; the new meeting point is v.

Procedure explore-only-child($v, next$)
    case 2.1: there is an unknown edge incident to $w \in children(v)$, $w \neq L(v)$
        split($L(v), H(w)$);
        $next := w$
    case 2.2: every edge incident to any $w \in children(v)$, $w \neq L(v)$ is explored
  (* $L(v)$ must be a leaf *)
        case 2.2.1: there are at least 2 unknown edges left
          let a be the deepest ancestor of v such that:
          $D(a) :=$ the closest descendant of a with incident unknown edges;
          split($H(D(a)), L(v)$);
          $next := D(a)$
        case 2.2.2: there is only 1 unknown edge left
          probe($L(v)$);
          $next := v$

Notice that all edges of the tree (except possibly the last one if the number of edges is odd) are explored by calling procedure split. Observe that in any bushy tree, there are only *red* and *green* edges. By definition, in every red edge $e_r = (u_r, v_r)$, node v_r has at least two children and every leaf of the tree is an endpoint of a green edge $e_g = (u_g, v_g)$. Also u_g has at least two children.

Since all values $H(u)$ and $L(u)$ can be computed in linear time it is easy to see that time complexity of Algorithm Bushy-Tree is linear.

Theorem 3. *Algorithm Bushy-Tree produces a fastest BHS-scheme for any bushy tree.*

Sketch of the proof: The scheme produced by Algorithm Bushy-Tree traverses any red edge 6 times and any green edge 2 times. Moreover every phase is a 2-phase (i.e. the two agents traverse edges in parallel), except possibly the last phase (in the case when the number of edges is odd), and no agent waits in any 2-phase.

5.2   An Approximation Algorithm for Trees

In this section we give an approximation algorithm with ratio $\frac{5}{3}$ for the black hole search problem, working for arbitrary trees (i.e. an algorithm which produces a BHS-scheme whose time is at most $5/3$ of the shortest possible time, for every input).

The high-level description of Algorithm Tree is the following. Let v be the meeting point of the two agents after a phase (initially $v = s$); the edges with upper node v are explored by calling procedure split until either all such edges are explored or there is at most one remaining unknown edge incident to v, which is explored by calling procedure probe; this is repeated for any child of v. The precise formulation of the algorithm is given below. Apart from procedures split and probe it uses function relocate defined in the previous section. The time-complexity of Algorithm Tree is linear.

Algorithm. Tree
   explore(s)

Procedure explore(v)
   for every pair of unknown edges $(v, x), (v, y)$ incident to v **do**
      split(x, y);
   end for
   if there is only one remaining unknown edge (v, z) incident to v **then**
      probe(z);
   end if
   if every edge is explored **then**
      repeat walk(s) **until** both agents are at s
   else
      $next$:= relocate(v);
      explore($next$)
   end if

Lemma 7. *Let u be a node which is neither a leaf nor a middle of a branch of blue edges. Let d be the down degree of u. Let β be the number of branches of blue edges with upper node u, ρ the number of red edges with upper node u and γ the number of green edges with upper node u. Algorithm Tree spends at most $d + 4\beta + 2\rho$ time units if d is even, and $d + 1 + 4\beta + 2\rho$ time units if d is odd for the traversals of all the above edges.*

Theorem 4. *Algorithm Tree achieves $\frac{5}{3}$ approximation ratio.*

Proof. If the tree consists of a single edge, then the ratio is one. Otherwise, suppose that the tree has k nodes $u_1, u_2, ..., u_k$ such that $\forall u_i \exists v_j \ (e_{ij} = (u_i, v_j))$ is a red edge, a green edge or an upper blue edge in a branch of blue edges. In any case, $\forall u_i \neq s\ u_i$ has at least two descendants, hence (u_i', u_i) is a red edge. Thus there are at least $k - 1$ red edges in the tree. Let d_i: $i = 1, ..., k$ be the down degree of u_i. Suppose that d_i: $i = 1, ..., l$ is odd and d_i: $i = l + 1, ..., k$ is even. Let β_i be the number of branches of blue edges with upper node u_i, ρ_i the number of red edges with upper node u_i and γ_i the number of green edges with upper node u_i. We have $d_i = \beta_i + \rho_i + \gamma_i$.

According to Lemma 6, any BHS-scheme must spend at least $3\beta_i + 3\rho_i + \gamma_i$ time units on the traversals of all red edges, green edges and branches of blue edges with upper node u_i. Hence in view of Lemma 7 the ratio between the time of our scheme and the fastest possible scheme is at most:

$$\frac{\sum_{i=1}^{l}(d_i + 1 + 4\beta_i + 2\rho_i) + \sum_{i=l+1}^{k}(d_i + 4\beta_i + 2\rho_i)}{\sum_{i=1}^{k}(3\beta_i + 3\rho_i + \gamma_i)} = \frac{\sum_{i=1}^{k}(5\beta_i + 3\rho_i + \gamma_i) + l}{\sum_{i=1}^{k}(3\beta_i + 3\rho_i + \gamma_i)}$$

The above ratio is $\leq \frac{5}{3}$ when $3l \leq 6\sum_{i=1}^{k}\rho_i + 2\sum_{i=1}^{k}\gamma_i$. Since $\sum_{i=1}^{k}\rho_i \geq k - 1$, this ratio is lower or equal to $\frac{5}{3}$ when

$$6(k - 1) + 2\sum_{i=1}^{k}\gamma_i \geq 3l \tag{1}$$

If $k - 1 \geq l$ (i.e. there is at least one node of even down degree) then inequality (1) is true.

If $k - 1 < l$ it means that $l = k$. This is the situation when every vertex u_i has an odd lower degree. If $k \geq 2$, inequality (1) still holds. If $k = 1$ then there is no red edge $(u_1 = s)$. As long as there are at least two green edges, inequality (1) is true. Otherwise one of the following holds:

- The tree consists of a block of β_1 branches of blue edges where β_1 is even, and one green edge. In this case the total number of edges in the tree is odd. Hence, in any BHS-scheme at least one edge must be explored in a 1-phase. We prove that any BHS-scheme has to spend at least $3\beta_1 + 2$ time units for all the traversals. According to Lemma 5 the total number of traversals needed is at least $6\beta_1 + 2$. At least 2 of the traversals are done during a 1-phase and require at least 2 time units. Therefore the time needed in this case is at least $\frac{6\beta_1}{2} + 2 = 3\beta_1 + 2$.
  According to Lemma 7, the scheme produced by Algorithm Tree uses $d_1 + 1 + 4\beta_1 = 5\beta_1 + 2$ time units. Thus the ratio is at most $\frac{5\beta_1 + 2}{3\beta_1 + 2} \leq \frac{5}{3}$.
- The tree consists of a block of β_1 branches of blue edges where β_1 is odd. If $\beta_1 = 1$ then the ratio is one. Otherwise we prove that any BHS-scheme has to spend in this case at least $3\beta_1 + 1$ time units for all traversals.
  - If there is an edge in a branch which has been traversed by both agents during a phase then the total number of edge traversals in that branch is 8. Therefore in view of Lemma 5, the total number of traversals is at least $6(\beta_1 - 1) + 8$ and the time needed is at least $\frac{6\beta_1 + 2}{2} = 3\beta_1 + 1$.

- Otherwise, if there is at least one edge that has been explored during a 1-phase then the total number of traversals done during *2-phases* is at most $6\beta_1 - 2$ by Lemma 5, while there are 2 traversals done in a 1-phase which requires 2 time units. Therefore the time needed is at least $\frac{6\beta_1-2}{2} + 2 = 3\beta_1 + 1$.

- The remaining case is that every edge is explored during a 2-phase and there is no edge which has been traversed by both agents during a phase. Since the number of upper edges in branches is odd, there must be a 2-phase ϕ during which an upper edge of a branch is explored together with a lower edge of another branch. The time needed for this phase is at least 4 time units since both agents cannot traverse the same edge. In view of Lemma 5 the total number of traversals in every phase except ϕ is at least $6(\beta_1 - 2) + 2 + 4$ (there is a branch on which only 2 traversals are done and a branch on which only 4 traversals are done). Hence the time needed in this case is at least $\frac{6\beta_1-6}{2} + 4 = 3\beta_1 + 1$.

According to Lemma 7, the time of the scheme produced by Algorithm Tree is $d_1 + 1 + 4\beta_1 = 5\beta_1 + 1$ time units. Thus in all three cases the ratio is at most $\frac{5\beta_1+1}{3\beta_1+1} \leq \frac{5}{3}$.

Notice that there exists a family of trees in which the approximation ratio achieved by Algorithm Tree is exactly 5/3. This family includes all trees which consist of an even number β of branches of blue edges. According to Lemma 7, the time of the scheme produced by Algorithm Tree is $\beta + 4\beta = 5\beta$ for such a tree, while the fastest BHS-scheme for this tree requires exactly 3β time units (for example, all upper edges are explored two by two by calling procedure split and then all lower edges are explored in the same way).

6   Conclusion

We presented algorithms for the black hole search problem on trees. For arbitrary trees we gave a 5/3-approximation algorithm, and for two classes of trees (lines and trees all of whose internal nodes have at least 2 children) we gave optimal algorithms, i.e., methods of constructing a shortest possible black hole search scheme for any input in the class. The time complexity of all our algorithms is linear in the size of the input.

It remains open if there exists a polynomial time algorithm to construct a fastest black hole search scheme for an arbitrary tree. More generally, we do not know if the problem is polynomial for arbitrary graphs. We conjecture that the answer to the latter question is negative. Hence it seems interesting to find good approximation algorithms for the black hole search problem on arbitrary graphs. It should be noted that a trivial scheme, proceeding along any spanning tree of the graph using walk-and-probe and returning to the starting node, provides a 4-approximation algorithm for this problem.

References

1. S. Dobrev, P. Flocchini, R. Kralovic, G. Prencipe, P. Ruzicka, N. Santoro, Black hole search by mobile agents in hypercubes and related networks, Proc. of Symposium on Principles of Distributed Systems (OPODIS 2002), 171-182.
2. S. Dobrev, P. Flocchini, G. Prencipe, N. Santoro, Mobile agents searching for a black hole in an anonymous ring, Proc. of 15th International Symposium on Distributed Computing, (DISC 2001), 166-179.
3. S. Dobrev, P. Flocchini, G. Prencipe, N. Santoro, Searching for a black hole in arbitrary networks: Optimal Mobile Agents Protocols, Proc. 21st ACM Symposium on Principles of Distributed Computing (PODC 2002), 153-161.
4. S. Dobrev, P. Flocchini, G. Prencipe, N. Santoro, Multiple agents rendezvous on a ring in spite of a black hole, Proc. Symposium on Principles of Distributed Systems (OPODIS 2003).
5. F. Hohl, Time limited black box security: Protecting mobile agents from malicious hosts, Proc. Conf. on Mobile Agent Security (1998), LNCS 1419, 92-113.
6. F. Hohl, A framework to protect mobile agents by using reference states, Proc. 20th Int. Conf. on Distributed Computing Systems (ICDCS 2000), 410-417.
7. S. Ng, K. Cheung, Protecting mobile agents against malicious hosts by intention of spreading, Proc. Int. Conf. on Parallel and Distributed Processing and Applications (PDPTA'99), 725-729.
8. T. Sander, C.F. Tschudin, Protecting mobile agents against malicious hosts, Proc. Conf. on Mobile Agent Security (1998), LNCS 1419, 44-60.
9. K. Schelderup, J. Ines, Mobile agent security – issues and directions, Proc. 6th Int. Conf. on Intelligence and Services in Networks, LNCS 1597 (1999), 155-167.
10. J. Vitek, G. Castagna, Mobile computations and hostile hosts, in: Mobile Objects, D. Tsichritzis, Ed., University of Geneva, 1999, 241-261.

Fast Localized Delaunay Triangulation*

Filipe Araújo and Luís Rodrigues

Universidade de Lisboa, Departamento de Informática,
Faculdade de Ciências, Campo Grande,
Edifício C6, 1749-016 Lisboa, Portugal
{filipius, ler}@di.fc.ul.pt

Abstract. A localized Delaunay triangulation owns the following interesting properties in a wireless *ad hoc* setting: it can be built with localized
information, the communication cost imposed by control information is
limited and it supports geographical routing algorithms that offer guaranteed convergence. This paper presents a localized algorithm that builds
a graph called planar localized Delaunay triangulation, *PLDel*, known
to be a good spanner of the unit disk graph, *UDG*. Unlike previous work,
our algorithm builds *PLDel* in a single communication step, maintaining a communication cost of $O(n \log n)$, which is within a constant of
the optimum. This represents a significant practical improvement over
previous algorithms with similar theoretical bounds. Furthermore, the
small cost of our algorithm makes feasible to use *PLDel* in real systems,
instead of the Gabriel or the Relative Neighborhood graphs, which are
not good spanners of *UDG*.

Keywords: Wireless *ad hoc* networks, Location-based routing schemes,
Delaunay triangulation.

1 Introduction

Wireless *ad hoc* networks are networks where nodes communicate with neighbors
within some range using a wireless link. Nodes of a wireless network typically
operate on batteries and thus have relatively few memory and energy resources.
It is therefore utterly important to rely on routing schemes with small state and
communication overhead. This requirement can be met by a *localized* routing
scheme, where nodes only maintain information about other nodes within a
limited neighborhood. On the other hand, for the sake of efficiency, a routing
scheme should be *competitive*, i.e., any path found by the scheme should be at
most c times longer than the shortest path. However, Kuhn *et al.* proved that no
localized scheme can be c-competitive [9]. Still, a localized routing scheme can
guarantee convergence, while achieving competitive path lengths in most cases.

---

* This work was partially supported by LaSIGE and by the FCT project INDIQoS
POSI/CHS/41473/2001 via POSI and FEDER funds.

T. Higashino (Ed.): OPODIS 2004, LNCS 3544, pp. 81–93, 2005.

One way of achieving competitive routing is to build a global Delaunay Triangulation [2]. Unfortunately, building such a graph is not a viable solution to the routing problem in *ad hoc* wireless networks, because: *i)* edges may be longer than communication range; *ii)* it cannot be built locally and therefore, communication cost is too high. Hence, our approach is to build a planar graph (i.e., without intersection of edges) as dense as possible ($O(n)$ edges), using Delaunay triangulations, but in a localized fashion. The point of having a dense graph is to use routing algorithms that achieve good hop count performance, while planarity is necessary to ensure convergence.

In literature, there are several algorithms that build Delaunay triangulations for routing purposes, e.g., [12, 13, 6, 10]. The algorithm in [13] builds a subgraph of the global Delaunay triangulation that only includes some of the edges within communication range of nodes; [12], [6] and [10] build a denser graph, with global communication cost of $O(n \log n)$, $O(n^2)$ and $O(n^2)$, respectively. While [6] and [10] are not optimal, [12] involves 4 communication steps to build the final subgraph, which may be prohibitive in practical systems. Hence, in this paper, we improve on the work of Li *et. al* [12], by presenting an algorithm that is considerably simpler and yet builds the same *Planar Localized Delaunay Triangulation* graph (*PLDel*), with the same asymptotic communication cost, but with just a single communication step (we define a communication step as the period required for sending and then receiving one or more messages which are not causally related).

Therefore, our algorithm is well suited to wireless environments for the following reasons: *i)* it is very efficient as it requires just one communication step; *ii)* it is applicable to dynamic and asynchronous settings (see Section 6); *iii)* it is localized, only requiring nodes to receive information broadcast by direct neighbors, thus requiring a communication cost within a small constant of the optimum (assuming that a beacon message of $O(\log n)$ bits in an n-node network is necessary per node); *iv)* it requires nodes to keep track of only a constant number of neighbors in the average; *v)* under the constraint of preserving planarity, it builds a graph with good density (see Section 5).

The rest of the paper is structured as follows. For self-containment we provide a short overview of necessary concepts in Section 2. In Section 3 we provide a survey on related work on wireless networks and Delaunay triangulations. In Section 4 we describe our algorithm and prove its correctness. In Section 5, we experimentally evaluate our algorithm. The appplication of the algorithm in dynamic settings is discussed in Section 6. Finally, Section 7 concludes the paper.

2   Preliminaries

We assume that nodes can determine their own position and the position of their neighbors. Given a set of nodes V in a two dimensional space, we model a wireless *ad hoc* network as a unit disk graph, $UDG(V)$, which is comprised of all nodes V and all edges connecting pairs of nodes of V whose distance is at most 1, i.e., in this model, two nodes A and B are direct neighbors (or simply *neighbors*) if and only if $||AB|| \leq 1$. Nodes A and B are k-hop neighbors if they can reach each other in k or fewer hops. Throughout this paper, we will use the following notation: a triangle defined by nodes A, B and C is represented as $\triangle ABC$; an angle $(< \pi)$ between edges AB and AC defined at A is interchangeably represented as $\angle BAC$ or $\angle CAB$; the circle whose diameter is defined by two nodes A and B is represented as $d(A,B)$; the circumcircle defined by node A, B and C is represented as $\bigcirc ABC$.

The *Gabriel graph (GG)* is comprised of all edges AB such that $d(A,B)$ does not contain any other node of V. The edges of a GG are called *Gabriel edges*. The *Relative neighborhood graph (RNG)* is comprised of all edges AB such that there is no node C for which $||AC|| < ||AB||$ and $||BC|| < ||AB||$ (i.e., node C, cannot be simultaneously closer to A and B than A and B are from each other). It should be noted that RNG is a subgraph of GG. The *Delaunay triangulation* (DT) of a node set V, represented as $Del(V)$, is the set of edges satisfying the "empty circle" property: edge AB belongs to the triangulation if and only if there is a circle containing A and B, but not containing any other node. An important property of $Del(V)$ that will be of use to us, states that the circumcircle of a triangle does not contain any node of V. Under the UDG model, a complete Delaunay triangulation may not exist, because some edges may be longer than 1 and therefore, we refer to $UDel(V) = Del(V) \cap UDG(V)$ instead.

In this paper we will use the definition proposed in [12] of k-*localized Delaunay graph over a node set* V, $LDel^{(k)}(V)$. $LDel^{(k)}(V)$ is comprised of two types of edges (not longer than 1): *i)* all edges from the GG; and *ii)* edges of all triangles ABC for which there are no nodes inside $\bigcirc ABC$ reachable by A, B or C in k or fewer hops. Li *et al.* [12] proved that $LDel^{(k)}(V)$ is planar for $k \geq 2$, but edges may intersect for $k = 1$. $PLDel(V)$ [12, 10] is defined as a planar graph comprised of all triangles of $LDel^{(1)}(V)$, *except* intersecting triangles that do not belong to $LDel^{(2)}(V)$. Moreover, Li *et al.* [12] proved that $UDel(V)$ is a $(4\sqrt{3}\pi)/9$-spanner of $UDG(V)$ and that $LDel^{(k)}(V) \supseteq UDel(V)$. Hence $PLDel(V)$ and $LDel^{(k)}(V)$, for all k, are also $(4\sqrt{3}\pi)/9$-spanners of $UDG(V)$.

3   Related Work

In literature, we can find several algorithms that build Delaunay triangulations, e.g. [11, 4, 16]. Of particular interest to us are the algorithms that allow Delaunay triangulations to be computed in an incremental way [1, 17], as new nodes that arrive later do not force a recomputation of the entire triangulation.

In [14], Liebeherr *et al.* proposed an algorithm to build a complete non-localized Delaunay triangulation that serves as an overlay network on top of IP. However, direct application of this algorithm to the more complex setting of a wireless environment is not possible since Delaunay neighbors may not be able to communicate if their distance is greater than 1. In the context of wireless networks, geographic routing algorithms like greedy and compass have received wide attention in literature [8, 18]: these algorithms are memoryless and may achieve excellent performance in dense graphs or even in graphs with $O(n)$ edges, based on Delaunay triangulations, as shown by experimental results of [12, 10]. Unfortunately, these algorithms are not guaranteed to converge. When they fail, one has to use alternative routing algorithms, such as algorithms based on the right-hand rule which are guaranteed to converge as long as the graph is planar. This commutation from greedy to perimeter routing was first proposed in [3] and later explored in a protocol called Greedy-Perimeter Stateless Routing (GPSR) [7]. To extract planar subgraphs from non-planar graphs, RNG, GG or variations of the Delaunay triangulation [19, 5, 2, 13], may be used. As density is important to achieve good routing performance, many authors have focused on increasing it, to create good spanners of $UDG(V)$ [6, 20, 10, 12]. Some of these approaches [6, 10, 12] are based on Delaunay triangulations, because efficient algorithms can be used to build graphs that are good spanners of $UDG(V)$.

Gao $et\ al.$ [6] use a triangulation algorithm that builds a planar graph called $restricted\ Delaunay\ graph$ (RDG). RDG is a graph that contains $UDel(V)$. Communication cost of their algorithm is $O(n^2)$ In [12], Li $et\ al.$ presented an algorithm that builds $PLDel(V)$ (also a supergraph of $UDel(V)$), with communication cost of $O\,(n \log n)$. Lan and Wen-Jing [10] also build $PLDel(V)$ but with higher communication cost ($O(n^2)$). In [13], Li $et\ al.$ presented algorithms that build subgraphs of $UDel(V)$ based on 1 and 2-hop neighbor information. Although their algorithms are simple, their graphs are less dense than any of the previous graphs and it is unclear whether they are good spanners of $UDG(V)$.

Our algorithm improves the results of Li $et\ al.$ [12]. Although the asymptotic communication cost of both algorithms is the same, namely $O(n \log n)$, our algorithm requires one communication step, while [12] requires 4 communication steps. Thus, our algorithm converges much faster. Furthermore, the total signaling cost of our algorithm is much smaller, as we will show in the evaluation section, because in FLDT nodes send only a subset of the Delaunay triangulation in their single communication step (if the subset is empty no message is sent).

4   Triangulation Algorithm

In this section we present a new Fast Localized Delaunay Triangulation (FLDT) algorithm that builds a $PLDel(V)$ graph.

4.1   Description

The FLDT algorithm is decentralized, as it does not rely on any centralized component, and localized, since nodes are only required to gather knowledge about some nodes in their 2-hop neighborhood. The algorithm builds a triangulation that ensures routing between any pair of nodes as long as $UDG(V)$ is connected. The algorithm consists of the following logical steps:

1. The *neighbor discovery* step. The purpose of this step is to allow nodes to discover their neighbors. For sake of clarity, we first describe and analyze the algorithm in the context of a fixed setting, where all nodes know their neighbors $a\ priori$. The discussion of the use of our algorithm in the context of dynamic settings (that may require the exchange of BEACON messages) is postponed to Section 6.

2. The _triangulation_ step. The purpose of this step is to let each node compute and advertise to its neighbors the relevant Delaunay triangulations. Based on the information collected during the neighbor discovery step, each node P locally computes a Delaunay triangulation. For convenience of exposition, we introduce the predicate $Delaunay\triangle_P(Q, R)$ that holds true at P if, according to the triangulation computed by node P, triangle $\triangle PQR$ should exist. $Delaunay\triangle PQR$ will also be used when referring to the predicate at no particular node. When $Delaunay\triangle_P(Q, R)$ holds at P, if $\angle QPR \geq \pi/3$, then P broadcasts a TRIANGULATE $\triangle PQR$ message to all nodes within range.

The purpose of the $\pi/3$ condition is to ensure that no node will issue more than 6 TRIANGULATE messages by its own initiative (as in [12]). Since no additional messages are sent in the following steps, total communication cost of FLDT is $O(n \log n)$. In practice, the constant involved in this bound is small, because, as we show in Section 5, each node announces less than 6 other nodes in average.

3. The _sanity_ step. The purpose of this step is to let neighbor nodes eliminate inconsistent Delaunay triangulations. They do so by comparing triangulations computed locally with the triangulations computed by their neighbors in Step 2, as advertised by TRIANGULATE messages. Note that by processing TRIANGULATE messages, nodes may learn about new nodes that are not their direct neighbors. This addititional information will never create new Delaunay triangulations, as triangulations must be formed with direct neighbors. However, TRIANGULATE messages may invalidate some of the triangulations computed in Step 2. This may happen at P if: $i)$ Q or R broadcast a TRIANGULATE message with some node T that invalidates $\triangle PQR$, i.e., $T \in \bigcirc PQR$, or $ii)$ some node W sends a TRIANGULATE message with an intersecting triangle WXZ, where either X or Z invalidate $\triangle PQR$, i.e., $X \in \bigcirc PQR$ or $Z \in \bigcirc PQR$. Case $i)$ ensures that a node only maintains a predicate if its neighbors are not aware of some node that invalidates it, while case $ii)$ avoids the existence of intersections[1].

4. The _Gabriel edges_ step. The purpose of this step is to add to the graph all missing Gabriel edges. Otherwise, despite always being correct, a Gabriel edge PQ for which no predicate $Delaunay\triangle_P(Q, R)$ holds at P (e.g., after switching to false in Step 3) would not be included by P. This will increase the density of the graph, while keeping $O(n)$ edges (note that a Gabriel edge always belongs to the Delaunay triangulation and can be determined locally without additional exchange of information).

Optimization. To simplify our algorithm, all TRIANGULATE messages should be sent in a single control message.   □

When comparing FLDT with previous solutions [12, 10] one must notice that the simplicity of our algorithm comes from two insights, that we later prove cor-

---

[1] Note that case $i)$ can also prevent some intersections.

rect in Section 4.2. First, proposals sent in TRIANGULATE messages, alone, suffice to confirm or reject triangulations proposed by neighbors in their own TRIANGU-LATE messages (and vice-versa), i.e., there is no need to dedicated replies. This insight builds on the observation that two Delaunay neighbors do not need to agree on some predicate $Delaunay \triangle PQR$. It can hold at P but not at Q and R if these two latter nodes are out of range of each other. The fundamental issue is, in fact, to ensure that two nodes P and Q always agree on whether edge PQ should exist (Lemma 4). Second, if three nodes P, Q and R wrongly assume the existence of $\triangle PQR$, intersected by $\triangle WXZ$, such that one of the nodes of $\triangle WXZ$ is inside $\bigcirc PQR$, then P, Q and R will listen to the same TRIANGU-LATE message on $\triangle WXZ$, thus commuting the predicate $Delaunay \triangle PQR$ to false simultaneously at P, Q, and R (Lemma 5).

4.2   FLDT Builds $PLDel(V)$ in a Single Communication Step

In this Section we show that, after a single communication step, our algorithm builds $PLDel(V)$. To see this, we reason as follows and present the necessary proofs afterward. The triangulation computed at step 2 of the algorithm is a super-graph of $LDel^{(1)}(V)$. Only step 3 of the algorithm removes edges from the graph: either edges from triangles that did not belong to $LDel^{(1)}(V)$ in the first place, and edges from all intersecting triangles that did not belong to $LDel^{(2)}(V)$. Therefore, the graph built by FLDT is a subgraph of $LDel^{(1)}(V)$ (Lemma 3), which is planar (Lemma 5). In fact, this graph is $PLDel(V)$ (Theorem 1).

In the proofs we assume that the network is static and that links are perfect (*i.e.*, no messages are lost). This assumption is made for sake of clarity. In Section 6 we discuss how lossy links can be addressed by the algorithm in practical dynamic settings (where nodes can join or leave). Note also that in the proofs we assume that no four nodes are co-circular (this scenario can be trivially addressed using simple tie-breaking rules).

Lemma 1. *In the $UDG(V)$ model, if two edges AB and CD of a given node set V intersect, then at least one of the nodes is within communication range of the other three.*

Proof. We first note that if AB intersects CD and if $d(A, B)$ includes C, C knows of A, B and D. Since AB intersects CD, $d(A, B)$ and $d(C, D)$ have overlapping areas (one may even contain the other) and hence it follows that at least one of the nodes (e.g., C) is inside the circle defined by the other pair of nodes (e.g. $d(A, B)$), thus proving the Lemma.   □

Lemma 2. *If after the Delaunay triangulation computed at step 2 of the FLDT algorithm, Delaunay $\triangle_A(B, C)$ holds, but edge AB cannot exist at B, B will send a TRIANGULATE message with at least one node $D \in \bigcirc ABC$.*

Proof. Refer to Figure 1. Since non-Gabriel edge AB exists at A, C must be inside $d(A, B)$ (e.g. see [10]). In this case, AB cannot exist at B if $Delau$-

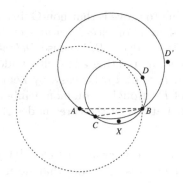

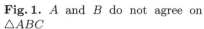

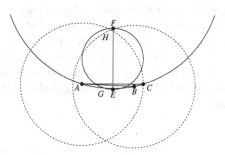

Fig. 1. A and B do not agree on $\triangle ABC$

Fig. 2. A, B and C wrongly agree on $\triangle ABC$

$nay\triangle_B(X, D)$ holds at B for some nodes X and D and XD intersects AB (assume w.l.o.g. that X and C are on the same side of AB, possibly with $X = C$). $D \in \bigcirc ABC$, because otherwise $\bigcirc BXD$, would contain A which would be a contradiction (D' in the figure must be outside $d(A, B)$ and closer to B than to A: $\bigcirc D'BC$ intersects $\bigcirc ABC$ at B and C, thus for $X = C$ it contains A; if $X \neq C$, $\bigcirc D'BX$ intersects $\bigcirc D'BC$ at B and D', thus containing the part of $\bigcirc D'BC$ that contains A). Since, $\angle XBD > \angle ABD > \pi/3$, B will send information of D in its TRIANGULATE messages. □

Corollary 1. *At the end of the FLDT algorithm, any node N, simultaneously neighbor of A and B in the conditions of Lemma 2, will know about some node $D \in \bigcirc ABC$.*

Lemma 3. *At the end of the FLDT algorithm, Delaunay$\triangle_A(B, C)$ holds at A only if there is no direct neighbor D of A, B or C such that $D \in \bigcirc ABC$.*

Proof. If edge AB cannot exist at B, the proof follows from Lemma 2. Hence, we will focus on the case where AB exists at A and B. The case where there is a common neighbor $C \in d(A, B)$ for which Delaunay$\triangle ABC$ holds at A and B, does not contradict the Lemma. Assume now that Delaunay$\triangle_A(B, C)$ holds, while Delaunay$\triangle_B(A, C)$ does not (Delaunay$\triangle_B(A, D)$ holds instead, with C and D lying on the same side of edge AB). Since $C, D \notin d(A, B)$ [10] we can use circumcircles to argue that either $D \in \bigcirc ABC$ with $\|DA\| > 1$ or $\|BC\| > 1$ (both cases can occur simultaneously). The latter case alone does not contradict the Lemma and, in the former case, since $\|AD\| > 1$, $\angle ABD > \pi/3$ and hence, B will send a TRIANGULATE message on $\triangle ABD$, thus making A switch Delaunay$\triangle_A(B, C)$ to false. The Lemma follows. □

Lemma 4. *At the end of the FLDT algorithm, if edge AB exists at A, it must exist at B, either because it is a Gabriel edge or because there is one predicate Delaunay$\triangle ACB$ holding at A and B for some common neighbor $C \in d(A, B)$.*

Proof. Given Lemma 2, the only not so trivial thing to prove is that non-Gabriel edge AB cannot be deleted by A and maintained by B or vice-versa at step 3 of the algorithm. Hence, assume that node A deletes edge AB, because $Delaunay\triangle_A(B, C)$ does not hold anymore due to some intersecting edge with node $D \in \bigcirc ABC$, which is not a direct neighbor of A, B or C. In this case, by Lemmas 1 and 3, A must have received information of D through a common neihbor of A, B and C and $Delaunay\triangle ABC$ will not hold at any of the three nodes A, B or C. ☐

As a consequence of the Lemma 3, the final graph is a subgraph of $LDel^{(1)}(V)$ (which may not be planar). The following Lemma serves to ensure that no intersection is possible.

Lemma 5. *Graph built by FLDT is planar.*

Proof. Refer to Figure 2 [12, 10]. Assume that $Delaunay\triangle ABC$ holds at A, B and C and that $\triangle ABC$ intersects EF (at AB and AC). If E has more than one intersecting edge with AB, assume w.l.o.g. that EF defines the minimum angle $\angle FEA$, with $F \in \bigcirc ABC$ (E cannot define an intersecting edge EF' if $F' \notin \bigcirc ABC$, because, in that case, any circle containing E and F' would have to include at lest one of the nodes A, B or C known by E). By Lemma 4, edge EF exists at E only if EF is a Gabriel edge or if some predicate $Delaunay\triangle EFG$ holds at E and F at the end of the algorithm (assume w.l.o.g. that G is at the left of EF). In the latter case, either EG or GF would also intersect AB and AC. Since by hypothesis F defines the smallest angle $\angle FEA$ it must be GF. By Lemma 1, in this case, G must be within communication range of A, B and C. $\angle AFB < \pi/3 \Rightarrow \angle EFG < \pi/3$, which means that A (the same goes for B and C) will always listen to some TRIANGULATE message with edge EF (from E or G) and will eliminate wrong edge AB (AC).

Now, consider the case where EF is a Gabriel edge. Then, there must be some node G, possibly $G = A$ for which $Delaunay\triangle_E(F, G)$ holds. By hypothesis AB and GE do not intersect. If $\angle FEG > \pi/3$ E sends a TRIANGULATE message and the Lemma follows. Otherwise, a new subdivision in cases is needed: GE exists at G and GE does not exist at G. In the first case, $Delaunay\triangle_G(E, H)$ holds and H may be, in fact, node F. For reasons similar to the ones given before, $H \in \bigcirc ABC$. $\angle AHB < \pi/3 \Rightarrow \angle GHE < \pi/3$. Since G knows of F, $H \neq F \Rightarrow ||HE|| > 1 \Rightarrow \angle HGE > \pi/3$. This means that either G or E or both will send a TRIANGULATE message with information of F or $H \in \bigcirc ABC$. In the second case, if the triangulation computed by G does not include non-Gabriel edge GE then, by Lemma 2, for some $X \in d(E, G)$, G will send information of $H \in \bigcirc EXG \Rightarrow H \in \bigcirc ABC$ above AB. Whether GE exists or not in G, by Lemma 1 and Corollary 1 A, B and C will hear about some intersecting edge with node $H \in \bigcirc ABC$, thus switching $Delaunay\triangle ABC$ to false. ☐

We know that since nodes can send their TRIANGULATE messages independently of each other in a single communication step, by Lemmas 3 and 5 and for the reasons explained before, it follows that FLDT builds a subgraph of

$PLDel(V)$. However, we still need to prove that it is not possible for some edge $AB \in LDel^{(1)}(V)$ to be incorrectly deleted due to the announcement of some other intersecting edge $EF \notin LDel^{(1)}(V)$.

Theorem 1. *After a single step of communication, FLDT builds the graph $PLDel(V)$.*

Proof. Refer to Figure 2. If $AB \in LDel^{(1)}(V)$ is deleted by existence of edge $EF \notin LDel^{(1)}(V)$ it cannot be a Gabriel edge, because a Gabriel edge is always correct. Hence, $\exists C \in d(A, B) \mid Delaunay \triangle ABC$ holds at A and B. However, w.l.o.g. $F \in \bigcirc ABC$. Since $EF \notin LDel^{(1)}(V)$, it is not a Gabriel edge and $\exists K_1 \in d(E, F)$ (not shown), such that $K_1 E$ or $K_1 F$ intersects AB (note that $||K_1 E|| < ||EF||$ and $||K_1 F|| < ||EF||$). Given that $A, B \notin d(E, F)$ and $A, B \notin d(K_1, E)$ if intersection is with $K_1 E$ ($d(K_1, F)$ if intersection is with $K_1 F$), it follows that even if the intersecting edge $\notin LDel^{(1)}(V)$, we can inductively repeat the reasoning until we find one intersecting edge $\in LDel^{(1)}(V)$. Hence, even if AB is deleted due to some edge $EF \notin LDel^{(1)}(V)$, there is some other edge $\in LDel^{(1)}(V)$ that would legitimately delete AB. Theorem follows. $\square$

5   Evaluation

In this section, we compare *i*) routing performance in each of the following graphs: RNG, GG, $PLDel$, UDG and DT and *ii*) signaling cost of FLDT versus the algorithm of [12]. Figure 3 illustrates the graphs in a network of 100 nodes. We have used the GPSR routing algorithm [7] in all graphs, except UDG, which is not planar. In UDG we have used the greedy routing algorithm. Results for DT are depicted only to serve as a reference, because, as we have discussed before, such triangulation is not possible in a wireless environment. Since node density has a crucial impact on the performance of routing algorithms, in our experiments, we have distributed a variable number of nodes (between 140 and 600) inside a square of fixed side (7.5 times the communication range). The reader should notice that density cannot be arbitrarily reduced, because disconnected topologies would result with high probability. On the other hand, increasing node density will benefit UDG, because greedy routing will converge with increasingly higher probability and, unlike the remaining graphs, paths will become shorter.

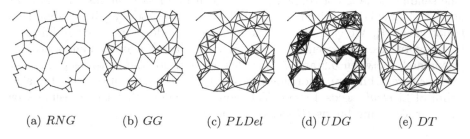

(a) *RNG*   (b) *GG*   (c) *PLDel*   (d) *UDG*   (e) *DT*

Fig. 3. Example of graphs

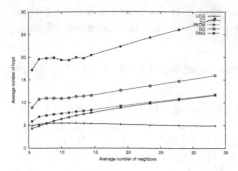
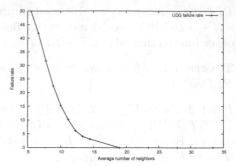

Fig. 4. Average number of hops   **Fig. 5.** Failure rate in the UDG

Figure 4 shows the average path length in number of hops (for paths where greedy did not failed), while Figure 5 depicts the percentage of failures for the greedy routing algorithm in the UDG graph. Both curves are functions of the average number of neighbors of a node[2]. From the figures, it is quite evident that when node density is high, no subgraph can do better than UDG, unless memory usage is an issue and a node does not want to maintain all its neighbors. In this case, $PLDel$ may be a good option, because nodes need to maintain only a constant number of neighbors in average. On the other hand, when node density decreases, $PLDel$ is definitely the preferable choice, because it achieves the best performance among the algorithms that ensure routing convergence. Since the possibility of a greedy routing failure always exists, no matter how large node density is, it may also be a good idea to maintain two graphs in memory: UDG and $PLDel$. The point is to use greedy in UDG whenever possible for performance reasons and switch back to a right-hand rule algorithm and to $PLDel$ in case greedy fails. Such solution has the advantage of being oblivious to node density. It is also interesting to observe that the number of hops obtained in $PLDel$ is typically quite close to that number in a DT, for high densities, where all edges are short, but the same is not true when node densities are small, because in these cases, DT uses long edges, thus saving many hops.

To complete our evaluation, we depict in Figure 6 the average number of neighbors announced by each node, in the algorithm of Li *et al.* and in our own algorithm. Note that whenever a triangle is announced, two nodes are counted (the sending node is not counted). The algorithm of Li *et al.* also needs to announce Gabriel edges, which are counted as only one node (again, sending node is not counted). We can see that the number of nodes announced stabilizes in both algorithms as the density increases, and that our algorithm announces approximately between 5.2 and 7 times fewer nodes for the densities of interest. Furthermore, while our algorithm needs a single communication step, the algorithm of Li *et al.* needs 4 steps. Therefore, we believe that these results show that our algorithm builds $PLDel$ very efficiently.

---

[2] For a node whose communication (unit) disk is entirely inside the simulation square.

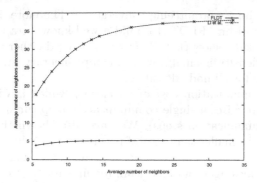

Fig. 6. Average number of neighbors announced by each node

6   Application in Dynamic Settings

So far, we have described the execution of our algorithm in a static setting, where a node knows *a priori* all its neighbors. We now discuss the application of our algorithm in dynamic settings.

The application of any graph building algorithm in a dynamic setting requires a complementary mechanism to discover new nodes and to detect the departure/failure of existing nodes. In an optimized implementation, the concrete mechanisms to be used may depend on the physical and data link layer technology. However, in the literature (for instance, [12, 10]) it is usually assumed that nodes periodically exchange BEACON messages. We would like to emphasize that our algorithm is particularly well suited for such setting, as TRI-ANGULATE messages can be easily piggybacked to (or even replace) BEACON messages. Therefore, when BEACON messages are required, our algorithm can be implemented with no additional messages, becoming extremely competitive with regard to the Gabriel or the Relative Neighborhood graphs, which are not good spanners of UDG.

Also, for sake of simplicity, we have assumed perfect channels in our exposition (i.e., no message losses). However, in a dynamic setting, BEACON messages have to be exchanged periodically. This means that, at no additional cost in terms of number of messages exchanged, our algorithm may retransmit periodically TRIANGULATE and recalculate $PLDel$ at the end of each period. Therefore, even if links are lossy, it can be shown that, as long as links are fair (*i.e.*, if a message is sent infinitely often by a process p then it can be received infinitely often by its receiver [15]), any new node will eventually participate in the triangulation.

7   Conclusions

Routing protocols for wireless *ad hoc* networks may benefit from using a planar and localized Delaunay triangulation to achieve good routing performance, while, at the same time, guaranteeing convergence. Therefore, in this paper we presented a new algorithm, FLDT, to build a well-known graph called *PLDel*. Our experimental results show that *PLDel* can be used either to substitute the *UDG*, when node density is small, or as a complementary graph that ensures routing convergence for all node densities.

FLDT has a communication cost of $O(n \log n)$, which is within a constant of the optimal and requires a single communication step (unlike previous work, that requires 4 communication steps). We have also shown that the signaling cost of FLDT is much smaller than that of previous approaches, due to the small number of control messages. Furthermore, in dynamic settings that require the exchange of beacon messages, our algorithm requires no more messages than the algorithms used to build the very simple but inefficient *GG* or *RNG*. Therefore, due to its efficiency, our algorithm is of practical relevance in location-based wireless *ad hoc* networks.

Acknowledgments

The authors are thankful to Antónia Lopes for her helpful comments on earlier versions of this paper.

References

1. Jean-Daniel Boissonnat and Monique Teillaud. On the randomized construction of the Delaunay tree. *Theoretical Computer Science*, 112(2):339–354, 1993.
2. Prosenjit Bose and Pat Morin. Online routing in triangulations. In *10th Annual Internation Symposium on Algorithms and Computation (ISAAC)*, 1999.
3. Prosenjit Bose, Pat Morin, Ivan Stojmenović, and Jorge Urrutia. Routing with guaranteed delivery in *ad hoc* wireless networks. In *International Workshop on Discrete Algorithms and Methods for Mobile Computing and Communications (DIALM)*, pages 48–55, 1999.
4. S. Fortune. A sweepline algorithm for Voronoi diagrams. *Algorithmica*, (2):153–174, 1987.
5. K. Gabriel and R. Sokal. A new statistichal approach to geographic variation analysis. *Systematic Zoology*, 18:259–278, 1969.
6. Jie Gao, Leonidas J. Guibas, John Hershberger, Li Zhang, and An Zhu. Geometric spanners for routing in mobile networks. In *2nd ACM Symposium on Mobile Ad Hoc Networking and Computing (MobiHoc 01)*, 2001.
7. Brad Karp and H. T. Kung. GPRS: Greedy perimeter stateless routing for wireless networks. In *ACM/IEEE International Conference on Mobile Computing and Networking*, 2000.
8. E. Kranakis, H. Singh, and J. Urrutia. Compass routing on geometric networks. In *11th Canadian Conference on Computation Geometry (CCCG 99)*, 1999.
9. Fabian Kuhn, Roger Wattenhofer, and Aaron Zollinger. Asymptotically optimal geometric mobile ad-hoc routing. In *6th International Workshop on Discrete Algorithms and Methods for Mobile Computing and Communications (DIALM'02)*, 2002.

10. Luan Lan and Hsu Wen-Jing. Localized Delaunay triangulation for topological construction and routing on manets. In *2nd ACM Workshop on Principles of Mobile Computing (POMC'02)*, 2002.

11. Der-Tsai Lee and Bruce J. Schachter. Two algorithms for constructing a Delaunay triangulation. *International Journal of Computer and Information Sciences*, 9(3):219–242, 1980.

12. Xiang-Yang Li, Gruia Calinescu, and Peng-Jun Wan. Distributed construction of a planar spanner and routing for ad hoc wireless networks. In *The 21st Annual Joint Conference of the IEEE Computer and Communications Societies (INFOCOM)*, 2002.

13. Xiang-Yang Li, Ivan Stojmenovic, and Yu Wang. Partial delaunay triangulation and degree limited localized bluetooth scatternet formation. *IEEE Transactions on Parallel and Distributed Systems*, 15(4):350–361, April 2004.

14. J. Liebeherr, M. Nahas, and W. Si. Application-layer multicasting with Delaunay triangulation overlays. Technical Report CS-2001-26, University of Virginia, Department of Computer Science, Charlottesville, VA 22904, 5 2001.

15. N. Lynch. Distributed algorithms. In *Data Link Protocols*, chapter 16, pages 691–732. Morgan-Kaufmann, 1996.

16. F. P. Preparata and M. I. Shamos. *Computational geometry: An introduction.* Springer-Verlag, New York, 1985.

17. R. Sibson. Locally equiangular triangulations. *The Computer Journal*, 21(3):243–245, 1977.

18. Ivan Stojmenovic. Position-based routing in ad hoc networks. *IEEE Communications Magazine*, July 2002.

19. G. Toussaint. The relative neighborhood graph of a finite planar set. *Pattern Recognition*, 4(12):261–268, 1980.

20. Yu Wang and Xiang-Yang Li. Geometric spanners for wireless ad hoc networks. In *The 22nd IEEE International Conference on Distributed Computing Systems*, 2002.

Robust Topology Control Protocols

Sukumar Ghosh, Kevin Lillis, Saurav Pandit,
and Sriram Pemmaraju

The University of Iowa, Iowa City, IA 52242-1419, USA
{ghosh, lillis, spandit, sriram}@cs.uiowa.edu

Abstract. Topology control protocols attempt to reduce the energy consumption of nodes in an ad-hoc wireless network while maintaining sufficient network connectivity. Topology control protocols with various features have been proposed, but they all lack robustness and are extremely sensitive to faulty information from neighbors. For example, the XTC protocol (R. Wattenhofer and A. Zollinger, XTC: A practical topology control algorithm for ad-hoc networks, *WMAN 2004*) can be forced to construct a disconnected network even if two nodes in the network receive slightly faulty distance information from one neighbor each. A key step in most localized topology control protocols is one in which each node establishes a total ordering on its set of neighbors based on information received from them. In this paper, we propose a metric for *robustness* of localized topology control protocols and define an r-robust topology control protocol as one that returns a correct output network even when its neighborhood orderings have been modified by up to $r-1$ adjacent swaps by a malicious adversary. We then modify XTC in a simple manner to derive a family of r-robust protocols for any $r > 1$. The price we pay for increased robustness is in terms of decreased network sparsity; however we can bound this decrease and we show that in transforming XTC from a 1-robust protocol (which it trivially is) into an r-robust protocol, the maximum vertex degree of the output network increases by a factor of $O(\sqrt{r})$. An extremely pleasant side-effect of our design is that the output network is both $\Omega(\sqrt{r})$-edge connected and $\Omega(\sqrt{r})$-vertex connected provided the input network is. Thus ensuring robustness of the protocol seems to give fault-tolerance of the output for free. Our r-robust version of XTC is almost as simple and practical as XTC and like XTC it only involves 2 rounds of communication between a node and its neighbors.

Keywords: Ad-hoc wireless networks, fault-tolerance, k-connectivity, robustness, topology control protocols.

1 Introduction

Ad-hoc wireless networks consist of autonomous devices or nodes communicating with each other by radio. Typically, each of these nodes has access to a tiny power source and this imposes stringent constraints on the amount of energy that a node

T. Higashino (Ed.): OPODIS 2004, LNCS 3544, pp. 94–109, 2005.

can use for communicating with other nodes. *Topology control* protocols attempt to reduce the power consumption of nodes in order to increase the life of the network. Typically, the energy required by a node s to transmit a message to a node t increases at least quadratically with the distance between s and t. As a consequence, power consumption is significantly reduced if messages from s to t were routed through a sequence of intermediate nodes, such that the distance between consecutive nodes in the path is small. Topology control protocols choose a transmission power level for each node so that a node communicates with just a few nearby nodes. Reducing transmission power level also reduces collisions and therefore saves energy by reducing the number of retransmissions. However, the local choice of transmission power level for each node has to be such that the induced network topology satisfies certain global properties such as connectivity and the presence of multiple short paths between pairs of nodes. The two primary goals of topology control: (i) reducing transmission power level to save energy and (ii) maintaining connectivity and redundancy of short paths to increase routing efficiency, are clearly in conflict with each other. Any satisfactory solution to the topology control problem needs to address this key difficulty.

Let $G = (V, E)$ denote the ad-hoc network with vertex set V denoting the set of nodes and edge set E denoting the set of communication links. Let $c : E \to \mathbf{R}^+$ be a cost function that associates a non-negative real cost to each edge $e \in E$. For each vertex $u \in V$, let $N(u)$ denote the neighbors of u in G. During the course of a topology control protocol P, each vertex $u \in V$ chooses a subset $N_P(u) \subseteq N(u)$ of vertices to transmit to. Letting E_P denote the set of directed edges $\{(u, v) \mid u \in V, v \in N_P(u)\}$, we can view the output of P as the directed spanning subgraph $G_P = (V, E_P)$ of G. Typically, it is desired that G_P satisfy the following properties.

Symmetry. If $v \in N_P(u)$ then $u \in N_P(v)$. As pointed out by [9, 11], without symmetry even the simple task of providing an ACK in response to a message received can become quite cumbersome. Symmetry implies that G_P can be viewed as an undirected graph. There is of course some cost to requiring symmetry, but this is not a property that is very difficult to impose. In describing the rest of the desired properties, we assume that G_P is undirected.

Sparseness. This property is typically quantified as $|E_P| = O(|V|)$. Often, a stronger property, that of bounded degree is desired. This property requires that for all vertices u, $|N(u)| \leq c$ for some constant c. Burkhart et. al. [2] point out that sparseness is often assumed to guarantee low interference, and while this may be true in an "average case" sense, it is not true in general. [2] also presents a reasonable definition of a metric for interference and one may, in addition to (or as an alternative to) sparseness, require that G_P minimize this interference metric.

Connectivity. G_P is required to be connected, provided G that is connected. Often, stronger versions of connectivity such as k-edge connectivity or k-vertex connectivity (for $k > 1$) are desired. These stronger versions of connectivity imply that G_P has multiple paths for routing between pairs of vertices and is more fault-tolerant to link or vertex failures.

Spanner Property. For any pair of vertices u and v, let $C(u,v)$ (respectively, $C_P(u,v)$) denote the cost of the cheapest path between u and v in G (respectively, G_P). Then, the spanner property requires the existence of a constant t such that $C_P(u,v) \leq t \cdot C(u,v)$ for all pairs of vertices $u,v \in V$. If such a constant t exists, then G_P is called a t-spanner of G.

Less typically, certain other properties such as planarity of G_P are also desired. If G_P is planar, then geometric routing algorithms such as **GOAFR$^+$** provide efficient routing in the network [3].

Definitions and Notation. In addition to costs, the edges of the input graph G may have associated non-negative real *lengths*. The cost of an edge is usually distinct from, but related to its length. Often it is assumed that the vertices of the input graph G are embedded in some metric space. In this case, the *length* of an edge $\{u,v\}$, denoted $|uv|$ is equal to the distance between u and v in that space. If the vertices of G are embedded in a Euclidean space, then G is called a *Euclidean graph*. A special case of a Euclidean graph is a *unit disk graph*. G is a unit disk graph if its vertices are embedded in the Euclidean plane and for any pair of vertices u and v, $\{u,v\}$ is an edge of G iff $|uv| \leq 1$. As mentioned in [11], unit disk graphs are usually used to model an ad-hoc network where all the network nodes are placed in an unobstructed plane and have equal (normalized) transmission power and isotropic antennas, that is, antennas transmitting with identical power in every direction of the plane. The cost of an edge $\{u,v\}$, $c(u,v)$, is typically used to denote the amount of energy that one endpoint of the edge has to expend in order to communicate with the other endpoint. For a Euclidean graph, it is reasonable to assume that $c(u,v) = |uv|^\alpha$ for some $\alpha \geq 2$. If G_P, the output of a topology control protocol satisfies the spanner property with respect to edge costs, then it is called an *energy spanner*. It G_P satisfies the spanner property with respect to edge lengths, then G_P is called a *distance spanner*.

Related Work. Various topology control protocols have been proposed, each guaranteeing some subset of the above mentioned properties. Here we mention the two protocols that seem to provide strongest guarantees. Wang and Li [10] have proposed a local protocol for construction of symmetric, bounded degree, planar spanners for networks modeled by unit disk graphs. We will call this the WL protocol. Wattenhofer and Zollinger [11] have proposed a much simpler protocol called XTC that constructs symmetric, bounded degree, planar networks for networks modeled by unit disk graphs. In addition, XTC returns a symmetric, connected network even for input networks that have arbitrary edge lengths. In favor of the WL protocol is the fact that this protocol is guaranteed to return a spanner, whereas XTC provides no such guarantees. [11] does present experiments to suggest that the output of XTC may be a good spanner in the "average case." In favor of the XTC protocol is its extreme simplicity and the fact that the output graph is connected even when the input graph is not a unit disk graph. This implies that it may be appropriate to use XTC even when the terrain on which the nodes are distributed is not the 2-dimensional plane and even when there are obstacles in the terrain.

Our Results. In this paper, we start by pointing out that existing protocols for the topology control problem, including the WL protocol and XTC, lack *robustness* and are extremely sensitive to faulty information from neighbors. For example, as we show in Section 2, the network constructed by XTC may end up becoming disconnected even when two nodes receive faulty distance information from one neighbor each. In a key step in the WL protocol, XTC, and other protocols such as the cone based protocol described in [5], each node u computes a total ordering $\prec_u$ on its neighborhood $N(u)$. In the WL protocol $\prec_u$ is based on degrees of vertices in $N(u)$, in XTC $\prec_u$ is based on the "quality" of the link between u and each vertex in $N(u)$, and in the cone based protocol $\prec_u$ is based on angles. In each case, correct information from neighbors is critical to the correctness of the neighborhood ordering and therefore critical to the correctness of the protocol itself.

Faulty or just incomplete information from neighbors is a common feature in ad-hoc wireless networks. An example of a protocol that works correctly in the presence of noisy distance information is the network localization protocol in [7]. Faulty information from neighbors could be due to signal interference, due to feeble power supply at the sender node, due to the receiver having an incorrect estimate of the transmission range at the sender, etc. Even if information from neighbors is not faulty, it could simply be out-of-date, because nodes may be mobile. Furthermore, it is also possible that nodes may only have approximate position awareness and as a result can only supply approximate distance information (see for example, the work in [8] on computing virtual coordinates). For all of these reasons, the total ordering $\widetilde{\prec}_u$ computed by a node u on its neighborhood $N(u)$ may be different from that actual ordering $\prec_u$ that u might have computed, had it been given accurate or complete information. Our goal is to devise a topology control protocols that work correctly even when each node u computes $\widetilde{\prec}_u$ (rather than $\prec_u$), provided each $\widetilde{\prec}_u$ is not too "far away" from $\prec_u$. A natural measure of distance between orderings (or permutations) of a set is the fewest number of swaps of adjacent elements it takes to get from one ordering to the other. We define (informally, for now) as *r-robust* protocol as one that can withstand a total of up to $r-1$ adjacent swaps performed on all the neighborhood ordering. We make this notion precise in Section 4. We point out that XTC is not even 2-robust. We then present a simple modification to XTC that can turn it into an r-robust protocol for any integer $r > 0$. The price we pay for the increase in robustness is in terms of a decrease in the sparsity of the network. However, we bound this decrease. More specifically, in transforming XTC from a 1-robust protocol (which it is, trivially) to a r-robust protocol, for any integer $r > 1$, we increase the maximum vertex degree of the output graph by a factor of $O(\sqrt{r})$. Even with these modifications, XTC continues to be extremely simple and practical. An extremely pleasant side-effect of our design is that the output network is both $\Omega(\sqrt{r})$-edge connected and $\Omega(\sqrt{r})$-vertex connected. In other words, ensuring robustness of the protocol seems to provide fault-tolerance of the output for free.

2   XTC is Not Robust

We start this section by reproducing the XTC protocol from [11].

    1. Establish order $\prec_u$ over u's neighbors in G
    2. Broadcast $\prec_u$ to each neighbor in G; receive orders from all neighbors
    3. Select topology control neighbors:
    4. $N_u := \{\ \}; \widetilde{N}_u := \{\ \}$
    5.   **while** ($\prec_u$ contains unprocessed neighbors)$\{$
    6. $v :=$ least unprocessed neighbor in $\prec_u$
    7.   **if**($\exists w \in N_u \cup \widetilde{N}_u : w \prec_v u$)
    8. $\widetilde{N}_u := \widetilde{N}_u \cup \{v\}$
    9.   **else**
    10. $N_u := N_u \cup \{v\}$
    11. $\}$

As mentioned in [11], the protocol consists of three main steps: (i) neighbor ordering (Line 1), (ii) neighbor order exchange (Line 2), and (iii) edge selection (Lines 3-11). In the edge selection step a vertex u decides to drop v from its set of neighbors if there is a vertex w that u and v both agree is mutually better. More precisely, u drops v from its neighborhood if there exists w such that $w \prec_u v$ and $w \prec_v u$. In the protocol, the variable N_u is the set of neighbors that u has chosen to retain and the variable $\widetilde{N}_u$ is the set of neighbors that u has chosen to drop. Let $E_{XTC} = \{(u,v) \mid v \in N_u\}$ and $G_{XTC} = (V, E_{XTC})$. Also, let $\prec = \{\prec_u \mid u \in V(G)\}$ denote the collection of neighborhood orderings. Note that the protocol leaves $\prec$ unspecified. Thus G_{XTC} is a function, not only of the input network G, but also of the neighborhood orderings $\prec$. This dependency will be important later and to emphasize this we use the notation $G_{XTC}(\prec)$ to denote the network constructed by the above protocol. In general, for a topology control protocol P, we use the notation $G_P(\prec)$ to denote the output of P. It is easily verified that $u \in N_v$ iff $v \in N_u$ and hence $G_{XTC}(\prec)$ can be thought of as undirected graph.

As mentioned in the introduction, XTC is extremely sensitive to small perturbations in the neighborhood orderings. In [11], it is shown that if G is a Euclidean graph and $\prec = \{\prec_u \mid u \in V(G)\}$, where $\prec_u$ is defined as

$$v \prec_u w \Leftrightarrow (|uv|, \min\{id_u, id_v\}, \max\{id_u, id_v\}) < (|uw|, \min\{id_u, id_w\}, \max\{id_u, id_w\}),$$

then $G_{XTC}(\prec)$ is symmetric and connected. We will call the above neighborhood ordering, a *distance-based* ordering. Note that in the distance-based ordering, ids are only used to break ties. We now present a simple example of a 4-vertex unit disk graph that illustrates the lack of robustness of XTC. We start with the neighborhood orderings $\prec$ as defined above, by Euclidean distance. We then make one swap each in the neighborhood orderings of two vertices to obtain new neighborhood orderings $\widetilde{\prec}$. We point out that $G_{XTC}(\widetilde{\prec})$ is not connected. Consider the unit disk graph shown in Figure 1. For the sake of being concrete, let the lengths of the edges be $|ab| = |dc| = \sqrt{3}/2$, $|ad| = |bc| = 1/2$, and $|ac| = |bd| = 1$. Then

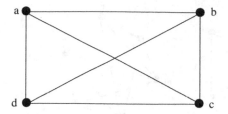

Fig. 1. A unit disk graph for showing the sensitivity of XTC to small perturbations

$$d \prec_a b \prec_a c$$
$$c \prec_b a \prec_b d$$
$$b \prec_c d \prec_c a$$
$$a \prec_d c \prec_d b$$

Now suppose that $\tilde{\prec}_a = \prec_a$, $\tilde{\prec}_d = \prec_d$, but

$$c \; \tilde{\prec}_b \; d \; \tilde{\prec}_b \; a$$
$$b \; \tilde{\prec}_c \; a \; \tilde{\prec}_c \; d$$

Note that $\tilde{\prec}_b$ and $\tilde{\prec}_c$ are obtained by swapping one pair of elements each in $\prec_b$ and $\prec_c$. If XTC is run on the unit disk graph shown below with $\tilde{\prec} = \{\tilde{\prec}_a, \tilde{\prec}_b, \tilde{\prec}_c, \tilde{\prec}_d\}$, then $G_{XTC}(\tilde{\prec})$ contains just the two edges $\{a, d\}$ and $\{b, c\}$ and is therefore disconnected. Thus a total of two adjacent swaps were sufficient to break connectivity. Later in the paper we modify XTC in a simple manner into an r-robust protocol, one that can tolerate a total of up to $r - 1$ adjacent swaps on its neighborhood orderings.

3   Characterizing Good Neighborhood Orderings

XTC's correctness and performance critically depends on $\prec$. Specifically, if $\prec$ is appropriately defined then the following two properties hold:

(i) For every triangle abc, $\prec_a$, $\prec_b$, and $\prec_c$ help vertices a, b, and c negotiate the dropping of one of the edges $\{a, b\}$, $\{b, c\}$, and $\{c, a\}$.
(ii) For every cut $(S, \overline{S})$ of G, $\prec$ prevents the dropping of some edge that crosses the cut $(S, \overline{S})$.

Property (i) implies that $G_{XTC}(\prec)$ is triangle-free, while (ii) implies that $G_{XTC}(\prec)$ is connected. Various properties of $G_{XTC}(\prec)$ proved separately in [11] immediately follow. Here we prove a general characterization of neighborhood orderings $\prec$ that guarantee properties (i) and (ii). It will be clear that the "distance-ordering" used in [11] satisfies this characterization. But more importantly, there are many other natural neighborhood orderings that also satisfy our characterization. For example, neighborhood orderings by increasing ids or by

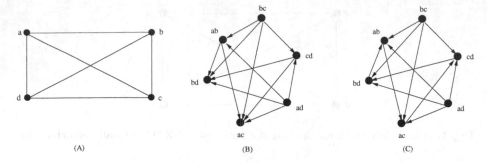

Fig. 2. On the left is the unit disk graph from Figure 1. In the middle is $L(G, \prec)$, where $\prec$ is the distance-based ordering. It is easily verified that this is acyclic. Vertices ad and bc are minimal vertices in $L(G, \prec)$. On the right is $L(G, \overset{\sim}{\prec})$, where $\overset{\sim}{\prec}$ is obtained from $\prec$ by swapping a and d in $\prec_b$ and $\prec_c$. Notice the cycle (ab, ac, cd, bd, ab) in $L(G, \overset{\sim}{\prec})$. This cycle is responsible for $G_{XTC}(\overset{\sim}{\prec})$ being disconnected

increasing angle also satisfy our characterization and therefore guarantee properties (i) and (ii).

The collection of neighborhood orderings $\prec$ induces a binary relation $\rightsquigarrow$ on the set of edges of G. For any two edges $e, e' \in E(G)$, $e \rightsquigarrow e'$ if e and e' share a common endpoint and if $e = \{u, v\}$ and $e' = \{u, w\}$, then $v \prec_u w$. Using this binary relation $\rightsquigarrow$ we can define a new (directed) graph $L(G, \prec)$ whose vertex set is the set of edges of G and whose set of (directed) edges is $\{(e, e') \mid e, e' \in E(G), e \rightsquigarrow e'\}$. We call $\prec$ *acyclic* if $L(G, \prec)$ is an acyclic graph. Note that if $L(G, \prec)$ is acyclic, then so is any subgraph of $L(G, \prec)$. Also note that any acyclic graph is guaranteed to contain at least one vertex with in-degree (respectively, out-degree) 0 and we call such a vertex, a *minimal* (respectively, *maximal*) vertex. Figure 2 illustrates the definitions of $\rightsquigarrow$, and $L(G, \prec)$.

Theorem 1. *Let G be an arbitrary connected graph and $\prec$ be a collection of neighborhood orderings of G. $G_{XTC}(\prec)$ is triangle-free and connected if $\prec$ is acyclic.*

Proof. To show that $G_{XTC}(\prec)$ is triangle-free, we consider an arbitrary triangle abc in G. Since $L(G, \prec)$ is acyclic there is a triangle edge, say $\{a, b\}$, such that $\{b, c\} \rightsquigarrow \{a, b\}$ and $\{c, a\} \rightsquigarrow \{a, b\}$. This implies that $c \prec_b a$ and $c \prec_a b$. As a result XTC will drop edge $\{a, b\}$ and therefore the triangle abc is not part of $G_{XTC}(\prec)$. Since the choice of abc was arbitrary, $G_{XTC}(\prec)$ is triangle-free.

To show that $G_{XTC}(\prec)$ is connected, we consider a cut $(S, \overline{S})$ of G. Let $L_S(G)$ be the subgraph of $L(G, \prec)$ induced by the edges of G crossing the cut. Since $L(G, \prec)$ is acyclic, so is $L_S(G)$. Let e be a minimal vertex of $L_S(G)$. We now show that e is retained in $G_{XTC}(\prec)$. Let $e = \{u, v\}$ and suppose that e is not retained in $G_{XTC}(\prec)$. Then there is a vertex $w \in V(G)$ that is a common neighbor of u and v such that $w \prec_u v$ and $w \prec_v u$. Since $\{u, v\}$ crosses the cut $(S, \overline{S})$, at least one of $e_u = \{u, w\}$ or $e_v = \{v, w\}$ also crosses the cut. Without loss of generality suppose that e_u crosses $(S, \overline{S})$. Therefore, e_u is a vertex in $L_S(G)$. Then, by the definition of $\leadsto$, $e_u \leadsto e$ and therefore e is not minimal in $L(G, \prec)$. This contradicts our choice of e as a minimal vertex in $L_S(G)$.

Thus we have shown that for every cut $(S, \overline{S})$ of G, there an edge in $G_{XTC}(\prec)$ crossing the cut. This shows that $G_{XTC}(\prec)$ is connected.

It is easy to see that the distance-based ordering is acyclic. Let G be a Euclidean graph and let $e = \{u, v\}$ be the edge in G such that the triple $(|uv|, \min\{id_u, id_v\}, \max\{id_u, id_v\})$ is first in the increasing lexicographic ordering of all such triples. From the definition of the distance-based ordering, it follows that e is minimal in $L(G, \prec)$. If we assume that $L(G - e, \prec)$ is acyclic, then by induction it follows that so is $L(G, \prec)$. Similar arguments show that the following alternate orderings are also acyclic.

1. The *id-based ordering* $\prec^{id}$. Let v and w be two neighbors of u. Then $v \prec_u^{id} w$ iff $id_v < id_w$. As before, $\prec^{id} = \{\prec_u^{id} \mid u \in V(G)\}$.
2. The *angle-based ordering* $\prec^a$. For any pair of vertices u and v in G, let $\alpha(u, v)$ denote the angle made by the line segment uv with the horizontal ray with origin u towards $+\infty$. For two neighbors v and w of u, $v \prec_u^a w$ iff

$$(\alpha(u, v), \min\{id_u, id_v\}, \max\{id_u, id_v\}) < (\alpha(u, w), \min\{id_u, id_w\}, \max\{id_u, id_w\}).$$

Of course, the id-based ordering is only well-defined when all vertices have (not necessarily distinct) ids and the angle-based ordering is only well defined when the vertices of G are embedded in Euclidean space and the vertices have ids. The latter is needed to break ties when angle comparison is not enough to distinguish neighbors.

The implication of the above characterization theorem is that XTC could have as well been run with the id-based ordering or the angle-based ordering instead of the distance-based ordering and the output graph would still have the properties: (i) symmetry, (ii) connectivity, and (iii) being triangle-free. However, it should be noted that ignoring distances completely and using the id-based ordering or angle-based ordering is not, in general, a good idea. Though symmetry

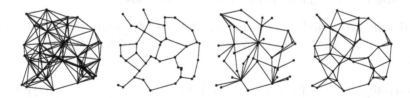

Fig. 3. The graph on the left is a unit disk graph obtained by dropping 40 points uniformly at random on a 3×3 grid. It contains 197 edges. The second graph from the left is the output of XTC using a distance-based ordering and it contains 47 edges. The third graph from the left is the output of XTC using an id-based ordering and it contains 55 edges. The rightmost graph is the output of k-XTC using a distance-based ordering, for $k = 2$. It contains 88 edges

and connectivity are preserved, the output graph may have other undesirable features. Some of these are apparent in the graph in Figure 3 (third from left) that is constructed by XTC using the id-based ordering. For example, the degrees of certain vertices are quite high and moreover these high degree vertices have several pendant edges incident on them. These nodes are therefore prone to high congestion and the network is vulnerable to the failure of such nodes. While we are not suggesting the use of id-based ordering as an alternative to distance-based ordering, the result in Theorem 1 does suggest the possibility of using id-based ordering when distances to neighbors are similar (not necessarily the same). This may be another way to increase robustness of the protocol.

4   *k*-XTC: A Robust Version of XTC

In this section, we propose a small modification to XTC that will turn it into a robust protocol. The protocol, which we will call k-XTC is obtained from XTC by changing Line 7 to the following.

$$\text{if } (\exists W \subseteq N_u \cup \tilde{N}_u \colon |W| = k \text{ and } \forall w \in W \colon w \prec_v u).$$

This modification simply means that the decision for u to drop v from its neighborhood needs the support of not one, but k other vertices that both u and v agree are mutually better. Let $G_{kXTC}(\prec)$ denote the output of k-XTC. Note that XTC is simply a special case of k-XTC with $k = 1$. A simple but important observation about the output of k-XTC is the following.

Proposition 1. *For any $k > 1$, for any j, $1 \leq j < k$, $G_{jXTC}(\prec)$ is a subgraph of $G_{kXTC}(\prec)$.*

The rightmost graph in Figure 3 shows the output of k-XTC for $k = 2$. This graph has the same rough "shape" as the output of XTC (the graph that is second from left) but is more dense and non-planar. As we will show later, this graph is k-edge connected as well as k-vertex connected. Therefore, every vertex in this graph has degree at least k.

We now quantify the notion of robustness as follows.

Definition: Let π and π' be two permutations of a finite, non-empty set S. We denote the fewest number of adjacent swaps needed to transform π to π' by $dist(\pi, \pi')$.

Definition: Let $\prec = \{\prec_u \mid u \in V(G)\}$ and $\tilde{\prec} = \{\tilde{\prec}_u \mid u \in V(G)\}$ be two collections of neighborhood orderings. Then we use $dist(\prec, \tilde{\prec})$ to denote $\sum_u dist(\prec_u, \tilde{\prec}_u)$.

Definition: A topology-control protocol P is said to be *r-robust for* $\prec$ if $G_P(\tilde{\prec})$ is connected for any collection of neighborhood orderings $\tilde{\prec}$, where $dist(\prec, \tilde{\prec}) < r$.

In other words, if P is r-robust for $\prec$, then P returns a connected subgraph even when executed with a collection of neighborhood orderings that is obtained from $\prec$ using at most $r - 1$ adjacent swaps. Measuring the "distance" between orderings by the number of adjacent swaps provides a clean abstraction for quantifying a variety of situations that might cause vertices to believe a "false" ordering on neighbors. For example, if a vertex u underestimates the distance to a neighbor v then v might appear earlier than it should in $\prec_u$. If the (incorrectly) estimated distance to v is much smaller than the actual distance, then v's place in $\prec_u$ may be many adjacent swaps away from its correct place in $\prec_u$. We now prove the main result of this paper. Note that the result is proved for any collection of acyclic neighborhood orderings and not just for the distance-based ordering. Showing that k-XTC is k-robust is not hard, but showing a quadratic robustness needs the more intricate argument presented below. The following theorem shows that to obtain an r-robust version of XTC, it is sufficient to use k-XTC for $k \geq \sqrt{2r}$.

Theorem 2. k-XTC is $\frac{k(k+1)}{2}$-robust for any collection $\prec$ of acyclic neighborhood orderings.

Proof. Let G be the input graph to k-XTC. Let $\prec$ be an arbitrary collection of *acyclic* neighborhood orderings and let $\tilde{\prec}$ be an arbitrary collection of neighborhood orderings. From Theorem 1 and Proposition 1, we know that $G_{kXTC}(\prec)$ is connected. We will show that if $G_{kXTC}(\tilde{\prec})$ is disconnected then $dist(\prec, \tilde{\prec}) \geq k(k+1)/2$. This will imply that k-XTC is $\frac{k(k+1)}{2}$-robust.

We start by supposing that $G_{kXTC}(\tilde{\prec})$ is disconnected and assuming for notational convenience, that $\tilde{H} = G_{kXTC}(\tilde{\prec})$. Since $\tilde{H}$ is disconnected there is a cut $C = (S, \overline{S})$ such that there is no edge of $\tilde{H}$ crossing $(S, \overline{S})$. On the other hand there is at least one edge in G crossing C. Let $E(C)$ be subset of edges in G crossing C. Since $L(G, \prec)$ is acyclic, the subgraph of $L(G, \prec)$ induced by edges in $E(C)$ is also acyclic. In the rest of the proof we use $L(C)$ to denote the subgraph of $L(G, \prec)$ induced by $E(C)$.

Our proof is constructive and what we now describe is the first iteration of the construction procedure. Let $e = \{u, v\}$ be a minimal edge in $L(C)$. Without loss of generality, suppose that $u \in S$ and $v \in \overline{S}$. The edge e does not appear in $\tilde{H}$ and this can only happen because there is a set W of k vertices such that for all $w \in W$, w is a common neighbor of u and v, $w \tilde{\prec}_u v$, and $w \tilde{\prec}_v u$. Let (W_u, W_v) be a partition of W such that $W_u \subseteq S$ and $W_v \subseteq \overline{S}$. Let $k_u = |W_u|$ and $k_v = |W_v|$. Note that $k_u + k_v = k$. Also note that for each $w \in W_v$, edge $\{u, w\}$ crosses C and similarly for each $w \in W_u$, edge $\{v, w\}$ crosses C. Also note that since $\{u, v\}$ is a minimal edge in $L(C)$, $v \prec_u w$ for all $w \in W_v$ and $u \prec_v w$ for all $w \in W_u$. Thus, we have (i) for all $w \in W_v$, $w \tilde{\prec}_u v$ and $v \prec_u w$ and (ii) for all $w \in W_u$, $w \tilde{\prec}_v u$ and $u \prec_v w$. See Figure 4 for an example. Item (i) implies that $dist(\prec_u, \tilde{\prec}_u) \geq k_v$ and item (ii) implies that $dist(\prec_v, \tilde{\prec}_v) \geq k_u$. These inequalities together imply that $dist(\prec, \tilde{\prec}) \geq k$.

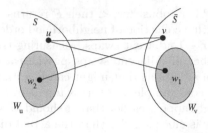

Fig. 4. The edges $\{u, w_1\}$ and $\{v, w_2\}$ cross the cut $(S, \overline{S})$. Furthermore, $v \prec_u w_1$ and $w_1 \overset{\sim}{\prec}_u v$. Also, $u \prec_v w_2$ and $w_2 \overset{\sim}{\prec} u$

Remark: Actually, something stronger can be claimed. Even if we wanted to transform $\prec_u$ into an ordering $\prec'_u$ such that $w \prec'_u v$ for all $w \in W_v$, but $\prec_u$ and $\prec'_u$ match in the pairwise ordering of all others pairs of elements, it would take at least k_v adjacent swaps. In other words, $\prec'_u$ is along the way between $\prec_u$ and $\overset{\sim}{\prec}_u$ and just getting to $\prec'_u$ from $\prec_u$ takes at least k_v adjacent swaps. Getting to $\overset{\sim}{\prec}_u$ from $\prec'_u$ may take additional adjacent swaps and we account for these separately in future iterations of the construction procedure. Similar remarks can be made about the "distance" between $\prec_v$ and $\overset{\sim}{\prec}_v$.

The choice of edge $e = \{u, v\}$ described above, ends the first iteration of our construction procedure. Let $B_1 = \{e\}$ and let $V_1 = \{u, v\}$. The set V_1 represents the endpoints of the edge in B_1. To state our induction hypothesis we need additional notation. For any set X of vertices, let $dist_X(\prec_u, \overset{\sim}{\prec}_u)$ be the minimum number of adjacent swaps we need to make on $\prec_u$ so that every element $v \in X \cap N(u)$ is in the same relative position in $\prec_u$ as in $\overset{\sim}{\prec}_u$. More precisely, $dist_X(\prec_u, \overset{\sim}{\prec}_u) = \min_{\prec'_u} dist(\prec_u, \prec'_u)$, where the min operation is over all $\prec'_u$ such that for any $v \in X \cap N(u)$ and for any $w \in N(u)$, $v \prec_u w \Leftrightarrow v \prec'_u w$. Here is a small example to illustrate this definition.

Example. Define the permutations $\pi = (54321)$ and $\pi' = (12345)$. It is easy to see that $dist(\pi, \pi') = 10$. Now let $X = \{1, 4\}$. What is $dist_X(\pi, \pi')$? It is again easy to verify that $dist_X(\pi, \pi') = dist(\pi, \pi'') = 9$, where $\pi'' = (13245)$. This is because $dist_X(\pi, \pi')$ is the number of adjacent swaps needed to transform π into a permutation in which 1 appears before all other elements and 4 appears after all other elements except 5. Thus the positions of elements 1, 4, and 5 are fixed.

For any collection $\prec$ of neighborhood orderings, let $dist_X(\prec, \overset{\sim}{\prec}) = \sum_{u \in X} dist_X(\prec_u, \overset{\sim}{\prec}_u)$. We also need the following two elementary facts about transforming one permutation into another via adjacent swaps.

Fact 1. For any $X \subseteq Y \subseteq N(u)$, $dist_X(\prec_u, \overset{\sim}{\prec}_u) \leq dist_Y(\prec_u, \overset{\sim}{\prec}_u)$.

Fact 2. Let $X \subseteq Y \subseteq N(u)$ and $x \in Y - X$. Suppose there is a set $W \subseteq N(u)$ such that for all $w \in W$, $x \prec_u w$ and $w \overset{\sim}{\prec}_u x$ then $dist_X(\prec_u, \overset{\sim}{\prec}_u) + |W| \leq dist_Y(\prec_u, \overset{\sim}{\prec}_u)$.

Our induction hypothesis is the following.

Induction hypothesis: For any $i \geq 1$, after i iterations of this procedure, we have a set B_i of i edges from $E(C)$ such that there are no edges from $E(C) - B_i$ into B_i, though there may be edges from B_i into $E(C) - B_i$. Let V_i be the set of endpoints of edges in B_i. Then $dist_{V_i}(\prec, \widetilde{\prec}) \geq k + (k-1) + \cdots + (k-i+1)$.

We have shown that at the end of the first iteration of the construction procedure, $|B_1| = 1$, there are no edges from $E(C) - B_1$ into B_1, and $dist_{V_1}(\prec, \widetilde{\prec}) \geq k$. This is the base case of our proof.

We now make the following claim about the $(i+1)$th iteration of our construction procedure. We will prove this claim later; for now we will assume that it holds and complete the proof of the induction step.

Claim: In the $(i+1)$th iteration it is possible to pick an edge $e' \in E(C) - B_i$ such that (i) e' has at least one endpoint not in V_i, and (ii) in-degree of e' in $L(C)$ is at most i.

Assuming this claim, we proceed in a manner that is similar to the argument for the first iteration. Let $e' = \{u', v'\}$, $u' \in S$, $v' \in \overline{S}$, and without loss of generality, $v' \notin V_i$. The fact that e' is not in $\widetilde{H}$ implies that there is a set W of k vertices such that for all $w \in W$, w is a common neighbor of u and v, $w \widetilde{\prec}_{u'} v'$ and $w \widetilde{\prec}_{v'} u'$. Using the fact (derived from the above claim) that the in-degree of e' in $L(C)$ is at most i, we conclude, using an argument similar to the one for the first iteration, that there exist subsets $W_{u'} \subseteq W \cap S$ and $W_{v'} \subseteq W \cap \overline{S}$, such that $|W_{u'}| + |W_{v'}| = (k - i)$ and

(i) for all $w \in W_{v'}$, $w \widetilde{\prec}_{u'} v'$ and $v' \prec_{u'} w$ and
(ii) for all $w \in W_{u'}$, $w \widetilde{\prec}_{v'} u'$ and $u' \prec_{v'} w'$.

Let $k_{u'} = |W_{u'}|$ and $k_{v'} = |W_{v'}|$, $B_{i+1} = B_i \cup \{e'\}$, and V_{i+1} be the endpoints of vertices in B_{i+1}. Item (i) along with Fact 2 implies that $dist_{V_{i+1}}(\prec_{u'}, \widetilde{\prec}_{u'}) \geq dist_{V_i}(\prec_{u'}, \widetilde{\prec}_{u'}) + k_{v'}$. Item (ii) implies that $dist_{V_{i+1}}(\prec_{v'}, \widetilde{\prec}_{v'}) \geq k_{u'}$. These inequalities together along with Fact 1 imply that $dist_{V_{i+1}}(\prec, \widetilde{\prec}) \geq dist_{V_i}(\prec, \widetilde{\prec}) + (k - i)$. This completes the induction step. If we repeat the induction step until $i = k$, then we have a set V_k of vertices such that $dist_{V_k}(\prec, \widetilde{\prec}) \geq k(k+1)/1$. Since $V_k \subseteq V$, by Fact 1 we have that $dist(\prec, \widetilde{\prec}) = dist_V(\prec, \widetilde{\prec}) \geq dist_{V_k}(\prec, \widetilde{\prec}) \geq k(k+1)/1$.

We now prove the above claim that guarantees the existence of e'.

Proof of Claim: Let T_i be the set of edges not in B_i, that have both endpoints in V_i. Consider the subgraph of $L(C)$ obtained by deleting $B_i \cup T_i$. Call this L_i. Since $L(C)$ is acyclic, L_i is also acyclic and let e' be a minimal vertex in L_i. If e' is not incident on any vertex in V_i, then e' is also minimal in $L(C)$ and we are done. So we assume that e' is incident on at least on vertex in V_i. Since, e' was picked from $L(C) - B_i - T_i$, e' cannot be incident on two vertices in V_i, because otherwise e' will be in T_i. Therefore, we are left with the case in which

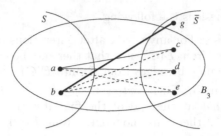

Fig. 5. This figure illustrates the proof of the Claim in the proof of Theorem 2. Here $B_3 = \{\{a,c\}, \{a,d\}, \{b,e\}\}$, $T_3 = \{\{b,d\}, \{b,c\}, \{a,e\}\}$, and $e' = \{b,g\}$. The set $V_3 = \{a,b,c,d,e\}$

e' is incident on one vertex in V_i. Now let $e' = \{b,g\}$ and suppose that $b \in V_i$ and $g \notin V_i$. Figure 5 illustrates the situation for $i = 3$. Suppose that there are x edges in B_i incident on b and y edges in T_i incident on b. In Figure 5, $x = 1$ and $y = 2$. The in-degree of e' in $L(C)$ is therefore bounded above by $x + y$ and since $x \leq |B_i| = i$, we get the upper bound $i + y$. Now note that for every edge $\{b, b'\}$ in T_i, there is an edge in B_i incident on b' that does not share any endpoints with edge $\{a, b\}$. In other words, for every edge e'' of T_i such that $e'' \rightsquigarrow e'$ there is a unique edge f in B_i such that $f \not\rightsquigarrow e'$. This gives the upper bound of i on the in-degree of e'.

An extremely pleasant side-effect of our design of k-XTC is the fault-tolerance of G_{kXTC}. We prove in the following two theorems that if G is k-edge connected (respectively, k-vertex connected) then G_{kXTC} is also k-edge connected (respectively, k-vertex connected). Localized protocols for constructing such fault-tolerant spanning subgraphs appear in [1, 6], but k-XTC is far simpler than these. Furthermore, k-XTC provides robustness, bounded degree in case the input is a unit disk graph, and also preserves k-connectivity for arbitrarily input graphs with arbitrary edge lengths. Also note that the following two theorems are proved for any acyclic collection of neighborhood orderings, not just for distance-based orderings.

Theorem 3. *For any collection of acyclic neighborhood orderings $\prec$, $G_{kXTC}(\prec)$ is k-edge connected provided G is k-edge connected.*

Proof. Suppose G is k-edge connected, but G_{kXTC} is not. For any cut $C = (S, \overline{S})$ of V, let $E(C)$ denote the edges in G crossing the cut and similarly, let $E_{kXTC}(C)$ denote the edges of G_{kXTC} crossing the cut C. Since G is k-edge connected, but G_{kXTC} is not, there there is a cut $C = (S, \overline{S})$ of V such that $|E(C)| \geq k$ and $|E_{kXTC}(C)| < k$. Let L be the subgraph of $L(G, \prec)$ induced by $E(C) - E_{kXTC}(C)$. Note that L is non-empty and since $L(G, \prec)$ is acyclic, so is L. Let $e = \{u, v\}$ be a minimal vertex in L. Since $\{u, v\} \in E - E_{kXTC}$, there exists a vertex set W, $|W| = k$, such that for all $w \in W$, w is a common neighbor of u and v and

$$w \prec_u v \text{ and } w \prec_v u. \tag{1}$$

Let $W_1 = W \cap S$ and $W_2 = W \cap \overline{S}$. Then, $\chi = \{\{u, x\} \mid x \in W_2\} \cup \{\{y, v\} \mid y \in W_1\}$ is a subset of $E(G)$ of edges that cross the cut $(S, \overline{S})$. Note that $|\chi| = k$ and therefore not all edges in χ can belong to $E_{kXTC}(C)$. Let $\{a, b\} \in \chi - E_{kXTC}(C)$. Thus $\{a, b\} \in E(C) - E_{kXTC}(C)$ and is therefore a vertex in L. Note that $\{a, b\}$ is either incident on u or incident on v. Without loss of generality, assume that $a = u$. Then, from (1) it follows that $b \prec_u v$. This means that $\{a, b\} \rightsquigarrow \{u, v\}$, contradicting that fact that $e = \{u, v\}$ is minimal in L.

Theorem 4. *For any collection of acyclic neighborhood orderings $\prec$, $G_{kXTC}(\prec)$ is k-vertex connected provided G is k-vertex connected.*

Proof. Suppose that G is k-vertex connected and G_{kXTC} is not. Since G_{kXTC} is not k-vertex connected, there exists $V' \subseteq V$ such that $|V'| = k - 1$ and $G'_{kXTC} = G_{kXTC} - V'$ is disconnected. Since G is k-vertex connected, $G' = G - V'$ is connected. Since G'_{kXTC} is disconnected, there exists cut $C = (S, \overline{S})$ of $V - V'$ such that no edges in G'_{kXTC} cross cut C. However, since G' is connected, there exists a non-empty set of edges E_C in G' that cross cut C. Let L be the subgraph of $L(G, \prec)$ induced by E_C. Let $e = \{u, v\}$ be a minimal vertex in E_C. Without loss of generality suppose that $u \in S$ and $v \in \overline{S}$. Since there are no edges in G'_{kXTC} that cross the cut C, e is not in G_{kXTC}. Hence, there exists $W \subseteq V$, $|W| = k$, such that for all $w \in W$, w is a common neighbor of both u and v, and $w \prec_u v$ and $w \prec_v u$. Since $|W| = k$ and $|V'| = k - 1$, there exists a vertex $w \in W - V'$. Therefore, w is a vertex in G' and in G'_{kXTC}. Without loss of generality assume that $w \in \overline{S}$. Therefore, edge $\{u, w\}$ crosses the cut C and belongs to E_C. Furthermore, since $w \prec_u v$, $\{u, w\} \rightsquigarrow \{u, v\}$ contradicting the fact that $\{u, v\}$ is minimal in L.

We use $\Delta(G)$ to denote the maximum degree of a vertex in G. We now show that the argument for the upper bound 6 [11] on $\Delta(G_{XTC})$ if G is a unit disk graph carries over cleanly to the k-XTC, giving an upper bound of $6k$ on $\Delta(G_{kXTC})$. Note that the argument is specific to distance-based orderings, and does not carry over to an arbitrary acyclic ordering. In fact, as mentioned before for the case of the id-based ordering, not all acyclic orderings will satisfy this upper bound result.

Theorem 5. *If G is unit disk graph and $\prec$ is the collection of distance-based neighborhood orderings, then $\Delta(G_{kXTC}(\prec)) \leq 6k$.*

Proof. To prove this theorem, we show that $k + 1$ adjacent edges in G_{kXTC} cannot enclose an angle less than $\frac{\pi}{3}$. More precisely, assume that a vertex u has $k + 1$ neighbors $v_0, v_1, \ldots, v_k$ in G_{kXTC}, listed in counterclockwise order starting at some arbitrary neighbor v_0. Further assume that $\angle v_0 u v_k < \frac{\pi}{3}$. Figure 6 illustrates the situation.

Suppose that among the neighbors $v_0, v_1, \ldots, v_k$, the neighbor v_i for some i, $0 \leq i \leq k$, is considered last by k-XTC. Since v_i is considered last we have

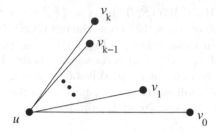

Fig. 6. The neighbors $v_0, v_1, \ldots, v_k$ of u. For the proof we suppose that $\angle v_0 u v_k < \pi/3$

$v_j \prec_u v_i$ for all $j \neq i$, $0 \leq j \leq k$. Since $\prec$ is the distance-based ordering, this implies that $|uv_j| \leq |uv_i|$, for all $j \neq i$, $0 \leq j \leq k$.

Now consider a triangle uv_iv_j, $j \neq i$, $0 \leq j \leq k$. Since $|uv_j| \leq |uv_i|$, uv_j is not the longest edge of the triangle. Also since $\angle v_j u v_i < \frac{\pi}{3}$, the line segment $v_i v_j$ is strictly shorter than at least one of the other two line segments in the triangle, namely uv_i and uv_j. Combining this with the fact that $|uv_j| \leq |uv_i|$, we have $|v_i v_j| < |uv_i|$, implying that $v_j \prec_{v_i} u$. Thus, we have $v_j \prec_u v_i$ and $v_j \prec_{v_i} u$ for all $j \neq i$, $0 \leq j \leq k$. This means that edge $\{u, v_i\}$ will not be included in G_{kXTC}, contradicting the fact that v_i is a neighbor of u in G_{kXTC}.

5   Future Directions

The spanner properties of G_{kXTC} remain unexplored and there are several interesting questions one could ask. For example, as k increases G_{kXTC} becomes more dense and we expect it to become a better spanner for G. One could ask if given any $t \geq 1$ and a unit disk graph G, whether there is a $k = k(t)$ such that G_{kXTC} is a t-spanner for G. In addition, one could focus on random unit disk graphs (those obtained by distributing points uniformly at random in a bounded planar region) and investigate spanner properties of G_{kXTC} in this setting. This would also be an attempt at analytically proving the conclusion, experimentally derived in [11], that G_{XTC} is a good spanner for random unit disk graphs.

Another direction we are interested in pursuing is relaxing the assumption that G is a unit disk graph and investigating k-XTC for for a more general class of graphs. For example, [4] defines a *quasi unit disk graph* a model that they claim is "close enough to reality as to represent existing networks." We are interested in investigating the performance of k-XTC for quasi unit disk graphs and for other realistic generalizations of unit disk graphs.

Acknowledgment. We thank Ted Herman for illuminating discussions on real world sensor and ad-hoc wireless networks.

References

1. M. Bahramgiri, M. Hajiaghayi, and V. S. Mirrokni. Fault-tolerant and 3-dimensional distributed topology control algorithms in wireless multi-hop networks. In *Proceedings of the 11th IEEE International Conference on Computer Communications and Networks (IC3N)*, pages 392–398, 2002.
2. M. Burkhart, P. von Rickenbach, R. Wattenhofer, and A. Zollinger. Does topology control reduce interference? In *Proceedings of the 4th ACM International Symposium on Mobile Ad-Hoc Networking and Computing (MOBIHOC)*, 2003.
3. F. Kuhn, R. Wattenhofer, Y. Zhang, and A. Zollinger. Geometric ad-hoc routing: Of theory and practice. In *Proceedings of the 22nd ACM Symposium on the Principles of Distributed Computing (PODC)*, 2003.
4. F. Kuhn, R. Wattenhofer, and A. Zollinger. Ad-hoc networks beyond unit disk graphs. In *DIAL-POMC 2003*, 2003.
5. L. Li, J. Halpern, P. Bahl, Y. Wang, and R. Wattenhofer. Analysis of a cone-based distributed topology control algorithm for wireless multi-hop networks. In *Proceedings of the ACM Symposium on Principles of Distributed Computing (PODC)*, pages 264–273, 2001.
6. N. Li and J.C. Hou. FLSS: A fault-tolerant topology control algorithm for wireless networks. In *Proceedings of MOBICOM*, 2004.
7. D. Moore, J. Leonard, D. Rus, and S. Teller. Robust distributed network localization with noisy range measurements. In *SenSys 2004*, 2004.
8. T. Moscibroda, R. O'Dell amd M. Wattenhofer, and R. Wattenhofer. Virtual coordinates for ad hoc and sensor networks. In *DIAL-POMC 2004*, 2004.
9. R. Prakash. Unidirectional links prove costly in wireless ad-hoc networks. In *Proceedings of the 3rd International Workshop on Discrete Algorithms and Methods for Mobile Computing and Communication (DIAL-M)*, 1999.
10. Y. Wang and X. Y. Li. Localized construction of bounded degree planar spanner for wireless ad hoc networks. In *Proceedings of the 2003 Joint Workshop on Foundations of Mobile Computing*, pages 59–68, 2003.
11. R. Wattenhofer and A. Zollinger. XTC: A practical topology control algorithm for ad-hoc networks. In *Proceedings of the 4th International Workshop on Algorithms for Wireless, Mobile, Ad Hoc and Sensor Networks (WMAN 04)*, 2004.

A Scheme Encouraging Mobile Nodes to Forward Packets via Multiple Wireless Links Aggregating System Between the Internet and Mobile Ad Hoc Networks

Yosuke Ito[1], Hiroshi Mineno[2], and Susumu Ishihara[3]

[1] Graduate School of Science and Technology, Shizuoka University,
3-5-1, Johoku, Hamamatsu, Shizuoka, 432-8561, Japan
Phone/Fax:+81-53-478-1265,
ito@ishilab.net
[2] Faculty of Information, Shizuoka University
mineno@cs.inf.shizuoka.ac.jp
[3] Faculty of Engineering, Shizuoka University
ishihara@ishilab.net

Abstract. We have proposed a system that achieves high-speed and high-quality communication between mobile nodes and the Internet by using multiple network interfaces of multiple mobile nodes. In this system, adjacent mobile nodes connect to each other with short-range high-speed links and establish temporary networks. A mobile node in a temporary network simultaneously uses multiple links owned by the nodes in the network when it communicates with nodes outside the network. In this system, a part of data packets for one node have to be relayed by the other nodes in the temporary network. However, other nodes might not relay data packets unless they receive some profit from their contribution. In this report, we introduce credits as an incentive to network nodes to relay packets. We propose a method that provides secure credit exchanges between nodes relaying packets and a node requesting the relays, and the method provides a trusted third party that assists those nodes exchanging credits.

Keywords: mobile computing, multiple paths, mobile IP, cooperation, incentive of forwarding, accounting, fairness, SHAKE, ad hoc network.

1 Introduction

In wireless communication environment, users demand to connect to the Internet comfortably at any time and place. In a previous report [1], we proposed SHAKE (a procedure for SHAring multiple paths to create a cluster networK Environment) to enable high-speed, reliable communication with multiple network interfaces for a temporal group of mobile devices. In SHAKE, mobile devices gathering in particular location establish a temporary network (we call this network an *alliance*) by establishing a short-range high-speed wireless link (e.g., wireless LAN). When a mobile device in an alliance accesses the Internet under a situation where the node has to use a slow link (e.g., 2G, 3G cellular), it uses not only its link to the Internet but also the links between

T. Higashino (Ed.): OPODIS 2004, LNCS 3544, pp. 110–123, 2005.

the other mobile devices in that location and the Internet. This improves the data transmission speed, reliability and connectivity of the communication between the mobile devices and the Internet.

In SHAKE, nodes must assist other nodes by using their own external link to relay traffic. If nodes refuse a relay connection because they have to use their own CPU power, memory, and battery to relay traffic for other nodes, communicating by using the SHAKE will be impossible. To solve this problem, we propose a scheme that uses credits as an incentive to encourage nodes to relay traffic for other nodes.

The rest of the paper is organized as follows. In Section 2, we review the SHAKE architecture, the issues, and the related work. In Section 3, we present architecture for motivating mobile nodes to perform relays. In Section 4, we discuss robustness and overhead of the proposed scheme. Section 5 summarizes this paper.

2   SHAKE

In this section, we provide an overview of SHAKE. In SHAKE, mobile nodes establish an alliance to enhance communication speed between them and the Internet. A node relaying data packets for another node in an alliance is described an Alliance Member (AM), and a node requesting the relay of data packets to AMs is described an Alliance Leader (AL). When an AL communicates outside of the alliance, it distributes traffic not only to its own external link but also to those of the AMs.

2.1   Mobile IP SHAKE

Mobile IP SHAKE [1] is an implementation of SHAKE on the IP layer. We assume the use of Mobile IP SHAKE in this paper. To establish SHAKE on the IP layer, a node that distributes traffic on the path between the correspondent node (CN) of an AL and the alliance including that AL is necessary. If no node distributes packets sent from the CN to the destination node (AL), the CN has to know all the addresses of the nodes in the alliance (AM). This is not ideal because it is not functionally practical for

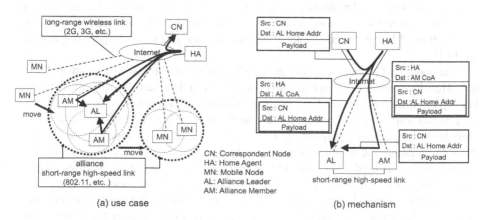

(a) use case   (b) mechanism

Fig. 1. Mobile IP SHAKE

ordinary hosts on the Internet to know the addresses of all AMs for a short time session. Mobile IP SHAKE exploits a feature that assures that the packets from the CN to a Mobile Node (MN) always go through the Home Agent (HA) of an MN on the Mobile IPv4 mechanism unless route optimization is used, and introduces a traffic-dispersion mechanisms into the HA. For this reason, Mobile IP SHAKE does not require any special mechanism for CNs.

Figure 1 provides an overview of Mobile IP SHAKE. An AL registers an AM's care-of address (CoA) as well as the AL's own CoA to the HA of the AL in advance. When the HA forwards packets sent from the CN, it encapsulates the packets and distributes them not only to the AL but also to the AMs. The AMs decapsulate the transmitted packets and forward them to the AL through the links in the alliance. When packets are transmitted from the inside of an alliance to the external link, the AL encapsulates and distributes packets to each AM. Then, each AM forwards the packets to the destination node or the AL's HA as in the reverse tunneling technology used in Mobile IPv4.

In the following section, we describe transmission from a node in an alliance to outside the cluster as '*uplink*', and transmission from outside the alliance into the alliance as '*downlink*'.

2.2   Issues in Using SHAKE

In SHAKE, AMs have to offer CPU resources, battery power, and link bandwidth to the AL. For this reason, AMs may refuse to relay packets for the AL unless mutual trust exists between the AL and the AMs or unless some reward is promised. Therefore, we introduce a mechanism for motivating AMs to relay packets for the AL by granting rewards to the AMs. We deal with this issue in this paper. Adding to this, the management of heterogeneous mobile nodes in the alliance and traffic distribution are important issues. These issues have been discussed in [2].

2.3   Related Work

The issues of cooperation of mobile nodes for packet forwarding have been investigated in ad hoc networks and multi-hop cellular networks. In [5, 7], reputation mechanisms for ad hoc networks were proposed. In [10], Eidenbenz et al. proposed game theory approach in ad hoc networks. Golle et al. analyzed the incentives in peer-to-peer networks [9].

Our approach for our special architecture SHAKE is credit-based mechanism. Credit-based mechanism is used in ad hoc networks [3, 6, 4], and in multi-hop cellular networks [11, 8]. In [3], Buttyan and Hubaux proposed virtual currency called *nuglets*. The sender of a packet loads *nuglets* on the packet, and the intermediate nodes acquire some *nuglets* from that packet by forwarding it. In [6], they proposed an improved mechanism. In [3, 6], to ensure the payment of the correct amount of *nuglets* to each node, tamper-proof hardware is used. Our system does not need any tamper-proof hardware at any node. Zhong et al. proposed a method relying on a central authority that collects receipts from the forwarding nodes [4]. In this method, intermediate nodes send receipts after forwarding data messages. Then, the central authority charges the source nodes and rewards the forwarding nodes based on the receipts.

The following are differences between these credit-based methods and our method. First, in [4, 11], authors use cryptographic functions based on public key cryptography, whereas our solution is based on symmetric key cryptography requiring less computation load. Secondly, some of above credit-based approaches do not solve a case in which the destination of a packet pays the reward. When SHAKE is used, an AL has to grant AMs the rewards in both cases when the AL is the transmission source and the destination, because the AL relies on AMs in both cases. So we designed a mechanism adapted to the both cases. Thirdly, these approaches assume only a rational malicious node that attempts to cheat if the expected benefit of doing so is greater than the expected benefit of acting honestly. In other words, they do not take care of the offenders for pleasure. We suppose that the existence of such offenders is one of serious problems. In addition to the cases that malicious nodes attack the system intentionally, cracked computers might attack other hosts unintentionally. This leads to collapse the systems and to loss service provider's confidence. The fourth difference is that above credit-based methods can not distinguish unintentional packet losses from packet drop of malicious node, and can not solve contradiction of charging arisen from packet losses. We also address this problem.

3   A Scheme Encouraging Mobile Nodes to Forward Packets on SHAKE

To encourage Alliance Members (AMs) to relay packets for an Alliance Leader (AL) in SHAKE, we introduce an incentive for AMs. We propose a method of using credit as the incentive. Each AM receives credit in compensation for the relay. Therefore, if an AL wants to send packets via an AM, the AL needs to pay credit for the AM. The amount of credit is proportional to the size of the packet. We assume that the credit can be converted into real money or can grant privilege to users in provider services. If a node wants to get more credit, the node can get by paying its debit or buy them using real money, or be remunerated by forwarding others' data traffic.

We introduce a trusted third party to maintain users' credit account, and we call this party a Credit Server (CS). We assume that the CS and the Home Agent (HA) are completely reliable and do not coalesce with other hosts. From a practical standpoint, HAs will be managed by ISP or carrier if Mobile IP is used for mobile phone. Because of this, it is considered to be reasonable that the HAs are completely reliable. The CS is the authority for managing credit, and the CS rewards AMs that have forwarded packets reliably and charges the ALs. The CS charges and rewards for the relay of packets forwarded successfully. We use Forward Reports (FRs) from an AM and a HA for judging whether packets have been successfully forwarded. Between the HA and the CS, and between the AM and the CS, the FRs are assumed not to be modified by a third party by using secure session like IPsec.

In the following discussion, we deal with the following malicious attacks.

– Forgery of credit:
  Individual nodes may illegitimately try to increase their own credit.

- Free riding (AL's refusal to pay to CS):
  An AL may claim that it did not initiate some communication despite being helped by AMs. The CS has to refuse these kinds of claims.
- AM's false charge for rewards:
  An AM may charge credit by sending a false FR to the CS. The CS has to refuse such kinds of charges.

3.1   Forwarding Uplink Packets

Overview. Figure 2 illustrates the flow of data packets and control messages for crediting procedures in uplink. In Section 2.1, in uplink on Mobile IP SHAKE, we pointed out that both the transitions of passing through HA and of not passing through HA could be used. However in this paper, we assume that packets from an AL to a CN are forwarded by the HA. The purpose of this is that we intend to enable the HA to confirm that AMs forward packets with certainty.

In uplink, the packets from an AL are delivered to the CN via an AM and an HA except packets sent directly from that AL's own external link. When the HA forwards a certain amount of packets via the AM, it generates a FR and sends it to the CS. We suppose that the HA sends the FRs to the CS via TCP for reliable transmission. When the CS receives the FRs from the HA, it judges whether each packet has been successfully forwarded. After this operation, the CS pays the reward to the AM and charges it to the AL for the successfully forwarded packets. This CS's payment is supposed to be levied as ISP or other service charges. When no FR is received from the HA, the CS judges that forwarding has failed, and does not charge or reward credit.

Protocol in Detail. In this section, we present details of the uplink protocol. The packets from an AL to a CN are distributed to a communication path via an AM (AL → AM → HA → CN) and another communication path using the AL's own external link (AL

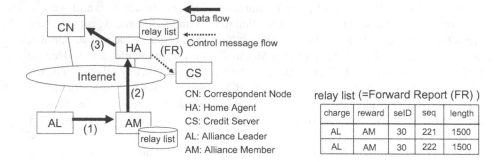

(1) $(payload, seID, seq, length, MAC_{K_{HA-AL}}(payload, seID, seq, length))$

(2) $(payload, seID, seq, length, MAC_{K_{HA-AM}}(seID, seq, length, MAC_{K_{HA-AL}}))$

(3) $(payload)$

Fig. 2. Uplink procedure

$\rightarrow$ HA $\rightarrow$ CN). Charging or rewarding credits is not processed for packets delivered directly from an AL to the HA rather than via an AM. Hereafter, we explain the protocol relating to the crediting procedure on the communication path via the AM.

To authenticate the sending node and the forwarding node of a packet, we use a message authentication code (MAC). In our proposal, an AL sends a packet with a session ID (*seID*), sequence number (*seq*), length (*length*) and its MAC. After an AM receives the packet, it forwards the packet to the HA with a new MAC computed with the MAC included in the received packet. The HA verifies the MAC in the received packet. The *seq* is used to resist replay attacks. The *length* is used for charging at the CS.

Symmetric session keys (K_{HA-AM}, K_{HA-AL}) must be established in advance through a suitable key exchange protocol between an HA and an AM via an AL, and between the HA and an AL, respectively. Hereafter, $MAC_{K_{HA-AM}}$, $MAC_{K_{HA-AL}}$ denote MACs, which are the keyed cryptographic hash values computed with the session key between the HA of the AL and an AM, and between the HA and the AL, respectively. Moreover, we assume that HAs have a *relay list* including a list of packets relayed for the AL. This *relay list* is used for generating FR for multiple relayed packets.

We explain the crediting procedure on Mobile IP SHAKE as described in Figure 2.

1. An AL generates the *seID* of the session, and distributes the packets to the AMs with their *seID*, *seq*, *length*, $MAC_{K_{HA-AL}}$. $MAC_{K_{HA-AL}}$ is the keyed cryptographic hash value of the content of the packet (i.e. *seID*, *seq*, *length*, *payload*) (Figure 2(1)). The session key K_{HA-AL} is used for computing $MAC_{K_{HA-AL}}$.
2. An AM receives the packet from the AL. It checks that the sequence number has not already been used. If the packet is not duplicated, the AM computes a new MAC with the received MAC and K_{HA-AM}, and forwards the packet to the HA adding the $MAC_{K_{HA-AM}}(seID, seq, length, MAC_{K_{HA-AL}})$ instead of the received MAC (Figure 2(2)).
3. The HA verifies whether the value of MAC added to the packet is correct by comparing it with the keyed cryptographic hash value using K_{HA-AL} and K_{HA-AM} stored in the HA. If it is not correct, the packet is dropped. Otherwise, the HA checks that the sequence number has not already been used. If the packet is not duplicated, the HA forwards the data packet to the CN (Figure 2(3)). After forwarding the packet, the HA adds the entry including the *seID*, *seq* and *length* of each packet to its *relay list*.
4. The HA sends a FR based on each *relay list* to the CS periodically or when the number of unsent entries of *relay list* reaches the upper limit (Figure 2).
5. The CS charges and rewards credit according to the amount of the packet reported from the HA.

3.2 Forwarding Downlink Packets

Overview. Figure 3 shows the flow of the data packets and the control messages in the crediting procedures in downlink. A data packet is delivered from the CN to an AL via the HA of the AL and an AM. When an AL receives a certain amount of packets

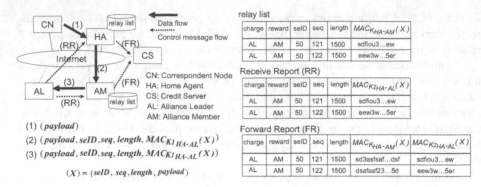

Fig. 3. Downlink procedure

forwarded by the AM, the AL sends a Receive Report (RR) of the forwarded packets to the HA and the AM. The RR is a list that contains the *seID*, *seq*, *length*, and $MAC_{K_{HA-AL}}$ of each packet. This RR is essential for confirming the success of forwarding. The RRs, as well as the FRs, are supposed to be sent through TCP connections. We assume that an AM and a HA require a $MAC_{K_{HA-AL}}$ contained in the RR to generate a FR. The AM and the HA generate their FR based on both the RR and their *relay list*, and send it to the CS. The CS compares the FRs from both the AM and the HA, and confirms that the packets were actually forwarded by the AM and the HA. If the FR is correctly collated, the charging and rewarding procedure is performed.

Protocol in Detail. In this section, we explain the details of the protocol in downlink according to Fig. 3. Symmetric session keys (K_{HA-AM}, K_{HA-AL}) are established in advance through a suitable key exchange protocol between the HA of the AL and an AM via the AL, and between the HA and the AL, respectively. Between the HA and the AL, two symmetric session keys are established. We name them $K1_{HA-AL}$, $K2_{HA-AL}$, respectively. One is used for authentication in communication, and the other is used for RRs.

1. The CN transmits the data packets destined for an AL (Figure 3(1)).
2. When the HA of the AL forwards the data packets to the AM, the HA generates the *seID* of the session, and attaches the *seID*, *seq*, *length* and $MAC_{K1_{HA-AL}}$ of the received packet (Figure 3(2)). After forwarding the packet, the HA adds an entry that consists of the *seID*, *seq*, *length* and the calculation result of $MAC_{K_{HA-AM}}(seID, seq, length, payload)$ to its *relay list*.
3. The AM receives the packet and then checks whether the sequence number has not already been used. The AM forwards the packet to the AL. After forwarding the packet, the AM adds an entry that consists of the *seID*, *seq*, *length*, and $MAC_{K_{HA-AM}}$ of the forwarded packet to its *relay list*.
4. When the AL receives the packet forwarded by the AM, the AL verifies whether the value of $MAC_{K1_{HA-AL}}$ added to the packet is correct. If the verification is successful, the AL adds an entry including the *seID*, *seq*, *length*, and the calculation result of $MAC_{K2_{HA-AL}}(seID, seq, length, payload)$ of the packet to its RR. When the AL

receives a certain amount of packets, the AL sends a RR to the HA and the AM. The HA and the AM generate FRs based on the RR and the *relay list* maintained by themselves, and send them to the CS. The content of the FRs is a list including the entries of the set of *seID*, *seq*, *length*, $MAC_{K_{HA-AM}}$ and $MAC_{K2_{HA-AL}}$ of forwarded packets as in Fig. 3.

5. The CS compares the entries in the FRs of the AM and the HA, and judges whether the packets were successfully forwarded. The CS charges and rewards credits according to the amount of correctly forwarded packets.

3.3   Mechanisms for the CS/HA to Resist Dishonest Claims

In order to resist dishonest claims by ALs and AMs, the CS and the HA perform the following procedures.

CS Operation. We assume that some CSs exist in the Internet. The CSs maintain a list of malicious nodes by mutually exchanging information or using a centralized information server. Specifically, the CSs record the nodes that refused to pay credits or falsely charged for rewards, and this information is shared by CSs. We assume that this information can be referred to all nodes when an alliance is established, and thus can be used to evaluate whether nodes are suitable to be included in an alliance. In addition, when the wrong MACs are submitted to the CS, the CS sends error messages containing the wrong MACs to the AL and the AM, which announces to the AL and the AM that the wrong MACs are sent. The error messages are assumed not to be modified by a third party by using secure session like IPsec.

HA Operation. In downlink, ALs are supposed to sent the RR to the HA and the AM if in fact they have received a packet from the CN via the HA and the AM. However the RR may not be sent from the AL in the following two cases. One is when the AL does not send the RR intentionally. The other is when some accidents occur on the link between the HA and AL via the AM, and the data packets from the CN do not reach the AL via the HA and the AM. In either case, we assume that the HA stops distributing packets to the route from which an RR was not delivered for a certain amount of time, and the HA distributes packets to other AMs' routes. Moreover, in the same way as CS, the HA sends error messages to the AL and the AM if wrong MACs are sent in uplink.

4   Analysis

In this section, we analyze the robustness and overhead of our proposed method.

4.1   Robustness Against Attacks of Malicious ALs

Here we consider the robustness against malicious attacks by Alliance Leaders (ALs).

Refusal of Payment by AL
Dishonset Act. An AL may refuse a payment claim from the Credit Server (CS) although it was actually supported by Alliance Members (AMs).

*Solution.*If the AL refuses payment, the CS records that the AL refused the payment. Because this recorded information is publicly open to the other nodes, the AL cannot maintain the confidence of other nodes using SHAKE afterwards. The payment refusal of the AL is prevented because payment refusal becomes disadvantageous when using SHAKE.

Transmission of Incorrect MAC by AL

Dishonest Act. In uplink, in order to escape charges, an AL might transmit a false MAC to the AM and the HA.

Solution. In uplink, the AL transmits $MAC_{K_{HA-AL}}$ with each packet. The MAC can be verified in the HA although it cannot be verified in the AM, because the MAC is made from the session key between the AL and the HA. If the HA's verification of the MAC is unsuccessful, the HA will drop the packet. Transmission of an incorrect MAC results in the packet undelivered to the CN. Therefore, the ALs will not transmit incorrect MACs.

Undelivered RR

Dishonest Act. In downlink transmission, an AL may not submit a Receive Report (RR) although it received packets via the AM accurately.

Solution. The HA will stop distributing packets to any route from which an RR is not submitted as described in Section 3.3. If an AL maliciously refuses to submit RRs, the HA will stop delivering packets to routes from which RRs are not submitted, and so the route will not be used. Therefore, all ALs will submit the RR faithfully if they want to use the route effectively.

Incorrect RR Submission

Dishonest Act. In two cases, incorrect RR may be submitted from an AL to refuse charging. One is that the AL submits incorrect RRs both to the HA and the AMs. The other is that the AL submits an incorrect RR either to the HA or the AM. The RRs can be verified in the HA though they cannot be verified in the AM, because the MACs contained in each entry of the RRs are made from the session key between the AL and the HA. Therefore, a problem exists when the AL submits a correct RR to the HA and an incorrect RR to the AM.

Solution. The Forward Report (FR) is supposed to contain the MAC generated by AL in the RR. If the CS cannot collate the FRs from the HA and the AM correctly, the CS sends error messages to the AL and the AM as described in Section 3.3. If the AM receives the error message, it stops forwarding of packets for the AL.

4.2 Robustness Against Malicious Attacks by AMs

In this section, we consider the ability of the proposal method to resist the malicious attacks of AMs.

Dishonest Rewards

Dishonest Act. An AM may charge for a reward for packets that it did not forward.

Solution. In uplink, if an AM wants to be rewarded, it must actually forward packets to the HA. The HA sends a FR to the CS for the only packets that arrived at the HA. Thus the AM cannot receive a reward for packets that it has not forwarded.

In downlink, the AM must send a FR to the CS to be rewarded for the forwarding of packets. When the AM generates the FR, the AM cannot generate the required MAC for the FR by itself because it needs the MAC computed for the forwarded packet with the session key between the HA and the AL owned by HA and AL. The MAC is included in a RR from the AL. Therefore, in downlink, an AM can generate a FR only when it has actually forwarded packets for the AL to the CN and received the corresponding RR from the AL.

Packet Drop in Forwarding

Dishonest Act. AM may intentionally drop packets for AL. *Solution.* An AM can easily drop packets intentionally. However, if a packet does not reach its forwarding destination node, the AM cannot be remunerated. If an AM drops only a few packets, the influence on the communication performance is a little, and this is common in mobile environment. Thus, any special operation is not performed. If the packet loss continues, the HA and the AL stop distributing packets to the route that is dropping packets as described in Section 3.3. Therefore, this dishonest act is insignificant.

Modification of MAC Generated by AL

Dishonest Act. In uplink, an AM forwards packets including MAC generated by the AL. In downlink, an AM receives a RR from the AL, then the AM sends a FR containing MAC generated by the AL and included in the RR. The AM can modify the AL's MACs, which intentionally damages the reputation of the AL.

Solution. If the CS and the HA receive wrong MACs, they send error messages to the AM and the AL as described in Section 3.3. If the AL receives the error message, it stops the distribution of packets to the AM and breaks the alliance with the AM.

4.3   Robustness Against Malicious Attacks by a Third Party

We assume that a HA is completely trustworthy. All dishonest behavior resulting from a conspiracy can be prevented by the tact that all packets must pass through the HA. For instance, if the HA cannot identify a third party that colludes with an AM or an AL, the HA does not forward packets and does not send a FR to the CS. Therefore, problems do not occur.

4.4   Robustness Against Malfunction Caused by Lost Packets on Links

In transmission on wireless links, packet loss may occur unexpectedly. We point out losses of data packets, and do not discuss losses of the RR and FR that are supposed to via TCP flow. We consider instances of both the uplink and downlink, and discuss the charging and rewarding rather than the influence on communication performance.

Uplink (AL → AM → HA → CN)

- Packet loss between AL and AM
  If the packet destined for the CN does not arrive at the AM, crediting procedure is not performed, and therefore problems do not occur.
- Packet loss between AM and HA
  In this case, the packet destined for the CN does not reach the HA even if the AM

actually forwards the packet to the HA. If the packet does not reach the HA, the AM cannot be remunerated though it was actually willing to forward the packet. We assume that the AM can be remunerated only when packet forwarding has succeeded. Contradictions related to rewards do not occur.

– Packet loss between HA and CN
  In this case, a packet from an AL to the CN does not reach the CN. However, an AM has in fact successfully forwarded the packet to the HA, and therefore the AL should send a reward to the AM. We assume that the AL sends the reward to the AM that has forwarded the packet successfully, and that the CS can confirm the AM's forwarding via the HA's FR. Therefore, contradictions related to rewards do not happen.

Downlink (CN → HA → AM → AL)

– Packet loss between CN and HA, Packet loss between HA and AM
  The charging and rewarding of credit will not occur if a packet does not reach the AM. Neither kind of packet losses causes problems.
– Packet loss between AM and AL
  In this case, even if an AM certainly forwarded the packet to the AL, whether the packet is dropped by the AM intentionally or not cannot be distinguished. In our proposed method, if an AM's successful forwarding cannot be confirmed, the rewarding procedure is not performed. Therefore, the contradictions to the rewarding procedure do not occur.

4.5   Overhead

SHAKE is a mechanism aiming at the improvement of the communication performance by using two or more links simultaneously. To maintain the very small overhead for the crediting procedure compared with the communication performance improvement is essential.

Computation Overhead. For each packet, MAC computations and MAC verifications have to be performed at the HA, AM, and AL. Cryptographic operations need energy and time to be performed. Regarding energy consumption, the energy required to perform the computation is negligible compared with the energy required to perform the transmission [12]. Moreover, the time required to compute the cryptographic hash function is also efficient. [13] shows numerical examples of speed benchmarks for some of the most commonly used cryptographic algorithms. For example, when being run on a Pentium 4 2.1 GHz processor under Windows XP SP 1.386, a MAC computation with HMAC/MD5 algorithm can be performed at 1.6 Gbps. According to this value, the MAC computation time for 1500 bytes packet would be approximately 7 microseconds. In the measurements of the Mobile IP SHAKE that we previously implemented, the time required to perform the forwarding at the HA was approximately 250 microseconds, the time required to perform the forwarding at the AM was approximately 24 microseconds. The MAC computation time (7 microseconds) is negligible compared with the forwarding time. Therefore, the overhead of MAC computations and MAC verifications at the HA, AM, and AL is acceptable.

Communication Overhead. In order to measure the communication overhead of each data packet, we have implemented a prototype of our scheme by adding an authentication header per packet on our Mobile IP SHAKE ([1]). We implemented this prototype on Linux, and realized the authentication header as a part of IP options. As mentioned in Section 3, we need seID, seq, length, and MAC for each packet. In this implementation, the MAC is computed by HMAC-MD5. In IP options format, option fields (1 byte) and option length field (1 byte) are prepared. We added *seID*(1 byte long), *length* (that is packet length, 1 byte long), *seq* (4 bytes long) and MAC (16 bytes long) to the IP options format. Additionally, we attached a 2-bytes long SPI (Security Parameter Index) field for the authentication algorithm and a 2-bytes long padding field. Thus, the total length of the authentication header is 28 bytes long.

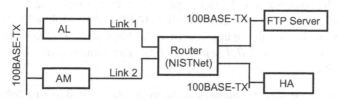

HA=Home Agent, AL=Alliance Leader, AM=Alliance Member

Fig. 4. Experimental network for emulating wireless network

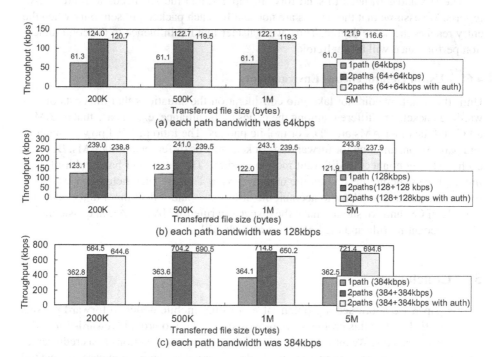

Fig. 5. Performance on an emulated network. Average of five trials

We measured the effect of the additional header to the throughput of the communication on the Mobile IP SHAKE. Figure 4 shows the network topology of the experimental network. An AL and an AM that have two fast Ethernet interfaces were connected, and they were also connected to a router with multiple network interfaces and runs NISTNET [14] network emulator. The HA of the AL and an FTP server were connected to the different network interfaces of the router. We measured the throughput when 200KB, 500KB, 1MB and 5MB files were transferred from the FTP server to the AL. The bandwidth and delay of the link between the AL and the router, and the AM and the router were set to 64, 128, 384 [kbps] and 100 [msec], respectively. The distribution ratio of AL to AM in the HA was 1:1. A case where only one AL was connected to the router was also tested for comparison.

Figure 5 shows the result of the experiments. We can see the influence to the throughput by addition of the authentication header is negligible. For example, in Fig. 5 (b), when 5MB file was transferred by normal Mobile IP SHAKE and the Mobile IP SHAKE with authentication header, the throughputs were 243.8 kbps and 237.9 kbps respectively. The ratio of 243.8 kbps to 237.9 kbps is 97.6 %. The communication overhead seems to be acceptable.

Other Overhead. In our system, the additional messages are required to establish symmetric keys between the HA and AL, and between the HA and AM. This is performed only once in a session.

The HA and AM need to send forward reports, and the AL needs to send receive reports. We assume that the reports are not sent for each packet, but sent only when the entry reaches the some degree. Thus, we consider that the influence to the communication performance will be negligible.

4.6   Use in Heterogeneous Environments

Until this point, we did not take into consideration the situations that the costs of forwarding packets are different among the nodes in the alliance, e.g., a case that an AM is a PC and the other AMs are PDA or mobile phones. The ratio of CPU power, memory and battery consumption for forwarding packets may be different among AMs. Besides, each AM may connect to different mobile carriers. The delay and bandwidth of each link and fee structure depend on the mobile carrier. Thus, in such heterogeneous environments, we have to take into account the differences and reflect them in the accounting rule of CS, and we should make the dispersion rule for HA and AL in consideration of the accounting rule and the link status of each AM.

5   Conclusion

In this paper, we addressed a problem of motivating mobile nodes to forward packets on SHAKE. To solve this problem, we proposed a method to provide rewards for nodes that forward packets. We introduced a trusted third party that functions as a credit server and manages members' credit accounts. We presented a charging/rewarding method based on Receive Reports (RRs) and Forward Reports (FRs). By using RRs and FRs, the charging/rewarding procedure works only for successfully forwarded packets, and our method can resist several kinds of dishonest attacks. Moreover, we showed that our system works even if unexpected packet losses occur on the link. We implemented the prototype of our system that deals with extension header per packet, and evaluated the communication overhead of the extension header. The result showed the overhead is acceptable for the use of SHAKE.

References

1. K. Koyama, Y. Ito, S. Ishihara, H. Mineno, "Performance evaluation of TCP on Mobile IP SHAKE," IPSJ journal, Vol. 45, No. 10, pp. 2270–2278, 2004.
2. H. Mineno, Y. Konishi, S. Ishihara, and T. Mizuno, "Implementation of cluster control manager for multiple wireless links sharing system," in proc. of PACRIM, 2003.
3. L. Buttyan and J.-P. Hubaux, "Enforcing Service availability in mobile ad-hoc WANs," in proc. of MobiHoc, 2000.
4. S. Zhong, Y. R. Yang, and J. Chen, "Sprite: A Simple, Cheat-Proof, Credit-Based System for Mobile Ad Hoc Netoworks," in proc. of INFOCOM. IEEE, 2003.
5. S. Marti, T. Giuli, K. Lai, and M. Baker, "Mitigating routing misbehavior in mobile ad hoc networks," in proc. of MobiCom, 2000.
6. Levente Buttyan, Jean-Pierre Hubaux, "Stimulating cooperation in self-organizing mobile ad hoc networks," Mobile Networks and Applications, v.8 n.5, p.579-592, 2003
7. Sonja Buchegger, Jean-Yves Le Boudec, "Performance analysis of the CONFIDANT protocol," in proc. of MobiHoc, 2002.
8. N. Ben Salem, L. Buttyan, J. P. Hubaux, and M. Jakobsson, "A Charging and Rewarding Scheme for Packet Forwarding in Multi-hop Cellular Networks," in proc. of MobiHoc, 2003.
9. P. Golle, K. Leyton-Brown, and I. Mironov, "Incentives in peer-topeer file sharing," in proc. of the ACM Symposium on Electronic Commerce (EC' 01) 2001, 2001.
10. Luzi Anderegg and Stephan Eidenbenz, "Ad hoc-VCG: a truthful and cost-efficient routing protocol for mobile ad hoc networks with selfish agents," in proc. of MobiCom, 2003.
11. B. Lamparter, K. Paul, and D. Westhoff, "Charging Support for Ad Hoc Stub Networks. Journal of Computer Communication," Technology and Applications, Elsevier Science, 2003.
12. G. J. Pottie and W. J. Kaiser. Wireless Integrated Network Sensors. Communications of the ACM, May, 2000.
13. Speed Comparison of Popular Crypto Algorithms, http://www.eskimo.com/~weidai/benchmarks.html
14. NIST Net, http://snad.ncsl.nist.gov/itg/nistnet

A Protocol for Recording Provenance in Service-Oriented Grids

Paul Groth, Michael Luck, and Luc Moreau

School of Electronics and Computer Science,
University of Southampton, Highfield,
Southampton SO17 1BJ, United Kingdom
{pg03r, mml, l.moreau}@ecs.soton.ac.uk

Abstract. Both the scientific and business communities, which are beginning to rely on Grids as problem-solving mechanisms, have requirements in terms of provenance. The provenance of some data is the documentation of process that led to the data; its necessity is apparent in
fields ranging from medicine to aerospace. To support provenance capture
in Grids, we have developed an implementation-independent protocol for
the recording of provenance. We describe the protocol in the context of a
service-oriented architecture and formalise the entities involved using an
abstract state machine or a three-dimensional state transition diagram.
Using these techniques we sketch a liveness property for the system.

Keywords: recording provenance, provenance, grids, web services,
lineage.

1 Introduction

A Grid is a system that coordinates computational resources not subject to centralized control using standard, open, general-purpose protocols and interfaces
to deliver non-trivial qualities of service [4]. By coordinating diverse, distributed
computational resources, Grids can be used to address large-scale problems that
might otherwise be beyond the scope of local, homogenous systems. Grids are
being developed to run a wide variety of applications for both the business and
science communities. Scientific applications include the analysis of data from the
Large Hadron Collider (lcg.web.cern.ch/LCG/), experiments in surface chemistry [3] and next generation climate research. Grids are used in the business
community to support aircraft simulation, seismic studies in the petroleum industry, and to provide faster portfolio recommendations in financial services
(www.ibm.com/grid).

These communities also have requirements in terms of *provenance*. We define
the provenance of some data as the documentation of the *process* that led to
the data. The necessity for provenance is apparent in a wide range of fields.
For example, the American Food and Drug Administration requires that the
provenance of a drug's discovery be kept as long as the drug is in use (up to 50

T. Higashino (Ed.): OPODIS 2004, LNCS 3544, pp. 124–139, 2005.

years sometimes). In chemistry, provenance is used to detail the procedure by which a material is generated, allowing the material to be patented. In aerospace, simulation records as well as other provenance data are required to be kept up to 99 years after the design of an aircraft. In financial auditing, the American Sarbanes-Oxley Act requires public accounting firms to maintain the provenance of an audit report for at least seven years after the issue of that report (United States Public Law No. 107-204). In medicine, the provenance of an organ is vital for its effective and safe transplantation. These are just some examples of the requirements for provenance in science and business. Provenance is particularly important when there is no physical record as in the case of a purely *in silico* scientific process.

Given the need for provenance information and the emergence of Grids as infrastructure for running major applications, a problem arises that has yet to be fully addressed by the Grid community, namely, how to record provenance in Grids? Some bespoke and ad-hoc solutions have been developed to address the lack of provenance recording capability within the context of specific Grid applications. Unfortunately, this means that such provenance systems cannot interoperate. Therefore, incompatibility of components prevents provenance from being shared. Furthermore, the absence of components for recording provenance makes the development of applications requiring provenance recording more complicated and onerous.

Another drawback to current bespoke solutions is the inability for provenance to be shared by different parties. Even with the availability of provenance-related software components, the goal of sharing provenance information will not be achieved. To address this problem, standards should be developed for how provenance information is recorded, represented, and accessed. Such standards would allow provenance to be shared across applications, provenance components, and Grids, making provenance information more accessible and valuable. In summary, the paucity of standards, components, and techniques for recording provenance is a problem that needs to be addressed by the Grid community. The focus of this work, the development of a general architecture and protocol for recording provenance, is a first step towards addressing these problems.

The rest of the paper is organised as follows: Section 2 presents a set of requirements that a provenance system should address. Then, Section 3 outlines a design for a provenance recording system in the context of service-oriented architectures. The key element of our system is the Provenance Recording Protocol described in Section 4. In Section 5, the actors in the system are formalised, and the formalisations are then used, in Section 6, to derive some important properties of the system. Finally, Section 7 discusses related work, followed by a conclusion. Given the length of this paper, we assume the reader is familiar with Grids, Virtual Organisations (VO), Web Services, and service-oriented architectures (SOA).

2   Requirements

We have identified a number of requirements that a provenance system should support through an initial requirements gathering process. The following seven requirements have been of particular importance in motivating the development of our architecture and protocol.

1. Verifiability. A provenance system should have the ability to verify a process in terms of the actors involved, their actions and their relationship with one another.

2. Accountability. Closely related to verifiability is accountability. An actor should be accountable for its actions in a process. Therefore, a provenance system should record in a non-repudiable manner any provenance generated by an actor.

3. Reproducibility. A provenance system should, at a minimum, be able to repeat a process and possibly reproduce a process from the provenance that it has stored.

4. Preservation. A provenance system should have the ability to maintain provenance information for an extended period of time. This is vital for applications run in the VO context because even after a VO disbands, provenance will typically need to be maintained.

5. Scalability. Given the large amounts of data that Grid applications handle, such as in the processing of data from the Large Hadron Collider, it is necessary that a provenance system be scalable. Another reason for scalability is that provenance information may be larger than the output data of an application.

6. Generality. Grids are designed to support a wide variety of applications, therefore, a provenance system should be general enough to record provenance from these varying applications.

7. Customisability. To allow for more application specific use of provenance information, a provenance system should allow for customisation. Aspects of customisability could include constraints on the type of provenance recorded, time constraints on when recording can take place, and the granularity of provenance to be recorded.

With these requirements in mind, we now detail our conceptual architecture for recording provenance in a SOA.

3   Conceptual Architecture

Figure 1(a) shows a typical workflow based service-oriented architecture. A client initiator invokes a workflow enactment engine which, in turn, invokes various services based on the workflow specified by the initiator, finally, a result is returned to the initiator. In essence, the architecture can be broken down into two types of actors: clients who invoke services and services that receive invocations and return results.

Given these types of actors and their method of communication, we have identified two kinds of provenance that exist in a service-oriented architecture.

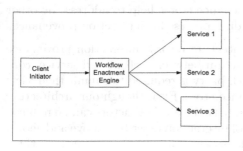

(a) Typical workflow based architecture

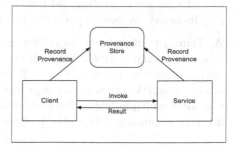

(b) The interaction between a client service and provenance store

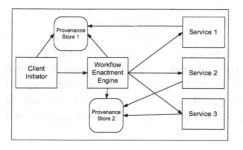

(c) Workflow based architecture with provenance recording

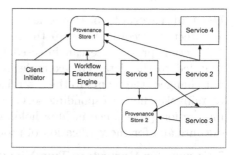

(d) Architecture with provenance recording and services invoking other services

Fig. 1. Architecture diagrams

The first kind of provenance is interaction provenance. For some data, interaction provenance is the documentation of interactions between actors that led to the data. In a SOA, interactions are, fundamentally, a client invoking a service. Therefore, interaction provenance can be obtained by recording the inputs and outputs of the various services involved in generating a result. The second type of provenance we have identified is actor provenance. For some data, actor provenance is documentation that can only be provided by a particular actor pertaining to the process that led to the data.

Within the context of these kinds of provenance, our architecture introduces a third type of actor, the provenance store.

Third Party Provenance Stores. We see third party provenance stores as key to fulfilling the requirements outlined above. In terms of preservation, placing the burden of maintaining provenance on third party stores means that neither clients nor services must maintain provenance information beyond the scope of any given application run. An additional benefit of third party provenance stores is that they provide a method for legacy applications to maintain provenance.

In order to better understand how provenance stores help to address the other requirements, we now explain the recording process for interaction provenance.

A Triangle of Interaction. Our architecture records interaction provenance in the following manner. For each interaction between a client and service, consisting of an invocation and a result, each party is required to submit their view of the interaction to a common provenance store. Even though our architecture considers multiple actors, the interaction between all these actors can be reduced down to a common 'triangular' pattern of interaction described above and shown in Figure 1(b). This reduction is possible because our system contains only three types of actors, the client, service and provenance store, where the store exists in order to record a copy of the simple one-to-one interaction of the client and service. The interaction of these three actors is governed by Provenance Recording Protocol, which we will detail later in the paper.

Uses of Interaction Provenance. The client-service interactions that our architecture records make up the interaction provenance for some data. This interaction provenance can be used to repeat or even reproduce the process that led to the data. For example, if the services involved in a process have not changed, the inputs to these services, stored in the provenance, can be used to reinvoke the corresponding services reproducing the process. Other uses of interaction provenance include holding actors to account for their inputs and outputs and for the verification of processes.

The case for Recording Two Views. However, if interaction provenance is to be used for reproduction, accountability or verification purposes, the interactions recorded must be agreed upon by the actors involved. Each actor has its own view of an interaction, which, at its most basic, is the input and output of the actor in an interaction. Therefore, in our architecture a client and service must submit their view of an interaction to a common provenance store, which can then check that the actors agree on their interaction. Without verification by the provenance store, several problems could arise, particularly in open environments.

For example, should the client be the only party recording the interaction in the provenance store, the service would be reliant on the client to submit provenance. In fact, without the submission of provenance from the service, there would be no evidence that the client invoked the service should the client not record the interaction. Given that a service can be held accountable for its actions recorded in the provenance store, this is unacceptable. In our system, the provenance store would know that a service was invoked because the service submits that information. The same problem would also exist in the case where the service was the only party submitting to the provenance store. We note that the requirement that both parties submit their views does not prevent collusion between parties, but it does allow the provenance store to detect when the two parties disagree about the record of an interaction.

Multiple provenance stores. Although a client and service are required to share a common provenance store for an interaction, different provenance stores can be used for different interactions even between the same client and service.

Figure 1(c) shows a typical workflow based architecture with multiple provenance stores. This architecture is assembled from the 'triangle' pattern pictured in Figure 1(b). One benefit of multiple provenance stores is the elimination of a central point of failure. Another benefit is that demand is spread across multiple services increasing the architecture's robustness. These benefits help to address the scalability requirement.

Advanced Architecture Support. As well as supporting typical workflow enactment based architectures, our system supports more advanced architectures like the one shown in Figure 1(d). In this architecture, services invoke other services to produce a result, in contrast to the previous architecture where the workflow enactment engine was the only actor invoking services. In order to maintain provenance across provenance stores, a client needs to inform the original provenance store when it uses a new provenance store. For example, in Figure 1(d), Service 1 must inform Provenance Store 1 that it has used Provenance Store 2 when invoking Service 3. This creates a link between provenance records stored in different stores that can be followed in order to provide the entire provenance trace for an application started by a client initiator.

Actor Provenance. We have mainly discussed how our system supports the recording of information about the interaction between actors in a service-oriented architecture. Our system also supports actor provenance, which could include anything from the workflow that an enactment engine runs to the disk and processing power a service used in a computation. This information can only be provided by the actor itself, so it cannot be verified like interaction provenance. We use a simple mechanism to store actor provenance by tying it to interaction provenance. The basis for our provenance recording system is the interaction between one client, one service and one provenance store. This interaction is specified by the Provenance Recording Protocol, which is presented next.

4   Recording Protocol

PReP is a four phase protocol consisting of negotiation, invocation, provenance recording and termination phases. The negotiation phase allows a client and service to agree on a provenance store to store a trace of their interaction. After this phase, the protocol enters the invocation phase, during which a client invokes a service and receives a result. Asynchronously, in the provenance recording phase, both the client and service submit their input and output data to the provenance store. When all data has been received by the provenance store, the termination phase occurs.

First, we discuss the messages and their parameters used by PReP, then we consider the four phases in detail. We model the protocol as an asynchronous message-passing system, in which all communication is expressed by an outbound message followed by a return message. The return message is either a result of the service invocation, a reply from the service during negotiation, or an

Name	Notation	Fields
propose	pro	ACTIVITYID, PSALLOWEDLIST, EXTRA
reply	reply	ACTIVITYID, PSACCEPTED, EXTRA
invoke	inv	ACTIVITYID, DATA, EXTRA
result	res	ACTIVITYID, DATA, EXTRA
record negotiation	rec_neg	ACTIVITYID, PSALLOWEDLIST, PSACCEPTED, EXTRA
record negotiation acknowledgement	rec_neg_ack	ACTIVITYID
record invocation	rec_inv	ACTIVITYID, EXTRA, DATA
record invocation acknowledgement	rec_inv_ack	ACTIVITYID
record result	rec_res	ACTIVITYID, DATA
record result acknowledgement	rec_res_ack	ACTIVITYID
submission finished	sf	ACTIVITYID, NUMOFMESSAGES
submission finished acknowledgement	sf_ack	ACTIVITYID
additional provenance	ap	ACTIVITYID, EXTRA
additional provenance acknowledgement	ap_ack	ACTIVITYID

Fig. 2. Protocol messages, their formal notation and message parameters

acknowledgement that the provenance store has received a particular message. Figure 2 lists the fourteen messages in our protocol. The usage of each message is described in more detail when we present the phases of the protocol. The message parameters shown in Figure 2 are detailed below.

The ACTIVITYID parameter identifies one exchange between a client and server. It contains: NONCEID, an identifier generated by the client to distinguish between other exchanges with the called service; SESSIONID, comprising all invocations that pertain to one result (the client originator of Figure 1(c) generates this identifier, which must be unique); THREADID, which allows clients to parse multiple interactions with the same service; CLIENT, which identifies the client; and SERVICE, which identifies the service.

Other parameters are: DATA, which contains data exchanged between a client and service; EXTRA, which is an envelope that can contain other messages related or not to the protocol allowing it to be extended; NUMOFMESSAGES, which indicates the total number of messages an entity sends to the provenance store; PSALLOWEDLIST, which is a list of approved provenance stores; and PSACCEPTED, which contains a reference to a provenance store that an entity accepts, or a rejection token.

PReP is divided into four phases: negotiation, invocation, provenance recording, and termination, which we now discuss in detail.

Negotiation. is the process by which a client and service agree on a provenance store to use. Typically, a client presents a list of provenance stores to the service via a *propose message*. The service then extracts the PSALLOWEDLIST from the propose message and selects a provenance store from the list. The service then replies with a *response message* containing the selected provenance store or a rejection in the PSACCEPTED parameter. Although the negotiation modelled here is simple, with only one request-response, the protocol is extensible through the use of the EXTRA parameter. Entities can encode more complicated messages into this envelope, providing a means for complex negotiations to take place. A client and service that have already negotiated and agreed on a provenance store might like to skip the negotiation phase of the protocol. Therefore, a message informing the service of the use of a previously agreed provenance store can be enclosed in the EXTRA envelope of the *invoke message*. However, the provenance store still needs to be informed of the agreement between the service and client via the *record negotiation message*.

Invocation. If a client has successfully negotiated with a service, it can then invoke the service and receive a result via the *invoke message* and *result message*. We have tried to limit the impact of PReP on normal invocation, the only extra parameters required to be sent are the ACTIVITYID and the EXTRA envelope. The ACTIVITYID is necessary to identify the exchange in relation to the provenance stored in the service, while the EXTRA envelope allows the protocol to be used without a negotiation phase and for later protocol extension.

Provenance Recording. is the key phase of the protocol. As discussed previously, the client and service are required to submit copies of all their sent and received messages to the provenance store. Submission is done through the various record messages with both the client and service sending *record negotiation*, *record invocation* and *record result* messages. Acknowledgement messages then inform the sender that each message has been received by the provenance store. The *record negotiation message* contains the list of provenance stores (PSALLOWEDLIST), the client proposed, and the provenance store accepted (PSACCEPTED) by the service. The *record invocation* and *record result* messages together contain the entire data transmitted between the client and service from the perspective of both entities. The requirement that all data be submitted allows the provenance store to have a complete view of the exchange. In order not to delay service invocation, the submission process can be done in a totally asynchronous fashion; for example, the client could send a *record invocation message* to the provenance store before or after receiving a *result message* from the service.

We cater for actor provenance instead of interaction provenance by the *additional provenance message*. With this message, an actor can record provenance about itself or other actors in the architecture by enclosing in the EXTRA envelope whatever information is pertinent. An important use of this capability is the linking of provenance records across provenance stores as described in Section 3. We note that there are no constraints on the data that can be submitted to the provenance store, allowing a wide variety of applications to be supported.

Termination. The final phase of the protocol is termination. The protocol terminates when the provenance store has received all expected messages from both the client and the service. The client and service are notified of termination through the acknowledgement to the *submission finished message*, which is returned after all expected messages are received from the client and service.

The number of expected messages is determined by the NUMOFMESSAGES parameter in the *submission finished message*. Because of the asynchronous nature of the protocol, the *submission finished message* can be sent any time after the negotiation phase.

5   Actors

We now consider how the provenance store, service and client act in response to the messages they send and receive. To understand the actions of these actors, we use complementary formalisation techniques, chosen because of the nature of the actors involved. First, we represent the provenance store as an abstract state machine (ASM). Second, we use a 3D state diagram to show the possible responses of the client and service. Both techniques assume asynchronous message passing. The importance of the internal functionality of the provenance store lends itself to an ASM formalisation whereas, given the importance of the external interactions of the client and service, a state transition diagram formalisation is more appropriate. We begin with the provenance store.

The Provenance Store. plays the central role in PReP. As far as recording is concerned, its interaction with the outside world is simple: it receives messages and sends acknowledgements. It does not initiate any communication and its purpose is to simply store messages. By formalising the provenance store, we can explain how the accumulation of messages dictates its actions.

To detail these actions, we model the provenance store as an ASM whose behaviour is governed by a set of transitions it is allowed to perform. The notation allows for any form of transition with no limits on complexity or granularity and has been used previously to describe a distributed reference counting algorithm [6].

The ASM State Space. The state space of the provenance store's ASM is shown in Figures 3 and 4. The System State Space models the space of messages and message channels that actors in the system use to communicate, whereas the Provenance Store State Space models the internal state space of provenance stores. We first describe the System State Space.

The System State Space considers a finite number of actors, A, which exchange messages. The set of messages is defined as the union of the sets RN, RI, RR, SF, and AP. All of these sets, excluding AP, are in turn defined by inductive types, whose constructors are named according to the messages in Figure 2. Communication between actors is modelled as a set of communication channels represented as bags of messages between pairs of actors.

An instance of a provenance store actor, p, is a tuple that consists of an element from the Client Message Store, CS, an element from the Service Message Store, SS, and an element from the set of communication channels, $\mathcal{K}$. The two tables are defined as functions whose argument is of type ACTIVITYID and consist of sets of messages that are from either the client or the service. On the other hand, AP is a set that contains all of the *additional provenance messages*. Note

$A = \{a_1, a_2, \ldots, a_n\}$ (Set of Actors)
CLIENT $\subset A$ (Set of Clients is a subset of Actors)
SERVICE $\subset A$ (Set of Services is a subset of Actors)
ACTIVITYID = SESSIONID × NONCEID × THREADID × CLIENT × SERVICE   (Activity Identification)

rec_neg:ACTIVITYID × PSALLOWEDLIST × PSACCEPTED × EXTRA → RN (Negotiation Messages)
rec_inv:ACTIVITYID × EXTRA × DATA → RI (Invocation Messages)
rec_res:ACTIVITYID × EXTRA × DATA → RR (Result Messages)
     sf:ACTIVITYID × NUMOFMESSAGES → SF (Submission Finished Messages)
     ap:ACTIVITYID × EXTRA → AP (Additional Provenance Messages)

$\mathcal{M} = RN \cup RI \cup RR \cup SF \cup AP$ (Messages)
Each message has a corresponding acknowledgement message, which is also a part of $\mathcal{M}$.

$\mathcal{K} = A \times A \to Bag(\mathcal{M})$ (Set of Message Bags)

Charateristic Variables:
$a \in A, k \in \mathcal{K}, ai \in$ ACTIVITYID$, rec\_neg \in RN, rec\_inv \in RI, rec\_res \in RR, sf \in SF, ap \in AP,$
$e \in$ EXTRA$, psal \in$ PSALLOWEDLIST$, psa \in$ PSACCEPTED$, d \in$ DATA$, nid \in$ NONCEID$, tid \in$ THREADID$,$
$client \in$ CLIENT$, service \in$ SERVICE$, nm \in$ NUMOFMESSAGES

If $ai = \langle sid, nid, tid, ts, client, service \rangle$ then
     $ai.sid = sid, ai.nid = nid, ai.tid = tid, ai.ts = ts, ai.client = client, ai.service = service$
If $sf = \langle ai, nm \rangle$ then $sf.ai = ai, sf.nm = nm$

Fig. 3. System State Space

$APL = \mathbb{P}(AP)$ (Set of Sets of Additional Provenance Messages)
$CN = RN$ (Client Negotiation Messages)
$CI = RI$ (Client Invocation Messages)
$CR = RR$ (Client Result Messages)
$CSF = SF$ (Client Submission Finished Messages)
$SN = RN$ (Service Negotiation Messages)
$SI = RI$ (Service Invocation Messages)
$SR = RR$ (Service Result Messages)
$SSF = SF$ (Service Submission Finished Messages)
$CS = $ ACTIVITYID $\to CN \times CI \times CR \times CSF \times APL$ (Client Records, a Client Message Store)
$SS = $ ACTIVITYID $\to SN \times SI \times SR \times SSF \times APL$ (Service Records, Service Message Store)
$PS = CS \times SS$ (Set of Provenance Stores)

Characteristic variables:
$p = \langle client\_T, service\_T, k \rangle, p \in A, apl \in APL, client\_T \in CS, service\_T \in SS, ps \in PS$
If $service\_T[ai] = \langle rec\_neg, rec\_inv, rec\_res, sf, apl \rangle$ then
     $service\_T[ai].rec\_neg = rec\_neg, service\_T[ai].rec\_inv = rec\_inv,$
     $service\_T[ai].rec\_res = rec\_res, service\_T[ai].sf = sf, service\_T[ai].apl = apl$
The same notation applies for $client\_T[ai]$.
Initial State:
$p_i = \langle client\_T_i, service\_T_i, k_i \rangle, client\_T_i = ai \to \emptyset, service\_T_i = ai \to \emptyset, k_i = \emptyset$

Fig. 4. Provenance Store State Space

that SS and CS are not defined using AP but with APL, the power set of AP. Informally, this shows that any number of *additional provenance messages* can be stored per ACTIVITYID.

Given the state space, the ASM is described by an initial state and a set of transitions. Figure 4 contains the initial state space, which can be summarised as empty client stores, empty service message stores, and empty communication channels. We use an arrow notation for a function taking an argument and returning a result. Therefore, $client\_T_i$ and $service\_T_i$ take an ACTIVITYID as an argument and return an empty state.

The ASM Rules. The transitions of the ASM are described through rules, which follow the format presented in Figure 5. Rules are identified by their name and a number of parameters that the rule operates over. Any number of conditions must be met in order for a rule to be fireable. A new state is achieved after applying all the pseudo-statements and functions to the state that met the conditions of the rule. The execution of a rule is atomic, so that no other rule may interrupt or interleave with an executing rule. This maintains the consistency of the ASM. A rule may contain *send, receive* or table update pseudo-statements. Informally, $send(a_1, a_2, m)$ inserts a message m into the channel from actor a_1 to actor a_2, and $receive(a_1, a_2, m)$ removes the message. A rule may also contain the *complete* function, which checks that none of the fields accessed by an ACTIVITYID are null. Formally, the pseudo-statements are defined as follows.

- If k is the set of message channels of a state $\langle \ldots, k \rangle$, then the expression $send(a_1, a_2, m)$ denotes the state $\langle \ldots, k' \rangle$, where [1] $k'(a_1, a_2) = k(a_1, a_2) \oplus \{m\}$, and $k'(a_i, a_j) = k(a_i, a_j), \forall (a_i, a_j) \neq (a_1, a_2)$.
- If k is the set of message channels of a state $\langle \ldots, k \rangle$, then the expression $receive(a_1, a_2, m)$ denotes the state $\langle \ldots, k' \rangle$, where $k'(a_1, a_2) = k(a_1, a_2) \ominus \{m\}$, and $k'(a_i, a_j) = k(a_i, a_j), \forall (a_i, a_j) \neq (a_1, a_2)$.
- If $table\_T$ is a component of state $\langle \ldots, table\_T, \ldots \rangle$, then the expression $table\_T[ai].y := V$ denotes the state $\langle \ldots, table\_T', \ldots \rangle$, where $table\_T[ai].x = table\_T'[ai].x$ if $x \neq y$, and $table\_T'[ai].y = V$.

$rule\_name(v_1, v_2, \cdots) :$
$\quad condition_1(v_1, v_2, \cdots)$
$\quad \wedge condition_2(v_1, v_2, \cdots) \wedge \cdots$
$\rightarrow \{$
$\quad pseudo\_statement_1;$
$\quad \cdots$
$\quad pseudo\_statement_n;$
$\}$

Fig. 5. Rule format

$receive\_neg(p, a, ai, psal, psa, e) :$
$\quad \mathsf{rec\_neg}(ai, psal, psa, e) \in \mathcal{K}(ps, a)$
$\rightarrow \{$
$\quad receive(p, a, \mathsf{rec\_neg}(ai, psal, psa, e));$
$\quad if \ (a = ai.client), \ then$
$\quad\quad client\_T[ai].rec\_neg :=$
$\quad\quad\quad \mathsf{rec\_neg}(ai, psal, psa, e);$
$\quad elif \ (a = ai.service), \ then$
$\quad\quad service\_T[ai].rec\_neg :=$
$\quad\quad\quad \mathsf{rec\_neg}(ai, psal, psa, e);$
$\quad send(p, a, \mathsf{rec\_neg\_ack}(ai));$
$\quad if \ complete[ai], \ then$
$\quad\quad send(p, a, \mathsf{sf\_ack}(ai));$
$\}$

Fig. 6. Receive negotiation rule

Likewise, the function *complete* is defined as follows:

- If $client\_T$ and $service\_T$ are components of a state $\langle client\_T, service\_T, \ldots \rangle$, then the expression $complete[ai]$ evaluates to true if $client\_T[ai].rec\_neg \neq$

---

[1] We use the operators $\oplus$ and $\ominus$ to denote union and difference on bags.

$\perp$, $client\_T[ai].rec\_inv \neq \perp$, $client\_T[ai].rec\_res \neq \perp$, $client\_T[ai].sf \neq \perp$, $client\_T[ai].sf.nm - 4 = |client\_T[ai].apl|$ and $service\_T[ai].rec\_neg \neq \perp$, $service\_T[ai].rec\_inv \neq \perp$, $service\_T[ai].rec\_res \neq \perp$, $service\_T[ai].sf \neq \perp$, $service\_T[ai].sf.nm - 4 = |service\_T[ai].apl|$.

Figure 6 shows one of the ASM's transition rules. *receive_neg* is the transition rule for the receipt of a record negotiation message. It specifies the behaviour of a provenance store actor when receiving, from actor a, a rec_neg message containing: an ACTIVITYID, a PSALLOWEDLIST, a PSACCEPTED parameter and an EXTRA envelope.

The condition placed on the rule states that for the rule to fire there must be a rec_neg message, which is part of the communication channel ($\mathcal{K}$) between a provenance store actor, p, and a. If this condition is satisfied, the message is consumed using the *receive* pseudo-statement. The rule then determines whether a is a client or service and puts the rec_neg message in the correct field of the appropriate table. After this table update, an rec_neg_ack is sent using the *send* pseudo-statement, which places the given message onto the communication channel between the specified entities. Finally, the *complete* functions tests to see if all messages have been received from both the client and the service. If all messages have been received, the *submission finished acknowledgement message* can be sent. The other four transitions follow the same pattern as the *receive_neg* rule, consuming a message and placing it into the the correct field of the appropriate table. The entire set of rules can be found at http://www.pasoa.org/protocol/rules.htm.

The Client and Service. We now formalise the actions of the client and the service. In this case, we have chosen not to use the ASM formalism because we have no knowledge of the decision algorithm a service would use when selecting a provenance store from the list proposed by the client. Furthermore, we want developers to be free to experiment with any sort of algorithm they deem best. However, we still want to formally investigate the actions of the client and service in response to PReP, so we represent the two entities with a 3D state transition diagram, which offers an intuitive yet rigorous means to describe the actions of the client and service based on sent and received messages.

Figure 7 shows the state transition diagram for both the client and service. It contains all the possible states of a client or service with regard to the PReP. Transitions between states are only permitted when messages are sent or received by the actor. These transitions are identified by the transition keys in the diagram. For example, transition (4) is the receipt of a *result message* and transition (5) is the sending of an *invoke message* in the case of the client. The diagram shows all possible ways that a client or service could send and receive messages.

We believe that these formalisations provide a firm basis for developers to implement the protocol. The ASM and 3D state transition diagram allow developers to understand the interaction of the client, service, and provenance store without prescribing a particular implementation technique. This gives developers the opportunity to choose the implementation mechanisms that fit their needs.

6   Properties

Given the above formal representations of the client, service and provenance store, we now can show an important property of PReP, namely, liveness. In distributed systems, it is common to refer to safety and liveness properties, to denote, respectively, that nothing bad will happen and that something good will eventually happen. In the case of PReP, liveness is that, ultimately, the *submission finished acknowledgement* message will be sent to both the client and the service.

To show that the protocol is indeed live, we first make some assumptions about the system implementing PReP. We assume that the client and service are live i.e. that they will eventually send and receive all the messages designated in the protocol. This entails that for any given invocation a service will always respond. Finally, we assume that all communication channels are live. Therefore, all sent messages will be delivered to the addressed party.

Given these assumptions, we now show that both the client and service will eventually end their interaction with the provenance store for one invocation of the service.

Lemma 1 (Termination). Given a finite number of exchanged messages, the actions of the client and service in relation to PReP will terminate for one invocation of a service. *Proof* Figure 7 shows, by definition, the actions of the

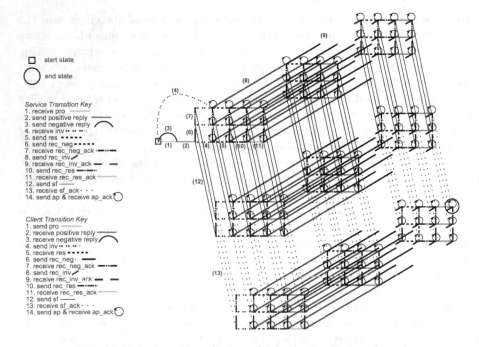

Fig. 7. State transition diagram for both the client and service

client and service in relation to PReP for one invocation of a service. We then derive the assumption that there are a finite number of *additional provenance messages*, because the *submission finished message* requires that a finite number of messages be specified. Next, we can determine a bound on the number of messages a client or service will exchange. Excluding *additional provenance messages*, we calculate this bound by enumerating all paths from the start state to the end state in the graph and selecting the longest, which is twelve transitions. This means that a client or service will exchange a maximum of twelve messages. Given this fixed bound and a finite number of *additional provenance messages*, the client and service will reach the end state shown in the graph and terminate.

Lemma 2 (Completeness). A provenance store can determine when it has a complete record of a service invocation. *Proof* We define a complete record as the function *complete* evaluating to true. An invocation is identified by an ACTIVITYID. Therefore, by definition, the provenance store can determine when it has a complete record for a service invocation.

Lemma 3 (PReP satisfies the liveness property). The *submission finished acknowledgement* message will be sent to both the client and the service. *Proof* Given that both the client and service will terminate (Lemma 1), both actors will send all their messages to the provenance store, which, as represented by the state machine, will fire the appropriate rule corresponding to the receipt of each message. These rules in turn update the state of the record referenced by an ACTIVITYID, *ai* and check for a complete record (Lemma 2) and, if it exists for *ai*, the *submission finished acknowledgement* is sent.

7   Related Work

Provenance recording also been investigated in the myGrid (www.mygrid.org.uk) project, whose goal is to provide a personalised "workbench" for bioinformaticians to perform *in-silico* experiments [7]. Although myGrid allows users to capture provenance data [10], it does not not address general architectures or protocols for recording provenance.

Ruth *et al.* present a system for recording provenance in the context of data sharing by scientists [8]. Each scientist has an e-notebook which records and digitally signs any input data or manipulations of data. When the data is shared via peer-to-peer communication, a scientist cannot refute the provenance of the data because of the digital signature process. The goal of the system is to generate a virtual community where scientists are accountable for their data. [8] focuses mainly on the trust aspect of the e-notebook system, rather than the protocols for distributing and storing provenance data.

Some work has focused on data provenance in databases. Buneman et al. [2] make the distinction between *why* (which tuples in a database contribute to a result) provenance and *where* (the location(s) of the source database that contributed to a result) provenance. In [1], a precise definition of provenance is given for both XML hierarchy and relational databases.

Szomszor and Moreau [9] argued for infrastructure support for recording provenance in Grids and presented a trial implementation of an architecture that was used to demonstrate several mechanisms for handling provenance data after it had been recorded. Our work extends [9] in several important ways. First, we consider an architecture that allows for provenance stores as well as composite services. Secondly, we model an implementation -independent protocol for recording provenance within the context of a service-oriented architecture, whereas, Szomszor and Moreau present an implementation specific service-oriented architecture.

The Chimera Virtual Data System [5] provides a data catalog along with a representation of derivation procedures in order to document data provenance. Chimera focuses on representing and querying data derivation information. We imagine that PReP could be used as the underlying protocol to store provenance information in a Chimera like system.

8   Conclusion

There are several avenues of future work we intend to pursue in the development of a provenance system. These avenues include, the further specification of PReP in terms of security, the implementation of PReP using Web Services and the integration of PReP into real world scenarios.

The necessity for storing, maintaining and tracking provenance is evident in fields ranging from biology to aerospace. As science and business embrace Grids as a mechanism to achieve their goals, recording provenance will become an ever more important factor in the construction of Grids. The development of common components, protocols, and standards will make this construction process faster, easier, and more interoperable. In this paper, we presented a stepping stone to the development of a common provenance recording system, namely, an implementation-independent protocol for recording provenance, PReP.

Acknowledgements

This research is funded in part by EPSRC PASOA project GR/S67623/01.

References

1. P. Buneman, S. Khanna, and W.-C. Tan. Data provenance: Some basic issues. In *Foundations of Software Technology and Theoretical Computer Science*, 2000.
2. P. Buneman, S. Khanna, and W.-C. Tan. Why and where: A characterization of data provenance. In *Int. Conf. on Databases Theory (ICDT)*, 2001.
3. M. Ford, D. Livingstone, J. Dearden, and H. V. der Waterbeemd, editors. *Comb-e-Chem: an e-science research project*. Blackwell, March 2002.
4. I. Foster. What is the grid? a three point checklist., July 2002.
5. I. Foster, J. Voeckler, M. Wilde, and Y.Zhao. Chimera: A virtual data system for representing, querying and automating data derivation. In *Proc. of the 14th Conf. on Scientific and Statistical Database Management*, July 2002.

6. L. Moreau and J. Duprat. A construction of distributed reference counting. *Acta Informatica*, 37:563–595, 2001.
7. L. Moreau and et. al. On the use of agents in a bioinformatics grid. In S. Lee, S. Sekguchi, S. Matsuoka, and M. Sato, editors, *Proc. of the 3rd IEEE/ACM CC-GRID'2003 Workshop on Agent Based Cluster and Grid Computing*, pages 653–661, Tokyo, Japan, 2003.
8. P. Ruth, D. Xu, B. K. Bhargava, and F. Regnier. E-notebook middleware for accountability and reputation based trust in distributed data sharing communities. In *Proc. 2nd Int. Conf. on Trust Management, Oxford, UK*, volume 2995 of *LNCS*. Springer, 2004.
9. M. Szomszor and L. Moreau. Recording and reasoning over data provenance in web and grid services. In *Int. Conf. on Ontologies, Databases and Applications of Semantics*, volume 2888 of *LNCS*, 2003.
10. J. Zhao, C. Goble, M. Greenwood, C. Wroe, and R. Stevens. Annotating, linking and browsing provenance logs for e-science. In *Proc. of the Workshop on Semantic Web Technologies for Searching and Retrieving Scientific Data*, October 2003.

Self-optimizing DHTs Using Request Profiling

Alina Bejan and Sukumar Ghosh*

Department of Computer Science,
University of Iowa, Iowa City, IA 52242, USA
{abejan, ghosh}@cs.uiowa.edu

Abstract. Various studies on request patterns in P2P networks have confirmed the existence of the interest-based clusters [11] and [12]. Some P2P networks that exhibit the small-world phenomenon contain clusters of peers that frequently communicate with one another [17]. The existence of interest-based clusters opens up the possibility of more efficient routing. In this paper we consider the problem of designing a *self-optimizing overlay network* and routing mechanisms to permit efficient location of resources by the *periodic profiling* of request patterns. Our self-optimization protocol uses selective replication of resources for restricting the sizes of the clusters, and proposes the deployment of inactive nodes for further reduction of the routing latency. The self-optimization protocol is demonstrated on the Chord network [22]. It leads to a routing latency that scales with the size of the clusters.

Keywords and Phrases: P2P network, overlay network, distributed hash tables, self-optimization, stabilization, clustering, routing latency.

1   Introduction

Motivation. A P2P network is an Internet-based distributed system for the efficient and scalable location of remote objects without any central authority. A large number of P2P networks uses distributed hash tables (DHT) – different parts of the hash table are managed by different servers spread around the Internet. Two metrics of the performance of DHT-based P2P networks are the space complexity for the individual nodes, and the routing distance for searching remote objects - both should be as small as possible. These two requirements conflict with one another - a sparse interconnection network like a ring has a constant size routing table, but the routing distance for queries may be as large as $O(n)$, whereas for a completely connected topology all queries are resolved in a single hop, but at the expense of a routing table of size $O(n)$. Existing P2P like CAN [19], Chord [22], Pastry [20], Tapestry [24] use interconnection topologies and routing mechanisms that strike a balance between these two extremes. These are the first set of deterministic models for DHTs. Except CAN, all the

---

* This research was supported in part by the National Science Foundation under grant CCR-9901391.

others provide $\log N$ routing latency with $\log N$ links per node. CAN adapts a d-dimensional torus to construct a DHT with a routing latency of $O(d.N^{\frac{1}{d}})$ using $O(d)$ links per node. Recently Naor and Wieder [18] showed how to use a De Bruijn network to construct a DHT with $O(\log N)$ routing latency and $O(1)$ links per node. De Bruijn graphs have also been used in the design of Koorde [13] and D2B [7]. Koorde introduces a new DHT based on Chord that provides $O(\log N)$ hops per lookup request, while nodes have only two neighbors. We do not take into account DHT organizations like Viceroy [14] that uses some randomization in the protocols for query routing.

Despite providing good solutions for meeting the conflicting goals of fast lookup and small number of states per process, these P2P networks provide a performance that is immune to variations in request patterns. However, in real life, such variations do exist. Many networks that exhibit the small-world phenomenon [17] also reveal the existence of interest-based clusters [11] and [12] (also see Stanford's Club Nexus project [2]). Numerous studies over the past few years have reinforced the existence of clusters [4], [11] and [12] in both grids and unstructured P2P environments, where user queries are confined to members of groups (not necessarily disjoint) whose sizes are much smaller than the network size. The goal of our paper is to design an adaptive P2P network that takes into consideration biases in the request patterns, and periods of inactivity of a fraction of the peers to self-optimize DHT routing tables, so that the routing latency and the space complexity scale as a logarithmic function of the size of the clusters, and is independent of the network size.

The task of adapting the overlay network to request patterns amounts to embedding a low diameter graph induced by the active source and the target nodes in the metric space. Let us start with the Chord ring [22] as a test case. Without loss of generality, assume that there are $N = 2^k$ nodes in the ring, with their keys ranging from 0 through $2^k - 1$. Each node i has $k = \log N$ fingers pointing to nodes with keys $(i+1), (i+2), \cdots (i+2^{k-1})$, and the routing distance between any pair of nodes is equal to the Hamming distance between their keys. However, if a pair of nodes with keys i and j frequently communicate with each other, and the Hamming distance between i and j is $\log N$, then there is no reason why they have to use $O(\log N)$ hops to communicate - each can set up a finger directly pointing to the other node and communicate in a single hop. Such optimizations are the cornerstones of our proposal. This improvement could come possibly at the expense of an increase in the routing distance between some other pair of nodes which do not frequently communicate with one another. Nevertheless, we consider our mission to be accomplished when (1) the routing distance between nodes within a cluster scales with the size of the cluster, and (2) the average routing distance between any pair of nodes is lower than that in the unoptimized Chord ring. Ideally cluster sizes should be small. Our work is different from [8] and [16], since small worlds do not necessarily lead to the existence of clusters.

The task of designing a self-optimizing overlay network reduces to periodically profiling the request patterns and adjusting the routing table fingers, so that the routing distance among nodes frequently communicating with one another goes down at the expense of the longer routes among nodes that communicate infrequently. A further scope of optimization stems from the existence of inactive nodes - nodes that are neither the source nor the destination of any query in a significant way. We demonstrate how active nodes in the clusters can acquire some of the inactive nodes and utilize a fraction of their links as surrogates to further reduce the routing latency within their own cluster.

Related Work. All DHT-based overlay networks like Chord, CAN, Pastry, Tapestry, Viceroy provide static guarantees about routing distances. Aspnes and Shah [3] introduced *skip graphs*, an alternative approach to designing P2P networks, by designing a tree structure that constantly balances itself to provide logarithmic routing distance among nodes, and some resilience against crash failures. Our approach is different from theirs, and based on DHTs. In [15], Manku presented an optimal routing scheme for Chord, where he expressed the routing distance as the difference of two binary integers with certain properties. His optimization method is static, and does not take into account user request profiles. Casanova [4], pointed out the crucial issue raised in [12] (but not answered) concerning potential protocols that would lead to a self-organizing overlay network by harnessing the clustering properties of a virtual network. This question was addressed in [21] for the unstructured Gnutella network. Ours is a different approach targeted to structured, DHT-based networks. In [6], Gnutella has been mapped on a structured overlay network - the resulting system reduces flooding as well as maintenance overhead. The idea of clustering used in conjunction with DHTs appears in more recent papers such as [9] and [10] – both solutions adopt a hierarchical organization of the DHT. Coral [9] employs proximity-based self-organizing clusters and sloppy hashing in order to enable nodes to locate and download files among peers without creating hot spots and without querying distant nodes. But the mechanisms of nodes joining clusters, and of merging and splitting clusters are based on criteria different from ours. Canon [10] is based on hierarchical DHTs that can be imposed on different P2P systems to improve caching and bandwidth usage for multicast, provide fault isolation, hierarchical storage of content and hierarchical storage control, while providing standard ratio of space complexity to routing latency. The clustering concept presented here is based on *domains*: each domain is organized as a DHT. The actual merge operation of domains and the lookup procedure are different from our approach.

Contributions. Our contributions in this paper are threefold. First, we demonstrate the feasibility of designing an adaptive P2P network that can self-optimize its performance. Second, we show that our adaptive P2P system indeed attains the optimal routing distance of $O(\log |W|)$ (W is the set of nodes in a cluster) when the nodes belong to disjoint clusters of size $|W|$ ($|W| < N$), and there are at most $\log N$ fingers per node. Even when a small fraction ϵ of all queries is directed towards nodes outside the cluster, the average routing distance between any pair of nodes is bounded from above by $(1-\epsilon). \log |W| + \epsilon. |W|. \log \frac{N}{|W|}$. Third, when the nodes in a cluster W discover B inactive nodes each with r fingers to spare for their cause, then the self-optimization algorithm can further reduce the average routing distance between nodes in the cluster to $(1 - \frac{B.r}{|W|}) . \log |W| + \frac{2.B.r}{|W|}$, which approaches a constant (namely two) as $B.r$ approaches $|W|$.

Organization. The paper is organized as follows. Section 2 introduces some preliminary definitions about DHT-based P2P networks and clarifies the goals of optimization. Section 3 presents the various pieces of the self-optimization algorithm, and explains how to put these pieces together. Section 4 discusses the complexities, and section 5 contains some concluding remarks and open questions.

2   The System Model

2.1   Preliminaries

The topology of a distributed hash table (DHT) based routing network is a directed graph $G = (V, E)$, where $V = \{0, 1, 2, \ldots, N-1\}$ denotes a set of nodes, and each edge $(i, j) \in E$ represents a link (also called a *finger*) from i to j. Each node contains a fraction of the keys. Both objects and node id's are hashed into the range $[0 \ldots N - 1]$ using the same hashing function, the outcome of which determines the distribution of keys among the different nodes. Each object is associated with at least two different nodes: one of these is the *owner* of that object, and the other is a *host* node (storing the object) chosen by the hashing function. Each object stored in a host node knows the identity of the owner. The set $\{j : (i, j) \in E\}$ defines the routing table of node i which is used to direct queries to the right destination node hosting an object. Space efficiency requires that the cardinality of the set $\{j : (i, j) \in E\}$ be small, whereas the routing efficiency requires the routing of each query from the source to the destination be completed in the fewest number of hops.

For the Chord network [22], without loss of generality, let $N = 2^k$. Each node i has a routing table with k fingers $f_i[0]$ through $f_i[k-1]$ pointing to nodes $(i+1), (i+2), \ldots (i+2^{k-1})$ respectively[1]. Thus the space complexity per node is O($\log N$), and the routing distance between any pair of nodes is also O($\log N$). These results are "flat guarantees" that hold regardless of variations in the request patterns of the individual nodes.

To optimize the routing tables for shortest routing distance, we take into consideration the request pattern $R(i)$ of each process i. Define the request pattern $R(i)$ of node i as a set $\{r(i, j), j : i \neq j\}$ where $r(i, j)$ denotes the frequency of requests from i to objects *owned* by node j, and is measured by the number of times node i sent requests to such objects during a predefined interval of time. On the basis of these frequencies, we classify the nodes in $R(i)$ into two categories: *preferred*, and *non-preferred*.

---

[1] When no real node exists in a target, the finger points to the *next* real node with a higher id.

Definition 1. A node j is a *preferred node* for node i, if $r(i, j) \geq t$, where t is a constant defined by the users.

For each node i, its preferred nodes form a set P_i. Clearly, the set P_i will vary over time. Our goal is to optimize the routing tables, so that every node can send queries to other nodes in its preferred list using the fewest number of hops. This may come at the expense of longer routes to some non-preferred nodes. However, this is acceptable as long as the average routing distance is smaller than the guaranteed routing distance in the unoptimized system.

2.2   Classification of Optimal Routing

There are two aspects of optimization: *local* and *global*. In local optimization, the average routing distance of *a single node* to the members in its preferred list is a minimum, whereas, in global optimization, the average routing distance of *all nodes* to the members in their preferred lists is a minimum. Note that local optimality of the individual nodes can conflict with one another, particularly when the space per node is small. Accordingly, various tradeoffs are possible. Two example situations are presented below.

Disjoint Clusters. A cluster is a subset W of nodes that satisfies the closure property $\forall i \in W : P_i \subseteq W$. The notation W_i will designate the cluster to which node i belongs. All nodes within a cluster share common interest in keeping the routing distance small among themselves. There can be several distinct clusters. When the clusters are disjoint, there is no conflict between local and global optimality.

Overlapped Clusters. Here the structure of the clusters can be identified on the basis of interest, and there are nodes that have multiple interests. The optimization of routing with respect to one interest group may conflict with that in the other interest group. Besides that, even if there is a tendency for nodes to cluster while serving their own interests – an outlier node in some cluster may frequently communicate with outliers in other clusters.

Apart from these, unusual request profiles are possible too, though quite rare. As an example, there may be several subsets $S_0, S_1, S_2, \ldots, S_{m-1}$ of nodes, $\cup_{i=0}^{m-1} S_i = V$ and $\forall i \in S_l, P_i \subseteq S_{(l+1) mod m}$. Some espionage networks are said to exhibit such behaviors[2]. When the improvement in routing for some interest group comes at the expense of a deterioration of routing distance for another interest group, the overall performance depends on the degree of overlap. In absence of any satisfactory optimization that benefits all interest groups, one can of course fall back to the unoptimized system and accept flat guarantees regardless of their request patterns.

3   The Self-optimization Algorithm

Our base case is the unoptimized Chord ring, where $\forall i : P_i = V$. Let $f_i[j]$ be the the jth entry in i's finger table. For the optimized system, by definition, $f_i[0] :=$

---

[2] It is mostly a folklore.

$i + 1 \bmod N$. This is chosen to guarantee connectivity between any pair of nodes in the ring. The goal of the optimization is to redefine the fingers $f_i[1]$ through $f_i[\log N - 1]$ for each node i, and specify a routing algorithm, such that the routing distance from i to the elements of P_i is as small as possible. In doing so, each node will dedicate a subset of fingers to provide *fast routes* to the members in the preferred list, and use the remaining fingers to communicate with nodes outside the preferred list.

Following established studies, assume that the request patterns reveal the existence of clusters involving the *owners* of the objects. Since every object is tagged with its owner's id, and every object also knows the identity of the originator of each request, clusters of owners frequently accessing objects owned by them can be easily identified. Let W_i designate a cluster to which node i belongs –it contains the preferred list of all nodes in W_i. For each node i, designate the set of non-preferred nodes $V \backslash W_i$ as Q_i. For each node i, arrange the nodes of W_i in the ascending order of keys. Also arrange the nodes of Q_i in the ascending order of keys. Let $W_i[k]$ be the kth element of W_i, and $Q_i[k]$ be the kth element of Q_i. If $w(i) = \lceil \log |W_i| \rceil$ and $q(i) = \lceil \log |Q_i| \rceil$, then, central to our routing algorithm are the following two rules for configuring the routing table of every process i:

Rule 1. for $j = 1$ to $w(i)$, $f_i[j] := W_i[l] : l = (i + 2^j) \bmod w(i)$

Rule 2. for $j = w(i) + 1$ to $\log N - 1$, $f_i[j] := Q_i[l] : l = (i + 2^{j-w(i)}) \bmod q(i)$

The guiding principle is to organize the nodes in W_i (respectively Q_i) as a mini-Chord ring to be accessed by the fingers 1 through $w(i)$ (respectively fingers $w(i) + 1$ through $\log N - 1$). Once the fingers are defined, the routing algorithm for node i will be as follows: Each node i will route queries to members of its cluster W_i using fingers 1 through $w(i)$, but use any finger to route queries to nodes that are not in its preferred list. Furthermore, in each step, only that finger will be chosen which leads to the query closest to the target node.

Routing rule for i (destination is j)

if $j \in W_i \rightarrow$ use $f_i[l]$: $0 < l \le w(i)$
$\qquad \qquad \qquad \wedge f_i[l] \le j < f_i[(l+1) \bmod w(i)]$
$\square \ j \in Q_i \rightarrow$ use $f_i[l]$: $f_i[l] \le j < f_i[(l+1) \bmod k]$
fi

Note that the routing rule is a refinement of the routing rule of Chord, where each node forwards requests to other nodes in the preferred list via a designated subset of its fingers only, and use the remaining ones to route to the non-preferred nodes. However, for routing to non-preferred nodes, our algorithm modifies the second part and takes the liberty to choose any finger that helps reach a node closest to the destination.

In the unoptimized Chord ring, if there are l fingers, and $l < \log N$, then the farthest node that a given node i can reach in a single hop is $(i + 2^{l-1})$. This leads to the following lemma:

Lemma 1. In a Chord ring, let there be N nodes, each with l fingers ($l \leq \log N$). There exists a routing mechanism such that the maximum routing distance is $\lceil \frac{N.l}{2^l} \rceil$ hops.

Proof. For every node i arrange its l fingers to point to nodes $i+1, i+2, i+4 \ldots$ $i + 2^{l-1}$. This guarantees that each node i can reach any other node in the range i to $i + 2^l - 1$ in at most l hops (based on Chord routing). Divide the ring into zones of size 2^l, so that there are $\lceil \frac{N}{2^l} \rceil$ zones (possibly including one truncated zone of smaller size). Within each zone, use the standard routing mechanism of Chord. Now any node should be reachable in at most $\lceil \frac{N.l}{2^l} \rceil$ hops. $\qquad \square$

Lemma 2. Let ϵ denote the fraction of times a request is directed to a node outside its cluster W. Then the average routing distance between any pair of nodes will not exceed $(1 - \epsilon).\log |W| + \epsilon.|W|.\log \frac{N}{|W|}$.

Proof. Of the $\log N$ fingers, $\log |W|$ are dedicated to routing to nodes within the cluster of size $|W|$, which will take $\log |W|$ hops. This happens $1 - \epsilon$ times. In the remaining ϵ times, one uses the remaining ($\log N$ - $\log |W|$) fingers to route requests to nodes outside W. Using the results of Lemma 1, each such routing can take at most $N.\log \frac{N}{|W|}/2^{\log \frac{N}{|W|}}$ hops which can be simplified to $|W|.$ $\log \frac{N}{|W|}$. $\qquad \square$

Identification of the clusters. Before the routing rules are applied, the clusters need to be identified, which means that each node should discover the membership of the cluster that it belongs to. The set of all nodes trivially satisfies the closure property $\forall i \in V : P_i \subseteq V$, but it is not "interesting". Also, the union of two clusters also satisfies the closure property and is a cluster. Our goal is to look for the *smallest subsets* of processes for which the closure property holds.

When a node accesses an object, the host node storing that object records the originating node's id. This happens during normal operation, which is also the profiling phase. At the end of the profiling phase, each node sends the ids of the requestors of all the objects stored in them to their respective owners. This sending operation becomes mandatory if the frequency of access of an object is above the chosen threshold t. No centralized sorting algorithm is required.

To formulate a mechanism by which each process discovers the members of its own cluster, we use a *request graph* $G_R = (V, E_R)$. Each node of the request graph represents a node of the network, and each directed edge $(i, j) \in E_R$ represents the fact that $j \in P_i$. Assuming that disjoint clusters exist, the task of finding the cluster amounts to finding the connected component to which a process belongs. Also note that every query from i to j will be followed by a response from j to i, so even if the request graph is not strongly connected, inclusion of the response path will provide a directed link from the destination to the source node. Therefore, we will replace each directed edge of the request graph by an undirected edge.

Let W_i denote the smallest size cluster that node i belongs to. The algorithm will initialize W_i to P_i – subsequently it will grow to the smallest cluster to which i belongs. In addition to W_i, each process i will maintain k sets $U_{i,0}$ through $U_{i,k-1}$ one per each link, which are initially empty. Whenever a node i receives a message (query or response) from another node and it contains the identity of members that node i has not yet seen, it appends them to W_i. The identity of these new members in the cluster are passed on to other members while sending out messages. The role of the sets $U_{i,j}$ is to memorize the identity of the current members that have already been passed on to others via link j. To update $U_{i,j}$ whenever a message (query or response) is sent out via finger j, the sender appends the set $W_i \backslash U_{i,j}$ (call it new_j) to the message. The program is as follows:

Identification of the clusters: program for node i

{Initially $W_i = P_i$, $\forall j : U_{i,j} = \phi$}
do msg received from k with a set new_i of ids $\rightarrow$ $W_i := W_i \cup new_i$
$\square$ message to be sent via $j \wedge W_i \neq U_{i,j} \rightarrow$
$\qquad\qquad$ append $new_j = W_i \backslash U_{i,j}$; $U_{i,j} := W_i$
od

At the end, both W_i and $U_{i,j}$ will contain the ids of all the nodes in the cluster to which node i belongs.

Theorem 1. The cluster identification algorithm converges to a fixed point where W_i contains the ids of all nodes of the smallest cluster to which node i belongs.

Proof. Initially $\forall i, j \in E_R$: $U_{i,j} \subseteq W_j$ holds. Also the condition holds every time the first action is completed, meaning this is an invariant. Since every W is bounded from above by the size max of the connected component, each W can grow at most max times, after which no new member in the cluster is discovered. After each node i sends out its $last$ message while the condition $U_{i,j} \subset W_i$ holds, $\forall j : U_{i,j} = W_i$. Therefore $\forall i, j \in E_R$: $W_i \subseteq W_j$. Furthermore, due to the propagation of the responses from j to i, $W_j \subseteq W_i$. Therefore $\forall i : |W_i| = max$. $\square$

What if no disjoint clusters exist? Apparently, for each node i, W_i eventually grows to V, and there is no scope of optimization. Of interest is the case of *weakly linked clusters*, where a cluster of larger size can be divided into two or more clusters of smaller size by removing a small number of edges in the request graph. Define a c-connected cluster as one that can be split into disjoint clusters by removing a minimum of c edges from the request graph. In reality, such removal of edges signals the need of caching the object into the local storage. An example is shown in Fig. 1a. The application of the cluster identification algorithm will cause each W to grow to V that will include all 12 nodes. However, the cluster is 2-connected (by removing the edges (8,9) and (12,1) one can split it into two

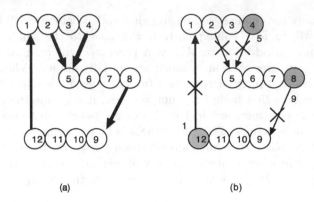

Fig. 1. Creating smaller clusters via replication and pruning

clusters). In fact, by replicating the objects in 1 into 12, the objects in 5 into 4, and the objects in 9 into 8, every node can satisfy its requests from a cluster of size 4, that is much smaller than V (Fig 1b). No node is required to cache *all* the objects from the other node, but only those that satisfy its own requests. Furthermore, this information should be made available to all members of the cluster, otherwise it can lead to unnecessary replication of the same objects within a small world. Such replication is useful if the number of objects to be copied is small. We will use an arbitrary metric $O(\log |P_i|)$ to quantify the smallness, but users can apply other standards too. The bottom line is that it leads to a reduction of the cluster size, and connsequently of the routing latency, at the expense of a minor increase in the space complexity.

Our goal is to let the self-optimization algorithm take care of this by itself, without external intervention, so that each process figures out how to leverage the available space for faster routing. This leads to our replica management protocol.

Replica management. Let $T_i = \{j : (j,i) \in E_R\}$. Assume that $|P_i \backslash T_i| \leq c$, where $c = \log |P_i \cap T_i|$. Then we propose that

(1) node i replicate the required objects from $P_i \backslash T_i$ into its own address space, and
(2) shrink P_i to $(P_i \cap T_i)$.

Eventually when the clusters are formed, the availability of the replicas must be known to other members belonging to the cluster. To deal with this, we will use a modification of the original hashing function.

We make the following claim regarding the replica management protocol:

Lemma 3. For some node i, let $|P_i \backslash T_i| \leq c$ hold. Then the replica management protocol will converge to a state in which $P_i \subseteq T_i$ holds at the expense of a space complexity of size c.

Proof. The action by node i reduces P_i to $(P_i \cap T_i)$, so the condition $P_i \subseteq T_i$ holds after i copies c objects from $P_i \backslash T_i$ into its own address space. Also, for each node $j \in T_i \backslash P_i$, $i \in P_j$. For such a node, if the precondition of the theorem holds, a similar action by node j will remove j from T_i (as well as from $T_i \backslash P_i$), further reducing the size of $T_i \backslash P_i$. This step will not invalidate the condition $P_i \subseteq T_i$. □

Notice that we are using the parameter c to strike a balance between two conflicting acts here. While the cluster identification algorithm expands W_i from P_i to the size of the cluster, the replica management protocol shrinks each P_i to a smaller value through limited replication of objects. In the interest of fast routing, we prefer to keep the size of the clusters as small as possible, if necessary at the expense of a minor increase in the space complexity. Since each node can independently initiate such replications, the average increase in the space complexity per node will be bounded from above by the value of c. After the replication is over, the system should start expanding their preferred lists for the identification of clusters. This is why we will allow the replica management protocol to take precedence over the cluster identification protocol.

One can make interesting observations in the dynamics of cluster identification. Even if an edge (i, j) is removed from the request graph via replication, the two nodes may end up in the same cluster due to a path existing between them via some node k. However the removal of enough number of edges (if they exist) is likely to divide the systems into smaller clusters, and expedite routing.

Once clusters are identified, at least one copy of the objects frequently accessed by its members should be available at some host node in that cluster. Per the routing algorithm, nodes should first try to locate the object within the cluster by treating the cluster as a miniature Chord ring. If it is not available inside the cluster, then searching continues outside the cluster, which is a slower process.

Utilizing inactive nodes. An interesting issue here is to explore whether the resources of inactive nodes (i.e. nodes for which both P_i and T_i are empty sets) can be utilized to enhance the routing performance of clustered networks. Such resources can be routing fingers that will serve as bypasses and shorten the routing distances, or these can consist of space donated by the inactive nodes to cache remote objects. We will explore the first possibility here. Assume that after the first phase, every inactive node sends out advertisements to the entire network about its inactivity, prompting one or more active nodes to grab the fingers of the inactive nodes for expediting its own routing. We will call it *finger stealing*. Let there be B such inactive nodes, each with $\log N$ fingers, and let these nodes spare r-out-of-$\log N$ fingers to expedite the routing within a cluster W. The issue is: How to orient these r fingers to reduce the worst-case (or the average) routing distances between a pair of nodes in the cluster?

Each node that grabs an inactive node as a router of its queries can reduce the routing distance to a node $\log |W|$ hops away to only two hops using one of the inactive node's fingers[3]. If there are B inactive nodes, then the $B.r$ fingers can shorten the average routing distance of all the nodes in the cluster to $\log|W|$ $-\frac{B.r.(\log|W|-2)}{|W|}$, which simplifies to $(1-\frac{B.r}{|W|}).(\log|W|)+\frac{2.B.r}{|W|}$. This leads to the following theorem:

Theorem 2. If there are B inactive nodes, and each inactive node contributes r fingers to expedite the routing about the nodes in a cluster of size $|W|$, then the average routing distance between the members will be $(1-\frac{B.r}{|W|}).(\log|W|)+\frac{2.B.r}{|W|}$.

Putting the pieces together. Assume that the nodes have their clocks approximately synchronized. Initially $\forall i : P_i = V$, and all fingers are oriented as in the traditional Chord ring. Divide the time into an infinite sequence of the three phases 0, 1, and 2. Each node i does the following schedule:

Phase 0. Profile the requests.

Phase 1. Determine P_i and T_i. Apply the *replica management protocol* to prune P_i whenever possible.

Phase 2. Use the *cluster identification protocol* to discover the clusters that each node possibly belongs to. Then configure the routing tables.

The duration of *Phase 0* will depend on the system dynamics [23]. The duration of *Phase 1* will be much shorter, and will be determined by the complexity of the replica management protocol. In each cycle, *Phase 0* will use the routing table generated from *Phase 2* of the previous cycle.

4   Performance

The routing distance $(1 - \epsilon)\log|W| + \epsilon.|W|.\log\frac{N}{|W|}$ is a definite improvement in performance when ϵ is much smaller than 1 (so that the second term of the expression is smaller than the first term). For example, when $N = 1,000,000$ and $W = 100$, ϵ has to be of the order of 0.001 or lower. In this case, the average routing distance will be $7+1 = 8$, as opposed to a routing distance of 20 in the unoptimized case. The scenario can be compared with page fault in virtual memory systems – each request to a node outside the cluster is an *access fault* that is comparable to a page fault, and is expected to occur infrequently.

The results of optimization shown here are specific to the Chord protocol, but similar techniques can be applied to other DHT architectures too. In [15], Manku proposed an optimization for the Chord ring using bidirectional routing, where he showed how the number of routing hops can be reduced by expressing the Hamming distance between pairs of nodes as the difference of two binary patterns. (For example, node i could communicate with node $i + 2^h - 1$ in only two hops, instead of the usual h hops, by first routing forward to $i + 2^h$ than backward to $i + 2^h - 1$.) Such route discovery methods are applicable to our method too, where this optimization can be used to further reduce the routing

---

[3] In that process, many routes to nodes outside the cluster are also shortened.

distance between preferred nodes to $\frac{1}{2}.\log|W|$. Moreover, these techniques of improvisation can also be used for routing outside the cluster.

As illustrated in the previous section, the inactive nodes offer new opportunities for performance enhancement. The maximum number B_{max} of inactive nodes that can be acquired by the active nodes is equal to $|W|/k$, in which case the routing distance between any pair of nodes will be reduced to a constant (namely *two*), and it will be unproductive to acquire any more inactive nodes. As another possibility, inactive nodes can allocate storage space to store a fraction of the objects required by the active nodes. With enough inactive nodes being available, the normal routing mechanism can be abandoned, and all routing can be done only through the inactive nodes, reducing the routing distance to one. Our self-optimization protocol does not yet have a mechanism to spontaneously deploy the inactive nodes for performance enhancement, but it is a topic for future investigation.

5   Conclusion

Each cluster is a league of owners. The DHT has been used as a tool to identify the clusters. The DHT also provides efficient routing within a cluster with a guaranteed routing latency of $\log|W|$. However, compared to Coral, the intercluster routing latency is higher. However, the clustering mechanism in Coral is messier, since clusters overlap, and each node is present in all the clusters.

Objects replicated by a node must be available to every node in its cluster. One approach will be to use an alternative hashing function to map objects to nodes within W. We however avoid the use of a second hashing function, and simply fold the key into a ring $[0..|W| - 1]$. This means that the replica of an object mapped originally into a node s will now be mapped into the node s $mod |W|$ in the cluster. In case such a node does not exist in the cluster, the replica will be placed in the *next node* in that cluster. Of course this requires each process to estimate the size of the cluster that it belongs to. However, only a crude estimate will suffice, since load balancing within the cluster is not an issue for now. One solution is to use $|P_i \cup T_i|$ as the size of W_i in the first cycle, and in the subsequent cycles, use the estimate of $|W_i|$ from the previous cycle. To locate an object, a node must first look for a replica of it in its own cluster, before locating it elsewhere.

To handle node join operations, we will allow the new node to join *any* cluster, modify the membership of that cluster, and update its preferred list accordingly. The profiling will begin from the next cycle, followed by optimization as explained earlier. To leave the network, a node must transfer its objects to the next node with a higher key *in the same cluster*. The periodic stabilization protocol will need an extra step - in addition to running the conventional stabilization protocol where each node verifies the correctness of its successor and predecessor pointers, it will also run a version of it within its own cluster.

The proposed protocol involves a few parameters whose choice is left to users, and need to be decided via experiments. In deciding the membership of the preferred list, one has to choose a value of t. However, if indeed clusters are present, then the choice of t will be natural, and it could be different for different nodes. In the case of weakly linked clusters, the choice of the parameter c will depend on how much cache each node is ready to spare.

An interesting variation in optimization takes a market-based approach, where nodes are allowed to bid for faster routes by making some payoffs. Nodes that receive these payoffs are ready to trade their resources for temporary degradation of their performance. Such market-oriented optimization algorithms are topics of future investigation.

References

1. Abraham, I., Awerbuch, B., Azar, Y., et al. *A generic scheme for building overlay networks in adversarial scenarios.* IPDPS 2003.
2. Adamic, L.A., Buyukkokten, O., and Adar, E. *A social network caught in the Web.* First Monday, volume 8, number 6 (June 2003),
3. Aspnes, J. and Shah, G. *Skip graphs.* Fourteenth Annual ACM-SIAM Symposium on Discrete Algorithms, January 2003, p. 384-393.
4. Casanova, H. *Distributed Computing Research Issues in Grid Computing.* ACM SIGACT News, Volume 33, Issue 3 (September 2002), p. 50-70.
5. Dabek, F., Li, J., et al. *Designing a DHT for low latency and high throughput.* NSDI 2004.
6. Castro, M., Costa, M., and Rowstron, A. *Should we build Gnutella on a structured overlay?.* HotNets 2003.
7. Fraigniaud, P. and Gauron, P. *An Overview of the Content-Addressable Network D2B.* PODC 2003.
8. Fraigniaud, P., Gavoille, C., and Paul, C. *Eclecticism shrinks even small worlds.* PODC 2004.
9. Freedman, M.J., and Mazieres, D. *Sloppy hashing and self-organizing clusters.* IPTPS 2003.
10. Ganesan, P., Gummadi, K., and Garcia-Molina, H. *Canon in G Major: Designing DHTs with Hierarchical Structure.* ICDCS 2004.
11. Iamnitchi, A., Ripeanu, M., Foster, I. *Small-World File-Sharing Communities.* IEEE InfoCom 2004, March 2004.
12. Iamnitchi, A., Ripeanu, M., Foster, I. *Locating Data in Peer-to-Peer Scientific Collaborations.* IPTPS 2002, March 2002.
13. Kaashoek, M.F. and Karger, D.R. *Koorde: a simple degree-optimal distributed hash table.* IPTPS 2003.
14. Malkhi, D., Naor, M., and Ratajczak, D. *Viceroy: A scalable and dynamic emulation of the butterfly.* ACM PODC 2002.
15. Manku, G.S. *Routing Networks for Distributed Hash Tables.* ACM PODC 2003.
16. Martel, C. and Nguyen, V. *Analyzing Kleinberg's (and other) small world Models.* PODC 2004.
17. Milgram, S. *The small world problem.* In Psychology Today 1, 61 (1967).
18. Naor,M. and Weider, U. *Novel Architectures for P2P Applications: the Continuous-Discrete Approach.* SPAA 2003.
19. Ratnasamy, S., Francis, P., Handley, M., Karp, R., Shenker,S. *A Scalable Content Addressable Network.* ACM SIGCOMM 2001.

20. Rowstron, A. and Druschel, P. *Pastry: Scalable, distributed object location and routing for large-scale peer-to-peer systems.* IFIP/ACM International Conference on Distributed Systems Platforms (Middleware) 2001, p. 329-350.
21. Sripanidkulchai, K., Maggs, B., and Zhang, H. *Efficient Content Location Using Internet-based Locality in Peer-to-Peer Systems.* Infocom 2003.
22. Stoica, I., Morris, R., Karger, D., Kaashoek, M.F. and Balakrishnan, H. *Chord: A Scalable Peer-to-Peer Lookup Protocol for Internet Applications.* IEEE Transactions on Networking 11 (1) 2003.
23. Watts, D.J., Strogatz, S.H. *Collective dynamics of 'small-world' networks.* Nature, vol. 393, 1998.
24. Zhao, B.Y., Kubiatowicz, J.D., and Joseph, A.D. *Tapestry: An Infrastructure for Fault-tolerant Wide-area Location and Routing.* Technical Report UCB/CSD-01-1141, Computer Science Division, U. C. Berkeley, April 2001.

Computing All the Best Swap Edges Distributively[*]

P. Flocchini[1], L. Pagli[2], G. Prencipe[2], N. Santoro[3],
P. Widmayer[4], and T. Zuva[5]

[1] University of Ottawa, Canada
flocchin@site.uottawa.ca
[2] Università di Pisa, Italy
{pagli, prencipe}@di.unipi.it
[3] Carleton University, Canada
santoro@scs.carleton.ca
[4] ETH, Zurich Switzerland
widmayer@inf.ethz.ch
[5] University of Botswana, Gaborone
zuvat@mopipi.ub.bw

1 Introduction

In systems using shortest-path routing tables, a single link failure is enough to interrupt the message transmission by disconnecting one or more shortest-path spanning trees. The on-line recomputation of an alternative path or of the entire new shortest path trees, rebuilding the routing tables accordingly, is rather expensive and causes long delays in the message's transmission [5, 10]. Hopefully, some of these costs will be reduced if the serial algorithms for dynamic graphs (e.g., those of [1]) could be somehow employed; to date, the difficulties of finding an efficient distributed implementation have not been overcome (e.g., see [9]).

An alternative approach is to precompute additional information and use it to augment the shortest-path routing tables so to make them operate when a failure occurs. Examples of this approach are techniques (e.g., see [4]) of pre-computing several edge-disjoint spanning trees for each destination. However, the alternative routes do not satisfy any optimization criterion (such as shortest path) even in the case when, at any time, only one link (not necessarily the same at all times) might be down.

A new strategy has been recently proposed [2, 5, 7, 8, 11]. It starts from the idea of precomputing, for each link in the tree, a single non-tree link (the *swap edge*) able to reconnect the network should the first fail. The strategy, called *point-of-failure swap rerouting* is simple: normal routing information will be used to route a message to its destination. If, however, the next hop is down, the

[*] Research partially supported by "Progetto ALINWEB", MIUR, Programmi di Ricerca Scientifica di Rilevante Interesse Nazionale, NSERC Canada, and the Swiss BBW 03.0378-1 for EC contract 001907 (DELIS).

T. Higashino (Ed.): OPODIS 2004, LNCS 3544, pp. 154–168, 2005.

message is first rerouted towards the swap edge; once this is crossed, normal routing will resume. Experimental results [11] show that the tree obtained from the swap edge is very close to the new shortest-path spanning tree computed from scratch.

Clearly, some swap edges are preferable to others. In [8], four main objective functions were defined, giving rise to four different problems. These functions have the goal to find a new tree that minimizes, respectively, the distance between the point of failure to the root (F_{dist}); the sum of distances (F_{sum}), the largest increment in the distance (F_{incr}), and the largest distance (F_{max}) of all nodes below the point of failure to the root.

In [8] they showed that these problems can be solved sequentially with different complexities: F_{dist} and F_{incr} in $O(m \cdot \alpha(m, n))$, F_{sum} in $O(n^2)$, and F_{max} in $O(n\sqrt{m})$, where $\alpha(m, n)$ is the functional inverse of Ackermann's function. These bounds are achieved using Tarjan's sophisticated technique of *transmuters* [12]. Unfortunately, there is currently no efficient distributed implementation of this sequential technique. From a distributed point of view, only the first of those problems, F_{dist}, has been investigated and solved. A simple but non-optimal solution has been developed in [5]. An efficient optimal solution has been recently proposed [3]. No efficient distributed solution exists to date for the problems F_{sum}, F_{incr}, and F_{max}. These problems appear to be rather important, since they minimize the average, the additional and the maximum delivery time of a message issued at any node. In this paper, we will be able to solve efficiently all three problems.

We propose two general distributed strategies, each solving the three problems with simple modifications. The first scheme uses $O(n_r^*)$ short messages, where n_r^* is the size of the transitive closure of $T_r \setminus \{r\}$; note that $0 \leq n_r^* \leq (n - 1)(n - 2)/2$. In the second scheme the number of messages decreases to $O(n)$ if long (i.e., $O(n)$ bits) messages are allowed. Both schemes use an overall complexity of $O(n_r^*)$.

2   Terminology and Problems

Let $G = (V, E)$ be a 2-connected undirected graph, with $n = |V|$ vertices and $m = |E|$ edges. A *label* of length $l \leq \log n$ is associated to each vertex of G. A non negative real *length* $w(e)$ is associated to each edge e. We say that the length of a path is the sum of the lengths of its edges, and the *distance* $d(x, y)$ between two vertices x and y is the length of a shortest path between them. Let $T = (V, E(T))$ be a spanning tree of graph G rooted in r. Let $T_q = (V(T_q), E(T_q))$ denote the subtree of T rooted in q.

Consider an edge $e = (x, y) \in E(T)$ with y closer to r; if such an edge is removed, the tree is disconnected in two subtrees: T_x and $T \setminus T_x$. A *swap* edge for $e = (x, y)$ is any edge $e' = (u, v) \in E \setminus \{e\}$ that connects the two subtrees and forms a new tree $T_{e/e'}$, called swap tree.

Let $\mathcal{S}_e$ be the set of all possible swap trees with respect to e. Depending on the goal of the swapping algorithm, some swap edges are preferable to others.

Given an objective function F over $\mathcal{S}_e$, an *optimal* or *best* swap edge for a link e is a swap edge e' such that $F(T_{e/e'})$ is minimum.

Let $d_T(u,v)$ (shortly $d(u,v)$) denote the distance between nodes u and v in T, and let $d_{T_{e/e'}}(u,v)$ (shortly $d_{e/e'}(u,v)$) denote their distance in $T_{e/e'}$. Given a subtree T_w of T, we denote by $W(T_w) = \sum_{t \in V(T_w)} d(t,w)$ the *weight* of T_w, and by $n(T_w)$ the number of nodes in T_w.

Given a rooted tree S, let $C(x, S)$ denote the set of children of node x in tree S, let $p(x, S)$ be the parent of node x in S, and $A(x, S)$ denote the ancestors of x in S. When $S = T$ we will simply write $C(x)$, $p(x)$ and $A(x)$. We consider the main problems studied in [8]:

1) F_{sum}-**problem:** $\min_{T_{e/e'} \in \mathcal{S}_e} \{F_{sum}(T_{e/e'})\}$, where $F_{sum}(T_{e/e'}) = \sum_{t \in V(T_x)} d_{e/e'}(t, r)$. Choose one of the swap edges e' that minimizes the sum of the distances $F_{sum}(T_{e/e'})$ from all nodes in T_x to r.

2) F_{incr}-**problem:** $\min_{T_{e/e'} \in \mathcal{S}_e} \{F_{incr}(T_{e/e'})\}$ where $F_{incr}(T_{e/e'}) = \max_{t \in V(T_x)} (d_{e/e'}(t, r) - d(t, r))$. Choose the swap edge that minimizes the maximum increment of the distance from r to any node in T_x.

3) F_{max}-**problem:** $\min_{T_{e/e'} \in \mathcal{S}_e} \{F_{max}(T_{e/e'})\}$ where $F_{max}(T_{e/e'}) = \max_{t \in V(T_x)} d_{e/e'}(t, r)$. Choose the swap edge that minimizes the maximum distance from the nodes in T_x to r.

3 Algorithmic Shell and Computational Tools

3.1 A Generic Algorithm

Consider the problem of computing the best swap edge for link $e = (x, p(x)) \in E(T)$, where $p(x)$ denotes the parent of x in T. We now present a generic distributed algorithm to perform this computation; the details of its modules depend on the objective function F and will be described later.

The algorithm is started by x; during its execution each node $z \in V(T_x)$ will determine the best, according to the objective function, local swap edge (z, z') for $(x, p(x))$. Among the local swap edges of all nodes, the swap edge yielding the global minimum cost will be then selected. More precisely, we define:

PROCEDURE BSE$(F, (x, p(x))$

- Node x determines, among its local swap edges for $(x, p(x))$, the one that minimizes F. As we will see, x is the only node that can do so without any additional information.
- After this, x sends to each child the *enabling information* it needs to compute the best among its local swap edges for $(x, p(x))$.
- Upon receiving the enabling information from its parent, a node computes the best among its local swap edge for $(x, p(x))$; it then sends enabling information to its children. This process terminates once the leaves of T_x are reached.
- The leaves then start a *minimum finding* process to determine, among the swap edges chosen by the nodes in T_x, the one that minimizes the objective function F.
- The optimal swap edge for $(x, p(x))$ is thus determined at node x.

This procedure finds the best swap edge for link $(x, p(x))$ (according to F). Thus, the generic algorithm to find all the best swap edges is

---

ALGORITHM BEST F-SWAP

1. PRE-PROCESSING(F)
2. $\forall x \neq r$: BSE $(F, (x, p(x)))$

---

where PRE-PROCESSING(F) is a preliminary process to be executed only if the nodes do not have the required initial information.

3.2   Identifying Swap Edges

Before proceeding with the instantiation of the generic algorithm for each of the objective functions, we describe a tool that allows a node to distinguish, among its incident edges, the ones that are swap edges for a given edge $(x, p(x))$.

Consider the following labeling of the nodes $\lambda : V \rightarrow \{1, \ldots, n\}^2$. Given T, for $x \in V$ let $\lambda(x) = (a, b)$, where a is the numbering of x in the *preorder* traversal of T; and b is the numbering of x in the *inverted preorder* traversal of T, i.e., when the order of the visit of the children is inverted. The pairs given by the labeling form a partial order $(\lambda, \geq)$ of dimension 2 (let $\lambda(z) = (z_1, z_2)$ and $\lambda(w) = (w_1, w_2)$, then $\lambda(z) \geq \lambda(w)$ if $z_1 \geq w_1$ and $z_2 \geq w_2$). The "dominance" relationship between these pairs completely characterizes the relationship "descendant" in the tree:

Property 1. *A node z is descendant of a node w in T if and only if $\lambda(z) \geq \lambda(w)$.*

In our algorithms, we assume that each node z knows its own pair $\lambda(z)$ as well the pairs of its neighbors. If not available, this information can be easily acquired by having each node exchange the information with its neighbors. Such a labeling will be given to the tree in a preprocessing phase. Based on Property 1, we can now see how the labeling can be used by a node u to recognize its incident swap edges for a given link $(x, p(x))$.

Property 2. *An edge $(u, v) \in E \setminus E(T)$ is a swap for $(x, p(x)) \in E(T)$ if and only if only one of u and v is a descendant of x in T.*

Thus, node $u \in T_x$ will be able to tell whether its incident edge (u, v) is a swap edge for $(x, p(x))$ simply by comparing $\lambda(v)$ with $\lambda(x)$; if $\lambda(v) \geq \lambda(x)$, then (u, v) is not a swap edge for $(x, p(x))$.

4   The F_{sum}-problem

In Problem F_{sum}, the *optimal swap edge* for link $e = (x, p(x))$ is one which minimizes the sum of the distances from all nodes in T_x to the root r, in the new spanning tree $T' = T_{e/e'}$. A swap edge (u, v) solving F_{sum} will also minimize the *average distance* of all the nodes belonging to T_x from the root r, since the size of T_x is the same for all the swap edges for x.

For solving the F_{sum}-problem (known also as *average stretch factor* [2]), we require each node z to possess the following a-priori information: its distance $d(z, r)$ from the root; the sum of the distances of all nodes in T_q to z for each of the children q of z; and the number of nodes $n(T_q)$ in T_q for each of its children q. If this information is not initially available, it can be easily acquired by the nodes in a pre-processing phase, composed by the following simple convergecast in T, executed only once at the beginning of the algorithm.

Given a subtree T_w and an edge (a, b), with $a \in V(T_w)$ and $b \in V \setminus V(T_w)$, let $sum(T_w, (a, b))$ denote the sum of distances in $T_w \cup (a, b)$ from all nodes of T_w to b.

PRE-PROCESSING(F_{sum})

1. The root r sends down a message to each child q containing a `request-for-sum` and a value $k = w(r, q)$.
2. The message is propagated down to the leaves (adding to k the weight of each traversed edge so that each node z knows its distance $d(z, r)$ to the root).
3. When a leaf l receives the message it starts a convergecast up to the root to propagate the requested information.
4. A leaf l with parent $p(l)$ sends up $sum(T_l, (l, p(l))) = w(l, p(l))$ and $n(T_l) = 1$
5. An internal node z receiving from each of its children q, the values $W(T_q)$ and $n(T_q)$, will compute:

$$n(T_z) = \sum_{q \in C(z)} n(T_q) + 1, \text{ and } sum(T_z, (z, p(z))) = W(T_z) + n(T_z) \cdot w(z, p(z))$$

and will send up the information $[sum(T_z, (z, p(z))), n(T_z)]$.

The correctness of the pre-processing is proven by the following:

Lemma 1. *Let z be a node in T.*

1. *The total number of nodes in T_z is: $n(T_z) = \sum_{q \in C(z)} n(T_q) + 1$.*
2. *The sum of the distances from all nodes in T_z to $p(z)$ is:*

$$sum(T_z, (z, p(z))) = W(T_z) + n(T_z) \cdot w(z, p(z)).$$

Proof. Part 1. is obvious. Let us consider Part 2. By definition, $sum(T_z, (z, p(z))) = \sum_{u \in V(T_z)} d(u, p(z))$. Thus,

$$sum(T_z, (z, p(z))) = \sum_{u \in V(T_z)} d(u, z) + \sum_{u \in V(T_z)} w(z, p(z))$$
$$= W(T_z) + n(T_z) \cdot w(z, p(z)).$$

Once all the information is available to the nodes, each node will exchange its local information with the neighbors in G. The number of messages exchanged during the preprocessing phase is then: $O(|E|)$.

Let z be a node in T_x that needs to compute the cost of a candidate swap edge $e' = (z, z')$ for e. Let $T' = T_{e/e'}$.

Lemma 2. *The sum of the distances in T' from all nodes in T_x to r is:*

$$F_{sum}(T') = W(T'_z) + n(T'_z) \cdot w(z, z') + n(T_x) \cdot d(z', r).$$

Proof. By definition we know that $F_{sum}(T') = \sum_{t \in V(T_x)} d_{e/e'}(t, r)$ $= \sum_{t \in T_x} [d_{e/e'}(t, z') + d(z', r)] = \sum_{t \in T_x} d_{e/e'}(t, z') + \sum_{t \in T_x} d(z', r)$, which is equal to $sum(T'_z, (z, z')) + n(T_x) \cdot d(z', r)$. Noticing that $sum(T'_z, (z, z')) = W(T'_z) + n(T'_z) \cdot w(z, z')$, the lemma follows.

Notice that $W(T'_z) = W(T_z) + sum(T_x \setminus T_z, (p(z), z))$ and $n(T'_z) = n(T_z) + n(T_x \setminus T_z)$ (see Figure 1). Thus, of the information required to compute the cost of the candidate swap edge (z, z'), there are two components that a node z ($z \neq x$) does not have locally available: $sum(T_x \setminus T_z, (p(z), z))$ and $n(T_x \setminus T_z)$. Only x has all the information immediately available and can locally compute the cost of its candidate swap edges; any other node z in T_x requires this additional information.

To instantiate algorithm BSE for F_{sum} we have to specify what is the *enabling information* to be propagated. On the basis of the above reasoning, the enabling information that any node z has to send down to its child q is composed of: the sum $sum(T_x \setminus T_q, (z, q))$ of the distances from q to the nodes in the subtree $T_x \setminus T_q$; and the number $n(T_x \setminus T_q)$ of nodes in this subtree.

The algorithm for finding the best swap edge for $(x, p(x))$ according to F_{sum} is as follows:

BSE$(F_{sum}, (x, p(x)))$

(* Algorithm for node z *)
1. *If* $z = x$
   - Compute cost of each local candidate swap edge:
     (for each $e' = (x, x')$, $F_{sum}(T_{e/e'}) = sum(T_x, (x, x')) + n(T_x) \cdot d(x', r)$)
   - select best candidate
   - for each child q: compute the enabling information $sum(T_x \setminus T_q, (x, q))$ and $n(T_x \setminus T_q)$ and send it to q. It will be shown that this information can be computed locally.
   - wait for the result of *minimum finding*; determine the best swap edge for $(x, p(x))$

2. *Else* $\{z \neq x\}$ – *Receiving enabling info* (s, n) *for* $(x, p(x))$
   - Compute cost of each local candidate swap edge:
     (for each $e' = (z, z')$, $F_{sum}(T_{e/e'}) = s + sum(T_z, (z, z')) + (n + n(T_z)) \cdot d(z', r) + n \cdot w(z, z')$. It will be shown that this information can be computed locally.
   - select best candidate
   - if I am a leaf: start *minimum finding*
   - if I am not a leaf
     - for each child q: compute the enabling information $sum(T_x \setminus T_q, (z, q))$, and $n(T_x \setminus T_q)$ and send it to q.
     - participate in *minimum finding* (wait for info from all children, select the best and send to parent)

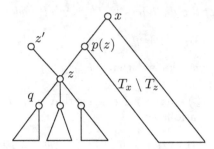

Fig. 1. Structure of the subtree T_x with respect to the swap edge (z, z')

Lemma 3. *Let $e = (x, p(x))$. Each node $z \in T_x$ can correctly compute: 1) the best local swap edge for e, 2) the value $sum(T_x \setminus T_q, (z, q))$ for each $q \in C(z)$, 3) the value $n(T_v \setminus T_q)$ for each $q \in C(z)$.*

Proof. First observe that, by Lemma 1, after the preprocessing phase, a node z has available: the labeling $\lambda(y)$ of each of its neighbors y; the distance $d(y, r)$ to r from each of its neighbors y; the sum of the distances $sum(T_q, (q, z))$ of all nodes in T_q to itself and the number of nodes $n(T_q)$ in T_q for each of its children q. The proof is by induction on the number of nodes in the path from z to of x.

Basis. $z = x$; i.e., the link to be swapped is $(z, p(z))$. By Lemma 2 we know that, for each swap edge (x, x'), $\sum_{t \in V(T_x)} d_{e/e'}(t, r) = sum(T_x, (x, x')) + n(T_x) \cdot d(x', r)$. Since x is the root of T_x, all the needed information is available at x after the preprocessing phase. Thus, x can locally compute all the swap edges and choose the minimum. Moreover x can compute, by using local information only, $sum(T_x \setminus T_q, (x, q))$ and $n(T_x \setminus T_q)$ for each $q \in C(x)$.

Induction step. Let it be true for a node and consider its child z in T. By Lemma 2 we know that, for each swap edge (z, z'),
$\sum_{t \in V(T_x)} d_{e/e'}(t, r) = sum(T'_z, (z, z')) + n(T_x) \cdot d(z', r)$. Moreover,
$sum(T'_z, (z, z')) = \sum_{q \in C(z, T')} sum(T'_q, (q, z))$
$+ (\sum_{q \in C(z, T')} n(T_q) + 1) \cdot w(z, z')$.

Notice that the children of z in T' consists of all the children of z in T plus the parent of z in T (i.e., $C(z, T') = C(z) \cup \{(z, p(z))\}$. The values of $sum(T'_q, (q, z))$, and $n(T'_q)$ for $q \in C(z)$ have been computed in the preprocessing phase and are locally available. Since, by induction hypothesis, $p(z)$ has computed the locally best swap edge and the values of $s(T_x \setminus T_z, (p(z), z))$ and $n(T_x \setminus T_z)$, and since it has sent to z these information, z can now correctly compute the cost of all its local swap edge and choose the minimum. Moreover, it can now compute $s(T_x \setminus T_q, (z, q))$ and $n(T_x \setminus T_q)$ for each of its children $q \in C(z)$.

5   The F_{max} and F_{incr} Problems

In Problem F_{max}, the *optimal swap edge* e' for link $e = (z, p(z))$ is any swap edge such that the longest distance of all the nodes in T_z from the root r is minimized in the new spanning tree $T_{e/e'}$; in F_{incr}, it is any swap edge such that the maximum increment in the distance from the nodes in T_z to the root r is minimized in the new spanning tree $T_{e/e'}$.

The algorithm for computing the best swap edges with respect to F_{max} and F_{incr} have the same structure as the one for F_{sum}. What differs is: (i) the information propagated in the preprocessing phase, and (ii) the "enabling information" to be sent to the children during the algorithm.

For solving the F_{max} and the F_{incr} problems we require each node z to possess the following information: its distance $d(z, r)$ from the root, and the maximum distance $mD(T_q, z)$ to z from a node in T_q for each $q \in C(z)$. This will be accomplished with a basic convergecast like in the previous section. In this case, Lines 4. and 5. of protocol PRE-PROCESSING change as follows:

IN THE PRE-PROCESSING

4. a leaf l with parent $p(l)$ sends up $max(T_l, p(l)) = w(l, p(l))$
5. an internal node z receiving from each of its children q, the values $max(T_q, z)$ will compute

$$max(T_z, p(z)) = \max\{max(T_q, z)\} + w(z, p(z))$$

and will send up the information $max(T_z, p(z))$.

Let z be a node in T_x that needs to compute the cost of a candidate swap edge $e' = (z, z')$ for $e = (x, p(x))$. Let $T' = T_{e/e'}$.

Lemma 4. *The maximum distance $F_{max}(T')$ and the maximum distance increment $F_{incr}(T')$ in T' from a node z in T_x to r are:*

$$F_{max}(T') = \max_{q \in C(z, T')} \{mD(T_q, z) + w(z, z') + d(z', r)\}$$

$$F_{incr}(T') = \max_{q \in C(z, T')} \{mD(T_q, z) + w(z, z') + d(z', r)\} - d(z, r)$$

To instantiate the generic algorithm of Section 3 for the F_{max} and the F_{incr} objective functions we have now to specify what is the *enabling information* that needs to be propagated so that all the nodes can make their local choice. As it will be shown, in both cases the enabling information that a node z has to send down to its child q is composed of the maximum distance $mD(T_x \setminus T_q, q)$ of the nodes in the subtree $T_x \setminus T_q$ to q. The algorithm for node z is then the same as the one for F_{sum}, where the computation of the cost of the local candidate swap edges and the enabling information change as follows:

CHANGES: MAX ALGORITHM

1. *If $z = x$, the cost of each local candidate swap edge is computed as follows: for each $e' = (z, z')$,*
$$F_{max}(T_{e/e'}) = \max_{q \in C(x)}\{mD(T_q, x) + w(x, x') + d(x', r)\}$$
$$F_{incr}(T_{e/e'}) = \max_{q \in C(x)}\{mD(T_q, x) + w(x, x') + d(x', r)\} - d(x, r).$$
2. *Else $\{z \neq x\}$ – Receiving enabling info m for $(x, p(x))$, the cost of each local candidate swap edge is computed as follows:*
$$F_{max}(T') = \max\{m, \max_{q \in C(z)}\{mD(T_q, z)\}\} + \{w(z, z') + d(z', r)\}$$
$$F_{incr}(T') = \max\{m, \max_{q \in C(z)}\{mD(T_q, z)\}\} + \{w(z, z') + d(z', r) - d(z, r)\}.$$
3. *The enabling information to be sent is $mD(T_x \setminus T_q, q)$.*

Lemma 5. *Given $e = (x, p(x))$, each node $z \in T_x$ correctly computes: 1) the local best swap edges for e, 2) the value $mD(T_q, z)$ for each $q \in C(z)$.*

Proof. The values $w(z, z')$ and $d(z', r))$ are locally available because they have been computed in the preprocessing phase. We know that $C(z, T') = C(z) \cup \{(z, p(z))\})$. If $q \in C(z)$, then $max(T_q, z)$ is locally available because it has also been computed in the preprocessing phase. On the other hand, if $q = p(z)$, $max(T_q, z)$ has to be computed during the algorithm. By definition, this is the *enabling information* sent to z by $p(z)$.

6 Correctness and Complexity

Lemma 6. *Algorithms $BSE(F_{sum})$,$BSE(F_{max})$, and $BSE(F_{incr})$, find the best swap edge for $e = (x, p(x))$ according to the corresponding objective function.*

Proof. By Lemmas 3, and 5 respectively, every node correctly computes its local best swap edge for e. By the correctness of the minimum finding, the global best swap edge will be communicated to x.

Theorem 1. *Independently executing Algorithms $BSE(F_{sum})$,$BSE(F_{max})$, and $BSE(F_{incr})$ for each edge, the problems $\{r, \sum\}$, $\{r, \delta\}$, and $\{r, \max\}$ are solved.*

Let us now examine the complexity of the proposed algorithm. Let n^* be the number of edges of the transitive closure of $T_r \setminus \{r\}$.

Theorem 2. *The message complexity of the Algorithms is at most $3n^*$.*

Proof. The preprocessing phase is executed only once and its complexity is $O(|E|)$. During the swap algorithm for $(x, p(x))$ the number of messages exchanged is $2|V(T_x)|$, thus, in total we have: $\sum_x 2|V(T_x)| = 2n^*$.

Since each message contains only a constant number of units of information (i.e., node, edge, label, weight, distance), the overall information complexity is of the same order of magnitude, i.e., $O(n^*)$.

7   An O(n) Messages Algorithm

7.1   Algorithmic Shell

The idea is that each node x simultaneously computes the "best" swap edges, not only for $(x, p(x))$, but also for each $(a, p(a))$, where a is an ancestor of x in T. At an high level, the algorithm consists simply of a *broadcast* phase started by the children of the root, followed by a *convergecast* phase started by the leaves.

BEST F-SWAP-LONG (BSL)

[Broadcast.]

1. Each child x of the root starts the broadcast by sending to its children a list containing its name and its distance from the root.
2. Each node y, receiving a list of names and distances from its parent, appends its name and $d_T(y, r)$ to the received list and sends it to its children.

[Convergecast.]

1. Each leaf z first computes the best local swap for $(z, p(z))$; then, for each a in the received list, it computes the best candidate swap for $(a, p(a))$; finally, sends the list of those edges to its parent (if different from r).
2. An internal node y waits until it receives the list of best swap edges from each of its children. Based on the received information and on its local swap edges, it computes its best swap edge for $(y, p(y))$; it then computes for each ancestor a the best candidate for $(a, p(a))$; finally, it sends the list of those edges to its parent (if different from r).

To show how this generic algorithmic structure can be used to solve the three studied problems, we need to specify how the convergecast part is done. The differences in three solutions are: (i) the computation of the best swap edge in the convergecast phase, and (ii) the additional information, of constant size, to be communicated to the ancestors together with the swap edge.

In the following, we will denote by $SL(x)$ the *Swap List* associated to node x; it is defined as a list of records *(edge, value, attributes)*, where *edge* indicates a swap edge for $(x, p(x))$; *value* the value of the objective function computed in the tree where $(x, p(x))$ has been substituted with *edge*; and *attributes* a list of parameters to be specified for the particular problem being solved. Moreover, let $ASL(x)$ be the swap list associated to the ancestors of x; it is a list of records *(edge, value, attributes, node)* indicating for each node $a \in A(x)$ (stored in the field *node*) the best candidate for $(a, p(a))$ (stored in *edge*), and the value of the objective function *(value)*; *attributes* is as in $SL(x)$.

Let us describe in details the operations executed by node x. First of all x computes the best swap edge for $(x, p(x))$ by considering the set $InS(x)$ of all local swap edges for $(x, p(x))$ and the set of swap edges transmitted to it from its children (Algorithm MYBSE). Then for each ancestor a it computes, among the swap edges in T_x, the best candidate for $(a, p(a))$ (Algorithm MYABSE). Note that the swap edges x computes for its ancestors can be worse than the final swap edges computed by its ancestors when *they* execute Algorithm MYBSE.

MYBSE

(* Algorithm for node x, where $e = (x, p(x))$ is the link to be swapped *)

1. Determine which of x's incident edges are swap edges for $(x, p(x))$; i.e., x constructs the set $InS(x)$.
2. For each swap edge $e_i = (x, y_i) \in InS(x)$, compute the value of the objective function via e_i, and the value of the other attributes and insert them together with e_i in $SL(x)$.
3. If x is not a leaf, from each $ASL(x_j)$ received from $x_j \in C(x)$, extract $(e_j, value, attributes, x)$ (or NIL, if no such record exists), and insert $(e_j, value, attributes)$ in $SL(x)$ (or NIL).
4. Sort $SL(x)$ in non decreasing order of $value$. The minimal element of $SL(x)$ gives one of the best swap edges for x and the value which minimizes the objective function.

MYABSE

(* Algorithm for node x *) For each ancestor node $a \in A(x)$:

1. Select the swap edge $e_i \in SL(x)$ which is also a swap edge for $(a, p(a))$, if any, with the minimal value of $value$, and consider its record $(e_i, v_i, attributes, a)$.
2. For $x_j \in C(x), 1 \le j \le h$, let $(e_j, v_j, attributes, a)$ be the record from $ASL(x_j)$. Update the values of v_j and of the *attributes* in relation to node x. Consider the set of the updated records $\{(e_j, v_j, attributes, a) \cup (e_i, v_i, attributes, a)\}$, $1 \le j \le h$, where $(e_i, v_i, attributes, a)$ is the record computed in Step 1. Select from this set the record $(\overline{e}, \overline{v}, attributes, a)$ with minimal $value$, if any, and insert it, in $ASL(x)$ (to be sent to x's parent); if no record can be selected, insert NIL in $ASL(x)$.

7.2   Identifying a Swap Edge

In order for a node to decide if one of its incident edge is a swap edge it is sufficient to check, during the convergecast phase, the information collected in the broadcast phase.

Property 3. *The fact that an edge $(u, v) \in E \setminus E(T)$ with $u \in T_u$ and $v \in T \setminus T_u$ is a swap edge for $(x, p(x))$, with $x \in A(u)$, can be checked at node u, and no communication is needed.*

Property 3 derives from the fact that, after the broadcast phase, u knows all its ancestors. Observe that if an edge is not a swap edge for $e = (x, p(x))$, it is not feasible for none of $a \in A(x)$.

8   The F_{sum} Problem with O(n) Messages

Problem F_{sum} is solved with minor modifications of the Convergecast Phase of Algorithm BSL.

To compute, each node z need some additional information: the distance $d_{T'}(z, r)$ in $T_{e/e'}$ for each considered swap edge e' for $(z, p(z))$; the weight $W(T_z)$ of the subtree T_z; the number of nodes $n(T_z)$ in such a subtree. The records of the list $SL(z)$ will thus have the form: $(edge, F_{sum}(T_z),$ $\{d_{T'}(z, r), W(T_z), n(T_z)\})$; the same three items (plus the field *node* indicating the ancestor) are stored in the records of $ASL(z)$.

The parameters $n(T_z)$ and $W(T_z)$ are easily computed inductively from the values sent to z by its children z_j, and from the weight of the edge (z_j, z). Namely: $n(T_z) = \sum_{z_i \in C(z)} n(T_{z_i}) + 1$; and $W(T_z) = \sum_{z_i \in C(z)} W(T_{z_i}) + \sum_{z_i \in C(z)} n(T_{z_i})$ $w(z, z_i)$. If z is a leaf $n(T_z) = 1$ and $W(T_z) = 0$.

Let us now show how to compute the new values of $F_{sum}(T_z)$, and of $d_{T'}(z, r)$ (Step 2 of MYBSE and of MYABSE).

Lemma 7. Let $(z, y) \in InS(z)$. Then

(i) $F_{sum} = W(T_z) + n(T_z) \cdot (w(z, y) + d_{T'}(y, r))$.
(ii) For each record $(e_i \neq NIL, F_{sum}(T_{z_i}), \{d_{T'}(z_i, r), W(T_{z_i}), n(T_{z_i})\}, z)$ re- ceived from child z_i, $d_{T'}(z, r) = w(z, z_i) + d_{T'}(z_i, r)$, and
$F_{sum}(T_z) = F_{sum}(T_{z_i}) + d_{T'}(z, r) + \sum_{j=1, j \neq i}^{h}(W(T_{z_j}) + n(T_{z_j})(w(z, z_i) + w(z, z_i) + d_{T'}(z_i, r)))$.

Proof. Assume that the children of z have already terminated their computation and transmitted their lists to z. Case (i) follows by Lemma 2.

The scenario of Case (ii) is better understood looking at Figure 2. If a swap edge e_i belonging to T_{z_i} is considered, all the nodes in T_{z_i} maintain their distance

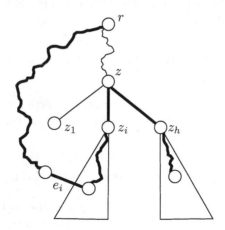

Fig. 2. Case (ii) in Lemma 7: the computation of $F_{sum}(T_z)$ via the swap edge e_i. The thick line represents the path to the root via e_i

from the root, hence they contribute to $F_{sum}(T_z)$ only for $F_{sum}(T_{z_i})$. Node z contributes for $d_{T'}(z, r)$. All the other nodes in $T_{z_j}, 1 \leq j \leq h, j \neq i$, to get the root, follow a path through edges (z_j, z), (z, z_i) and finally through the swap edges e_i.

The messages used in the convergecast phase are now longer with respect to the messages used in the approach of Section 4, but still of constant size. We finally have:

Theorem 3. *Each node $z \neq r$:*
(i) correctly computes its best swap edge:
(ii) determines for each ancestor $a \neq r$ the best swap edge for a in T_z.

Proof. First observe that, as result of the broadcast, every node receives the label of its ancestors (except r) and it can determine which edges are swap edges for itself and its ancestors (Property 2 and 3). The proof is by induction on the height $h(z)$ of the subtree T_z.

Basis. $h(z) = 0$; i.e., z is a leaf. In this case, one component contains only z, while the other contains all the other nodes. In other words, the only possible swap edges are incident on z. Thus, z can correctly compute its best swap edge by computing the value of the distance as stated in point (i) of Lemma 7, thus proving (i). It can also immediately determine the swap edges with respect to all of its ancestors and compute for them the value of the parameters as stated in point (ii) of Lemma 7, and select, for each ancestor, the best candidate.

Induction step. Let the theorem hold for all nodes z with $0 \leq h(z) \leq k - 1$; we will now show that it holds for z with $h(z) = k$. By inductive hypothesis, it receives from each child y the best candidate for each ancestor of $y \in C(z)$, including z itself. Hence, based on these lists and on the locally available set $InS(z)$, z can correctly determine its optimal swap edge, as well as its best feasible swap edge for each of its ancestors.

Theorem 4. F_{sum} *can be solved with the $O(n)$ message complexity and $O(n_r^*)$ data complexity.*

Proof. The theorem follows immediately from Properties 2 and 3, and from the fact that, by Lemma 7, the messages still have constant size.

9   The F_{max} and F_{incr} Problems with O(n) Messages

We will show how F_{max} is solved by BSL. The value to be minimized is the maximal distance from the nodes in T_z to the root via a swap edge e_i. Similarly to F_{sum}, we need to compute inductively two values; namely, the distance from z to the root via e_i, $d_{T'}(z, r)$, and the maximal distance from the nodes in T_z to z, that is $mD(T_q, z)$, with $q \in C(z)$. The list $SL(z)$ is now composed of records of four elements; namely: $(edge, F_{max}(T_z), \{d_{T'}(z, r), mD(T_q, z)\}); ASL(z)$ contains the same information, plus the field *node*.

Let us now show how to compute the new values of the parameters along a new swap edge e_i (Step 2 of MYBSE) and how to compute the same values when a swap edge transmitted from a child is considered. The same operations are performed also in Step 2 of MYABSE. We have:

Lemma 8. *Let T_{z_k} be the subtree of T_z containing the node at the maximal distance from r. Moreover, let $mD_2(z) = max_{q \neq k}(mD(T_q, z)$ be the maximal distance of the nodes in T_{z_j} to z, with $z_j \in \{C(z) \setminus z_k\}$. For $(z, l) \in InS(z)$, we have*

(i) $F_{max}(T_z) = max_{q \in C(z, T)}(mD(T_q, z) + w(z, l) + d_{T'}(l, r))$.
(ii) For each record $(e_s \neq NIL, F_{max}(T_{z_s}), \{d_{T'}(z_s, r), mD(z_s)\}, z)$ received from child z_s, $d_{T'}(z, r) = (w(z, z_s) + d_{T'}(z_s, r))$. Moreover, if $s = k$, then $F_{max}(T_z) = max(F_{max}(T_{z_s}), mD_2s(z) + d_{T'}(z, r))$; otherwise, $F_{max}(T_z) = max(F_{max}(T_{z_s}), mD(z) + d_{T'}(z, r))$.

Proof. Assume that the children of z have already terminated their computation and transmitted their lists to z. From these values z can compute the maximum distance of a node in T_z, and Case (i) follows immediately. For Case (ii), if the swap edge e_s does not belongs to T_{x_k}, the maximal distance is given by the maximal value among $F_{max}(T_{z_s})$ and $(mD(z) + d_{T'}(z, r))$. Otherwise, all the nodes in T_{x_k} maintain their distance from the root; for all the other nodes (in $T_j, 1 \leq j \leq h, j \neq k$), called *far* nodes, to get to the root the path goes through edges $(z_j, z), (z, z_k)$, and finally through the swap edge z_s. Hence, in this case, to compute the distance of the far nodes we have to consider the node at the maximal distance not belonging to T_{x_k}, whose distance is $mD_2(z)$.

Thus, it follows that:

Theorem 5. *Each node $x \neq r$:*

(i) correctly computes the best swap edge for $(x, p(x))$ according to F_{max};
(ii) determines for each ancestor $a \neq r$ the best swap edge for v in T_u.

F_{incr} can be solved with a simple extension of the solution of F_{max}.

Theorem 6. *Problems F_{max} and F_{incr} can be solved with $O(n)$ messages and an overall $O(n_r^*)$ information complexity.*

Proof. It follows immediately from Properties 2 and 3, and from Lemma 8.

References

1. D. Eppstein, Z. Galil, and G.F. Italiano. Dynamic graph algorithms. *CRC Handbook of Algorithms and Theory, CRC Press, 1997.*
2. A. Di Salvo and G. Proietti. Swapping a failing edge of a shortest paths tree by minimizing the average stretch factor. *Proc. of 10th Colloquium on Structural Information and Communication Complexity* (SIROCCO 2004) 2004.

3. P. Flocchini, T. Mesa, L. Pagli, G. Prencipe, and N. Santoro. Efficient protocols for computing optimal swap edges. *In Proc. of 3rd IFIP International Conference on Theoretical Computer Science* (TCS 2004), 2004, to appear.

4. A. Itai and M. Rodeh. The multi-tree approach to reliability in distributed networks. *Information and Computation*, 79:43-59, 1988.

5. H. Ito, K. Iwama, Y. Okabe, and T. Yoshihiro. Polynomial-time computable backup tables for shortest-path routing. *Proc. of 10th Colloquium on Structural Information and Communication Complexity* (SIROCCO 2003), 163–177, 2003.

6. H. Mohanty and G.P.Bhattacharjee. A distributed algorithm for edge-disjoint path problem *Proc. of 6th Conference on Foundations of Software Technology and Theoretical Computer Science* (FSTTCS), 44-361, 1986.

7. E. Nardelli, G. Proietti, and P. Widmayer. Finding all the best swaps of a minimum diameter spanning tree under transient edge failures. *Journal of Graph Algorithms and Applications*, 2(1):1–23, 1997.

8. E. Nardelli, G. Proietti, and P. Widmayer. Swapping a failing edge of a single source shortest paths tree is good and fast. *Algoritmica*, 35:56–74, 2003.

9. P. Narvaez, K.Y. Siu, and H.Y. Teng. New dynamic algorithms for shortest path tree computation *IEEE Transactions on Networking*, 8:735–746, 2000.

10. L. L. Peterson and B. S. Davie. *Computer Networks: A Systems Approach, 3rd Edition*. Morgan Kaufmann, 2003.

11. G. Proietti. Dynamic maintenance versus swapping: An experimental study on shortest paths trees. *Proc. 3rd Workshop on Algorithm Engineering* (WAE 2000), 207–217 2000

12. R. E.Tarjan. Application of path compression on balanced trees. *Journal of ACM*, 26:690–715, 1979.

SRF TCP: A TCP-Friendly and Fair Congestion Control Method for High-Speed Networks

Masahiko Fukuhara[1], Fumiaki Hirose[1], Tomoya Hatano[2],
Hiroshi Shigeno[1], and Ken-ichi Okada[1]

[1] Faculty of Science and Technology, Keio University,
3-14-1 Hiyoshi, Kohoku-ku, Yokohama, Kanagawa, Japan
{fukuhara, hirose, shigeno, okada}@mos.ics.keio.ac.jp
[2] NTT Access Network Service Systems Laboratories,
1-6 Nakase, Mihama-ku, Chiba-shi, Chiba, Japan
hatano.tomoya@ansl.ntt.co.jp

Abstract. TCP Reno congestion control carries two issues. First, its performance is poor in high-speed networks. To solve this TCP Reno drawback, HighSpeed TCP and Scalable TCP were proposed. However, the fairness between these proposed TCP and TCP Reno is not considered, when both connections coexist. Second, TCP Reno connections share bandwidth unfairly, when TCP flows with different RTTs use the same link. Many approaches have been proposed to solve this issue. However, no single method has been proposed to solve both issues. In this paper, we propose Square Root Fair TCP (SRF TCP). SRF TCP congestion control (1) sends packets efficiently in high-speed networks, (2) is TCP-friendly with TCP Reno and (3) shares fair bandwidth between flows with different RTTs. We evaluate the capabilities of SRF TCP through computer simulations and compare it with TCP Reno, High-Speed TCP and Scalable TCP.

1 Introduction

Recently, an infrastructure which enables high-speed transmission has been made by the evolution of the optical network. And the cost of the service using such an infrastructure is falling year by year. Many services which realize various demands will appear from now on and high-speed transmission is spreading widely. Moreover, satellite and wireless links with high latency are becoming more general. TCP congestion control is needed to be efficient even if bandwidth-delay product increases.

When current TCP, TCP Reno, is used in high-speed networks, it cannot use the link bandwidth effectively. In order to solve this problem at end hosts, HighSpeed TCP[1] and Scalable TCP[2] were proposed. These proposals have the problem of fairness with TCP Reno. When TCP Reno connections and proposed TCP connections coexist in the same link, the proposed TCP connections obtain the bandwidth aggressively.

T. Higashino (Ed.): OPODIS 2004, LNCS 3544, pp. 169–183, 2005.

In TCP Reno, the difference in flow's RTT causes unfair bandwidth allocation to each flow. Many mechanisms which improve fairness at end hosts have been developed. However, these mechanisms disregard fairness with TCP Reno and adaptation to high-speed transmission.

As the solution of these problems, a lot of research focusing on AQM[3, 4] are proposed. CSFQ[5], which is a queuing system at a network, is also proposed. Another approach for high-speed networks, taken by XCP[6], uses explicit feedback from routers for congestion control. However, these proposals need to make changes of both end hosts and networks. We have the idea that the problem by TCP congestion control should be improved in TCP, that is at only end hosts.

TFRC[7], Binomial congestion control[8] and many AIMD mechanisms[9, 10] are researched for TCP-friendly congestion control method. However, these mechanisms cannot transmit efficiently in high-speed networks.

In this paper, we propose Square Root Fair TCP (SRF TCP), which solves the problems of TCP Reno. In SRF TCP, when an ACK is received, the window increases proportional to the flow's RTT and inversely proportional to the square root of its congestion window. When a packet is lost, the window decreases proportional to the square root of its congestion window. SRF TCP is desirable for high-speed transmission, improves fairness with TCP Reno and improves unfair bandwidth allocation by the difference in flow's RTT.

The paper is organized as follows. In section 2, we describe TCP Reno congestion control and its problems. We describe the related works on TCP congestion control mechanism for high-speed transmission in section 3, and on unfairness by the difference in flow's RTT in section 4. Section 5 proposes SRF TCP. In section 6, we present simulation results of SRF TCP. Section 7 concludes the paper.

2   TCP Reno

2.1   Congestion Control

TCP Reno increases the congestion window (W) by $1/W$ for each received ACK and decreases it in half for each loss event. TCP Reno controls the congestion window as follows:

$$\text{Increase: } W = W + \frac{1}{W}, \tag{1}$$

$$\text{Decrease: } W = W - \frac{1}{2}W. \tag{2}$$

Based on received ACK and packet loss, TCP congestion control mechanism controls the congestion window to transmit packets effectively. As a result, a packet loss event arises periodically. The congestion window and throughput (T) are related to packet loss rate (p) and TCP Reno response function is computed as follows[11]:

$$W_{reno} = \frac{1.22}{p^{0.5}}, \tag{3}$$

$$T_{reno} = \frac{Size_{pac}}{RTT} \frac{1.22}{p^{0.5}}, \tag{4}$$

where packet size is $Size_{pac}$.

2.2   Problem in High-Speed Networks

From equation (3), TCP Reno places a serious constraint on the congestion window that can be achieved by TCP in realistic environments. For example, for a TCP Reno connection with 1500-byte packets and a 100 ms RTT, achieving a steady-state throughput of 10 Gbps would require an average congestion window of 83000 segments, and an average packet drop rate of 2×10^{-10} at most[1]. This is an unrealistic requirement for current networks. It takes more than 40000 RTTs to recover the congestion window after the loss event to make efficient use of the link bandwidth. The reason why TCP Reno cannot achieve high throughput is that its congestion window is increased by a significantly small size of 1 packet per RTT at most, while it is decreased by half the size of it at a packet loss.

2.3   Fairness Between Flows with Different RTTs

For TCP Reno, the window increase is inversely proportional to RTT. A TCP Reno connection with longer RTT increases the congestion window slowly. A connection with slow increasing window cannot adapt the sending rate to the network condition promptly, while a connection with faster increasing window takes more available bandwidth. As a result, TCP Reno congestion control mechanism lacks the mechanism to share fair bandwidth. In addition, from equation (4), the fact that the throughput is inversely proportional to its RTT proves that this issue arises.

3   TCP Congestion Control Mechanism for High-Speed Networks

3.1   HighSpeed TCP

HighSpeed TCP is proposed to transmit data efficiently in high-speed networks. It uses three parameters, W_L, W_H, and P_H. To ensure TCP compatibility, it uses the same response function as TCP Reno when the current congestion window is at the maximum W_L, and uses the HighSpeed response function when the current congestion window is greater than W_L. HighSpeed TCP keeps average congestion window W_H, when packet loss rate is P_H. To simplify, it sets the property that the response function gives a straight line on a log-log scale. This results in the following response function, for values of the average congestion window greater than W_L:

$$logW = \frac{logW_H - logW_L}{logP_H - logP_L}(logp - logP_L) + logW_L. \tag{5}$$

HighSpeed TCP can be translated into increase and decrease functions. They use $a(W)$ as the window increase per RTT and $b(W)W$ as the window decrease for each loss event. Given decrease parameters of $b(W) = b_H$ for $W = W_H$, the value of $b(W)$ for other values of $W > W_L$ can be specified. HighSpeed TCP lets $b(W)$ vary linearly as the log of W, and $a(W)$ can be computed as follows:

$$b(W) = \frac{logW - logW_L}{logW_H - logW_L}(b_H - 0.5) + 0.5. \tag{6}$$

$$a(W) = 2W^2 p(W)\frac{b(W)}{2 - b(W)}. \tag{7}$$

In this proposal, $W_L = 38$, $W_H = 83000$, $P_H = 10^{-7}$ and $b_H = 0.1$ are recommended. On these occasions, HighSpeed TCP response function is computed as follows:

$$W_{hs} = \frac{0.119}{p^{0.835}}, \tag{8}$$

$$T_{hs} = \frac{Size_{pac}}{RTT}\frac{0.119}{p^{0.835}}. \tag{9}$$

This is how HighSpeed TCP realizes efficient transmission in high-speed networks. However, inverse proportion to RTT in equation (9) proves that High-Speed TCP has unfairness by the difference in flow's RTT. Moreover, it is indicated that HighSpeed TCP is more aggressive than TCP Reno and it arises unfair bandwidth allocation with TCP Reno. From equation (4) and (9), the proportion of throughput between TCP Reno and HighSpeed TCP is computed as follows:

$$\frac{T_{hs}}{T_{reno}} = \frac{0.0971}{p^{0.335}}. \tag{10}$$

For example, for packet drop rates of 10^{-6}, the proportion of throughput is 10.0, which is unfair.

3.2   Scalable TCP

Scalable TCP also improves the TCP performance in high-speed wide area networks. Scalable TCP controls the congestion window as follows:

$$\text{Increase: } W = W + 0.01, \tag{11}$$

$$\text{Decrease: } W = W - 0.125W. \tag{12}$$

For Scalable TCP, the congestion window is increased by $0.01W$ proportional to its congestion window per RTT. According to [2], the recovery time after a packet loss is 13.42RTT, which is proportional to the RTT and independent of the congestion window. On the other hand, for TCP Reno, the congestion window is increased by 1 segment per RTT and the recovery time after a packet loss is proportional to both the RTT and the congestion window. A Scalable TCP connection recovers its congestion window in a short time even when it has a large congestion window. Therefore, Scalable TCP makes efficient use of the bandwidth in high-speed networks. Scalable TCP response function is computed as follows:

$$W_{sca} = \frac{0.0745}{p} \qquad (13)$$

$$T_{sca} = \frac{Size_{pac}}{RTT} \frac{0.0745}{p} \qquad (14)$$

Scalable TCP also has unfairness by the difference in flow's RTT according to equation (14). Moreover, from equation (4) and (14), the proportion of throughput between TCP Reno and Scalable TCP is computed as follows:

$$\frac{T_{sca}}{T_{reno}} = \frac{0.0608}{p^{0.5}}. \qquad (15)$$

For example, for packet drop rates of 10^{-6}, the proportion of throughput is 60.9. The unfairness with TCP Reno is more serious than that of HighSpeed TCP and it is fatal to spread in the world.

3.3   The Relationship Between the Congestion Window and p

Figure 1 shows the relation between p and W of TCP Reno, HighSpeed TCP and Scalable TCP. At the same p, the window difference between TCP Reno and HighSpeed TCP is smaller than that of TCP Reno and Scalable TCP. It shows that HighSpeed TCP is more TCP-friendly than Scalable TCP. However, when p gets smaller, HighSpeed TCP causes unfair bandwidth allocation. To improve fairness with TCP Reno compared to HighSpeed TCP, the congestion window of new TCP method in Figure 1 should be kept less than HighSpeed TCP congestion window.

4   Unfairness by the Difference in Flow's RTT

4.1   Needs for Improvement

Satellite links are becoming more general and gigabit transmission with these links will also be required extremely. However, satellite links have longer round trip propagation delay. For TCP Reno, it takes too much time for a connection with longer RTT to recover the halved congestion window, especially in gigabit networks. HighSpeed TCP also needs 123 seconds for a connection with 1 second RTT to recover the decreased congestion window in 10 Gbps networks. On this occasion, recovery time is too long to make efficient use of link bandwidth. In order for a connection with longer RTT to recover the decreased congestion window and make efficient use of high-speed networks, the window increase and decrease algorithm independent of RTT is needed.

4.2   Related Works

Many methods have been proposed to solve unfairness by the difference in flow's RTT. Fang et al. [12] set TCP window increase at a constant rate and removed

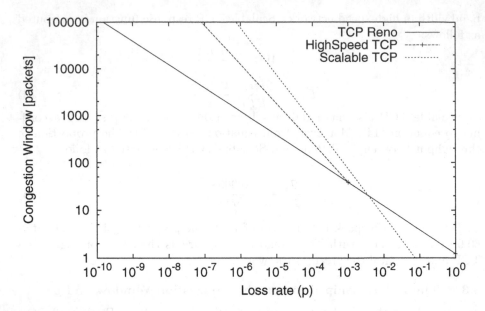

Fig. 1. The relation between p and W of TCP Reno, HighSpeed TCP and Scalable TCP

the influence of RTT differences. In this proposal, the unfair problem with TCP Reno remains.

Hamann et al. [13] proposed a congestion control method which increases the congestion window for each received ACK as follows:

$$W = W + \frac{1}{W} S_{wnd}, \tag{16}$$

$$S_{wnd} = S_{wnd} + \beta RTT^2. \tag{17}$$

The window increase is proportional to RTT^2 to share fair bandwidth between flows with different RTTs. Although the proposed congestion control keeps fairness with TCP Reno, no improvement is made to realize efficient transmission in high-speed networks.

5   Proposed Congestion Control Method

We propose Square Root Fair TCP (SRF TCP) which can transmit data with efficient use of the link bandwidth in high-speed networks, resolves unfairness by the difference in flow's RTT and improves fairness with TCP Reno.

In this paper, for a new congestion control method, let the congestion window increase and decrease as follows:

$$\text{Increase: } W = W + aW^\alpha, \tag{18}$$

$$\text{Decrease: } W = W - bW^\beta. \tag{19}$$

5.1   Resolution of α and β

To transmit data efficiently in high-speed networks, values of α and β are specified at first. TCP Reno, which is the Additive Increase Multiplicative Decrease (AIMD) congestion control, adopts $\beta - \alpha = 2$. And TFRC and Binomial congestion control also adopts $\beta - \alpha = 2$. In high-speed networks, the AIMD congestion control decreases its congestion window significantly while the window increase is small. According to [14], $\beta - \alpha = 1$ is recommended for ideal response function. When $\beta - \alpha = 1$, the packet loss rate is independent of the congestion window and is dependent on only RTT, which is desirable for high-speed data transmission.

The choices of α and β to be considered are $(\alpha, \beta) = (-1, 0), (0, 1), (-1/2, 1/2)$. When $(\alpha, \beta) = (-1, 0)$, the window decrease is *constant*. For large congestion window, the window decrease gets relatively too small, while the window decrease gets relatively too large for small congestion window. Thus, $(-1, 0)$ is not desirable to use the link bandwidth efficiently in both normal and high-speed networks.

When $(\alpha, \beta) = (0, 1)$, which is adopted by Scalable TCP, the window increase per RTT gets relatively too large at large congestion window. When the coefficient of increase is changed to a smaller value, the window increase per RTT gets relatively too small at small congestion window.

For $(\alpha, \beta) = (-1/2, 1/2)$, the window increase grows steadily and the window decrease drops steadily. The window increase and decrease can be adjusted to the desirable value for every congestion window. This system can be used efficiently for transmission in both normal and high-speed networks. Therefore, we adopt $(\alpha, \beta) = (-1/2, 1/2)$ for the new congestion control method. On these occasions, the response function is computed as follows:

$$W = \frac{a}{bp}, \tag{20}$$

$$T = \frac{Size_{pac}}{RTT} \frac{a}{bp}. \tag{21}$$

5.2   Resolution of a and b

The congestion control of $(\alpha, \beta) = (-1/2, 1/2)$ increases the congestion window by $aw^{\frac{1}{2}}$ per RTT and decreases it by $bw^{\frac{1}{2}}$ for each loss event. From equation (21), the average throughput is inversely proportional to RTT. In order for throughput to be independent of RTT, $b/a \propto RTT$ is required.

When the window increase is set proportional to RTT, the window increase and decrease become same value, independent of flow's RTT. Thus $a = a'RTT$ seems to be desirable.

The values of a' and b are specified from the following factors. (1) $b = 15$ is needed for window decrease to be more than $0.05W$ for 10 Gbps data transfer. (2) In order to control at the same performance as HighSpeed TCP at 10 Gbps link, $p = 10^{-7}$ is desirable when $W = 83000$. From equation (20), we set $b/a' = 12$. Then the recovery time will be $12[sec]$ and $a' = 1.25$ is specified. When $a' = 1.25$, the window increase per 1 RTT is 36 packets for 10 Gbps data transfer, which is not a too large window increase. Thus, the window increase and decrease in SRF TCP is set as follows:

$$\text{Increase: } W = W + 1.25RTTW^{-\frac{1}{2}}, \tag{22}$$

$$\text{Decrease: } W = W - 15W^{\frac{1}{2}}. \tag{23}$$

And SRF TCP response function is computed as follows:

$$W_{srf} = \frac{0.0833RTT}{p}, \tag{24}$$

$$T_{srf} = \frac{0.0833Size_{pac}}{p}. \tag{25}$$

In equation (25), T_{srf} is independent of RTT and SRF TCP shares fair bandwidth between flows with different RTTs.

From equation (4) and (25), the proportion of throughput between TCP Reno and SRF TCP is computed as follows:

$$\frac{T_{srf}}{T_{reno}} = \frac{0.00694}{p^{0.5}}, \tag{26}$$

where $RTT = 100ms$ is set. For packet drop rates of 10^{-6}, the proportion of throughput is 7.0. The fairness of SRF TCP with TCP Reno is improved in comparison to that of HighSpeedTCP or Scalable TCP.

5.3   Comparison to TCP Reno

SRF TCP is set to perform better than TCP Reno. When $W \leq \frac{0.64}{RTT^2}$, the window increase of SRF TCP ($1.25RTTW^{-\frac{1}{2}}$) is less than $1/W$, which is the window increase of TCP Reno. When $W \leq 900$, the window decrease of SRF TCP ($15W^{\frac{1}{2}}$) is more than $0.5W$, which is the window decrease of TCP Reno. On these occasions, SRF TCP performs worse than TCP Reno. Therefore, the window increase and decrease of SRF TCP are set to the same value as TCP Reno.

When $\frac{0.64}{RTT^2} \leq W \leq 900$, SRF TCP increases the congestion window by $1.25RTTW^{-\frac{1}{2}}$ for every received ACK and decreases it by $0.5W$ for each loss event. SRF TCP response function is computed as follows:

$$W_{srf} = \frac{1.67RTT^{0.667}}{p^{0.667}}, \tag{27}$$

$$T_{srf} = \frac{Size_{pac}}{RTT^{0.333}} \frac{1.67}{p^{0.667}}. \tag{28}$$

When $\frac{0.64}{RTT^2} \leq W \leq 900$, the proportion of throughput between TCP Reno and SRF TCP is computed as follows:

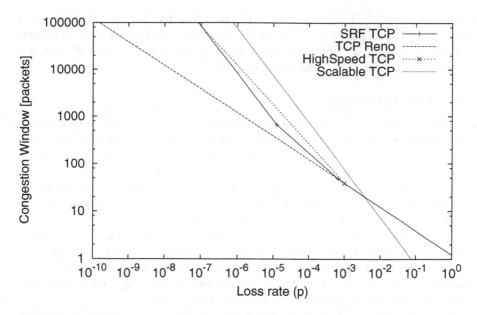

Fig. 2. The relation between p and W of SRF TCP

$$\frac{T_{srf}}{T_{reno}} = \frac{0.438}{p^{0.166}},\tag{29}$$

where $RTT = 100ms$ is set.

We name the congestion control method in equation (30) and (31) as SRF TCP.

$$\text{Increase: } W = W + max(1.25RTTW^{-\frac{1}{2}}, \frac{1}{W}),\tag{30}$$

$$\text{Decease: } W = W - min(15W^{\frac{1}{2}}, \frac{1}{2}W).\tag{31}$$

5.4   Comparison to HighSpeed TCP and Scalable TCP

Figure 2 shows the relation between p and the congestion window of SRF TCP. From the figure, at every p, the window difference between TCP Reno and SRF TCP is smaller than the window difference between TCP Reno and the other TCPs. Therefore, SRF TCP is considered to improve fairness with TCP Reno.

Additionally, the congestion window of SRF TCP is close to that of High-Speed TCP to make efficient use of link bandwidth at smaller p.

6   Evaluation

We evaluate the proposed SRF TCP through computer simulations in comparison to TCP Reno, HighSpeed TCP and Scalable TCP with Network Simulator version 2 (ns-2) [15]. The simulation topology is shown in Figure 3. In this model, the link bottleneck bandwidth, the round trip propagation delay and the number of TCP connections are changed. All simulations were run long enough to ensure the system has reached a consistent behavior.

6.1   Link Utilization

Figures 4 and 5 show the link utilization when a varying number of flows are transmitted in 100 Mbps and 1 Gbps bottleneck link, respectively. The round trip propagation delay is 100 ms. From figure 4, SRF TCP utilizes the link bandwidth more efficiently than TCP Reno and less efficiently than HighSpeed TCP and Scalable TCP in 100 Mbps when only one flow is transmitted. As the number of flows increases, the difference between SRF TCP and HighSpeed TCP gets small, while Scalable TCP utilizes bandwidth efficiently.

As shown in figure 5, SRF TCP utilizes the link bandwidth as efficiently as HighSpeed TCP and more than TCP Reno, regardless of the number of flows. On the other hand, Scalable TCP cannot utilize link bandwidth at the smaller number of flows, because Scalable TCP increases much congestion window at a time and leads much packet loss and longer recovery time.

Figure 6 shows the link utilization when one flow is transmitted as the bottleneck bandwidth increases. Shown in figure 6, SRF TCP makes efficient use of the link bandwidth at wider bandwidth. In figure 2, SRF TCP gets close to HighSpeed with larger congestion window, and at this simulation, the performance of SRF TCP is almost the same as that of HighSpeed TCP. At narrower

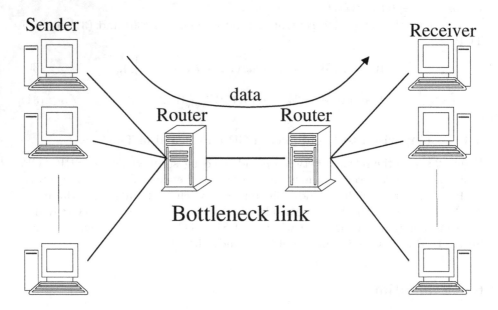

Fig. 3. Simulation model

bandwidth, SRF TCP utilizes as much bandwidth as TCP Reno in order to retain TCP compatibility.

Therefore, SRF TCP utilizes the link bandwidth at wider bandwidth and retains TCP compatibility at narrower bandwidth. The high performance is observed notably at the smaller number of flows.

6.2   Fairness with TCP Reno

Figure 7 shows fairness when one TCP Reno flow and one SRF TCP, HighSpeed TCP or Scalable TCP flow are transmitted together as the bottleneck bandwidth

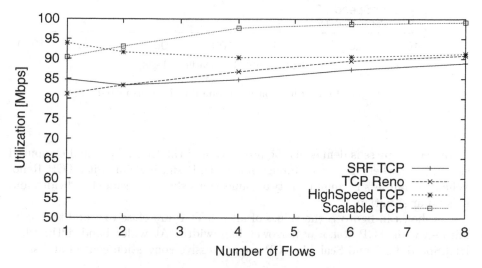

Fig. 4. Link utilization of 100 Mbps bottleneck link

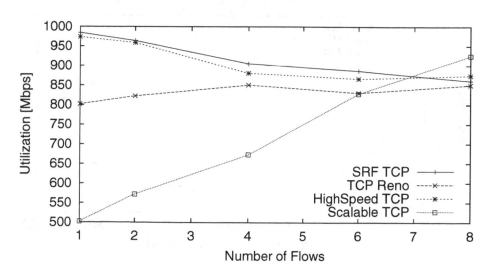

Fig. 5. Link utilization of 1 Gbps bottleneck link

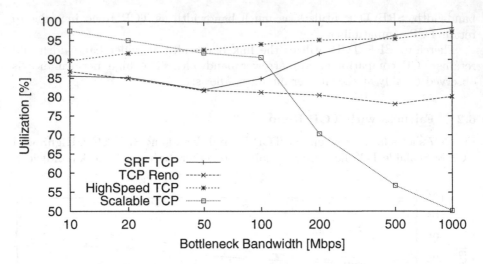

Fig. 6. Link utilization when one flow is transmitted

increases. Fairness is defined as the proportion of the throughput and computed as T/T_{reno}, where T is the throughput of TCP sharing link with TCP Reno. When the fairness is equal to 1, two connections share the same bandwidth and it is a fair situation.

As shown in figure 7, the values of all the TCP are close to 1 and they keep fairness with TCP Reno at narrower bandwidth. At wider bandwidth, while HighSpeed TCP and Scalable TCP are aggressive congestion control and share

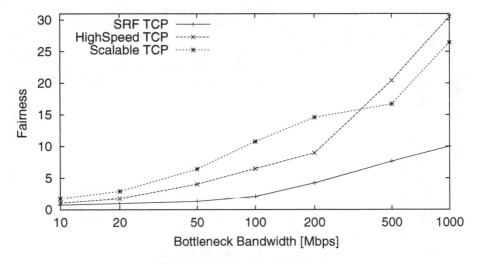

Fig. 7. Fairness with TCP Reno

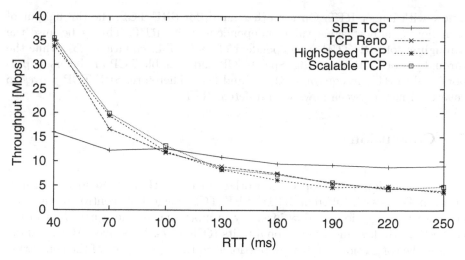

Fig. 8. Each throughput of flows with different RTTs in 100 Mbps

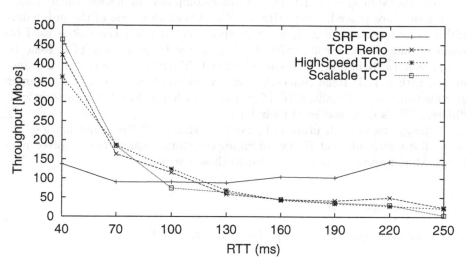

Fig. 9. Each throughput of flows with different RTTs in 1 Gbps

unfair bandwidth with TCP Reno, SRF TCP improves fairness with TCP Reno. From these results, SRF TCP proves to ensure compatibility with TCP Reno.

6.3   Fairness Between Flows with Different RTTs

Figures 8 and 9 show the throughput of 8 flows with different RTTs in 100 Mbps and 1 Gbps bottleneck bandwidth, respectively. RTTs of the flow #1 to #8 are 40, 70, 100, 130, 160, 190, 220 and 250 ms, respectively.

From these figures, the throughput of TCP Reno, HighSpeed TCP and Scalable TCP are dispersed; a flow with shorter RTT gets more bandwidth than a flow with longer RTT. On the other hand, for SRF TCP, the throughput of each flow is almost same value independent of its RTT. This is because the throughput of SRF TCP is independent of its RTT in equation (25), while the throughput of TCP Reno, HighSpeed TCP and Scalable TCP are inversely proportional to RTT in equation (4), (9) and (14). Therefore, SRF TCP proves to ensure fairness between flows with different RTTs.

7   Conclusion

In this paper, we proposed Square Root Fair TCP (SRF TCP) to realize efficient data transmission in high-speed networks, fairness with TCP Reno and fairness between flows with different RTTs. SRF TCP congestion control method increases the congestion window inversely proportional to the square root of the congestion window and proportional to its RTT for each received ACK, and decreases the congestion window proportional to the square root of the congestion window for each loss event.

From the evaluation of SRF TCP through computer simulation, the following three points are proved. First, SRF TCP makes efficient use of the link bandwidth at wider bandwidth. It is obviously observed when the link is used by smaller connections. Second, SRF TCP improves fairness with TCP Reno in comparison to HighSpeed TCP and Scalable TCP when the connection is transmitted with a TCP Reno connection. Effectiveness of improvement gets larger at wide bandwidth. Finally, SRF TCP shares fair bandwidth between flows with different RTTs independent of their RTTs.

Although bandwidth utilization, fairness with TCP Reno and fairness between flows with different RTTs are improved, all the issues are not solved perfectly. More improvements are needed to these issues.

Acknowledgement

This work was supported by a special grant from COE.

References

1. S. Floyd, "HighSpeed TCP for Large Congestion Windows", Internet Draft draft-floyd-tcp-highspeed-02.txt, February 2003.
2. Tom Kelly, "Scalable TCP: Improving Performance in HighSpeed Wide Area Networks", December 2002. http://www-lce.eng.cam.ac.uk/ ctk21/scalable/.
3. T. J. Ott, T. V. Lakshman, and L. H. Wong, "SRED: Stabilized RED," in Proceedings of the IEEE INFOCOM '99, March 1999.
4. M. Christiansen, K. Jeffay, D. Ott, and F. D. Smith, "Tuning RED for web traffic," in Proceedings of the ACM SIGCOMM 2000, August 2000.
5. I. Stoica, S. Shenker, and H. Zhang. "Core-stateless fair queuing: A scalable architecture to approximate fair bandwidth allocations in high speed networks," In Proc. of ACM SIGCOMM '98, August 1998.

6. D. Katabi, M. Handley and C. Rohrs. "Congestion Control for High Bandwidth-Delay Product Networks," ACM SIGCOMM 2002, August 2002.
7. Mark Handley, Jitendra Padhye, Sally Floyd, and Joerg Widmer, "TCP Friendly Rate Control (TFRC): Protocol Specification," RFC 3448, January 2003.
8. D. Bansal and H. Balakrishnan, "Binomial Congestion Control Algorithms," In Proceedings of IEEE INFOCOM 2001, April 2001.
9. Y. Richard Yang and Simon S. Lam, "General AIMD congestion control," in Proceedings of ICNP, November 2000.
10. S. Floyd, M. Handley, J. Padhye, and J. Widmer. "Equation-based congestion control for unicast applications," in Proceedings of the ACM SIGCOMM 2000, August 2000.
11. J. Padhye, V. Firoiu, D. Towsley and J. Krusoe, "Modeling TCP Throughput: A Simple Model and its Empirical Validation," ACM SIGCOMM '98, P303–314, 1998.
12. Fang, W. and Peterson, L.: TCP mechanisms for Diff-Serv Architecture, *Princeton University, CS Dept., Technical Report TR-605-99* (1999).
13. T. Hamann, J. Walrand, "A New Fair Window for ECN Capable TCP (New-ECN)," in Proceedings of IEEE INFOCOM 2000, March 2000.
14. T. J. Ott, "ECN protocols and the TCP paradigm," in Proceedings' of IEEE INFOCOM 2000, March 2000.
15. The network simulator ver.2 - ns-2. http://www.isi.edu/nsnam/ns/

Embedded Systems
- Challenges and Work Directions

Joseph Sifakis

Verimag and ARTIST2 European Network of Excellence

Abstract. Embedded Systems are components integrating software and hardware jointly and specifically designed to provide given functionalities. These components may be used in many different types of applications, including transport (avionics, space, automotive, trains), electrical and electronic appliances (cameras, toys, television, washers, dryers, audio systems, cellular phones), power distribution, factory automation systems, etc.

Their extensive use and integration in everyday products marks a significant evolution in information science and technology. A main trend is the proliferation of embedded systems, that should work in seamless interaction while respecting real-world constraints.

Embedded systems have a number of specific characteristics, which play a role in structuring the technical domain including criticality, reactivity and autonomy.

The coming generations of embedded systems - primarily used in mass-market products - need development methods and tools allowing to jointly consider functionality, quality, physical implementation, and market constraints: The need to jointly consider functional and extra-functional constraints leads to a system-centric approach to development. Here, the main focus is the end result: a system as the combination of hardware and software, in interaction with its physical environment.

Current methods and tools do not allow system-centric approaches. These approaches raise difficult, fundamental research problems, which are the basis of an emerging theory that should bring together information and physical sciences. Information sciences consider models of computation based on abstract notions of machines (e.g., automata, complexity and computability theory, algorithms, etc.), that do not take into account physical properties of computation (e.g., execution times, delays, latency, etc.). There is no unified theory allowing to predict the behavior of an application software on a given execution platform which determines execution speed and other dynamic properties of the application.

System-centric approaches raise two grand challenges common to all the activities of system development. The first is theory and tools for rigorous component-based engineering. This determines our ability to build complex systems from simpler ones by mastering their complexity. The second is intelligence, a long term vision for systems that are able to analyze and adapt their behavior according to changes of their environment.

T. Higashino (Ed.): OPODIS 2004, LNCS 3544, pp. 184–185, 2005.

We discuss specific work directions in system development activities to meet these challenges, including modeling, programming and compilation, operating systems design, controller synthesis, testing and verification.

Reference

1. ARTIST: "Selected Topics in Embedded Systems Design: Roadmaps for Research", http://www.artist-embedded.org/Roadmaps/

Comparison of Failures and Attacks on Random and Scale-Free Networks

Jean-Loup Guillaume[1], Matthieu Latapy[1], and Clémence Magnien[2]

[1] LIAFA – CNRS – Université Paris 7 – 2 place Jussieu,
75251 Paris Cedex 05, France
Fax : 33 (0)1 44 27 68 49
{guillaume, latapy}@liafa.jussieu.fr
[2] CREA – CNRS – École Polytechnique – 1, rue Descartes,
75005 Paris, France
Fax : 33 (0)1 55 55 90 40
magnien@shs.polytechnique.fr

Abstract. It appeared recently that some statistical properties of complex networks like the Internet, the World Wide Web or Peer-to-Peer systems have an important influence on their resilience to failures and attacks. In particular, scale-free networks (*i.e.* networks with power-law degree distribution) seem much more robust than random networks in case of failures, while they are more sensitive to attacks.

In this paper we deepen the study of the differences in the behavior of these two kinds of networks when facing failures or attacks. We moderate the general affirmation that scale-free networks are much more sensitive than random networks to attacks by showing that the number of links to remove in both cases is similar, and by showing that a slightly modified scenario for failures gives results similar to the ones for attacks. We also propose and analyze an efficient attack strategy against links.

Keywords: Internet, Complex Networks, Random Graphs, Scale-Free Graphs, Resilience, Fault tolerence, Reliability, Network Topology.

Introduction

In a random network [1, 2] with n nodes, each of the $\frac{n \cdot (n-1)}{2}$ possible links exists with a given probability p. In other words, a random network is constructed from n nodes by choosing $m = p \cdot \frac{n \cdot (n-1)}{2}$ links at random. In such a network, the degree distribution p_k follows a Poisson law: $p_k = e^{-z} \frac{z^k}{k!}$ where z is the average degree. Intuitively, such a distribution means that most nodes have a degree close to the average, and that the number of nodes with a given degree decays exponentially fast away from the mean degree.

However, it has been shown recently that most real-world complex networks [3, 4, 5, 6, 7, 8, 9], in particular the Internet [10], the World Wide Web [7, 11] and Peer-to-Peer systems [12], have a power-law degree distribution: $p_k \sim k^{-\alpha}$. In

T. Higashino (Ed.): OPODIS 2004, LNCS 3544, pp. 186–196, 2005.

the cases we have cited, α is close to 2.5. Intuitively, such a distribution means that, despite most nodes have a low degree, the number of nodes with (very) high degree is not negligible.

Since this difference between random networks and real-world complex networks has been discovered, a strong effort has been put on the understanding of its consequences. One of the most famous is that it significantly influences the robustness of networks [7, 13, 14, 15, 16, 17], which can be observed as follows. Given a network, one can model a series of failures by a random removal of nodes (or links), whereas an attack is modeled by the targeted removal of a series of chosen nodes (or links). The way the nodes (or links) are chosen during an attack is called an *attack strategy*. The quality of the service provided by the network under consideration can be roughly evaluated by the size of its largest connected component (*i.e.* the number of machines which can communicate in the Internet, for instance). The resilience of the network to failures or attacks can then be analyzed by studying how the size of the largest connected component varies as a function of the number of removed nodes (or links). In particular, the network is said to have a *giant connected component* if it has a component of size linear with respect to the size of the network. In other words, a constant proportion (with respect to the network size) of the whole network is connected. Other criteria for measuring network efficiency have been proposed, see for instance [16, 17, 18, 19].

The most widely studied attack strategy has been introduced independently in [7] and [13]. It consists in removing nodes by decreasing order of their degree. We will refer to this attack as the *classical* attack strategy. The effects of this attack strategy are plotted in Figure 1, together with the effect of failures.

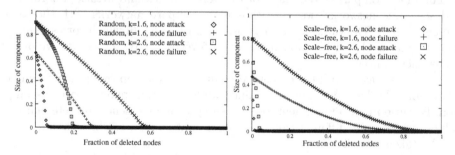

Fig. 1. Effects of random failures and attacks on random networks (left) and scale-free networks (right). The plots represent the size of the largest connected component as a function of the fraction of removed nodes. Different values of the mean degree k are considered

From these experiments the following observations can be derived [7, 13]. First, there is a qualitative difference in the behavior of random and scale-free networks in case of failures: for random networks, the size of the largest connected component drops to zero when a finite fraction of the nodes are removed (this fraction represents a *threshold value*), whereas for scale-free networks, it decreases very slowly, and reaches 0 only when most nodes have been removed. Thus scale-free networks appear to be much more resilient to failures than random networks. However, the opposite seems true for attacks: scale-free networks collapse much more quickly than random networks. The power-law distribution of degrees in the Internet, which might therefore make it very resilient to failures but extremely sensitive to attacks, has even been called the *Achilles's heel of the Internet* [20].

Although attacks remove a very large fraction of the links, we show in Section 1 that this is not sufficient to explain the qualitative difference between failures and attacks for scale-free networks. We then investigate further this difference (Section 2) by proposing two new attack strategies, one against nodes and the other against links, and comparing their effects with those of the classical attacks and failures.

Before entering in the core of the paper, let us say a word on our plots. The plots for experimental results obtained by simulation are the average of simulations over a large number of samples. This is in general representative of the mean behavior, but it must be noted that the actual simulation result obtained on one instance may be significantly different in some cases (in particular in what concerns threshold values for scale-free networks).

Concerning the thresholds values, we considered that the threshold was reached whenever the size of the largest connected component of the network becomes smaller than 5% of the whole. The plots representing the thresholds are in function of the mean degree for random networks, and the degree exponent for scale-free networks, which are the main parameters in these contexts. A scale-free network is connected if $\alpha \leq 3.48$, therefore we will not be interested in the case where α is greater than this value.

For plots comparing the effect of different failures and attacks for random and scale-free networks, we have chosen to compare networks with the same average degree. The values we have chosen are 1.6 and 2.6, which corresponds to scale-free networks with exponents 3 and 2.5 respectively, representative of the values met in practice.

In several cases, we plot numerical evaluations for approximation formulæ. These formulæ have often been obtained under the continuous degree assumption. Because in our experimentations the degree is by essence discrete, empiric values may be quite different from the approximation values, which should therefore be taken as indicative.

All scale-free networks have been generated using the algorithm for obtaining networks with a prescribed degree distribution described in [21]. We have generated scale-free networks with N nodes and exponent α by drawing N degrees between 1 and N, following a power-law with exponent α. Then pairs of stubs are randomly connected. Some proofs in the following use the fact that links are pairs of randomly chosen stubs.

We also need to introduce a few notations: $\zeta(\alpha)$ is the Riemann ζ function, defined by $\zeta(\alpha) = \sum_{k=1}^{\infty} k^{-\alpha}$. the K-th harmonic number, denoted by $H_K^{(\alpha)}$, is equal to $H_K^{(\alpha)} = \sum_{k=0}^{K} k^{-\alpha}$. Finally, given a degree distribution p_k, we denote by $\langle k \rangle$ and $\langle k^2 \rangle$ the mean of the degree and the square degree respectively: $\langle k \rangle = \sum_{k=0}^{\infty} k p_k$ and $\langle k^2 \rangle = \sum_{k=0}^{\infty} k^2 p_k$.

1   The Links Point of View

The classical attack strategy removes high-degree nodes first. Since in a scale-free network there is a high heterogeneity between nodes, highest degree nodes have a very large number of links attached to them. Therefore, one may wonder if the efficiency of attacks on these networks is a consequence of the fact that the number of *links* removed is much larger than in the case of failures. Likewise, one may wonder if the fact that the attack results in the removal of much more links in a scale-free network than in a random one is the cause of the difference between the two. These explanations actually have been proposed by some authors to give an intuitive explanation of the results presented above.

The aim of this section is to evaluate these ideas by the study of classical attacks under the links point of view. Indeed, the classical attack strategy can be viewed as a strategy targeting links, where links adjacent to high degree nodes are removed first. Then, the size of the giant component can be plotted as a function of the number of removed links, see Figure 2. In this figure, the behavior of these networks under random link removal, *i.e. link* failure, is also plotted as a comparison.

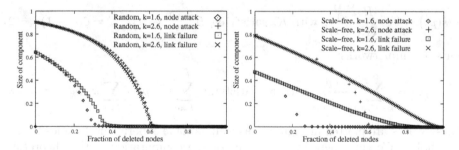

Fig. 2. The effects of the classical node attack when considering links, and of link failure, for random networks (left) and scale-free networks (right)

At first glance, this link attack strategy seems much more efficient than random removal. This can be confirmed formally with the same kind of arguments that have been developed in [14, 15]. From this, one obtains that the threshold m_c of links that have to be randomly removed to break the network is:

$$m_c = 1 - \frac{\langle k \rangle}{\langle k^2 \rangle - \langle k \rangle}$$

This result can be obtained by the following reasoning: when links are removed, this changes the degree distribution of the network. The new degree distribution can be explicitely computed. Since links are removed at random, the network is a random network with the new degree distribution. There exists a criterion [21] for deciding if such a network has a giant component or not, and the above formula is obtained from the application of this criterion to the new degree distribution of the network.

It turns out that this quantity is the same as the threshold p_c for *nodes* failure [14, 22]. This means in particular that link failures do not make scale-free networks collapse. Therefore, the fact that a scale-free network collapses using the classical attack means that the efficiency of this attack strategy is *not* due to the fact that it removes many links. If the same number of links are removed randomly, then the network does not collapse.

Let us now try to evaluate precisely the efficiency of this link attack. The fraction m_c of links that must be removed to break the network can be computed in the same manner as what has been done in [14, 22] for the number of nodes. For any network, the fraction $m(p_c)$ of links removed in an attack is equal to $s(p_c)^2 + 2s(p_c)(1 - s(p_c))$, where $s(p_c)$ represents the number of stubs (links' endpoints) attached to the removed nodes. $s(p_c)$ can be evaluated by the following equations [15, 14].

For scale-free networks:

$$s(p_c) - 2 = \frac{2 - \alpha}{3 - \alpha} \left(s(p_c)^{(3-\alpha)/(2-\alpha)} - 1 \right), \tag{1}$$

or

$$s(p_c) = 1 - \frac{H_{K_c-1}^{(\alpha-1)}}{\zeta(\alpha - 1)}, \text{ with } K_c \text{ satisfying } H_{K_c}^{(\alpha-2)} - H_{K_c}^{(\alpha-1)} = \zeta(\alpha - 1). \tag{2}$$

For random networks:

$$s(p_c) = \sum_{k=K_c+1}^{\infty} \frac{k \cdot p_k}{z}, \text{ with } K_c \text{ satisfying } \sum_{k=0}^{K_c} k^2 \cdot p_k - \sum_{k=0}^{K_c} k \cdot p_k = z \tag{3}$$

These values are plotted in Figure 3, as well as some experimental values for the thresholds. We enter here in the details of the computation of the theoretical value of the threshold for random networks, obtained by solving Equation 3. Solving this equation gives the value of $K(p)$, the maximal degree in the network after the attack, in function of the mean degree z of the network. By definition, $K(p)$ can only take integer values. But since, in random networks, the degrees of the nodes are all gathered in a small set of values around n, it is not always possible to obtain values of $K(p)$ that statisfy exactly the equation. We have chosen the points obtained at the values of z that yield the least error, the other values of z forbidding any accurate computation of the theoretical threshold. It is nonetheless interesting to observe that the experimental values for the threshold follow the curve that is suggested by these few theoretical dots.

We can now conclude precisely on the efficiency of the classical attack strategy. First, althoug the number of links removed during such an attack on scale-free networks is huge, it is not sufficient to explain the collapse of the network:

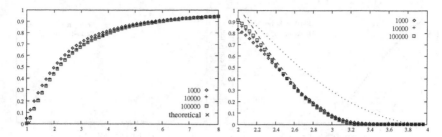

Fig. 3. Experimental values of the critical fraction $m(p_c)$ of links that must be removed in a classical node attack to disconnect random networks as a function of the mean degree (left), and scale-free networks as a function of the degree exponent (right). We have represented theoretical and experimental values. For scale-free networks, the values obtained from Equation 1 (dotted line) and from Equation 2 (dashed line) are plotted

if the same number of links is randomly removed, then the network does not collapse. However, the number of removed links during a classical attack of a random network and of a scale-free network are very similar, for the values of the mean degree we are interested in. This moderates the conclusion that scale-free networks are particularly sensitive to classical attacks: in terms of links, they are as robust as random networks.

2   New Attack Strategies

In [21] a criterion for a network to almost surely have a giant component is given:

$$\langle k^2 \rangle - 2\langle k \rangle > 0 \iff p_1 < \sum_{k=3}^{\infty} k(k-2)p_k$$

The key point is therefore the proportion of nodes of degree 1 in the network. Therefore, it seems that any strategy aiming at increasing this proportion should quickly break the network. Using this remark, we propose two new attack strategies (one against nodes and the other against links) which give more insight on the actual efficiency of classical attacks.

2.1   Almost-Failures Attack

Our first attack strategy simply consists in randomly removing nodes of degree at least 2. This decreases the number of nodes of degree higher than 1 and increases the number of nodes of degree 0 or 1. The effect of this attack is shown in Figure 4.

Notice that this attack is barely different from node failure, and yet it is much more efficient. It actually is qualitatively different from failures, since it displays a threshold.

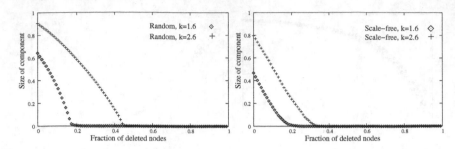

Fig. 4. The effect of the new node attack strategy on random networks (left) and scale-free networks (right)

We can easily prove this by providing an upper bound for this threshold: when all nodes that had initially a degree higher that one have been removed, then the network surely does not have a giant component anymore, since all nodes have degree at most 1. Therefore the giant component is destroyed when a fraction $1 - p_1 - p_0$ of the nodes has been removed.

For scale-free networks with exponent α, this quantity is equal to $1 - 1/\zeta(\alpha)$. For random networks with mean degree z, it is equal to $1 - e^{-z}(z+1)$. The plots for these quantities are shown in Figure 5, together with experimental values.

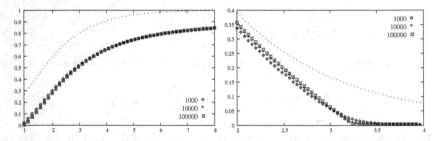

Fig. 5. The plots for the upper bound for the new node attack strategy (lines), and for experimental values of the threshold for networks of size 10^3, 10^4 and 10^5, for random networks (left) and scale-free networks (right). The lines represent the theoretical upper bound

Notice that the values of the threshold are quite large (one has to remove a large fraction of the nodes do destroy the network). Our aim here, though, is not to obtain an efficient attack strategy, but to show that the qualitative difference between the classical attack strategy and node failures on scale-free networks relies on the fact that, in an attack, no nodes of degree 1 are removed: if nodes of degree higher than 1 are randomly removed, then the same qualitative behavior is recovered.

2.2   Efficient Link Attack

We have seen in Section 1 that, although the classical attack displays a threshold when considered from the links point of view, it is not efficient in this regard. Still based on the fact that increasing the proportion of nodes of degree 1 collapses the network, we now propose the following attack strategy on links: we remove at random links between nodes of degree at least 2. The effect of this attack is shown in Figure 6.

As expected, this attack strategy displays a threshold m_c. Again, we can show this by providing an upper bound as follows.

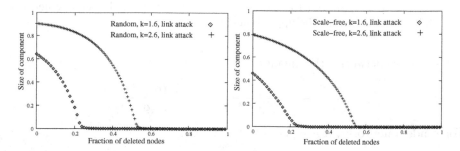

Fig. 6. The effect of the new link attack strategy on random networks (left) and scale-free networks (right)

When all the links between nodes of degree at least 2 have been removed, the network is decomposed in a set of disjoint stars (each central node is connected to nodes of degree 1). Since the maximal degree of a node in a finite scale-free network with N nodes can be evaluated as $N^{\frac{1}{\alpha-1}}$ [22], the size of the largest connected component (*i.e.* the largest star) is sublinear with respect to N whenever $\alpha > 2$.

An upper bound for m_c is therefore given by the fraction of links between nodes of degree at least 2. This quantity is 1 minus the fraction of links incident to at least one node of degree 1. The number of such links is given by the number of nodes of degree 1, minus the number of links between two nodes of degree 1.

This last number can be computed as follows. There are Np_1 nodes of degree 1, each of them having a probability $Np_1/2|E|$ of being connected to another node of degree 1[1] ($|E| = N\langle k\rangle/2$ denotes the number of links in the network). Therefore the number of *nodes* of degree 1 adjacent to another node of degree 1 is $N^2 p_1^2/2|E| = Np_1^2/\langle k\rangle$ on average. Finally, the number of links between two such nodes is therefore $Np_1^2/2\langle k\rangle$.

From this we have that the number of links adjacent to at least one node of degree 1 is: $Np_1 - Np_1^2/2\langle k\rangle$, and the number of links *not* adjacent to any node of degree 1 is: $|E| - Np_1 + Np_1^2/2\langle k\rangle$. The fraction of such links therefore is:

$$1 - \frac{2p_1}{\langle k\rangle} + \frac{p_1^2}{\langle k\rangle^2}.$$

---

[1] This is accurate in the limit of large N.

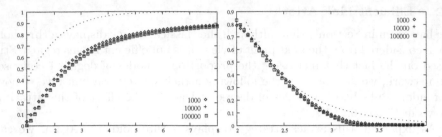

Fig. 7. Experimental values for the threshold for the new link attack strategy, for networks of size 10^3, 10^4 and 10^5, for random networks (left) and scale-free networks (right). The lines represent the upper bounds

For scale-free networks, this quantity is equal to:

$$1 - \frac{2}{\zeta(\alpha - 1)} + \frac{1}{\zeta^2(\alpha - 1)} = 1 - \frac{2\zeta(\alpha - 1) - 1}{\zeta^2(\alpha - 1)}.$$

For random networks, it is equal to:

$$1 - 2e^{-z} + e^{-2z}.$$

This upper bound can be evaluated numerically. The result of this evaluation is shown in Figure 7, together with experimental values.

If we compare these results to the ones obtained in Section 1, then we can observe that our attack strategy is more efficient than the classical one, viewed from the links point of view. This is not surprising since in the classical attack strategy one may remove many links attached to nodes of degree 1, which does not help in destroying the network. Our strategy, on the opposite, focuses on those links which really disconnect the network.

3   Conclusion and Discussion

In this contribution, we provided a detailed comparison of the impact of failures and classical attacks on random and scale-free networks. Our aim was to give a more precise insight on the actual efficiency of attacks on scale-free compared to random networks, and compared to failures.

To achieve this, we investigated the often claimed affirmation that the efficiency of attacks on scale-free networks is due to the large number of links they remove. We show that removing the same number of links at random has much less impact, contradicting this affirmation. However, when the number of removed links is considered, scale-free networks are not more fragile than random ones. Finally, we used a classical criterion for network connectivity to design two new attack strategies. The first one is very close to a series of failures but behaves qualitatively like classical attacks (there is a threshold for scale-free networks). This tends to show that the presence of a threshold for classical attacks is not due to a high efficiency, but rather to the fact that they do not remove nodes of degree 1. The second strategy we propose, based on links removal, shows that one can design attack strategies more efficient than the classical one, with respect to the fraction of removed links.

These results lead us to the conclusion that, despite failures and classical attacks clearly behave differently and although the random or scale-free nature of the network strongly influences this, one should be careful in driving conclusions from this. The sensitivity of scale-free networks to attacks relies on the fact that they have many low-degree nodes. Their robustness relies on the fact that when we choose a node at random, we choose such a node with high probability. Moreover, the fact that a classical attack on a scale-free network removes many links may be considered as partly but not fully responsible for its rapid breakdown.

This work may be pursued in many directions. First, the accuracy of the evaluation of the various thresholds should be improved. Likewise, the impact of the finite size of real-world network is in general not understood and should be studied. Moreover, other properties of real-world complex networks, like clustering or degree correlations, should be taken into account. From a more general point of view, the impact of failures and attacks on the actual networks of interest, like the Internet, the World Wide Web and Peer-to-Peer systems, but also biological or social networks, should be deepened. It is likely that these networks have some hidden properties which render them very resilient to failures, and maybe sensitive to certain attack strategies.

Acknowledgments. This work was partly funded by the *Metrosec : Metrology for Security and Quality of Service* project. (`http://www.laas.fr/~owe/METROSEC/`) We warmly thank Alessandro Vespignani for useful comments and discussions.

References

1. B. Bollobás. *Random Graphs.* Academic Press, 1985.
2. P. Erdös and A. Rényi. On random graphs I. *Publ. Math. Debrecen,* 6:290–297, 1959.
3. M.E.J. Newman. The structure and function of complex networks. *SIAM Review,* 45(2):167–256, 2003.
4. A.-L. Barabási, Z. Deszo, E. Ravasz, S.H. Yook, and Z. Oltvai. Scale-free and hierarchical structures in complex networks. In *Sitges Proceedings on Complex Networks,* 2004.
5. S.N. Dorogovtsev and J.F.F. Mendes. Evolution of networks. *Adv. Phys. 51, 1079-1187,* 2002.
6. S.N. Dorogovtsev and J.F.F. Mendes. *Evolution of Networks: From Biological Nets tou the Internet and WWW.* Oxford University Press, 2000.
7. A.Z. Broder, S.R. Kumar, F. Maghoul, P. Raghavan, S. Rajagopalan, R. Stata, A. Tomkins, and J.L. Wiener. Graph structure in the web. *WWW9 / Computer Networks,* 33(1-6):309–320, 2000.
8. A.Z. Broder, R. Kumar, F. Maghoul, P. Raghavan, S. Rajagopalan, R. Stata, A. Tomkins, and J.L. Wiener. Graph structure in the web. In *Proceedings of*

the 9th international World Wide Web conference on Computer networks : the international journal of computer and telecommunications netowrking, pages 309–320. North-Holland Publishing Co., 2000.

9. M.E.J. Newman. Random graphs as models of networks. In Stefan Bornholdt and Heinz Georg Schuster, editors, Hankbook of Graphs and Networks: From the Genome to the Internet. Wiley-vch, 2003.

10. M. Faloutsos, P. Faloutsos, and C. Faloutsos. On power-law relationships of the internet topology. In SIGCOMM, pages 251–262, 1999.

11. L. Adamic and B. Huberman. Power-law distribution of the world wide web. Science, 287, 2000.

12. M. Ripeanu, I. Foster, and A. Iamnitchi. Mapping the gnutella network: Properties of large-scale peer-to-peer systems and implications for system design. IEEE Internet Computing Journal special issue on peer-to-peer networking, 6(1), 2002.

13. R. Albert, H. Jeong, and A.-L. Barabási. Error and attack tolerance in complex networks. Nature, 406:378–382, 2000.

14. D.S. Callaway, M.E.J. Newman, S.H. Strogatz, and D.J. Watts. Network robustness and fragility: Percolation on random graphs. Phys. Rev. Lett., 85:5468–5471, 2000.

15. R. Cohen, K. Erez, D. ben Avraham, and S. Havlin. Breakdown of the internet under intentional attack. Phys. Rev. Lett., 86:3682–3685, 2001.

16. S.-T. Park, A. Khrabrov, D.M. Pennock, S. Lawrence, C. Lee Giles, and L.H. Ungar. Static and dynamic analysis of the internet's susceptibility to faults and attacks. In IEEE Infocom 2003, San Francisco, CA, April 1–3 2003.

17. A. Broido and K. Claffy. Topological resilience in ip and as graphs. 2002. http://www.caida.org/analysis/topology/resilience/

18. V. Latora and M. Marchiori. Efficient behavior of small-world networks. Phys. Rev. Lett., 87, 2001.

19. P. Crucitti, V. Latora, M. Marchiori, and A. Rapisarda. Efficiency or scale-free networks: error and attack tolerance. Physica A, 320:622–642, 2003.

20. R. Pastor-Satorras and A. Vespignani. Evolution and Structure of the Internet: A Statistical Physics Approach. Cambridge University Press, 2003. To appear.

21. M. Molloy and B. Reed. A critical point for random graphs with a given degree sequence. Random Structures and Algorithms, 6:161, 1995.

22. R. Cohen, K. Erez, D. ben Avraham, and S. Havlin. Resilience of the internet to random breakdown. Phys. Rev. Lett., 85:4626, 2000.

Firewall Queries

Alex X. Liu[1], Mohamed G. Gouda[1], Huibo H. Ma[2], and Anne HH. Ngu[2]

[1] Department of Computer Sciences, The University of Texas at Austin,
Austin, Texas 78712-0233, U.S.A.
{alex, gouda}@cs.utexas.edu
[2] Department of Computer Science, Texas State University,
San Marcos, Texas 78666-4616, U.S.A.
{hm1034, angu}@txstate.edu

Abstract. Firewalls are crucial elements in network security, and have been widely deployed in most businesses and institutions for securing private networks. The function of a firewall is to examine each incoming and outgoing packet and decide whether to accept or to discard the packet based on a sequence of rules. Because a firewall may have a large number of rules and the rules often conflict, understanding and analyzing the function of a firewall have been known to be notoriously difficult. An effective way to assist humans in understanding and analyzing the function of a firewall is by issuing firewall queries. An example of a firewall query is "Which computers in the private network can receive packets from a known malicious host in the outside Internet?". Two problems need to be solved in order to make firewall queries practically useful: how to describe a firewall query and how to process a firewall query. In this paper, we first introduce a simple and effective SQL-like query language, called the Structured Firewall Query Language (SFQL), for describing firewall queries. Second, we present a theorem, called the Firewall Query Theorem, as a foundation for developing firewall query processing algorithms. Third, we present an efficient firewall query processing algorithm, which uses firewall decision trees as its core data structure. Experimental results show that our firewall query processing algorithm is very efficient: it takes less than 10 milliseconds to process a query over a firewall that has up to 10,000 rules.

Keywords: Network Security, Firewall Queries, Firewalls.

1 Introduction

Serving as the first line of defense against malicious attacks and unauthorized traffic, firewalls are crucial elements in securing the private networks of most businesses, institutions, and even home networks. A firewall is placed at the point of entry between a private network and the outside Internet so that all incoming and outgoing packets have to pass through it. A packet can be viewed as a tuple with a finite number of fields; examples of these fields are source/destination IP address, source/destination port number, and protocol type. A firewall maps

T. Higashino (Ed.): OPODIS 2004, LNCS 3544, pp. 197–212, 2005.
© Springer-Verlag Berlin Heidelberg 2005

each incoming and outgoing packet to a decision according to its configuration. A firewall configuration defines which packets are legitimate and which are illegitimate by a sequence of rules. Each rule in a firewall configuration is of the form

$$\langle predicate \rangle \rightarrow \langle decision \rangle$$

The $\langle predicate \rangle$ in a rule is a boolean expression over some packet fields and the physical network interface on which a packet arrives. For the sake of brevity, we assume that each packet has a field that contains the identification of the network interface on which a packet arrives. The $\langle decision \rangle$ of a rule can be *accept*, or *discard*, or a combination of these decisions with other options such as the logging option. For simplicity, we assume that the $\langle decision \rangle$ in a rule is either *accept* or *discard*.

A packet *matches* a rule if and only if (*iff*) the packet satisfies the predicate of the rule. The predicate of the last rule in a firewall is usually a tautology to ensure that every packet has at least one matching rule in the firewall. The rules in a firewall often conflict. Two rules in a firewall *conflict* iff they have different decisions and there is at least one packet that can match both rules. Due to conflicts among rules, a packet may match more than one rule in a firewall, and the rules that a packet matches may have different decisions. To resolve conflicts among rules, for each incoming or outgoing packet, a firewall maps it to the decision of the first (i.e., highest priority) rule that the packet matches.

The function (i.e., behavior) of a firewall is specified in its configuration, which consists of a sequence of rules. The configuration of a firewall is the most important component in achieving the security and functionality of the firewall [24]. However, most firewalls on the Internet are poorly configured, as witnessed by the success of recent worms and viruses like Blaster [6] and Sapphire [7], which could easily be blocked by a well-configured firewall [26]. It has been observed that most firewall security breaches are caused by configuration errors [5]. An error in a firewall configuration means that some illegitimate packets are identified as being legitimate, or some legitimate packets are identified as being illegitimate. This will either allow unauthorized access from the outside Internet to the private network, or disable some legitimate communication between the private network and the outside Internet. Neither case is desirable. Clearly, a firewall configuration should be well understood and analyzed before being deployed.

However, due to the large number of rules in a firewall and the large number of conflicts among rules, understanding and analyzing the function of a firewall have been known to be notoriously difficult [21]. The implication of any rule in a firewall cannot be understood without examining all the rules listed above that rule. There are other factors that contribute to the difficulties in understanding and analyzing firewalls. For example, a corporate firewall often consists of rules that are written by different administrators at different times and for different reasons. It is difficult for a new firewall administrator to understand the implication of each rule that is not written by herself.

An effective way to assist humans in understanding and analyzing firewalls is by issuing firewall queries. Firewall queries are questions concerning the function of a firewall. Examples of firewall queries are "Which computers in the outside Internet cannot send emails to the mail server in a private network?" and "Which computers in the private network can receive BOOTP[1] packets from the outside Internet?". Figuring out answers to these firewall queries is of tremendous help for a firewall administrator to understand and analyze the function of the firewall. For example, assuming the specification of a firewall requires that all computers in the outside Internet, except a known malicious host, are able to send emails to the mail server in the private network, a firewall administrator can test whether the firewall satisfies this requirement by issuing a firewall query "Which computers in the outside Internet cannot send emails to the mail server in the private network?". If the answer to this query contains exactly the known malicious host, then the firewall administrator is assured that the firewall does satisfy this requirement. Otherwise the firewall administrator knows that the firewall fails to satisfy this requirement, and she needs to reconfigure the firewall. As another example, suppose that the specification of a firewall requires that any BOOTP packet from the outside Internet is to be blocked from entering the private network. To test whether the firewall satisfies this requirement, a firewall administrator can issue a firewall query "Which computers in the private network can receive BOOTP packets from the outside Internet?". If the answer to this query is an empty set, then the firewall administrator is assured that the firewall does satisfy this requirement. Otherwise the firewall administrator knows that the firewall fails to satisfy this requirement, and she needs to reconfigure the firewall.

Firewall queries are also useful in a variety of other scenarios, such as firewall maintenance and firewall debugging. For a firewall administrator, checking whether a firewall satisfies certain conditions is part of daily maintenance activity. For example, if the administrator detects that a computer in the private network is under attack, the firewall administrator can issue queries to check which other computers in the private network are also vulnerable to the same type of attacks. In the process of designing a firewall, the designer can issue some firewall queries to detect design errors by checking whether the answers to the queries are consistent with the firewall specification.

To make firewall queries practically useful, two problems need to be solved: how to describe a firewall query and how to process a firewall query. The second problem is technically difficult. Recall that the rules in a firewall are sensitive to the rule order and the rules often conflict. The naive solution is to enumerate every packet specified by a query and check the decision for each packet. Clearly,

---

[1] The Bootp protocol is used by workstations and other devices to obtain IP addresses and other information about the network configuration of a private network. Since there is no need to offer the service outside a private network, and it may offer useful information to hackers, usually Bootp packets are blocked from entering a private network.

this solution is infeasible. For example, to process the query "Which computers in the outside Internet cannot send any packet to the private network?", this naive solution needs to enumerate 2^{88} possible packet and check the decision of the firewall for each packet, which is infeasible.

In this paper, we present solutions to both problems. First, we introduce a simple and effective SQL-like query language, called the Structured Firewall Query Language (SFQL), for describing firewall queries. This language uses queries of the form "*select...from...where...*". Second, we present a theorem, called the Firewall Query Theorem, as the foundation for developing firewall query processing algorithms. Third, we present an efficient query processing algorithm that uses firewall decision trees as its core data structure. For a given firewall of a sequence of rules, we first construct an equivalent firewall decision tree by a construction algorithm. Then the firewall decision tree is used as the core data structure of this query processing algorithm for answering each firewall query. Experimental results show that our firewall query processing algorithm is very efficient: it takes less than 10 milliseconds to process a query over a firewall that has up to 10,000 rules. Clearly, our firewall query processing algorithm is fast enough in interacting with firewall administrators.

Note that firewalls that we consider in this paper are static firewalls, not stateful firewalls in which the function of a firewall changes dynamically as packets pass by. Also note that the queries of a firewall are intended primarily for the administrator of the firewall to use. For a firewall that protects a private network, neither normal users in the private network nor the outsiders of the private network are able to query the firewall. Since the focus of this paper is firewall configurations, in the rest of this paper, we use "firewall" to mean "firewall configuration" if not otherwise specified.

2   Related Work

There is little work that has been done on firewall queries. In [21,25], a firewall analysis system that uses some specific firewall queries was presented. In [21,25], a firewall query is described by a triple (a set of source addresses, a set of destination addresses, a set of services), where each service is a tuple (protocol type, destination port number). The semantics of such a query are "which IP addresses in the set of source addresses can send which services in the set of services to which IP addresses in the set of destination addresses?". We go beyond [21,25] in the following two major aspects.

1. No algorithm for processing a firewall query over a sequence of rules was presented in [21] or [25]. Consequently, how fast and scalable that a firewall query can be processed remains unknown, while the efficiency of a firewall query processing algorithm is crucial in order to interact with a human user. In contrast, we present an efficient algorithm for processing a firewall query over a sequence of rules. Our firewall query algorithm takes less than 10 milliseconds to process a query over a firewall that has up to 10,000 rules.

2. The query language described in [21] and [25] is too specific: it is only applicable to IP packets and it only concerns the four fields of source address, destination address, protocol type and destination port number. This makes the expressive power of the query language in [21, 25] limited. For example, even only considering IP packets, it cannot express a firewall query concerning source port numbers or application fields. In contrast, our Structured Firewall Query Language is capable of expressing firewall queries with arbitrary fields.

In [18], some ad-hoc "what if" questions that are similar to firewall queries were discussed. However, no algorithm was presented for processing the proposed "what if" questions.

In [9], expert systems were proposed to analyze firewall rules. Clearly, building an expert system just for analyzing a firewall is overwrought and impractical.

Detecting potential firewall configuration errors by conflict detection was discussed in [3, 8, 17, 22]. Similar to conflict detection, six types of so-called "anomalies" were defined in [1]. Examining each conflict or anomaly is helpful in reducing potential firewall configuration errors; however, the number of conflicts or anomalies in a firewall is typically large, and the manual checking of each conflict or anomaly is unreliable because the meaning of each rule depends on the current order of the rules in the firewall, which may be incorrect.

Some firewall design methods have been proposed in [4, 16, 20, 13]. These works aim at creating firewall rules, while we aim at analyzing firewall rules.

Firewall vulnerabilities are discussed and classified in [19, 11]. However, the focus of [19, 11] are the vulnerabilities of the packet filtering software and the supporting hardware part of a firewall, not the configuration of a firewall.

There are some tools currently available for network vulnerability testing, such as Satan [10, 12] and Nessus [23]. These vulnerability testing tools scan a private network based on the current publicly known attacks, rather than the requirement specification of a firewall. Although these tools can possibly catch errors that allow illegitimate access to the private network, it cannot find the errors that disable legitimate communication between the private network and the outside Internet.

3   Structured Firewall Query Language

3.1   Firewalls

In this section, we present the actual syntax of the firewall query language and show how to use this language to describe firewall queries.

We first define a *packet* over the fields $F_1, \cdots, F_d$ as a d-tuple $(p_1, \cdots, p_d)$ where each p_i is in the domain $D(F_i)$ of field F_i, and each $D(F_i)$ is an interval of nonnegative integers. For example, the domain of the source address in an IP packet is $[0, 2^{32})$. For the brevity of presentation, we assume that all packets are over the d fields $F_1, \cdots, F_d$, if not otherwise specified. We use Σ to denote the set of all packets. It follows that Σ is a finite set and $|\Sigma| = |D(F_1)| \times \cdots \times |D(F_n)|$.

Given a firewall f, each packet p in Σ is mapped by f to a decision, denoted $f.p$, in the set $\{accept, discard\}$. Two firewalls f and f' are equivalent, denoted $f \equiv f'$, iff for any packet p in Σ, $f.p = f'.p$ holds. This equivalence relation is symmetric, self-reflective, and transitive.

A firewall consists of a sequence of rules. Each rule is of the following format:

$$(F_1 \in S_1) \wedge \cdots \wedge (F_d \in S_d) \rightarrow \langle decision \rangle$$

where each S_i is a nonempty subset of $D(F_i)$, and the $\langle decision \rangle$ is either $accept$ or $discard$. If $S_i = D(F_i)$, we can replace $(F_i \in S_i)$ by $(F_i \in all)$, or remove the conjunct $(F_i \in D(F_i))$ altogether. Some existing firewall products, such as Linux's ipchain, require that S_i be represented in a prefix format such as 192.168.0.0/16, where 16 means that the prefix is the first 16 bits of 192.168.0.0 in a binary format. In this paper, we choose to represent S_i as a nonempty set of nonnegative integers because of two reasons. First, any set of nonnegative integers can be automatically converted to a set of prefixes (see [15]). Second, set representations are more convenient in mathematical manipulations.

A packet $(p_1, \cdots, p_d)$ *matches* a rule $(F_1 \in S_1) \wedge \cdots \wedge (F_d \in S_d) \rightarrow \langle decision \rangle$ iff the condition $(p_1 \in S_1) \wedge \cdots \wedge (p_d \in S_d)$ holds. Since a packet may match more than one rule in a firewall, each packet is mapped to the decision of the first rule that the packet matches. The predicate of the last rule in a firewall is usually a tautology to ensure that every packet has at least one matching rule in the firewall.

Here we give an example of a simple firewall. In this example, we assume that each packet only has two fields: S (source address) and D (destination address), and both fields have the same domain $[1, 10]$. This firewall consists of the sequence of rules in Figure 1. Let f_1 be the name of this firewall.

$$
\begin{array}{llll}
r_1: & S \in [4, 7] & \wedge & D \in [6, 8] & \rightarrow & accept \\
r_2: & S \in [3, 8] & \wedge & D \in [2, 9] & \rightarrow & discard \\
r_3: & S \in [1, 10] & \wedge & D \in [1, 10] & \rightarrow & accept
\end{array}
$$

Fig. 1. Firewall f_1

3.2 Query Language

A *query*, denoted Q, in our Structured Firewall Query Language (SFQL) is of the following format:

> **select** F_i
> **from** f
> **where** $(F_1 \in S_1) \wedge \cdots \wedge (F_d \in S_d) \wedge (\textbf{decision} = \langle dec \rangle)$

where F_i is one of the fields $F_1, \cdots, F_d$, f is a firewall, each S_j is a nonempty subset of the domain $D(F_j)$ of field F_j, and $\langle dec \rangle$ is either $accept$ or $discard$.

The result of query Q, denoted $Q.result$, is the following set:

$\{p_i|(p_1, \cdots, p_d)$ *is a packet in* Σ, *and*
$\quad (p_1 \in S_1) \wedge \cdots \wedge (p_d \in S_d) \wedge (f.(p_1, \cdots, p_d) = \langle dec \rangle)\}$

Recall that Σ denotes the set of all packets, and $f.(p_1, \cdots, p_d)$ denotes the decision to which firewall f maps the packet $(p_1, \cdots, p_d)$.

We can get the above set by first finding all the packets $(p_1, \cdots, p_d)$ in Σ such that the following condition

$$(p_1 \in S_1) \wedge \cdots \wedge (p_d \in S_d) \wedge (f((p_1, \cdots, p_d)) = \langle dec \rangle)$$

holds, then projecting all these packets to the field F_i.

For example, a question to the firewall in Figure 1, "Which computers whose addresses are in the set $[4, 8]$ can send packets to the machine whose address is 6?", can be formulated as the following query using SFQL:

> **select** S
> **from** f_1
> **where** $(S \in \{[4, 8]\}) \wedge (D \in \{6\}) \wedge (\textbf{decision} = accept)$

The result of this query is $\{4, 5, 6, 7\}$.

As another example, a question to the firewall in Figure 1, "Which computer cannot send packets to the computer whose address is 6?", can be formulated as the following query using SFQL:

> **select** S
> **from** f_1
> **where** $(S \in \{all\}) \wedge (D \in \{6\}) \wedge (\textbf{decision} = discard)$

The result of this query is $\{3, 8\}$.

Next we give more examples on how to use SFQL to describe firewall queries.

4   Firewall Query Examples

In this section, we describe some example firewall queries using SFQL. Let f be the name of the firewall that resides on the gateway router in Figure 2. This gateway router has two interfaces: interface 0, which connects the gateway router to the outside Internet, and interface 1, which connects the gateway router to the

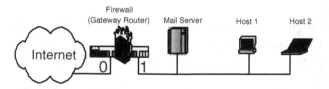

Fig. 2. Firewall f

inside local network. In these examples, we assume each packet has the following five fields: I (Interface), S (Source IP), D (Destination IP), N (Destination Port), P (Protocol Type).

Question 1:

Which computers in the private network protected by the firewall f can receive BOOTP[2] packets from the outside Internet?

Query Q_1:

select D
from f
where $(I \in \{0\}) \wedge (S \in \{all\}) \wedge (D \in \{all\}) \wedge (N \in \{67, 68\})$
$\wedge (P \in \{udp\}) \wedge (\textbf{decision} = accept)$

Answer to question 1 is $Q_1.result$.

Question 2:

Which ports on the mail server protected by the firewall f are open?

Query Q_2:

select N
from f
where $(I \in \{0, 1\}) \wedge (S \in \{all\}) \wedge (D \in \{Mail\ Server\} \wedge (N \in \{all\})$
$\wedge (P \in \{all\}) \wedge (\textbf{decision} = accept)$

Answer to question 2 is $Q_2.result$.

Question 3:

Which computers in the outside Internet cannot send SMTP[3] packets to the mail server protected by the firewall f?

Query Q_3:

select S
from f
where $(I \in \{0\}) \wedge (S \in \{all\}) \wedge (D \in \{Mail\ Server\}) \wedge (N \in \{25\})$
$\wedge (P \in \{tcp\}) \wedge (\textbf{decision} = discard)$

Answer to question 3 is $Q_3.result$.

Question 4:

Which computers in the outside Internet cannot send any packet to the private network protected by the firewall f?

Query Q_4:

select S
from f
where $(I \in \{0\}) \wedge (S \in \{all\}) \wedge (D \in \{all\}) \wedge (N \in \{all\}) \wedge (P \in \{all\})$
$\wedge (\textbf{decision} = accept)$

Answer to question 4 is $T - Q_4.result$, where T is the set of all IP addresses outside of the private network

---

[2] Bootp packets are UDP packets and use port number 67 or 68.

Question 5:
  Which computers in the outside Internet can send SMTP packets to both
  host 1 and host 2 in the private network protected by the firewall f?
Query Q_{5a}:
  select S
  from f
  where $(I \in \{0\}) \wedge (S \in \{all\}) \wedge (D \in \{Host\ 1\}) \wedge (N \in \{25\})$
        $\wedge (P \in \{tcp\}) \wedge (\mathbf{decision} = accept)$
Query Q_{5b}:
  select S
  from f
  where $(I \in \{0\}) \wedge (S \in \{all\}) \wedge (D \in \{Host\ 2\}) \wedge (N \in \{25\})$
        $\wedge (P \in \{tcp\}) \wedge (\mathbf{decision} = accept)$
Answer to question 5 is $Q_{5a}.result \cap Q_{5b}.result$.

5   Firewall Query Processing

In this section, we discuss how to process a firewall query for consistent firewalls.
Consistent firewalls and inconsistent firewalls are defined as follows:

Definition 1 (Consistent Firewalls). A firewall is called a consistent firewall
iff any two rules in the firewall do not conflict.

Definition 2 (Inconsistent Firewalls). A firewall is called an inconsistent
firewall iff there are at least two rules in the firewall that conflict.

Recall that two rules in a firewall conflict iff they have different decisions and
there is at least one packet that can match both rules. For example, the first
two rules in the firewall in Figure 1, namely r_1 and r_2, conflict. Note that for
any two rules in a consistent firewall, if they overlap, i.e., there is at least one
packet can match both rules, they have the same decision. So, given a packet
and a consistent firewall, all the rules in the firewall that the packet matches
have the same decision. Figure 1 shows an example of an inconsistent firewall,
and Figure 3 shows an example of a consistent firewall. In these two firewall
examples, we assume that each packet only has two fields: S (source address)
and D (destination address), and both fields have the same domain $[1, 10]$.

Our interest in consistent firewalls is twofold. First, each inconsistent firewall
can be converted to an equivalent consistent firewall, as described in Section 6.
Second, as shown in the following theorem, it is easier to process queries for
consistent firewalls than for inconsistent firewalls.

Theorem 1 (Firewall Query Theorem). Let Q be a query of the following
form:

---

[3] SMTP stands for Simple Mail Transfer Protocol. SMTP packets are TCP packets
   and use port number 25.

$$r'_1 : \quad S \in [4,7] \qquad\qquad \wedge\, D \in [6,8] \qquad\qquad \rightarrow a$$
$$r'_2 : \quad S \in [4,7] \qquad\qquad \wedge\, D \in [2,5] \cup [9,9] \qquad \rightarrow d$$
$$r'_3 : \quad S \in [4,7] \qquad\qquad \wedge\, D \in [1,1] \cup [10,10] \rightarrow a$$
$$r'_4 : \quad S \in [3,3] \cup [8,8] \quad \wedge\, D \in [2,9] \qquad\qquad \rightarrow d$$
$$r'_5 : \quad S \in [3,3] \cup [8,8] \quad \wedge\, D \in [1,1] \cup [10,10] \rightarrow a$$
$$r'_6 : \quad S \in [1,2] \cup [9,10] \wedge\, D \in [1,10] \qquad\quad \rightarrow a$$

Fig. 3. Consistent firewall f_2

select F_i
from f
where $(F_1 \in S_1) \wedge \cdots \wedge (F_d \in S_d) \wedge (\mathbf{decision} = \langle dec \rangle)$

If f is a consistent firewall that consists of n rules $r_1, \cdots, r_n$, then we have

$$Q.result = \bigcup_{j=1}^{n} Q.r_j$$

where each rule r_j is of the form

$$(F_1 \in S'_1) \wedge \cdots \wedge (F_d \in S'_d) \rightarrow \langle dec' \rangle$$

and the quantity of $Q.r_j$ is defined as follows:

$$Q.r_j = \begin{cases} S_i \cap S'_i & \text{if } (S_1 \cap S'_1 \neq \emptyset) \wedge \cdots \wedge (S_d \cap S'_d \neq \emptyset) \wedge (\langle dec \rangle = \langle dec' \rangle), \\ \emptyset & \text{otherwise} \end{cases}$$

$\square$

The Firewall Query Theorem implies a simple query processing algorithm: given a consistent firewall f that consists of n rules $r_1, \cdots, r_n$ and a query Q,

Rule – based Firewall Query Processing Algorithm
Input : (1) A consistent firewall f that consists of n rules: $r_1, \cdots, r_n$,
          (2) A query Q:
              select F_i
              from f
              where $(F_1 \in S_1) \wedge \cdots \wedge (F_d \in S_d) \wedge (\mathbf{decision} = \langle dec \rangle)$
Output: Result of query Q
Steps:
1. $Q.result := \emptyset$;
2. **for** $j := 1$ **to** n **do** /*Let $r_j = (F_1 \in S'_1) \wedge \cdots \wedge (F_d \in S'_d) \rightarrow \langle dec' \rangle$*/
   if $(S_1 \cap S'_1 \neq \emptyset) \wedge \cdots \wedge (S_d \cap S'_d \neq \emptyset) \wedge (\langle dec \rangle = \langle dec' \rangle)$
   then $Q.result := Q.result \cup (S_i \cap S'_i)$;
3. **return** $Q.result$;

Fig. 4. Rule-based Firewall Query Processing Algorithm

compute $Q.r_j$ for each j, then $\bigcup_{j=1}^{n} Q.r_j$ is the result of query Q. We call this algorithm the *rule-based firewall query processing algorithm*. Figure 4 shows the pseudocode of this algorithm.

6   FDT-Based Firewall Query Processing Algorithm

Observe that multiple rules in a consistent firewall may share the same prefix. For example, in the consistent firewall in Figure 3, the first three rules, namely r_1', r_2', r_3', share the same prefix $S \in [4, 7]$. Thus, if we apply the above query processing algorithm in Figure 4 to answer a query, for instance, whose "where clause" contains the conjunct $S \in \{3\}$, over the firewall in Figure 3, then the algorithm will repeat three times the calculation of $\{3\} \cap [4, 7]$. Clearly, repeated calculations are not desirable for efficiency purposes.

In this section, we present a firewall query processing method that has no repeated calculations and can be applied to both consistent and inconsistent firewalls. This method consists of two steps. First, convert the firewall (whether consistent or inconsistent) to an equivalent firewall decision tree (short for FDT). Second, use this FDT as the core data structure for processing queries. We call the algorithm that uses an FDT to process queries the *FDT-based firewall query processing algorithm*. Firewall decision trees are defined as follows. Note that firewall decision trees are a special type of firewall decision diagrams, which are introduced in [13] as a useful notation for specifying firewalls.

Definition 3 (Firewall Decision Tree). A Firewall Decision Tree t over fields $F_1, \cdots, F_d$ is a directed tree that has the following four properties:

1. Each node v in t has a label, denoted $F(v)$, such that

$$F(v) \in \begin{cases} \{F_1, \cdots, F_d\} & \text{if } v \text{ is nonterminal,} \\ \{accept, discard\} & \text{if } v \text{ is terminal.} \end{cases}$$

2. Each edge e in t has a label, denoted $I(e)$, such that if e is an outgoing edge of node v, then $I(e)$ is a nonempty subset of $D(F(v))$.
3. A directed path in t from the root to a terminal node is called a *decision path* of t. Each decision path contains d nonterminal nodes, and the i-th node is labelled F_i for each i that $1 \le i \le d$.

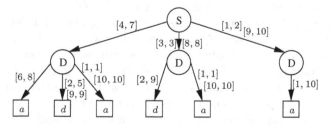

Fig. 5. Firewall Decision Tree t_3

4. The set of all outgoing edges of a node v in t, denoted $E(v)$, satisfies the following two conditions:
   (a) *Consistency*: $I(e) \cap I(e') = \emptyset$ for any two distinct edges e and e' in $E(v)$,
   (b) *Completeness*: $\bigcup_{e \in E(v)} I(e) = D(F(v))$ □

Figure 5 shows an example of an FDT named t_3. In this example, we assume that each packet only has two fields: S (source address) and D (destination address), and both fields have the same domain $[1, 10]$. In the rest of this paper, including this example, we use "a" as a shorthand for *accept* and "d" as a shorthand for *discard*.

A decision path in an FDT t is represented by $(v_1 e_1 \cdots v_k e_k v_{k+1})$ where v_1 is the root, v_{k+1} is a terminal node, and each e_i is a directed edge from node v_i to node v_{i+1}. A decision path $(v_1 e_1 \cdots v_k e_k v_{k+1})$ in an FDT defines the following rule:

$$F_1 \in S_1 \wedge \cdots \wedge F_n \in S_n \rightarrow F(v_{k+1})$$

where

$$S_i = \begin{cases} I(e_j) & \text{if the decision path has a node } v_j \text{ that is labelled with field } F_i, \\ D(F_i) & \text{if the decision path has no node that is labelled with field } F_i. \end{cases}$$

For an FDT t, we use $\Gamma(t)$ to denote the set of all the rules defined by all the decision paths of t. For any packet p, there is one and only one rule in Γ_t that p matches because of the consistency and completeness properties; therefore, t maps p to the decision of the only rule that p matches in Γ_t. Considering the FDT t_3 in Figure 5, Figure 3 shows all the six rules in Γ_{t_3}.

Given an FDT t, any sequence of rules that consists of all the rules in Γ_t is equivalent to t. The order of the rules in such a firewall is immaterial because the rules in Γ_t are non-overlapping. Given a sequence of rules, an equivalent FDT can be constructed using the construction algorithm described in [20]. Therefore, an inconsistent firewall can be converted to an equivalent consistent firewall using the following two steps: first, construct an equivalent FDT from the original inconsistent firewall; second, generate one rule for each decision path of the FDT. Then any sequence that consists of all the rules defined by the decision paths of the FDT is the resulting equivalent consistent firewall.

The pseudocode of the FDT-based firewall query processing algorithm is shown in Figure 6. Here we use $e.t$ to denote the (target) node that the edge e points to, and we use $t.root$ to denote the root of FDT t.

The above FDT-based firewall query processing algorithm has two inputs, an FDT t and an SFQL query Q. The algorithm starts by traversing the FDT from its root. Let F_j be the label of the root. For each outgoing edge e of the root, we compute $I(e) \cap S_j$. If $I(e) \cap S_j = \emptyset$, we skip edge e and do not traverse the subgraph that e points to. If $I(e) \cap S_j \neq \emptyset$, then we continue to traverse the subgraph that e points to in a similar fashion. Whenever a terminal node is encountered, we compare the label of the terminal node and $\langle dec \rangle$. If they are the same, assuming the rule defined by the decision path containing the terminal node is $(F_1 \in S_1') \wedge \cdots \wedge (F_d \in S_d') \rightarrow \langle dec' \rangle$, then we add $S_i \cap S_i'$ to $Q.result$.

FDT – based Firewall Query Processing Algorithm
Input : (1)An FDT t,
          (2)A query Q: **select** F_i
                         from t
                         where $(F_1 \in S_1) \wedge \cdots \wedge (F_d \in S_d) \wedge (\textbf{decision} = \langle dec \rangle)$
Output : Result of query Q
Steps:
1. $Q.result := \emptyset$;
2. **CHECK**($t.root$, $(F_1 \in S_1) \wedge \cdots \wedge (F_d \in S_d) \wedge (\textbf{decision} = \langle dec \rangle$)
3. **return** $Q.result$;

CHECK(v, $(F_1 \in S_1) \wedge \cdots \wedge (F_d \in S_d) \wedge (\textbf{decision} = \langle dec \rangle)$)
1. **if** (v is a terminal node) and ($F(v) = \langle dec \rangle$) **then**
   (1) Let $(F_1 \in S_1') \wedge \cdots \wedge (F_d \in S_d') \rightarrow \langle dec' \rangle$ be the rule
       defined by the decision path containing node v;
   (2) $Q.result := Q.result \cup (S_i \cap S_i')$;
2. **if** (v is a nonterminal node) **then** /*Let F_j be the label of v*/
      for each edge e in $E(v)$ **do**
        if $I(e) \cap S_j \neq \emptyset$ **then**
           CHECK($e.t$, $(F_1 \in S_1) \wedge \cdots \wedge (F_d \in S_d) \wedge (\textbf{decision} = \langle dec \rangle)$)

Fig. 6. FDT-based Firewall Query Processing Algorithm

7 Experimental Results

So far we have presented two firewall query processing algorithms, the rule-based algorithm in Section 5 and the FDT-based algorithm in Section 6. In this section, we evaluate the efficiency of both algorithms. In the absence of publicly available firewalls, we create synthetic firewalls according to the characteristics of real-life packet classifiers discussed in [2, 14]. Note that a firewall is also a packet classifier. Each rule has the following five fields: interface, source IP address, destination IP address, destination port number and protocol type. The programs are implemented in SUN Java JDK 1.4. The experiments were carried out on a SunBlade 2000 machine running Solaris 9 with 1Ghz CPU and 1 GB of memory.

    Figure 7 shows the average execution time of both algorithms versus the total number of rules in the original (maybe inconsistent) firewalls. The horizontal axis indicates the total number of rules in the original firewalls, and the vertical axis indicates the average execution time (in milliseconds) for processing a firewall query. Note that in Figure 7, the execution time of the FDT-based firewall query processing algorithm does not include the FDT construction time because the conversion from a firewall to an equivalent FDT is performed only once for each firewall, not for each query. Similarly, the execution time of the rule-based firewall query processing algorithm does not include the time for converting an inconsistent firewall to an equivalent consistent firewall because this conversion is performed only once for each firewall, not for each query.

From Figure 7, we can see that the FDT-based firewall query processing algorithm is much more efficient than the rule-based firewall query processing algorithm. For example, for processing a query over an inconsistent firewall that has 10,000 rules, the FDT-based query processing algorithm uses about 10 milliseconds, while the rule-based query processing algorithm uses about 100 milliseconds. The experimental results in Figure 7 confirm our analysis that the FDT-based query processing algorithm saves execution time by reducing repeated calculations.

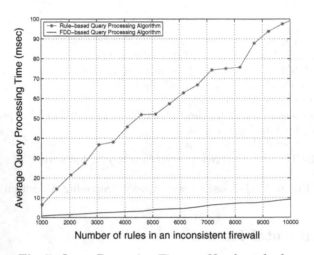

Fig. 7. Query Processing Time vs. Number of rules

8   Concluding Remarks

Our contributions in this paper are three-fold. First, we introduce a simple and effective SQL-like query language, the Structured Firewall Query Language, for describing firewall queries. Second, we present a theorem, the Firewall Query Theorem, as the foundation for developing firewall query processing algorithms. Third, we present an efficient algorithm that uses firewall decision trees as its core data structure for processing firewall queries. Given a firewall of a sequence of rules, we first construct an equivalent firewall decision tree. Then the firewall decision tree is used as the core data structure of this query processing algorithm to answer each firewall query. Our experimental results show that this query processing algorithm is very efficient.

To keep our presentation simple, we have described a somewhat watered-down version of the firewall query language where the "select" clause in a query has only one field. In fact, the "select" clause in a query can be extended to have more than one field. The results in this paper, e.g., the Firewall Query Theorem and the two firewall query processing algorithms, can all be extended accordingly to accommodate the extended "select" clauses.

References

1. E. Al-Shaer and H. Hamed. Discovery of policy anomalies in distributed firewalls. In *IEEE INFOCOM'04*, March 2004.
2. F. Baboescu, S. Singh, and G. Varghese. Packet classification for core routers: Is there an alternative to cams? In *Proc. of IEEE INFOCOM*, 2003.
3. F. Baboescu and G. Varghese. Fast and scalable conflict detection for packet classifiers. In *Proc. of the 10th IEEE International Conference on Network Protocols*, 2002.
4. Y. Bartal, A. J. Mayer, K. Nissim, and A. Wool. Firmato: A novel firewall management toolkit. *Technical Report EES2003-1, Dept. of Electrical Engineering Systems, Tel Aviv University*, 2003.
5. CERT. Test the firewall system. http://www.cert.org/security-improvement/practices/p060.html.
6. CERT Coordination Center. http://www.cert.org/advisories/ca-2003-20.html.
7. D. Moore et al. http://www.caida.org/outreach/papers/2003/sapphire/sapphire.html.
8. D. Eppstein and S. Muthukrishnan. Internet packet filter management and rectangle geometry. In *Symp. on Discrete Algorithms*, pages 827–835, 2001.
9. P. Eronen and J. Zitting. An expert system for analyzing firewall rules. In *Proc. of the 6th Nordic Workshop on Secure IT Systems (NordSec 2001)*, pages 100–107, 2001.
10. D. Farmer and W. Venema. Improving the security of your site by breaking into it. *http://www.alw.nih.gov/Security/Docs/admin-guide-to-cracking.101.html*, 1993.
11. M. Frantzen, F. Kerschbaum, E. Schultz, and S. Fahmy. A framework for understanding vulnerabilities in firewalls using a dataflow model of firewall internals. *Computers and Security*, 20(3):263–270, 2001.
12. M. Freiss. *Protecting Networks with SATAN*. O'Reilly & Associates, Inc., 1998.
13. M. G. Gouda and A. X. Liu. Firewall design: consistency, completeness and compactness. In *Proc. of the 24th IEEE International Conference on Distributed Computing Systems (ICDCS'04)*, pages 320–327.
14. P. Gupta. *Algorithms for Routing Lookups and Packet Classification*. PhD thesis, Stanford University, 2000.
15. P. Gupta and N. McKeown. Algorithms for packet classification. *IEEE Network*, 15(2):24–32, 2001.
16. J. D. Guttman. Filtering postures: Local enforcement for global policies. In *Proc. of IEEE Symp. on Security and Privacy*, pages 120–129, 1997.
17. A. Hari, S. Suri, and G. M. Parulkar. Detecting and resolving packet filter conflicts. In *Proc. of IEEE INFOCOM*, pages 1203–1212, 2000.
18. S. Hazelhurst, A. Attar, and R. Sinnappan. Algorithms for improving the dependability of firewall and filter rule lists. In *Proc. of the International Conference on Dependable Systems and Networks (DSN'00)*, pages 576–585, 2000.
19. S. Kamara, S. Fahmy, E. Schultz, F. Kerschbaum, and M. Frantzen. Analysis of vulnerabilities in internet firewalls. *Computers and Security*, 22(3):214–232, 2003.
20. A. X. Liu and M. G. Gouda. Diverse firewall design. In *Proc. of the International Conference on Dependable Systems and Networks (DSN'04)*, pages 595–604, June 2004.
21. A. Mayer, A. Wool, and E. Ziskind. Fang: A firewall analysis engine. In *Proc. of IEEE Symp. on Security and Privacy*, pages 177–187, 2000.
22. J. D. Moffett and M. S. Sloman. Policy conflict analysis in distributed system management. *Journal of Organizational Computing*, 4(1):1–22, 1994.

23. Nessus. http://www.nessus.org/. March 2004.
24. A. D. Rubin, D. Geer, and M. J. Ranum. *Web Security Sourcebook*. Wiley Computer Publishing, 1th edition, 1997.
25. A. Wool. Architecting the lumeta firewall analyzer. In *Proc. of the 10th USENIX Security Symposium*, pages 85–97, August 2001.
26. A. Wool. A quantitative study of firewall configuration errors. *IEEE Computer*, 37(6):62–67, 2004.

Self-tuning Reactive Distributed Trees
for Counting and Balancing

Phuong Hoai Ha, Marina Papatriantafilou, and Philippas Tsigas

Department of Comp. Science, Chalmers University of Technology,
SE-412 96 Göteborg, Sweden
{phuong, ptrianta, tsigas}@cs.chalmers.se

Abstract. The main contribution of this paper is that it shows that it *is* possible to have reactive distributed trees for counting and balancing with no need for the user to fix manually any parameters. We present a data structure that in an on-line manner balances the trade-off between the tree traversal latency and the latency due to contention at the tree nodes. Moreover, the fact that our method can expand or shrink a subtree several levels in any adjustment step, has a positive effect in the efficiency: this feature helps the self-tuning reactive tree minimize the adjustment time, which affects not only the execution time of the process adjusting the size of the tree but also the latency of all other processes traversing the tree at the same time with no extra memory requirements. Our experimental study compared the new trees with the reactive diffracting ones on the SGI Origin2000, a well-known commercial ccNUMA multiprocessor. This study showed that the self-tuning reactive trees i) select the same tree depth as the reactive diffracting trees do; ii) perform better and iii) react faster.

1 Introduction

Distributed data structures suitable for synchronization that perform efficiently across a wide range of contention conditions are hard to design. Typically, "small", "centralized" such data structures fit better low contention levels, while "bigger", "distributed" such data structures can help in distributing concurrent processor accesses to memory banks and in alleviating memory contention.

Diffracting trees [1] are distributed data structures. Their most significant advantage is the ability to distribute a set of concurrent process accesses to many small groups locally accessing shared data, in a coordinated manner. Each process(or) accessing the tree can be considered as leading a *token* that follows a path from the root to the leaves. Each node is a computing element receiving tokens from its single input (coming from its parent node) and sending out tokens to its outputs; it is called *balancer* and acts as a *toggle mechanism* which, given a stream of input tokens, alternately forwards them to its outputs, from left to right (sending them to the left and right child nodes, respectively). The result is an even distribution of tokens at the leaf nodes. Diffracting trees have been introduced for *counting-problems*, and hence the leaf nodes are counters, assigning numbers to each token that exits from them. Moreover, the number of tokens that are output at the leaves, satisfy the *step property*, which states that: when there are no tokens present inside the tree and if out_i denotes the number of tokens that have been output at leaf i, $0 \le out_i - out_j \le 1$ for any pair i and j of leaf-nodes such that $i < j$ (i.e.

T. Higashino (Ed.): OPODIS 2004, LNCS 3544, pp. 213–228, 2005.

if one makes a drawing of the tokens that have exited from each counter as a stack of boxes, the combined outcome will have the shape of a single step).

The fixed-size diffracting tree is optimal only for a small range of contention levels. To solve this problem, Della-Libera and Shavit proposed the *reactive diffracting trees*, where each node can shrink (to a counter) or grow (to a subtree with counters as leaves) according to the current load, in order to attain optimal performance [2]. The algorithm in [2] uses a set of parameters to make its decisions, namely folding/unfolding thresholds and the time-intervals for consecutive reaction checks. The parameter values depend on the multiprocessor system in use, the applications using the data structure and, in a multiprogramming environment, on the system utilization by the other programs that run concurrently. The programmer has to fix these parameters manually, using experimentation and information that is commonly not easily available (future load characteristics). A second characteristic of this scheme is that the reactive part is allowed to shrink or expand the tree only one level at a time, making the cost of a multi-adjustment phase on a reactive tree become high.

In this work we show that reactiveness and these two characteristics are not tied together: in particular, we present a tree-type distributed data structure that has the same semantics as the reactive trees that can expand or shrink many levels at a time, without need for manual tuning. To circumvent the need for manually setting parameters, we have analyzed the problem of balancing the trade-off between the two key measures, namely the contention level and the depth of the tree, in a way that enabled the use of efficient on-line methods for its solution. The new data structure is also considerably faster than the reactive diffracting trees, because of the low-overhead, multilevel reaction part: the new reactive trees can shrink and expand many levels at a time without using clock readings. The self-tuning reactive trees[1], like the reactive diffracting trees, are aimed in general for applications where such distributed data structures are needed. Since the latter were introduced in the context of counting problems, we use similar terms in our description, for reasons of consistency.

The rest of this paper is organized as follows. Section 2 presents the key idea and the algorithm of the self-tuning reactive tree. Section 3 describes the implementation of the tree. Section 4 presents an experimental evaluation of the self-tuning reactive trees, compared with the reactive diffracting trees, on the Origin2000 platform, and elaborate on a number of properties of our algorithm. Section 5 concludes this paper. Due to the space constraint, the correctness proof of our algorithm is presented in [3].

2   Self-tuning Reactive Trees

2.1   Problem Description

The problem we are interested in is to construct a tree that satisfies the following requirements:

---

[1] We do not use term *diffracting* in the title of this paper since our algorithmic implementation does not use the *prism* construct, which is in the core of the algorithmic design of the (reactive) diffracting trees.

1. It must evenly distribute a set of concurrent process accesses to many small groups locally accessing shared data (counters at leaves), in a coordinated manner like the (reactive) diffracting trees. The step-property must be guaranteed.

2. Moreover, it must automatically and efficiently adjust its size according to its load in order to gain performance. It must not require any manually tuning parameters.

In order to satisfy these requirements, we have to tackle the following algorithmic problems:

1. Design a dynamic mechanism that would allow the tree to predict when and how much it should resize in order to obtain good performance whereas the load on it changes unpredictably. Moreover, the overhead that this mechanism will introduce should not exceed the performance benefits that the dynamic behavior itself will bring.

2. This dynamic mechanism should not only adjust the size of the tree in order to improve performance, but, more significantly, adjust it in a way that the tree still guarantees the fundamental properties of the structure, such as the step property.

2.2 Key Idea

The ideal reactive tree is the one in which each leaf is accessed by only one process(or) –holding a token [2] – at a time and the cost to traverse it from the root to the leaves is kept minimal. However, these two latency-related factors are opposite to each other, i.e. if we want to decrease the contention at the leaves, we need to expand the tree and so the cost to traverse from the root to the leaves increases.

What we are looking for is a tree where the *overall overhead*, including the *latency due to contention* at the leaves and the *latency due to traversal* from the root to the leaves, is minimal and with *no manual tuning*. In addition to this, an algorithm that can achieve the above, must also be able to cope with the following difficulties: If the tree expands immediately when the contention level increases, then it will pay the expensive cost for travel and this cost is going to be unnecessary if after that the contention level suddenly decreases. On the other hand, if the tree does not expand in time when the contention-level increases, it has to pay the large cost of contention. If the algorithm knew in advance about the changes of contention-levels at the leaves in the whole time-period that the tree operates, it could adjust the tree-size at each time-point in a way such that the overall overhead is minimized. As the contention-levels change unpredictably, there is no way for the algorithm to know this kind of information, i.e. the information about the future.

To overcome this problem, we have designed a reactive algorithm based on the online techniques that are used to solve the online currency trading problem [4].

Definition 1. *Let* surplus *denote the number of processors that exceeds the number of leaves of the self-tuning reactive tree, i.e. the subtraction of the number of the leaves from the maximal number of processors in the system that potentially want to access*

---

[2] For reasons of brevity, throughout the paper, instead of using the phrase "process(or) holding a token" we use simply the term process or processor.

the tree. The surplus *represents the contention level on the tree because the surplus processors cause contention on the leaves.*

Definition 2. *Let* latency *denote the latency due to traversal from the root to the leaves.*

Our challenge is to balance the trade-off between *surplus* and *latency*. Our solution for the problem is based on an optimal competitive algorithm called *threat-based algorithm* [4]. The algorithm is an optimal solution for the one-way trading problem, where the player has to decide whether to accept the current exchange rate as well as how many of his/her dollars should be exchanged to yens at the current exchange rate without knowledge on how the exchange rate will vary in the future.

2.3   The New Algorithm

In the self-tuning reactive trees, to adapt to the changes of the contention efficiently, a leaf should be free to shrink or grow to any level suggested by the reactive scheme in one adjustment step. With this in mind, we designed a data structure for the trees such that the time used for the adjustment and the time in which other processors are blocked by the adjustment are kept minimal. Figure 1 illustrates the self-tuning reactive tree data structure. Each balancer has a *matching* leaf with corresponding identity. Symmetrically, each leaf that is not at the lowest level of the tree has a *matching* balancer with corresponding identity. The squares in the figure are balancers and the circles are leaves. The numbers in the squares and circles are their identities. Each balancer has two outputs, $left$ and $right$, each of them being a pointer that can point to either a leaf or a balancer. A shrink or expand operation is essentially a switch of such a pointer (from the balancer to the matching leaf or from the leaf to the matching balancer, respectively). The solid arrows in the figure represent the present pointer contents.

Assume the tree has the shape as in Figure 1, where the solid arrows are the pointers' current contents. A processor p_i first visits the tree at its root IN, then following the root pointer visits balancer 1. When visiting a balancer, p_i switches the balancer's toggle-bit

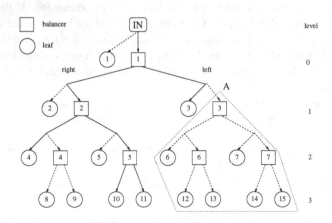

Fig. 1. A self-tuning reactive tree

to the other position (i.e. from left to right and vise-versa) and then continues visiting the next node according to the toggle-bit. When visiting a leaf L, p_i before taking an appropriate counter value and exiting, checks the *reaction condition* according to the current load at L. The reaction condition estimates which tree level is the best for the current load.

The reaction procedure. In order to balance the trade-off between *surplus* and *latency*, the procedure can be described as a game, which evolves in *load-rising* and *load-dropping transaction phases*.

Definition 3. *A* load-rising *(resp.* load-dropping*) transaction phase is a maximal sequence of subsequent visits at a leaf-node with monotonic non-decreasing (resp. non-increasing) estimated contention-level over the entire tree. A load-rising phase ends when a decrease in contention is observed; at that point a load-dropping phase begins.*

During a load-rising phase, a processor traversing that leaf may decide to expand the leaf to a subtree of depth that depends on the amount of the rising contention-level. That value is computed using the *threat-based on-line* method of [4], following the principle: "expand *just enough* to guarantee a bounded competitive ratio, even in the case that contention may drop to minimum at the next measurement". Symmetric is the case during a load-dropping phase, where the reaction is to shrink a subtree to the appropriate level, depending on the measurement. The computation of the level to shrink to or to expand to uses the number of processors in the system as an upper bound of contention. The reaction procedure is described in detail in Section 3.2.

Depending on the result of checking the reaction condition, the processor acts as follows:

Recommended reaction: Grow to level l_{lower}, i.e. the current load is too high for the leaf L and L should expand to level l_{lower}. The processor, before exiting the tree through L, must help in carrying out the expansion task. To do so, the corresponding subtree must be constructed (if it was not already existent), the subtree's counters' (leaves') values must be set, and the pointer pointing to L must switch to point to its corresponding balancer, which is the root of the subtree resulting from the expansion.

Recommended reaction: Shrink to level l_{higher}, the current load at the leaf L is too low and thus L would like to cause a shrink operation to a higher level l_{higher}, in order to reduce the latency of traversing from the root to the present level. This means that the pointer to the corresponding balancer (i.e. ancestor of L) at level l_{higher} must switch to point to the matching counter (leaf) and the value of that counter must be set appropriately. Let B denote that balancer. The sub-tree with B as a root contains more leaves than just L, which might not have decided to shrink to l_{higher}, and thus the processor must take this into account. To enable processors do this check, the algorithm uses an asynchronous vote-collecting scheme: when a leaf L decides to shrink to level l_{higher}, it adds its *weighted vote* for that shrinkage to a corresponding vote-array at balancer B.

Definition 4. *The weight of the vote of leaf L is the number of lowest-level leaves in the subtree rooted at the balancer matching L.*

As an example in Figure 1 the weight of the vote of leaf 4 is 2. Note that when voting for balancer B, the leaf L is not concerned about whether B has shrunk into its matching leaf or not. The processor that helps L write its vote to B's vote-array, will then check whether there are enough votes collected at B's vote-array. If there are enough votes collected at B' vote-array, i.e. if the sum of their weights is more than half of the total possible weight of the sub-tree rooted at B (i.e. if more than half of that subtree wants to shrink to the leaf matching B), the shrinkage will happen. After completing the shrinkage task, the processor increases and returns the counter value of L, thus exiting the tree. In the checking process, the processor will abort if the balancer B has shrunk already by a concurrent operation.

In the shrinkage procedure, the leaf matching B and the leaves of the sub-tree rooted at B must be locked in order to (i) collect their counters' values, (ii) compute the next counter value for the leaf matching B and (iii) switch the pointer from B to its matching leaf. Note that all the leaves of subtree B need to be locked *only if* the load on the subtree is *so small that it should be shrunk to a leaf*. Therefore, locking the subtree in this case effectively behaves as if locking a leaf (i.e. as it is done in the classical reactive diffracting trees) from the performance point of view.

Example of executing grow: Consider a processor p_i visiting leaf 3 in Figure 1, and let the result of the check be that the leaf should grow to sub-tree A with leaves $12, 13, 14$ and 15: The processor first constructs the sub-tree, whereas at the same time other processors may continue to access leaf 3 to get the counter values and then exit the tree without any disturbance. After that, it locks leaf 3 in order to (i) switch the pointer to balancer 3 and (ii) assign the proper values to counters $12, 13, 14$ and 15, then it releases leaf 3. At this point, the new processors following the left pointer of balancer 1 will traverse through the new sub-tree, whereas the old processors that were directed to leaf 3 before, will continue to access leaf 3's counter and exit the tree. After completing the expansion task, p_i continues its normal task to access leaf 3's counter and exits the tree.

Example of executing shrink: Consider a processor p_i visiting leaf 10 in Figure 1 and let the result of the reaction condition be that the subtree should shrink to leaf 2. Because the sub-tree rooted at balancer 2 contains more leaves besides 10, which might not have decided to shrink to 2, processor p_i will check the votes collected at 2 for shrinking to that level. Assume that leaf 4 has voted for balancer 2, too. The weight of leaf 4's vote is two because the vote represents leaves 8 and 9 at the lowest level. Leaf 10's vote has weight 1. Therefore, the sum of the weights of the votes collected at balancer 2 is 3. In this case, processor p_i will help balancer 2 to perform the shrinkage task because the weight of votes, 3, is more than half of the total possible weight of the sub-tree (i.e. more than half of 4, which is the number of the leaves at the lowest level of the subtree – $8, 9, 10$ and 11). Then p_i locks leaf 2 and all the leaves of the sub-tree rooted at balancer 2, collects the counter values at them, computes the next counter value for leaf 2 and switches the pointer from balancer 2 to leaf 2. After that, all the leaves of the sub-tree are released immediately so that other processors can continue to access their counters. As soon as the counter at leaf 2 is assigned the new value, the new processors going along the right pointer of balancer 1 can access the counter and exit the tree whereas the old processors are traversing in the old sub-tree. After completing the shrinkage task, the processor exits the tree, returning the value from counter 10.

Space needs of the algorithm. In a system with n processors, the algorithm needs $n - 1$ balancer nodes and $2n - 1$ leaf nodes. Note that it may seem that the data structure for the self-tuning reactive trees uses more memory space than the data structure for the reactive diffracting trees, since it introduces an auxiliary node (matching leaf) for each balancer of the tree. However, this is actually splitting the functionality of a node in the reactive diffracting trees into two components, one that is enabled when the node plays the role of a balancer and another that is enabled when the node plays the role of a leaf (cf. also Section 3.3 and Section 3.4). In other words, the corresponding memory requirements are similar. From the structure point of view, splitting the node functionality is a fundamental difference between the self-tuning trees and the reactive diffracting trees. The voting arrays' space needs at each balancer are $O(k)$, which are similar to the space needs for the prism at each balancer of the reactive diffracting trees, where k is the number of leaves of the subtree rooted at the balancer.

3   Implementation

3.1   Preliminaries

Data structure and shared variables: Figure 3 describes the tree data structure and the shared variables used in the implementation.

The synchronization primitives used for the implementation are *test-and-set (TAS)*, *fetch-and-xor (FAX)* and *compare-and-swap (CAS)*. Their semantics are described in [3]. Moreover, in order to simplify the presentation and implementation of our algorithm, we define, implement and use advanced synchronization operations: *read-and-follow-link* and *conditionally-acquire-lock*. The read-and-follow-link operations and the conditionally-acquire-lock operation are outlined in pseudo-code in Fig. 2. The way

---

$NodeType$ ASSIGN($NodeType * trace_i, NodeType * child$)
A0 $*trace_i := child$;/*mark $trace_i$ under update,*clearing mask-bit*/
A1 $temp := *child$; /*get the expected value*/
A2 $temp.mask := 1$;/*set the mask-bit*/
A3   **if** $(local := CAS(trace_i, child, temp)) = child$ **then return** $temp$;
A4   **else return** $local$;

$NodeType$ READ($NodeType * trace_i$)
R0   **do**
R1 $local := *trace_i$;
R2   **if** $local.mask = 0$ **then** /*$*trace_i$ is marked*/
R3 $temp := *local$; /*help corresponding Assign() ... */
R4 $temp.mask := 1$;
R5 $CAS(trace_i, local, temp)$;
R6   **while**$(local.mask = 0)$; /*... until the Assign() completes*/
R7   **return** $local$;

boolean ACQUIRELOCK_COND(**int** $lock$, **int** Nid)
AL0   **while** $((CurOccId := CAS(lock, 0, Nid)) \neq 0)$ **do**
AL1   **if** $IsParent(CurOccId, Nid)$ **then return** $Fail$;
AL2   *Delay using exponential backoff*;
AL3   **return** $Success$;

Fig. 2. The read-and-follow-link operations (Assign/Read) and conditionally-acquire-lock operation (AcquireLock_cond)

---

type $NodeType$ = **record** $Nid : [1..MaxNodeId]$; $kind : \{BALANCER, LEAF\}$; $mask$: **bit**; **end**;
    $BalancerType$ = **record** $state : \{ACTIVE, OLD\}$; $level$: **int**; $toggleBit$: **boolean**;
        $parent : [1..MaxNodeId]$; $leftChild, rightChild : NodeType$;
        $votes$: **array**$[1..SizeOfMySubtree]$ **of int**; **end**;
    $LeafType$ = **record** $state : \{ACTIVE, OLD\}$; $level, count, init$: **int**;
        $parent : [1..MaxNodeId]$; $lock : \{0..MaxNodeId\}$; $contention, totLoadEst$: **int**;
        $transPhase : \{RISING, DROPPING\}$;
        $latency, baseLatency, surplus, baseSurplus, oldSugLevel, sugLevel$: **int**; **end**;
shared variables
    $Balancers$: **array**$[0..MaxNodeId]$ **of** $BalancerType$;
    $Leaves$: **array**$[1..MaxNodeId]$ **of** $LeafType$;
    $TokenToReact$: **array**$[1..MaxNodeId]$ **of boolean**;
    $Tracing$: **array**$[1..MaxProcs]$ **of** $[1..MaxNodeId]$;
private variables
    $MyPath$: **array**$[1..MaxLevel]$ **of** $NodeType$; /*one for each processor*/

int CHECKCONDITION($LeafType\ L$)
C0 $TotLoadEst := MIN(MaxProcs, L.contention * 2^{L.level})$;
C1 $FirstInPhase := False$;
C2   **if** $(L.transPhase = RISING)$ **and** $(TotLoadEst < L.totLoadEst)$ **then**
        $L.transPhase := DROPPING$; $L.baseLatency := L.latency$; $FirstInPhase := True$;
C3   **else if** $(L.transPhase = DROPPING)$ **and** $(TotLoadEst > L.totLoadEst)$ **then**
        $L.transPhase := RISING$; $L.baseSurplus := L.surplus$; $FirstInPhase := True$;
C4   **if** $L.transPhase = RISING$ **then** $Surplus2Latency(L, TotLoadEst, FirstInPhase)$;
C5   **else** $Latency2Surplus(L, \frac{1}{TotLoadEst}, FirstInPhase)$;
        $L.totLoadEst := TotLoadEst$; $L.oldSugLevel := L.sugLevel$;
C6 $L.sugLevel := log_2(MaxProcs - L.surplus)$;
        if $L.sugLevel < L.level$ **then return** $SHRINK$;
        else if $L.sugLevel > L.level$ **then return** $GROW$;
        else return $NONE$;

SURPLUS2LATENCY($L, TotLoadEst, FirstInPhase$)
SL0 $X := L.surplus$; $baseX := L.baseSurplus$; $Y := L.latency$;
SL1 $rXY := TotLoadEst$; $LrXY := L.totLoadEst$;
SL2   **if** $FirstInPhase$ **then**
        if $rXY > mXY * C$ **then** $deltaX := baseX * \frac{1}{C} * \frac{rXY - mXY * C}{rXY - mXY}$; /*C: comp. ratio*/
SL3   **else** $deltaX := baseX * \frac{1}{C} * \frac{rXY - LrXY}{rXY - mXY}$;
SL4 $L.surplus := L.surplus - deltaX$; $L.latency := L.latency + deltaX * rXY$;

LATENCY2SURPLUS($L, \frac{1}{TotLoadEst}, FirstInPhase$)
/* symmetric to the above with: $X := L.latency$; $baseX := L.baseLatency$; $Y := L.surplus$;
    $rXY := \frac{1}{TotLoadEst}$; $LrXY := \frac{1}{L.totLoadEst}$; */

Fig. 3. The tree data structure and CheckCondition, Surplus2Latency and Latency2Surplus procedures

these locking mechanisms interact and ensure safety and liveness in our data structure accesses is explained in the descriptions of the implementations of the $Grow$ and $Shrink$ procedures and is proven in [3].

3.2   Reaction Conditions

As mentioned in section 2.3, each leaf L of the self-tuning reactive tree estimates which level is the best for the current load. The leaf estimates the total load of tree by using the following formula:

$$TotLoadEst = L.contention * 2^{L.level}$$

line C0 in $CheckCondition()$ in Figure 3, where $MaxProcs$ is the maximum number of processors potentially wanting to access the tree and $L.contention$, the contention of a leaf, is the number of processors that currently visit the leaf. $L.contention$ is increased by one every-time a processor visits the leaf L and is decreased by one when a processor leaves the leaf. Because the number of processors accessing the tree cannot be greater than $MaxProcs$ we have an upper bound for the load: $TotLoadEst \leq MaxProcs$.

At the beginning, the initial tree is just a leaf, so the the initial $surplus$, $base$ $Surplus$, is $MaxProcs - 1$ and the initial $latency$, $baseLatency$, is 0. Then, based on the contention variation on each leaf, the values of $surplus$ and $latency$ are updated according to the online trading algorithm. Procedure $Surplus2Latency()$ (respectively $Latency2Surplus()$) is invoked (lines C4, C5) to adjust the number of surplus processors that the tree should have at that time. The surplus value will be used to compute the number of leaves the tree should have and consequently the level the leaf L should shrink/grow to. .

Procedure $Surplus2Latency(L, TotLoadEst, FirstInPhase)$ in Figure 3 exchanges $L.surplus$ to $L.latency$ according to the *threat-based algorithm* [4] using $TotLoadEst$ as exchange rate. For self-containment, the computation implied by this algorithm is explained below. In a load-rising transaction phase, the following rules must be followed:

1. The tree is expanded only when the estimated current total load is the highest so far in the present transaction phase.
2. When expanding, expand *just enough* to keep the competitive ratio $c = \varphi - \frac{\varphi - 1}{\varphi^{1/(\varphi-1)}}$, where $\varphi = \frac{MaxProcs}{2}$, even if the total load drops to the minimum possible in the next measurement.

Following these, the number of leaves the tree should have more is:

$$deltaSurplus = baseSurplus * \frac{1}{C} * \frac{TotLoadEst - TotLoadEst^-}{TotLoadEst - 2}$$

where $TotLoadEst^-$ is the highest observed total load before the present measurement and $baseSurplus$ is the number of surplus processors at the beginning of the present transaction phase (line SL3, where mXY is the lower bound of the estimated total load). Everytime a new transaction phase starts, the value $baseSurplus$ is set to the last value of $surplus$ in the previous transaction phase (line C3). The parameter $FirstInPhase$ is used to identify whether this is the first exchange of the transaction phase. At the beginning,

$$surplus = baseSurplus = MaxProcs - 1$$

i.e. the tree degenerates to a node. Both variables $TotLoadEst^-$ and $baseSurplus$ are stored in fields $TotLoadEst$ and $baseSurplus$ of the leaf data structure, respectively.

Symmetrically, when the tree should shrink to reduce the traversal latency, the exchange rate is the inverse of the total load, $rXY = \frac{1}{TotLoadEst}$, which is increasing. In this case, the value of $surplus$ increases and that of $latency$ decreases.

3.3   Expanding a Leaf to a Sub-tree

A grow operation of a leaf L to a subtree T, whose root is L's matching balancer B and whose depth is $L.SugLevel - L.level$, essentially needs to (i) set the counters at the new leaves in T to proper values to ensure the step property; (ii) switch the corresponding child pointer of L's parent from L to B; and (iii) activate the nodes in T. (Figure 5 illustrates the steps taken in procedure grow, which is given in pseudocode in Figure 4.) Towards (i), it needs to:

GROW(int Nid) /*Leaves[Nid] becomes OLD;Balancers[Nid] and its subtree become ACTIVE*/
G0 $L := Leaves[Nid]; B := Balancers[Nid]$;
G1   **forall** i, $Read(Tracing[i])$ /* Can't miss any processors since the current ones go to Leaves[Nid]*/
      if $\exists$ pending processors in the subtree rooted at B **then** return; /*abort*/
G2   **for each** balancer B' in the subtree rooted at B,up to level $L.sugLevel - 1$
      forall entries $i : B'.votes[i] := 0; B'.toggleBit = 0$;
G3   **for each** leaf L' at level $L.sugLevel$ of the subtree rooted at B,in decreasing order of nodeId **do**
      if not $AcquireLock\_cond(L'.lock, Nid)$ **then** Release all acquired locks; **return**; /*abort*/
G4   **if** (**not** $AcquireLock\_cond(L.lock, Nid)$) **or** ($L.state = OLD$) **then**
      /*1st: an ancestor activated an overlapping $Shrink$; 2nd:someone already made the expansion*/
      Release all acquired locks; **return**; /*abort*/
G5   Switch parent's pointer from L to B;
G6   **forall** i, $Read(Tracing[i])$ /*Can't miss any since the new ones go to B*/
      $ppL := \#(pending\ processors\ at\ L)$;
G7 $CurCount := L.count; L.state := OLD$;
G8 $Release(L.lock)$;
G9   **for each** balancer B' as described in step $G2$ **do** $B'.state := ACTIVE$;
G10   **for each** leaf L' as described in step $G3$ **do**
      update $L'.count$ using ppL and $CurCount$; $L'.state := ACTIVE$; $Release(L'.lock)$;
      return;/*Success*/

ELECT2SHRINK(**int** Nid, $NodeType\ MyPath[]$)
E0 $L := Leaves[Nid]$;/*the leaf asks to shrink*/
      if $L.oldSugLevel < L.sugLevel$ **then** /*new suggested level islower than older suggestion*/
E1   **for**$(i := L.oldSugLevel; i < L.sugLevel; i++)$ **do** $Balancers[MyPath[i].Nid].votes[Nid] := 0$;
      else for ($i := L.sugLevel; i < L.oldSugLevel; i++$) **do**
E2 $B := Balancers[MyPath[i].Nid]$;
E3 $B.votes[Nid] := 2^{MaxLevel-L.level}; bWeight := 2^{MaxLevel-B.level}$; /*weight of B's subtree*/
E4   **if** $\frac{\sum_i B.votes[i]}{bWeight} > 0.5$ **then** $Shrink(i)$; **break**;

SHRINK (**int** Nid)/*Leaves[Nid] becomes ACTIVE; Balancers[Nid] and its subtree become OLD*/
S0 $B := Balancers[Nid]; L := Leaves[Nid]$;
S1   **if** ($TAS(TokenToReact[Nid]) = 1$) **then return**; /*abort, someone is doing the shrinkage*/
S2   **forall** $i : Read(Tracing[i])$ /*can't miss any since the currentones go to B*/
      if $\exists$ pending processor at L **then return**;/*abort*/
S3   **if** (**not** $AcquiredLock\_cond(L.lock, Nid)$) **or** ($B.state = OLD$) **then**
      /*1st: some ancestor is performing Shrink; 2nd: someone already made the shrinkage*/
      Release possibly acquired lock; **return**; /*abort*/
S4 $L.state := OLD$;/*avoid reactive adjustment at L*/
S5   **forall** leaf L' in B's subtree, in increasing order of nodeId **do**
      $AcquireLock\_cond(L'.lock, Nid)$; /*No fails expected since Grow operations by ancestors
                                           will abort at G1*/
S6   Switch the parent's pointer from B to L
S7   **forall** $i : Read(Tracing[i])$; $eppB := \#(effective\ pending\ processors\ in\ B's\ subtree)$;
      /*can't miss any since the new ones go to L*/
S8   **for each** balancer B' in the subtree rooted at B **do** $B'.state := OLD$;
      $SL := \emptyset; SLCount := \emptyset$;
S9   **for each** leaf L' in the subtree rooted at B **do**
      if ($L.state = ACTIVE$) **then** $SL := \cup L'; SLCount := \cup L'.count; L'.state := OLD$;
      $Release(L'.lock)$;
S10 $L.count := f(eppB, SL, SLCount)$;
S11 $L.state := ACTIVE$;
S12 $Release(L.lock)$;
S13 $Reset(TokenToReact[Nid])$;

Fig. 4. The Grow, Elect2Shrink and Shrink procedures

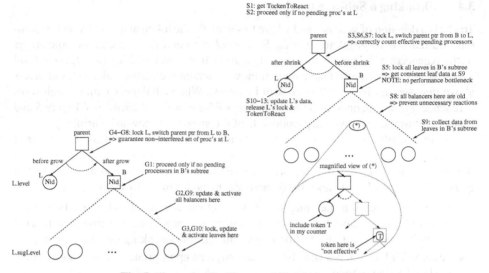

Fig. 5. Illustration for Grow and Shrink procedures

- make sure there are no pending tokens in T. If there are any, *Grow* aborts (step G1 in *Grow*), since it should not cause "old" tokens get "new" values (that would cause "holes" in the sequence of numbers received by all tokens in the end). A new grow operation will be activated anyway by subsequent tokens visiting L, since L has high contention.
- acquire the locks for the new leaves, to be able to assign proper counter values to them (step G3 in *Grow*) to ensure the step property.
- make a consistent measurement of the number of pending processors in L and $L.count$ to use in the computation of the aforementioned values for the counters. Consistency is ensured by acquiring L's lock (step G4) and by switching L's parent's pointer from L to B (i.e. performing action (ii) described above; step G5 in *Grow*), since the latter leaves a "non-interfered" set of processors in L.

Each of these locks' acquisition is *conditional*, i.e. if some ancestor of L holds it, the attempt to lock will return fail. In such a case the grow procedure aborts, since the failure to get the lock means that there is an overlapping shrink operation by an ancestor of L. (Note that overlapping grow operations by an ancestor of L would have aborted, due to the existence of the token (processor) at L (step G1 in *Grow*).) Furthermore, the new leaves' locks are requested in *decreasing* order of node-id, followed by the request of $L.lock$, to avoid deadlocks.

Towards action (iii) from above, the grow procedure needs to reset the tree's T balancers' toggle bits and vote arrays (before switching L's parent's pointer from L to B; step G2) and set the state values of all balancers and bottom-level leaves in T to ACTIVE (after having made sure that the growing will not abort; step G9-G10).

3.4   Shrinking a Sub-tree to a Leaf

Towards a decision of whether and where to shrink to, the token at a leaf L_0 with recommended reaction to shrink to level $L_0.SugLevel$ must add L_0's vote in the vote arrays of the balancers of its path from the root, starting from level $L_0.SugLevel$, up to level $L_0.level - 1$ (it must also take care to remove potentially existing older votes at layers above that; step E1 in $Elect2Shrink$ in Figure 4). When a balancer with enough votes is reached, the shrink operation will start (steps E3-E4 in $Elect2Shrink$). Figure 5 and Figure 4 illustrate and give the pseudocode of the steps taken towards shrinking.

Symmetrically to a grow operation, a shrink from a subtree T rooted at balancer B (with enough votes) to B's matching leaf L, essentially needs to (i) set the counter at L to the proper value to ensure the step property; (ii) switch the corresponding child pointer of B's parent from B to L; and (iii) de-activate the nodes in T. Towards (i), it needs to:

- make sure there are no pending tokens in L. If there are any, shrink aborts (step S2 in $Shrink$), since it should not cause "old" tokens get "new" values. Subsequent tokens' checking of the reaction condition may reinitiate the shrinking later on anyway.
- acquire L's lock (step S3), to be able to assign an appropriate counter value to it, to ensure the step property.
- make a consistent measurement of (1) the number of pending processors in T and (2) the values of counters of each leaf L' in T. Consistency is ensured by acquiring $L'.lock$ for all L' in T (step S5) and by switching B's parent's pointer from B to L (i.e. performing action (ii) described above; step S6 in $Shrink$), since the latter leaves a "non-interfered" set of processors in T.

Similarly to procedure grow, these locks' acquisition is conditional. Symmetrically with grow, the requests are made first to $L.lock$ and then to the locks of the leaves in T, in *increasing* order of node-id, to avoid deadlocks. Failure to get $L.lock$ implies an overlapping shrink operation by an ancestor of L. Note that overlapping grow operations by an ancestor of L would have aborted, due to the existence of the token at B (step G1 in $Grow$). Note also that an overlapping shrink by some of L's ancestors cannot cause any of the attempts to get some $L'.lock$ to fail, since that shrink operation would have to first acquire the lock for L (and if it had succeeded in getting that, it would have caused the shrink from B to L to abort earlier, at step S3 of $Shrink()$).

Towards action (iii) from above, the shrink procedure sets the balancers' and leaves' states in T to OLD (steps S8-S9 in $Shrink$), after having made sure that the shrink will not abort.

4   Evaluation

In this section, we evaluate the performance of the self-tuning reactive trees proposed here. We used the reactive diffracting trees of [2] as a basis of comparison since they are the most efficient reactive counting constructions in the literature.

The source code of [2] is not publicly available and we implemented it following exactly the algorithm as it is presented in the paper. We used the full-contention benchmark, the index distribution benchmark [2] and the surge load benchmark [2] on the SGI Origin2000, a popular commercial ccNUMA multiprocessor.

In [2], besides running the benchmarks on a non-commercially availiable machine with 32 processors (Alewife), the authors also ran them on the simulator simulating a multiprocessor system similar to Alewife with up to 256 processors.

The most difficult issue in implementing the reactive diffracting tree is to find the best folding and unfolding thresholds as well as the number of consecutive timings called *UNFOLDING_LIMIT, FOLDING_LIMIT* and *MINIMUM_HITS* in [2]. However, subsection *Load Surge Benchmark* in [2] described that the reactive diffracting tree sized to a depth 3 tree when they ran index-distribution benchmark [1] with 32 processors in the highest possible load ($work = 0$) and the number of consecutive timings was set at 10. According to the description, we run our implementation of the reactive diffracting tree on the ccNUMA Origin 2000 with 32 MIPS R10000 processors and the result is that folding and unfolding thresholds are 4 and 14 microseconds, respectively. This selection of parameters did not only keep our experiments consistent with the ones presented in [1] but also gave the best performance for the diffracting trees in our system. Regarding the prism size (prism is an algorithmic construct used in diffracting process in the reactive diffracting trees), each node has $c2^{(d-l)}$ prism locations, where $c = 0.5$, d is the average value of the reactive diffracting tree depths estimated by processors passing the tree and l is the level of the node [2,5]. The upper bound for adaptive spin *MAXSPIN* is 128 as mentioned in [1].

In order to make the properties and the performance of the self-tuning reactive tree algorithm presented here accessible to other researchers and to help reproducibility of our results, C code for the tested algorithms is available at http://www.cs.chalmers.se/~phuong/sat_jul04.tar.gz.

4.1 Full-Contention and Index Distribution Benchmarks

The system used for our experiments was a ccNUMA SGI Origin2000 with sixty four 195MHz MIPS R10000 CPUs with 4MB L2 cache each. The system ran IRIX 6.5. We ran the reactive diffracting tree *RD-tree* and the self-tuning reactive tree *ST-tree* in the full-contention benchmark, in which each thread continuously executed only the function to traverse the respective tree, and in the index distribution benchmark with $work = 500\mu s$ [2][1]. Each experiment ran for one minute and we counted the average number of operations per second.

Results: The results are shown in Figure 6 and Figure 7. The right charts in both the figures show the average depth of the ST-tree compared to the RD-tree. The left charts show the proportion of the ST-tree throughput to that of the RD-tree.

The most interesting result is that when the contention on the leaves increases, the ST-tree automatically adjusts its size close to that of the RD-tree that requires three experimental parameters for each specific system.

Regarding throughput and scalability, we observed that the ST-tree performs better than the RD-tree. This is because the ST-tree has a faster and more efficient reactive scheme. The surge load benchmark in the next subsection shows that the reactive trees *continuously* adjust their current size slightly around the average size corresponding to a certain load (cf. Figure 8). Therefore, an efficient adjustment procedure will significantly improve the performance of the trees.

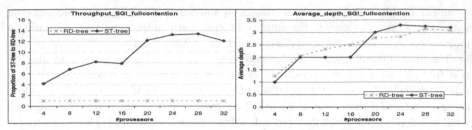

Fig. 6. Throughput and average depth of trees in the full-contention benchmark on SGI Origin2000

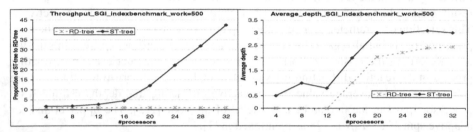

Fig. 7. Throughput and average depth of trees in the index distribution benchmark with $work = 500\mu s$ on SGI Origin2000

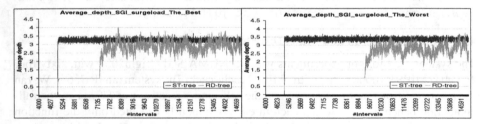

Fig. 8. Average depths of trees in the surge benchmark on SGI Origin2000, best and worst measurements. In a black-and-white printout, the darker line is the ST-tree

Studing the figures closer, in the full-contention benchmark (Figure 6), we can observe the scalability properties of the ST-tree, which shows increased throughput with increasing number of processors (as expected using the aforementioned arguments) in the left chart. The right chart shows that the average depth of the ST-trees is nearly the same as that of the RD-tree, i.e. the reaction decisions are pretty close.

In the index distribution benchmark with $work = 500\mu s$, which provides a lower-load environment, the ST-tree can be observed to show very desirable scalability behavior as well, as shown in Figure 7. The charts of the average depths of both trees have approximately the same shapes again, but the ST-tree expands from half to one depth unit more than RD-tree. This is because the throughput of the former was larger, hence the contention on the ST-tree leaves was higher than that on RD-tree leaves, and this made the ST-tree expand more.

4.2   Surge Load Benchmark

The benchmark shows how fast the trees react to contention variations. The benchmark is run on a smaller but faster machine[3], ccNUMA SGI2000 with thirty 250MHz MIPS R10000 CPUs with 4MB L2 cache each. On the machine the optimal folding and unfolding thresholds, which keep our experiments consistent with the ones presented in [1], are 3 and 10 microseconds, respectively. All other parameters are kept the same as the benchmarks discussed in the previous subsection.

In this benchmark we measured the average depth of each tree in each interval of 400 microseconds. The measurement was done by a monitor thread. At interval 5000, the number of threads was changed from four to twenty eight. The average depth of the trees at the interval 5001 was measured after synchronizing the monitor threads with all the new threads, i.e. the period between the end of interval 5000 and the beginning of interval 5001 was not 400 microseconds. Figure 8 shows the average depth of both trees from interval 4000 to interval 15000. The left chart shows the best reaction time figures for the RD-tree and the ST-tree; the right one shows the worst reaction time figures for the RD-tree and the ST-tree. In the benchmark, the ST-tree reached the suitable depth 3 for the case of 28 threads at interval 5004 in the best case and 5008 in the worst case, i.e. only after 5 to 8 intervals since the time all 28 threads started to run. The RD-tree reached level 3 at interval 7447 in the best case and at interval 9657 in the worst case. That means the reactive scheme introduced in this paper and used by the ST-tree makes the same decisions as the RD-tree, and, moreover, it reacts to contention variations much faster than the latter.

5   Conclusion

The self-tuning reactive trees presented in this work distribute the set of processors that are accessing them, to many smaller groups accessing disjoint critical sections in a coordinated manner. They collect information about the contention at the leaves (critical sections) and then they adjust themselves to attain adaptive performance. The self-tuning reactive trees extend a successful result in the area of reactive concurrent data structures, the reactive diffracting trees, in the following way:

- The reactive adjustment policy does not use parameters which have to be set manually and which depend on experimentation.
- The reactive adjustment policy is based on an efficient adaptive algorithmic scheme.
- They can expand or shrink many levels at a time with small overhead.
- Processors pass through the tree in only one direction, from the root to the leaves and are never forced to go back.

Moreover, the self-tuning reactive trees:

- have space needs comparable with that of the classical reactive diffracting trees

---

[3] This is because the first machine was replaced with that one at our computer center while this experimental evaluation was still in progress.

- exploit low contention cases on subtrees to make their locking process as efficient as in the classical reactive diffracting trees although the locking process locks more nodes at the same time.

Therefore, the self-tuning reactive trees can react quickly to changes of the contention levels, and at the same time offer a good latency to the processes traversing them and good scalability behavior. We have also presented an experimental evaluation of the new trees, on the SGI Origin2000, a well-known commercial ccNUMA multiprocessor. We think that it is of big interest to do a performance evaluation on modern multiprocessor systems that are widely used in practice.

Last, we would like to emphasize an important point. Although the new trees have better performance than the classical ones in the experimental evaluation conducted and presented here, this is not the main contribution of this paper. What we consider as main contribution is the ability of the new trees to self-tune their size efficiently without any need of manual tuning.

References

1. Shavit, N., Zemach, A.: Diffracting trees. ACM Trans. Comput. Syst. **14** (1996) 385–428
2. Della-Libera, G., Shavit, N.: Reactive diffracting trees. J. Parallel Distrib. Comput. **60** (2000) 853–890
3. Ha, P.H., Papatriantafilou, M., Tsigas, P.:   Self-adjusting trees.   Technical Report 2003-09, Computing Science, Chalmers University of Technology (2003) http://www.cs.chalmers.se/~phuong/ SAT_TR.ps.gz.
4. El-Yaniv, R., Fiat, A., Karp, R.M., Turpin, G.: Optimal search and one-way trading online algorithms. Algorithmica **30** (2001) 101–139
5. Shavit, N., Upfal, E., Zemach, A.: A steady state analysis of diffracting trees. Theory of Computing Systems **31** (1998) 403–423

Optimal Resilience Asynchronous Approximate Agreement

Ittai Abraham, Yonatan Amit, and Danny Dolev

School of Computer Science and Engineering,
The Hebrew University of Jerusalem, Israel
{ittaia, mitmit, dolev}@cs.huji.ac.il

Abstract. Consider an asynchronous system where each process begins with an arbitrary real value. Given some fixed $\epsilon > 0$, an approximate agreement algorithm must have all non-faulty processes decide on values that are at most ϵ from each other and are in the range of the initial values of the non-faulty processes.

Previous constructions solved asynchronous approximate agreement only when there were at least $5t + 1$ processes, t of which may be Byzantine. In this paper we close an open problem raised by Dolev et al. in 1983. We present a deterministic optimal resilience approximate agreement algorithm that can tolerate any t Byzantine faults while requiring only $3t + 1$ processes.

The algorithm's rate of convergence and total message complexity are efficiently bounded as a function of the range of the initial values of the non-faulty processes. All previous asynchronous algorithms that are resilient to Byzantine failures may require arbitrarily many messages to be sent.

Keywords: approximate agreement, Byzantine agreement, asynchronous systems.

1 Introduction

In the classical Byzantine Generals problem a set of processes begin with some initial value and must reach agreement on one of the initial values is spite of having some faulty processes. In the approximate version it is required that the values of all non-faulty processes eventually converge to a range that is bounded by some predefined $\epsilon > 0$.

It is well know that in asynchronous communication models reaching agreement is impossible under the possibility of having even one faulty process [8]. In sharp contrast, Dolev et al. [3, 4], show that approximate agreement is possible in asynchronous systems that have $5t+1$ processes, t of which may be Byzantine.

In this paper we solve the open question raised by [3, 4]. We show that Approximate Agreement can be reached with $3t + 1$ processes, t of which may be Byzantine. Fischer et al. [7] show that there is no approximate agreement protocol with $3t$ or less processes that can tolerate t Byzantine failure. Hence our algorithm has optimal resilience.

T. Higashino (Ed.): OPODIS 2004, LNCS 3544, pp. 229–239, 2005.
© Springer-Verlag Berlin Heidelberg 2005

The results are further strengthened by bounding the total number of rounds and the total number of messages sent. We bound the number of rounds until termination as a function of the range of initial values of the non-faulty processes. Our round and message efficiency is in contrast to all previous asynchronous solutions [4] in which the faulty processes can cause the protocol to run for an arbitrarily high (yet final) number of rounds.

The results presented in this paper are obtained using two building blocks. One is an asynchronous version of the Reliable-Broadcast protocol of Srikanth and Toueg [11]. The other building block is a novel *witness* technique. The witness technique limits the ability of faulty processes to lie about the range of values they were able to collect. This building block seems to be very powerful and it enables the non-faulty processes to rapidly converge their values.

There is a large body of work on stronger assumptions or weaker properties of the Approximate Agreement problem. In the synchronous version of approximate agreement, Mahaney and Schneider [10] improve the time complexity by using the Crusader Agreement protocol of Dolev [2] as a building block. Fekete [5] gives algorithms with asymptotically optimal convergence rates for the synchronous version of the problem. Fekete [6] also gives efficient algorithms for the asynchronous approximate agrement problem that is resilient against weaker adversaries of failure by omission and crash-failures. Kieckhafer and Azadmanesh [9] give a hybrid synchronous algorithm that can withstand both Byzantine and benign failures.

Another alternative for weakening the properties of Agreement is to require a probabilistic termination property that only guarantees a finite expectancy of termination (but there may exist infinite executions). Bracha [1] presents a randomized $3t + 1$ resilient Byzantine Agreement protocol with probabilistic termination. In contrast, our protocol is deterministic and always guarantees termination.

1.1   Model and Problem Definition

Consider a set of n processes. Processes communicate by a fully connected asynchronous network with reliable FIFO channels. Messages sent will eventually arrive after a finite unbounded amount of time. The channels between any two processes maintain FIFO property, if p sends to q message m and later sends message m' then q will first receive m and only later receive m'.

We assume that t of the processes may be Byzantine. All other processes follow the algorithm and are denoted as non-faulty.

Assume each non-faulty process begins with an arbitrary real input value and fix some (arbitrarily small) pre-agreed $\epsilon > 0$. An *Approximate Agreement Algorithm* must satisfy the following two conditions:

Agreement. All non-faulty processes eventually halt with output values that are within ϵ of each other;

Validity. The value output by each non-faulty process must be within the range of the initial values of non-faulty processes.

1.2   Notations

Let V denote the set of processes, and G the set of non-faulty processes. Hence $n = |V|$ and $|G| \geq n - t$.

Let S denote a finite multiset of reals. Intuitively S can be thought of as a set of real numbers in which repetitions are considered. For example $\{1, 1, 3\}$ equals $\{1, 3, 1\}$ but differs from $\{1, 3\}$. Formally let $\mathbb{R}$ denote the set of reals and $\mathbb{N}$ the set of natural numbers then S is a function $S : \mathbb{R} \mapsto \mathbb{N}$ such that $\{r \in \mathbb{R} \mid S(r) \neq 0\}$ is finite. Define $|S| = \sum_{r \in \mathbb{R}} S(r)$, $\min S = \min_{S(r) \neq 0}\{r \in \mathbb{R}\}$, $\max S = \max_{S(r) \neq 0}\{r \in \mathbb{R}\}$, and the *range* of S as $\delta(S) = \max S - \min S$.

Given a multiset S denote $s_1, s_2, \ldots, s_{|S|}$ the values of S ordered in a non decreasing order. For any $t < |S|/2$, define $trim(S, t)$ as the multiset containing the values $s_{t+1}, s_{t+2}, \ldots, s_{|S|-t-1}$ (removing the t largest and t smallest values from S). Define

$$reduce(S, t) = \frac{\max(trim(S, t)) + \min(trim(S, t))}{2}.$$

Given a set of processes V, let P be a set of (process,value) pairs. Formally, $P \subset (V \times \mathbb{R})$. Define $P_{|2}$ as the multiset of values of the second coordinate in P. To shorten notations, we extend the multiset operators to P, for example $\max P = \max P_{|2}$, $reduce(P, t) = reduce(P_{|2}, t)$.

We use the following conventions for defining the value of a variable during the execution of a protocol. All our protocols have explicit round numbers starting with 1 and incrementing by one each iteration. Given a variable x we denote x_p^h as the value of the variable x on process p when p completes its h-th round.

2   Reliable Broadcast and a $4t + 1$ Resiliency

The basic idea of [4] is to gather at least $n - t$ values, trim the t largest and t smallest of the gathered values, and then compute some averaging function of the remaining values as the next approximation. We begin by noting why the algorithm of Dolev et al. [4] fails for $4t + 1$ processes of which at most t may be Byzantine. Suppose $t + 1$ non faulty processes begin with 0 and another $2t$ non faulty processes begin with 1. The problem is that the remaining t Byzantine processes may send conflicting values to different processes. Specifically, all processes that begin with value $i \in \{0, 1\}$ may gather at least $2t + 1$ values that equal i so the trimming will cause them to see the same value i and never to converge. We overcome this difficulty by using Reliable-Broadcast.

Instead of gathering directly $n - t$ values, the simple $4t + 1$ algorithm gathers $n - t$ values that have been sent by Reliable-Broadcast.

The properties of the Reliable-Broadcast above are a variation of the asynchronous Reliable-Broadcast of [11]:

Correctness. If a non-faulty process p with a message m on round h performs Reliable-Broadcast(m, h) then all non-faulty processes will eventually Reliable-Accept(p, m, h).

Reliable-Broadcast code for process p with message m on round h:
　　send (p, m, h) to all processes;

Echo() method for process q:
　　upon receiving (p, m, h) from p
　　　　if q never sent a message of the form $(p, \cdot, h)$ then
　　　　　　send (p, m, h) to all processes;
　　upon receiving (p, m, h) from at least $t + 1$ unique processes;
　　　　if q never sent a message of the form $(p, \cdot, h)$ then
　　　　　　send (p, m, h) to all processes;

Condition for **Reliable-Accept**(p, m, h) at process q:
　　Received (p, m, h) from at least $n - t$ unique processes;

Fig. 1. Code for Reliable-Broadcast(m) and Reliable-Accept(p, m)

Non-forgeability. If a non-faulty process p does not perform at round h the task Reliable-Broadcast(m, h) then no non-faulty process will ever perform Reliable-Accept(p, m, h).

Uniqueness. If a non-faulty process performs Reliable-Accept(p, m, h) and another non-faulty process performs Reliable-Accept(p, m', h) then $m = m'$;

Lemma 1. *The algorithm in Figure 1 realizes Correctness, Non-forgeability, and Uniqueness.*

Proof. Non-forgeability holds since non-faulty processes will never receive the non existent message directly and hence may receive at most t indirect messages. Therefore a non-faulty process will never echo a nonexisting messages and clearly will never accept such a message.

Correctness holds since eventually every non-faulty process will receive either a direct message from p or $t + 1$ indirect messages and due to non-forgeability these are the only two options.

For uniqueness, suppose that the condition Reliable-Accept(p, m, h) holds for a non-faulty process q then at least $t + 1$ non-faulty processes have sent (p, m, h) hence any other non-faulty process can gather at most $n - (t + 1)$ messages of the form (p, m', h) with $m' \neq m$, hence such m' will never be accepted.   □

Given the Reliable-Broadcast primitive we present a simple $4t + 1$ resilient Approximate Agreement protocol. In each round, each process waits until it performs Reliable-Accept on $n - t$ different values.

Theorem 1. *Let U denote the multiset of initial values of non-faulty processes. If all non-faulty processes run the algorithm in Figure 2 for at least $\log_2(\delta(U)/\epsilon)$ rounds then their values are at most ϵ for each other and in the range of the initial values.*

Code for process p:

Local variables:
 $values \subset (V \times \mathbb{R})$ initially $values = \bot$;
 $init \in \mathbb{R}$; // the initial value;
 $val \in \mathbb{R}$ initially $val = init$;
 $round \in \mathbb{N}$ initially $round = 1$;

repeat:
 Reliable-Broadcast('value', $p, val, round$);
 $values := \bot$;
 repeat
  upon Reliable-Accept('value', q, u, h) and $h = round$ // the first time
    $values := values \cup (q, u)$;
 until $|values| \geq n - t$;
 $val := reduce(values, t)$;
 $round := round + 1$;

Fig. 2. The simple $4t + 1$ algorithm

The proof of this theorem can be derived as a simple exercise from the lemmata given for the $3t + 1$ algorithm and the fact that due to the Reliable-Broadcast mechanism, every two non-faulty processes accept at least $n - 2t \geq 2t+1$ common values in each round.

3   The $3t + 1$ Algorithm

We note that for $3t+1$ resilience, simply using Reliable-Broadcast and trimming is not enough. In the worst case, two processes may accept a multiset of values that intersect only at one value, and after trimming the resulting multisets will not intersect. For example, suppose $n = 4, t = 1$ and let the values be $0, 0, 1, 1$; the faulty process can arrange that all processes with value $i \in \{0, 1\}$ will receive 3 values and after trimming the median will equal i and no progress will be made.

Hence, for the $3t + 1$ resilient algorithm we use an additional mechanism of gathering witnesses. A witness for process p is a process whose first $n - t$ accepted values were also accepted by p. Process p waits to gather $n - t$ witnesses. Since each process gathers $n - t$ witnesses, every two processes have at least $t + 1$ common witnesses, and thus at least one non-faulty witness. Having a common non-faulty witness implies that every pair of non-faulty processes have at least $n - t$ commonly accepted values.

Each message is associated with a specific round. Given a message with a higher round number than the current round, the receiving process saves it and will treat it as a new message when the process will reach the relevant round.

We also need a mechanism that allows processes to know when to decide on their value and halt. Let U denote the multiset of initial values of non-faulty processes, ideally we aim to bound the number of rounds (and hence the number of messages sent) as a function of $\delta(U)$, the range of the initial values of the non-faulty processes (non-faulty range).

We note that in the asynchronous algorithm of [4] the Byzantine process can induce arbitrarily high and low values that will cause the protocol to run for an arbitrarily large (but finite) number of rounds.

In order to achieve round and message efficiency we employ a special initial round protocol that estimates the non-faulty range. The idea is to force all processes (even Byzantine ones) to Reliable-Broadcast the vector of values they gathered. This enforces a process to send values that are all inside the range of the initial values U. We show that the estimation of $\delta(U)$ by any non-faulty process is adequate to ensure that the resulting values are within ϵ of each other.

Different processes may have different estimations on the number of rounds required. Hence, care should be taken so that processes do not halt too early and cause others never to terminate. Specifically, a process waits until it Reliable-Accepts at least $t + 1$ 'halt' messages and it reaches a round larger

---

Local variables:
    $values \subset (V \times \mathbb{R})$ initially $values = \bot$;
    $init \in \mathbb{R}$; // the initial value;
    $val \in \mathbb{R}$ initially $val = init$;
    $(\forall x \in V) :\ report[x], proof[x] \subset (V \times \mathbb{R})$ initially $proof[x] := \bot$;
    $witnesses, proven \subset V$;
    $round, enough \in \mathbb{N}$ initially $round = 1$;
    $L \subset \mathbb{N}$ initially $L = \bot$;

Code for process p:
init();
repeat
    Reliable-Broadcast('value', $p, val, round$);
    $values := \bot$;
    $(\forall x \in V) :\ report[x] := \bot$;
    repeat
        // delay high round messages, discard low round messages
        upon Reliable-Accept('value', q, u, h) and $h = round$
            FIFO-Broadcast('report', q, u, h) to all;
            $values := values \cup (q, u)$;
        upon FIFO-Accept('report', q, u, h) from process r and $h = round$
            $report[r] := report[r] \cup (q, u)$;
        $witnesses := \{x \in V \mid report[x] \subseteq values$ and $|report[x]| \geq n - t\}$;
        check/decide();
    until $|witnesses| \geq n - t$;
    $val := reduce(values, t)$;
    $round := round + 1$;

Fig. 3. The $3t + 1$ algorithm

Code for **init()**
    Reliable-Broadcast('init', p, val);
    repeat
       upon Reliable-Accept('init', q, u) (The first value from q)
          then $values := values \cup (q, u)$;
    until $|values| \geq n - t$;
    Reliable-Broadcast('proof', $p, values$);
    repeat
       upon Reliable-Accept('init', q, u) (The first value from q)
          then $values := values \cup (q, u)$;
       upon Reliable-Accept('proof', $q, vals$) (The first proof from q)
          then $proof[q] := vals$;
      $proven := \{v \in V \mid proof[v] \neq \perp$ and $proof[v] \subseteq values\}$;
    until $|proven| \geq n - t$;
    $values := \{(q, reduce(proof[q], t)) \mid q \in proven\}$;
    $val := reduce(values, t)$;
    $enough := \lceil \log_2(\delta(values)/\epsilon) \rceil + 1$;

Code for **check/decide()**
    if $(round = enough)$ then Reliable-Broadcast('halt', $p, round$) to all;
    upon Reliable-Accept('halt', q, h) (the first halt from q) then $L := L \cup \{h\}$;
    if $|L| \geq t + 1$ and $round > \min(trim(L, t))$ then **decide** val and **halt**;

Fig. 4. The **init()** and **check/decide()** methods for process p

than the estimation of at least one non-faulty process whose 'halt' message it accepted.

The code for the $3t + 1$ algorithm appears in Figure 3 and Figure 4.

4   Analysis

4.1   Informal Properties of Witness:

In order to advance in a round a process p requires at least $n - t$ witnesses. Process x is a witness for process p if the first $n - t$ values that x claimed to accept were accepted by p.

Since 'report' messages are sent via FIFO-Broadcast then if x is a non-faulty witness for both p, q then both p and q must have accepted the *first* $n - t$ values that x has accepted.

4.2   Liveness

Lemma 2. *If no non-faulty process halts before or during round h and all of them reach round h, then all non-faulty processes eventually advance to round $h + 1$.*

Proof. Seeking a contradiction, let $S \subseteq G$ be the set of non-faulty processes that never advance to round $h + 1$.

Eventually every $p \in G$ will Reliable-Broadcast its value. Hence eventually every $p \in G$ will Reliable-Accept at least $n - t$ values. Therefore every $p \in G$ will send at least $n - t$ 'report' messages. Hence eventually all $p \in S$ will Reliable-Accept each value in these 'report' messages. Hence all $p \in G$ will eventually have at least $n - t$ witnesses, and must advance.   □

Lemma 3. *All non-faulty processes eventually decide and halt.*

Proof. Seeking a contradiction, suppose some set of non-faulty processes $S \subseteq G$ never decides.

We begin by showing that at least one process must halt. Eventually by Lemma 2 the round number will be higher than the *enough* values of $t + 1$ non-faulty processes and so at least $t + 1$ 'halt' messages will be sent. Recall that a process p halts when its round number is larger than $\min(trim(L_p, t))$ and $|L_p| \geq t + 1$ (see the last line of the *check/decide* method). Hence eventually some non-faulty process will halt.

Let h be the minimum round that some process $p \in G$ halts at, hence by Lemma 2 all non-faulty processes will eventually reach round h. Since 'halt' messages are sent via Reliable-Broadcast, all other non-faulty processes will eventually receive the same set of 'halt' messages (with the same round values) that caused p to halt. Hence all non-faulty processes will eventually have $\min(trim(L_p, t)) \leq h$ and so must eventually halt.   □

4.3   Safety

Lemma 4 (Validity). *For all $p \in G$ and round h,*

$$\min U \leq val_p^h \leq \max U .$$

Proof. The proof is by induction on round numbers. Clearly the initial values are in U by definition. Assuming that all the values of the previous round (or the initial values for $h = 1$) for all $p \in G$ are in the range, then the next value val^h is a product of $reduce(values^{h-1}, t)$ for some set of values that were sent by Reliable-Broadcast (or in the **init** method, their proofs were sent via Reliable-Broadcast). Since there are at most t Byzantine processes, and *reduce* trims the t largest and t smallest accepted values, the maximal and minimal remaining values will always be inside the range of the maximal and minimal values of set of values of the non-faulty processes at the previous round. Hence the averaging in $reduce(values, t)$ will be on values that are in the range of U by the induction hypothesis.   □

The witness property is stated as follows:

Lemma 5. *Every pair of non-faulty processes p, q that complete round h, maintain that*

$$\left| values_p^h \cap values_q^h \right| \geq n - t .$$

Proof. If non-faulty processes p, q finish round h, they have at least $t+1$ common witnesses. This follows from the fact that each has at least $n - t$ witnesses, and every $n - t$ quorum has a $t + 1$ intersection with every other quorum. Hence p, q have at least one common non-faulty witness r.

By the definition of witnesses and the FIFO properties of the 'report' messages, the first $n - t$ values accepted by r will appear both in $values_p$ and in $values_q$.   □

Define $U_i = \bigcup_{p \in G} val_p^i$ be the multiset containing the *val* values of all the non-faulty processes after they all completed round i. We now show an exponential decrease in the range.

Lemma 6. *The range of non-faulty processes is cut by at least a half*

$$\delta(U_i) \leq \frac{\delta(U_{i-1})}{2} .$$

Proof. By Lemma 5 we know that every two processes have in common at least $n - t$ accepted values. Let p, q be two arbitrary non-faulty processes, with $values_p^i, values_q^i$ as their multiset of values. Without loss of generality we assume that $val_p^i \geq val_q^i$. Denote $m = \min(U_{i-1})$ and $M = \max(U_{i-1})$. It is sufficient to prove the following:

Claim: $val_p^i - val_q^i \leq \frac{M-m}{2}$

Proof: Denote $R = values_p^i \cap values_q^i$, thus $|R| \geq n - t$ and denote $V_p = trim(values_p^i, t)$, $V_q = trim(values_q^i, t)$.

Let x be the median of R, then $x \in V_q$ because R has at least $n - t$ elements and we only trim t from each side. Hence $\max(V_q) \geq x$. In addition, $\min(V_q) \geq m$ because *trim* removes the t smallest elements in $values_q^i$. Therefore $val_q \geq \frac{m+x}{2}$.

In a similar fashion, $x \in V_p$, which implies $\min(V_p) \leq x$ and $\max(V_p) \leq M$ and thus $val_p \leq \frac{M+x}{2}$. Combining with the above we get $val_p - val_q \leq \frac{M-m}{2}$.
                                                                                     □

4.4   Termination Detection

We now show that the algorithm runs for sufficiently many rounds to ensure non-faulty values are at most ϵ of each other.

Lemma 7. *Let k denote the minimal round estimation $k = \min\{enough_r \mid r \in G\}$. Then if all $p \in G$ complete round k then*

$$(\forall p, q \in G)\ |val_p^k - val_q^k| \leq \epsilon .$$

Proof. Let p be a process such that $enough_p = k$. Examine the $n - t$ values in $values_p$ at the end of the **init** method. Consider a non-faulty process q, it also gathers $values_q$ by the end of its **init** method. Due to the fact that the values and proofs are sent via Reliable-Broadcast, process q can receive and accept at most t values that are not in $values_p$, all other values that q accepts must agree with $values_p$. Hence if we trim the t largest and t smallest values in $values_q$ the range of the remaining values is inside the range of $values_p$. Formally, we have

$$\min values_p \leq reduce(values_q, t) \leq \max values_p .$$

Then by iteratively applying Lemma 6, after all non-faulty processes run for $\log_2(\delta(values_p)/\epsilon)$ rounds, their values will be close enough. $\square$

Let U be the set of initial values of non-faulty processes and A be the set of all the initial values that are eventually accepted by Reliable-Accept by the end of the initial round (so $U \subseteq A$). Let $C = trim(A, t)$. Clearly $\delta(C) \leq \delta(U)$ because removing the t largest and t smallest elements from A results in a range that is at most the range of U.

Lemma 8. *The number of rounds that any non-faulty process completes is at most*

$$\log_2\left(\frac{\delta(U)}{\epsilon}\right).$$

Proof. For any process q, and prover $r \in proven_q$ we have

$$\min C \leq reduce(proof[r]_q, t) \leq \max C$$

Notice that r may be faulty. This is true since $proof[r]$ is a set of $n - t$ values that were sent by Reliable-Broadcast, hence $proof[r] \subseteq A$ and trimming $proof[r]$ results in a range that is smaller than $\delta(C)$. Hence $\min U \leq \min values_q$ and $\max values_q \leq \max U$, because $values_q$ is set in **init** to be the set of $reduce(proof[r], t)$, for all $r \in proven_q$. Therefore $enough_p \leq \log_2\left(\frac{\delta(U)}{\epsilon}\right)$ for all $p \in G$.

Let $E = \bigcup_{p \in G} enough_p$ then all $p \in G$ halt after at most $\min(trim(E, t))$ rounds. This is true because they will eventually receive $t + 1$ 'halt' messages and decide. However after round $\min(trim(E, t))$ no process can gather $n - t$ replies and hence cannot advance further. $\square$

Theorem 2. *All non-faulty processes terminate after at most $\log_2(\delta(U))/\epsilon)$ rounds, with values that are at most ϵ of each other, in the range of the initial values.*

Proof. All non-faulty processes halt by Lemma 3. Termination is in at most $\log_2(\delta(U)/\epsilon)$ rounds, deduced from Lemma 8. Since termination requires $t + 1$ *halt* messages, it occurs at a round that is larger than $enough_p$ for some $p \in G$, hence from Lemma 6 and Lemma 7 the decision values are ϵ from each other. Finally, Lemma 4 proves that the decision values are inside the initial values of the non-faulty processes. $\square$

5   Conclusions

In this paper we solve the open question left from the original paper solving the Approximate Agreement problem. The protocol presented limits the ability of the faulty processes to influence the convergence of the non-faulty processes.

The novel witness technique used in the paper seems to be very powerful. We wonder how useful it is in solving other problems. For example, what impact can it have for solving clock synchronization problems?

An interesting topic is the bounds on the rate of convergence. Now that it is only depends on the range of values of the non-faulty processes, one can look for an optimal convergence rate.

References

1. G. Bracha. An asynchronous $\lfloor (n-1)/3 \rfloor$-resilient consensus protocol. In *Proceedings of the third annual ACM symposium on Principles of distributed computing*, pages 154–162. ACM Press, 1984.
2. D. Dolev. The byzantine generals strike again. *J. Algorithms*, 3(1), 1982.
3. D. Dolev, N. A. Lynch, S. S. Pinter, E. W. Stark, and W. E. Weihl. Reaching approximate agreement in the presence of faults. In *Proceedings of the 3rd Symposium on Reliability in Distributed Systems*, 1983.
4. D. Dolev, N. A. Lynch, S. S. Pinter, E. W. Stark, and W. E. Weihl. Reaching approximate agreement in the presence of faults. *J. ACM*, 33(3):499–516, 1986.
5. A. D. Fekete. Asymptotically optimal algorithms for approximate agreement. In *Proceedings of the fifth annual ACM symposium on Principles of distributed computing*, pages 73–87. ACM Press, 1986.
6. A. D. Fekete. Asynchronous approximate agreement. In *Proceedings of the sixth annual ACM Symposium on Principles of distributed computing*, pages 64–76. ACM Press, 1987.
7. M. J. Fischer, N. A. Lynch, and M. Merritt. Easy impossibility proofs for distributed consensus problems. In *Proceedings of the fourth annual ACM symposium on Principles of distributed computing*, pages 59–70. ACM Press, 1985.
8. M. J. Fischer, N. A. Lynch, and M. S. Paterson. Impossibility of distributed consensus with one faulty process. *Journal of the ACM*, 32(2):374–382, 1985.
9. R. M. Kieckhafer and M. H. Azadmanesh. Reaching approximate agreement with mixed-mode faults. *IEEE Trans. Parallel Distrib. Syst.*, 5(1):53–63, 1994.
10. S. R. Mahaney and F. B. Schneider. Inexact agreement: accuracy, precision, and graceful degradation. In *Proceedings of the fourth annual ACM symposium on Principles of distributed computing*, pages 237–249. ACM Press, 1985.
11. T. K. Srikanth and S. Toueg. Simulating authenticated broadcasts to derive simple fault-tolerant algorithms. *Distributed Computing*, 2(2):80–94, 1987.

Lock-Free and Practical Doubly Linked List-Based Deques Using Single-Word Compare-and-Swap

Håkan Sundell and Philippas Tsigas

Department of Computing Science,
Chalmers University of Technology and Göteborg University,
412 96 Göteborg, Sweden
{phs, tsigas}@cs.chalmers.se
http://www.cs.chalmers.se/~{phs, tsigas}

Abstract. We present an efficient and practical lock-free implementation of a concurrent deque that supports parallelism for disjoint accesses and uses atomic primitives which are available in modern computer systems. Previously known lock-free algorithms of deques are either based on non-available atomic synchronization primitives, only implement a subset of the functionality, or are not designed for disjoint accesses. Our algorithm is based on a general lock-free doubly linked list, and only requires single-word compare-and-swap atomic primitives. It also allows pointers with full precision, and thus supports dynamic deque sizes. We have performed an empirical study using full implementations of the most efficient known algorithms of lock-free deques. For systems with low concurrency, the algorithm by Michael shows the best performance. However, as our algorithm is designed for disjoint accesses, it performs significantly better on systems with high concurrency and non-uniform memory architecture. In addition, the proposed solution also implements a general doubly linked list, the first lock-free implementation that only needs the single-word compare-and-swap atomic primitive.

1 Introduction

A deque (i.e. double-ended queue) is a fundamental data structure. For example, deques are often used for implementing the ready queue used for scheduling of tasks in operating systems. A deque supports four operations, the *PushRight*, the *PopRight*, the *PushLeft*, and the *PopLeft* operation. The abstract definition of a deque is a list of values, where the *PushRight/PushLeft* operation adds a new value to the right/left edge of the list. The *PopRight/PopLeft* operation correspondingly removes and returns the value on the right/left edge of the list.

To ensure consistency of a shared data object in a concurrent environment, the most common method is mutual exclusion, i.e. some form of locking. Mutual exclusion degrades the system's overall performance [1] as it causes blocking,

T. Higashino (Ed.): OPODIS 2004, LNCS 3544, pp. 240–255, 2005.

i.e. other concurrent operations can not make any progress while the access to the shared resource is blocked by the lock. Mutual exclusion can also cause deadlocks, priority inversion and even starvation.

In order to address these problems, researchers have proposed non-blocking algorithms for shared data objects. Non-blocking algorithms do not involve mutual exclusion, and therefore do not suffer from the problems that blocking could generate. Lock-free implementations are non-blocking and guarantee that regardless of the contention caused by concurrent operations and the interleaving of their sub-operations, always at least one operation will progress. However, there is a risk for starvation as the progress of some operations could cause some other operations to never finish. Wait-free [2] algorithms are lock-free and moreover they avoid starvation as well, as all operations are then guaranteed to finish in a limited number of their own steps. Recently, some researchers also include obstruction-free [3] implementations to the non-blocking set of implementations. These kinds of implementations are weaker than the lock-free ones and do not guarantee progress of any concurrent operation.

The implementation of a lock-based concurrent deque is a trivial task, and can preferably be constructed using either a doubly linked list or a cyclic array, protected by either a single lock or by multiple locks where each lock protects a part of the shared data structure. To the best of our knowledge, there exists no implementations of wait-free deques, but several lock-free implementations have been proposed. However, all previous lock-free deques lack in several important aspects, as they either only implement a subset of the operations that are normally associated with a deque and have concurrency restrictions[1] like Arora et al. [4], or are based on atomic hardware primitives like Double-Word Compare-And-Swap (CAS2)[2] which is not available in modern computer systems. Greenwald [5] presented a CAS2-based deque implementation as well as a general doubly linked list implementation [6], and there is also a publication series of a CAS2-based deque implementation [7],[8] with the latest version by Martin et al. [9]. Valois [10] sketched out an implementation of a lock-free doubly linked list structure using Compare-And-Swap (CAS)[3], though without any support for deletions and is therefore not suitable for implementing a deque. Michael [11] has developed a deque implementation based on CAS. However, it is not designed to allow parallelism for disjoint accesses as all operations have to synchronize, even though they operate on different ends of the deque. Secondly, in order to support dynamic maximum deque sizes it requires an extended

---

[1] The algorithm by Arora et al. does not support push operations on both ends, and does not allow concurrent invocations of the push operation and a pop operation on the opposite end.

[2] A CAS2 operations can atomically read-and-possibly-update the contents of two non-adjacent memory words. This operation is also sometimes called DCAS in the literature.

[3] The standard CAS operation can atomically read-and-possibly-update the contents of a single memory word.

CAS operation that can atomically operate on two adjacent words, which is not available[4] on all modern platforms.

In this paper we present a lock-free algorithm for implementing a concurrent deque that supports parallelism for disjoint accesses (in the sense that operations on different ends of the deque do not necessarily interfere with each other). An earlier description of this algorithm appeared as a technical report [12] in March 2004. The algorithm is implemented using common synchronization primitives that are available in modern systems. It allows pointers with full precision, and thus supports dynamic maximum deque sizes (in the presence of a lock-free dynamic memory handler with sufficient garbage collection support), still using normal CAS-operations. The algorithm is described in detail later in this paper, together with the aspects concerning the underlying lock-free memory management. In the algorithm description the precise semantics of the operations are defined and a proof that our implementation is lock-free and linearizable [13] is also given.

We have performed experiments that compare the performance of our algorithm with two of the most efficient algorithms of lock-free deques known; [11] and [9], the latter implemented using results from [14] and [15]. Experiments were performed on three different multiprocessor systems equipped with 2,4 or 29 processors respectively. All three systems used were running different operating systems and were based on different architectures. Our results show that the CAS-based algorithms outperforms the CAS2-based implementations[5] for any number of threads and any system. In non-uniform memory architectures with high contention our algorithm, because of its disjoint access property, performs significantly better than the algorithm in [11].

The rest of the paper is organized as follows. In Section 2 we describe the type of targeted systems. The actual algorithm is described in Section 3. The experimental evaluation is presented in Section 4. We conclude the paper with Section 5.

2   System Description

Each node of the shared memory multi-processor system contains a processor together with its local memory. All nodes are connected to the shared memory via an interconnection network. A set of co-operating tasks is running on the system performing their respective operations. Each task is sequentially executed on one of the processors, while each processor can serve (run) many tasks at a time. The co-operating tasks, possibly running on different processors, use shared

---

[4] It is available on the Intel IA-32, but not on the Sparc or MIPS microprocessor architectures. It is neither available on any currently known and common 64-bit architecture.

[5] The CAS2 operation was implemented in software, using either mutual exclusion or the results from [15], which presented an software CASn (CAS for n non-adjacent words) implementation.

data objects built in the shared memory to co-ordinate and communicate. Tasks synchronize their operations on the shared data objects through sub-operations on top of a cache-coherent shared memory. The shared memory may not though be uniformly accessible for all nodes in the system; processors can have different access times on different parts of the memory.

3   The New Lock-Free Algorithm

The algorithm is based on a doubly linked list data structure, see Figure 1. To use the data structure as a deque, every node contains a value. The fields of each node item are described in Figure 5 as it is used in this implementation. Note that the doubly linked list data structure always contains the static head and tail dummy nodes.

In order to make the doubly linked list construction concurrent and non-blocking, we are using two of the standard atomic synchronization primitives, Fetch-And-Add (FAA) and Compare-And-Swap (CAS). Figure 2 describes the specification of these primitives which are available in most modern platforms.

To insert or delete a node from the list we have to change the respective set of prev and next pointers. These have to be changed consistently, but not necessarily all at once. Our solution is to treat the doubly linked list as being a singly linked list with auxiliary information in the prev pointers, with the next pointers being updated before the prev pointers. Thus, the next pointers always form a consistent singly linked list, but the prev pointers only give hints for where to find the previous node. This is possible because of the observation that a "late" non-updated prev pointer will always point to a node that is directly or some steps before the current node, and from that "hint" position it is always

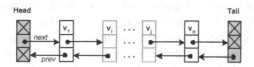

Fig. 1. The doubly linked list data structure

```
procedure FAA(address:pointer to word, number:integer)
    atomic do
        *address := *address + number;

function CAS(address:pointer to word, oldvalue:word, newvalue:word):boolean
    atomic do
        if *address = oldvalue then *address := newvalue; return true;
        else return false;
```

Fig. 2. The Fetch-And-Add (FAA) and Compare-And-Swap (CAS) atomic primitives

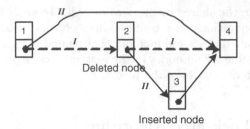

Fig. 3. Concurrent insert and delete operations can delete both nodes

possible to traverse[6] through the next pointers to reach the directly previous node.

One problem, that is general for non-blocking implementations that are based on the singly linked list data structure, arises when inserting a new node into the list. Because of the linked list structure one has to make sure that the previous node is not about to be deleted. If we are changing the next pointer of this previous node atomically with a CAS operation, to point to the new node, and then immediately afterwards the previous node is deleted - then the new node will be deleted as well, as illustrated in Figure 3. There are several solutions to this problem. One solution is to use the CAS2 operation as it can change two pointers atomically, but this operation is not available in any modern multiprocessor system. A second solution is to insert auxiliary nodes [10] between every two normal nodes, and the latest method introduced by Harris [16] is to use a deletion mark. This deletion mark is updated atomically together with the next pointer. Any concurrent insert operation will then be notified about the possibly set deletion mark, when its CAS operation will fail on updating the next pointer of the to-be-previous node. For our doubly linked list we need to be informed also when inserting using the prev pointer.

In order to allow usage of a system-wide dynamic memory handler (which should be lock-free and have garbage collection capabilities), all significant bits of an arbitrary pointer value must be possible to be represented in both the next and prev pointers. In order to atomically update both the next and prev pointer together with the deletion mark as done by Michael [11], the CAS-operation would need the capability of atomically updating at least $30 + 30 + 1 = 61$ bits on a 32-bit system (and $62 + 62 + 1 = 125$ bits on a 64-bit system as the pointers are then 64 bit). In practice though, most current 32 and 64-bit systems only support CAS operations of single word-size.

However, in our doubly linked list implementation, we never need to change both the prev and next pointers in one atomic update, and the pre-condition associated with each atomic pointer update only involves the pointer that is changed. Therefore it is possible to keep the prev and next pointers in separate

---

[6] As will be shown later, we have defined the deque data structure in a way that makes it possible to traverse even through deleted nodes, as long as they are referenced in some way.

words, duplicating the deletion mark in each of the words. In order to preserve the correctness of the algorithm, the deletion mark of the next pointer should always be set first, and the deletion mark of the prev pointer should be assured to be set by any operation that has observed the deletion mark on the next pointer, before any other updating steps are performed. Thus, full pointer values can be used, still by only using standard CAS operations.

3.1   The Basic Steps of the Algorithm

The main algorithm steps, see Figure 4, for inserting a new node at an arbitrary position in our doubly linked list will thus be as follows: *I)* Atomically update the next pointer of the to-be-previous node, *II)* Atomically update the prev pointer of the to-be-next node. The main steps of the algorithm for deleting a node at an arbitrary position are the following: *I)* Set the deletion mark on the next pointer of the to-be-deleted node, *II)* Set the deletion mark on the prev pointer of the to-be-deleted node, *III)* Atomically update the next pointer of the previous node of the to-be-deleted node, *IV)* Atomically update the prev pointer of the next node of the to-be-deleted node. As will be shown later in the detailed description

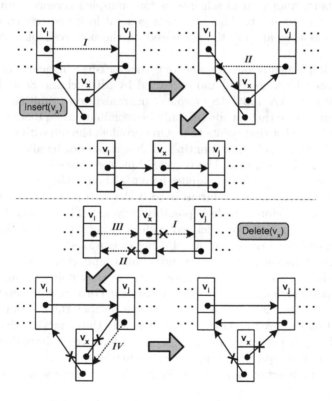

Fig. 4. Illustration of the basic steps of the algorithms for insertion and deletion of nodes at arbitrary positions in the doubly linked list, as described in Section 3.1

of the algorithm, helping techniques need to be applied in order to achieve the lock-free property, following the same steps as the main algorithm for inserting and deleting.

3.2   Memory Management

As we are concurrently (with possible preemptions) traversing nodes that will be continuously allocated and reclaimed, we have to consider several aspects of memory management. No node should be reclaimed and then later re-allocated while some other process is (or will be) traversing that node. For efficiency reasons we also need to be able to trust the prev and the next pointers of deleted nodes, as we would otherwise be forced to re-start the traversing from the head or tail dummy nodes whenever reaching a deleted node while travers-ing and possibly incur severe performance penalties. This need is especially important for operations that try to help other delete operations in progress. Our demands on the memory management therefore rule out the SMR or ROP methods by Michael [17] and Herlihy et al. [18] respectively, as they can only guarantee a limited number of nodes to be safe, and these guarantees are also re-lated to individual threads and never to an individual node structure. However, stronger memory management schemes as for example reference counting would be sufficient for our needs. There exists a general lock-free reference counting scheme by Detlefs et al. [14], though based on the non-available CAS2 atomic primitive.

For our implementation, we selected the lock-free memory management scheme invented by Valois [10] and corrected by Michael and Scott [19], which makes use of the FAA and CAS atomic synchronization primitives. Using this scheme we can assure that a node can only be reclaimed when there is no prev or next pointer in the list that points to it. One problem though with this scheme, a general problem with reference counting, is that it can not handle cyclic garbage (i.e. 2 or more nodes that should be recycled but reference each other, and there-fore each node keeps a positive reference count, although they are not referenced by the main structure). Our solution is to make sure to break potential cyclic references directly before a node is possibly recycled. This is done by changing the next and prev pointers of a deleted node to point to active nodes, in a way that is consistent with the semantics of other operations.

The memory management scheme should also support means to de-reference pointers safely. If we simply de-reference a next or prev pointer using the means of the programming language, it might be that the corresponding node has been reclaimed before we could access it. It can also be that the deletion mark that is connected to the prev or next pointer was set, thus marking that the node is deleted. The scheme by Valois et al. supports lock-free pointer de-referencing and can easily be adopted to handle deletion marks.

The following functions are defined for safe handling of the memory manage-ment:

> **function** MALLOC_NODE() :**pointer to** Node
> **function** DEREF(address:**pointer to** Link) :**pointer to** Node
> **function** DEREF_D(address:**pointer to** Link) :**pointer to** Node

function COPY(node:**pointer to** Node) :**pointer to** Node
procedure REL(node:**pointer to** Node)

The functions *DEREF* and *DEREF_D* atomically de-references the given link and increases the reference counter for the corresponding node. In case the deletion mark of the link is set, the *DEREF* function then returns NULL. The function *MALLOC_NODE* allocates a new node from the memory pool. The function *REL* decrements the reference counter on the corresponding given node. If the reference counter reaches zero, the function then calls the *TerminateNode* function that will recursively call *REL* on the nodes that this node has owned pointers to, and then it reclaims the node. The *COPY* function increases the reference counter for the corresponding given node.

As the details of how to efficiently apply the memory management scheme to our basic algorithm are not always trivial, we will provide a detailed description of them together with the detailed algorithm description in this section.

3.3   Pushing and Popping Nodes

The *PushLeft* operation, see Figure 5, inserts a new node at the leftmost position in the deque. The algorithm first repeatedly tries in lines L4-L14 to insert the new node (*node*) between the head node (*prev*) and the leftmost node (*next*), by atomically changing the next pointer of the head node. Before trying to update the next pointer, it assures in line L5 that the *next* node is still the very next node of head, otherwise *next* is updated in L6-L7. After the new node has been successfully inserted, it tries in lines P1-P13 to update the prev pointer of the next node. It retries until either i) it succeeds with the update, ii) it detects that either the next or new node is deleted, or iii) the next node is no longer directly next of the new node. In any of the two latter, the changes are due to concurrent Pop or Push operations, and the responsibility to update the prev pointer is then left to those. If the update succeeds, there is though the possibility that the new node was deleted (and thus the prev pointer of the *next* node was possibly already updated by the concurrent Pop operation) directly before the CAS in line P5, and then the prev pointer is updated by calling the *HelpInsert* function in line P10. The linearizability point of the *PushLeft* operation is the successful CAS operation in line L11.

The *PushRight* operation, see Figure 5, inserts a new node at the rightmost position in the deque. The algorithm first repeatedly tries in lines R4-R13 to insert the new node (*node*) between the rightmost node (*prev*) and the tail node (*next*), by atomically changing the next pointer of the *prev* node. Before trying to update the next pointer, it assures in line R5 that the *next* node is still the very next node of *prev*, otherwise *prev* is updated by calling the *HelpInsert* function in R6, which updates the prev pointer of the *next* node. After the new node has been successfully inserted, it tries in lines P1-P13 to update the prev pointer of the next node, following the same scheme as in the *PushLeft* operation. The linearizability point of the *PushRight* operation is the successful CAS operation in line R10.

```
union Link
   _: word
   ⟨p, d⟩: ⟨pointer to Node, boolean⟩

structure Node
   value: pointer to word
   prev: union Link
   next: union Link

// Global variables
head, tail: pointer to Node
// Local variables
node,prev,prev2,next,next2: pointer to Node
last,link1: union Link

function CreateNode(value: pointer to word)
  :pointer to Node
C1     node:=MALLOC_NODE();
C2     node.value:=value;
C3     return node;

procedure TerminateNode(node: pointer to
Node)
RR1   REL(node.prev.p);
RR2   REL(node.next.p);

procedure PushLeft(value: pointer to word)
L1     node:=CreateNode(value);
L2     prev:=COPY(head);
L3     next:=DEREF(&prev.next);
L4     while T do
L5        if prev.next ≠ ⟨next,F⟩ then
L6           REL(next);
L7           next:=DEREF(&prev.next);
L8           continue;
L9        node.prev:=⟨prev,F⟩;
L10       node.next:=⟨next,F⟩;
L11       if CAS(&prev.next,⟨next,F⟩
  ,⟨node,F⟩) then
L12          COPY(node);
L13          break;
L14       Back-Off
L15    PushCommon(node,next);

procedure PushRight(value: pointer to word)
R1     node:=CreateNode(value);
R2     next:=COPY(tail);
R3     prev:=DEREF(&next.prev);
R4     while T do
R5        if prev.next ≠ ⟨next,F⟩ then
R6           prev:=HelpInsert(prev,next);
R7           continue;
R8        node.prev:=⟨prev,F⟩;
R9        node.next:=⟨next,F⟩;
R10       if CAS(&prev.next,⟨next,F⟩
  ,⟨node,F⟩) then
R11          COPY(node);
R12          break;
R13       Back-Off
R14    PushCommon(node,next);

procedure MarkPrev(node: pointer to Node)
MP1    while T do
MP2       link1:=node.prev;
MP3       if link1.d = T or CAS(&node.prev
  ,link1,⟨link1.p,T⟩) then break;
```

```
procedure PushCommon(node, next: pointer
to Node)
P1     while T do
P2        link1:=next.prev;
P3        if link1.d = T or node.next ≠
  ⟨next,F⟩ then
P4           break;
P5        if CAS(&next.prev,link1
  ,⟨node,F⟩) then
P6           COPY(node);
P7           REL(link1.p);
P8           if node.prev.d = T then
P9              prev2:=COPY(node);
P10             prev2:=HelpInsert(prev2,next);
P11             REL(prev2);
P12          break;
P13       Back-Off
P14    REL(next);
P15    REL(node);

function PopLeft(): pointer to word
PL1    prev:=COPY(head);
PL2    while T do
PL3       node:=DEREF(&prev.next);
PL4       if node = tail then
PL5          REL(node);
PL6          REL(prev);
PL7          return ⊥;
PL8       link1:=node.next;
PL9       if link1.d = T then
PL10         HelpDelete(node);
PL11         REL(node);
PL12         continue;
PL13      if CAS(&node.next,link1
  ,⟨link1.p,T⟩) then
PL14         HelpDelete(node);
PL15         next:=DEREF_D(&node.next);
PL16         prev:=HelpInsert(prev,next);
PL17         REL(prev);
PL18         REL(next);
PL19         value:=node.value;
PL20         break;
PL21      REL(node);
PL22      Back-Off
PL23   RemoveCrossReference(node);
PL24   REL(node);
PL25   return value;

function PopRight(): pointer to word
PR1    next:=COPY(tail);
PR2    node:=DEREF(&next.prev);
PR3    while T do
PR4       if node.next ≠ ⟨next,F⟩ then
PR5          node:=HelpInsert(node,next);
PR6          continue;
PR7       if node = head then
PR8          REL(node);
PR9          REL(next);
PR10         return ⊥;
PR11      if CAS(&node.next,⟨next,F⟩
  ,⟨next,T⟩) then
PR12         HelpDelete(node);
PR13         prev:=DEREF_D(&node.prev);
PR14         prev:=HelpInsert(prev,next);
PR15         REL(prev);
PR16         REL(next);
```

Fig. 5. The algorithm, part 1(2)

The *PopLeft* operation, see Figure 5, tries to delete and return the value of the leftmost node in the deque. The algorithm first repeatedly tries in lines PL2-PL22 to mark the leftmost node (*node*) as deleted. Before trying to update the next pointer, it first assures in line PL4 that the deque is not empty, and secondly in line PL9 that the node is not already marked for deletion. If the deque was detected to be empty, the function returns. If *node* was marked for deletion, it tries to update the next pointer of the *prev* node by calling the *HelpDelete* function, and then *node* is updated to be the leftmost node. If the prev pointer of *node* was incorrect, it tries to update it by calling the *HelpInsert* function. After the node has been successfully marked by the successful CAS operation in line PL13, it tries in line PL14 to update the next pointer of the *prev* node by calling the *HelpDelete* function, and in line PL16 to update the prev pointer of the *next* node by calling the *HelpInsert* function. After this, it tries in line PL23 to break possible cyclic references that includes *node* by calling the *RemoveCross-Reference* function. The linearizability point of a *PopLeft* operation that fails, is the read operation of the next pointer in line PL3. The linearizability point of a *PopLeft* operation that succeeds, is the read operation of the next pointer in line PL3.

The *PopRight* operation, see Figure 5, tries to delete and return the value of the rightmost node in the deque. The algorithm first repeatedly tries in lines PR2-PR19 to mark the rightmost node (*node*) as deleted. Before trying to update the next pointer, it assures i) in line PR4 that the node is not already marked for deletion, ii) in the same line that the prev pointer of the tail (*next*) node is correct, and iii) in line PR7 that the deque is not empty. If the deque was detected to be empty, the function returns. If *node* was marked for deletion or the prev pointer of the *next* node was incorrect, it tries to update the prev pointer of the *next* node by calling the *HelpInsert* function, and then *node* is updated to be the rightmost node. After the node has been successfully marked it follows the same scheme as the *PopLeft* operation. The linearizability point of a *PopRight* operation that fails, is the read operation of the next pointer in line PR4. The linearizability point of a *PopRight* operation that succeeds, is the CAS sub-operation in line PR11.

3.4   Helping and Back-Off

The *HelpDelete* sub-procedure, see Figure 6, tries to set the deletion mark of the prev pointer and then atomically update the next pointer of the previous node of the to-be-deleted node, thus fulfilling step 2 and 3 of the overall node deletion scheme. The algorithm first ensures in line HD1 that the deletion mark on the prev pointer of the given node is set. It then repeatedly tries in lines HD6-HD38 to delete (in the sense of a chain of next pointers starting from the head node) the given marked node (*node*) by changing the next pointer from the previous non-marked node. First, we can safely assume that the next pointer of the marked node is always referring to a node (*next*) to the right and the prev pointer is always referring to a node (*prev*) to the left (not necessarily the first). Before trying to update the next pointer with the CAS operation in line HD34, it assures in line HD6 that *node* is not already deleted, in line HD7 that the *next* node is not marked, in line HD14 that the *prev* node is not marked, and in HD28 that *prev* is the previous node of *node*. If *next* is marked, it is updated to be the next node. If *prev* is marked we might need to delete it before we can update

```
PR17        value:=node.value;
PR18        break;
PR19        Back-Off
PR20    RemoveCrossReference(node);
PR21    REL(node);
PR22    return value;

procedure HelpDelete(node: pointer to Node)
HD1     MarkPrev(node);
HD2     last:=⊥;
HD3     prev:=DEREF_D(&node.prev);
HD4     next:=DEREF_D(&node.next);
HD5     while T do
HD6         if prev = next then break;
HD7         if next.next.d = T then
HD8             MarkPrev(next);
HD9             next2:=DEREF_D(&next.next);
HD10            REL(next);
HD11            next:=next2;
HD12            continue;
HD13        prev2:=DEREF(&prev.next);
HD14        if prev2 = ⊥ then
HD15            if last ≠ ⊥ then
HD16                MarkPrev(prev);
HD17                next2:=DEREF_D(&prev.next);
HD18                if CAS(&last.next,⟨prev,F⟩
        ,⟨next2,F⟩) then REL(prev);
HD19                else REL(next2);
HD20            REL(prev);
HD21            prev:=last;
HD22            last:=⊥;
HD23        else
HD24            prev2:=DEREF_D(&prev.prev);
HD25            REL(prev);
HD26            prev:=prev2;
HD27            continue;
HD28        if prev2 ≠ node then
HD29            if last ≠ ⊥ then REL(last);
HD30            last:=prev;
HD31            prev:=prev2;
HD32            continue;
HD33        REL(prev2);
HD34        if CAS(&prev.next,⟨node,F⟩
        ,⟨next,F⟩) then
HD35            COPY(next);
HD36            REL(node);
HD37            break;
HD38        Back-Off
HD39    if last ≠ ⊥ then REL(last);
HD40    REL(prev);
HD41    REL(next);
```

```
function HelpInsert(prev, node: pointer to
Node): pointer to Node
HI1     last:=⊥;
HI2     while T do
HI3         prev2:=DEREF(&prev.next);
HI4         if prev2 = ⊥ then
HI5             if last ≠ ⊥ then
HI6                 MarkPrev(prev);
HI7                 next2:=DEREF_D(&prev.next);
HI8                 if CAS(&last.next,⟨prev,F⟩
        ,⟨next2,F⟩) then REL(prev);
HI9                 else REL(next2);
HI10            REL(prev);
HI11            prev:=last;
HI12            last:=⊥;
HI13        else
HI14            prev2:=DEREF_D(&prev.prev);
HI15            REL(prev);
HI16            prev:=prev2;
HI17            continue;
HI18        link1:=node.prev;
HI19        if link1.d = T then
HI20            REL(prev2);
HI21            break;
HI22        if prev2 ≠ node then
HI23            if last ≠ ⊥ then REL(last);
HI24            last:=prev;
HI25            prev:=prev2;
HI26            continue;
HI27        REL(prev2);
HI28        if link1.p = prev then break;
HI29        if prev.next = node and CAS(
        &node.prev,link1,⟨prev,F⟩) then
HI30            COPY(prev);
HI31            REL(link1.p);
HI32            if prev.prev.d ≠ T then break;
HI33        Back-Off
HI34    if last ≠ ⊥ then REL(last);
HI35    return prev;

procedure RemoveCrossReference(
    node: pointer to Node)
RC1     while T do
RC2         prev:=node.prev.p;
RC3         if prev.prev.d = T then
RC4             prev2:=DEREF_D(&prev.prev);
RC5             node.prev:=⟨prev2,T⟩;
RC6             REL(prev);
RC7             continue;
RC8         next:=node.next.p;
RC9         if next.prev.d = T then
RC10            next2:=DEREF_D(&next.next);
RC11            node.next:=⟨next2,T⟩;
RC12            REL(next);
RC13            continue;
RC14        break;
```

Fig. 6. The algorithm, part 2(2)

prev to one of its previous nodes and proceed with the current deletion. This extra deletion is only attempted if a next pointer from a non-marked node to *prev* has been observed (i.e. *last* is valid). Otherwise if *prev* is not the previous node of *node* it is updated to be the next node.

The *HelpInsert* sub-function, see Figure 6, tries to update the prev pointer of a node and then return a reference to a possibly direct previous node, thus fulfilling step 2 of the overall insertion scheme or step 4 of the overall deletion scheme. The algorithm repeatedly tries in lines HI2-HI33 to correct the prev pointer of the given node (*node*), given a suggestion of a previous (not necessarily the directly previous) node (*prev*). Before trying to update the prev pointer with the CAS operation in line HI29, it assures in line HI4 that the *prev* node is not marked, in line HI19 that *node* is not marked, and in line HI22 that *prev* is the previous node of *node*. If *prev* is marked we might need to delete it before we can update *prev* to one of its previous nodes and proceed with the current deletion. This extra deletion is only attempted if a next pointer from a non-marked node to *prev* has been observed (i.e. *last* is valid). If *node* is marked, the procedure is aborted. Otherwise if *prev* is not the previous node of *node* it is updated to be the next node. If the update in line HI29 succeeds, there is though the possibility that the *prev* node was deleted (and thus the prev pointer of *node* was possibly already updated by the concurrent Pop operation) directly before the CAS operation. This is detected in line HI32 and then the update is possibly retried with a new *prev* node.

Because the *HelpDelete* and *HelpInsert* are often used in the algorithm for "helping" late operations that might otherwise stop progress of other concurrent operations, the algorithm is suitable for pre-emptive as well as fully concurrent systems. In fully concurrent systems though, the helping strategy as well as heavy contention on atomic primitives, can downgrade the performance significantly. Therefore the algorithm, after a number of consecutive failed CAS operations (i.e. failed attempts to help concurrent operations) puts the current operation into back-off mode. When in back-off mode, the thread does nothing for a while, and in this way avoids disturbing the concurrent operations that might otherwise progress slower. The duration of the back-off is initialized to some value (e.g. proportional to the number of threads) at the start of an operation, and for each consecutive entering of the back-off mode during one operation invocation, the duration of the back-off is changed using some scheme, e.g. increased exponentially.

3.5   Avoiding Cyclic Garbage

The *RemoveCrossReference* sub-procedure, see Figure 6, tries to break cross-references between the given node (*node*) and any of the nodes that it references, by repeatedly updating the prev and next pointer as long as they reference a fully marked node. First, we can safely assume that the prev or next field of *node* is not concurrently updated by any other operation, as this procedure is only called by the main operation that deleted the node and both the next and prev pointers are marked and thus any concurrent update using CAS will fail.

Before the procedure is finished, it assures in line RC3 that the previous node (*prev*) is not fully marked, and in line RC9 that the next node (*next*) is not fully marked. As long as *prev* is marked it is traversed to the left, and as long as *next* is marked it is traversed to the right, while continuously updating the prev or next field of *node* in lines RC5 or RC11.

3.6   General Operations of Doubly Linked Lists and Correctness Proofs

Due to page restrictions, the detailed description of the general operations of a doubly linked list (i.e. traversals and arbitrary inserts and deletes) as well as detailed proofs of correctness of the lock-free and linearizability criteria are described in an extended version of this paper [20].

4   Experimental Evaluation

In our experiments, each concurrent thread performed 1000 randomly chosen sequential operations on a shared deque, with a distribution of 1/4 *PushRight*, 1/4 *PushLeft*, 1/4 *PopRight* and 1/4 *PopLeft* operations. Each experiment was repeated 50 times, and an average execution time for each experiment was estimated. Exactly the same sequence of operations were performed for all different implementations compared. Besides our implementation, we also performed the same experiment with the lock-free implementation by Michael [11] and the implementation by Martin et al. [9], two of the most efficient lock-free deques that have been proposed. The algorithm by Martin et al. was implemented together with the corresponding memory management scheme by Detlefs et al. [14]. However, as both [9] and [14] use the atomic operation CAS2 which is not available in any modern system, the CAS2 operation was implemented in software using two different approaches. The first approach was to implement CAS2 using mutual exclusion (as proposed in [9]). The other approach was to implement CAS2 using one of the most efficient software implementations of CASN known that could meet the needs of [9] and [14], i.e. the implementation by Harris et al. [15].

A clean-cache operation was performed just before each sub-experiment using a different implementation. All implementations are written in C and compiled with the highest optimization level. The atomic primitives are written in assembly language.

The experiments were performed using different number of threads, varying from 1 to 28 with increasing steps. Three different platforms were used, with varying number of processors and level of shared memory distribution. To get a highly pre-emptive environment, we performed our experiments on a Compaq dual-processor Pentium II PC running Linux, and a Sun Ultra 80 system running Solaris 2.7 with 4 processors. In order to evaluate our algorithm with full concurrency we also used a SGI Origin 2000 system running Irix 6.5 with 29 250 MHz MIPS R10000 processors. The results from the experiments are shown in

Figure 7. The average execution time is drawn as a function of the number of threads.

Our results show that both the CAS-based algorithms outperform the CAS2-based implementations for any number of threads. For the systems with low or medium concurrency and uniform memory architecture, [11] has the best performance. However, for the system with full concurrency and non-uniform memory architecture our algorithm performs significantly better than [11] from 2 threads and more, as a direct consequence of the nature of our algorithm to support parallelism for disjoint accesses.

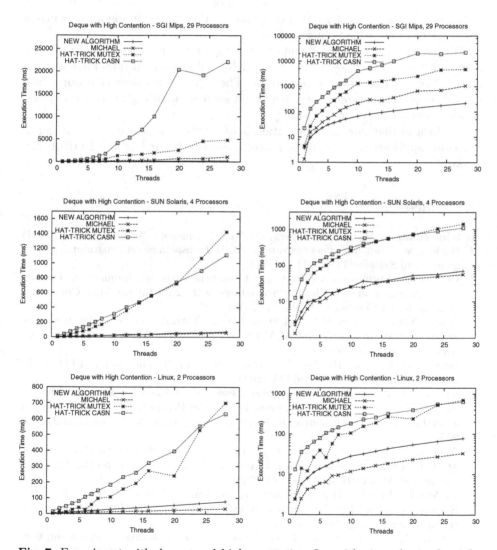

Fig. 7. Experiment with deques and high contention. Logarithmic scales in the right column

5   Conclusions

We have presented the first lock-free algorithmic implementation of a concurrent deque that has all the following features: i) it supports parallelism for disjoint accesses, ii) uses a fully described lock-free memory management scheme, iii) uses atomic primitives which are available in modern computer systems, and iv) allows pointers with full precision to be used, and thus supports dynamic deque sizes. In addition, the proposed solution also implements all the fundamental operations of a general doubly linked list data structure in a lock-free manner. The doubly linked list operations also support deterministic and well defined traversals through even deleted nodes, and are therefore suitable for concurrent applications of linked lists in practice.

We have performed experiments that compare the performance of our algorithm with two of the most efficient algorithms of lock-free deques known, using full implementations of those algorithms. The experiments show that our implementation performs significantly better on systems with high concurrency and non-uniform memory architecture.

We believe that our implementation is of highly practical interest for multiprocessor applications. We are currently incorporating it into the NOBLE [21] library.

References

1. Silberschatz, A., Galvin, P.: Operating System Concepts. Addison Wesley (1994)
2. Herlihy, M.: Wait-free synchronization. ACM Transactions on Programming Languages and Systems **11** (1991) 124–149
3. Herlihy, M., Luchangco, V., Moir, M.: Obstruction-free synchronization: Double-ended queues as an example. In: Proceedings of the 23rd International Conference on Distributed Computing Systems. (2003)
4. Arora, N.S., Blumofe, R.D., Plaxton, C.G.: Thread scheduling for multiprogrammed multiprocessors. In: ACM Symposium on Parallel Algorithms and Architectures. (1998) 119–129
5. Greenwald, M.: Non-Blocking Synchronization and System Design. PhD thesis, Stanford University, Palo Alto, CA (1999)
6. Greenwald, M.: Two-handed emulation: how to build non-blocking implementations of complex data-structures using DCAS. In: Proceedings of the twenty-first annual symposium on Principles of distributed computing, ACM Press (2002) 260–269
7. Agesen, O., Detlefs, D., Flood, C.H., Garthwaite, A., Martin, P., Shavit, N., Steele Jr., G.L.: DCAS-based concurrent deques. In: ACM Symposium on Parallel Algorithms and Architectures. (2000) 137–146
8. Detlefs, D., Flood, C.H., Garthwaite, A., Martin, P., Shavit, N., Steele Jr., G.L.: Even better DCAS-based concurrent deques. In: International Symposium on Distributed Computing. (2000) 59–73
9. Martin, P., Moir, M., Steele, G.: DCAS-based concurrent deques supporting bulk allocation. Technical Report TR-2002-111, Sun Microsystems (2002)
10. Valois, J.D.: Lock-Free Data Structures. PhD thesis, Rensselaer Polytechnic Institute, Troy, New York (1995)

11. Michael, M.M.: CAS-based lock-free algorithm for shared deques. In: Proceedings of the 9th International Euro-Par Conference. Lecture Notes in Computer Science, Springer Verlag (2003)
12. Sundell, H., Tsigas, P.: Lock-free and practical deques using single-word compare-and-swap. Technical Report 2004-02, Computing Science, Chalmers University of Technology (2004)
13. Herlihy, M., Wing, J.: Linearizability: a correctness condition for concurrent objects. ACM Transactions on Programming Languages and Systems **12** (1990) 463–492
14. Detlefs, D., Martin, P., Moir, M., Steele Jr, G.: Lock-free reference counting. In: Proceedings of the 20th Annual ACM Symposium on Principles of Distributed Computing. (2001)
15. Harris, T., Fraser, K., Pratt, I.: A practical multi-word compare-and-swap operation. In: Proceedings of the 16th International Symposium on Distributed Computing. (2002)
16. Harris, T.L.: A pragmatic implementation of non-blocking linked lists. In: Proceedings of the 15th International Symposium of Distributed Computing. (2001) 300–314
17. Michael, M.M.: Safe memory reclamation for dynamic lock-free objects using atomic reads and writes. In: Proceedings of the 21st ACM Symposium on Principles of Distributed Computing. (2002) 21–30
18. Herlihy, M., Luchangco, V., Moir, M.: The repeat offender problem: A mechanism for supporting dynamic-sized, lock-free data structure. In: Proceedings of 16th International Symposium on Distributed Computing. (2002)
19. Michael, M.M., Scott, M.L.: Correction of a memory management method for lock-free data structures. Technical report, Computer Science Department, University of Rochester (1995)
20. Sundell, H.: Efficient and Practical Non-Blocking Data Structures. PhD thesis, Department of Computing Science, Chalmers University of Technology (2004)
21. Sundell, H., Tsigas, P.: NOBLE: A non-blocking inter-process communication library. In: Proceedings of the 6th Workshop on Languages, Compilers and Runtime Systems for Scalable Computers. (2002)

A Dynamic Reconfiguration Tolerant Self-stabilizing Token Circulation Algorithm in Ad-Hoc Networks

Hirotsugu Kakugawa[1,*] and Masafumi Yamashita[2,**]

[1] Faculty of Engineering, Hiroshima University,
1-4-1 Kagamiyama, Higashi Hiroshima, Hiroshima, Japan
h.kakugawa@computer.org
[2] Graduate School of Information Science and Electrical Engineering,
Kyushu University, 6-10-1 Hakozaki, Fukuoka, Japan
mak@csce.kyushu-u.ac.jp

Abstract. Ad-hoc networks do not provide an infrastructure for communication such as routers and are characterized by 1) quick changes of communication topology and 2) unstable system behaviors. Self-stabilizing algorithms have been studied well to design stable distributed algorithms on unstable systems, but they are not requested to be adaptive to dynamic topology changes. We in this paper propose a new concept of dynamic reconfiguration tolerant (DRT for short) self-stabilizing algorithm, which is a self-stabilizing algorithm that is also robust against dynamic changes of topology. We next propose a DRT self-stabilizing token circulation algorithm. It deterministically circulates a token through a spanning tree edges in an asymptotically optimal time $O(n)$, once the system is stabilized. The spanning tree will converge to the minimum spanning tree, if the network remains static.

Keywords: token circulation, self-stabilization, ad-hoc network, spanning tree.

1 Introduction

Ad-hoc networks consist of mobile terminals with wireless communication devices. There is no pre-existing infrastructure for communication, and a terminal is connectable to an ad-hoc network without configuring it. This is a fascinating feature for end-users, but is a seed of the following technical difficulties, when to implement applications in ad-hoc networks; (a) since there are no access points that route messages among mobile terminals, the mobile terminals must route

---

* This work is partially supported by the Ministry of Education, Culture, Sports, and Technology, Grant-in-Aid 15700017.
** This work is partially supported by the Ministry of Education, Culture, Sports, and Technology, Grants-in-Aid 14085204 and 14380145.

T. Higashino (Ed.): OPODIS 2004, LNCS 3544, pp. 256–266, 2005.
© Springer-Verlag Berlin Heidelberg 2005

messages by themselves, (b) since the network topology rapidly changes as "mobile" terminals migrate, communication protocols must be adaptive to dynamic changes of topology, and (c) since a terminal may join or even leave the ad-hoc network while participating in an application job, communication protocols must be robust against communication faults such as a network partition. Algorithms on ad-hoc networks are hence requested to be adaptive to communication topology changes, in addition to the fault tolerant ability expected for general distributed algorithms.

Self-stabilizing systems, which tolerate any finite number of transient faults, have been discussed as an ideal model of fault tolerance [1, 2]. However, they are not necessarily robust against dynamic changes of topology and thus may not correctly work on ad-hoc networks. We hence introduce a new concept of fault tolerance: For a given constraint C on dynamic changes of the network topology, we say that a system is *dynamic reconfiguration tolerant* (DRT for short) self-stabilizing under C, if the system works as a correct self-stabilizing system as long as network changes do not violate C. When C claims that no topological changes happen, a DRT self-stabilizing algorithm for C is just a self-stabilizing algorithm, and the concept of DRT self-stabilization is an extension of self-stabilization. Note that the introduction of condition C to make the limitation of the adaptiveness explicit is the heart of our proposal, since many algorithms would be able to adapt to slight topological changes, but non-trivial algorithms would be unable to adapt to extremely quick changes. We then propose a *DRT self-stabilizing token circulation algorithm* for ad-hoc networks, under some moderate network reconfiguration constraint C.

Self-stabilizing token circulation algorithms have been extensively studied [3, 4, 5, 6]. Among them is the work by Chen and Welch [7] the closest from our work. They proposed a deterministic distributed mutual exclusion algorithm for ad-hoc networks, which is in essence a self-stabilizing token circulation algorithm. Their algorithm however requires a system to remain static while the system is converging to a legitimate configuration; it is not a DRT self-stabilizing algorithm for a non-trivial C.[1] This is a fundamental difference between theirs and ours; our algorithm converges to a legitimate configuration, even if the system is not static (as long as the system satisfies a moderate condition C).

Our algorithm has some other advantages; one of them arises from the fact that it is stateless in the sense that non-initiators do not need to maintain the status of the protocol. Let Δ and D be the maximum degree and the diameter of the network, respectively. Then in Chen and Welch's algorithm, every process maintains a local variable of $O(\log(n\Delta^D))$ bits, while in our algorithm, non-initiators do not need to maintain local variables. One might consider that our token would need to carry more information than theirs. As a matter of fact, our token carries information of $O(n \log n)$ bits, while theirs n timestamps of $O(\log(n^2\Delta^D))$ bits each, or $O(n^2 \log n)$ bits altogether in the worst case. Another

---

[1] Note that mutual exclusion is guaranteed in the presence of arbitrary mobility, once the system is stabilized.

advantage comes from the fact that a token is circulated along the set of spanning tree edges. Their algorithm requires $O(\log(n\Delta^D))$ time per round of circulation, which is $O(n \log n)$ in the worst case, while ours is $O(n)$.

Finally our algorithm guarantees that the convergence time is deterministically bounded by $O(n)$, and the spanning tree along which the token is circulated converges to the minimum spanning tree in $O(n^2)$-time, if the network remains static.

2   The Model

We consider a system consisting of n mobile terminals with wireless communication devices. We model such a system by a set of processes $V = \{p_1, p_2, ..., p_n\}$ ($n \geq 2$) with unique identifiers. For each process p_i, let N_i be the set of neighbor processes that p_i can *directly* communicate with. We assume that every communication channel is bidirectional; $p_j \in N_i$ iff $p_i \in N_j$. N_i's for all $p_i \in V$ define a network $G = (V, E)$, where $(p_i, p_j) \in E$ if and only if $p_j \in N_i$. For each edge $(p_i, p_j) \in E$, we assign a positive *weight* (or cost) denoted by $w_{i,j}(= w_{j,i})$. We say that p_j is *smaller* than p_k (or p_j has *priority* over p_k) if $w_{i,j} < w_{i,k}$. The weight of an edge can be defined based on bandwidth, distance, or reliability, for example.

Since processes (i.e., terminals) may change their locations, N_i may dynamically change and so may G accordingly. The weight $w_{i,j}$ may also dynamically change. We can however assume that the weights $w_{i,j}$ are unique without loss of generality, since otherwise, we can use triples $(w_{i,j}, p, q)$ as unique weights instead, where $p = \min\{p_i, p_j\}$ and $q = \max\{p_i, p_j\}$. The minimum spanning tree is thus uniquely determined. We assume that each p_i knows up-to-date values of N_i and $w_{i,j}$ for all $p_j \in N_i$. We assume that N_i never changes while a token is visiting p_i.

Suppose that the system is partitioned into several sub-networks and this situation continues forever. Then all what a process in a sub-network can hope is to circulate a token among the processes in the sub-network. A change of network topology may be viewed from the process as a join or a leave of another process to or from the (sub-)network. We thus consider V as the set of all processes that have chances to participate in the system, and assume that upper bound of the network size $|V| = n$ is also known to the processes.

Our network is synchronous in the sense that 1) the local clock of each process shows the same speed, 2) there is an upper bound δ on the communication delay between two neighboring processes, 3) δ is known to the processes, and 4) processing time at each process is negligible. Without loss of generality, we assume that $\delta = 1$ (unit time).

A system is a *dynamic reconfiguration tolerant* (DRT for short) self-stabilizing system with respect to a specification P under a dynamic network reconfiguration constraint C if the following conditions are satisfied.

(1) Convergence: For any initial configuration and for any computation starting from it, the system eventually satisfies P, as long as network configuration changes follow C.

(2) Safety: For any initial configuration that satisfies P and for any computation starting from it, the system remains to satisfy P, as long as network configuration changes follow C. If we take a constraint "neither transient error nor network reconfiguration occurs" for C, a DRT self-stabilizing system with respect to P under C is a conventional self-stabilizing system with respect to P.

3   The Algorithm

This section presents a stateless and DRT self-stabilizing algorithm for circulating a token along the minimum spanning tree edges in an ad-hoc network. The algorithm has three parameters M, α and τ, which affect the correctness and the performance. Section 4 shows some values are sufficient for the algorithm to be correct, and then we analyze the performance.

A process that is interested in token circulation becomes an initiator. Hence more than one process may become an initiator. The algorithm consists of two threads, *"initiator thread"* for an initiator (Figure 1) and *"token thread"* for all processes who receives a token (Figure 3). Hence these two threads are executed in a single process of the initiator.

When a process becomes an initiator, the initiator thread generates a token and sends it in a depth-first graph search manner to one of its neighbors. As part of its information, the token carries a tree that spans the processes it has visited in terms of the set of tree edges. Hence it carries an empty edge set, i.e., empty tree, at the initiation time. If a process p_j receives the token from a process p_i, the token thread updates the tree edge set in the token by adding an edge (p_i, p_j) and forwards it to a neighbor p_ℓ of p_j. Note that p_ℓ is selected so that the addition of edge (p_j, p_ℓ) does not create a cycle in the tree (carried by the token). After a while, the token will carry a spanning tree edge set T, which however may not be the minimum spanning tree. The cost of a spanning tree is gradually improved, and we eventually obtain the minimum spanning tree.

Since our algorithm is stateless, a token t needs to carry all of the following data for circulation, some of which may be temporarily inconsistent because of failures and/or topology changes.

- $t.type \in \{\mathsf{probe}, \mathsf{echo}\}$: The direction of traversal. If t is being sent toward a leaf (resp. the root), $t.type = \mathsf{probe}$ (resp. echo).
- $t.tree$: A set of ordered edges that represents a rooted tree, along which t is circulated. The root of $t.tree$ is the initiator of t ($= t.ini$).
- $t.wgt$: The weights of edges in $t.tree$.
- $t.age$: The age of t, whose value is initially 0 and is incremented by one whenever t makes a move.
- $t.id$: The identifier of t assigned by the initiator selected from an integer set $\{0, 1, \ldots, M - 1\}$.[2]

---

[2] Ideally, M should be selected so that more than M tokens never exist in the network at a time. However, this assumption is removable and M can be set any value ≥ 2, at the expense of the convergence time.

Variables of an initiator p_i :
   m : **integer initially** 0;   — *Token identifier.*

Code for an initiator p_i :
```
 1:  while {          — Initiate new circulation by generating a new token.
 2:     try {
 3:        wait;       — Wait for a token to arrive (with timeout). Token is handled by the token thread.
 4:     } catch (Signal) {    — A token visits this process. This event is notified by the token thread.
 5:        ;           — Do nothing. Wait for next arrival of a token.
 6:     } catch (TimeoutException) {
 7:        m := (m + 1) mod M;      — Assign new token identifier.
 8:        t := ⟨probe, 0, 0, 0, m, p_i, ⊥, ∞⟩
 9:        Let p_k be a process in N_i such that w_{i,k} is the smallest;
10:        send t to p_k;
11:     }
12:  }
```

Fig. 1. Initiator thread: the code for an initiator

```
 1:  macro UpdateToken ≡
 2:  {
 3:     // IMPROVE THE SPANNING TREE.
 4:     if (t.alte ≠ ⊥) {      — There is an edge to improve the spanning tree.
 5:        t.tree := t.tree ∪ {t.alte};      — Temporarily t.tree has a cycle.
 6:        Find an edge e in t.tree such that
 7:              t.tree − {e} is a spanning tree and its weight is the smallest;
 8:        t.tree := t.tree − {e};
 9:        Delete from t.wgt the weight of edge e;
10:        Add into t.wgt edge t.alte with weight t.altw;
11:     }
12:     // REFRESH THE TOKEN FOR THE NEXT ROUND OF TOKEN CIRCULATION.
13:     if (p_i = t.ini) {
14:        m := (m + 1) mod M;
15:        t.id := m;      — Assign new token identifier.
16:        t.age := 0;     — Reset token age.
17:     }      — If p_i (= the root of t.tree) is not the initiator of t, t.age and t.id are unchanged.
18:     t := ⟨probe, t.tree, t.wgt, t.age, t.id, t.ini, ⊥, ∞⟩;
19:     — Assign new token identifier and reset the token age.
20:  }

21:  macro FindCandidate ≡
22:  {
23:     if (t.alte = ⊥)
24:        Let T be t.tree;
25:     else
26:        Let T be the spanning tree with the smallest weight among subgraphs of t.tree ∪ t.alte;
27:     Let T' be the spanning tree with the smallest weight among subgraphs of
28:        T ∪ {(p_i, p_ℓ) : p_ℓ ∈ N_i − TreeNeighbors(t)};
29:     if (weight of T' < weight of T){
30:        Let p_ℓ be a process that yields T';
31:        return p_ℓ;
32:     }
33:     return ⊥;
34:  }
```

Fig. 2. Macro definitions for token thread

— $t.ini$: The identifier of initiator.
— $t.alte$: The current candidate edge e for improving the weight of $t.tree$.
— $t.altw$: The weight of $t.alte$.

When a token t **arrives at** p_i **from** p_j **:**

```
1:   t := receive;
2:   t.age := t.age + 1;        — Increment the age by one.
3:   if (p_i is an initiator) ∧ ((t.ini > p_i) ∨ ((t.ini = p_i) ∧ (t.id ≠ m))) {
4:         Discard t;           — Discard the token based on priority.
5:   } else if (¬Alive(t))      — The token is too old to alive.
6:         Discard t.
7:   } else {
8:         if (p_i is an initiator)
9:               notify;        — Restart timeout timer of the initiator thread.
10:        // EXTEND THE SPANING TREE IF p_i IS NOT YET INCLUDED.
11:        if (t.type = probe) ∧ ((p_j, p_i) ∉ t.tree){      — This is the first visit to p_i.
12:              t.tree := t.tree ∪ {(p_j, p_i)};  t.wgt := t.wgt ∪ {(p_j, p_i, w_i(p_j))};      — Extend the tree.
13:              t.alte = ⊥;  t.altw = ∞;      — Reset the candidate for improving the spanning tree.
14:              if (t.ini = p_i)    — The token visits initiator p_i which was disconnected from t.tree.
15:                    t := ⟨probe, ∅, 0, m, p_i, ⊥, ⊥, ∞⟩      — Reset t and start a new round.
16:        }
17:        // CHECK IF NETWORK TOPOLOGY AND EDGE WEIGHTS ARE CHANGED.
18:        for each p_k ∈ (Children(t, p_i) − N_i)      — A child p_k is disconnected from p_i.
19:              Delete a subtree rooted at p_k from t.tree, and update t.wgt accordingly;
20:        if (Parent(t, p_i) ∉ N_i)    — Parent process is disconnected from p_i.
21:              t.tree := a subtree of t.tree rooted at p_k, and update t.wgt accordingly;
22:        for each p_k ∈ TreeNeighbors(t, p_i) {
23:              if (the weight of (p_k, p_i) in t.wgt is different from w_i(p_k))
24:                    Update the weight of (p_k, p_i) in t.wgt to be w_i(p_k);
25:        }
26:        // FIND A CANDIDATE EDGE TO IMPROVE THE SPANNING TREE.
27:        if (N_i − Procs(t) = ∅) {
28:              p_ℓ := FindCandidate;      — p_ℓ is in N_i − TreeNeighbors(t) or equals ⊥.
29:              if (p_ℓ ≠ ⊥) {    — Better candidate is found.
30:                    t.alte = (p_i, p_ℓ);  t.altw = w_i(p_ℓ);
31:              }
32:        }
33:        // FIND A DESTINATION OF THE TOKEN.
34:        if (N_i − Procs(t) ≠ ∅) {    — There is a neighbor process not in the spanning tree.
35:              t.type := probe;  p_k := a process such that w_i(p_k) is the smallest among p_k ∈ N_i − Procs(t);
36:        } else if (p_i is a leaf process of t.tree) {
37:              t.type := echo;  p_k := Parent(t, p_i);      — t will be sent back to the parent (p_k = p_j).
38:        } else {
39:              if (t.type = probe) {    — t was received from the parent.
40:                    p_k := FirstChild(t, p_i);      — t will be sent to the first child.
41:              } else {    — t was received from a child (t.type = echo).
42:                    p_k := NextChild(t, p_i, p_j);      — t will be sent to the next child.
43:              }
44:              if (p_k ≠ ⊥) {    — There is a child to forward.
45:                    t.type := probe;      — t will be sent as a probe token to the child.
46:              } else {    — No more child to forward t (p_k = ⊥).
47:                    if (p_i = Root(t)) {    — The end of a round. p_i may not be t.ini. (See lines 20–21.)
48:                          UpdateToken;      — Improve the spanning tree, and prepare for the next round.
49:                          p_k := FirstChild(t, p_i);      — t will be sent to the first child.
50:                    } else {
51:                          p_k := Parent(t, p_i);      — t will be sent back to the parent.
52:                    }
53:              }
54:        }
55:        // FORWARD THE TOKEN.
56:        send t to p_k;
57:   }
```

Fig. 3. Token thread: the code for a process who receives a token

The algorithm makes use of the following functions:

– $Procs(t)$: The process set of $t.tree$.
– $Root(t)$: The root of $t.tree$.

- $Parent(t, p_i)$: The parent of p_i in $t.tree$. If p_i is the root then $Parent$ $(t, p_i) = \perp$.
- $Children(t, p_i)$: The set of children of p_i in $t.tree$.
- $FirstChild(t, p_i)$: The smallest child of p_i in $t.tree$. If p_i has no children in $t.tree$, then $FirstChild(t, p_i) = \perp$.
- $NextChild(t, p_i, p_j)$: The smallest child among those of p_i in $t.tree$ larger than p_j.
- $TreeNeighbors(t, p_i)$: The set of neighbors of p_i in $t.tree$.
- $Alive(t)$: The predicate that returns **true** if and only if $t.age \leq \alpha$.

3.1   Initiator Thread

The roles of initiator thread are to create a new token and to recreate it when it does not return within τ ticks and is suspected to be lost. We will show in Section 4 that the timeout value $\tau = 6(n-1)$ is sufficient to guarantee that timeout implies no tokens being circulated. The initiator thread maintains a local integer variable $m \in \{0, \ldots, M-1\}$ for token identifier. When a timeout occurs, the initiator increments m by one (modulo M), and creates a new token carrying the initial data. Initiator then sends it to the smallest neighbor to start its circulation. The initiator thread does nothing, as long as a timeout does not occur. Note that an arrival of the token is captured by the token thread concurrently executed in the initiator, and is notified to the initiator thread by using communication primitives **notify** and **wait**.

3.2   Token Thread

The token thread is responsible for the following four functions (A)-(D):

(A) Token Elimination: A token t continues to travel among nodes in a depth-first fashion, unless it is eliminated with suspicion of its being redundant, since 1) its age $t.age$ has exceeded a constant α, or 2) t arrives at an initiator p who has priority. As for 1), parameter α should be selected so that a correct circulation always finishes less than α edge traversals (when the network is static). We particularly take $\alpha = 2(n-1)$ in Section 4. As for 2), the priority of t defined by $(t.int, t.id)$ is alphabetically compared with that of p defined by (p, m), where m is the current version number.

(B) Token Circulation: A token t is circulated in a depth-first graph search manner. Initially $t.tree$ is empty, and it grows as it visits a new process. As long as the network is static, an implementation of circulation is straightforward, although it consists of 2 phases. In the first phase, a standard depth-first graph search algorithm is executed, and t will be returned back to its initiator with a spanning tree $t.tree$.

In the second phase, t repeatedly makes a preorder traversal of the spanning tree $t.tree$, where the children are traversed in the order of their weights. During the traversal, t gathers information to improve $t.tree$, but we leave this issue in Items (C) and (D).

Recall however that the network may not be static. When the token reaches a node p_i, the data of token may be inconsistent with its current neighbors N_i and/or the weights $w_{i,j}$. We recover consistency simply by keeping data consistent with N_i and $w_{i,j}$ and by discarding the rest. For example, if we discover $p_k \notin N_i$ for some $(p_i, p_k) \in t.tree$, then update $t.tree$ by removing edge (p_i, p_k), and then remove all connected components in $t.tree$ that does not contain p_i. We then update $t.wgt$ accordingly.

Note that the root of $t.tree$ changes if the parent of p_i leaves the network. Even so, the token continues to travel, as long as its age is less than α. If t happens to return its initiator $t.ini$, then the initiator initiates a new round, otherwise, t is eliminated by age.

(C) Searching for Candidate Edge: The spanning tree $t.tree$ of t is not always minimum when the first phase ends. In further rounds of traversals, we try to improve $t.tree$ by replacing an edge e' in $t.tree$ with another edge $t.alte$ that encounters during the last traversal, to eventually attain the minimum spanning tree. Here e' is the node with the largest weight in the unique cycle in $t.tree \cup \{t.alte\}$. Note that it is easy to maintain $t.alte$, since it is obvious for a node p_i to check if there is such an e' for a particular e incident on it.

(D) Initiating Next Traversal: When token t returns to the initiator, the initiator improves the spanning tree $t.tree$ by replacing the edge e' in $t.tree$ with $t.alte$, and initializes t by incrementing the version number $t.id$ and resetting the age $t.age$ to 0.

4   Correctness and Performance

Consider an arbitrary initial configuration such that there are some initiators in the network. Suppose that there will be no transient failures and that no other process will not become an initiator. We show that eventually an exactly one token is circulated among the processes along a spaning tree, as long as network topology changes satisfy some condition given below. Because of the page limit, we only describe a scenario for the proofs. Recall that α is the lifetime of a token, and τ is the timeout interval for token recreation.

Since $t.tree$ dominates the amount of information carried by a token t, we obviously have:

Theorem 1. *The amount of information that a token needs to carry is $O(n \log n)$ bits.*   □

Regardless of how the network topology changes (as long as the conditions described in Section 2 hold), we can show the followings:

Lemma 1. *If there are no tokens initially, a token will be generated.*   □

Let p^* be the smallest initiator. Recall Token Elimination policy of the token thread. Since p^* always eliminates tokens generated by other initiators, p^* eventually initiates a token. If there are more than one token initiated by p^*, all but the one with $p^*.m = t.id$ are eliminated. Hence we can assume without loss of generality that there is a single token t in the network initiated by p^* such that $p^*.m = t.id$, and t is never eliminated, unless its age reaches α or the timeout timer of p^* expires at τ.

Suppose first that **the network is static**. Since there remains an exactly one token with $p^*.m = t.id$ by the above observations and $(n-1)$ improvements of $t.tree$ always make $t.tree$ minimum, we obviously have:

Theorem 2. *A token t such that $t.id = p^*.m$ will eventually return to p^* with the minimum spanning tree in $t.tree$, and will continue to traverse $t.tree$ since then. The cover time is hence $2(n-1)$. Furthermore, the convergence time to the minimum spanning tree is at most $2(n-1)^2$, after t constructing a spanning tree.* $\square$

Next suppose that **the network topology may change only by edge augmentations**. Since the network will not be partitioned, we have:

Theorem 3. *Let $\alpha = 2(n-1)$ and $\tau = 4(n-1)$. Then the algorithm is DRT self-stabilizing token circulation algorithm, if no edges are removed from the network.* $\square$

By combining it with Theorem 2, we can conclude that t eventually carries the minimum spanning tree in $2(n-1)^2$ time.

Finally, we consider **general network topology changes**. Let us emphasize that we cannot even require the token to carry a spanning tree or to circulate all the processes in general, since the network may be partitioned, and what the algorithm can guarantee vary, depending on the condition on possible topology changes.

The first constraint C_1 on the network change we consider is the following: 1) no two edge disconnections occur within $6(n-1)$ time, and 2) the network is not partitioned.

Theorem 4. *Let $\alpha = 6(n-1)$ and $\tau = 12(n-1)$. Then the algorithm is a DRT self-stabilizing token circulation algorithm under a dynamic network reconfiguration constraint C_1. The token can visit all processes in each traversal, but the cover time is $6(n-1)$.*

Proof (Sketch). Consider the following worst case scenario: Suppose that immediately after its initiation by an initiator p^*, a token t leaves p^* to a child q, and that the edge e between p^* and q disconnects immediately after this move. The token circulation then continues until t finds e disconnection at the last moment of this circulation when it is about to be sent back to p^* from q.

Then q starts the second circulation of t as a temporally root. Note that this circulation starts by time $2(n-1)$. Since the network is not partitioned and no edges (except e) disconnect by $6(n-1)$ time, t always returns to p^* by time $4(n-1)$. It is worth noting that there may be a process such that t has not visited yet. It is however clear that the third circulation will visit all processes since no edges except e still will not disconnect next $2(n-1)$ time, and $2(n-1)$ additional steps are sufficient to complete the circulation.

Hence the cover time is $6(n-1)$, and $\tau = 12(n-1)$ is sufficient for other initiators not to issue new tokens by timeouts.   □

Let C_2 be a condition that is the same as C_1 except that the minimum time interval between two edge disconnections is reduced to $4(n-1)$.

Theorem 5. *Let $\alpha = 6(n-1)$ and $\tau = 12(n-1)$. Under a dynamic network reconfiguration constraint C_2, the algorithm is a DRT self-stabilizing token circulation algorithm in a weak sense; a token of the highest priority is circulated and remains to be circulated forever, but it may not visit all processes in each circulation and initiators with lower priorities (if any) may issue tokens.*   □

Readers might be interested in network partition. Suppose that a network is partitioned into two sub-networks, each of which contains an initiator. Then a token will be circulated forever in each of the sub-networks, our algorithm cannot stabilize this situation. This shows that Condition (2) of C_1 and C_2 are inevitable.

5   Conclusion

In this paper, we proposed the concept of dynamic reconfiguration tolerant (DRT) self-stabilization as a theoretical framework of distributed algorithm for dynamic ad-hoc networks. We then proposed a deterministic and stateless DRT self-stabilizing token circulation algorithm under some network topology change constraint. What the algorithm can guarantee depends on what we can assume to network topology changes. If the network is stable, an exactly one token is circulated along the minimum spanning tree in $O(n)$ time. Obviously it guarantees nothing if the network topology quickly changes. But it can guarantee a single token circulation even if edge disconnections occur (as long as their occurrences are not so frequent).

In this paper, we have assumed that each p_i knows up-to-date values of N_i and $w_{i,j}$ for all $p_j \in N_i$. This assumption however is not so realistic; in real systems, the message sent to a neighbor simply fails if the neighbor is no longer within the transmission range. We however believe that we can modify our algorithm so that it works under the above more realistic assumption by repeatedly recomputing destination of a token until token passing succeeds.

A challenging problem we leave as a future work is to extend the definition of token circulation so that there can be a correct token circulation algorithm, even if the network is partitioned, and to propose a DRT self-stabilizing token circulation algorithm based on the new definition.

References

1. Dijkstra, E.W.: Self-stabilizing systems in spite of distributed control. Communications of the ACM **17** (1974) 643–644
2. Dolev, S.: Self-stabilization. The MIT Press (2000)

3. Datta, A.K., Johnen, C., Petit, F., Villan, V.: Self-stabilizing depth first token circulation in arbitrary rooted networks. In: Proceedings of the 5th International Colloquium on Structual Information and Communication Complexity (SIRROCO). (1998) 119–131
4. Malpani, N., Vaidya, N.H., Welch, J.L.: Distributed token circulation on mobile ad hoc networks. In: Proceedings of the 9th International Conference on Network Protocols (ICNP). (2001)
5. Israeli, A., Jalfon, M.: Token management schemes and random walks yield self stabilizing mutual exclusion. In: Proceedings of the 9th ACM Symposium on Principles of Distributed Computing, ACM (1990) 119–131
6. Dolev, S., Schiller, E., Welch, J.: Random walk for self-stabilizing group communication in ad-hoc networks. In: the 21st IEEE Symposium on Reliable Distributed Systems (SRDS). (2002) 70–79
7. Chen, Y., Welch, J.L.: Self-stabilizing mutual exclusion using tokens in mobile ad hoc networks. In: Proceedings of the Sixth International Workshop on Discrete Algorithms and Methods for Mobile Computing and Communications (DIALM). (2002)

Snap-Stabilizing Depth-First Search on Arbitrary Networks*

Alain Cournier, Stéphane Devismes, Franck Petit, and Vincent Villain

LaRIA, CNRS FRE 2733,
Université de Picardie Jules Verne, Amiens (France)

Abstract. A *snap-stabilizing protocol*, starting from any arbitrary initial configuration, always behaves according to its specification. In this paper, we present a snap-stabilizing depth-first search wave protocol for arbitrary rooted networks. In this protocol, a wave of computation is initiated by the root. In this wave, all the processors are sequentially visited in depth-first search order. After the end of the visit, the root eventually detects the termination of the process. Furthermore, our protocol is proven assuming an unfair daemon, i.e., assuming the weakest scheduling assumption.

keywords: Distributed systems, fault-tolerance, stabilization, depth-first search.

1 Introduction

A distributed system is a network where processors execute local computations according to their state and the messages from their neighbors. In such systems, a *wave protocol* [1] is a protocol where at least one processor (called *initiator*) initiates cycles of computations (also called *wave*). At the ending of each cycle, each initiator is abled to determine a result depending on both the terminal configuration and the history of the cycle's computation.

In an arbitrary rooted network, a Depth-First Search (*DFS*) wave is initiated by the root. In this wave, all the processors are sequentially visited in depth-first search order. This scheme has many applications in distributed systems. For example, the solution of this problem can be used to solve mutual exclusion, spanning tree computation, constraint programming, routing, or synchronization.

The concept of *self-stabilization* [2] is the most general technique to design a system to tolerate arbitrary transient faults. A self-stabilizing system, regarless of the initial states of the processors and messages initialy in the links, is guaranteed to converge to the intented behavior in finite time. *Snap-stabilization* was introduced in [3]. A *snap-stabilizing* protocol guaranteed that it always behaves according to its specification. In other words, a snap-stabilizing protocol is also a

---

* The full version is available at www.laria.u-picardie.fr/~devismes/tr2004-9.ps

T. Higashino (Ed.): OPODIS 2004, LNCS 3544, pp. 267–282, 2005.

self-stabilizing protocol which stabilizes in 0 step. Obviously, a *snap-stabilizing* protocol is optimal in stabilization time.

Related Works. There exists several (non self-stabilizing) distributed algorithms solving this problem, e.g., [4, 5]. In the area of self-stabilizing systems, a silent algorithm (i.e., using this algorithm, the system converges to a fix point) which computes a DFS spanning tree for arbitrary rooted networks is given in [6]. Several self-stabilizing (but not snap-stabilizing) wave algorithms based on the *depth-first token circulation* $(DFTC)$ have been proposed for arbitrary rooted networks. The first one was proposed in [7]. It requires $O(\log(N) + \log(\Delta))$ bits per processors where N is the number of processors and Δ the degree of the network. Subsequently, several other self-stabilizing protocols were proposed, e.g., [8, 9, 10]. All these papers attempted to reduce the memory requirement to $O(\log(\Delta))$ bits per processor. The algorithm proposed in [8] offers the best space complexity. All these above solutions [8, 7, 9, 10] have a stabilization time in $O(N \times D)$ rounds where D is the diameter of the network. The solution proposed in [11] stabilizes in $O(N)$ rounds using $O(\log(N) + \log(\Delta))$ bits per processor. Until now, this is the best solution (for arbitrary networks) in term of trade-off between time and space complexities. The correctness of the above algorithms is proven assuming a (weakly) fair daemon. Roughly speaking, a daemon is considered as an adversary which tries to prevent the protocol to behave as expected, and fairness means that the daemon cannot prevent forever a processor to execute an enabled action. The first snap-stabilizing $DFTC$ has been proposed in [12] for tree networks. In arbitrary networks, a *universal transformer* providing a snap-stabilizing version of any (neither self- nor snap-) protocol is given in [13]. Obviously, combining this protocol with any $DFTC$ algorithm, we obtain a snap-stabilizing $DFTC$ algorithm for arbitrary networks. However, the resulting protocol works assuming a weakly fair daemon only. Indeed, it generates an infinite number of snapshots, independently of the token progress. Therefore, the number of steps per wave cannot be bounded.

Contributions. In this paper, we present the first snap-stabilizing depth-first search wave protocol for arbitrary rooted networks assuming an unfair daemon, i.e., assuming the weakest scheduling assumption. Indeed, using our protocol, the execution of a DFS wave is bounded by $O(N^2)$ steps. The protocol does not use any pre-computed spanning tree but requires identities on processors. The snap-stabilizing property guarantees that as soon as the protocol is initiated by the root, every processor of the network will be visited in DFS order. After the end of the visit, the root eventually detects the termination of the process.

Outline of the paper. The rest of the paper is organized as follows: in Section 2, we describe the distributed systems and the model in which our protocol is written. Moreover, in the same section, we give a formal statement of the Depth-First Search Wave Protocol solved in this paper. In Section 3, we present the Depth-First Search Wave Protocol. In the following section (Section 4), we give the proof of snap-stabilization of the protocol and some complexity results. Finally, we make concluding remarks in Section 5.

2   Preliminaries

Distributed System. We consider a *distributed system* as an undirected connected graph $G = (V, E)$ where V is a set of *processors* ($|V| = N$) and E is the set of *bidirectional communication links*. We consider networks which are *asynchronous* and *rooted*, i.e., among the processors, we distinguish a particular processor called *root*. We denote the root processor by r. A communication link (p, q) exists if and only if p and q are neighbors. Every processor p can distinguish all its links. To simplify the presentation, we refer to a link (p, q) of a processor p by the *label* q. We assume that the labels of p, stored in the set $Neig_p$[1], are locally ordered by $\prec_p$. We assume that $Neig_p$ is a constant, $Neig_p$ is shown as an input from the system. Moreover, we assume that the network is identified, i.e., every processor has exactly one identity which is unique in the network. We denote the identity of a processor p by Id_p. We assume that Id_p is a constant. Id_p is also shown as an input from the system.

Computational Model. In the computation model that we use, each processor executes the same program except r. We consider the local shared memory model of communication. The program of every processor consists of a set of *shared variables* (henceforth, referred to as variables) and a finite set of actions. A processor can only write to its own variables, and read its own variables and variables owned by the neighboring processors. Each action is constituted as follows:

$$< label > :: < guard > \rightarrow < statement > .$$

The guard of an action in the program of p is a boolean expression involving the variables of p and its neighbors. The statement of an action of p updates one or more variables of p. An action can be executed only if its guard is satisfied. We assume that the actions are atomically executed, meaning, the evaluation of a guard and the execution of the corresponding statement of an action, if executed, are done in one atomic step.

The *state* of a processor is defined by the value of its variables. The *state* of a system is the product of the states of all processors ($\in V$). We will refer to the state of a processor and system as a *(local) state* and *(global) configuration*, respectively. Let $\mathcal{C}$, the set of all possible configurations of the system. An action A is said to be *enabled* in $\gamma \in \mathcal{C}$ at p if the guard of A is true at p in γ. A processor p is said to be *enabled* in γ ($\gamma \in \mathcal{C}$) if there exists an enabled action A in the program of p in γ.

Let a distributed protocol $\mathcal{P}$ be a collection of binary transition relations denoted by $\mapsto$, on $\mathcal{C}$. A *computation* of a protocol $\mathcal{P}$ is a *maximal* sequence of configurations $e = (\gamma_0, \gamma_1, ..., \gamma_i, \gamma_{i+1}, ...)$, such that for $i \geq 0$, $\gamma_i \mapsto \gamma_{i+1}$ (called a *step*) if γ_{i+1} exists, else γ_i is a terminal configuration. *Maximality* means that the sequence is either finite (and no action of $\mathcal{P}$ is enabled in the terminal configuration) or infinite. All computations considered in this paper are assumed to be maximal. The set of all possible computations of $\mathcal{P}$ is denoted as $\mathcal{E}$.

---

[1] Every variable or constant X of a processor p will be noted X_p.

We consider that any processor p executed a *disabling action* in the computation step $\gamma_i \mapsto \gamma_{i+1}$ if p was *enabled* in γ_i and not enabled in γ_{i+1}, but did not execute any action between these two configurations. (The disabling action represents the following situation: at least one neighbor of p changes its state between γ_i and γ_{i+1}, and this change effectively made the guard of all actions of p false.)

In a step of computation, first, all processors check the guards of their actions. Then, some *enabled* processors are chosen by a *daemon*. Finally, the "elected" processors execute one or more of theirs *enabled* actions. There exists several kinds of *daemon*. Here, we assume a *distributed daemon*, i.e., during a computation step, if one or more processors are enabled, the daemon chooses at least one (possibly more) of these enabled processors to execute an action. Furthermore, a daemon can be *weakly fair*, i.e., if a processor p is continuously enabled, p will be eventually chosen by the daemon to execute an action. If the daemon is *unfair*, it can forever prevent a processor to execute an action except if it is the only enabled processor.

In order to compute the time complexity, we use the definition of *round* [14]. This definition captures the execution rate of the slowest processor in any computation. Given a computation e ($e \in \mathcal{E}$), the *first round* of e (let us call it e') is the minimal prefix of e containing the execution of one action (an action of the protocol or the disabling action) of every enabled processor from the first configuration. Let e'' be the suffix of e such that $e = e'e''$. The *second round* of e is the first round of e'', and so on. We say that a round is *finite* if it is constituted of a finite number of steps.

Snap-stabilizing Systems. The concept of *snap-stabilization* was introduced in [3]. In this paper, we restrict this concept to the wave protocols only.

Definition 1 (Snap-stabilization for Wave Protocols). *Let $\mathcal{T}$ be a task, and $\mathcal{SP}_\mathcal{T}$ a specification of $\mathcal{T}$. A wave protocol $\mathcal{P}$ is snap-stabilizing for the specification $\mathcal{SP}_\mathcal{T}$ if and only if:*

1. *At least one processor (called initiator) eventually executes a particular action of $\mathcal{P}$ (called initialization action).*
2. *The result obtained with $\mathcal{P}$ from this initialization action always satisfies $\mathcal{SP}_\mathcal{T}$.*

Theorem 1. *Let $\mathcal{T}$ be a task and $\mathcal{SP}_\mathcal{T}$ be a specification of $\mathcal{T}$. Let $\mathcal{P}$ be a protocol such that, assuming a weakly fair daemon, $\mathcal{P}$ is self-stabilizing for $\mathcal{SP}_\mathcal{T}$. If, for every execution of $\mathcal{P}$ assuming an unfair daemon, each round is finite, then $\mathcal{P}$ is also self-stabilizing for $\mathcal{SP}_\mathcal{T}$ assuming an unfair daemon.*

Proof. Let e be an execution of $\mathcal{P}$ assuming an unfair daemon. By assumption, every round of e is finite. Then, as every round of e is finite, each enabled processor (in e) executes an action (either a disabling action or an action of $\mathcal{P}$) in a finite number of steps. In particular, every continuously enabled processor executes an action of $\mathcal{P}$ in a finite number of steps. So, e is also an execution of

$\mathcal{P}$ assuming a weakly fair daemon. Since $\mathcal{P}$ is self-stabilizing for $\mathcal{SP}_T$ assuming a weakly fair daemon, e stabilizes to $\mathcal{SP}_T$. Hence, $\mathcal{P}$ is self-stabilizing for $\mathcal{SP}_T$ even if the daemon is unfair.   □

Specification of the Depth-First Search Wave Protocol. Before giving the specification of the Depth-First Search Wave Protocol, we propose some definitions.

Definition 2 (Path). *The sequence of processors $p_1, ..., p_k$ ($\forall i \in [1... k]$, $p_i \in V$) is a path of $G = (V, E)$ if $\forall i \in [1...k-1]$, $(p_i, p_{i+1}) \in E$. The path $p_1, ..., p_k$ is referred to as an elementary path if $\forall i, j$ such that $1 \leq i < j \leq k$, $p_i \neq p_j$. The processors p_1 and p_k are termed as initial and final extremities, respectively.*

Definition 3 (First Path). *For each elementary path of G from the root, $P = (p_1=r), ..., p_i, ...,p_k$, we associate a word $l_1, ..., l_i, l_{k-1}$ (noted $word(P)$) where, $\forall i \in [1...k-1]$, p_i is linked to p_{i+1} by the edge labelled l_i on p_i. Let $\prec_{lex}$ be a lexicographical order over these words. For each processor p, we define the set of all elementary paths from r to p. The path of this set with the minimal associated word by $\prec_{lex}$ is called the first path of p (noted $fp(p)$).*

Using this notion, we can define the *first DFS order*:

Definition 4 (First DFS Order). *Let $p, q \in V$ such that $p \neq q$. We can define the first DFS order $\prec_{dfs}$ as follows: $p \prec_{dfs} q$ if and only if $word(fp(p)) \prec_{lex} word(fp(q))$.*

Specification 1 (fDFS Wave). *Let $Visited$ be a predicate. A finite computation $e \in \mathcal{E}$ is called a fDFS wave (i.e., first DFS wave) if and only if the following tree conditions are true:*

1. *r initiates the fDFS wave by initializing the set of processors satisfying Visited with r.*
2. *During a fDFS wave, the other processors are sequentially included in the set of processors satisfying Visited following the first DFS order.*
3. *r eventually detects the ending of a fDFS wave and if r detects the ending of a fDFS wave then $\forall p \in V$, p satisfies Visited.*

Remark 1. In order to prove that our protocol is snap-stabilizing for Specification 1, we must show that every execution of the protocol satisfies these both conditions:

1. r eventually initiates a fDFS wave.
2. From any configuration where r has initiated a fDFS wave, the system always satisfies Specification 1.

3   Algorithm

In this section, we present a DFS wave protocol referred to as Algorithm *snapDFS* (see Algorithms 1. and 2.). We first present the normal behavior. We then explain the method of error correction.

Algorithm 1. Algorithm $snapDFS$ for $p = r$

Input: $Neig_p$: set of neighbors (locally ordered); Id_p: identity of p;
Constant: $Par_p = \bot$;
Variables: $S_p \in Neig_p \cup \{idle, done\}$; $Visited_p$: set of identities;
Macros:
$Next_p \qquad = (q = \min_{\prec_p}\{q' \in Neig_p :: (Id_{q'} \notin Visited_p)\})$ if q **exists**,
$\qquad\qquad\qquad done$ **otherwise**;
$ChildVisited_p = Visited_{S_p}$ if $(S_p \notin \{idle, done\})$, $\emptyset$ **otherwise**;
Predicates:
$Forward(p) \qquad \equiv (S_p = idle)$
$Backward(p) \quad \equiv (\exists q \in Neig_p :: (S_p = q) \land (Par_q = p) \land (S_q = done))$
$Clean(p) \qquad\quad \equiv (S_p = done)$
$SetError(p) \quad\; \equiv (S_p \neq idle) \land [(Id_p \notin Visited_p)$
$\qquad\qquad\qquad\qquad \lor (\exists q \in Neig_p :: (S_p = q) \land (Id_q \in Visited_p))]$
$Error(p) \qquad\quad \equiv SetError(p)$
$ChildError(p) \equiv (\exists q \in Neig_p :: (S_p = q) \land (Par_q = p) \land (S_q \neq idle)$
$\qquad\qquad\qquad\quad \land \neg(Visited_p \subsetneq Visited_q))$
$LockedF(p) \qquad \equiv (\exists q \in Neig_p :: (S_q \neq idle))$
$LockedB(p) \qquad \equiv [\exists q \in Neig_p :: (Id_q \notin ChildVisited_p) \land (S_q \neq idle)] \lor Error(p)$
$\qquad\qquad\qquad\qquad \lor ChildError(p)$

Actions:
$F :: Forward(p) \land \neg LockedF(p) \quad \rightarrow Visited_p := \{Id_p\}$; $S_p := Next_p$;
$B :: Backward(p) \land \neg LockedB(p) \rightarrow Visited_p := ChildVisited_p$; $S_p := Next_p$;
$C :: Clean(p) \lor Error(p) \qquad\qquad \rightarrow S_p := idle$;

Normal Behavior. From a normal configuration, we distinguish two phases in our protocol: the *visiting phase* where the protocol visits all the processors in the *first DFS order* and the *cleaning phase* which cleans the trace of the *visiting phase* so that the root is eventually ready to initiate a new *visiting phase*. These both phases work in parallel. In its normal behavior, Algorithm $snapDFS$ uses three variables for each processor p:

1. S_p designates the *successor* of p in the visiting phase, i.e., if there exists $q \in Neig_p$ such that $S_p = q$, then q (resp. p) is said to be a *successor* of p (resp. a *predecessor* of q),
2. $Visited_p$ is the set of processors which have been visited during the visiting phase,
3. Par_p designates the processor which has pointed out p as one of its successors during the visiting phase (as r has no predecessor, Par_r is the constant $\bot$).

Consider the configurations where $[(S_r = idle) \land (\forall p \in Neig_r , S_p = idle) \land (\forall q \in V \setminus (Neig_r \cup \{r\}), S_q \in \{idle, done\})]$. We refer to these configurations as *normal initial configurations*. In these configurations, every processor $q \neq r$ such that $S_q = done$ is enabled to perform its cleaning phase (see Predicate $Clean(p)$). Processor q performs its cleaning phase by executing Action C, i.e., it assigns $idle$ to S_q. Moreover, in this configuration, the root (r) is enabled to initiate a visiting phase (Action F). Processor r can initiate a visiting phase by initializing $Visited_r$ with its identity (Id_r) and pointing out (with S_r) its minimal neighbor in the local order $\prec_r$ (see Macro $Next_r$). In the worst case, every processor q, such that $S_q = done$, executes its cleaning phase, after, r is the only enabled processor and initiates a visiting phase. From this point on, r is the only $visited$ processor.

When a processor $p \neq r$ such that $S_p = idle$ is pointed out with S_q by a neighboring processor q, then p waits until all its neighbors p', such that $S_{p'} = done$ and $Id_{p'} \notin PredVisited_p$ (here, $Visited_q$), execute their cleaning phase. After, p can execute Action F. Then, p also designates q with Par_p and assigns $PredVisited_p \cup \{Id_p\}$ (here, $Visited_q \cup \{Id_p\}$) to $Visited_p$. Informally, the $Visited$ set of the last visited processor contains the identities of all the visited processors. Finally, p chooses a new successor, if any. For this earlier task, two cases are possible (see Macro $Next_p$):

1. $\forall\, p' \in Neig_p$, $Id_{p'} \in Visited_p$, i.e., all neighbors of p have been visited; the visiting phase from p is now terminated, so, S_p is set to $done$,
2. otherwise, p chooses as a successor the minimal processor by $\prec_p$ in $\{p' :: p' \in Neig_p \wedge Id_{p'} \notin Visited_p\}$ and p is now in the visiting phase.

In both cases, p is now considered as $visited$.

When q is the successor of p and $S_q = done$, p knows that the visiting phase from q is terminated. Thus, p must continue the visiting phase using another neighboring processor which is still not visited, if any: p executes Action B and it assigns $ChildVisited_p$ to $Visited_p$. Hence, it knows exactly which processors have been visited and it can designate another successor, if any, as in Action F (see Macro $Next_p$). Processor q is, now, enabled to execute its cleaning phase (Action C).

Finally, $S_r = done$ means that the visiting phase is terminated for all the processors and so, r can execute its cleaning phase. Thus, the system eventually reaches a $normal\ initial\ configuration$ again.

Error Correction. First, from the normal behavior, we can remark that, if $p \neq r$ is in the visiting phase and the visiting phase from p is still not terminated, then p must have a predecessor and must designate it with its variable Par_p, i.e., each processor $p \neq r$ must satisfy: $(S_p \notin \{idle, done\}) \Rightarrow (\exists q \in Neig_p :: S_q = p \wedge Par_p = q)$. The predicate $NoRealParent(p)$ allows to determine if this condition is not satisfied by p. Then, during the normal behavior, each processor maintains properties based on the value of its $Visited$ set and that of its predecessors, if any. Thus, in any configuration, p must respect the following conditions (see Action F):

1. $(S_p \neq idle) \Rightarrow (Id_p \in Visited_p)$ because when p is visited, it includes its identity in its $Visited$ set.
2. $(S_p \in Neig_p) \Rightarrow (Id_{S_p} \notin Visited_p)$, i.e., p must not point out a previously visited processor.
3. $((p \neq r) \wedge (S_p \neq idle) \wedge (\exists q \in Neig_p :: (S_q = p) \wedge (Par_p = q))) \Rightarrow (Visited_q \subsetneq Visited_p)$ because while $p \neq r$ is in the visiting phase, $Visited_p$ must strictly include the $Visited$ set of its parent.

Algorithm 2. Algorithm $snapDFS$ for $p \neq r$

Input: $Neig_p$: set of neighbors (locally ordered); Id_p: identity of p;
Variables: $S_p \in Neig_p \cup \{idle, done\}$; $Visited_p$: set of identities; $Par_p \in Neig_p$;
Macros:
$Next_p$ $= (q = \min_{\prec_p} \{q' \in Neig_p :: (Id_{q'} \notin Visited_p)\})$ if q **exists**,
               $done$ **otherwise**;
$Pred_p$ $= \{q \in Neig_p :: (S_q = p)\}$;
$PredVisited_p$ $= Visited_q$ if $(\exists! \; q \in Neig_p :: (S_q = p))$, $\emptyset$ **otherwise**;
$ChildVisited_p = Visited_{S_p}$ if $(S_p \notin \{idle, done\})$, $\emptyset$ **otherwise**;
Predicates:
$Forward(p)$ $\equiv (S_p = idle) \wedge (\exists q \in Neig_p :: (S_q = p))$
$Backward(p)$ $\equiv (\exists q \in Neig_p :: (S_p = q) \wedge (Par_q = p) \wedge (S_q = done))$
$Clean(p)$ $\equiv (S_p = done) \wedge (S_{Par_p} \neq p)$
$NoRealParent(p) \equiv (S_p \notin \{idle, done\}) \wedge \neg(\exists q \in Neig_p :: (S_q = p) \wedge (Par_p = q))$
$SetError(p)$ $\equiv (S_p \neq idle) \wedge [(Id_p \notin Visited_p)$
                     $\vee (\exists q \in Neig_p :: (S_p = q) \wedge (Id_q \in Visited_p))$
                     $\vee (\exists q \in Neig_p :: (S_q = p) \wedge (Par_q = p) \wedge \neg(Visited_q \subsetneq Visited_p))]$
$Error(p)$ $\equiv NoRealParent(p) \vee SetError(p)$
$ChildError(p)$ $\equiv (\exists q \in Neig_p :: (S_p = q) \wedge (Par_q = p) \wedge (S_q \neq idle)$
                     $\wedge \neg(Visited_p \subsetneq Visited_q))$
$LockedF(p)$ $\equiv (|Pred_p| \neq 1) \vee (\exists q \in Neig_p :: (Id_q \notin PredVisited_p) \wedge (S_q \neq idle))$
                     $\vee (Id_p \in PredVisited_p)$
$LockedB(p)$ $\equiv (|Pred_p| \neq 1) \vee (\exists q \in Neig_p :: (Id_q \notin ChildVisited_p) \wedge (S_q \neq idle))$
                     $\vee Error(p) \vee ChildError(p)$
Actions:
$F :: Forward(p) \wedge \neg LockedF(p)$ $\rightarrow Visited_p := PredVisited_p \cup \{Id_p\}$;
                                   $S_p := Next_p$; $Par_p := (q \in Pred_p)$;
$B :: Backward(p) \wedge \neg LockedB(p)$ $\rightarrow Visited_p := ChildVisited_p$; $S_p := Next_p$;
$C :: Clean(p) \vee Error(p)$ $\rightarrow S_p := idle$;

If one of these conditions is not satisfied by p, p satisfies $SetError(p)$. So, Algorithm $snapDFS$ detects if p is in an abnormal state, i.e., $(((p \neq r) \wedge NoRealParent(p)) \vee SetError(p))$ with the predicate $Error(p)$. In the rest of the paper, we call *abnormal processor* a processor p satisfying $Error(p)$. If p is an abnormal processor, then we must correct p and all the processors visited from p. We simply correct p by setting S_p to $idle$ (Action C). So, if, before p executes Action C, there exists a processor q such that $(S_p = q \wedge Par_q = p \wedge S_q \notin \{idle, done\} \wedge \neg Error(q))$, then after p executes Action C, q becomes an abnormal processor too (replacing p). These corrections are propagated until the visiting phase from p is completely corrected. However, during these corrections, the visiting phase from p can progress by the execution of Actions F and B. But, we can remark that the $Visited$ set of the last processor of a visiting phase grows by the execution of Actions F and B and the last processor of a visiting phase can only extend the propagation using processors which are not in its $Visited$ set. Thus, the visiting phase from an abnormal processor cannot run indefinitely. Hence, we will see later that the visiting phase from an abnormal processor will be eventually corrected.

Finally, we focus on the different ways to stop (or slow down) the propagation of the erroneous behaviors. Actions F and B allow a processor p to execute its visiting phase. However, by observing its state and that of its neighbors, p can detect some fuzzy behaviors and stop them: that is the goal of the predicates $LockedF(p)$ and $LockedB(p)$ in Actions F and B, respectively. A processor p is *locked* (i.e., p cannot execute Action B or Action F) when it satisfies at least one of the five following conditions:

1. p has several predecessors.
2. p is an abnormal processor.
3. p has a successor q such that $((S_q \neq idle) \wedge (Par_q = p) \wedge \neg(Visited_p \subsetneq Visited_q))$, i.e., q is abnormal.
4. p $(S_p = idle)$ is designated as a successor by q but Id_p is in $Visited_q$, i.e., q is abnormal.
5. some non-visited neighbors q of p are not cleaned, i.e., $S_q \neq idle$ (also used in a normal behavior).

4 Correctness and Complexity Analysis

4.1 Basic Definitions and Properties

Let $p \in V$. p is *pre-clean* if and only if $(Clean(p) \vee (S_p = done \wedge Error(p)))$. We recall that p is *abnormal* if and only if it satisfies $Error(p)$. A processor p is *linked* to a processor q if and only if $(S_p = q) \wedge (Par_q = p) \wedge \neg SetError(q) \wedge (S_q \neq idle)$. In this case p is called the *parent* of q and q the *child* of p. We can also remark that S_p (resp. Par_q) guarantees that q (resp. p) is the only child (resp. parent) of p (resp. q). As $Par_r = \perp$, obviously, r never has any parent.

A *linked path* of G is a path $P = p_1, ..., p_k$ such that $S_{p_1} \notin \{idle, done\}$ and $\forall i, 1 \leq i \leq k-1$, p_i is linked to p_{i+1}. We will note $IE(P)$ the *initial extremity* of P (i.e., p_1) and $FE(P)$ the *final extremity* of P (i.e., p_k). Moreover, the *length* of P (noted $length(P)$) is equal to k. Obviously, in any configuration, every linked path of G is elementary. So, from now on and until the end of the paper, we only consider maximal non-empty linked paths. The next lemma gives an important property of such linked paths.

Lemma 1. *Every linked path P satisfies $Visited_{FE(P)} \supseteq \{Id_p :: p \in P \wedge p \neq IE(P)\}$.*

We call abnormal linked path, a linked path P satisfying $Error(IE(P))$. Respectively, we call normal linked path, every linked path which is not abnormal. Obviously, a normal linked path P satisfies $IE(P) = r$.

Lemma 2. *A normal linked path P satisfies $Visited_{FE(P)} \supseteq \{Id_p :: p \in P\}$.*

Now, we introduce the notion of *future* of a linked path. We call *future* of a linked path P the evolution of P during a computation. In particular, the *immediate future* of P is the transformation supported by P after a step. Note that, after a step, P may disappear. Thus, by convention, we denote by $Dead_P$ the fact that P has disappeared after a step.

Definition 5 (Immediate Future of a Linked Path). *Let $\gamma_i \mapsto \gamma_{i+1}$ be a step. Let P be a linked path in γ_i. We call $F(P)$ the immediate future of P in γ_{i+1} and we define it as follows.*

1. **If** *there exists a linked path P' in γ_{i+1} which satisfies one of the following conditions: (a) $P \cap P' \neq \emptyset$, or (b) in γ_i, $S_{FE(P)} = IE(P')$ and $IE(P')$ executes Action F in $\gamma_i \mapsto \gamma_{i+1}$ then $F(P) = P'$,*
2. **else,** $F(P) = Dead_P$.

By convention, we state $F(Dead_P) = Dead_P$.

Figure 1 depicts two types of immediate future. Consider first Configurations i and ii. Configuration i contains one linked path only: $P = $ r, 1, 2. Moreover, Processor 3 has Action F enabled in i and executes it in $i \mapsto ii$ (i.e., 3 hooks on to P). Thus, the step $i \mapsto ii$ illustrates the case 1.(a) of Definition 5: in this execution, $F(P) = $ r, 1, 2, 3. Configuration iii also contains one linked path only: $P' = 1$. Then, in iii, Processor 1 has Action C enabled and Processor 2 has Action F enabled. These two processors execute C and F respectively in $iii \mapsto iv$ (1 unhooks from P' and 2 hooks on to P'). So, we obtain Configuration iv which illustrates the case 1.(b) of Definition 5: in this execution, $F(P') = 2$. Note that if only Processor 1 executes Action C from iii, P' disappears, i.e., $F(P') = Dead_P$.

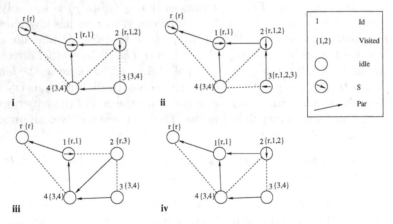

Fig. 1. Instances of Immediate Futures

Definition 6 (Future of a Linked Path). *Let $e \in \mathcal{E}$. Let $\gamma_i \in e$. We define $F^k(P)$ ($k \in \mathbb{N}$), the future of P in e after k steps of computation from γ_i, as follows:*

1. $F^0(P) = P$,
2. $F^1(P) = F(P)$ *(immediate future of P)*,
3. $F^k(P) = F^{k-1}(F(P))$ *(future of P after k steps of computation)*, **if** $k > 1$.

The following remarks and lemmas give some properties of linked paths and their futures.

Remark 2. Let $\gamma_i \mapsto \gamma_{i+1}$ be a step. Let P be a linked path in γ_i. $\forall p \in V$, p hooks on to P in $\gamma_i \mapsto \gamma_{i+1}$ if and only if p executes Action F in $\gamma_i \mapsto \gamma_{i+1}$ and $p = FE(F(P))$ in γ_{i+1}. As Par_r is a constant equal to $\bot$, r cannot hook on to any linked path.

Remark 3. Let $\gamma_i \mapsto \gamma_{i+1}$ be a step such that there exists a linked path P in γ_i. A processor p unhooks from P in $\gamma_i \mapsto \gamma_{i+1}$ in the three following cases only:

1. P is an abnormal linked path, $IE(P) = p$ and p executes Action C,
2. $S_p = done$ and its parent in P executes Action B ($p \neq r$),
3. $p = r$, its child q satisfies $S_q = done$, and r sets S_r to $done$ by executing Action B. In this case, q is also unhooked from P (Case 2.); moreover, since r never has any parent, $IE(P) = r$ and setting S_r to $done$ involves that P disappears, i.e., $F(P) = Dead_P$.

The following lemma allows us to claim that, during a computation, the identities of processors which hook on to a linked path P and its future are included into the $Visited$ set of the final extremity of the future of P. By checking Actions B and F of Algorithms 1. and 2., this lemma is easy to verify:

Lemma 3. *Let P be a linked path. While $F^k(P) \neq Dead_P$ (with $k \in \mathbb{N}$), $Visited_{FE(F^k(P))}$ contains exactly $Visited_{FE(P)}$ union the identities of every processor which hooks on to P and its future until $F^k(P)$.*

By checking Action F of Algorithms 1. and 2., follows:

Lemma 4. *For all linked path P, $\forall p \in V$ such that $Id_p \in Visited_{FE(P)}$, p cannot hook on to P.*

By Lemmas 3 and 4, we deduce the next lemma.

Lemma 5. *For all linked path P, if $p \in V$ hooks on to P, then p cannot hook on to $F^k(P)$, $\forall k \in \mathbb{N}^+$.*

In the rest of the paper, we study the evolution of the paths. So, a lot of results concern P and $F^k(P)$ with $k \in \mathbb{N}$. From now on, when there is no ambiguity, we replace "P and $F^k(P)$, $\forall k \in \mathbb{N}$" by P only.

4.2   Proof Assuming a Weakly Fair Daemon

Now, we assume a weakly fair daemon. Under this assumption, the number of steps of any round is finite. So, as we have defined the future of a linked path in terms of steps, we can also evaluate the future of a linked path in terms of rounds. Let $e \in \mathcal{E}$. Let P be a linked path in γ_i ($\in e$). We note $F_R^K(P)$ the future of P, in e, after K rounds from γ_i.

We now show that the network contains no abnormal linked path in at most N rounds, i.e., every abnormal path P of the initial configuration satisfies $F_R^N(P)$ $= Dead_P$.

Theorem 2. *The system contains no abnormal linked path in at most N rounds.*

Sketch of Proof. It is easy to see that the number of abnormal linked paths cannot increase. Moreover, if Action C is enabled at p, then it remains enabled until p executes it. So, let P be an abnormal linked path. As the daemon is weakly fair, after each round, at least one processor unhooks from P (while P exists). By Lemmas 1, 4 and 5 and Remark 2, the number of processors which can hook on to P is at most $N - length(P)$. So, in the worst case, N rounds are necessary to unhook the processors of P and those which will hook on. Thus, $F_R^N(P) = Dead_P$. □

The following lemmas and theorems allow to prove that r eventually executes Action F.

Lemma 6. *For every normal linked path P, the future of P is $Dead_P$ after at most $2N - 2$ actions on it.*

Proof. Let $e \in \mathcal{E}$. Let $\gamma_i \in e$. Assume that there exists a normal linked path P in γ_i. First, we can remark that the future of P is either a normal linked path or $Dead_P$. Moreover, obviously, each action on P is either Action F or Action B. By Lemmas 4 and 5, only processors p such that $Id_p \notin Visited_{FE(P)}$ (in γ_i) can hook on to P at most one during the execution. By Lemma 2, in the worst case, the number of processors which hook on to P during the execution is $N - length(P)$. Then, after $N - 2$ processors unhooked from P (i.e., $length(P)$ $+ (N - length(P)) - 2$ actions B on P), P satisfies $length(P) = 2$. In this case, only one action can be executed on P: the parent of $FE(P)$ (i.e., $IE(P)$) can execute Action B. Now, by Lemma 3, $Visited_{FE(P)} = \{Id_q :: q \in V\}$. So, by executing Action B, $IE(P)$ sets $S_{IE(P)}$ to $done$ ($Next_{IE(P)}$). Thus, as explained in Remark 3, P disappears. Hence, in the worst case, the future of P is $Dead_P$ after $N - length(P) + (N - 2) + 1$ actions which is maximal if initialy $length(P) = 1$, i.e., $2N - 2$ actions. □

If there exists no abnormal linked path, we can remark that, after at most one round, there always exists at least one continuously enabled action on the normal linked path. Thus, by Lemma 6 follows:

Lemma 7. *Let P be a normal linked path. If there exists no abnormal linked path, $F_R^{2N-1}(P) = Dead_P$.*

Theorem 2 and Lemma 7 prove the following theorem.

Theorem 3. *For all normal linked path P, $F_R^{3N-1}(P) = Dead_P$.*

Theorem 4. *From any initial configuration, r executes Action F after at most 3N rounds.*

Proof. By Theorems 2 and 3, from any initial configuration, the system needs at most $3N - 1$ rounds to reach a configuration γ_i satisfying $\forall p \in V$, $S_p \in \{idle, done\}$. In γ_i, $\forall p \in V$ such that $S_p = done$, we have, $S_{Par_p} \neq p$. So, every p has Action C continuously enabled. As the daemon is weakly fair, after one round, $\forall p \in V$, $S_p = idle$. Thus, r is the only enabled processor and Action F is the only enabled action of r. Hence, from any initial configuration, the root executes Action F after at most 3N rounds. □

From the explanation provided in Section 3, it is easy to verify that when the system starts from a configuration where $\forall p \in V$, $S_p = idle$ (let us call it the *idle* configuration) it performs a traversal of the network according to Specification 1. Now, if the system starts from an arbitrary configuration, then it can contain some pre-clean processors and abnormal linked paths. We can remark that the pre-clean processors and the abnormal linked paths can only slow down the progression of the normal linked path. But the system keeps even so a normal behavior because the normal linked path progresses in the same way than if it starts from a *idle* configuration. So, the normal linked path eventually visits all the processors in the *first DFS* order and, after, r eventually detects the termination of the wave when r sets S_r to *done* (because $\forall p \in V, Id_p \in Visited_r$). Hence:

Theorem 5. *From any configuration where r executes Action F, the execution satisfies Specification 1.*

From Remark 1, Theorems 4 and 5, follows:

Theorem 6. *Algorithm snapDFS is snap-stabilizing for Specification 1 with a weakly fair daemon.*

4.3   Proof Assuming an Unfair Daemon

From now on, we do not make any fairness assumption. The two next lemmas allow to prove that, in any execution of Algorithm *snapDFS*, each round is finite.

Lemma 8. *The future of an abnormal linked path P is $Dead_P$ after at most $2N - 1$ actions on it.*

Proof. The reasonning is similar to the proof of Lemma 6. □

Lemma 9. *Every round of Algorithm snapDFS has a finite number of steps.*

Proof. Let $e \in \mathcal{E}$. Assume that a round R of e has an infinite number of steps. Let γ_R be the first configuration of R.

First, assume that some abnormal linked paths of γ_R never disappear. So, the system eventually reaches a configuration $\gamma_i \in R$ in which there exists only abnormal linked paths which never disappear. Now, as every abnormal linked path disappears after a finite number of actions on it (see Lemma 8), there exists a configuration γ_j ($j \geq i$) from which no action will be executed on these abnormal linked paths. Then, every pre-clean processor is clean after one Action C and a normal linked path can only generate a finite number of pre-clean processors. Indeed, the pre-clean processors generated by the normal linked path has belong to it before and, until the normal linked path disappears, only a finite number of processors can hook on to it (see Lemma 5). Then, the pre-clean processors cannot prevent forever actions to be executed on a normal linked path. Now, by Lemma 6, every normal linked path disappears after a finite number of steps. So, the root processor executes Action F infinitively often to create normal linked paths. But, if r executes Action F, then, by Theorem 5, r creates a new normal linked path P and every processor ($\neq r$) eventually hooks on to P during the execution (in particular, the processors of abnormal linked paths). Now, a processor p can hook on to P if $S_p = idle$ (see Remark 2 and Predicate $Forward(p)$). Thus, P is eventually locked because the processors of the abnormal linked paths never hook on to it. So, r cannot execute Action F infinitively often, a contradiction. Thus, there exists a step $\gamma_{j'} \mapsto \gamma_{j'+1}$ with $j' \geq j$ in which at least one action is executed on an abnormal linked path, a contradiction. Hence, the abnormal linked paths eventually disappear.

So, there exists a configuration γ_k in which there exists no abnormal linked path. From this configuration, there always exists at most one linked path, the normal linked path. Assume that there exists no normal linked path in γ_k. Then, after a finite number of steps, r executes Action F and creates a normal linked path P (in the worst case, after $O(N)$ Actions C, every pre-clean processor becomes idle and r is the only enabled processor). As explained above, the pre-clean processors cannot prevent forever actions to be executed on P. By Lemma 6, the future of P is $Dead_P$ after a finite number of actions on it. Now, by Theorem 5, before disappearing, every processor hooks on to it by executing Action F. So, Round R is eventually done, a contradiction. Finally, if there exists a normal linked path P' in γ_k, by a similar reasonning, after a finite number of steps, the future of P' is $Dead_{P'}$ and we retrieve the previous case, a contradiction.

Hence, after a finite number of steps, every enabled processor of γ_R has executed one action. □

By Theorems 1 and 6, and Lemma 9, the following theorem holds.

Theorem 7. *Algorithm snapDFS is snap-stabilizing for Specification 1 even if the daemon is unfair.*

4.4   Complexity Analysis

Space Complexity. By checking Algorithms 1. and 2., follows:

Lemma 10. *The space requirement of Algorithm snapDFS is $O(N \times \log(N) + \log(\Delta))$ bits per processor.*

Time Complexity.

Lemma 11. *From any initial configuration, r executes Action F in $O(N^2)$ steps.*

Proof. In the initial configuration, the system can contain $O(N)$ pre-clean processors and $O(N)$ linked paths. Then, every linked path can generate $O(N)$ pre-clean processors. Indeed, the pre-clean processors generated by a linked path has belong to it before and, until a linked path disappears, every processor can hook on to it at most once (see Lemma 5). Finally, every pre-clean processor cleans it by executing Action C. And, every linked path disappears after $O(N)$ actions on it (see Lemmas 6 and 8). Hence, in the worst case, after $O(N^2)$ steps, r is the only enabled processor and executes Action F in the next step.   □

The following lemma can be deduced from Lemma 11.

Lemma 12. *From any initial configuration, a complete fDFS wave is executed in $O(N^2)$ steps.*

By Lemma 7, and Theorems 2 and 4, we can deduce the following result.

Lemma 13. *From any initial configuration, a complete fDFS wave is executed in at most $5N - 1$ rounds.*

5   Conclusion

We presented a snap-stabilizing depth-first search wave protocol for arbitrary rooted networks. The protocol does not use any pre-computed spanning tree but requires identities on processors. The snap-stabilizing property guarantees that as soon as the root initiates the protocol, every processor of the network will be visited in DFS order. After the end of the visit, the root eventually detects the termination of the process. Furthermore, as our protocol is snap-stabilizing, by definition, it is also a self-stabilizing protocol which stabilizes in 0 round (resp. 0 step). Obviously, our protocol is optimal in stabilization time. We also showed that the proposed protocol works correctly assuming an unfair daemon, i.e., assuming the weakest scheduling assumption. Finally, note that our protocol executes a complete traversal of the network in $O(N)$ rounds and $O(N^2)$ steps, respectively. The memory requirement of our solution is $O(N \times \log(N) + \log(\Delta))$ bits per processor. In a future work, we would like to design a snap-stabilizing DFS wave protocol (for arbitrary rooted networks) with a memory requirement independent of N.

Acknowledgements. We would like to thank the anonymous referees for their suggestions and contructives comments on the earlier version of the paper. Their suggestions have greatly enhanced the readability of the paper.

References

1. Tel, G.: Introduction to distributed algorithms. Cambridge University Press (Second edition 2001)
2. Dijkstra, E.: Self stabilizing systems in spite of distributed control. Communications of the Association of the Computing Machinery **17** (1974) 643–644
3. Bui, A., Datta, A., Petit, F., Villain, V.: State-optimal snap-stabilizing PIF in tree networks. In: Proceedings of the Forth Workshop on Self-Stabilizing Systems, IEEE Computer Society Press (1999) 78–85
4. Awerbuch, B.: A new distributed depth-first-search algorithm. Information Processing Letters **20** (1985) 147–150
5. Cheung, T.: Graph traversal techniques and maximum flow problem in distributed computation. IEEE Transactions on Software Engineering **SE-9(4)** (1983) 504–512
6. Collin, Z., Dolev, S.: Self-stabilizing depth-first search. Information Processing Letters **49(6)** (1994) 297–301
7. Huang, S., Chen, N.: Self-stabilizing depth-first token circulation on networks. Distributed Computing **7** (1993) 61–66
8. Datta, A., Johnen, C., Petit, F., Villain, V.: Self-stabilizing depth-first token circulation in arbitrary rooted networks. Distributed Computing **13(4)** (2000) 207–218
9. Johnen, C., Beauquier, J.: Space-efficient distributed self-stabilizing depth-first token circulation. In: Proceedings of the Second Workshop on Self-Stabilizing Systems. (1995) 4.1–4.15
10. Petit, F., Villain, V.: Color optimal self-stabilizing depth-first token circulation. In: I-SPAN'97, Third International Symposium on Parallel Architectures, Algorithms and Networks Proceedings, IEEE Computer Society Press (1997) 317–323
11. Petit, F.: Fast self-stabilizing depth-first token circulation. In: Proceedings of the Fifth Workshop on Self-Stabilizing Systems, Lisbonne (Portugal), LNCS 2194 (October 2001) 200–215
12. Petit, F., Villain, V.: Time and space optimality of distributed depth-first token circulation algorithms. In: Proceedings of DIMACS Workshop on Distributed Data and Structures, Carleton University Press (1999) 91–106
13. Cournier, A., Datta, A., Petit, F., Villain, V.: Enabling snap-stabilization. In: 23th International Conference on Distributed Computing Systems (ICDCS 2003). (2003) 12–19
14. Dolev, S., Israeli, A., Moran, S.: Uniform dynamic self-stabilizing leader election. IEEE Transactions on Parallel and Distributed Systems **8** (1997) 424–440

A Self-stabilizing Link-Coloring Protocol Resilient to Byzantine Faults in Tree Networks

Yusuke Sakurai[1], Fukuhito Ooshita[2], and Toshimitsu Masuzawa[2]

[1] Information and Communication Systems Group,
Sharp Corporation Yamatokoriyama-shi, 639-1186 Japan
sakurai.yuhsuke@sharp.co.jp
[2] Graduate School of Information Science and Technology,
Osaka University, Toyonaka-shi, 560-8531 Japan
{f-oosita, masuzawa}@ist.osaka-u.ac.jp

Abstract. Self-stabilizing protocols can tolerate any type and any number of transient faults. But self-stabilizing protocols have no guarantee of their behavior against permanent faults. Thus, investigation concerning self-stabilizing protocols resilient to permanent faults is important.

This paper proposes a self-stabilizing link-coloring protocol resilient to (permanent) Byzantine faults in tree networks. The protocol assumes the central daemon, and uses $\Delta + 1$ colors where Δ is the maximum degree in the network. This protocol guarantees that, for any nonfaulty process v, if the distance from v to any Byzantine ancestor of v is greater than two, v reaches its desired states within three rounds and never changes its states after that. Thus, it achieves fault containment with radius of two. Moreover, we prove that the containment radius becomes $\Omega(\log n)$ when we use only Δ colors, and prove that the containment radius becomes $\Omega(n)$ under the distributed daemon. These lower bound results prove necessity of $\Delta + 1$ colors and the central daemon to achieve fault containment with a constant radius.

1 Introduction

Self-stabilization[5] is one of the most effective and promising paradigms for fault-tolerant distributed computing[6]. A self-stabilizing protocol is guaranteed to achieve its desired behavior eventually regardless of the initial network configuration (i.e., global state). This implies a self-stabilizing protocol is resilient to any number and any type of transient faults since it can converge to its desired behavior from any configuration resulted by transient faults. However the convergence to the desired behavior is guaranteed only on the assumption that no further fault occurs during the convergence. Thus, a self-stabilizing protocol is not guaranteed to achieve its desired behavior in the presence of a permanent fault. Thus, it is strongly desired to design self-stabilizing protocols resilient to permanent faults.

T. Higashino (Ed.): OPODIS 2004, LNCS 3544, pp. 283–298, 2005.

There are some researches about self-stabilizing protocols resilient to permanent faults [1, 4, 10, 16, 3, 15, 17, 19]. Most of these researches treat only crash faults, and these self-stabilizing protocols guarantee that each nonfaulty process achieves its desired behavior regardless of the initial network configuration. Nesterenko et al.[17] treat Byzantine faults as permanent faults. The main difficulty in tolerating Byzantine faults is caused by arbitrary and unbounded state changes of the Byzantine process: processes around the Byzantine processes may change their states in response to the state changes of the Byzantine processes, and processes next to the processes changing their states may also changes their states. This implies that the influence of the Byzantine processes expands to the whole system, and then no process can achieve its desired behavior. Nesterenko et al.[17] give a novel definition of a self-stabilizing protocol resilient to Byzantine faults. The protocol guarantees, by containing the influence of Byzantine processes to only processes near them, the other processes can achieve their desired behaviors eventually. They introduce the containment radius as the distance between a Byzantine process and processors affected by the Byzantine process. They also propose self-stabilizing protocols resilient to Byzantine faults for the vertex coloring problem and the dining philosophers problem. The containment radius is one for the vertex coloring problem and two for the dining philosophers problem.

The concept of fault containment is very popular in the field of self-stabilizing protocol[7, 8, 9, 13, 12, 2]. However, these papers aim to contain the influence of a transient fault, and they do not consider Byzantine faults.

In this paper, we consider a self-stabilizing link-coloring protocol resilient to Byzantine faults in tree networks. Link-coloring of the distributed system is an assignment of colors to the communication links such that no two communication links with the same color share a process in common. Link-coloring has many applications in distributed systems, e.g., scheduling data transfer and assigning frequency band in wireless networks. Thus, many distributed protocols for link-coloring are proposed[11, 14, 18]. However, the fault tolerance is not considered in these protocols.

In this paper, we propose a self-stabilizing link-coloring protocol resilient to Byzantine faults. The protocol assumes the central daemon, i.e., exactly one process can execute an operation at each time, and uses $\Delta + 1$ colors, where Δ is the maximum degree of the network. The protocol guarantees that any nonfaulty process v reaches its desired states within three rounds and never changes its state after that if v has no Byzantine ancestor with the distance of two or less. Moreover, we show that, for any self-stabilizing link-coloring protocol resilient to Byzantine faults, when it uses only Δ colors, the containment radius becomes $\Omega(\log n)$ if $\Delta \geq 3$, and $\Omega(n)$ if $\Delta = 2$, where n is the number of processes. Thus, our proposed protocol attains the minimality in the number of colors for achieving fault containment of Byzantine processes with a constant containment radius. Next, for any self-stabilizing link-coloring protocol that assumes the distributed daemon, i.e., an arbitrary number of processes can execute operations at each time, even when it can use arbitrary number of colors, we show that the containment radius becomes $\Omega(n)$. This lower bound result implies that the assumption of the central daemon is reasonable to attain the fault containment against Byzantine faults with a constant containment radius.

2   Preliminaries

2.1   Distributed System

A *distributed system* $S = (P, L)$ consists of a set $P = \{v_1, v_2, \ldots, v_n\}$ of processes and a set L of communication links (simply called links). A link is an unordered pair of distinct processes and processes v and w are called *neighbors* if $(v, w) \in L$. A distributed system S can be regarded as a graph with a vertex set P and a link set L, and thus, we use some graph terminologies to a distributed system S.

We consider *rooted tree networks* in this paper. For each process $v \in P$, N_v denotes the set of neighbors of v, prt_v denotes the parent of v, and Ch_v denotes the set of children of v. We do not assume existence of a unique identifier of each process. Instead we assume each process can identify its parent from them, and distinguish each of its children by local ordering on its children. The x-th child of process v is denoted by $ch_v(x)$ $(1 \le x \le |Ch_v|)$. The distance from the root process to process v is called the depth of v. The maximum degree of a tree network is denoted by Δ, i.e., the root process has at most Δ children and any other process has at most $\Delta - 1$ children.

Each process is modeled by a state machine that can communicate with its neighbors through link registers. For each pair of neighboring processes, u and v, there are two link registers $r_{u,v}$ and $r_{v,u}$. Message transmission from u to v is realized as follows: u writes a message to link register $r_{u,v}$ and then v reads it from $r_{u,v}$.

For each process v, let $In_v = \{r_{u,v} | u \in N_v\}$ be the input register set of v and $Out_v = \{r_{v,u} | u \in N_v\}$ be the output register set of v. For convenience, we use variables to denote the states of a process and a link register, and use *guarded actions* (simply called *actions*) to denote the state transition function of a process. Each action is of the following form:

$< guard > \rightarrow < statement >$

The guard of an action of a process v is a boolean expression consisting of the variables of v and all input registers r $(r \in In_v)$. The statement of an action of v updates one or more variables of v and all output registers r $(r \in Out_v)$. The values assigned to the variables of v and r $(r \in Out_v)$ depend only on the values of variables of v and r $(r \in In_v)$. The statement of an action can be executed only if its guard is evaluated to true. When guards of multiple actions are evaluated to true, one of these actions is deterministically selected and executed. We assume that each action is atomically executed: the evaluation of the guard and the execution of the corresponding statement of the action, if executed, are done in one atomic step. The execution of an action of v is called a *step* of v.

A global state of a distributed system is called a *configuration* and is denoted by a product of states of all processes and all link registers. We define C as the set of all possible configurations of a distributed system S. For each configuration $\rho \in C$, $\rho|v$ and $\rho|r$ denote the states of process v and link register r in configuration ρ respectively.

When a process v has a guarded action whose guard is true at configuration ρ, we say v is *enabled* at ρ. Let $En(\rho, v)$ be a predicate such that $En(\rho, v) = true$ iff v is enabled at ρ. Letting Q be any set of processes, when configuration ρ changes to configuration ρ' by executing actions of every enabled process in Q, we denote $\rho \overset{Q}{\mapsto} \rho'$.

A *schedule* of a distributed system is an infinite sequence of sets of processes. Let $\mathcal{Q} = Q_1, Q_2, \ldots$ be a schedule. An infinite sequence of configurations $e = \rho_0, \rho_1, \ldots$ is called an *execution* from an initial configuration ρ_0 by a schedule $\mathcal{Q}$, if e satisfies $\rho_i \overset{Q_{i+1}}{\mapsto} \rho_{i+1}$ for each i ($i \geq 0$). Notice that the execution e is uniquely determined from its initial configuration and a schedule $\mathcal{Q}$ since the executed action of each process is deterministically selected (even when a process has two or more actions with true guards). The set of possible schedules in a distributed system is sometimes modeled by a scheduler called a daemon. In this paper, we consider two kinds of daemons, the *distributed daemon* and the *central daemon*. Under the distributed daemon, each Q_i can be an arbitrary set of processes. That is, the distributed daemon allows two or more processes execute their actions simultaneously. By contrast, the central daemon is a special case of the distributed daemon. Under the central daemon, $|Q_i| = 1$ holds for each i, i.e., no two processes execute their actions simultaneously. Under the central daemon, when $Q_i = \{q_i\}$ for each i, we simply describe a schedule as $\mathcal{Q} = q_1, q_2, \ldots$ and describe a configuration transition as $\rho_i \overset{q_{i+1}}{\mapsto} \rho_{i+1}$ instead of $\rho_i \overset{Q_{i+1}}{\mapsto} \rho_{i+1}$. The set of all possible executions from an initial configuration $\rho_0 \in C$ is denoted by E_{ρ_0}. The set of all possible executions is denoted by E, that is, $E = \bigcup_{\rho_0 \in C} E_{\rho_0}$.

We consider *asynchronous* distributed systems where we can make no assumption on schedules except that any schedule is *weakly fair*: every process appears in the schedule infinitely often.

In this paper, we consider two kinds of permanent faults: crash faults and Byzantine faults.

- *crash faults*: A crash process (i.e., a process with the crash fault) prematurely stops execution of its actions. If v is a crash process, v does not change states of v and r ($r \in Out_v$) after certain time even when there is an action with true guard. Before that time, v acts as a nonfaulty process and correctly executes its actions.
- *Byzantine faults*: A Byzantine process (i.e., a process with the Byzantine fault) can arbitrarily behave independently from its actions. If v is a Byzantine process, v can repeatedly change states of v and r ($r \in Out_v$) arbitrarily.

We define BF and CF as the sets of Byzantine processes and crash processes respectively. Since a crash fault can be regarded as a special case of the Byzantine fault, $BF \supseteq CF$ holds. However, in what follows, we assume without loss of generality that $BF \cap CF = \emptyset$ holds by excluding crash processes from the set BF.

Let $CF = \{f_1, f_2, \ldots, f_c\}$. In distributed systems where faults can occur, an infinite sequence of configurations $e = \rho_0, \rho_1, \ldots$ is called an *execution* by a schedule $\mathcal{Q} = Q_1, Q_2, \ldots$, if there exists $t_1, t_2, \ldots, t_c$ such that the following conditions hold for any i $(i \geq 0)$:

- For any $v \in Q_{i+1} - (BF \cup CF)$, execution of an action of v changes v's state from $\rho_i|v$ to $\rho_{i+1}|v$ (possibly $\rho_i|v = \rho_{i+1}|v$) and changes the state of every $r \in Out_v$ from $\rho_i|r$ to $\rho_{i+1}|r$ (possibly $\rho_i|r = \rho_{i+1}|r$).
- For any $f_j \in Q_{i+1} \cap CF$, if $i \geq t_j$, the states of f_j and each output register $r \in Out_{f_j}$ remain unchanged from ρ_i to ρ_{i+1}: $\rho_i|f_j = \rho_{i+1}|f_j$ and $\forall r \in Out_{f_j} : \rho_i|r = \rho_{i+1}|r$ hold. If $i < t_j$, execution of an action of f_j changes its state from $\rho_i|f_j$ to $\rho_{i+1}|f_j$ (possibly $\rho_i|f_j = \rho_{i+1}|f_j$) and changes the state of every $r \in Out_{f_j}$ from $\rho_i|r$ to $\rho_{i+1}|r$ (possibly $\rho_i|r = \rho_{i+1}|r$). Notice that t_j implies that process f_j becomes crashed between ρ_{t_j-1} and ρ_{t_j}.
- For any $v \notin Q_{i+1}$, $\rho_i|v = \rho_{i+1}|v$ and $\forall r \in Out_v : \rho_i|r = \rho_{i+1}|r$ hold.

Notice that, for any process $v \in Q_{i+1} \cap BF$, $\rho_{i+1}|v$ and $\rho_{i+1}|r$ $(r \in Out_v)$ can be arbitrary states.

In asynchronous distributed systems, time is usually measured by *asynchronous rounds* (simply called *rounds*). Let $e = \rho_0, \rho_1, \ldots$ be an execution from configuration ρ_0 by a schedule $\mathcal{Q} = Q_1, Q_2, \ldots$. The first round of e is defined to be the minimum prefix of e, $e' = \rho_0, \rho_1, \ldots, \rho_k$, such that $\bigcup_{i=1}^{k} Q_i = P$. Round t $(t \geq 2)$ is defined recursively, by applying the above definition of the first round to $e'' = \rho_k, \rho_{k+1}, \ldots$. Intuitively, every process has a chance to update its state in every round.

2.2   Self-stabilizing Protocol Resilient to Byzantine Faults

In this paper, we treat only *static problems*, i.e., once the system reaches a desired configuration, the configuration remains unchanged forever. For example, the spanning-tree construction problem is a static problem, and the mutual exclusion problem is not a static problem[6]. A static problem can be defined by a *specification predicate*, $spec(v)$, for each process v, which specifies the condition that v should satisfy at the desired configuration. A specification predicate $spec(v)$ is a boolean expression consisting of the variables of $P_v \subseteq P$ and link registers $R_v \subseteq R$, where R is the set of all link registers.

A self-stabilizing protocol is a protocol that guarantees each process v satisfies $spec(v)$ eventually regardless of the initial configuration. By this property, a self-stabilizing protocol can tolerate any number and any type of transient faults. However, since we consider permanent faults such as Byzantine faults and crash faults, faulty processes cannot satisfy $spec(v)$. In addition, nonfaulty processes near the faulty processes can be influenced by the faulty processes and cannot satisfy $spec(v)$. Thus, Nesterenko et al.[17] define a self-stabilizing protocol resilient to these faults. Informally, the protocol requires each nonfaulty process v far from any faulty process to satisfy $spec(v)$ eventually. They also propose concepts of strict tolerance and strict stabilization to define some classes of protocols resilient to Byzantine faults. We combine the above two concepts, and propose $(\mathcal{B}, \mathcal{C})$-self-stabilization with radius (τ, μ), where $\mathcal{B}$ and $\mathcal{C}$ represent Byzantine faults and crash faults respectively. In the following definition, let $\Gamma(v, l)$ be the set of processes whose distance to v is at most l.

Definition 1. *A configuration ρ_0 is a $(\mathcal{B}, \mathcal{C})$-stable configuration with radius (τ, μ) if and only if, for any execution $e = \rho_0, \rho_1, \ldots$ and any process v, the following condition holds:*

If the distance from v to any Byzantine process is more than τ ($\forall w \in \Gamma(v, \tau) : w \notin BF$) and the distance from v to any crash process is more than μ ($\forall u \in \Gamma(v, \mu) : u \notin CF$), for any i, i) v satisfies spec(v) in ρ_i, ii) $\rho_i|v = \rho_{i+1}|v$ holds, iii) $\rho_i|r = \rho_{i+1}|r$ ($r \in Out_v$) holds.

Definition 1 states, once the system reaches a stable configuration, a process v sufficiently far from any faulty process satisfies spec(v) and never changes the states of v and r ($r \in Out_v$) forever.

Definition 2. *A protocol A is a $(\mathcal{B}, \mathcal{C})$-self-stabilizing protocol with radius (τ, μ) if and only if, for any execution $e = \rho_0, \rho_1, \ldots$ of A starting from any configuration ρ_0, there exists ρ_i that is a $(\mathcal{B}, \mathcal{C})$-stable configuration with radius (τ, μ). We say that the stabilizing time of A is k for the minimum k such that the last configuration of the k-th round is a stable configuration in any execution of a protocol A.*

Definition 2 states a $(\mathcal{B}, \mathcal{C})$-self-stabilizing protocol guarantees that the system eventually reaches a $(\mathcal{B}, \mathcal{C})$-stable configuration from any initial configuration. If a protocol A is a $(\mathcal{B}, \mathcal{C})$-self-stabilizing protocol with radius (τ, μ), where τ and μ are constant, A is strictly $\mathcal{C}$-tolerant[17] and strictly stabilizing[17].

2.3   Link-Coloring Problem

A link-coloring problem is to find an assignment of colors to links such that no two links with the same color share a process in common. In the following, let $CSET$ be a given set of colors, and let $Color((u, v)) \in CSET$ be a color of link (u, v). We define the distributed link-coloring problem as follows.

Definition 3. *In the distributed link-coloring problem, the specification predicate spec(v) for a process v is given as follows:*

$$\forall x, y \in N_v : x \neq y \Longrightarrow Color((v, x)) \neq Color((v, y))$$

In the following, we define a *b-link-coloring protocol* as a link-coloring protocol using b colors.

3   Link-Coloring Protocol Under the Central Daemon

In this section, we propose a $(\mathcal{B}, \mathcal{C})$-self-stabilizing $(\Delta + 1)$-link-coloring protocol with radius $(2, 1)$. Our protocol uses at most $\Delta + 1$ colors for link-coloring, and thus, we assume $CSET = \{1, 2, \ldots, \Delta + 1\}$.

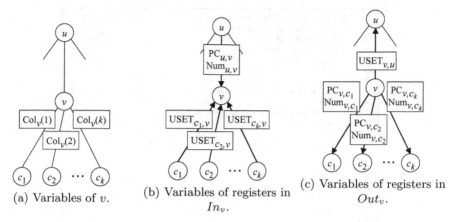

Fig. 1. Variables of v, link registers in In_v, and link registers in Out_v, where $u = prt_v$ and $c_x = ch_v(x)$ $(1 \leq x \leq |Ch_v|)$

Let v be any process, $u = prt_v$, and x_v be an integer satisfying $v = ch_u(x_v)$. First, we explain variables on a process and a link register (See Fig. 1).

- Process v has variables $\mathtt{Col}_v(x)$ $(1 \leq x \leq |Ch_v|)$. Variable $\mathtt{Col}_v(x)$ denotes a color of link $(v, ch_v(x))$. Notice that v does not have the variable to store the color of link (u, v) for its parent u. The color of the link is stored in $\mathtt{Col}_u(x_v)$ of u.
- Link register $r_{u,v}$ has variables $\mathtt{Num}_{u,v}$ and $\mathtt{PC}_{u,v}$. Process u assigns x_v to $\mathtt{Num}_{u,v}$, and assigns $\mathtt{Col}_u(x_v)$ to $\mathtt{PC}_{u,v}$. Process v can learn the color of link (u, v) by reading $\mathtt{PC}_{u,v}$. The value of $\mathtt{Num}_{u,v}$ is used to determine $\mathtt{Col}_v(x)$ $(1 \leq x \leq |Ch_v|)$.
- Link register $r_{v,u}$ has a variable $\mathtt{USET}_{v,u}$. Process v assigns $\left\{\mathtt{Col}_v(x) \big| 1 \leq x \leq |Ch_v|\right\}$ to $\mathtt{USET}_{v,u}$. Process u can learn the colors assigned to links $(v, ch_v(x))$ $(1 \leq x \leq |Ch_v|)$ by reading $\mathtt{USET}_{v,u}$.

For simplicity, we assume that $\mathtt{Col}_v(x) \in CSET$ $(1 \leq x \leq |Ch_v|)$, $1 \leq \mathtt{Num}_{u,v} \leq \Delta$, $\mathtt{PC}_{u,v} \in CSET$, and $\mathtt{USET}_{v,u} \subseteq CSET$ are always satisfied at any configuration even when there exist some Byzantine processes.

Process v executes the following step atomically:

1. Process v reads variables on all link registers in In_v.
2. Process v locally determines colors $\mathtt{Col}_v(x)$ for all x $(1 \leq x \leq |Ch_v|)$.
3. For each x $(1 \leq x \leq |Ch_v|)$, letting $w = ch_v(x)$, process v writes x and $\mathtt{Col}_v(x)$ to $\mathtt{Num}_{v,w}$ and $\mathtt{PC}_{v,w}$ on link register $r_{v,w}$ respectively.
4. Letting $u = prt_v$, process v writes $\left\{\mathtt{Col}_v(x) \big| 1 \leq x \leq |Ch_v|\right\}$ to $\mathtt{USET}_{v,u}$ on link register $r_{v,u}$.

We show the protocol LINKCOLORING in Fig. 2. For simplicity, we show the protocol by giving the pseudo-code. The function LINKCOLORING is executed in one atomic step.

```
 1:    function LINKCOLORING {
 2:    // v is the root process
 3:    if v = root then
 4:       for k := 1 to |Ch_v| {
 5:          Col_v(k) := k
 6:       }
 7:
 8:    // v is not the root process
 9:    else
10:       // assign colors to Col_v(k) (k < Num_{u,v})
11:       u := prt_v
12:       c := 1
13:       for k := 1 to min({Num_{u,v} - 1, |Ch_v|}) {
14:          if PC_{u,v} = c then
15:             c + +
16:          endif
17:          Col_v(k) := c
18:          c + +
19:       }
20:
21:       // assign colors to Col_v(k) (k > Num_{u,v})
22:       c := |Ch_v|
23:       for k := |Ch_v| downto Num_{u,v} + 1 {
24:          if PC_{u,v} = c then
25:             c − −
26:          endif
27:          Col_v(k) := c
28:          c − −
29:       }
30:
31:       // assign colors to Col_v(k) (k = Num_{u,v})
32:       if |Ch_v| ≥ Num_{u,v} then
33:          k := Num_{u,v}
34:          if Col_v(k) ∉ {k, k + 1, k + 2} or
35:             PC_{u,v} = Col_v(k) or
36:             Col_v(k − 1) = Col_v(k) or
37:             Col_v(k + 1) = Col_v(k) then
38:             C := {k, k + 1, k + 2} − {PC_{u,v}} − USET_{ch_v(k),v}
39:             if C ≠ ∅ then
40:                Col_v(k) := min(C)
41:             else
42:                Col_v(k) := min({k, k + 1, k + 2} − {PC_{u,v}})
43:             endif
44:          endif
45:       endif
46:    endif
47:
48:    // write colors to link registers
49:    for k := 1 to |Ch_v| {
50:       Num_{v,ch_v(k)} := k
51:       PC_{v,ch_v(k)} := Col_v(k)
52:    }
53:    if v ≠ root then
54:       USET_{v,u} := { Col_v(k) | 1 ≤ k ≤ |Ch_v| }
55:    endif
56: }
```

Fig. 2. The protocol LINKCOLORING: the action of v

To explain how each process v determines $\texttt{Col}_v(x)$, we define candidate color sets and preference colors. For each process v and each x $(1 \leq x \leq |Ch_v|)$, we define the *candidate color set* $CCol_v(x)$ as follows:

$$CCol_v(x) = \{x, x+1, x+2\}$$

For each process v (v is not the root) and each x ($1 \leq x \leq |Ch_v|, x \neq \text{Num}_{prt_v,v}$), we define the *preference color* $PCol_v(x)$ as follows:

$$PCol_v(x) = \begin{cases} x & (x < \text{Num}_{prt_v,v}) \\ x+2 & (x > \text{Num}_{prt_v,v}) \end{cases}$$

In the protocol LINKCOLORING, nonfaulty process v assigns colors to links with the following policies: 1) v always assigns colors to links so that no two links with the same color share v, 2) v always assigns color $c \in CCol_v(x)$ to $Col_v(x)$, and 3) if possible, v assigns color $PCol_v(x)$ to $Col_v(x)$. According to these policies, v assigns a color to $Col_v(x)$ as follows:

- Case where v is the root process. Process v assigns x to $Col_v(x)$ ($1 \leq x \leq |Ch_v|$) (See line 4 to 6).
- Case where v is not the root process. Let $u = prt_v$ and $w = ch_v(\text{Num}_{u,v})$.
  1. Case where $PC_{u,v} \in CCol_v(\text{Num}_{u,v}) = \{\text{Num}_{u,v}, \text{Num}_{u,v}+1, \text{Num}_{u,v}+2\}$
     - For each x ($x < \text{Num}_{u,v}$), v assigns x to $Col_v(x)$ (See line 10 to 19).
     - Let $C = CCol_v(\text{Num}_{u,v}) - \{PC_{u,v}\}$. If there exists c such that $c \in C - \text{USET}_{w,v}$, v assigns c to $Col_v(\text{Num}_{u,v})$. Otherwise, v assigns any color $c \in C$ to $Col_v(\text{Num}_{u,v})$ (See line 30 to 44).
     - For each x ($x > \text{Num}_{u,v}$), v assigns $x+2$ to $Col_v(x)$ (See line 21 to 29).
  2. Case where $PC_{u,v} < \text{Num}_{u,v}$.
     - For each x ($x < PC_{u,v}$), v assigns x to $Col_v(x)$ (See line 10 to 19).
     - For each x ($PC_{u,v} \leq x < \text{Num}_{u,v}$), v assigns $x+1$ to $Col_v(x)$(See line 10 to 19).
     - Let $C = CCol_v(\text{Num}_{u,v}) - \{\text{Num}_{u,v}\}$. If there exists c such that $c \in C - \text{USET}_{w,v}$, v assigns c to $Col_v(\text{Num}_{u,v})$. Otherwise, v assigns any color $c \in C$ to $Col_v(\text{Num}_{u,v})$ (See line 31 to 45).
     - For each x ($x > \text{Num}_{u,v}$), v assigns $x+2$ to $Col_v(x)$ (See line 21 to 29).
  3. Case where $PC_{u,v} > \text{Num}_{u,v} + 2$.
     - For each x ($x < \text{Num}_{u,v}$), v assigns x to $Col_v(x)$ (See line 10 to 19).
     - Let $C = CCol_v(\text{Num}_{u,v}) - \{\text{Num}_{u,v} + 2\}$. If there exists c such that $c \in C - \text{USET}_{w,v}$, v assigns c to $Col_v(\text{Num}_{u,v})$. Otherwise, v assigns any color $c \in C$ to $Col_v(\text{Num}_{u,v})$ (See line 31 to 45).
     - For each x ($\text{Num}_{u,v} < x \leq PC_{u,v} - 2$), v assigns $x+1$ to $Col_v(x)$ (See line 21 to 29).
     - For each x ($PC_{u,v} - 2 < x$), v assigns $x+2$ to $Col_v(x)$ (See line 21 to 29).

After v executes an action, the guards of actions of v become false and $spec(v)$ becomes true. Notice that the guards of actions of v and $spec(v)$ do not include variables $\text{USET}_{w,v}$ ($w \in Ch_v$). Thus, once v executes an action, even when $w \in Ch_v$ is a Byzantine process and changes $\text{USET}_{w,v}$ arbitrarily, the guards of actions of v remain false and $spec(v)$ remains true unless prt_v changes $PC_{prt_v,v}$.

Assume v and $u = prt_v$ are nonfaulty processes, and prt_u is a Byzantine process. In what follows, we explain how the influence of a Byzantine process prt_u is contained in the candidate color sets and the preference colors.

Since u is a nonfaulty process, by the protocol, u assigns a color in $CCol_u(x)$ to $Col_u(x)$ in the first round. Thus, process u reduces the influence of Byzantine process prt_u in the sense that the change of $Col_u(x)$ is constrained in $CCol_u(x)$ although the change of $PC_{prt_u,u}$ is completely unconstrained.

As described above, u always assigns a color in $CCol_u(x)$ to $Col_u(x)$ ($1 \leq x \leq |Ch_u|$). Consequently, letting $C = \{Num_{u,v}, Num_{u,v} + 1, Num_{u,v} + 2\}$, $PC_{u,v} = Col_u(Num_{u,v}) \in CCol_u(Num_{u,v}) = C$ holds at any configuration after the first round. Then, when v executes a step after the first round, v assigns $PCol_v(x)$ to $Col_v(x)$ for each x ($x \neq Num_{u,v}$), and assigns a color in $CCol_v(Num_{u,v})$ to $Col_v(Num_{u,v})$. This implies v never changes $Col_v(x)$ ($x \neq Num_{u,v}$) even when u changes $PC_{u,v}$. However, v may have to change $Col_v(Num_{u,v})$ in response to change of $PC_{u,v}$. Letting $w = ch_v(Num_{u,v})$, since w also assigns $PCol_w(x)$ to $Col_w(x)$ for each x ($x \neq Num_{v,w}$) after the second round, links that can be assigned colors in C to and connects to either v or w are only (u,v), (v,w), and $(w, ch_w(Num_{u,v}))$. Thus, v can assign a color in C to $Col_v(Num_{u,v})$ so that no two links with the same color share either v or w. Therefore, w, a process apart from the Byzantine ancestor by distance of three, is not affected by the Byzantine process, and we attain the fault containment against the Byzantine faults. About the protocol LINKCOLORING, we have the following theorem.

Theorem 1. *The protocol* LINKCOLORING *is a* $(\Delta + 1)$-*link-coloring protocol satisfying the following property:*

- *Let* $e = \rho_0, \rho_1, \ldots$ *be any execution,* $v \in P$ *be any nonfaulty process, and* ρ_s *be the last configuration of the third round. When* v *has no Byzantine ancestor with the distance of two or less and has no crash parent, for any* t ($t \geq s$), *i)* v *satisfies* $spec(v)$ *in* ρ_t, *ii) both* $\rho_t|v = \rho_{t+1}|v$ *and* $\forall r \in Out_v : \rho_t|r = \rho_{t+1}|r$ *hold.*

Corollary 1. *The protocol* LINKCOLORING *ia a* $(\mathcal{B}, \mathcal{C})$-*self-stabilizing* $(\Delta + 1)$-*link-coloring protocol with radius* $(2,1)$. *The stabilization time of* LINKCOLORING *is three.*

In addition, we define that a process v is in a *consistent state* if $PC_{v,ch_v(x)} = Col_v(x)$ holds for any x ($1 \leq x \leq |Ch_v|$). Notice that, for any process $v \notin BF$, once v executes an action, v is in a consistent state forever. For nonfaulty process v apart from any Byzantine ancestor by distance of three, when prt_v is a crash process, we cannot guarantee that v satisfies $spec(v)$. However, if prt_v crashes in a consistent state, we can guarantee that.

Theorem 2. *The protocol* LINKCOLORING *is a* $(\Delta + 1)$-*link-coloring protocol satisfying the following property:*

- *Let* $e = \rho_0, \rho_1, \ldots$ *be any execution,* $v \in P$ *be any nonfaulty process* v, *and* ρ_s *be the last configuration of the third round. When* v *has no Byzantine* *ancestor with the distance of two or less and has the crash parent that crashes in a consisten state, for any t $(t \geq s)$, i) v satisfies spec(v) in ρ_t, ii) both $\rho_t|v = \rho_{t+1}|v$ and $\forall r \in Out_v : \rho_t|r = \rho_{t+1}|r$ holds.*

4   Impossibility of Link-Coloring Using Δ Colors Under the Central Daemon

In this section, we consider a self-stabilizing Δ-link-coloring protocol. We can link-color tree networks with Δ colors. However, we show that, for any self-stabilizing Δ-link-coloring protocol, the containment radius is $\Omega(\log n)$ if $\Delta \geq 3$, and $\Omega(n)$ if $\Delta = 2$, where n is the number of processes. Thus, the protocol LINKCOLORING attains the minimality in the number of colors for achieving fault containment of Byzantine processes with a constant containment radius. To show the lower bounds, we define the *view* of v as the states of v and all link registers in In_v, and $view(\rho, v)$ denotes the view of process v in configuration ρ.

Theorem 3. *Assume $\Delta \geq 3$. For any $(\mathcal{B}, \mathcal{C})$-self-stabilizing Δ-link-coloring protocol with radius $(\tau(n), \mu(n))$, $\tau(n) = \Omega(\log n)$ holds, where n is the number of processes.*

Proof. We assume that the color of a link (u, v) is determined (or coded) by the states of u, v, $r_{u,v}$, and $r_{v,u}$. Assume that A is a $(\mathcal{B}, \mathcal{C})$-self-stabilizing Δ-link-coloring protocol with radius $(\tau(n), \mu(n))$.

Let a system $S = (P, L)$ be a complete $(\Delta - 1)$-ary tree such that each non-leaf process has $\Delta - 1$ children and all leaf processes have the same depth, say h. Then, $n = \sum_{k=0}^{h}(\Delta - 1)^k$ holds. Let $P = \{v_1, v_2, \ldots, v_n\}$, and let $ch_{v_i}^S(x)$ be the x-th child of v_i in S. Let v_l be a process with depth of $\lceil h/2 \rceil$, $v_m = prt_{v_l}$, and c be an integer satisfying $v_l = ch_{v_m}^S(c)$.

We assume the set of Byzantine processes $BF = \{v_l\}$ and the set of crash processes $CF = \emptyset$. First, we assume that there exists a $(\mathcal{B}, \mathcal{C})$-stable configuration ρ satisfying the following Condition $\mathcal{A}$. (We show existence of ρ in the latter part of this proof.)

Condition $\mathcal{A}$: 1) For any $v_i \in P - \{v_m, v_l\}$, all links incident to v_i have different colors, 2) letting E_l and E_m be the sets of all links incident to v_l and v_m respectively, $\left\{Color(e) \middle| e \in (E_l \cup E_m) - \{(v_l, v_m)\}\right\} = CSET$.

Notice that, in ρ, whatever color is assigned to link (v_l, v_m), a link incident to v_l or v_m has the same color as link (v_l, v_m).

We consider the execution from ρ such that a Byzantine process v_l behaves as a nonfaulty process, that is, all processes behave correctly. The execution is the same as the execution from ρ in the case all processes are nonfaulty. Thus, the system reaches a configuration ρ' where any process v satisfies spec(v). Remind that, in ρ, whatever color is assigned to link (v_l, v_m), a link incident to v_l or v_m has the same color as link (v_l, v_m). Thus, there exists $v_{a_1} \in \{v_l, v_m\}$ and $v_{a_2} \in N_{v_{a_1}} - \{v_l, v_m\}$ such that the color of link (v_{a_1}, v_{a_2}) in ρ' is difffernt from that in ρ. Since all links incident to v_{a_2} have different colors in ρ, if the degree of v_{a_2} is Δ, there exists neighbor v_{a_3} of v_{a_2} such that the color of link (v_{a_2}, v_{a_3}) in ρ' is different from that in ρ. In the similar way, we can construct a sequence of links, $(v_{a_1}, v_{a_2}), (v_{a_2}, v_{a_3}), \ldots, (v_{a_{f-1}}, v_{a_f})$, whose colors in ρ' are different from those in ρ. Notice that the degree of v_{a_f} is not Δ. Consequently, the state of either $v_{a_{f-1}}$, v_{a_f}, r_{a_{f-1},a_f}, or $r_{a_f,a_{f-1}}$ in ρ is different from that in ρ'. Since the degree of v_{a_f} is not Δ and the system S is a complete $(\Delta-1)$-ary tree, v_{a_f} is the root process or a leaf process. Thus, the distance from $v_{a_{f-1}}$ (or v_{a_f}) to a Byzantine process v_l is $\Omega(h) = \Omega(\log n)$. Since ρ is a $(\mathcal{B}, \mathcal{C})$-stable configuration with radius $(\tau(n), \mu(n))$, processes whose distance to v_l is more than $\tau(n)$ do not change any state. Therefore, $\tau(n) = \Omega(\log n)$.

In the following, we prove existence of a $(\mathcal{B}, \mathcal{C})$-stable configuration satisfying Condition $\mathcal{A}$. To prove it, we construct a system $T = (P', L')$ as follows. Let $P' = P \cup \{u_1, u_2, \ldots, u_{\Delta-1}\}$, where $u_i \notin P$ $(1 \le i \le \Delta - 1)$, and L' is defined as follows (See Fig. 3):

1. $ch^T_{v_i}(x) = ch^S_{v_i}(x)$ $(i \ne m)$
2. $ch^T_{v_m}(x) = \begin{cases} u_1 & (x = c) \\ ch^S_{v_m}(x) & (x \ne c) \end{cases}$
3. $ch^T_{u_1}(x) = \begin{cases} u_{x+1} & (x < c) \\ v_l & (x = c) \\ u_x & (x > c) \end{cases}$

For the system T, let $\mathcal{Q}_T = p_1, p_2, \ldots$ be a schedule, and let $e_T = \sigma_0, \sigma_1, \ldots$ be an execution by schedule $\mathcal{Q}_T$ in the case that $BF = \emptyset$ and $CF = \emptyset$. Then, in

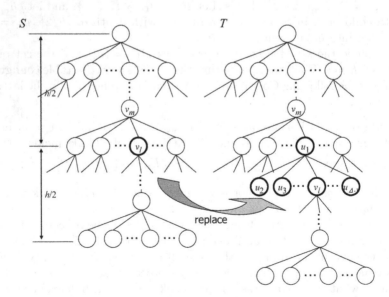

Fig. 3. Two systems

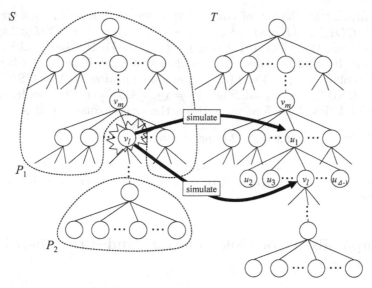

Fig. 4. Byzantine process v_l in S behaves as u_1 for P_1 and as v_l for P_2

e_T, there exists a configuration σ_s such that any process v satisfies $spec(v)$ and never changes any state after σ_s.

Next, for the system S, we construct a schedule $\mathcal{Q}_S = q_1, q_2, \ldots$ and an execution $e_S = \rho_0, \rho_1, \ldots$ in the case that $BF = \{v_l\}$ and $CF = \emptyset$. We define the initial configuration ρ_0 so that $view(\rho_0, v_i) = view(\sigma_0, v_i)$ holds for any v_i. We construct the schedule $\mathcal{Q}_S$ in which v_i $(i \neq l)$ executes a step in the same order as in $\mathcal{Q}_T$, and v_l executes a step immediately before each step of neighbors of v_l. In e_S, the Byzantine process v_l simulates the behavior of u_1 and v_l in e_T (See Fig. 4). That is, if $q_\alpha = v_l$, $q_{\alpha+1} = v_m$, and $q_{\alpha+1}$ is the k-th step of v_m in e_S, v_l changes the states of itself and link register r_{v_l, v_m} so that $\rho_\alpha|v_l = \sigma_\beta|v_l$ and $view(\rho_\alpha, v_m) = view(\sigma_\beta, v_m)$, where σ_β is the configuration such that $p_{\beta+1}$ is the k-th step of v_m in e_T. And, if $q_\alpha = v_l$, $q_{\alpha+1} = ch^S_{v_l}(x)$, and $q_{\alpha+1}$ is the k-th step of $ch^S_{v_l}(x)$ in e_S, v_l changes the states of itself and its output registers so that $\rho_\alpha|v_l = \sigma_\beta|v_l$ and $view(\rho_\alpha, ch^S_{v_l}(x)) = view(\sigma_\beta, ch^T_{v_l}(x))$, where σ_β is the configuration such that $p_{\beta+1}$ is the k-th step of $ch^T_{v_l}(x)$ in e_T. Then, any v_i $(i \neq l)$ changes the states of itself and its output registers in the same way in e_T. By the definition of e_T, there exists a configuration ρ_t such that, any process v_i $(i \neq l)$ never changes its state after ρ_t. Since A is a $(\mathcal{B}, \mathcal{C})$-self-stabilizing protocol with radius $(\tau(n), \mu(n))$, the system eventually reaches a $(\mathcal{B}, \mathcal{C})$-stable configuration $\rho_{t'}$ with radius $(\tau(n), \mu(n))$. Let t'' be the integer such that $t'' \geq \max\{t, t'\}$ and $q_{t''+1} \in Ch_{v_l}$. By the definition of t'', $\rho_{t''}$ is a $(\mathcal{B}, \mathcal{C})$-stable configuration with radius $(\tau(t), \mu(t))$.

Since colors of links except for (v_m, v_l) in $\rho_{t''}$ are the same as those in σ_s, $\rho_{t''}$ satisfies the first condition of $\mathcal{A}$.

In the following, we show that $\rho_{t''}$ also satisfies the second condition of $\mathcal{A}$. Let $E_S(v)$ and $E_T(v)$ be the sets of all links incident to v in S and in T respectively.

Let $COL(\rho, E)$ be the set of colors that links in E have in configuration ρ. Let $U = COL(\rho_{t''}, (E_S(v_l) \cup E_S(v_m)) - \{(v_l, v_m)\})$, $V = COL(\sigma_s, E_T(v_l) - \{(v_l, u_1)\})$, and $W = COL(\sigma_s, E_T(v_m) - \{(v_m, u_1)\})$. By the definition of $\rho_{t''}$, $U = V \cup W$ holds. Then, since degrees of v_l and v_m in T are Δ, letting χ_1 and χ_2 be the colors of (v_l, u_1) and (v_m, u_1) in configuration σ_s, $V = CSET - \{\chi_1\}$ and $W = CSET - \{\chi_2\}$ hold. Since $\chi_1 \neq \chi_2$, $V \cup W = CSET$ holds, and thus, $U = CSET$ holds. Therefore, $\rho_{t''}$ satisfies the second condition of $\mathcal{A}$.   □

Similarly, we can get the following theorem.

Theorem 4. *Assume $\Delta = 2$. For any $(\mathcal{B}, \mathcal{C})$-self-stabilizing Δ-link-coloring protocol with radius $(\tau(n), \mu(n))$, $\tau(n) = \Omega(n)$ holds, where n is the number of processes.*

5   Impossibility of Link-Coloring Under the Distributed Daemon

In this section, we consider a self-stabilizing link-coloring protocol under the distributed daemon. The distributed daemon allows two or more processes to execute their actions simultaneously, while the central daemon does not. Thus, the distributed daemon is usually regarded as a more practical model. However in this section, we show that, for any self-stabilizing link-coloring protocol, the influence of a Byzantine process expands to a process whose distance to the Byzantine process is $\Omega(n)$ even when it can use arbitrarily large number of colors. This lower bound result implies that the assumption of the central daemon is reasonable to attain the fault containment against Byzantine faults with a constant containment radius.

Theorem 5. *Let n be the number of processes, and A be a link-coloring protocol under the distributed daemon. If A is a $(\mathcal{B}, \mathcal{C})$-self-stabilizing protocol with radius $(\tau(n), \mu(n))$, $\tau(n) = \Omega(n)$ holds.*

Proof. We assume that the color of a link (u, v) is determined by the states of u, v, $r_{u,v}$, and $r_{v,u}$. Assume that A is a $(\mathcal{B}, \mathcal{C})$-self-stabilizing protocol with radius $(\tau(n), \mu(n))$.

We consider a distributed system $S = (P, L)$ in the form of a line graph: Let $P = \{v_1, v_2, \ldots, v_n\}$ and $L = \{(v_i, v_{i+1}) | 1 \leq i \leq n - 1\}$, where v_1 is the root process. Let $BF = \{v_1, v_n\}$ and $CF = \emptyset$.

We consider an execution $e = \rho_0, \rho_1, \ldots$ by a schedule $\mathcal{Q} = Q_1, Q_2, \ldots$, where $Q_i = P$ for any i. We assume that $view(\rho_0, v_2) = view(\rho_0, v_3) = \cdots = view(\rho_0, v_{n-1}) = s_0$. Since processes $v_2, v_3, \ldots, v_{n-1}$ execute the same step, $view(\rho_1, v_3) = view(\rho_1, v_4) = \cdots = view(\rho_1, v_{n-2}) = s_1$. Then, we assume that Byzantine processes v_1 and v_n change the states so that $view(\rho_1, v_2) = view(\rho_1, v_{n-1}) = s_1$ can hold. This implies $view(\rho_1, v_2) = view(\rho_1, v_3) = \cdots = view(\rho_1, v_{n-1}) = s_1$. When Byzantine processes execute a step similarly, we have $view(\rho_i, v_2) = view(\rho_i, v_3) = \cdots = view(\rho_i, v_{n-1}) = s_i$ for any i. It shows that, for any ρ_i, $Color((v_2, v_3)) = Color((v_3, v_4)) = \cdots = Color((v_{n-2}, v_{n-1}))$ holds. Thus, letting $h = \lceil \frac{n}{2} \rceil$, a process v_h cannot satisfy $spec(v_h)$. Since the distance from v_h to any Byzantine process is $\Omega(n)$, $\tau(n) = \Omega(n)$. $\square$

6 Conclusion

In this paper, we considered a self-stabilizing link-coloring protocol resilient to Byzantine faults in rooted tree networks. First, under the central daemon, we proposed a self-stabilizing link-coloring protocol resilient to Byzantine faults. The protocol uses $\Delta + 1$ colors, where Δ is the maximum degree of the network, and guarantees that any nonfaulty process v reaches its desired states within three rounds and never changes its state after that if v has no Byzantine ancestor with the distance of two or less. Furthermore, we showed that, for any self-stabilizing link-coloring protocol using Δ colors, the containment radius becomes $\Omega(\log n)$ if $\Delta \geq 3$, and $\Omega(n)$ if $\Delta = 2$, where n is the number of processes. Thus, our proposed protocol attains the minimality in the number of colors for achieving fault containment of Byzantine processes with a constant containment radius. Next, under the distributed daemon, we show that, for any self-stabilizing link-coloring protocol, the containment radius becomes $\Omega(n)$ even when it can use arbitrary number of colors. This lower bound result implies that the assumption of the central daemon is reasonable to attain the fault containment against Byzantine faults with a constant containment radius.

Acknowledgement

This work is supported in part by a JSPS, Grant-in-Aid for Scientific Research ((B)(2)15300017), and "The 21st Century Center of Excellence Program" of the Ministry of Education, Culture, Sports, Science and Technology, Japan.

References

1. E. Anagnostou and V. Hadzilacos. Tolerating transient and permanent failures. *Lectures Notes in Computer Science, Vol 725 (Springer-Verlag)*, pages 174–188, 1993.
2. A. Arora and H. Zhang. Lsrp: Local stabilization in shortest path routing. In *Proceedings of the 2003 International Conference on Dependable Systems and Networks*, pages 139–148, 2003.
3. J. Beauquier and S. Kekkonen-Moneta. Fault-tolerance and self-stabilization: impossibility results and solutions using self-stabiling failure detectors. *International Journal of Systems Science*, 28(11):1177–1187, 1997.
4. J. Beauquier and S. Kekkonen-Moneta. On ftss-solvable distributed problems. In *Proceedings of the 6th Annual ACM Symposium on Principles of Distributed Computing*, page 290, 1997.
5. E. W. Dijkstra. Self stabilizing systems in spite of distributed control. *Communications of the Association of the Computing Machinery*, 17:643–644, 1974.

6. S. Dolev. *Self-Stabilization*. MIT Press, 2000.
7. S. Ghosh and A. Gupta. An exercise in fault-containment: self-stabilizing leader election. *Information Processing Letters*, 59(5):281–288, 1996.
8. S. Ghosh, A. Gupta, T. Herman, and S. V. Pemmaraju. Fault-containing self-stabilizing algorithms. In *Proceedings of the 15th Annual ACM Symposium on Principles of Distributed Computing*, pages 45–54, 1996.
9. S. Ghosh and S. V. Pemmaraju. Tradeoffs in fault-containing self-stabilization. In *Proceedings of the 3rd Workshop on Self-Stabilizing Systems*, pages 157–169, 1997.
10. A. S. Gopal and K. J. Perry. Unifying self-stabilization and fault-tolerance. In *Proceedings of the 12th Annual ACM Symposium on Principles of Distributed Computing*, pages 195–206, 1993.
11. D. A. Grable and A. Panconesi. Nearly optimal distributed edge colouring in o(log log n) rounds. In *Proceedings of the 8th Annual ACM-SIAM Symposium on Discrete Algorithms*, pages 278–285, 1997.
12. Y. Katayama and T. Masuzawa. A fault-containing self-stabilizing protocol for constructing a minimum spanning tree. *IEICE Transactions*, J84-D-I(9):1307–1317, 2001.
13. S. Kutten and B. Patt-Shamir. Stabilizing time-adaptive protocols. *Theoretical Computer Science*, 220(1):93–111, 1999.
14. M. V. Marathe, A. Panconesi, and L. D. Risinger. An experimental study of a simple, distributed edge coloring algorithm. In *Proceedings of the 12th Annual ACM Symposium on Parallel Algorithms and Architectures*, pages 166–175, 2000.
15. T. Masuzawa. A fault-tolerant and self-stabilizing protocol for the topology problem. In *Proceedings of the 2nd Workshop on Self-Stabilizing Systems*, pages 1.1–1.15, 1995.
16. H. Matsui, M. Inoue, T. Masuzawa, and H. Fujiwara. Fault-tolerant and self-stabilizing protocols using an unreliable failure detector. *IEICE Transactions on Information and Systems*, E83-D(10):1831–1840, 2000.
17. M. Nesterenko and A. Arora. Tolerance to unbounded byzantine faults. In *Proceedings of 21st IEEE Symposium on Reliable Distributed Systems*, pages 22–29, 2002.
18. A. Panconesi and A. Srinivasan. Fast randomized algorithms for distributed edge coloring. In *Proceedings of the 11th Annual ACM Symposium on Principles of Distributed Computing*, pages 251–262, 1992.
19. S. Ukena, Y. Katayama, T. Masuzawa, and H. Fujiwara. A self-stabilizing spanning tree protocol that tolerates non-quiescent permanent faults. *IEICE Transaction*, J85-D-I(11):1007–1014, 2002.

A Hierarchy-Based Fault-Local Stabilizing Algorithm for Tracking in Sensor Networks

Murat Demirbas[1], Anish Arora[1], Tina Nolte[2], and Nancy Lynch[2]

[1] Computer Science & Engineering, The Ohio State University,
Columbus, OH 43210, USA
[2] MIT Computer Science & Artificial Intelligence Laboratory,
Cambridge, MA 02139, USA

Abstract. In this paper, we introduce the concept of *hierarchy-based fault-local stabilization* and a novel self-healing/fault-containment technique and apply them in STALK. STALK is an algorithm for tracking in sensor networks that maintains a data structure on top of an underlying hierarchical partitioning of the network. Starting from an arbitrarily corrupted state, STALK satisfies its specification within time and communication cost proportional to the size of the faulty region, defined in terms of levels of the hierarchy where faults have occurred. This local stabilization is achieved by slowing propagation of information as the levels of the hierarchy underlying STALK increase, enabling more recent information propagated by lower levels to override misinformation at higher levels before the misinformation is propagated more than a constant number of levels. In addition, this stabilization is achieved without reducing the efficiency or availability of the data structure when faults don't occur: 1) Operations to *find* the mobile object distance d away take $O(d)$ time and communication to complete, 2) Updates to the tracking structure after the object has moved a total of of d distance take $O(d * log$ network diameter) amortized time and communication to complete, 3) The tracked object may relocate without waiting for STALK to complete updates resulting from prior moves, and 4) The mobile object can move while a *find* is in progress.

Keywords: Sensor networks, self-stabilization, fault-containment, tracking, distributed data structures.

"Everything is related to everything else, but near things are more related than distant things".

Waldo Tobler's First Law of Geography

1 Introduction

In a distributed system, faults can occur that might be propagated throughout the system. In some systems, this propagation of errors might be unacceptable.

T. Higashino (Ed.): OPODIS 2004, LNCS 3544, pp. 299–315, 2005.

Fault-containment or error confinement is concerned with preventing this propagation of faults beyond a small region. Exactly what is meant by "small" is defined as a polynomial of the *perturbation size*, an error severity measure. Previously, the perturbation size of a failure was defined in terms of the number of errors that occurred. This measure is convenient for expressing the seriousness of a processor fault in the execution of an algorithm as long as the algorithm does not incorporate use of processor hierarchies.

Hierarchies have long been imposed on networks of processors to facilitate design of efficient and scalable protocols. For example, Awerbuch and Peleg's tracking paper [6] described distributed directory servers to store location information for mobile objects. The directory servers were composed of a hierarchy of geographically defined regional directories where directories at higher levels of the hierarchy were responsible for maintaining information for larger regions of a network.

Another example of geographically defined hierarchies used in distributed systems are clusterings based on *hierarchical partitionings*. In such a system, all processes are divided into level zero clusters. Each of these clusters contain members that are close to one another geographically and have a defined clusterhead. These level zero clusterheads are then partitioned into level one clusters, again containing members that are close to one another, and so on.

Using traditional definitions of perturbation size, a fault that occurs at a single level zero process during execution of a hierarchy-based algorithm has the same size as that of a fault of a single level ten process. As a result, a fault-containing algorithm would have to prevent propagation of information beyond an area whose size is a polynomial based on perturbation size one. This kind of level-blind fault-containment is not always possible. Instead, it can be useful to define perturbation size and fault-containment in terms of the hierarchy. Perturbation size would be defined in terms of levels where errors occurred, and a fault-containing algorithm would be required to not propagate faults more than a small number of levels in the hierarchy. In this paper, we define such a notion and use it to evaluate an algorithm for tracking a mobile object.

Because of the recent growth of applications in mobile computing, cellular telephony, and military contexts, tracking of mobile objects has recently received significant attention [6, 20, 22, 8, 12]. The DARPA Network Embedded Software Technology (NEST) program posed tracking as a challenge problem in wireless sensor networks, and several groups have delivered small-scale (100 node networks) tracking demonstrations: pursuer-evader tracking with one human controlled evader and three autonomous pursuers is showcased in [21], and detection, classification, and tracking of various intruders, such as persons and cars, are demonstrated in [3].

In addition to the opportunities they provide for tracking of objects, wireless sensor networks also impose additional challenges. Sensor nodes are energy-constrained, and algorithms that require excessive communication are unacceptable since they drain battery power quickly. Sensor networks are fault-prone, message losses and corruptions and node failures are frequent, nodes can lose synchrony and programs can reach arbitrary states [17]. On-site maintenance is infeasible and hence sensor networks should be self-healing. Moreover self-healing should achieve fault-containment to prevent a fault in one region of the network from contaminating the entire network and requiring a global correction, wasting the energy of the nodes and reducing the availability of the tracking service.

Contributions. Our novel contribution is to present a hierarchy-based self-healing/fault-containment technique and then demonstrate the concept with an algorithm for tracking in sensor networks, which we call STALK (Stabilizing Tracking viA Layered linKs). To achieve scalability, STALK employs a hierarchical tracking structure. The tracking structure is a path imposed on an underlying hierarchical partitioning of the sensor network into clusters, such as those provided by the self-stabilizing algorithm described in [18]. We implement updates to the tracking structure by means of two local actions, *grow* and *shrink*. The grow action enables a path to grow from the new location of the mobile object to increasingly higher levels of the hierarchy and connect to the original path. The shrink action cleans branches deserted by the object. Shrinking also starts at the lowest level and climbs to increasingly higher levels. Despite the fact that grow and shrink occur concurrently, we complete the move operation successfully by using suitably-chosen timers to determine when these actions are performed.

STALK is hierarchy-based fault-containing, preventing propagation of faults in the tracking structure beyond a small number of levels in the hierarchy. Starting from an arbitrarily corrupted state, it satisfies its specification in time and work proportional to perturbation size, defined in terms of levels (as defined by the underlying hierarchy) where faults have occurred. We achieve fault-containment by slowing propagation of information as the levels of the hierarchy underlying STALK increase, enabling the more recent information propagated by lower levels to override misinformation at higher levels.

STALK provides good locality guarantees; a *move* of the object being tracked to distance d away requires $O(d * logD)$ time and communication (work) to update the tracking structure, where D is the network diameter. In the full version of our paper [11] we also describe a *find* operation using the tracking structure. A find operation invoked at a process queries neighboring processes at increasingly higher levels of the clustering hierarchy until it encounters a process on the tracking path. Once the path is found, the find operation follows it to its leaf to reach the mobile object. In the full version we also show that a *find* invoked within distance d of the mobile object requires $O(d)$ work to reach the object and that when no faults occur, our scheme for achieving fault-containment does not increase the complexity of tracking or finding. Furthermore, we show that STALK achieves seamless tracking of a continuously moving object by allowing concurrent tracking and finding operations. For space reasons, we refer the reader to the full version [11] for these results and instead concentrate here on the tracking program actions of STALK and fault-containment.

Related work. The idea of employing a hierarchical structure for achieving scalability of tracking has been extensively researched. The idea of using a partial information strategy to optimize both finds and moves in a relatively static point-to-point network was investigated in [6]. In [6], a hierarchy of regional directories is constructed so that each level l directory enables a node to find a mobile object within 2^l distance from itself. The communication cost of a find for an object d away is $O(d * log^2N)$ and that of a move of distance d is $O(d * logD * logN + log^2D/logN)$ (where N is the number of nodes and D is network diameter). However, a topology change, such as a node failure, necessitates a global reset of the system since the regional directories depend on a non-local clustering program [5] that constructs a sparse cover of a graph.

In [9], the tracking problem is considered for a geometric network model similar to ours, and cost complexity similar to ours is achieved. However, the tracking structure maintained is not available during moves of mobile objects and the program for finding a mobile object is only implicitly defined. This algorithm is also not fault-tolerant. Papers such as [2, 23] are concerned with non-stabilizing solutions for personal communication systems and the mobile Internet Protocol, not sensor networks. A location service for ad hoc networks is described in [1] and provides attractive worst case and average case costs and provides some fault-tolerance, though it is not fault-containing.

There has been work on self-stabilizing, though not fault-containing, tracking algorithms [15, 12, 10]. The distributed arrow protocol [15] is one such algorithm but suffers from the dithering problem —where an object moving back and forth across a multi-level hierarchy boundary may lead to nonlocal updates. The protocols in [10] do not exploit the hierarchy idea and are not scalable for large networks. In [12], using a hierarchy of location servers, a stabilizing location management protocol is presented. However, the protocol in [12] does not ensure locality of finds. In [14] another self-stabilizing algorithm using hierarchies to solve a problem close to tracking is presented, though it too is not fault-containing.

Fault-containment of self-stabilizing algorithms in general has received growing interest [13, 19, 7, 4], though none of these algorithms use a hierarchy-based concept of fault-containment. The notion of fault containment within the context of stabilization was first formalized in [13]; algorithms were proposed to contain state-corruption of a single node in a stabilizing spanning tree protocol. In [19] fault-containment of Byzantine nodes was studied in dining philosophers and graph coloring algorithms; this work required the range of contamination to be constant and is too limiting for problems such as tracking and routing where locality is not constant. In [7], a broadcast protocol was proposed to contain observable variables in the presence of state corruptions, but the protocol allowed for global propagation of internal protocol variables. Another protocol that achieved fault-local stabilization in shortest path routing was presented in [4]. To achieve fault-containment the protocol used privileged containment actions that were a constant time faster than the fault-intolerant program actions.

Organization of the paper. After presenting the model in the next section, we present the specifications of STALK and a definition for hierarchy-based fault-localization in Section 3. In Section 4, we present the move operation. Fault local stabilization actions for the tracking path are discussed in Section 5. Finally we conclude our paper in Section 6. For space reasons, we relegate detailed proofs to the Technical Report [11].

2 Model

We consider a sensor network consisting of multiple sensor locations. Each sensor location plays host to (possibly) multiple processes with identifiers from a set P. In this paper, as a convention, i and j refer to process identifiers, and $i.x$ refers to the value of variable x at i.

We denote the location of a process i with $loc(i)$ (and for convenience the set of locations of process set I with $loc(I)$). The Euclidean distance between the locations of i and j is denoted by $dist(i, j)$.

Hierarchical partitioning. Assume a hierarchical partitioning of processes over locations. Consider a tree with levels 0 through MAX of all processes P. For each process i we define:

1. $lvl(i)$, the level of process i in the tree,
2. $h(i)$, i's parent in the tree (for convenience, we define $h(i)$ to be i if $lvl(i) = MAX$),
3. $h^n(i)$, the iterated parent, defined as $h(i)$ if $n = 1$ and $h(h^{n-1}(i))$ otherwise,
4. $children(i)$, i's children in the tree. We assume a one-to-one correspondence

between the level 0 processes in the tree and sensor locations. For a location v we denote the level 0 process residing at v as $proc_0(v)$. We also assume that for any i such that $lvl(i) > 0$, i's location $loc(i)$ is equal to $loc(j)$ of one of its children j.

This partitioning yields *clusters*. For i such that $lvl(i) = k+1$, $0 \le k < MAX$, $children(i)$ together form a cluster C at level k whose clusterhead, $head(C)$, is i. $Radius(C)$ is the maximum distance from $head(C)$ to any process in C.

Next we introduce the symmetric neighbor relation. For level 0 processes i, j, $i \ne j$, $j \in nbr(i) \iff dist(i, j) \le 1$. For level $k > 0$ processes i, j, that are clusterheads of level $k - 1$ clusters C_i and C_j, i and j are neighbors if C_i and C_j contain two processes that are neighbors.

Geometry assumptions. We fix the following assumptions about the hierarchical partitioning:

1. We define a real constant $r \ge 3$ to denote the cluster dilation factor; the radius of a level l cluster is at least r^l,
2. We define a real maximum cluster radius constant $m \ge 2/\sqrt{3}$ to bound the radius of a level l cluster to be at most mr^l,

3. We define a real minimum cluster breadth constant q satisfying $\frac{2m+r-1}{r-1} \leq q \leq 2m$ to restricts the locations in *non-neighboring* level l clusters to be greater than qr^l apart.

The constraints imply a bound, ω, on the number of neighbors at any level $l > 0$. They also imply that, for $l > 0$, the distance between two neighboring level l processes is within $2r^{l-1}$-to-$2mr^{l-1}$, and the distance between a level l process and its children in the hierarchy is at most mr^{l-1}. This clustering does not necessarily imply a uniform tiling of the network, as radii of clusters at the same level are not required to be the same. The network diameter, D, is the maximum distance between any two locations in the network. Each node in the network is deployed with $O(MAX)$ storage where $MAX \leq log_r D$.

An example of the clustering geometry with $r = 3$ can be found in Section 4. Our hierarchical partitioning constraints can be realized by using a distributed and fault-local stabilizing clustering protocol, LOCI [18].

3   System Specification

Here we describe the specification for the system.

Mobile object. The mobile object **Evader** resides at exactly one sensor location. We model the **Evader** using **object** and **no_object** inputs at processes: An **object**$_i$ occurs at all processes residing at the object's current location and **no_object**$_j$ occurs for all other locations. When moving, the object nondeterministically moves to a neighboring location.

STALK. STALK consists of two parts, **Tracker** and **Finder**, as seen in Figure 1. **Tracker** maintains a tracking structure by propagating mobile object information obtained through **object** and **no_object** inputs. **Finder** answers client **finds** by outputting **found** at the mobile object's current location. **Finder** would query **Tracker** for location information through **cpq** requests and **Tracker** would answer with **cpointer** responses.

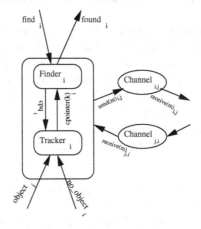

Fig. 1. STALK architecture at process i

STALK is implemented distributively by individual processes communicating through channels. Each process is assumed to have access to its own local timer, that advances at the same rate at all processes. We do not assume time synchronization across processes.

Channels. We use a communication abstraction of a (possibly) multi-hop channel $\mathbf{Channel}_{i,j}$ between any two processes i and j. Such channels are accessed using $\mathbf{send(m)}_{i,j}$ to send from i and $\mathbf{receive(m)}_{i,j}$ to receive at j. The cost of sending a message through $\mathbf{Channel}_{i,j}$ is $dist(i,j)$, and in the absence of faults a message is removed from the channel by at most $\delta * dist(i,j)$ time where δ is a known message delay factor.

Fault model and tolerance specification. Processes can suffer from arbitrary state corruption. These faults may occur at any time and in any finite number and order. Channels may suffer faults that corrupt, manufacture, duplicate, or lose messages.

We say a system is *self-stabilizing* iff starting from an arbitrary state the system eventually recovers to a consistent state, a state from where its specification is satisfied. In Section 4 we characterize consistent states for our implementation.

A perturbation count for a given system state is the minimum number of processes whose state must change to achieve a consistent state of the system. For work and time calculations the level of "perturbed" processes are important; a fault hitting a level l process affects the entire level l cluster and hence its size is r^l. We define the *perturbation size* of a system to be a weighted sum of the sizes of perturbed processes. A stabilizing system is *fault local stabilizing* if the time and work required for stabilization are bounded by functions of perturbation size rather than system size.

Complete system. The complete system is the composition of all channels, **Evader** and STALK. We require the system be fault-local stabilizing to a consistent state. Starting from a consistent state we then require that if the object moves d distance, the amortized time and work to update the tracking structure is $O(d * log(D))$. (Other guarantees and requirements relating to *find*s and concurrent tracking and finding are discussed in the Tech Report [11].)

4   Tracker

Here we describe how **Tracker** updates the tracking path after a move, assuming that the mobile object does not relocate until the updates are completed. In [11], we relax this restriction and allow the object to relocate while effects of its previous moves are still rippling through the path.

Updates to the tracking path are implemented by two local actions, grow and shrink. The grow action enables a new path to grow to increasingly higher levels of the clustering hierarchy and connect to the original path at some level. The shrink action cleans old branches deserted by the mobile object starting from the lowest levels.

A hierarchical partitioning of a network inevitably results in multi-level cluster boundaries: even though two processes are neighbors they might be contained in different clusters at all levels (except the top) of the hierarchy. If a process were to always propagate grows and shrinks to its clusterhead, a small movement of the object back and forth across a multi-level cluster boundary could result in work proportional to the size of the network rather than the distance of the move. To resolve this "dithering" problem, we allow one *lateral link* per level in our tracking path. A process occasionally connects to the original path with a lateral link to a neighboring process rather than by propagating a link to its parent in the hierarchy.

To implement **Tracker**, each process i maintains a child pointer c, a parent pointer p, a grow timer $gtime$, and a shrink timer $stime$. In the initial states, $i.c = i.p = \bot$ and $i.gtime = i.stime = \infty$ for all i. We assume the use of grow and shrink constants g and s that satisfy:

$$s \geq 10.5\delta m \tag{1}$$

$$\frac{s + \delta m}{r} < g \leq s - \delta m \tag{2}$$

A grow or shrink timer is set at i for $g * r^{lvl(i)}$ or $s * r^{lvl(i)}$ time respectively. The values for the timers are chosen to satisfy the requirements on both the work calculations in Section 4.4 and the fault-containment proofs in Section 5.

Signature:	State:
Input: **object**$_i$	$c \in P \cup \{\bot\}$, initially $\bot$
no_object$_i$	$p \in P \cup \{\bot\}$, initially $\bot$
cpq$_i$	$gqack \in P \cup \{\bot\}$, initially $\bot$
receive$(msg^*)_{j,i}, j \in P$	$gnbrquery \subseteq P$, initially $\emptyset$
	$update$, a Boolean, initially $false$
Output: **send**$(msg^*)_{i,j}, j \in P,$	$gtime \in \Re$, a timer, initially ∞
cpointer$(j)_i, j \in P \cup \{\bot\}$	$stime \in \Re$, a timer, initially ∞
$^*msg \in \{$gquery, ack_gquery, grow, shrink$\}$	$now \in \Re$, a timer indicating current time

Fig. 2. Signature and state of **Tracker**$_i$

Tracker$_i$ answers a **cpq**$_i$ input (an information request from **Finder**$_i$) with a **cpointer**$(i.c)_i$ output, providing the value of its child pointer. The **send**s and **receive**s propagate grows and shrinks as explained in detail below for process i.

4.1 Grow Action

A grow updates a path to point to the new location of the object.

If i is at level 0, the object is at the same location as i, and i's child pointer c does not point to itself, then i becomes the leaf of the tracking path by setting c to i and setting its grow timer, $gtime$, scheduling a **grow** to be sent when $gtime$ expires.

Input: **object**$_i$
eff: if $c \neq i$ $\wedge$ $lvl(i) = 0$ then
         $c := i$
         $gtime := now + g$

Output: **send** (**gquery**)$_{i,j}$
pre: $j \in gnbrquery$
eff: $gnbrquery := gnbrquery - \{j\}$
         if $gnbrquery = \emptyset$ then
             $gtime := now + g * r^{lvl(i)}$

Input: **receive** (**gquery**)$_{j,i}$
eff: if $p = h(i)$ then
             $gqack := j$

Output: **send** (**ack_gquery**)$_{i,j}$
pre: $gqack = j$
eff: $gqack := \bot$

Input: **receive** (**ack_gquery**)$_{j,i}$
eff: if $c \neq \bot$ $\wedge$ $p = \bot$ then
             $p := j$

Output: **send** (**grow**)$_{i,j}$
pre: $now = gtime$ $\wedge$ $c \neq \bot$ $\wedge$
         $((j = p$ $\wedge$ $p \in nbr(i))$ $\vee$
         $(j = h(i)$ $\wedge$ $p = \bot))$
eff: if $p = \bot$ then
             $p := h(i)$
         $gtime := \infty$

Input: **receive** (**grow**)$_{j,i}$
eff: $c := j$
         if $lvl(i) = MAX$ then
             $p := i$
         if $p = \bot$ then
             $gnbrquery := nbr(i)$

Fig. 3. Grow actions at process i

If i is above level 0 and receives a **grow** message, it sets its c pointer to the sender, sets *gtime* scheduling a **grow** to be sent to its prospective parent. i also sends a **gquery** message to its neighbors to check if the tracking path is reachable through a neighbor. The tracking path allows the use of one lateral link per level. A neighbor j that receives the **gquery** sends an **ack_gquery** back if j is on the tracking path and there isn't already a lateral link pointing to j, i.e., if $j.p$ points to its own clusterhead, $h(j)$. If i receives such an **ack_gquery** from j then it sets p to point to j, in preparation for adding a lateral link at j.

When *gtime* expires, if c is still non-$\bot$, meaning that the path has not shrunk while i's grow timer was counting down, then a **send** (**grow**) is performed to extend the tracking path. If $i.p$ points to a neighbor j then the grow message is sent to j, inserting a lateral link. Otherwise, if $p = \bot$, i sets p to point to its own clusterhead $h(i)$ and sends a **grow** message to $h(i)$, propagating the grow one level up in the hierarchy. In either case *gtime* is set to ∞, and i's role in updating the tracking path is complete.

If a **grow** message is received at i but i already has a parent in the tracking path or is the MAX level process, then i does not propagate the grow (it is already on the tracking path).

4.2   Shrink Action

A shrink cleans old, deserted branches of the tracking path.

If i is at level 0 and has a non-$\bot$ child pointer, but the mobile object is not at i's location, then i removes itself from the leaf of the tracking path. It sets its child pointer c to $\bot$ and sets the shrink timer *stime*, scheduling a **shrink** to be sent upon expiration of *stime*.

Input: **no_object**$_i$
eff: if $lvl(i) = 0 \ \wedge \ c \neq \bot$ then
           $c := \bot$
           $stime := now + s$

Input: **receive(shrink)**$_{j,i}$
eff: if $c = j$ then
           $c := \bot$
           $stime := now + s * r^{lvl(i)}$

Output: **send (shrink)**$_{i,j}$
pre: $now = stime \ \wedge \ c = \bot \ \wedge \ j = p$
eff: $p := \bot$
           $stime := \infty$

Fig. 4. Shrink actions at process i

If i receives a **shrink** message from another process j, i checks to see whether its child pointer c points to j (c might not point to j; it may have been updated to point to a process on a newer path). If $c = j$ then i removes itself from the path by setting c to $\bot$ and then sets its shrink timer, scheduling a **shrink** message to be sent to its parent p. Otherwise, if $c \neq j$, i ignores the message, ensuring that shrink actions clean only deadwood and not the entire tracking path.

When $stime$ expires, if c is still $\bot$, meaning no newer path has connected at i while $stime$ was counting down, i sends a **shrink** message to its parent p in the path and then sets p to $\bot$.

Example. Figure 5 depicts a sample tracking path. The path is seen pointing to a level 2 clusterhead, which points to one of its hierarchy children, a level 1 clusterhead. That clusterhead has a lateral link to another level 1 clusterhead that points to a level 0 cluster where the object **e** is located. Deadwood is denoted by the dotted path.

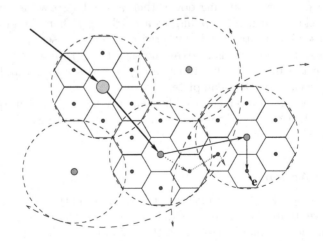

Fig. 5. Tracking path example

4.3   Correctness

Here we present system invariants and define consistent states of the system.

In the absence of faults, every process i satisfies I, the following five conditions, at all times:

I0. If $lvl(i) = 0$ and **object**$_i$ occurs then $i.c = i$,

I1. If $i.c \neq \perp$ then one of the following holds:

  (a) $i.c = i$ and the object is at i,

  (b) $i.c$ points to one of its children in the clustering hierarchy, or

  (c) $i.c$ points to a neighbor and $i.p$ points to

  its parent in the clustering hierarchy,

I2. If $i.p \neq \perp$ then either $i.c \neq \perp$ or i is executing a shrink action and will send a **shrink** to $i.p$,

I3. The dual: if $i.c \neq \perp$ then $i.p \neq \perp$ or i is executing a grow action and will send a **grow** to its prospective parent,

I4. If $i.c \neq i$ and $i.c \neq \perp$ then $(i.c).p$ is either i or $\perp$. In the latter case a **shrink** from $i.c$ is in transit to i.   □

A *tracking path* is a sequence $\{i_x, \ldots, i_1\}$ where

  1. i_1 is a leaf and contains the object,

  2. Every process but i_1 points to the next
     process as its child, and

  3. I is satisfied at all processes in the sequence.

A *complete tracking path* is a tracking path $\{i_x, \ldots, i_1\}$ where $lvl(i_x) = MAX$ and $i_x.p = i_x$.

A *consistent state* is a state where a complete tracking path exists and $i.c = i.p = \perp$ for every process i not in the tracking path.

Using invariant I it follows from the program actions that an execution starting from an initial state eventually reaches a consistent state and that consistent states are closed under moves of the object.

In the case where the evader can relocate before updates have been completed it is necessary to relax the definition of a tracking path and instead define a more general *tracking structure* describing path segments that satisfy certain reachability conditions. Details can be found in the Technical Report.

4.4   Work

In order to prove our work claims, we must show that the timing of changes to the new and old tracking paths satisfy certain relationships to ensure that the old path is reused (via insertion of a lateral link) to the extent possible. More specifically, it follows from the assumptions on timer constants s and g that an old path being cleaned bottom-up from level 0 will not clean one of its level l pointers before a grow starting at level 0 in the new path reaches level l and has an opportunity to query one of those pointers, allowing for the addition of a lateral link.

This allows us to reason that the new path (which grows by propagating pointers straight up the hierarchy until it connects to the old path) connects to the pre-shrink old path at the lowest level process that is either an iterated clusterhead of the new object location or a neighbor of such a clusterhead that is not itself connected to the tracking path via a lateral link. In the latter case, the new path would connect via a lateral link.

We then prove the following theorem.

Theorem 1. *Starting from a consistent state, move operations of the mobile object to a total of distance d away require at most $O(d * \omega m r * MAX)$ amortized work and $O(d * g r^2 * MAX)$ amortized time to update the tracking path.*

Proof sketch. The above reasoning implies a level l pointer in the path is updated as often as every $\sum_{j=1}^{l-2} q r^j$ distance because of the required use of lateral links at all levels below l (note that $q r^l$ is the minimum distance between two non-neighboring level l clusters). An $O(m r^{l-1})$ work and $O(g r^l)$ time cost is incurred each time a level l pointer is updated. The costs, multiplied by frequency of updates, are summed for each level for the result. $\square$

5   Fault-Containment

After state corruption of a region of (potentially all) processes, our tracking path heals itself in a fault-local manner within work proportional to perturbation size. Here we discuss correction actions enabling fault-local stabilization of the path.

Through faults a shrink action can be mistakenly initiated. For example, when a portion of a tracking path is hit by faults, higher level processes of the path, unaware a healthy lower path exists, start a shrink action. If "growth" at lower levels lags behind "shrinking" of upper levels, faults can propagate through the entire upper path. For fault-containment, grow actions started at lower levels must contain shrink actions.

Similarly, grow actions can be mistakenly initiated. Consider a garbage path with no object at its leaf. The topmost process of this path, unaware that the path does not lead to the object, starts a grow action. If "shrinking" from lower levels lags behind "growing" of upper levels, faults can contaminate the entire network. Thus shrinks started at lower levels must contain grows.

The above requirements are both satisfied by giving priority to actions with more recent information regarding the path; actions from lower levels are privileged over ones at higher levels. We achieve this by delaying shrink/grow for longer periods as the level of the process executing the action increases. This way, propagation actions coming from below are subject to lesser delays and can arrest mistakenly initiated propagation actions; hierarchy-based fault-local stabilization is achieved. We note that the latency imposed by delaying is a constant factor of the communication delay to higher levels and does not affect the quality of tracking.

Stabilization. Here we present correction actions for re-establishing the tracking path invariant I starting from an arbitrarily corrupted state.

Internal: **start-grow**$_i$
pre: $(c \neq \perp \;\wedge\; p = \perp \;\wedge$
$\qquad gtime \notin [now, now + g * r^{lvl(i)}])$
eff: if $lvl(i) = MAX$ then
$\qquad p = i$
$\quad$ if $p = \perp$ then
$\qquad gnbrquery := nbr(i)$

Internal: **start-shrink**$_i$
pre: $(c = \perp \;\wedge\; p \neq \perp \;\wedge$
$\qquad stime \notin [now, now + s * r^{lvl(i)}])$
$\qquad \vee\; [p \in nbr(i) \;\wedge\; c \in nbr(i)]$
eff: $c := \perp$
$\qquad stime := now + s * r^{lvl(i)}$

Fig. 6. Starting grow/shrink at process i

Output: **send (heartbeat)**$_{i,j}$
pre: $now = next \;\wedge\; j = p$
eff: $next := now + b * r^{lvl(i)}$

Internal: **heartbeat_set**$_i$
pre: $p \neq \perp \;\wedge\; next \notin [now, now + b * r^{lvl(i)}]$
eff: $next := now + b * r^{lvl(i)}$

Input: **receive (heartbeat)**$_{j,i}$
eff: if $c = \perp$ then $c := j$
$\quad$ if $c = j$ then $timeout :=$
$\qquad now + (b + 2\delta m/r) * r^{lvl(i)}$

Internal: **timeout_set**$_i$
pre: $(c \neq \perp \;\wedge\; c \neq i \;\wedge\; timeout \notin$
$\qquad [now, now + (b + 2\delta m/r) * r^{lvl(i)}])$
eff: $timeout := now + (b + 2\delta m) * r^{lvl(i)}$

Internal: **timeout_expire**$_i$
pre: $now = timeout \;\wedge\; c \neq \perp \;\wedge\; c \neq i$
eff: $c := \perp$

Fig. 7. Heartbeat actions at process i

Correction actions for $I0$ and $I1$. $I0$ is established trivially by **object** and **no_object** inputs. The correction of $I1$ follows from the domain assumptions we make on non-$\perp$ c, p and $gnbrquery$ variables for $i \in P$. We require that $i.c \neq \perp \Rightarrow i.c \in \{nbr(i) \cup children(i)\}$: $i.c$ points to either a neighbor of i or to a child of i. Similarly, we restrict the domain of non-$\perp$ $i.p$ variables to $\{nbr(i) \cup \{h(i)\}\}$ and $i.gnbrquery$ to subsets of $nbr(i)$. These assumptions are reasonable since the clustering provides a process with the identifiers of its neighbors, children, and clusterhead; a process can locally check and set these variables to $\perp$ if their values are outside their respective domains.

Correction action for $I2$. If i has a valid parent but no valid child, then $I2$ is corrected at i by setting $i.c = \perp$ and scheduling a **shrink** message to be sent to $i.p$.

Correction action for $I3$. If i has a valid child but no parent, then a **gquery** message is sent to i's neighbors and a **grow** message is scheduled to be sent to the future parent of i.

Correction actions for $I4$. To correct $I4$ we use heartbeat messages and two timers: *next* for periodically sending heartbeats to the parent and a *timeout* for dissociating a child if no heartbeat is heard. The correction actions use a constant b for calculating the frequency of heartbeat messages, whose periodicity are tunable to achieve less communication or faster detection. We require that b is more than twice s, the shrink timer constant:

$$b \geq 2s \tag{3}$$

Intuitively, this condition serves to prevent a scenario where aggressively scheduled heartbeats shrink the original path before a new growing path can reconnect to the original.

Every i with a non-$\perp$ valued parent sends a **heartbeat** message to its parent every $b * r^{lvl(i)}$ time by setting *next*. Every time i receives a **heartbeat** or **grow** message from its child, *i.c*, i resets its *timeout* variable to $(b + 2\delta m/r) * r^{lvl(i)}$ (it is also reset upon receipt of a **grow** to prevent the scenario where the heartbeat timeout of i expires scheduling a shrink just after i receives a **grow** message from a process in a newly growing path). If i receives a heartbeat from j but $i.c = \perp$ then i sets $i.c := j$. Otherwise, a **heartbeat** message received from a process other than $i.c$ is ignored.

If i has a non-$\perp$ valued child, is not a leaf, and has not received a **heartbeat** message in a $(b + 2\delta m/r) * r^{lvl(i)}$ time interval, then $i.c$ is set to $\perp$.

Stabilization of the *next* and *timeout* variables of the corrector is ensured by keeping their values within their respective domains.

Using the correction actions described above, we prove in Theorem 2, that STALK is self-stabilizing to a consistent state, where a complete tracking path exists.[1]

Theorem 2. STALK *is self-stabilizing.*   □

Fault-local stabilization. To prove hierarchy-based fault-local stabilization we first give a bound on arresting distance of grow/shrink actions in Lemmas 1 and 2. In these lemmas, $l_1 + 1$ and l_2 are respectively the lowest and highest perturbed levels: faults occur only from level $l_1 + 1$ through level l_2. We prove fault containment by showing that due to our timing assumptions, a correction propagated from l_1 catches propagation of bad information at a level $l > l_2$, leaving levels above l untouched by faults. The proofs for both lemmas are done by comparing the maximum time the propagation of a lower wave takes to reach level l versus the minimum time the higher wave takes to pass it.

Lemma 1. *Propagation of a shrink action started at level $l_1 + 1$ catches propagation of a grow action started at level l_2 by level l where*

$$l = l_2 + \lceil \log_r \frac{br - b + sr + gr - 2s + 3\delta m}{gr - s - \delta m} \rceil.$$ □

Lemma 2. *Propagation of a grow action started at level l_1 catches propagation of a shrink action started at level l_2 by level l where*

$$l = l_2 + \lceil \log_r \frac{br - b + sr^2 - gr - \delta m}{sr - gr - 3\delta m} \rceil.$$ □

---

[1] In the case where the evader can relocate before updates are completed, the algorithm self-stabilizes to a state where a more general tracking structure exists, as mentioned in Section 4.3.

The size, $l - l_2$, of contamination due to fault propagation is independent of the network size and is tunable via grow and shrink timer settings. In [11] we provide values that satisfy these requirements, as well as a number of others ($g = 5\delta m, s = 11\delta m, b = 11\delta mr$).

Finally, the above two lemmas allow us to prove the following theorem:

Theorem 3 (Fault-local stabilization). *For a perturbation size S and a highest level L of corruption, our program self-stabilizes in $O(S)$ work and $O(r^L)$ time.* ☐

Proof sketch. Even though there may be many different scenarios for corruption, since they all lead to either mispropagation of a shrink or a grow, they all can be cast to the below two cases for a perturbed process i: 1) i can be corrupted to think it has a child and i grows up, 2) i can be corrupted to think it has no child and i shrinks up.

In either case i learns the correct information within at most $O(r^{lvl(i)})$ time and from the containment arguments in Lemmas 1 and 2 this correction wave contains previous misinformed waves within a constant number of levels in the hierarchy, or $O(r^{lvl(i)})$ time and work.

The work for fault-containment is additive: summation of the work for all perturbed processes gives the work for the system. However, since fault-containment takes place concurrently for all perturbed processes, the fault-containment time $O(r^L)$ for the highest level perturbed process (at level L) dominates, giving at most $O(r^L)$ time. ☐

6   Concluding Remarks

We presented STALK, a hierarchy-based fault-local stabilizing tracking service for sensor networks. We use two concepts to achieve hierarchy-based fault locality: hierarchical partitioning and level-based timeouts for execution of actions. The key idea is to wait longer before updating a wider region's view by employing larger timeouts when propagating an update to higher levels of the hierarchy. This way, more recent updates from lower levels can catch-up to and override the misinformed updates at higher levels within a constant number of levels above the fault. While achieving fault-local stabilization STALK also adheres to the locality of tracking operations. Moreover, by enabling concurrent move and concurrent find operations STALK achieves seamless and continuous tracking of the mobile object. This last point is described more fully in our Technical Report [11].

STALK has applications in message routing to mobile units and in pursuer/evader games. As part of our efforts to develop sensor network services in the DARPA/NEST program, we are implementing STALK on the Mica mote platform [16]. For future work, we are examining other problems that could benefit from our hierarchy-based local stabilization technique.

References

1. I. Abraham, D. Dolev, and D. Malkhi. LLS: a locality aware location service for mobile ad hoc networks. *Manuscript*, 2004.
2. I.F. Akyildiz, J. McNair, J.S.M. Ho, H. Uzunalioglu, and W. Wang. Mobility management in next-generation wireless systems. *Proceedings of the IEEE*, 87:1347–1384, 1999.
3. A. Arora and et. al. Line in the sand: A wireless sensor network for target detection, classification, and tracking. *To appear in Computer Networks (Elsevier)*, 2004.
4. A. Arora and H. Zhang. LSRP: Local stabilization in shortest path routing. In *IEEE-IFIP DSN*, pages 139–148, June 2003.
5. B. Awerbuch and D. Peleg. Sparse partitions (extended abstract). In *IEEE Symposium on Foundations of Computer Science*, pages 503–513, 1990.
6. B. Awerbuch and D. Peleg. Online tracking of mobile users. *Journal of the Association for Computing Machinery*, 42:1021–1058, 1995.
7. Y. Azar, S. Kutten, and B. Patt-Shamir. Distributed error confinement. In *ACM PODC*, pages 33–42, 2003.
8. A. Bar-Noy and I. Kessler. Tracking mobile users in wireless communication networks. In *INFOCOM*, pages 1232–1239, 1993.
9. Y. Bejerano and I. Cidon. An efficient mobility management strategy for personal communication systems. *MOBICOM*, pages 215–222, 1998.
10. M. Demirbas, A. Arora, and M. Gouda. A pursuer-evader game for sensor networks. *Sixth Symposium on Self-Stabilizing Systems(SSS'03)*, 2003.
11. M. Demirbas, A. Arora, T. Nolte, and N. Lynch. STALK: A self-stabilizing hierarchical tracking service for sensor networks. Technical Report OSU-CISRC-4/03-TR19, The Ohio State University, April 2003.
12. S. Dolev, D. Pradhan, and J. Welch. Modified tree structure for location management in mobile environments. In *INFOCOM (2)*, pages 530–537, 1995.
13. S. Ghosh, A. Gupta, T. Herman, and S.V. Pemmaraju. Fault-containing self-stabilizing algorithms. *ACM PODC*, pages 45–54, 1996.
14. M. Herlihy and Y. Sun. A location-aware concurrent mobile object directory for ad-hoc networks. *Manuscript*, 2004.
15. M.P. Herlihy and S. Tirthapura. Self-stabilizing distributed queueing. In *Proceedings of 15th International Symposium on Distributed Computing*, pages 209–219, oct 2001.
16. J. Hill, R. Szewczyk, A. Woo, S. Hollar, D. Culler, and K. Pister. System architecture directions for network sensors. *ASPLOS*, pages 93–104, 2000.
17. M. Jayaram and G. Varghese. Crash failures can drive protocols to arbitrary states. *ACM Symposium on Principles of Distributed Computing*, 1996.
18. V. Mittal, M. Demirbas, and A. Arora. LOCI: Local clustering in large scale wireless networks. Technical Report OSU-CISRC-2/03-TR07, The Ohio State University, February 2003.

19. M. Nesterenko and A. Arora. Local tolerance to unbounded byzantine faults. In *IEEE SRDS*, pages 22–31, 2002.
20. E. Pitoura and G. Samaras. Locating objects in mobile computing. *Knowledge and Data Engineering*, 13(4):571–592, 2001.
21. B. Sinopoli, C. Sharp, L. Schenato, S. Schaffert, and S. Sastry. Distributed control applications within sensor networks. *Proceeding of the IEEE, Special Issue on Sensor Networks and Applications*, August 2003.
22. A. P. Sistla, O. Wolfson, S. Chamberlain, and S. Dao. Modeling and querying moving objects. In *ICDE*, pages 422–432, 1997.
23. J. Xie and I.F. Akyildiz. A distributed dynamic regional location management scheme for mobile ip. *IEEE INFOCOM*, pages 1069–1078, 2002.

The Quorum Deployment Problem
(Extended Abstract)

Seth Gilbert[1] and Grzegorz Malewicz[2]

[1] Massachusetts Institute of Technology,
Computer Science and Artificial Intelligence Laboratory, Cambridge, MA
sethg@mit.edu
[2] University of Alabama, Computer Science Department, Tuscaloosa, AL
greg@cs.ua.edu

Abstract. Quorum systems are commonly used to maintain the consistency of replicated data in a distributed system. Much research has been devoted to developing quorum systems with good theoretical properties, such as fault tolerance and high availability. However, even given a theoretically good quorum system, it is not obvious how to efficiently deploy such a system in a real network. This paper introduces a new combinatorial optimization problem, the *Quorum Deployment Problem*, and studies its complexity. We demonstrate that it is NP-hard to approximate the Quorum Deployment Problem within any factor of n^δ, where n is the number of nodes in the distributed network and $\delta > 0$. The problem is NP-hard in even the simplest possible distributed network: a one-dimensional line with metric cost. We begin to study algorithms for variants of the problem. Some variants can be solved optimally in polynomial time and some NP-hard variants can be approximated to within a constant factor.

Keywords: quorum systems, combinatorial optimization, fault-tolerance.

1   Introduction

The most common technique for ensuring fault-tolerance in a distributed system is replication: the data or code is replicated at a large number of nodes in the network, thus ensuring that no small number of failures can derail the computation. The primary difficulty with this approach is ensuring the consistency of replicas, without increasing the cost of accessing the data too much. There is a fundamental trade-off between the fault-tolerance of the data and the cost of maintaining consistency.

Quorum systems have long been used (e.g., [1, 2, 3, 4]) to solve the problem of replica consistency. A *quorum*, q, is a set of nodes in the network, and a

* This work is supported by MURI–AFOSR SA2796PO 1-0000243658, USAF–AFRL #FA9550-04-1-0121, NSF Grant CCR-0121277, NSF-Texas Engineering Experiment Station Grant 64961-CS, and DARPA F33615-01-C-1896.

T. Higashino (Ed.): OPODIS 2004, LNCS 3544, pp. 316–330, 2005.
© Springer-Verlag Berlin Heidelberg 2005

quorum system is a set of quorums, Q, such that every two quorums in Q share at least one node. That is, given two quorums, $q, q' \in Q$, there exists some node $i \in q \cap q'$; the intersection of these two quorums is non-empty.

In order to ensure the consistency of the data, when a node chooses to modify the data, it notifies some quorum, say, $q \in Q$, of the modification; when a node wants to access the data, it contacts some quorum, say, $q' \in Q$. Since the two quorums, q and q', intersect at some node, we can be sure that the read operation that accesses the data learns about the earlier modification. Variations on this technique are frequently used to implement data replication (e.g., [5, 6, 7, 8]). For example, Attiya et al. use this technique to construct a read/write shared memory ([9]), and this is later extended to construct a reconfigurable read/write shared memory ([10, 11]). A similar technique has been used for mutual exclusion protocols (e.g., [3, 12]) and secure access protocols (e.g., [13]).

Much of the original work on quorum systems assumes that each quorum consists of a majority of the nodes in the network. In this way, the intersection property is immediately guaranteed, and optimal fault-tolerance is achieved. (See, for example, [14, 1, 15].) More recently, however, there has been much research developing more complicated quorum systems with a variety of interesting properties, such as improved availability, faster responses, and more flexibility to respond to dynamic systems. (See, for example, [16, 17, 18, 19, 20].)

Typically, an algorithm designer first constructs quorums with these types of good properties, and only then decides which network node will use which quorum so as to achieve low cost of network communication. Tsuchiya et al. [21] and Fu [22], on the other hand, have taken a different approach; their algorithms begin with a network, and determine a quorum system that is optimized under certain performance metrics. Unfortunately, the resulting quorum systems do not necessarily guarantee good fault tolerance, availability, etc. By first designing the quorum system, and then determining a good deployment, it seems possible to obtain both good network performance as well as good quorum system properties.

Let us illustrate this process in an example. Consider the quorum system in Figure 1(a) (originally described in [16]). The nodes in the network are arranged in a grid with $\sqrt{n}$ nodes in each row and column. Each quorum consists of one row and one column. Any two quorums, then, intersect at two nodes; for example, in Figure 1(a) quorums q and q' intersect at node i. Figure 1(b) represents an arbitrary network embedded in a two-dimensional plane in which the cost of communication between any two nodes is proportional to the distance between the nodes. In order to use the quorum system, each node in the real network must be mapped to a node in the grid, as in Figure 1(c). Then, each node chooses one of the quorums to use. For example, node i might choose to use quorum q, while node j might choose to use quorum q'. In an optimal world, each node is close to all the nodes in the quorum that is chooses.

If the quorum system is badly deployed, the cost of maintaining consistent replicas may be prohibitively expensive. It turns out that for completely natural quorum systems – and real world networks – the difference between an optimal

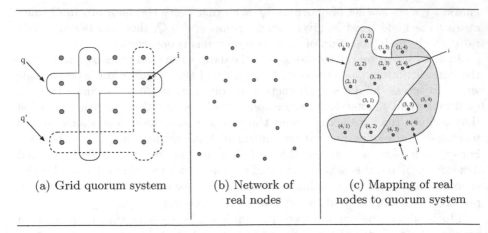

(a) Grid quorum system	(b) Network of real nodes	(c) Mapping of real nodes to quorum system

Fig. 1. Figure 1(a) represents an abstract quorum system of 16 nodes, where q and q' are two possible quorums, and i is a node in the intersection. Figure 1(b) is an example of a network of nodes, embedded in a two-dimensional plane; communication time between two nodes is proportional to their distance. Figure 1(c) is a mapping of the real nodes in the network onto the abstract nodes in the quorum system

deployment and a sub-optimal deployment can be quite large. In fact, we can show that for *every* non-trivial quorum system, there is some network in which an optimal deployment is much better than a bad deployment. If there are two nodes connected by an expensive communication link (for example, the network is occasionally partitioned), a sub-optimal deployment may require the nodes to communicate while an optimal deployment may not.

In this paper, we introduce the *Quorum Deployment Problem*, the problem of using a quorum system optimally. We assume that the set of quorums is fixed, and that the cost of sending a message between any two nodes is known in advance. The cost for some node, i, of using a quorum system is defined to be the cost of sending a message to every node in some quorum. Our goal is to determine the mapping from the real nodes in the network to the abstract nodes in the quorum specification, and the choice of which quorum each node should use during an operation. We present the problem more formally in Section 2.

Summary of Results

Our goal in this paper is to determine when the Quorum Deployment Problem can and cannot be efficiently solved. We first notice that a more constrained version of the problem, the *Partial Deployment Problem*, is solvable in polynomial time (see Section 3). The general version of the Quorum Deployment Problem, though, is quite hard. Even in the simplest possible distributed network – where the nodes are arranged in a line – the problem is NP-hard.

The natural question, then, is whether it is possible to determine an *approximately* optimal deployment. We show in Section 4 that it is NP-hard to approximate an optimal deployment within any constant factor. In fact, it is hard to approximate an optimal deployment within any factor of n^δ for any $\delta > 0$, where n is the number of nodes in the network.

Finally, in Section 5, we explore special cases (that are still NP-hard) in which the problem can be approximately solved, and in Section 6, we conclude and discuss future work.

2   The Quorum Deployment Problem

In this section, we formally define the *Quorum Deployment Problem*. The goal of the Quorum Deployment Problem is to determine, given a quorum system and a distributed network, how best to make use of that quorum system.

More formally, assume we are given a distributed network consisting of n nodes, connected by a message-passing network. We are given an n by n matrix, C, that specifies the cost of sending a message from node i to node j: $C_{i,j}$ is assumed to be the latency of the network connecting i and j. In this paper, we assume that the communication network is fixed. Anytime the network changes, the deployment must be recalculated, resulting in a quorum reconfiguration.

We are also given a quorum system, Q. For concreteness, we assume that Q consists of exactly n quorums, one for each node in the network. While quorum systems with more – and fewer – quorums may be interesting, we discover that the problem is quite hard even with this restriction. We assume that the quorum system is specified as an n by n matrix, where the columns represent the nodes in the quorums and the rows represent the quorums. Each entry in the matrix is either a 0 or a 1. Quorum p contains node j if (and only if) $Q_{p,j} = 1$. (See Figure 3(b) for an example of a quorum system in matrix form.)

Recall that the original notion of a quorum system assumes that every pair of quorums intersect. Occasionally in this paper, we relax this restriction, and allow the matrix Q to contain quorums that do not share a node. It turns out that the relaxed version of the problem is polynomially equivalent to the strict version of the problem.

A quorum deployment, then consists of two components. First, recall that each column in the quorum matrix represents a node; therefore each column in the quorum matrix must be assigned to a node in the network. This determines which real nodes are in each quorum. If node i is assigned to column j, then $Q_{p,j}$ determines whether node i is in quorum p. (Recall that each row of Q represents a quorum.)

Second, each node is assigned a quorum to use. Typically when using a quorum system, a node performing an operation must send a message to every node in some quorum, or receive a message from every node in some quorum. If, for example, node i is assigned quorum p, then whenever an operation occurs at node i, it first attempts to contact quorum p. If this fails (due to the failure of nodes in quorum p, for example), then node i may contact other quorums. (It is a separate – and harder – problem to determine a sequence of quorums to contact.) In this paper, we attempt to optimize for the common case, where quorum p has not failed. For each node i, the cost of the deployment is determined by the cost of accessing each node in its assigned quorum. For example, if node i is assigned quorum p, then the cost of the quorum deployment for i is:

$$\sum_{j \in p} C_{i,j}$$

We express each of the two components of quorum deployment as a permutation on $[1, n]$. We refer to the first component, the assignment of a node to a column in the quorum matrix, as the permutation β. That is, node i is assigned to column j if $\beta(i) = j$. Therefore, if node i is assigned quorum p, then the cost of the quorum deployment for i is:

$$\sum_{j=1}^{n} C_{i,j} \cdot Q_{p,\beta(j)}$$

The first term determines the cost of accessing node j, and the second term determines whether node j is in quorum p: the term $Q_{p,\beta(j)}$ is 1 if the column assigned to j is part of quorum p.

We refer to the second component of the quorum deployment, the assignment of a quorum to each node, as the permutation α. Node i is assigned quorum p if $\alpha(i) = p$. Therefore, the cost of quorum deployment for node i is:

$$\sum_{j=1}^{n} C_{i,j} \cdot Q_{\alpha(i),\beta(j)}$$

The total cost of a quorum deployment is the total cost of deployment for all the nodes in the network. Therefore, the total cost of deployment, $D(C, Q, \alpha, \beta)$ is:

$$D(C, Q, \alpha, \beta) = \sum_{i=1}^{n} \sum_{j=1}^{n} C_{i,j} \cdot Q_{\alpha(i),\beta(j)}$$

Our goal is to minimize this cost: given matrices C and Q, find two permutations α and β on $\{1, \ldots, n\}$ that minimize $D(C, Q, \alpha, \beta)$ across all possible choices for α and β. We call this optimization problem the Quorum Deployment Problem.

Throughout the paper, we occasionally consider variants and restricted versions of the Quorum Deployment Problem. We describe these in more detail as they arise. The following is a brief preview of the variants:

- *Relaxed Quorum Deployment*: In this variant, the "quorums" are not required to intersect[1]. We may at times refer to the original problem as the *strict* deployment problem.

---

[1] In this case, referring to the sets as "quorums" is a misuse of terminology, since the defining features of a set of quorums is that they intersect. For simplicity, however, we continue to use this term.

- *Partial Quorum Deployment*: In this variant, one of the two permutations, α or β, is given in advance as part of the problem instance.
- *Linear Quorum Deployment*: In this variant, the communication network is restricted to be a linear network. That is, all the nodes in the distributed network are embedded on a line.
- *Metric Cost Quorum Deployment*: In this variant, the cost matrix defines a metric. In particular, the distances between the nodes satisfies the triangle inequality.

3   Partial Quorum Deployment

We first consider the restricted problem of *Partial Quorum Deployment*. In the general Quorum Deployment Problem, we are given a quorum, Q, and a distributed network, C, and our goal is to determine a deployment, $\langle \alpha, \beta \rangle$, that has optimal cost. In the *Partial Quorum Deployment* problem, we assume that one of the two permutations in the deployment is fixed. That is, we assume that either α or β is given.

In one case, the permutation α may be fixed in advance. For example, α may be fixed as the identity: node 1 uses quorum 1, node 2 uses quorum 2, etc. The goal is to determine the permutation β, the assignment of nodes to the columns of the quorum matrix.

In the second case, the permutation β is fixed in advance. The goal, then, is to determine the permutation α, the assignment of which quorum each node should use.

Both cases of the Partial Deployment Problem can be reduced to the *Assignment Problem*, which has been well studied and can be solved in polynomial time (see, for example, [23]).

In the *Assignment Problem*, we are given a weighted bipartite graph, consisting of $2n$ nodes – n left nodes, L, and n right nodes, R – and a weight function $w_{i,j} \geq 0$ for all $i \in L$ and $j \in R$. The goal is to choose a matching consisting of n edges with minimum weight.

Theorem 1. *Given an instance of the Partial Deployment Problem, consisting of C, Q, and α, we can determine an instance of the Assignment Problem (in $O(n^2)$ time) where the solution to the Assignment Problem is the permutation β that minimizes the cost of the deployment. The same holds if the Partial Deployment Problem is specified to include β; the solution to the resulting Assignment Problem is the permutation α that minimizes the cost of the deployment.*

Proof. Assume that the permutation α is given. We construct a bipartite graph for the Assignment Problem where the left nodes, L, represent the nodes and the right nodes, R, repesent the columns in the quorum matrix, Q. The weight of an edge connecting $i \in L$ and $j \in R$ is the cost of assigning i to column j in Q. That is:

$$w_{i,j} = \sum_{\ell=1}^{n} C_{\ell,i} \cdot Q_{\alpha(\ell),j} \, .$$

The Assignment Problem results in a permutation that minimizes the cost of the weights. The resulting permutation minimizes the cost of the quorum deployment.

Equivalently, if the permutation β is given, the left nodes in the bipartite graph represent the nodes and the right nodes represent the quorums; the weight of an edge represents the cost of a node using a given quorum. In this case:

$$w_{i,j} = \sum_{\ell=1}^{n} C_{i,\ell} \cdot Q_{j,\beta(\ell)} \ .$$

Again, the Assignment Problem minimizes the weights, resulting in a permutation that minimizes the cost of the quorum deployment.   □

4   Hardness of the Quorum Deployment Problem

While the Partial Deployment Problem is readily solvable, the general Quorum Deployment Problem is quite hard. In this section, we first show in Section 4 that it is NP-hard to approximate the general Quorum Deployment Problem within *any* constant factor. In fact, for any $\delta > 0$, it is hard to approximate within a factor of n^{δ}, where n is the number of nodes in the network. We then show that another variant, the Metric Cost Deployment problem, is NP-hard, and that the relaxed version (where the quorums are not required to intersect) is also NP-hard to approximate.

Hardness of Approximation

Our main hardness result is derived from a gap-creating reduction from the Balanced Complete Bipartite Subgraph (BCBS) Problem (see [24] for a statement of the problem, and [25] for recent results). In this problem, we are given a bipartite graph, $G = (V, E)$, consisting of left nodes, L, and right nodes, R. We are also given a constant, k. The goal is to find a balanced complete bipartite subgraph of size $2k$, with k left nodes and k right nodes.

Throughout this section, we use the bipartite graph in Figure 2 as an example. Notice that this graph has a balanced, complete subgraph of size two, consisting of nodes 2 and 3 on the left (in L) and nodes 5 and 8 on the right (in R). However, there is no such subgraph of size three.

In our reduction, we produce an instance of the Quorum Deployment Problem that has an efficient deployment if and only if the graph G contains a balanced complete bipartite subgraph of size k.

First, we define the reduction, $Cost(G, k) = C$ and $Quorums(G, k) = Q$, that transforms an instance of the BCBS problem into an instance of the Quorum Deployment Problem. We choose $n = |V| + 1$. The first $n - 1$ columns encode the original BCBS problem; the last column ensures that all the quorums intersect.

The cost matrix, C, is related to the "complement" of the incidence matrix for the graph, G: each edge in the matrix G results in a cheap link in the matrix C, while two disconnected nodes in G are connected by an expensive link in the

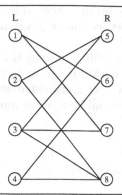

L   R

Fig. 2. Example instance of the Balanced Complete Bipartite Subgraph problem, where $k = 2$

$$\begin{pmatrix} n^x & n^x & n^x & n^x & n^x & 1 & 1 & n^x & 1 \\ n^x & n^x & n^x & n^x & 1 & n^x & n^x & 1 & 1 \\ n^x & n^x & n^x & n^x & 1 & n^x & 1 & 1 & 1 \\ n^x & n^x & n^x & n^x & n^x & 1 & n^x & 1 & 1 \\ n^x & 1 & 1 & n^x & n^x & n^x & n^x & n^x & 1 \\ 1 & n^x & n^x & 1 & n^x & n^x & n^x & n^x & 1 \\ 1 & n^x & 1 & n^x & n^x & n^x & n^x & n^x & 1 \\ n^x & 1 & 1 & 1 & n^x & n^x & n^x & n^x & 1 \\ 1 & 1 & 1 & 1 & 1 & 1 & 1 & 1 & 1 \end{pmatrix}$$

(a) Cost Matrix, $Cost(G, k)$

$$\begin{pmatrix} 1 & 1 & 0 & 0 & 0 & 0 & 0 & 0 & 1 \\ 1 & 1 & 0 & 0 & 0 & 0 & 0 & 0 & 1 \\ 0 & 0 & 0 & 0 & 0 & 0 & 0 & 0 & 1 \\ 0 & 0 & 0 & 0 & 0 & 0 & 0 & 0 & 1 \\ 0 & 0 & 0 & 0 & 0 & 0 & 0 & 0 & 1 \\ 0 & 0 & 0 & 0 & 0 & 0 & 0 & 0 & 1 \\ 0 & 0 & 0 & 0 & 0 & 0 & 0 & 0 & 1 \\ 0 & 0 & 0 & 0 & 0 & 0 & 0 & 0 & 1 \\ 1 & 1 & 1 & 1 & 1 & 1 & 1 & 1 & 1 \end{pmatrix}$$

(b) Quorum Matrix,
$Quorums(G, k)$

Fig. 3. An example of a reduction from the Balanced Complete Bipartite Subgraph problem in Figure 2 to the Quorum Deployment Problem

matrix C. For the purposes of the reduction, we fix x so that n^x is sufficiently large. The size of x depends on the desired value of δ. (That is, $x = O(\delta)$.) Formally:

$$Cost(G, k)_{i,j} = \begin{cases} 1 & \text{if } (i, j) \in E \text{ and } i, j < n \\ n^x & \text{if } (i, j) \notin E \text{ and } i, j < n \\ 1 & \text{if } i = n \text{ or } j = n \end{cases}$$

Consider the example in Figure 3(a). The submatrix delimited by the first four rows and first four columns represents the edges between nodes in L. Notice that because there are no edges between nodes in L, all the entries are n^x. The submatrix delimited by rows five through eight and columns five through eight represents edges between nodes in R, and therefore consists only of entries n^x. The last row and the last column contain the value 1. The remaining entries represent the edges between nodes in L and nodes in R. For example, the entry at $(3,5)$ represents the edge between node 3 and node 5. Observe that the cost matrix is symmetric.

Notice that the existence of high-cost links is important in the reduction. If the ratio of the maximum communication cost to the minimum cost is bounded by a constant, then any deployment approximates optimal to within a constant factor. Therefore, any inapproximability result must allow the ratio to grow as n grows.

The quorum matrix, Q, consists of k quorums containing the first k nodes, and the extra node, n. It also contains a single quorum that contains all the nodes. The rest of the quorums contain only node n. Formally:

$$
Quorums(G, k)_{i,j} = \begin{cases} 1 & \text{if } i, j \leq k \\ 1 & \text{if } i = n \\ 1 & \text{if } j = n \\ 0 & \text{otherwise} \end{cases}
$$

Consider again the example in Figure 3(b). The first two rows and two columns contains the value 1, representing the complete bipartite graph of size two. The last row and the last column contain the value 1, as well.

We show that if the original bipartite graph contains a balanced, complete bipartite subgraph of size k, then the derived Quorum Deployment Problem has a small cost. Alternatively, if the original bipartite graph does not contain such a subgraph, then the derived Quorum Deployment Problem results in a high cost deployment. A full proof is contained in the full version [26].

Lemma 1. *Fix any $x > 1$. Let $G = (V, E)$ be a bipartite graph, and let $1 \leq k \leq |V|$. Let $C = Cost(G, k)$ and $Q = Quorums(Q, k)$. Then the following holds:*

$$
(G, k) \in BCBS \Rightarrow \exists \alpha, \exists \beta, \ D(C, Q, \alpha, \beta) \leq n^2
$$
$$
(G, k) \notin BCBS \Rightarrow \forall \alpha, \forall \beta, \ D(C, Q, \alpha, \beta) > n^x
$$

That is, if there is a size k balanced, complete, bipartite subgraph in G, then the minimum cost of the resulting deployment is less then or equal to n^2. If there is not a size k balanced, complete, bipartite subgraph in G, then the minimum cost of the resulting deployment is greater than n^x.

Proof (sketch). The proof consists of two parts. In the first, we assume that $(G, k) \in BCBS$. In the second, we assume that $(G, k) \notin BCBS$.

Case 1 – $(G, k) \in BCBS$: First, suppose that there is a balanced complete bipartite subgraph on $2k$ nodes in G. We determine a deployment, (α, β) that has a small cost. Let $L' \subseteq L$ be the left partition of the subgraph and $R' \subseteq R$ the right partition of the subgraph. Choose α to map the nodes in L' to the first k rows, and choose β to map the nodes in R' to the first k columns. Node n is mapped to row n and column n. Then each of the quorum entries in the first k rows and k columns is mapped to one of the edges in the complete bipartite subgraph, and as a result, has cost 1. Each of the quorum entries in row n and column n is mapped to an entry in the cost matrix of cost 1. Therefore, the total cost of the deployment is $k^2 + 2n - 1 \leq n^2$, as desired.

Case 2 – $(G, k) \notin BCBS$: On the other hand, suppose that there is no complete bipartite subgraph on $2k$ nodes in G. We shall see that any deployment has cost larger than n^x. In particular, every deployment must include at least one expensive edge. It is clear that node n can, without loss of generality, be mapped to row n and column n: given an optimal assignment where this is not the case, it is possible to permute the assignment so that this is the case, without increasing the cost. Then notice that if there is a deployment that does not include any entry of n^x, then this implies that there exists a complete bipartite subgraph of size k, which we assumed was not the case. □

We conclude that the Quorum Deployment Problem is hard to approximate:

Theorem 2. *For any $\delta > 0$, it is NP-hard to approximate the Quorum Deployment problem with factor n^δ.*

Hardness of Metric Cost Quorum Deployment

In the Metric Cost Quorum Deployment Problem, the cost matrix is restricted to be symmetric and satisfy the triangle inequality. In this case, the cost of i sending a message to j is the same as the cost of j sending a message to i, and the cost of sending a message from i to j is no larger than the cost of sending a message from i to k and from k to j. It is clear from the reduction in Lemma 1 that this version of the problem is NP-hard:

Theorem 3. *The Metric Cost Quorum Deployment Problem is NP-hard.*

Proof. We use the same reduction as in Lemma 1, except instead of constructing the matrix $Cost(G, k)$ by setting non-edge costs to n^x, we set non-edge costs to 2. The matrix immediately satisfies the requirements of a metric. The correctness follows by the same argument as in Lemma 1, where if $(G, k) \in BCBS$ then the optimal cost of deployment is $k^2 + 2n - 1$; otherwise, if $(G, k) \notin BCBS$, then cost of any deployment is at least $k^2 + 2n$. □

Hardness of Relaxed Metric Quorum Deployment

If we do not require that the "quorums" intersect, then we can show that such relaxed deployment problem is inapproximable even when the cost matrix is symmetric and satisfies the triangle inequality. The proof is inspired by the reduction from a strongly NP-complete 3-Partition Problem (see [24], SP15) to the Quadratic Assignment Problem (QAP) (see [24], ND43) given by Queyranne [27]. Our reduction extends the result of Queyranne. Since the deployment algorithm allows two degrees of freedom, α and β, as compared to QAP that has only one degree of freedom ($\alpha = \beta$ in QAP), we construct an instance of the deployment problem that reduces this flexibility, ensuring that when there is no 3-partition the cost of deployment is high. The proof is presented in the full version [26].

Theorem 4. *The Relaxed Metric Quorum Deployment Problem (with symmetric cost matrix that satisfies the triangle inequality and quorums that do not have to intersect) is NP-hard to approximate to within any constant factor.*

We note that the proof of this theorem implies that when the quorum matrix is a block diagonal matrix (ones inside blocks and zeros everywhere else) and the number of blocks can be as large as a polynomial fraction of n, then the deployment problem is inapproximable to within any constant factor. We also note that if the quorum matrix contains just one block, then it is NP-hard to optimally solve the problem. This follows from the proof of Theorem 3, where the bottom row and right column are trimmed from the matrices.

5   Approximation Algorithms for Metric Costs and Restricted Quorums

We have seen that if we allow arbitrary relaxed quorum matrix, then there is no constant factor approximation algorithm for the deployment problem even if we assume that the cost matrix is symmetric and satisfies the triangle inequality. It seems that the intricacy of the quorum matrix plays an important role in the ability to approximate the problem. Therefore, in this section, we establish a family of somewhat contrived quorum matrices that admit constant factor approximation for metric cost networks. Solving deployment optimally for this family, however, is still NP-hard.

We give a constant factor approximation algorithm for the Quorum Deployment Problem with a *block diagonal hyperbolic quorum matrix* and a symmetric cost matrix that satisfies the triangle inequality. The quorum matrix is composed of a constant number p of *hyperbolas* placed on the diagonal. Each hyperbola i is contained inside a constant number k_i of nested squares (see Figure 4, and a formal definition in the full version [26]). The approximation factor is $c = 4 \cdot \max_{1 \le r \le p} k_r$. The algorithm runs in $O(n^{k_1 + \cdots + k_p + 3p})$ time.

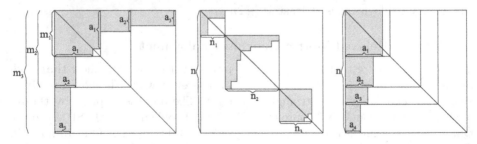

Fig. 4. Left: example of a hyperbola contained in $k = 3$ nested squares. Middle: example of a block diagonal hyperbolic quorum matrix with $p = 3$ hyperbolas with $k_1 = 1$, $k_2 = 3$ and $k_3 = 2$ nested squares respectively. Right: a quorum matrix composed of a part, called vertical telescope, of a single hyperbola. Note that any two quorums intersect in this matrix

Theorem 5. *There is a c-approximation algorithm for the Quorum Deployment Problem with a block diagonal hyperbolic quorum matrix and symmetric cost matrix that satisfies the triangle inequality, where $c = 4 \cdot \max_{1 \leq r \leq p} k_r$. The algorithm runs in $O(n^{k_1 + \cdots + k_p + 3p})$ time.*

The proof sketch that follows presents an overview of the approximation algorithm and our key observations. A detailed proof of the theorem is given in the full version [26]. For convenience of the presentation, we specify the permutations α and β to rearrange rows and columns of the *cost* matrix rather than the *quorum* matrix. This of course yields an equivalent optimization problem.

Proof (sketch). Suppose for a moment that the quorum matrix has ones inside a submatrix $U \times U$, and zeros everywhere else. Let $m = |U|$. An optimal deployment will place some rows $\tilde{U}'$ and some columns $\tilde{V}'$ of the cost matrix inside $U \times U$. When we pick a row i and m columns V, that minimize the sum of costs at the intersection of the row and the columns, then by the triangle inequality and symmetricity of the cost matrix, we can conclude that the sum of costs inside the submatrix $V \times V$ is at most twice the cost of the optimal deployment. We notice that the conclusion is true even though the optimal deployment may have $\tilde{U}' \neq \tilde{V}'$, i.e., may indeed take advantage of two degrees of freedom to lower the cost. This observation extends the technique of Krumke et al. [28] developed for the Quadratic Assignment Problem where we would have $\tilde{U}' = \tilde{V}'$ (in QAP rows and columns are permuted in the same way).

Now suppose that the quorum matrix has the richer structure of a single hyperbola. Then an optimal deployment has extra ability to avoid high costs due to "holes" in the quorum matrix, as compared to the $U \times U$ case just discussed. We can show, however, how to effectively deal with these holes by appropriately rearranging rows and columns to "push" low costs to the areas occupied by the hyperbola, and leave high costs behind. The hyperbola is contained in k nested squares. The square h has size m_h by m_h and the hyperbola has thickness a_h at the edge of the square (cf. Figure 4). For each h, we can find a row i_h and m_h columns V_h that minimize the sum of costs at the intersection of this row and the columns. Since we have selected a row and columns that minimize the sum, clearly, the cost of any optimal deployment is at least $1/k \sum_{1 \leq h \leq k} a_h \sum_{j \in V_h} C_{i_h, j}$. This simplistic bound leaves too big a freedom in the choice of subsets V_h, and so the submatrices $V_h \times V_h$ would not be useful for approximation because the submatrices would not have to be nested. Recall that the k squares are nested in the optimal deployment, so we can still bound from below the cost of the deployment if we introduce a constraint that $V_1 \subset V_2 \subset \ldots \subset V_k$. With this constraint though, there are dependencies between V_h's. Hence we cannot perform the minimization of the sum $\sum_{j \in V_h} C_{i_h, j}$ across the choices of i_h and V_h independent from the minimization of the corresponding sums across other rows and other subsets of columns because we could get stuck in a local minimum. What we need to do instead, is to minimize the value of the entire bound across all possible choices under the constraint. We can find the nested subsets V_h and rows i_h that minimize the bound

$\sum_{1 \le h \le k} a_h \sum_{j \in V_h} C_{i_h,j}$ using an appropriately adjusted polynomial time algorithm of Tokuyama and Nakano [29], in a fashion resembling the method used by Guttmann-Beck and Hassin [30]. After V_h's and i_h's have been found, we rearrange rows and columns. Using the triangle inequality and symmetricity of the cost matrix, we conclude that the costs inside submatrix $V_h \times V_h$ can be bounded from above by $2m_h$ times the costs at the intersection of row i_h and columns V_h. If we move the a_h lowest cost rows to the top part of the submatrix, then the sum of costs accumulated there is proportionally reduced, and so it is at most a a_h/m_h fraction of the sum of costs inside the entire submatrix. We rearrange rows of the submatrix $V_1 \times V_1$, then rows of $V_2 \times V_2$ and so on, and then columns. When rearrangements are done carefully, we can ensure that one rearrangement does not destroy the upper bounds on costs created by the prior rearrangements. After the rearrangements, the sum of costs inside the parabola will be at most $4 \sum_{1 \le h \le k} a_h \sum_{j \in V_h} C_{i_h,j}$. This completes approximation argument for a single parabola.

Finally, assume that the quorum matrix is a block diagonal hyperbolic quorum matrix composed of p hyperbolas. We modify the algorithm for finding nested subsets of columns, so that now the algorithm minimizes across p collections of nested subsets of columns. After we have found the collections, we apply, to each of the p collections of nested submatrices, the algorithm for rearranging rows and columns. This yields the desired approximation result and completes the proof.   □

We contrast our approximation results with the inapproximability results from the previous section. When the number of hyperbolas can be as big as a polynomial fraction of n, then the deployment problem is inapproximable to within any constant factor, even when each hyperbola i is just a single square completely filled in with ones. However, we can approximate the problem to within a constant factor when the number of hyperbolas is constant, and even if each hyperbola is contained in more than one square.

6   Conclusions and Future Work

In this paper, we have introduced the Quorum Deployment problem, a natural problem that arises when attempting to efficiently replicate data. We have examined the complexity of a number of variants of the problem, showing that the Partial Deployment Problem can be solved in polynomial time, while the general Quorum Deployment Problem and the Relaxed Metric Deployment problem are inapproximable. Finally, we presented some special NP-hard cases in which the problem can be approximated and other cases that admit optimal polynomial time solution.

While many of the results presented in this paper are negative, we believe it is important to continue examining cases for which quorums may be efficiently deployed, as the problem has significant practical import. Most previous research has focused on developing quorum systems that have good robustness to various failure modes; future research should also take into account the difficulty of deploying the quorums. While we conjecture that most currently developed quorum systems (such as the grid quorum system) cannot be deployed efficiently, we would like to develop families of quorum systems that are both robust and can be deployed efficiently.

References

1. Gifford, D.K.: Weighted voting for replicated data. In: Proceedings of the seventh symposium on operating systems principles. (1979) 150–162
2. Thomas, R.H.: A majority consensus approach to concurrency control for multiple copy databases. Transactions on Database Systems **4** (1979) 180–209
3. Garcia-Molina, H., Barbara, D.: How to assign votes in a distributed system. Journal of the ACM **32** (1985) 841–860
4. Herlihy, M.: A quorum-consensus replication method for abstract data types. ACM Transactions on Computer Systems **4** (1986) 32–53
5. Agrawal, D., Abbadi, A.E.: Resilient logical structures for efficient management of replicated data. Technical report, University of California Santa Barbara (1992)
6. Bearden, M., Jr., R.P.B.: A fault-tolerant algorithm for decentralized on-line quorum adaptation. In: Proceedings of the 28th International Symposium on Fault-Tolerant Computing Systems, Munich, Germany (1998)
7. El Abbadi, A., Toueg, S.: Maintaining availability in partitioned replicated databases. Transactions on Database Systems **14** (1989) 264–290
8. El Abbadi, A., Skeen, D., Cristian, F.: An efficient fault-tolerant protocol for replicated data management. In: Proc. of the 4th Symp. on Principles of Databases, ACM Press (1985) 215–228
9. Attiya, H., Bar-Noy, A., Dolev, D.: Sharing memory robustly in message-passing systems. Journal of the ACM **42** (1995) 124–142
10. Lynch, N., Shvartsman., A.: RAMBO: A reconfigurable atomic memory service for dynamic networks. In: Proc. of the 16th Intl. Symp. on Distributed Computing. (2002) 173–190
11. Gilbert, S., Lynch, N., Shvartsman, A.: RAMBO II:: Rapidly reconfigurable atomic memory for dynamic networks. In: Proc. of the Intl. Conference on Dependable Systems and Networks. (2003) 259–269
12. Maekawa, M.: A $\sqrt{N}$ algorithm for mutual exclusion in decentralized systems. ACM Tranactions on Computer Systems **3** (1985) 145–159
13. Naor, M., Wieder, U.: Access control and signatures via quorum secret sharing. IEEE Transactions on Parallel and Distributed Systems **9** (1998) 909–922
14. Upfal, E., Wigderson, A.: How to share memory in a distributed system. Journal of the ACM **34** (1987) 116–127
15. Vitányi, P.M.B., Awerbuch, B.: Atomic shared register access by asynchronous hardware. In: Proceedings 27th Annual IEEE Symposium on Foundations of Computer Science, New York, IEEE (1986) 233–243
16. Cheung, S.Y., Ammar, M.H., Ahamad, M.: The grid protocol: A high performance scheme for maintaining replicated data. Knowledge and Data Engineering **4** (1992) 582–592
17. Peleg, D., Wool, A.: Crumbling walls: a class of high availability quorum systems. In: Proceedings of the 14th ACM Symposium on Principles of Distributed Computing. (1995) 120–129

18. Malkhi, D., Reiter, M.: Byzantine quorum systems. In: Proceedings of the 29th Symposium on Theory of Computing. (1997) 569–578
19. Naor, M., Wool, A.: The load, capacity, and availability of quorums systems. SIAM Journal on Computing **27** (1998) 423–447
20. Naor, M., Wieder, U.: Scalable and dynamic quorum systems. In: Twenty-Second ACM Symposium on Principles of Distributed Computing. (2003)
21. Tsuchiya, T., Yamaguchi, M., Kikun, T.: Minimizing the maximum delay for reaching consensus in quorum-based mutual exclusion schemes. IEEE Transactions on Parallel and Distributed Systems **10** (1999) 337–345
22. Fu, A.W.: Delay-optimal quorum consensus for distributed systems. IEEE Transactions on Parallel and Distributed Systems **8** (1997) 59–69
23. Schrijver, A.: 17. In: Combinatorial Optimization. Volume A. Springer (2003)
24. Gary, M.R., Johnson, D.S.: Computers and Intractability. Freeman (1979)
25. Peeters, R.: The maximum edge biclique problem is NP-complete. Discrete Applied Mathematics **131** (2003) 651–654
26. Gilbert, S., Malewicz, G.: The quorum deployment problem. Technical Report CSAIL-TR-972, MIT (2004)
27. Queyranne, M.: Performance ratio of polynomial heuristics for triangle inequality quadratic assignment problems. Operations Research Letters **4** (1986) 231–234
28. Krumke, S.O., Marathe, M.V., Noltemeier, H., Radhakrishnan, V., Ravi, S.S., Rosenkrantz, D.J.: Compact location problems. Theoretical Computer Science **181** (1997) 379–404
29. Tokuyama, T., Nakano, J.: Geometric algorithms for the minimum cost assignment problem. Random Structures and Algorithms **6** (1995) 393–406
30. Guttmann-Beck, N., Hassin, R.: Approximation algorithms for min-sum p-clustering. Discrete Applied Mathematics **89** (1998) 125–142

A Constraint-Based Formalism for Consistency in Replicated Systems

Marc Shapiro[1], Karthikeyan Bhargavan[1], and Nishith Krishna[2]

[1] Microsoft Research, Cambridge, United Kingdom
[2] Compter Science Department, Courant Institute,
New York University, USA

Abstract. We present a formalism for modeling replication in a distributed system with concurrent users sharing information. It is based on actions, which represent operations requested by independent users, and constraints, representing scheduling relations between actions. The formalism encompasses semantics of shared data, such as commutativity or conflict between actions, and user intents such as causal dependence or atomicity. It enables us to reason about the consistency properties of a replication protocol or of classes of protocols. It supports weak consistency (optimistic protocols) as well as the stronger pessimistic protocols. Our approach clarifies the requirements and assumptions common to all replication systems. We are able to prove a number of common properties. For instance consistency properties that appear different operationally are proved equivalent under suitable liveness assumptions. The formalism enables us to design a new, generalised peer-to-peer consistency protocol.

1 Introduction

Replicating data in a distributed system improves availability at the cost of maintaining consistency, since each site's view may be partial or stale. It is well accepted that replication can be made more efficient by taking semantics into account, but it is difficult to reason about the correctness of such weaker protocols. Partial replication constitutes an further complication. Despite a large body of previous work [1], we lack a formal framework for understanding, reasoning about, and comparing replication protocols. This paper presents such a framework.

We model a distributed system as a replicated database and a replication protocol. Users independently submit queries and updates to the database, abstracted as *actions*. End users, applications and data types (together abstracted as clients in this framework) also submit scheduling *constraints* to express important intents or semantic properties.

Each site has a local view (called multilog) of known actions and constraints. The site executes a schedule, which completely determines the state of the replica. Sites converge if they execute the same actions in the same order, which a replication protocol ensures, if necessary, by adding more constraints.

T. Higashino (Ed.): OPODIS 2004, LNCS 3544, pp. 331–345, 2005.

Our contributions are the following. We propose a novel framework for reasoning about replicated systems. It is the first that unifies: data semantics such as commutativity and conflicts, application semantics such as causal dependence, user intents such as atomicity, and protocol decisions about which operations to execute and in which order. Our framework is simple, and gives a semantics of replication in terms of constrained sets.

Our results clarify the requirements and assumptions of a replication system. As an example, we will model different systems in our framework, e.g., Bayou and ESDS, and prove them consistent.

We are able to prove interesting properties for classes of replication protocols. For instance, we identify four different notions of consistency, which seem to differ in their operational requirements. We are able to prove that, under sufficiently strong liveness assumptions, they are equivalent.

The framework can guide the design of new replication protocols. We propose a new distributed replication algorithm generalising Bayou, whose design is directly guided by the framework. It shows that constraints can be used as an implementation mechanism as well as specification framework.

The paper proceeds as follows. Section 2 overviews the basic formalism. Section 3 defines and compares consistency properties. We examine some decision algorithms from the literature and rules for local decision in Section 4. We derive a novel decentralised replication algorithm in Section 5. Section 6 compares with related work, and we conclude in Section 7 with a summary of contributions and future work.

A separate technical report [2] provides a complete formal treatment. Here we focus on presenting the intuitions and keep the formalism to a minimum.

2   Formal Framework

Each site in a replicated system maintains a local view called *multilog*.[1] The current state results from executing a *sound* (i.e., valid) schedule computed from the multilog. Over time the multilog grows (and conceptually never shrinks) by addition of actions and constraints, either *submitted* by local clients or received from remote sites. The set of sound schedules grows with the number of actions and shrinks as the number of constraints increases.

2.1   Actions and Schedules

Slightly more formally, A is the set of unique actions INIT, $\alpha, \beta, \ldots$. Actions are assumed deterministic[2] but are otherwise uninterpreted. The *non-action* $\overline{\alpha}$ is a placeholder with no effect (non-actions will be useful when discussing liveness). Action INIT represents the initial state and has no effect.

---

[1]   We call it a multilog and not a log, because it contains actions submitted at several sites and the actions are not ordered.

[2]   Executing the same action from two equivalent input states yields equivalent output states.

A *schedule* is a non-empty sequence of actions and non-actions, for instance $S = \text{INIT}.\alpha.\overline{\beta}.\gamma$. In this example, α is *executed* (noted $\alpha \in S$), and β is non-executed (noted $\overline{\beta} \in S$); all four actions are said *scheduled* (noted $sched(\alpha, S)$). A given action may appear only once in a schedule, either as executed or as non-executed. The ordering is noted $<_S$. Every schedule starts with INIT. Intuitively, a non-action in a schedule indicates that the scheduler is aware of the action but does not execute it, e.g., because of a constraint.

Actions commute unless specified otherwise by the notation $\alpha \nleftrightarrow \beta$ (read "non-commuting"). A non-action commutes with every action and non-action. Two schedules are *equivalent* ($S_1 \equiv S_2$) if they execute the same actions, and non-commuting pairs of actions execute in the same order.

Commutativity allows us to model a number of real-world cases of schedule equivalence:

- Classically, actions commute if both are reads, or if they access independent variables.
- Overwriting: in some systems an out-of-order write has no effect; then writes effectively commute. For instance in timestamped replication (Last Writer Wins) [1], writing a file tests whether the write timestamp is greater than the file's; if so the write takes effect, otherwise it is a no-op [2].
- Reconciliation: An example of a reconciliation algorithm is Operational Transformation [3]. Two actions submitted concurrently execute in arbitrary order. The second one to execute is transformed to ignore the effect of the first, in effect rendering them commutative.
- Failure or aborts: An action that fails or aborts becomes *dead*, i.e., appears as a non-action in all schedules, which commutes with all actions.

2.2 Multilogs and Sound Schedules

Multilog $M = (K, \rightarrow, \triangleright)$ represents a site's view. K is the set of known actions ($K \subseteq A$); $\rightarrow$ and $\triangleright$ are the set of known constraints. The relation $\rightarrow \subseteq A \times A$ (pronounced Before) is not necessarily acyclic, nor reflexive, nor transitive. Relation $\triangleright \subseteq A \times A$ (pronounced MustHave) is transitive and reflexive. By convention, for any $\alpha \in A$, $\text{INIT} \rightarrow \alpha$ and $\alpha \triangleright \text{INIT}$; this is left implicit in the rest of the paper.

Figure 1 gives some examples of constraints and of common combinations. Intuitively, $\alpha \rightarrow \beta$ indicates that a scheduler must maintain an ordering between the two actions: no schedule may execute β before α. A schedule that executes neither α nor β, or only α, or only β, or both α and β in that order (but not necessarily adjacent) is correct with respect to this constraint. Relation $\alpha \triangleright \beta$ is an implication: if α executes in a schedule, then β must also execute somewhere in the same schedule, although not necessarily in that order. A schedule that executes only β, or that executes neither α nor β, is correct with respect to this constraint. Conversely, if the schedule non-executes β, then α may not execute.

The set of sound schedules of M is noted $\Sigma(M)$; M is said sound if $\Sigma(M) \neq \emptyset$. Schedule $S \in \Sigma(M)$ iff:

- Every action in K is either executed or non-executed in S: $\alpha \in K \Rightarrow$ $sched(\alpha, S)$.
- Actions that execute in S are ordered by $\rightarrow$: $\alpha, \beta \in S \wedge \alpha \rightarrow \beta \Rightarrow \alpha <_S \beta$.
- MustHave behaves like implication: $\alpha \in S \wedge \alpha \rhd \beta \Rightarrow \beta \in S$.

For instance, the multilogs $M1 = (\{\alpha\}, \emptyset, \{\text{INIT} \rhd \alpha\})$ and $M2 = (\{\alpha\}, \{\alpha \rightarrow \alpha\}, \emptyset)$ are both sound. Their sound schedules are $\Sigma(M1) = \{\text{INIT}.\alpha\}$ and $\Sigma(M2) = \{\text{INIT}.\overline{\alpha}\}$. Their union $M3 = (\{\alpha\}, \{\alpha \rightarrow \alpha\}, \{\text{INIT} \rhd \alpha\})$ is not sound. Although it contains a $\rightarrow$ cycle, multilog $M4 = (\{\alpha, \beta\}, \{\alpha \rightarrow \beta, \beta \rightarrow \alpha\}, \emptyset)$ is sound, since $\Sigma(M4) = \{\text{INIT}.\overline{\alpha}.\overline{\beta}, \text{INIT}.\alpha.\overline{\beta}, \text{INIT}.\overline{\alpha}.\beta\}$. (We do not need to consider the sound schedules $\text{INIT}.\overline{\beta}.\alpha$ and $\text{INIT}.\beta.\overline{\alpha}$ since they are equivalent to the previous ones.)

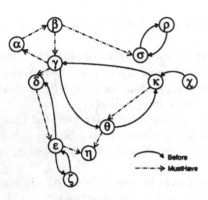

Fig. 1. Example constraints. α, β and γ form a *parcel*, an atomic (i.e., all-or-nothing) execution. γ executes only if δ also executes. δ is *causally dependent* on ϵ. ϵ and ζ conflict with (i.e., mutually exclude) each other. Only two actions out of the three γ, θ and κ can execute. If both χ and κ execute, χ comes first

We say that two multilogs are equivalent if they generate the same set of sound schedules: $M_1 \equiv M_2$ iff $\Sigma(M_1) = \Sigma(M_2)$. Note that $\Sigma(M)$ is closed with respect to schedule equivalence. Hereafter, we identify a multilog with its equivalence class.

This limited constraint language is surprisingly expressive. We have used it to express the semantics of applications as diverse as a shared calendar, a travel reservation system and a replicated file system [4, 5]. For instance if α creates a directory and β a file in that same directory, the file system submits $\beta \rhd \alpha \wedge \alpha \rightarrow \beta$ (causal dependence) along with β.

A set of actions c is said to *conflict* if the actions in c form a $\rightarrow$ cycle. Intuitively, this means that no sound schedule can execute all the actions in c. For example, if $\alpha \rightarrow \beta$ and $\beta \rightarrow \alpha$, then α and β conflict, i.e., there can be no sound schedule that executes both of them.

2.3   Significant Subsets and Events of a Replication Protocol

Execution strategies vary widely between replication protocols: in some, actions execute immediately, in others they are deferred; execution order may be pre-established or computed; actions might roll back. However a protocol would be useless if it did not reach some final decision for every action. We represent decisions as constraints; the following *significant subsets* capture the possible stages of irrevocable decision:

- **Guaranteed** actions execute in every schedule. $Guar(M)$ is the smallest set satisfying: (1) INIT $\in Guar(M)$. (2) $\forall\beta \in A$: If $\alpha \in Guar(M)$ and $\alpha \triangleright \beta$ then $\beta \in Guar(M)$.
- **Dead** actions non-execute in every schedule. $Dead(M)$ is the smallest set satisfying: (1) $\forall\alpha \in A$: If $\beta_1, \ldots, \beta_m \in Guar(M)$, where m is any natural integer, and $\alpha \rightarrow \beta_1 \rightarrow \ldots \rightarrow \beta_m \rightarrow \alpha$, then $\alpha \in Dead(M)$. (2) $\forall\alpha \in A$: If $\beta \in Dead(M)$ and $\alpha \triangleright \beta$, then $\alpha \in Dead(M)$.
- A **serialised** action is one that is ordered with respect to all non-commuting actions that execute. $Serialised(M) \stackrel{\text{def}}{=} \{\alpha \in A | \forall\beta \in A, \alpha \bowtie \beta \Rightarrow \alpha \rightarrow \beta \vee \beta \rightarrow \alpha \vee \beta \in Dead(M)\}$
- An action is **decided** once it is either dead, or both guaranteed and serialised.
  $$Decided(M) \stackrel{\text{def}}{=} Dead(M) \cup (Guar(M) \cap Serialised(M))$$
- An action is **stable** when its effects cannot change, i.e., it is either dead, or it is guaranteed and serialised and all preceding actions are themselves stable. (In practice, stable actions can be pruned from multilogs.) $Stable(M)$ is the smallest set satisfying: (1) INIT $\in Stable(M)$, (2) $Dead(M) \subseteq Stable(M)$, (3) If $(\alpha \in Guar(M) \cap Serialised(M)) \wedge (\forall\beta \in A : \beta \rightarrow \alpha \Rightarrow \beta \in Stable(M))$ then $\alpha \in Stable(M)$.

Note that if M is sound, every guaranteed action must be known: $Guar(M) \subseteq K$. Also note that $\alpha \rightarrow \alpha \Rightarrow \alpha \in Dead(M)$ and that INIT $\triangleright \alpha \Rightarrow \alpha \in Guar(M)$. M is sound iff the guaranteed and dead sets are disjoint.

3   Replication and Consistency

In this section, we describe liveness and safety properties that we require of replication systems, stated in terms of our action-constraint framework.

3.1   Site Schedules and Transition Rules

Different replication systems (such as ESDS and Bayou) differ by the actions and constraints they accept, and by the decisions they make. We summarise a replication protocol by rules describing how the system changes from time t to $t + 1$.

The current state of site i is the result of running a *site schedule* $S_i(t) \in \Sigma(M_i(t))$. In our framework, if $|\Sigma(M_i(t))| > 1$, then the choice between sound schedules is irrelevant for consistency, although individual replication systems may carefully pick a schedule for optimality.

Each site i has its own view $M_i(t) = (K_i, \rightarrow_i, \triangleright_i)(t)$, evolving over time t, called its *site multilog*.[3] Multilogs are monotonically non-shrinking, which implies that the significant subsets of Section 2.3 are non-shrinking, and that an unsound multilog remains unsound forever.

---

[3] For simplicity we assume discrete time and use a global time notation. The theory does not assume that a site can observe the global time.

All protocols obey a Universal Transition Rule, which says simply that a site may receive actions and constraints from a local client or from a remote multilog.

A specific protocol may have additional transition rules. As an example, let us encode a linearisable protocol, i.e., one in which an action takes effect at some instant in time, and actions execute in taking-effect order. We translate this to the following transition rule: "Only one action may be submitted per unit of time; if α is submitted at time t, then for any action $\beta \neq \alpha$: if $\beta \in \bigcup_j K_j(t-1)$ then $\beta \to \alpha$, otherwise $\alpha \to \beta$."

A replicated system based on pessimistic concurrency control, or *pessimistic system*, has transition rules that ensure that at every site and every time $S_i(t)$ is a prefix of $S_i(t+1)$. Otherwise the system is said *optimistic*.

3.2   Liveness Conditions

While different replication algorithms maintain different consistency invariants, all of them must satisfy some liveness conditions for convergence. We identify two liveness conditions, one for the propagation protocol that distributes actions and constraints, the other for the decision algorithm that stabilises actions and multilogs.

The propagation protocol must ensure that all actions and constraints submitted to the system eventually reach all nodes.

Property 1 (Eventual Propagation). *A replicated system has the Eventual Propagation (EP) property iff every submitted action and constraint is eventually known everywhere:*

- $\alpha \in K_i(t) \Rightarrow \forall j : \exists t' : \alpha \in K_j(t')$
- $\alpha \rhd_{i,(t)} \beta \Rightarrow \forall j : \exists t' : \alpha \rhd_{j,(t')} \beta$
- $\alpha \to_{i,(t)} \beta \Rightarrow \forall j : \exists t' : \alpha \to_{j,(t')} \beta$

The decision algorithm must ensure that all locally known actions are eventually decided:

Property 2 (Eventual Decision). *A replicated system has the Eventual Decision (ED) property iff every submitted action is eventually decided:* $\alpha \in K_i(t) \Rightarrow \exists t' : \alpha \in Decided(M_i(t'))$.

ED implies that every action eventually becomes stable [2]. ED does not preclude the trivial implementation that makes every action dead; our framework does not rule this out, since it is a valid strategy if actions fail.

3.3   Mergeability and Uniform Local Soundness

We now discuss different definitions of consistency in our framework. The first one, Mergeability, captures the intuition that sites must not make conflicting decisions: a hypothetical omniscient observer would not see anything wrong. Mergeability generalises the classical *serialisability* property.

Property 3. *A system has the Mergeability property if, given any arbitrary collection of sites $i, i', i'' \dots$ and any arbitrary collection of times $t, t', t'' \dots$:* $M_i(t) \cup M_{i'}(t') \cup M_{i''}(t'') \dots$ *is sound.*

Mergeability is not easy to ensure in a distributed setting. For instance, consider Site 1 has multilog $(\{\alpha\}, \emptyset, \{\text{INIT} \rhd \alpha\})$ and Site 2 has multilog $(\{\alpha\}, \{\alpha \to \alpha\}, \emptyset)$. They are both sound but not mergeable, as their union $(\{\alpha\}, \{\alpha \to \alpha\}, \{\text{INIT} \rhd \alpha\})$ is not sound.

Mergeability suggests that for safety, it is enough if all sites agree upon a deterministic decision strategy. For instance, a simple timestamp-based protocol can guarantee mergeability by ensuring that all sites order actions uniformly, using a global timestamp.

Under the EP liveness assumption, every submitted action and constraint is eventually received everywhere, so in effect every site becomes an omniscient observer. Then Mergeability reduces to the simpler Uniform Local Soundness (ULS) invariant that site multilogs are sound at all times: $\forall i, t : \Sigma(M_i(t)) \neq \emptyset$.

3.4   Eventual Consistency

A classical consistency property for optimistic replication systems is Eventual Consistency. It has been used to argue informally about the correctness of Grapevine [6] or Bayou [7].

Property 4. *A system is Eventually Consistent if, if every client stops submitting, and submitted actions are decided, then eventually every site will execute the same schedule, up to equivalence, and hence have the same final value:*

$$\exists T : \forall i, t > T \Rightarrow \text{No actions are submitted at } i$$
$$\Longrightarrow$$
$$\exists T', \forall t', t'', i, j : t' > T' \wedge t'' > T'$$
$$\wedge\, S_i(t') \in \Sigma(M_i(t')) \wedge S_j(t'') \in \Sigma(M_j(t''))$$
$$\Rightarrow S_i(t') \equiv S_j(t'')$$

Although eventual consistency simply captures the notion of replica convergence, it says little about the safety invariants satisfied by the algorithm before the system stabilises; these properties are captured by mergeability.

3.5   Common Monotonic Strong Prefix (CMSP)

Lamport's replicated state machine approach [8] mandates that all site execute exactly the same schedule. Clearly such a system is consistent, but this does not work for optimistic protocols where $S_i(t)$ is not necessarily a prefix of $S_i(t+1)$. However, even in an optimistic system, over time some actions will stabilise and form a prefix of all schedules. Such a system is consistent if the stable prefixes of different sites are equivalent. The system makes progress if the prefix grows.

Formally, a schedule P is a prefix of schedule S, written $P \ll S$, if $S \equiv S'$ where S' is a schedule of the form $P.Q$ for some sequence of actions Q.

Property 5. *A replicated system $M_i(t)$ (i varying over sites, t over time) satisfies the Common Monotonic Strong Prefix (CMSP) Property if there exists a function $\pi(i, t)$ such that:*

1. $\pi(i,t)$ *is a prefix of* all *sound schedules:* $\forall S \in \Sigma(M_i(t)) \Rightarrow \pi(i,t) \ll S$.
2. *The prefix is equivalent at all sites:* $\pi(i,t) \equiv \pi(j,t)$
3. *The prefix is monotonically non-shrinking over time:* $t < t' \implies \pi(i,t) \ll \pi(i,t')$
4. *Every known action eventually reaches the prefix:* $\forall \alpha \in K_i(t) \implies \exists t' : sched(\alpha, \pi(i,t'))$

We show that the actions in a CMSP are stable, and that the set of stable actions forms a CMSP [2].

3.6   Summary

We have presented four definitions of consistency, along with two liveness conditions. An interesting result is that under uniform assumptions, these definitions of consistency are equivalent. This may come as a surprise, since the operational definitions appear so different. In particular, under the eventual propagation and eventual decision liveness conditions, uniform local soundness (and hence mergeability) guarantees eventual consistency and the common monotonic strong prefix property. We provide a formal proof in our technical report [2].

4   Replication Systems and Decision Strategies

Consistency requires an agreement between all sites, which in the general case entails a consensus. For instance, mergeability forbids different sites from making conflicting decisions, thus requiring a consensus between deciding sites. Yet some practical protocols manage without this complexity, primarily by making assumptions about the distribution of constraints across actions. Here, we survey a few replication algorithms and their decision strategies.

Timestamped Replication. In timestamped replication, all actions are assumed to have a unique timestamp. This timestamp induces a total $\rightarrow$ order on all actions even before they are submitted to the system. No decisions need to be made since all actions are guaranteed and ordered, hence stable, when submitted. Hence mergeability is guaranteed by default. The replication algorithm thus reduces to a simple propagation protocol that must satisfy the EP property.

A variation on the timestamped replication algorithm is one that uses the "last-writer wins" decision strategy. It assumes that each action modifies a single variable and when two actions modify the same variable, the action with the later timestamp should be effectively executed last. So, when two actions are received out of order, either they commute, or the one received later is converted to a no-op (identity action). As we argued in Section 2.1, this strategy makes all actions effectively commute, and trivially guarantees mergeability, while allowing sites to execute actions without delay.

ESDS. The ESDS protocol [9] assumes that actions only have acyclic causal constraints between them, of the form $\alpha \triangleright \beta, \beta \rightarrow \alpha$. All actions are guaranteed at submission, the only requirement is that their causal predecessors must execute first. ESDS again reduces to a propagation algorithm that must satisfy the EP property, while maintaining the invariant that whenever α is propagated to a site, all β such that $\alpha \rhd \beta$ have already been propagated. This enables each site to easily keep track of the actions it can safely execute. Since actions do not commute, ESDS requires a distributed agreement for serialisation. All the sites participate in computing a total order for actions that is consistent with the causal order.

Bayou. Many systems centralise consensus at a primary site. Bayou [7] assumes that the shared data can be partitioned into independent databases, each with its own primary site. Actions on different partitions commute and are assumed to have no constraints between each other. Primaries make decisions for their own actions and order them. Hence, the replication system consists of a propagation protocol satisfying EP that ensures that all actions reach their primaries, a primary decision strategy that ensures ED, and a propagation protocol that distributes the primary decisions to all sites. By centralizing the decision-making for each partition, mergeability for actions and constraints on a single partition are ensured, and by disallowing constraints between partitions, all site multilogs are mergeable.

Sufficient Conditions for Local Decision. If the constraint graph has some well-behaved properties, some decisions can be safely decentralised; in Section 5 we will derive an efficient decision protocol from the following observations. Consider for instance an action α that is involved in a single constraint $\alpha \rhd \beta$: then it is always safe to make α dead, regardless of the decision for β. Conversely, if α is only involved in $\gamma \rhd \alpha$, it is always safe to make α guaranteed, regardless of γ. This can be generalised to any acyclic $\rhd$ graph. Taking the example of a chain $\alpha_1 \rhd \ldots \rhd \alpha_n$ it is safe to either: make α_1 dead, then move on to α_2, left to right; or make α_n guaranteed, then move on to α_{n-1}, right to left. Since users don't like to see their actions aborted, guaranteeing in the right-left direction is preferable.

The decision regarding each α_i must consider $\rightarrow$ constraints. If α_i is not part of a $\rightarrow$ cycle, the decision may be either guarantee or make dead (although guaranteeing is preferable). If it is part of a $\rightarrow$ cycle, and all other actions in the cycle are guaranteed, the only sound decision is to make α_i dead; otherwise either decision is allowed.

Such local decisions may be sub-optimal. To ensure optimality, viz., that the smallest possible number of actions is made dead, it is necessary to consider the whole graph as in IceCube [4].

5   A Decentralised Replication Algorithm

Consider a travel booking system, where airlines and hotels each manage their own primaries, but a user wants his hotel and flight bookings to happen atomically (all-or-nothing). Previous systems do not support this scenario: for instance Bayou imposes that all actions in a transaction have the same primary.

We present a new algorithm, derived from the safe decision conditions from Section 4, that works for arbitrary constraint graphs, hence does not suffer this restriction.

5.1   Input Assumptions

We assume the invariant that when α is in K_i, all constraints such that $\alpha \triangleright \beta$ and $\beta \to \alpha$ (for any β) are known at i. Each action in A is eventually submitted at some site. In addition, each action α is assigned a unique primary site, $P(\alpha)$. We assume that two actions commute if and only if they have different primaries. Conflicting (mutually-excluding) actions are represented by $\to$ cycles. We assume the existence of a function $victim(c)$ that deterministically chooses one action from a subset of actions C.

Note that Bayou relies on the independence of primaries to enable distributed decision making. Each primary waits for actions and makes them guaranteed or dead without coordinating with other primaries. In contrast, our algorithm must consider $\triangleright$ and $\to$ constraints between actions on different primaries.

5.2   Propagation Module

We re-use the standard Bayou anti-entropy algorithm for propagating actions and constraints to all sites. The algorithm satisfies the eventual propagation property: every action and constraint submitted at some site eventually reaches all other sites. In addition, it maintains the invariant from the previous section.

5.3   The Decision Algorithm

Every primary must know for every action whether it is guaranteed or dead, and its execution order with respect to other non-commuting actions. To represent these decisions, each site maintains a set G_i of guaranteed actions, a set D_i of dead actions, and a relation $O_i \subseteq G_i \times G_i$ that totally orders all actions belonging to the same primary. The normal propagation module reliably distributes decisions among all sites.

Given these sets, the schedule executed at a site is any schedule that contains all guaranteed actions, no dead actions, and obeys the MustHave constraints in $\triangleright_i$ and the ordering constraints in $\to_i$ and O_i. For uniform local soundness, such a schedule must always exist. For eventual decision to hold, all actions in K_i must eventually be included in G_i or D_i.

The decision algorithm runs concurrently with the propagation module. An action is first submitted to the system, then it becomes ready for a decision, it may become guaranteeable, and finally it becomes guaranteed or dead. We present the decision algorithm in terms of these states.

Ready Actions. An action α is said to be *ready* at its primary $P(\alpha)$ if

- All β such that $\alpha \triangleright \beta$ are known at $P(\alpha)$
- All β such that $\beta \to \ldots \to \alpha$ are known at $P(\alpha)$.

Each of these conditions imposes a wait before any decision on α can be taken. A primary has a set of ready actions from which it chooses the next action to make a decision on.

Guaranteeable Actions. Once all the constraints on an action α are collected, the primary begins the process of discovering whether α can be guaranteed. In particular, since it knows the closure of Before and MustHave relations, it can detect all the decision cycles between actions. For an action to be guaranteeable, all the actions it MustHave should be guaranteeable and at least one member of each $\rightarrow$ cycle it belongs to should be dead. This stage comprises the following steps:

- Compute the set M of all actions in a $\triangleright$ cycle with α. Let the set of remaining actions it MustHave be designated M'.
- Compute the set C of action sets representing cycles of $\rightarrow$ involving α.
- Wait for all the actions in M' to become guaranteed. If any of these actions becomes dead, α is now known to be dead; exit.
- For each cycle c in C, designate $victim(c)$ to be dead. If this action is α, exit.
- Designate α as guaranteeable.[4]
- Send messages to all primaries with actions in M saying that α is guaranteeable.

We again rely on the propagation module to distribute the guaranteeable actions to related primaries.

Guaranteed Actions. In the case of $\triangleright$ cycles, all members of the cycle must agree to either be guaranteed or be dead. The final steps before guaranteeing are as follows:

- Wait until either some action in M is dead, or all actions in M are guaranteeable. If the former, α is now known to be dead; exit.
- Wait until all β such that $\beta \rightarrow \ldots \rightarrow \alpha$ and $P(\beta) = P(\alpha)$ have been decided.
- Guarantee α and order it after all guaranteed β with $P(\beta) = P(\alpha)$

Dead Actions. In the process of computing guaranteeable and guaranteed actions, we identify two conditions in which an action becomes dead: either when one of the actions it MustHave is dead (either down a $\triangleright$ chain, or in a $\triangleright$ cycle), or when it is designated as the victim in a $\rightarrow$ cycle.

The choice of action to make dead in a $\rightarrow$ cycle can be arbitrary. In general it is safe to make one or more actions in such a cycle dead, as long as this is propagated up any $\triangleright$ chain. However, making too many actions dead, or choosing the wrong action to make dead, can have a negative impact on performance.

Summary of Decision Algorithm. We now summarize the steps for deciding action α. Assume α was submitted at site j.

---

[4] Some systems may elect to make α dead at this point according to their own strategies. For instance, Bayou checks a predicate, called the "dependency check," attached to each action.

1. Through epidemic (or other) communication, α is eventually known at its primary site i, $P(\alpha) = i$.
2. The propagation module at site i communicates with other sites, discovering all β such that: $\alpha \rhd \ldots \rhd \beta \vee \beta \to \ldots \to \alpha$. The action becomes ready.
3. For each cycle c of $\to$ involving α, if $victim(c) = \alpha$, then decide α is dead (e.g., add constraint $\alpha \to \alpha$) and exit.
4. Partition all β such that $\alpha \rhd \beta$, into subsets M and M', according to the following property: actions in M are such that $\beta \rhd \alpha$, those in M' are not.
5. Wait until: either some action in M' is known to be dead; or all actions in M' are known to be guaranteed. In the former case, α is now known to be dead; exit. In the latter, α is now guaranteeable.
6. To all actions in M, send a message saying that is α is guaranteeable.
7. Wait for either some action in M to be known to be dead, or for all actions in M to be guaranteeable. In the former case, α is now known to be dead; exit. In the latter, decide α is guaranteed (e.g., add INIT $\rhd \alpha$).
8. The final execution order of α is given by its $\to$ relations. Wait for all β such that $\beta \to \ldots \to \alpha \wedge P(\alpha) = P(\beta)$. Execute α after all such actions that are guaranteed.

5.4   Correctness

To prove the consistency and convergence of the algorithm, we rely on eventual propagation, on eventual decision, and on uniform local soundness.

The propagation module is fashioned on standard anti-entropy protocols and reliably delivers all actions, constraints, and decisions. To prove that the decision algorithm eventually decides every action, we show that all the wait conditions in the algorithm are eventually satisfied, i.e., there are no wait-for cycles. For uniform local soundness, we argue that every decision extends the set of constraints in a sound manner by performing a step-by-step case analysis on the algorithm.

5.5   Extensions for Partial Replication

Up to now we assumed that all data is replicated at every site. Let us now consider partial replication: shared data is partitioned into n disjoint *databases* $D^1, \ldots, D^n$, and we allow a site to replicate an arbitrary subset of the databases (as long as every database is present on at least one site). Actions are correspondingly partitioned into subsets $A^1, \ldots, A^n$. A site replicating D^i should receive submitted actions that are in A^i, and the constraints that involve such actions. It does not need to receive actions or constraints for databases it does not replicate.

Both our correctness conditions and our distributed algorithm extend naturally to partial replication with constraints across partitioned data. The analysis and presentation of this modified algorithm is left to a future paper; here we sketch some details.

The $\rhd$ constraint is not adequate for partial replication, because if $\alpha \rhd \beta$, then a site that executes α must also know β. Therefore we define a version that is "remotable" across partitions, Split MustHave, noted $\rhd\!\!\!> \subseteq A \times A$. The definitions of mergeability and eventual consistency can then be extended in terms of this new ▷ operator.

The distributed algorithm stated above uses full replication only in computing the closure (and cycles) of ▷ and →. Under partial replication, this computation must be done in a distributed manner. We adopt Manivannan and Singhal's distributed knot detection algorithm [10] for this purpose.

6   Related Work

IceCube is a general-purpose system supporting optimistic replication and co-operative work [4], based on actions and constraints. Experience with IceCube shows that relatively complex applications can be readily encoded in this framework. Its decision algorithm is centralised and computes an optimal schedule given an arbitrary graph of actions and constraints. Although the problem is NP-hard, IceCube uses efficient heuristics and manages to execute in almost linear time in the common case.

Our survey of optimistic replication [1] motivated us to understand the commonalities and differences between protocols.

Chong and Hamadi [11] proposed a decentralised decision algorithm based on constraint satisfaction principles, which inspired our algorithm in Section 5.

The relations between consistency and ordering have been well studied in the context the causal dependence relation [12]. Our simpler and modular primitives clarify and generalise this analysis. The primitives are common to all protocols, as are the significant events of actions becoming guaranteed, dead, serialised, decided and stable.

Lamport's state-machine replication [8] broadcasts actions to all sites and ensures consistency because each site executes exactly the same schedule. Our CMSP property generalises this definition. Sousa et al. [13] generalise Lamport's state-machine approach to the commitment of partially replicated databases.

Much formal work on consistency focuses on serialisability. Mergeability constitutes a generalisation of serialisability.

The X-Ability theory [14] allows an action to appear several times in the same schedule if it is idempotent; for instance, retrying a failed action is allowed. Schedules are tested for equivalence after filtering out such duplicates. It would be interesting to encode their approach in our formalism, and analyse their assumptions, which are quite strong. This is left for future work.

Our approach has many similarities with the Acta framework [15]. Acta provides a set of logical primitives over execution histories, including presence of an event, implication, and causal dependence and ordering between events. Acta makes assumptions specific to databases, such as the existence of transaction commit and abort primitives. The Acta description language is more powerful and is used to analyse protocols at a finer granularity. On the other hand, the action-constraint language is simpler; it is straightforward to translate most of the Acta dependencies into our language. Acta takes serialisability as the definition of consistency, and does not deal with partial replication.

7   Conclusions and Future Work

We presented a formalism for describing replication protocols and consistency. Our significant subsets are common to the many replication protocols that can be described in our language. We generalise a number of classical formulations of the consistency property and prove them equivalent. This underscores the deep commonalities between protocols that appear quite different on the surface. Although consistency entails global consensus in the general case, we exhibited sufficient conditions for making local decisions. We derived a new distributed decision algorithm, which supports multiple primaries, constraints across primaries, and can be extended to handle partial replication. Our results apply to a broad range of protocols, both pessimistic and optimistic.

This paper only presented the intuitions; the interested reader will find a fully formal treatment in our technical report [2]. That report also contains a detailed description for a variety of diverse classical replication protocols, including consistency proofs.

The formalism rests upon only two binary constraints. This makes it easy to prove properties, and is powerful enough to incorporate all the classical replication protocols. However the semantics of some applications (e.g., a shared bank account) demand more powerful primitives. A possible direction is to generalise constraints to be n-ary and our significant subsets to patterns. Then the crucial safety property would be that the guaranteed and dead subsets are disjoint.

Acknowledgments

We thank Fabrice le Fessant for his participation to early stages of this work, Yek Chong and Youssef Hamadi for their contributions on a decentralised decision algorithm, and Tony Hoare, Miguel Castro and Patrick Valduriez for their encouragement and suggestions.

References

1. Saito, Y., Shapiro, M.: Optimistic replication. Computing Surveys (2005).
2. Shapiro, M., Bhargavan, K.: The Actions-Constraints approach to replication: Definitions and proofs. Technical Report MSR-TR-2004-14, Microsoft Research (2004).
3. Sun, C., Jia, X., Zhang, Y., Yang, Y., Chen, D.: Achieving convergence, causality preservation, and intention preservation in real-time cooperative editing systems. Trans. on Comp.-Human Interaction 5 (1998) 63–108.
4. Preguiça, N., Shapiro, M., Matheson, C.: Semantics-based reconciliation for collaborative and mobile environments. In: Proc. Tenth Int. Conf. on Coop. Info. Sys. (CoopIS), Catania, Sicily, Italy (2003)
5. Shapiro, M., Preguiça, N., O'Brien, J.: Rufis: mobile data sharing using a generic constraint-oriented reconciler. In: Conf. on Mobile Data Management, Berkeley, CA, USA (2004).
6. Birell, A.D., Levin, R., Needham, R.M., Schroeder, M.D.: Grapevine: An exercise in distributed computing. Communications of the ACM 25 (1982) 260–274

7. Terry, D.B., Theimer, M.M., Petersen, K., Demers, A.J., Spreitzer, M.J., Hauser, C.H.: Managing update conflicts in Bayou, a weakly connected replicated storage system. In: Proc. 15th ACM Symposium on Operating Systems Principles, Copper Mountain CO (USA), ACM SIGOPS (1995).
8. Lamport, L.: Time, clocks, and the ordering of events in a distributed system. Communications of the ACM **21** (1978) 558–565
9. Fekete, A., Gupta, D., Luchangco, V., Lynch, N., Shvartsman, A.: Eventually-serializable data services. Theoretical Computer Science **220** (1999) 113–156
10. Manivannan, D., Singhal, M.: An efficient distributed algorithm for detection of knots and cycles in a distributed graph. IEEE Transactions on Parallel and Distributed Systems **14** (2003) 961–972
11. Chong, Y., Hamadi, Y.: Distributed IceCube. Private communication (2004)
12. Ramamritham, K., Chrysanthis, P.K.: A taxonomy of correctness criteria in database applications. VLDB Journal **5** (1996) 85–97
13. Sousa, A., Oliveira, R., Moura, F., Pedone, F.: Partial replication in the database state machine. In: Int. Symp. on Network Comp. and App. (NCA'01), Cambridge MA, USA, IEEE (2001) 298–309
14. Frølund, S., Guerraoui, R.: X-Ability: A theory of replication. In: Symp. on Principles of Dist. Comp. (PODC 2000), Portland, Oregon, USA, ACM SIGACT-SIGOPS (2000)
15. Chrysanthis, P.K., Ramamritham, K.: ACTA: The SAGA continues. In Elmagarmid, A.K., ed.: Database Transaction Models for Advanced Applications. Morgan Kaufmann (1992) 349–397

Analyzing Convergence in Consistency Models for Distributed Objects

Francisco J. Torres-Rojas[1] and Esteban Meneses[2]

[1] Costa Rica Institute of Technology (I.T.C.R.) and
University of Costa Rica (U.C.R.)
torres@ic-itcr.ac.cr
[2] Costa Rica Institute of Technology and PrediSoft,
Costa Rica
emeneses@ic-itcr.ac.cr

Abstract. At instant t, two or more sites could perceive different values for the same distributed object X. However, depending on the consistency protocol used, it might be expected that, after a while, every site in the system should see the same value for this object. In this paper, we present a formalization of the concept of *convergence* and analyze its relationships with several consistency models. Among other things, we claim that, by itself, *sequential consistency* is not a convergent protocol.

1 Introduction

In order to deal with several, possibly different, copies or replicas of the same objects in diverse sites of a distributed systems, it is necessary to define a consistency protocol. One would expect that the consistency protocol should offer some kind of guarantees about the convergence, at the end of the day, of the shared objects. Thus, convergence is almost understood as a requirement for the correctness of a distributed computation. However, a consistency model such as *sequential consistency* [15], which is usually referred as "strong consistency", does **not** contain nor imply, by itself, convergence of the shared objects. It is our feeling that many excellent implementations of this consistency model are actually aiming at accomplishing convergence of the shared information, and not to just satisfying the strict (and minimal) mathematical requirements of sequential consistency, which might have blurred out the line between convergence and consistency. In this paper, we establish precise definitions of what we understand by convergence and analyze several well-known consistency models to the light of these definitions.

Convergence is an idea found in multiple areas of science. It is often related to some kind of stability. Although operations made in the past could have created certain disorganization in the arrangement of the analyzed system, there is comfort in knowing that our object of study achieves a stable behavior after a given instant. Mathematically, the definition of convergence is usually associated to a *sequence* of terms. For example, in real numbers, the sequence $\{x_n\}$ converges

T. Higashino (Ed.): OPODIS 2004, LNCS 3544, pp. 346–356, 2005.
© Springer-Verlag Berlin Heidelberg 2005

to x if, for every $\epsilon > 0$ there exist some natural number m such that for $n \geq m$ it happens that $|x_n - x| < \epsilon$. As it can be observed, the number m imposes the limit after which, everything seems to be "stable". In this case, the stability of the sequence is characterized by being sufficiently close to number x.

In the context of groupware systems, some authors [9, 18] define convergence by looking at the final result of a work session. Operations made by users could arrive at different times to the other sites, executing possibly in different orders. However, it is required that the final result be exactly the same for every user. It is also important offering convergence in mobile computing applications [10], specially when disconnection periods are considered. In this case, after operations (possibly conflicting) are made over different replicas of the same object, it is required that all replicas converge to the same state after all the processes have been reconnected for sufficiently long. This is one of the key ideas that we explore in this paper: *convergence* in the values of the shared objects in a distributed system for a *lapse of time*. Moreover, we consider subsets of shared objects and also unbounded time ranges.

Our approach to understanding convergence in distributed systems is introduced in Section 2. We study the convergence properties of some consistency models in Section 3. Finally, the conclusions of this paper are presented in Section 4.

2   Convergence Model

Consider the distributed history shown in Figure 1. After X is updated by one of the sites, the new value is communicated, with some delay, to the other site. Site *1* updates X at time t_1 giving it the value 3 (which was 0 initially). It is not until time t_2 that Site *2* discovers that X has been updated. However, at time t_3 Site *2* makes a new change to X, giving it the value of 7. Let's say that news of this change arrive too late to Site *1*, and by time t_4, Site *1* has updated again X to value 4. Similarly, Site *2* does not perceive this last change and updates X at time t_5 to value 6. At time t_6 Site *1* realizes that X has a new value and from here on, both sites agree on the value of X. Thus, finally, convergence has been reached.

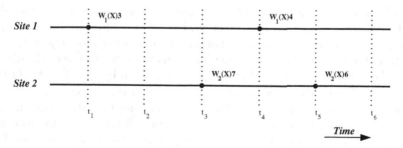

Fig. 1. Two sites in a convergent execution

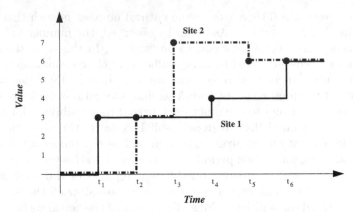

Fig. 2. Convergence of two sites

Figure 2 plots the values that X takes at every instant, as perceived by each site, and it shows that there is convergence after time t_6. Nevertheless, it could be claimed that the time intervals $[0,t_1],[t_2,t_3]$ and $[t_6,+\infty]$ form a set of ranges where convergence was achieved, we refer to these time ranges as *convergence frames* (see Section 2.3). Our formal definition for convergence will capture these two kinds of stability ranges: the one obtained after the *last* update to some distributed object, and the time frames where two or more sites agree on the same value for a particular object.

2.1   Trivial Convergence

Definition 1. *An execution in a distributed system is* **trivially convergent over object** X *if all sites have agreed to assign a particular value for* X *after time t. If the execution is trivially convergent over every possible object, we say that the execution is* **trivially convergent.**

This is the less interesting case for convergence, since a situation like this hardly represents the general case, and even though the system is reaching convergence in the value of X, this does not imply correctness in the execution.

2.2   Absolute Convergence

Figure 3 shows a simple distributed computation, with 2 sites and one shared object X. There are a series of **writes** and **reads** executed by both sites, and, at several times during execution, sites see different values for object X. But, at some time t after event $\mathbf{w}_1(\mathtt{X})4$, which happens to be the last actualization to X in the whole execution, all **reads** to object X executed by any site *should* return the value 4. Thus, after time t, this system has converged regarding the value of object X. The intuition behind *absolute convergence* is that, at the end of the day, after the **writes** stop, every site involved in a distributed computation will agree on the same values for the same objects. Notice that this is similar to the concept of eventual consistency, but it is our purpose to distinguish between convergence and consistency.

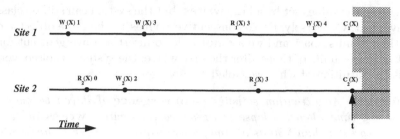

Fig. 3. Convergent cut

Following the lines of *consistent cuts* [16], we define a *convergent cut* this way:

Definition 2. *We say that a* **convergent cut over object** X *is a set of phantom events* $\mathcal{C} = \{C_1, C_2, ..., C_N\}$, *where every* C_i *is inserted in local history* $\mathcal{H}_i$, *all at the same time* t. *All the* C_i *are* **read** *operations over* X *that would return exactly the value written by the latest* **write** *into object* X *that occurred before* t.

Definition 3. *An execution in a distributed system is* **absolutely convergent over object** X *if at any arbitrary time after* t, *which itself occurs after the last* **write** *to object* X, *a convergent cut over object* X *can be inserted. If the execution is absolutely convergent over every possible distributed object, we say that the execution is* **absolutely convergent**.

If an execution is absolutely convergent over object X at time t, i.e., we can insert a convergent cut $\mathcal{C}$ at time t, it must be true that the same cut $\mathcal{C}$ can be inserted, with identical results, at any time $u > t$. Now, if there are M shared objects X_j, $1 \leq j \leq M$, and the execution is absolutely convergent for all the M objects, then for every object we associate a minimum time t_j where its corresponding convergence cut can be inserted. Therefore, the distributed system is absolutely convergent at any time after $t = max(t_1, t_2, ..., t_M)$.

2.3 δ-Convergence

It is typically desirable that the lapse before an update is communicated to everybody else in a distributed system be as short as possible. However, in a very active system with frequent **writes** to the same shared objects, it is normal that the values of these objects diverge during execution. Even under these circumstances, we could expect that after the "last" **write**, as mentioned in the previous section, the system reaches *absolute convergence*. Besides, if the system, after considering factors such as overhead, communication delays, and consistency protocols, can guarantee that an update is known to the complete system (either by updating or by invalidations) in at most δ units of time, the execution might manifest intervals where the system is evidently convergent in relation to some objects.

Now, we claim that if the lapses between multiple consecutive **writes** to the same object are shorter than the parameter δ, there was not enough time for propagating the values set by all the **writes**, but the system can still be classified as convergent. Conversely, if two consecutive **writes** to the same object X occur more than δ units apart and we are **not** able to insert a convergent cut for this object at least δ units of times after the first **write**, the system is not convergent. This is the intuition of what we called δ-convergence:

Definition 4. *An execution satisfies δ-**convergence** if it can be guaranteed that, at any time when the lapse between two consecutive **writes** to the same object X is greater than δ units of time, a convergent cut over X can be inserted δ units of time after the first **write**.*

Thus, in a δ-convergent execution, if X is updated at time t and the next update to this object, anywhere in the system, occurs at time u, with $t + \delta < u$, there is an interval $[t + \delta, u]$ where all sites in the system would perceive, if they read it, the very same value for object X. We call this interval a *convergence frame* for object X. On the other hand, if $t + \delta > u$, we might not define such a convergence frame, but we still claim that the system is δ-convergent. In other words, the system is allowed to be "unstable" for at most δ units of time after a **write**, without being considered non-convergent.

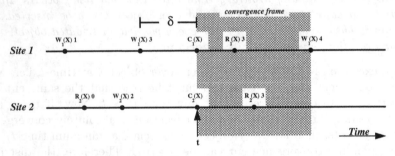

Fig. 4. Convergence frame

Figure 4 shows some of the previous concepts. If δ units of time after operation $w_1(X)3$ occurred, we are able to insert a convergent cut associated to object X (which means that if every site in the system would read X all they would find the same value), this establishes a convergence frame for object X. Of course, another update to object X can be made thereafter, but until that new update the system has converged on the value of X. Extending this concept to several objects is straightforward.

3   Convergence and Consistency Models

Consider a distributed system with N sites sharing objects. The *global history* $\mathcal{H}$ of this system is the partially ordered set of all operations occurring at all sites. $\mathcal{H}_i$ is the total ordered set or sequence of operations that are executed on site *i*. In order to simplify, we assume that all operations are either **read** or **write**, that each value written is unique, and that all the objects have an initial value of zero.

If $\mathcal{D}$ is a set of operations, then a *serialization* of $\mathcal{D}$ is a linear sequence S containing exactly all the operations of $\mathcal{D}$ such that each **read** operation to a particular object returns the value written by the most recent (in the order of S) **write** operation to the same object. If $\prec$ is an arbitrary partial order relation over $\mathcal{D}$, we say that serialization S *respects* $\prec$ if $\forall$ **a**, **b** $\in \mathcal{D}$ such that **a** $\prec$ **b** then **a** precedes **b** in S.

3.1 Convergence and Linearizability

The **read** and **write** operations $\in \mathcal{H}$ take a finite, non-zero time to execute, so there is a time elapsed from the instant when a **read** or **write** "starts" to the moment when such operation "finishes". Nevertheless, for the purposes of this paper, we associate to each operation an instant (at some point between the start and the end), called the *effective time* of the operation. If **a** has an effective time previous to the effective time of **b** we denote this as **a** $<_{E-T}$ **b**.

Definition 5. *History* $\mathcal{H}$ *satisfies* Linearizability (**LIN**) *if there is a serialization* S *of* $\mathcal{H}$ *that respects the order* $<_{E-T}$ [11].

If serialization S respects the order $<_{E-T}$, this means that any **read** to a shared object X returns a value corresponding to the most recent **write** on X. Therefore, **LIN** is an inherently convergent protocol. It is easy to see that, under **LIN**, a convergent cut associated to each object can always be inserted right after the last **write** into that object, which proves that the execution is *absolutely convergent* (see Definition 3). Similarly, no matter how close two **writes** to the same object are, convergent cuts can always be inserted immediately after every **write**, which proves that the execution satisfies δ-convergence for any value of δ.

3.2 Convergence and Sequential Consistency

If **a** occurs before **b** in $\mathcal{H}_i$ we say that **a** precedes **b** in *program order*, and denote this as **a** $<_{PROG}$ **b**.

Definition 6. *History* $\mathcal{H}$ *satisfies* Sequential Consistency (**SC**) *if there is a serialization* S *of* $\mathcal{H}$ *that respects the order* $<_{PROG}$ *for every site in the system* [15].

Thus, **SC** does not require that a **read** operation returns the most recent value with respect to real-time, but just that the result of any execution is the same as if the operations of all sites can be arranged in a serialization S that respects the partial order $<_{PROG}$.

We claim that **SC** does not imply convergence. Given the nonexistence of real-time requirements in this consistency model, sites are not actually forced to update or invalidate its local objects unless that this is required to build S correctly. However, there is the very common misconception of assuming that

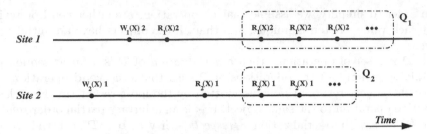

Fig. 5. A sequentially consistent history that does not converge

SC guarantees convergence. Normally, we use the terms "sequential consistency" and "strong consistency" interchangeably, but this probably is because many of the protocols used to induce **SC** on the execution are actually imposing more requirements (with additional overhead) than what really are needed to satisfy the definition of **SC** in [15].

Figure 5 presents a simple example of a distributed execution that satisfies **SC**, but whose shared objects never converge. Site *2* writes value 1 into object X, and, some time later, Site *1* writes value 2 into object X. The following **read** on Site *1* returns 2, while the next **read** operation on Site *2* returns the old value 1. Notice that, considering only these four events, the history, so far, satisfies **SC**: just take $S = \mathbf{w}_1(X)2, \mathbf{r}_1(X)2, \mathbf{w}_2(X)1, \mathbf{r}_2(X)1$. This serialization does not respect real-time, but fulfills the requirements for **SC** [15]. Now, nothing forces Site *1* and Site *2* to agree, at any point in the future, on the value of X. Consider operation sets $\mathcal{Q}_1$ and $\mathcal{Q}_2$, both containing just **reads** over object X, one executing on Site *1* and the other executing on Site *2*, respectively. The value retrieved by operations in $\mathcal{Q}_1$ is 2, while the value retrieved by operations in $\mathcal{Q}_2$ is 1. It can be proved by induction over $|\mathcal{Q}_1|$ and $|\mathcal{Q}_2|$ that this distributed history is sequentially consistent. A possible serialization is $S = \mathbf{w}_1(X)2, \mathbf{r}_1(X)2, \{\mathcal{Q}_1\}, \mathbf{w}_2(X)1, \mathbf{r}_2(X)1, \{\mathcal{Q}_2\}$. Thus, Sites *1* and *2* can execute an infinite number of **reads** over object X, satisfy **SC**, and never converge to the same value. In this example, *absolute convergence* is not guaranteed by **SC**, and, if we choose $\mathbf{w}_1(X)2$ and $\mathbf{w}_2(X)1$ as occurring more than δ units of time apart, neither δ-convergence is satisfied. It is easy to build an example more complex than Figure 5, involving multiple sites, shared objects and values written, where **SC** is respected, and where absolute convergence and δ-convergence are never met.

3.3   Convergence and Causal Consistency

Let $\mathcal{H}_{i+w}$ be the set of all the operations in $\mathcal{H}_i$ plus all the **write** operations in $\mathcal{H}$. The partially ordered *happens-before* relationship "$\rightarrow$" for message passing systems as defined in [14] can be modified to order the operations of $\mathcal{H}$. Let $\mathbf{a}, \mathbf{b}$ and $\mathbf{c} \in \mathcal{H}$, we say that $\mathbf{a} \rightarrow \mathbf{b}$, i.e., $\mathbf{a}$ happens-before (or *causally precedes*) $\mathbf{b}$, if one of the following holds:

1. **a** and **b** are executed on the same site and **a** is executed before **b**.
2. **b** reads an object value written by **a**.
3. **a** → **c** and **c** → **b**.

Definition 7. *History $\mathcal{H}$ satisfies* Causal Consistency (**CC**) *if for each site i there is a serialization S_i of the set $\mathcal{H}_{i+w}$ that respects causal order "→"* [3].

CC is a consistency model weaker than **SC**, i.e., every sequentially consistent execution is also causally consistent, but the reverse is not true. It can be implemented efficiently [3, 19]. **CC** requires that all causally related operations be seen in the same order by all sites, while different sites could perceive concurrent operations in different orders [3]. **CC** has been shown to be sufficient for applications that support asynchronous sharing among distributed users. It has been explored both in message passing systems [8] and in shared memory and object systems [2, 4, 5, 12, 13, 19]. Relations between **SC** and **CC** have been studied in [3, 17]. Given the existence of concurrent writes in an execution, **CC** can not guarantee absolute convergence nor δ-convergence.

3.4 Convergence and Timed Consistency

Timed Consistency (**TC**), as proposed in [20], requires that if the effective time of a **write** is t, the value written by this operation must be visible to all sites in the distributed system by time $t + \Delta$, where Δ is a parameter of the execution.

Definition 8. *Let* **a**, **b** $\in \mathcal{D} \subseteq \mathcal{H}$ *with effective times t_1 and t_2, respectively, be two operations over the same object* X. *We say that* **a** $<_\Delta$ **b** *if:*

1. *Both* **a** *and* **b** *are* **write** *operations and $t_1 < t_2$, or*
2. **a** *is a* **write** *operation,* **b** *is a* **read** *operation and $t_1 < (t_2 - \Delta)$.*

Definition 9. *History $\mathcal{H}$ satisfies* Timed Consistency (**TC**) *if there is a serialization S of $\mathcal{H}$ that respects the partial order $<_\Delta$* [20].

Under **TC**, a **read** does not return stale values if there are more recent values that have been available for more than Δ units of time. It can be seen that when $\Delta = 0$, **TC** becomes **LIN**. So, **TC** can be considered as a generalization or weakening of **LIN**. Ordering and time are two different aspects of consistency. One avoids conflicts between operations, the other addresses how quickly the effects of an operation are perceived by the rest of the system [6, 20].

The execution showed in Figure 6 satisfies **SC** and **CC**. Up to the second operation of Site *1*, the execution satisfies **TC** for the value of Δ presented in this figure, but, by that same instant, **LIN** is no longer satisfied. After this point, the execution neither satisfies **TC** because there are **read** operations in Site *1* that start more than Δ units of real-time after Site *0* writes the value **7** into object X and these **read** operations do not return this value.

Definition 10. *History $\mathcal{H}$ satisfies* Timed Sequential Consistency (**TSC**) *if there is a serialization S of $\mathcal{H}$ that simultaneously respects the partial order $<_{PROG}$ and the partial order $<_\Delta$* [20].

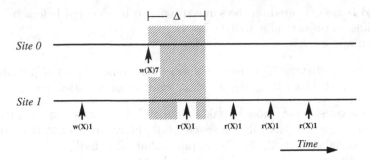

Fig. 6. Distributed History does not satisfy **TC**

Definition 11. *History* $\mathcal{H}$ *satisfies* Timed Causal Consistency (**TCC**) *if for each site* i *there is a timed serialization* S_i *of* $\mathcal{H}_{i+w}$ *that simultaneously respects causal order* → *and the partial order* $<_\Delta$ [20].

We claim that **TC**, **TSC** and **TCC** do guarantee convergence. Figure 7 shows the same execution presented previously in Figure 5, but including the requirements of **TC**. As it can be appreciated, after operation $w_1(X)2$ there is an interval of Δ units of time units before Site 2 must, necessarily, be aware of this change. However, after this point both sites know the actual value of X, and, therefore, all the **reads** in $\mathcal{Q}_1$ and $\mathcal{Q}_2$ will report the value **2**.

Theorem 1. *TC satisfies* absolute convergence *and* δ-convergence.

Proof. At most Δ units of time after the last **write** for every shared object, **TC** guarantees that the updated value is known to every site in the distributed system, therefore, we can insert a convergent cut over each shared object Δ units of time after the corresponding last **write** operation, which according to Definition 3 proves that the execution satisfies *absolute convergence*. Now, it should be easy to see that δ-convergence is guaranteed for the value $\delta = \Delta$.

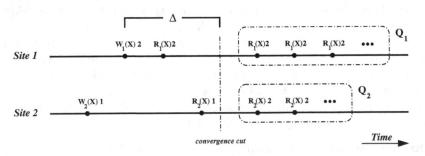

Fig. 7. A timed consistent history

4   Conclusions and Future Work

Convergence is a very useful and important notion in distributed systems. In this paper, we present a formalization of the concept and use our definitions to analyze the behavior of several well-known consistency protocols. We found that *Linearizability* and the variants of *Timed Consistency*, due to real-time considerations included in the definition of these models, guarantee *absolute convergence* and *δ-convergence* as defined in this paper. On the other hand, *Causal Consistency* and *Sequential Consistency* can not make such a claim.

Given the popularity of **SC**, the last affirmation can be surprising. This can be handled in a pessimistic way (i.e., worrying because a protocol that induces **SC**, not necessarily implies convergence unless that it explicitly includes such considerations), or in an optimistic way (i.e., taking advantage of the lack of mandatory convergence of **SC** to obtain more efficient consistency protocols that guarantee the correctness of applications that only require the minimal version of **SC**).

For future work we want to explore efficient implementations of **TC**. We must also study the implications of our notions of convergence in several applications such as distributed shared memories, collaborative systems, mobile computing and distributed databases. Besides, we still need to fully understand the behavior of a protocol such as **TCC**, because, obviously there is a performance impact when we move from **CC** to **TCC**.

References

1. Adve, S. and Gharachorloo, K., *Shared Memory Consistency Models: A Tutorial.* Western Research Laboratory, Research Report 95/7, 1995.
2. Ahamad, M., Torres-Rojas, F., Kordale, R., Singh, J. and Smith, S.,*Detecting Mutual Consistency of Shared Objects*, Proc. of International Workshop on Mobile Systems and Applications, 1994.
3. Ahamad, M., Neiger, G., Burns, J., Kohli., P. and Hutto, P. *Causal memory: definitions, implementation and programming.* Distributed Computing. September, 1995.
4. Ahamad, M., Bhola, S., Kordale, R. and Torres-Rojas, F., *Scalable Information Sharing in Large Scale Distributed Systems*, Proceedings of the Seventh SIGOPS Workshop, August 1996.
5. Ahamad, M., Raynal,M. and Thiakime, G., *An adaptive architecture for causally consistent services*, Proc. ICDCS98, Amsterdam. 1998.
6. Ahamad, M. and Raynal, M., *Ordering and Timeliness: Two Facets of Consistency?*, Future Directions in Distributed Computing, 2003.
7. Attiya, H and J. Welch, J., *Sequential Consistency vs. Linearizability*, ACM Transactions on Computer Systems. Vol 12, Number 12. May 1994.
8. Birman,K., Schiper, A. and Stephenson, P.,*Lightweight Causal and Atomic Group Multicast*, ACM Transactions on Computer Systems, Vol 9, No. 3, pp. 272-314, Aug. 1991.
9. Ellis, C.A. and Gibbs, S.J. *Concurrency Control in Groupware Systems.* In ACM SIGMOD'89 proceedings,pages 399-407, 1989.

10. Guerraoui, R. and Hari, C. *On the Consistency Problem in Mobile Distributed Computing*. ACM POMC, 2002.
11. Herlihy, M. and Wing, J. *Linearizability: A Correctness Condition for Concurrent Objects*. ACM Transactions on Programming Languages and Systems. Vol 12(3), July 1990.
12. Kordale, R. and Ahamad, M. *A Scalable Technique for Implementing Multiple Consistency Levels for Distributed Objects*, Proceedings of the 16th. International Conference in Distributed Computing Systems. May 1996.
13. Kordale, R. *System Support for Scalable Services*, Ph.D. dissertation, College of Computing, Georgia Institute of Technology. January 1997.
14. Lamport, L. *Time, Clocks and the Ordering of Events is a Distributed System*. Communications of the
15. Lamport, L. *How to make a Multiprocessor Computer that correctly executes Multiprocess Programs*. IEEE Transactions on Computer Systems, C-28(9), 1979.
16. Mattern, F. *Virtual Time and Global States of Distributed Systems*. Proceedings of the International Workshop on Parallel and Distributed Algorithms, 215-226, 1989.
17. Raynal, M. and Schiper, A., *From Causal Consistency to Sequential Consistency in Shared Memory Systems*, Proceedings 15th Int. Conference FST & TCS (Foundations of Software Technology and Theoretical Computer Science), Springer-Verlag LNCS 1026, pp. 180-194. Bangalore, India, Dec. 1995.
18. Sun, C. et al. *Achieving convergence, causality-preservation, and intention-preservation in real-time cooperative editing systems*. ACM Transactions in Computer-Human Interaction, 5(1):63-108, 1998.
19. Torres-Rojas, F. J., Ahamad, M. and Raynal, M. *Lifetime Based Consistency Protocols for Distributed Objects*. Proc. 12th International Symposium on Distributed Computing, DISC'98, Andros, Greece, September 1998.
20. Torres-Rojas, F. J., Ahamad, M. and Raynal, M. *Timed Consistency for Shared Distributed Objects*. Annual ACM Symposium on Principles of Distributed Computing PODC'99, Atlanta, Georgia, 1999.

Directional Versus Omnidirectional Antennas for Energy Consumption and k-Connectivity of Networks of Sensors*

Evangelos Kranakis[1], Danny Krizanc[2], and Eric Williams[2]

[1] School of Computer Science, Carleton University,
Ottawa, Ontario, K1S 5B6, Canada
[2] Department of Mathematics and Computer Science,
Wesleyan University, Middletown CT 06459, USA

Abstract. A network is k-connected if it remains connected after the removal of any $k - 1$ of its nodes. Assume that n sensors, modeled here as (omni)directional antennas, are dropped randomly and independently with the uniform distribution on the interior of a unit length segment or a unit square. We derive sufficient conditions on the beam width of directional antennas so that the energy consumption required to maintain k-connectivity of the resulting network of sensors is lower when using directional than when using omnidirectional antennas. Our theoretical bounds are shown by experiment to be accurate under most circumstances. For the case of directional antennae, we provide simple algorithms for setting up a k-connected network requiring low energy.

1 Introduction

Communications networks are eliminating the barriers of distance and time by providing rapid access to information. New sensor systems currently under development add to these characteristics by providing the ability to function, autonomously, in unusually extreme and complex environments. They also have numerous applications in tele-medicine, transportation, tracking endangered species, detecting toxic agents, as well as monitoring the security of civil and engineering infrastructures.

Sensors are low power communication and sensing devices that can be embedded in the physical world (see Kahn et al [8], Sohrabi et al [21], Estrin et al [5]). Large scale sensor networks are formed by sensors that can be automatically configured after being dropped over a given region. It is expected that the cost of such devices will drop significantly in the near future (see [14], Agre et al [1], and Warneke et al [24]). Sensor nodes enable autonomy, self-configurability, and

---

* Research of the first author supported in part by NSERC (Natural Sciences and Engineering Research Council of Canada) and MITACS (Mathematics of Information Technology and Complex Systems) grants.

T. Higashino (Ed.): OPODIS 2004, LNCS 3544, pp. 357–368, 2005.

self-awareness, in the sense that they can assemble themselves automatically, adapt dynamically to failures, manage movement, and react to changes in network requirements. However, malfunctioning of individual sensors may well lead to operational failures resulting either in a disconnected network or failing to monitor a certain subregion.

Our paper addresses the problem of comparing the energy consumption between networks of omnidirectional and directional sensors under the assumption of maintaining network connectivity. Assume n sensors are dropped randomly and independently with the uniform distribution over a region (which here we consider either a unit length segment or a unit square). A network is k-connected if it remains connected after the removal of any $k-1$ of its nodes. We investigate the impact of the size of the reachability radius of the sensors (given as a function of the total number n of sensors and the number k of faults) on the k-connectivity of the sensor system. We use this analysis to compare the energy consumption required for the k-connectivity of the resulting sensor network when using omnidirectional versus directional sensors. Our results show that significant savings are possible when directional antennae are used over omni-directional antennae, assuming the beam width of the directional antennae is sufficiently small. We compute theoretical bounds on the maximum beam width allowable in order to save energy and compare our theoretical results to experimentally derived bounds. As part of the derivation of our upper bound for directional antennae, we present simple algorithms for achieving k-connectivity in sensor networks.

1.1   Model of Sensors

We consider two types of antennas: omnidirectional and directional. The former transmit their signal over a 360 degree angle and, for the purposes of this paper, any sensor within the reachability radius of this sensor will receive the signal. The latter are directional antennas that can be aimed and have a given beam width α. They can be thought of as either being on a "swivel" that can be oriented towards a target or equivalently that each such sensor has multiple antennas each occupying a sector with beam width α so as to cover a 360 degree angle (in fact $\lceil 2\pi/\alpha \rceil$ of these antennas would suffice). However, the sensor does not necessarily have to activate all these antennas at the same time. Instead, it will aim at a neighboring "target region or node" by activating the appropriate antenna so as to cover a region in a given direction.

1.2   Energy Consumption

In any wireless network signals must be transmitted and received with sufficient strength in order to be properly detected and interpreted. For any kind of unguided, wireless media the signal disperses and falls off with distance over the transmission medium. Although attenuation is in general a complex function of the distance and the makeup of the atmosphere, a significant cause of signal degradation is simply *free space loss* which is due to the fact that the signal spreads over an ever larger area. For an ideal isotropic antenna free space loss is measured as the ratio of the transmitted to received power and is equal to $\frac{(4\pi d)^2}{\lambda^2}$, where λ is the carrier wavelength, and d is the propagation distance between antennas. In particular, the energy required by an antenna to reach all hosts within its radius is proportional to the area covered. Thus, with a reachability radius r an omnidirectional antenna will consume power proportional to πr^2 (the area of a circle with radius r) while a directional antenna with beam width α radians will consume power proportional to $\frac{\alpha}{2}r^2$, whereby we assume that the signal is transmitted over the primary lobe and the power consumed by the remaining lobes is negligible. For additional information on antenna performance see Ramanathan [18] and on antenna theory see Balanis [2].

1.3   Results of the Paper

The core of the paper is divided into two sections. First, in Section 2 we consider the case where the sensors are dropped on a unit length line segment. In Section 3 we consider the case where the sensors are dropped on a unit square. In both cases first we provide a sensor orientation algorithm and subsequently we study the energy consumption of the resulting sensor network. We also give a sufficient condition on the beam width of the antenna so that directional sensors consume less energy to achieve the same connectivity of the resulting sensor network. Table 1 summarizes our theoretical results. In Section 4 we provide experimental analysis.

Table 1. For the threshold value of the beam width indicated in the right column the energy consumption of a sensor network of n directional sensors is below the energy consumption of a sensor network of n omnidirectional sensors so as to achieve $(k + 1)$-connectivity with probability at least $e^{-e^{-c}} - e^{-e^{c}}$

	Threshold beam width
Unit Segment	$\frac{\pi}{2} \cdot \left(\frac{\ln n + k \ln\ln n + \ln(k!) - c}{\ln n + (2k+1)\ln\ln n + c} \right)^2$
Unit Square	$\frac{2}{5(k+1)} \cdot \left(\frac{\ln n + k \ln\ln n + \ln(k!)}{\ln n + k \ln\ln n + c} \right)$

1.4   Related Work and Preliminaries

Directional antennas have not been explored widely in the context of ad-hoc networks. Some recent papers exploring multiple beam antennas in order to increase throughput, and reduce delay and routing overhead include [9, 13, 18, 22]. To date, however, we are not aware of any work that has considered a comparison of the energy efficiency of omnidirectional versus directional antennas with respect to connectivity properties of the network. Related to our work is the paper of Shakkottai et al [20] which addresses coverage and connectivity for a restricted model of omnidirectional sensors occupying the vertices of a unit square grid and to the paper of Kranakis et al [10] which investigates the more general model of directional sensors with given beam width occupying arbitrary positions (as opposed to grid points) in the interior of the unit square.

Useful for our analysis is the coupon collector's problem and its extensions. In particular, an extension of the coupon collectors problem is that of determining the threshold for the number (denoted by $X^{(k)}$) of selections (coupons) required in order to collect at least $k + 1$ copies of each coupon type. It is well-known (see Motwani et al. [12][Exercise 3.11]) that the sharp threshold is centered at $n(\ln n + k \ln \ln n)$, i.e., for any integer $k \geq 0$ and constant c,

$$\lim_{n \to \infty} \Pr[X^{(k)} > n(\ln n + k \ln \ln n + c)] = e^{-e^{-c}}. \tag{1}$$

It is useful to note for $c > 0$ large enough the term $e^{-e^{-c}}$ in the righthand side of Equation 1 is arbitrarily close to 1 and for $c < 0$ large enough it is arbitrarily close to 0.

Valuable for our theoretical analysis are also the studies on thresholds for the connectivity and minimum node degree, as well as general thresholds for monotone properties in geometric disk graphs that can be found in the work of Penrose [15, 16, 17]. Related bounds can be found in [6, 7, 19, 23]

2   Sensors on a Unit Length Line Segment

In this section we limit our region to the unit length segment. We consider $(k + 1)$-connectivity and contrast the energy consumption of omnidirectional versus directional antennas. For clarity of exposition, we separate the connectivity analysis for omnidirectional and directional antennas.

2.1   Omnidirectional Sensors

Assume that n omnidirectional sensors are dropped randomly and independently with the uniform distribution on the interior of a unit segment. For any integer $k \geq 1$ and real number constant c let the sensors have identical radius r, given by the formula

$$r = \frac{\ln n + k \ln \ln n + \ln(k!) - c}{n}. \tag{2}$$

The main result of Penrose [15][Theorems 1.1 and 1.2] states that for the *toroidal distance metric* on a unit segment and the radius given by Identity 2

$$\lim_{n \to \infty} \Pr[\text{network is } (k + 1)\text{-connected}] = e^{-e^c}. \tag{3}$$

The toroidal distance metric differs from the usual distance metric on a unit segment only in the wraparound boundary effects. Therefore Formula 3 gives an upper bound on the probability of achieving $(k + 1)$-connectivity on a unit segment with the usual distance metric. Therefore we have the following theorem.

Theorem 1. *Consider omnidirectional antennas, with reachability radius r given by Formula 2, and suppose that $k \geq 0$ is an integer and $c > 0$ is a real. Assume n omnidirectional antennas are dropped randomly and independently with the uniform distribution on the interior of a unit segment. Then*

$$\lim_{n \to \infty} \Pr[\text{network is } (k + 1)\text{-connected}] \leq e^{-e^c}. \tag{4}$$

Thus, for the radius chosen by Formula 2 the network is $(k+1)$-connected with probability as indicated by Equation 4.

2.2 Directional Sensors

Consider the case of directional sensors each with a single antennae of beam width α that may be oriented in any direction. (We note that in the case of multiple antennae, an energy saving is trivially possible for any beam width by using two opposing antennae that cover the segment using the same radius as required by the omnidirectional case.) It is fairly easy to show that by aiming alternately $k+1$ antennae to the right along the segment followed by $k+1$ antennae to the left and insuring that each sensor reaches at least $2k+2$ other sensors, the resulting network is k-connected. For each sensor, we choose the radius to be

$$r = 2 \cdot \frac{\ln n + (2k+1)\ln\ln n + c}{n} \tag{5}$$

and partition the unit interval into $\frac{2}{r}$ subintervals each of length $\frac{r}{2}$. We must aim their beam in such a way that k-connectivity of the resulting network is guaranteed. Using Equation 1, it is easy to establish that each subinterval contains $2k+2$ sensors with probability at least $e^{-e^{-c}}$. Next we divide the sensors in each subinterval into two (approximately) equal size parts: the leftmost half and the rightmost half (see Figure 1). For each subinterval we direct the leftmost half

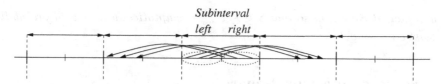

Subinterval

left   right

Fig. 1. Alternating the beam direction of the sensors from one subinterval to the next

of the sensors (at least $k+1$) to the right and the rightmost half of the sensors (also at least $k+1$) to the left. We can prove the following theorem.

Theorem 2. *Consider directional antennas with given beam width α, reachability radius r given by Formula 5, and suppose that $k \geq 0$ is an integer and $c > 0$ is a real. Assume n directional antennas are dropped randomly and independently with the uniform distribution on the interior of a unit length segment. Then*

$$\lim_{n\to\infty} \Pr[\text{network is } (k+1)\text{-connected}] \geq e^{-e^{-c}}. \tag{6}$$

2.3 Comparison of Energy Consumption

Omnidirectional sensors transmit the signal over an angle 2π. In order to achieve $(k+1)$-connectivity the resulting energy consumption $\mathcal{E}_{\text{OMNI}}^{(k)}$ of the network satisfies

$$\mathcal{E}_{\text{OMNI}}^{(k)} \geq n \cdot \pi \cdot \left(\frac{\ln n + k\ln\ln n + \ln(k!) - c}{n}\right)^2,$$

asymptotically in n with probability at least $1 - e^{-e^c}$. This can be contrasted with the energy consumption $\mathcal{E}_{\mathrm{DIRE}}^{(k)}$ required to achieve $k + 1$-connectivity of a network of directional sensors with beam width α (measured in radians). In particular, $\mathcal{E}_{\mathrm{DIRE}}^{(k)}$ satisfies

$$\mathcal{E}_{\mathrm{DIRE}}^{(k)} \leq n \cdot \frac{\alpha}{2} \cdot \left(2 \cdot \frac{\ln n + (2k + 1)\ln\ln n + c}{n} \right)^2,$$

asymptotically in n with probability at least e^{-e^c}. A simple calculation yields that asymptotically in n if

$$n \cdot \frac{\alpha}{2} \cdot \left(2 \cdot \frac{\ln n + (2k + 1)\ln\ln n + c}{n} \right)^2 \leq n \cdot \pi \cdot \left(\frac{\ln n + k \ln\ln n + \ln(k!) - c}{n} \right)^2$$

then $\mathcal{E}_{\mathrm{DIRE}}^{(k)} \leq \mathcal{E}_{\mathrm{OMNI}}^{(k)}$. We get the following result.

Theorem 3. *Consider an experiment in which n sensors are dropped randomly and independently in the interior of a unit length segment. Suppose that $k \geq 0$ is an integer and $c > 0$ is a real. Then*

$$\alpha \leq 2\pi \cdot \left(\frac{\ln n + k \ln\ln n + \ln(k!) - c}{\ln n + (2k + 1)\ln\ln n + c} \right)^2 \tag{7}$$

is a sufficient condition so that $\mathcal{E}_{\mathrm{DIRE}}^{(k)} \leq \mathcal{E}_{\mathrm{OMNI}}^{(k)}$ asymptotically in n with probability at least $e^{-e^{-c}} - e^{-e^c}$.

3   Sensors on a Unit Square

In this section we limit our region to the unit square. We consider $(k + 1)$-connectivity and contrast the energy consumption of omnidirectional versus directional antennas. We consider connectivity separately for omnidirectional and directional antennas.

3.1   Omnidirectional Sensors

Assume that n omnidirectional sensors are dropped randomly and independently with the uniform distribution on the interior of a unit square. For any integer $k \geq 0$ and real number constant c let the sensors have identical radius r, given by the formula

$$r = \sqrt{\frac{\ln n + k \ln\ln n + \ln(k!) - c}{n\pi}}. \tag{8}$$

The main result of Penrose [15][Theorems 1.1 and 1.2] states that for the *toroidal distance metric* on a unit square and the radius given by Identity 8

$$\lim_{n \to \infty} \Pr[\text{network is } (k + 1)\text{-connected}] = e^{-e^c}. \tag{9}$$

The toroidal distance metric differs from the usual distance metric on a unit square only in the wraparound boundary effects. Therefore Formula 9 gives an upper bound on the probability of achieving $(k+1)$-connectivity on a unit square with the usual distance metric. Therefore we have the following theorem.

Theorem 4. *Consider omnidirectional antennas, with reachability radius r given by Formula 8, and suppose that $k \geq 0$ is an integer and $c > 0$ is a real. Assume n omnidirectional antennas are dropped randomly and independently with the uniform distribution on the interior of a unit square. Then*

$$\lim_{n \to \infty} \Pr[network\ is\ (k+1)\text{-}connected] \leq e^{-e^c}. \tag{10}$$

Thus, for the radius chosen by Formula 8 the network is $(k+1)$-connected with probability as indicated by Equation 10.

3.2   Directional Sensors

Consider the case of directional sensors with $k+1$ beams, where $k \geq 0$ is an integer. Fix k and a constant $c > 0$. Partition the unit square into $\frac{1}{r^2}$ subsquares or blocks each of side r, where

$$r = \sqrt{\frac{\ln n + k \ln \ln n + c}{n}}. \tag{11}$$

Let the reachability radius r' of the directional sensors be equal to the length of the diagonal of a rectangle with dimensions $r \times (2r)$ (see Figure 2), i.e.,

$$r' = \sqrt{\frac{5(\ln n + k \ln \ln n + c)}{n}} = r\sqrt{5}. \tag{12}$$

Let $N^{(k)}$ be the random variable that counts the number of sensors to be dropped so that each subsquare contains $k+1$ sensors. In view of Identity 1,

$$\lim_{n \to \infty} \Pr\left[N^{(k)} > \frac{1}{r^2}\left(\ln\left(\frac{1}{r^2}\right) + k \ln \ln\left(\frac{1}{r^2}\right) + c\right)\right] = e^{-e^{-c}}. \tag{13}$$

Now assume that n sensors each of radius r (given in Equation 11) are dropped on the interior of the unit square. Since $n > 1/r^2$, we have that

$$n = \frac{n(\ln n + k \ln \ln n + c)}{\ln n + k \ln \ln n + c} > \frac{1}{r^2}\left(\ln\left(\frac{1}{r^2}\right) + k \ln \ln\left(\frac{1}{r^2}\right) + c\right).$$

By Equation 1 we have that each subsquare will have $k+1$ sensors with probability at least $e^{-e^{-c}}$. Now we must provide an "antenna orientation" algorithm to direct the sensor beams in such a way that connectivity in the unit square is guaranteed.

Number the sensors in a given square $1, \ldots, t+1$. (Assume sensors have unique identities and so they can order themselves. This set up phase can be done using broadcast in all directions.) For $i = 1, \ldots, t+1$ the sensors numbered i in each square form themselves into a hamiltonian cycle that visits every square using one of their $k + 1$ antennae. Sensor i in each square then uses its k remaining antennae to point at sensor $j \neq i$ in its square. We claim the result is $k + 1$-connected. Say sensor i in block B wants to talk to sensor j in block C. If k sensors fail, there is still a hamiltonian cycle (say nodes numbered m) that is completely alive. Node i sends its message to node m in block B, node m in block B sends the message to node m in block C, which in turn sends it to node j in block C. Therefore the network is $(k + 1)$-connected. Two important points are the following

1. Some blocks have more than k sensors. These sensors can be distributed arbitrarily among the cycles.
2. The longest any antennae has to reach is $r\sqrt{5}$, where r is the side length required to have $k+1$ nodes per square. (Note: in the worst case an antennae must reach across the diagonal of a $2r$ by r rectangle.)

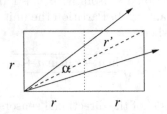

Fig. 2. The radius r' of the directional sensors is determined by the geometry of two adjacent subsquares. in particular it must be chosen so that $r' \geq r\sqrt{5}$

In particular, regardless of the beam width, the resulting system of directional antennas must be $k + 1$-connected with high probability. We can prove the following theorem.

Theorem 5. *Consider directional antennas with given beam width α, reachability radius r given by Formula 12, and suppose that $k \geq 0$ is an integer and $c > 0$ is a real. Assume n directional antennas are dropped randomly and independently with the uniform distribution on the interior of a unit square. Then*

$$\lim_{n \to \infty} \Pr[network\ is\ (k + 1)\text{-}connected] \geq e^{-e^{-c}}. \tag{14}$$

We note that if we assume that the nodes have unique identities (e.g., if they can compute their geographic location through a GPS system) then the algorithm in Theorem 5 can be implemented fairly easily in a distributed manner. We further note that by using a small number of extra antennae aimed at sensors in the other adjacent subsquares can lead to an improvement in the diameter of the resulting sensor system from approximately n/k to $\sqrt{n/k}$.

3.3 Comparison of Energy Efficiency

In this section we compare the energy consumption of a sensor network of n omnidirectional versus n directional sensors to attain $(k + 1)$-connectivity. Let $\mathcal{E}_{\text{OMNI}}^{(k)}$ and $\mathcal{E}_{\text{DIRE}}^{(k)}$ be the energy consumption in the omnidirectional and directional case respectively, to attain $(k + 1)$-connectivity.

Omnidirectional sensors transmit the signal over an angle 2π. In order to achieve $(k + 1)$-connectivity n omnidirectional sensors are necessary and the resulting energy consumption of the network satisfies

$$\mathcal{E}_{\text{OMNI}}^{(k)} \geq n \cdot \pi \cdot \frac{\ln n + k \ln \ln n + \ln(k!) - c}{n\pi},$$

asymptotically in n with probability at least $1 - e^{-e^c}$. This can be contrasted with the energy consumption $\mathcal{E}_{\text{DIRE}}^{(k)}$ of a network of directional sensors with beam width α (measured in radians) which may transmit the signal over an angle α. In this case, $\mathcal{E}_{\text{DIRE}}^{(k)}$ satisfies

$$\mathcal{E}_{\text{DIRE}}^{(k)} \leq n(k + 1) \cdot \frac{\alpha}{2} \cdot \frac{5(\ln n + k \ln \ln n + c)}{n},$$

asymptotically in n with probability at least $e^{-e^{-c}}$. It is clear that, with high probability asymptotically in n if

$$\frac{5(k + 1)\alpha}{2} \cdot (\ln n + k \ln \ln n + c) \leq \ln n + k \ln \ln n + \ln(k!) - c$$

then $\mathcal{E}_{\text{DIRE}}^{(k)} \leq \mathcal{E}_{\text{OMNI}}^{(k)}$. A simple calculation yields the following theorem comparing the energy consumption of a sensor network of n omnidirectional versus n directional sensors to attain $(k + 1)$-connectivity.

Theorem 6. *Consider an experiment in which n sensors are dropped randomly and independently in the interior of a unit square. Assume $k \geq 0$ is an integer and $c > 0$ is a real. Then*

$$\alpha \leq \frac{2}{5(k + 1)} \cdot \left(\frac{\ln n + k \ln \ln n + \ln(k!) - c}{\ln n + k \ln \ln n + c} \right) \tag{15}$$

is a sufficient condition so that $\mathcal{E}_{\text{DIRE}}^{(k)} \leq \mathcal{E}_{\text{OMNI}}^{(k)}$ asymptotically in n with probability at least $e^{-e^{-c}} - e^{-e^c}$.

4 Experimental Results

The theoretical results presented above, while providing a true bound on α, are based in part upon approximations and hold only asymptotically in n. In order to get an idea of how accurate our estimates are we provide the results of some simulations we performed on our simple model.

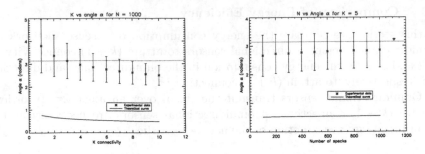

Fig. 3. Simulation results for unit segment

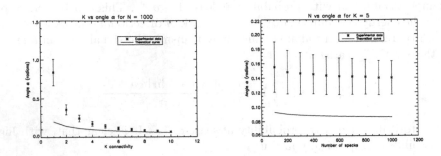

Fig. 4. Simulation results for unit square

For both the one dimensional and two dimensional cases we considered values of k ranging from 1 to 10 and values of n ranging from 100 to 1000 by 100. Figure 3 depicts simulation results for unit segments. Figure 4 depicts simulation results for unit squares. Each experiment consisted of dropping n sensors at random on either the unit segment or the unit square. For a given k, a lower bound on the radius required to achieve k-connectivity for omnidirectional antennae was obtained by finding the distance to the k-th nearest neighbor and an upper bound on the radius required to achieve k-connectivity using directional antennae was obtained using the algorithms described above. Each experiment was repeated 10,000 times and the average of all 10,000 runs along with error estimates were reported. The energy requirements in each case were computed using the model above and the ratios of the energy were plotted and compared to the theoretical result. We present the results of plotting α (the maximum beam width allowable to achieve energy savings) versus n for $k = 5$ as well as plotting α versus k for $n = 1000$. Plots for the other values of k and n are similar.

We observe that the theoretical bounds predict the shape of the curves quite well although for small values of n and k they significantly underestimate the value of α sufficient to ensure lower energy for the directional case. For the two dimensional case, we see that the theoretical curve approximates the experimental results quite well as k increases. While the theoretical predictions should improve in accuracy as n increases, it seems clear that a gap will always exist.

We suspect that this is due to approximations made in our upper bounds for the directional case that may be improved using a better analysis.

References

1. J. Agre and L. Clare, An integrated architecture for cooperative sensing networks, IEEE Computer, vol. 33, no. 5, May 2000, 106-108.
2. C. A. Balanis, Antenna Theory: Analysis and Design, 2nd ed. New York: Wiley, 1997.
3. D. Braginsky and D. Estrin, Rumor routing algorithm for sensor networks, 2001. Available at http://lecs.cs.ucla.edu/ estrin/.
4. L. Doherty, L. E. Ghaoui, and K. S. J. Pister, Convex position estimation in wireless sensor networks, in Proceedings of IEEE Infocom, (Anchorage, AK), April 2001.
5. D. Estrin, R. Govindan, J. Heidemann and S. Kumar: Next Century Challenges: Scalable Coordination in Sensor Networks. In Proc. 5th ACM/IEEE International Conference on Mobile Computing, MOBICOM'1999.
6. A. Goel, S. Rai, B. Krishnamachari, Sharp Thresholds for Monotone Properties in Random Geometric Graphs. Stanford University, Manuscript, 2003.
7. P. Gupta and P. R. Kumar, Critical Power for Asymptotic Connectivity in Wireless Networks. Stochastic Analysis, Control, Optimization, and Applications, Birkhauser, 1998.
8. J. M. Kahn, R. H. Katz, and K. S. J. Pister, Mobile networking for smart dust, in Proceedings of MobiCom 99, (Seattle, WA), August 1999.
9. Y. B. Ko, V. Shankarkumar, and N. H. Vaidya, Medium access control protocols using directional antennas in ad-hoc networks, Proc. IEEE INFOCOM'2000, March 2000.
10. E. Kranakis, D. Krizanc, J. Urrutia, Coverage and Connectivity in Networks with Directional Sensors. In proceedings Euro-Par Conference, Pisa, Italy, August 31-September 3, 2004, Danelutto M., Vanneschi M., Laforenza D. (Eds.), Vol. 3149, Springer Verlag, LNCS.
11. S. Meguerdichian, F. Koushanfar, M. Potkonjak, and M. Srivastava, Coverage problems in wireless ad-hoc sensor networks, in Proceedings of IEEE Infocom, (Anchorage, AK), 2001.
12. R. Motwani, P. Raghavan, Randomized Algorithms, Cambridge University Press, 1995.
13. A. Nasipuri, S. Ye, J. You, and R. E. Hiromoto, A MAC protocol for mobile ad hoc networks using directional antennas, Proc. IEEE Wireless Communications and Networking Conference (WCNC'2000), 2000.
14. National Research Council, Embedded, Everywhere: A Research Agenda for Systems of Embedded Computers, Committee on Networked Systems of Embedded Computers, for the Computer Science and Telecommunications Board, Division on Engineering and Physical Sciences, Washington, DC, 2001.
15. M. D. Penrose, On k-Connectivity for a Geometric Random Graph, Random Structures and Algorithms, 15, 145-164, 1999.
16. M. D. Penrose, The Longest Edge of the Random Minimal Spanning Tree, The Annals of Applied Probability, 7(2) 1997, 340-361.
17. M. D. Penrose, Random Geometric Graphs, Oxford University Press, 2003.
18. R. Ramanathan, On the Performance of Ad Hoc Networks with Beamforming Antennas, In the Proceedings of ACM Symposium on Mobile Ad hoc Networking and Computing (MobiHoc'2001), 2001.

19. P. Santi and D. Blough, The Critical Transmitting Range for Connectivity in Sparse Wireless Ad Hoc Networks, IEEE Transactions on Mobile Computing, to appear.
20. S. Shakkottai, R. Srikant, N. Shroff, Unreliable Sensor Grids: Coverage, Connectivity and Diameter, In proceedings of IEEE INFOCOM, 2003, held in San Francisco, March 30 to April 2, 2003.
21. K. Sohrabi, J. Gao, V. Ailawadhi, and G. Pottie, Protocols for self- organization of a wireless sensor network, IEEE Personal Communications, vol. 7, pp. 16-27, October 2000.
22. A. Spyropoulos, and C.S. Raghavendra, Energy Efficient Communications in Ad Hoc Networks Using Directional Antennas, in proceedings of INFOCOM 2002, New York, June 23-27, 2002.
23. P.-J. Wan and C.-W. Yi, Asymptotic Critical Transmission Radius and Critical Neighbor Number for k-connectivity in Wireless Ad Hoc Networks, Mobihoc, 2004, to appear.
24. B. Warneke, M. Last, B. Leibowitz, and K. Pister, SmartDust: communicating with a cubic-millimeter computer, IEEE Computer, vol. 34, no. 1, January 2001, 44-51.
25. W. Ye, J. Heidemann, and D. Estrin, An energy-efficient MAC protocol for wireless sensor networks, in Proceedings of IEEE Infocom, (New York, NY), June 2002.

Secure Location Verification
Using Radio Broadcast

Adnan Vora and Mikhail Nesterenko*

Computer Science Department,
Kent State University, Kent, OH, 44242
avora@cs.kent.edu, mikhail@cs.kent.edu

Abstract. *Secure location verification* is a recently stated problem that has a number of practical applications. The problem requires a wireless sensor network to confirm that a potentially malicious *prover* is located in a designated area. The original solution to the problem, as well as solutions to related problems, exploits the difference between propagation speeds of radio and sound waves to estimate the position of the prover. In this paper, we propose a solution that leverages the broadcast nature of the radio signal emitted by the prover and the distributed topology of the network. The idea is to separate the functions of the sensors. Some sensors are placed such that they get the signal from the prover if it is inside the protected area. The others are positioned so that they can only get the signal from the prover outside the area. Hence the latter sensors reject the prover if they hear its signal. Our solution is versatile and deals with provers using either omni-directional or directional propagation of radio signals without requiring any special hardware besides a radio transceiver. We estimate the bounds on the number of sensors required to protect the areas of various shapes and extend our solution to handle complex radio signal propagation, optimize sensor placement and operate without precise topology information.

Keywords: location verification, wireless sensor networks, security.

1 Introduction

The problem of secure location verification is stated by Sastry et al [1]. The problem is to confirm the physical presence of the principal (prover) in a protection zone. Location verification has a number of uses such as target tracking, smart inventory, location-based access control, etc. For example, once the presence of the prover has been confirmed, it can be granted access privileges such as connection to a private wireless network, starting a car, opening doors to a restricted area or disabling an alarm.

---

* This research was supported in part by DARPA contract OSU-RF#F33615-01-C-1901 and by NSF CAREER Award 0347485.

T. Higashino (Ed.): OPODIS 2004, LNCS 3544, pp. 369–383, 2005.

Related work. The close interaction of computing devices with the physical environment requires novel approaches to security. Naik et al. [2] adopt security techniques to the constraints and demands of such systems. Alternatively, in this paper we exploit the properties of the environment to solve the security task.

A number of researchers commented on the importance of location verification in wireless sensor networks [3, 4, 1]. There are many protocols that achieve location verification by exploiting the difference between radio signal propagation and ultra-sound, etc. Particularly, Hu et al. use temporal packet leashes [5], Brands et al. use a time-bounded challenge-response protocol [6]. A limitation of these schemes is the necessity of highly accurate time measurement capabilities and possibly non-RF communication hardware on the sensor nodes.

Balfanz et al. [3] use location-limited channels for location verification; however, the lack of location-limited channels may abridge the suitability of this method. Moreover, this method does not provide any strong security guarantees [1]. Corner and Noble [7] use short-range communication to verify proximity. However, their scheme fails if a malicious user is able to send data from a distance using a powerful transmitter. Kindber et al. [8] use constrained channels to limit transmission range of the prover, but their protocol does not provide strong security guarantees either. Tamper-resistant hardware is used in the industry to provide location authentication [9].

Our contribution and paper organization. We propose a location verification protocol that relies on the broadcast nature of radio communication and cooperation of the sensor nodes. Intuitively, once the prover issues a radio signal, sensors in its vicinity will receive the signal, while remote sensors will not. The sensor nodes can then compare their readings to estimate the reception area, and thus determine the presence of the prover. Our protocol is resource efficient, and it does not require extended sensor capabilities needed for time-of-flight location estimation approaches.

In the presentation of the paper we strive to make the material as accessible as possible. Thus, we first discuss the solution to the simplest problem with the strongest assumptions about the environment and security threats (e.g. perfect signal reception, omni-directional antennas of the attackers). At first we do not discuss the distributed implementation of our algorithm. We then relax each assumption and extend our solution to more a realistic specification. To keep our paper focused we do not present a complete system that is capable of protecting against a wide spectrum of security threats such as node compromise. However, in the end of the paper we discuss how our protocol can be incorporated into such a system.

The specific contributions of this paper are as follows. We restate the location verification problem [1] in Section 2, in a way that allows its formal treatment and suggests a range of solutions. Using this as a basis, we present a generic protocol for location verification. We outline its properties in Section 3.

In Section 4, we demonstrate that an arbitrary polygonal protection zone can be completely secured with $O(n)$ sensors where n is the number of sides in the polygon. The basic protocol may leave out certain portions of the protection zone where the prover may or may not be accepted (ambiguity zone). In the same section, we also show that an arbitrary (non-polygonal) zone can be secured with $O(S + P)$ sensors such that the ambiguity zone occupies a band of constant thickness around the border, where S and P are the zone's area and perimeter respectively.

In the basic protocol, the number of verification attempts before the prover is accepted is proportional to the size of the zone. In Section 6, we show that this number can be decreased to the logarithm of the zone size by using extra verifiers. In Section 7, we show how the prover can be accepted in the ambiguity zone with extra verification attempts, and we also estimate the number of such attempts to be proportional to the logarithm of the protection zone size.

We provide a few extensions to our basic protocol. In addition to the simple broadcast model using omni-directional radio signals, which defines a fixed-sized circular area of perfect reception around the radio source, in Section 8, we extend the protocol to deal with the complex broadcast model, which introduces a band of non-deterministic reception around the area of perfect reception. In Section 5, we provide further modifications to defend against adversaries that use directional radio signals to defeat the protocol. In this case the adversaries are capable of generating signals with non-zero gain, which distorts the shape of the signal propagation area. In Section 9, we provide the protocol for location verification where arbitrary verifier placement is used instead of a calculated, deterministic placement. In Section 10 we conclude the paper by discussing how our protocol can be extended to a complete security system.

2   Preliminaries

Definitions. The location verification problem requires a set of verifiers to accept a prover if it is located in a designated *protection zone*. A *verifier* is a sensor capable of communicating with the other verifiers as well as the prover. A *prover* is a mobile entity requesting access to the resources that are guarded by the verifiers. The verifiers *accept* the prover, if it is present in the protection zone and behaves according to the *communication rules*. Otherwise, the verifiers either *reject* the prover or issue no decision.

There are two kinds of verifiers: an *acceptor* and a *rejector*. The plane is divided into three zones according to the verifier's ability to locate the prover: the *acceptance zone* — a prover in this zone is always accepted if it behaves according to the communication rules; the *ambiguity zone* — a prover in this zone may or may not be accepted (regardless of the prover's adherence to the communication rules); and the *rejection zone* — a prover in this zone is never accepted.

For a particular protection zone a verification protocol is *secure* if every point outside the protection zone is also in the rejection zone. The verifiers *secure* the protection zone. *Protection gap* is the maximum distance between a point in the rejection zone and the nearest point outside the protection zone. Notice that this distance is only meaningful for points inside the protection zone. Hence, the protection gap is a measure of how much the rejection zone encroaches upon the protection zone. Protection is *complete* if the protection gap is zero.

Assumptions and threat model. The verifiers are able to communicate securely and reliably amongst themselves. The verifiers are trusted. That is, a malicious entity cannot either disrupt the communication between verifiers or impersonate a verifier. We do not focus on communication issues between verifiers. Throughout the rest of the paper, we assume that the data that one verifier records is available to the other verifiers as needed.

If the verifiers send a message to the prover, the prover is always able to receive it. Prover authentication is not required. That is, any entity that communicates with the verifiers is considered a prover. The prover is able to configure its radio transmitter so that the radio signal propagates to an arbitrary fixed distance. Both the signal transmission and reception are instantaneous.

We consider an *omni-directional* radio propagation model for the prover. In this model, if a prover sends a signal, every verifier within some fixed distance of the prover receives it, while no verifier that is further away does. This distance depends on the signal strength of the prover. We relax the omni-directionality assumption in Section 5 and the perfect circular reception assumption in Section 8.

The prover may be malicious. A malicious prover does not have to comply with the verification protocol. Multiple provers may collude to defeat the verification protocol. In the case of multiple provers, the provers may be able to synchronize their signals perfectly and time them with high accuracy. If all malicious provers are in the rejection zone, none of them is supposed to be accepted.

Problem statement. We adapt the problem statement from [1].

Problem 1 (Location Verification). Given a closed protection zone, specify a secure location verification protocol.

Observe that the only requirement on the protection zone is that it be closed, i.e. the zone does not have to be connected.

3   Location Verification Protocol

Verification protocol. Our verification protocol rules are as follows. *The prover remains stationary during verification. It sends a radio signal so that verifiers within the distance of the signal increment x can hear it. If the prover does not receive their decision, it increases its signal strength by x and rebroadcasts the signal. The procedure repeats until the verifiers respond. When one of the verifiers hears the prover, the verifiers form a decision. They accept the prover if none of the rejectors hear it and reject it otherwise.*

Basic Protocol Properties.

Lemma 1. *A certain point on the plane is in the rejection zone if and only if the distance from this point to the nearest acceptor is no less than that to the nearest rejector.*

Proof: **If:** We show that when multiple malicious provers are located as stated in the lemma, the only decision that the verifiers can make is reject. Note that the cardinality of the set of malicious provers is not limited. Also, since the signal transmission is instantaneous, we can consider that there is a stationary prover at every point from which a mobile prover sends a signal. Hence, we can ignore the mobility of the provers.

According to the communication rules, the accept decision is reached when at least one acceptor and no rejectors hear the prover's signal. For the acceptor to hear the signal, the signal strength should be high enough to cover the distance from the prover to the acceptor. However, every prover is no further from the nearest rejector than from an acceptor. Due to our signal propagation assumption, if an acceptor receives the signal from the prover, then at least one rejector must have also heard it. In this case, according to the communication rules, the verifiers reject the prover. Thus, each point that is at least as far away from the nearest acceptor as from the nearest rejector is in the rejection zone.

Only if: We prove the contrapositive. Suppose that for a certain point p on a plane, the distance to the nearest acceptor is less than that to the nearest rejector. Let the prover be located at p and broadcast with the minimal signal strength necessary for the acceptor to receive the signal. In this case, according to the signal propagation assumptions, the rejector does not hear the prover. By the communication rules of the protocol, the prover is accepted. By definition, a prover is never accepted in any point of the rejection zone. Hence, p is not in the rejection zone. Thus, for every point in the rejection zone it is necessary to be at least as far from the nearest acceptor as from the nearest rejector.   □

To state our results more formally, we define a few terms from computational geometry. By definition [10–Ch.5], a verifier's Voronoi cell is the area that is closer to this verifier than to any other verifier. Thus, any point in a rejector's cell (including the boundary) is at least as close to the rejector as to the nearest acceptor. The following theorem follows from Lemma 1.

Theorem 1. *For the location verification protocol to be secure it is necessary and sufficient that the union of the rejectors' Voronoi cells covers the area outside the protection zone.*

Recall that the statement of location verification problem requires that the protection zone be finite. A non-trivial solution to the problem needs at least one acceptor. From Theorem 1, it follows that the Voronoi cell of each acceptor must be finite. It can be easily shown that the minimum number of objects (verifiers) to form a finite Voronoi cell is four. Moreover, these four objects produce only one finite cell. Hence the following corollary.

Corollary 1. *A non-trivial solution to the location verification problem requires at least four verifiers (one acceptor and three rejectors).*

Lemma 2. *A certain point on the plane is in the acceptance zone if the nearest acceptor is at least one signal increment (x) closer to this point than the nearest rejector.*

Observe that the statement of this lemma is not symmetric to that of Lemma 1. The "only if" part of Lemma 2 in general does not hold.

Proof: Let the nearest acceptor and the nearest rejector be at the respective distances a and $b > a + x$ from the point of interest. According to the communication rules, the acceptor receives the signal from the prover after $\lceil a/x \rceil$ tries. Hence, the distance of the signal propagation is:

$$\left\lceil \frac{a}{x} \right\rceil x \;\leq\; \left(\frac{a}{x} + 1\right) x \;=\; a + x \;<\; b$$

Thus, when the nearest acceptor receives the signal from the prover, the rejectors are still too far from the prover to have also received the signal.   □

Observe that Lemmas 1 and 2 delineate acceptance and rejection zones only. Yet these two zones do not cover the whole plane. The remaining area is the ambiguity zone. In this zone, every point is closer to the nearest acceptor than to a rejector but the difference in the respective distances is less than the signal increment. The reason for the existence of this zone is the following. The prover increments its signal by x each time it broadcasts. For a prover in the ambiguity zone, it is possible that the signal is too weak for the verifiers to receive it. Yet when the signal is incremented by x and rebroadcast, both an acceptor and a rejector hear it. According to the protocol, the verifiers reject the prover. However, the points of the ambiguity zone are closer to an acceptor than to a rejector. Hence, a prover that does not follow the protocol may tune its signal strength such that an acceptor hears it even though none of the rejectors do. Thus, this prover is accepted.

In the solution that Corollary 1 suggests, the protection gap can be arbitrarily large. Indeed, since the number of verifiers is fixed, the shape of the acceptor's Voronoi cell is rather rigid and the boundary of the protection zone can deviate arbitrarily far from this shape. The following lemma allows complete protection of a polygonal protection zone.

Lemma 3. *Given an n-sided convex polygonal protection zone, it is possible to secure the protection zone completely using n + 1 verifiers.*

Proof: Let us place an acceptor at an arbitrary point in the protection zone. Also, we place each rejector so that the bisector of the line joining this rejector and the acceptor contains the side of the protection zone as a segment. Since the protection zone is convex, the Voronoi cell of the only acceptor matches the protection zone. Hence, the union of the rejectors' Voronoi cells covers the area outside the protection zone. According to Theorem 1, the protocol is secure. By definition, the protection provided by this placement of verifiers is complete. The total number of verifiers is $n + 1$.

Lemma 4. *Given an n-sided convex polygonal protection zone containing a circle of radius r, $n + 1$ verifiers can completely secure this protection zone such that the acceptance zone contains an open disk with radius $r - x/2$.*

Proof: To estimate the size of the acceptance zone, refer to Figure 1. The protection zone contains a circle of radius r. We position the acceptor at the center of the circle and the rejectors outside the protection zone, as described in the proof of Lemma 3. Note that Lemma 3 holds regardless of the exact position of the acceptor inside the polygon. Consider a concentric open disk of radius $r - x/2$. The distance between every point in this disk and its nearest rejector is greater than $r + x/2$. Hence, for every point of the disk, the distance to the acceptor is less than that to the nearest rejector by x. According to Lemma 2, the disk is inside the acceptance zone.   □

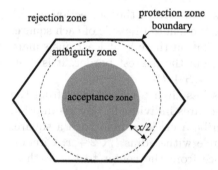

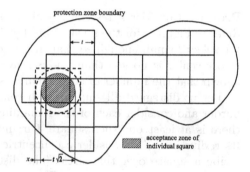

Fig. 1. Zone delineation in case of a polygonal protection zone. Illustration to the proof of Lemma 4

Fig. 2. Covering a zone of arbitrary shape with a constant ambiguity gap. Illustration for the proof of Theorem 3

4   Securing Arbitrary Zones

To address the security of arbitrary polygons, we expand our protocol as follows. A protection zone may be decomposed into a number of smaller sub-zones. The sub-zones are secured separately. In other words, the verifiers of one sub-zone do not interact with the verifiers of another. The prover is accepted in the aggregate zone if it is accepted by the verifiers of at least one of the constituent sub-zones. Using the expanded protocol, we derive the upper bound on the number of verifiers needed for protection zones of arbitrary shape. We state our results in the following two theorems.

Theorem 2. *An arbitrary n-sided polygonal protection zone can be completely secured by $O(n)$ verifiers.*

Proof: The number of triangles required to triangulate an n-sided polygon is $n-2$. According to Lemma 3, it takes 4 verifiers to secure a triangle completely. Thus, the total number of verifiers required to secure an n-sided protection zone is $4n-8$. The theorem follows.   □

Observe that the solution that the proof of Theorem 2 suggests, may potentially leave the aggregate acceptance zone disconnected. This may complicate the positioning of the prover for acceptance. The following theorem bounds the number of verifiers necessary to secure an arbitrary protection zone such that the acceptance zone is continuous and its boundary is within a constant distance from the boundary of the protection zone. To state this fact, we define *ambiguity gap* to be the maximum distance from a point in the ambiguity zone to the nearest point outside the protection zone.

Theorem 3. *The number of verifiers required to secure an arbitrary-shaped protection zone of area S and perimeter P with a constant ambiguity gap is in $O(S+P)$.*

Proof: Consider a tessellation of squares that covers the protection zone.[1] Refer to Figure 2 for the illustration. Let t be the length of a side of each square. We select t small enough so that in the tessellation there is at least one square whose center is no less than $t + x\sqrt{2}$ away from the nearest border. It is well-known that the number of such squares is in $O(S+P)$.

Let us disregard all squares with centers less than $t + x\sqrt{2}$ away from the border and consider each of the remaining squares individually. By assumption there is at least one such square. Circumscribe a circle around such a square. Its radius is $t/\sqrt{2}$. Consider a concentric circle with radius $t/\sqrt{2} + x$. Circumscribe a square over this circle. The distance from the center to the furthest point in this square is $t + x\sqrt{2}$. By construction, the square is completely inside the protection zone. According to Lemma 3, it takes 5 verifiers to secure this square completely. Moreover, from Lemma 4 the internal square will be inside the acceptance zone. Repeat the process for all the squares of the tessellation. The combined acceptance zone is continuous, and the ambiguity gap is no more than $t + x\sqrt{2}$. Since it takes a constant number of verifiers to cover each square, the total number of verifiers is in $O(S+P)$.   □

5   Directional Antennas

In the discussion thus far, we assume that the malicious provers follow the omni-directional broadcast model. Malicious provers, however, may be equipped with directional antennas, allowing them to add a non-zero gain in a particular direction, thereby distorting the shape of the reception area. A malicious prover

---

[1] The proof does not depend on the shape of the polygons. The squares are used for simplicity.

can exploit the directionality of the signal to defeat the verifiers. Such a prover directs a narrow beam of radio signal such that the signal avoids reception by the rejectors but targets acceptors. Thus, the prover may violate the security of the protocol.

Consider a maximal sector inside the propagation area of the emitted directional signal. A signal is definitely received in every point of this sector. *Beamwidth* β is the minimum angle among the sectors that correspond to propagation areas of various signal strengths. We assume that malicious provers cannot make their beamwidth arbitrarily small, i.e. β is constant.

The following lemma is equivalent to Lemma 1. It is proven similarly.

Lemma 5. *Provided that malicious provers are capable of using directional antennas with fixed minimum beamwidth β, a certain point on the plane is in the rejection zone if every sector of angle β originating in this point and containing an acceptor also contains a rejector.*

Observe that a benign prover uses only omni-directional antennas. Hence, the acceptance criterion of Lemma 2 applies to it.

Theorem 4. *It is possible to secure an arbitrary shaped protection zone against malicious provers with directional antennas using $O(r)$ verifiers where r is the size of the circle inscribed in the protection zone.*

Proof: Consider a circle of radius $r - k > 0$ that is concentric with the circle inscribed in the protection zone where is k is a constant independent of r. Refer to Figure 3 for illustration. Place a single acceptor in the middle of this circle and the rejectors on its circumference at a distance of $2k \cdot \tan(\beta/2)$ from each other. Observe that conditions of Lemma 5 are satisfied for every point outside the inscribed circle. Therefore, every point outside the protection zone is in the rejection zone. According to the specification of the location verification problem such a placement of the verifiers secures the protection zone.

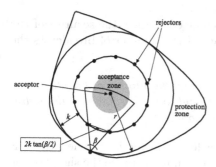

Fig. 3. Placing rejectors to protect against malicious provers with directional antennas. Illustration for the proof of Theorem 4

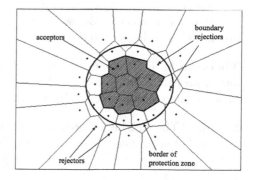

Fig. 4. Zone delineation with random verifier placement

The number of required verifiers is:

$$1 + \left\lceil \frac{2\pi(r-k)}{2k\tan(\beta/2)} \right\rceil$$

Since k and β are constant, the number of verifiers are in $O(r)$.   □

Observe that the verifier placement discussed in the proof of Theorem 4 can potentially yield an empty acceptance zone. For a non-trivial solution $r - k$ has to be large enough so that a circle with this radius contains a polygon satisfying the conditions of Theorem 4.

6   Logarithmic Verification Time

According to the communication rules of our protocol, the prover repeatedly broadcasts its signal until it hears from the verifiers. The prover increases its signal strength by x each time. Let d be the largest distance between any two points in the acceptance zone. Since the acceptors and the verifiers have to be inside the protection zone, the maximum number of broadcasts is $\lceil d/x \rceil$, i.e. it is proportional to the size of the protection zone. However, with a particular layout of the sensors and a modification of the protocol, this number can be made proportional to the logarithm of the size of the zone.

In order to do this, we put the following extra assumption on the placement of acceptors. *For every point in the acceptance zone, there exists an integer i, $(i \geq 0)$, such that there are no rejectors closer to this point than $x \cdot 2^{i+1}$, and at least one acceptor between $x \cdot 2^i$ and $x \cdot 2^{i+1}$.*

We also update the communication rules as follows. *The prover sends a radio signal so that the verifiers within distance x receive the signal. If the prover does not receive their decision it doubles its signal strength and rebroadcasts the signal. The procedure repeats until a verifier responds. When an acceptor hears a radio broadcast from a prover claiming to be in the acceptance zone, it accepts the prover if none of the rejectors hear the prover.*

Observe that the rejection rules are not changed. Hence, the security of the protocol is not affected. Below is our estimate of the number of broadcasts the prover needs to be accepted.

Theorem 5. *For the modified protocol, the maximum number of broadcasts required for the prover to get accepted is proportional to the logarithm of the radius of the circle circumscribed over the protection zone.*

Proof: The maximum broadcast distance for a prover is d. The prover is accepted after at most $i+2$ broadcasts. The maximum distance the signal of the prover covers is $x \cdot 2^{i+1}$. That is $x \cdot 2^{i+1} \leq d$. Taking the logarithm of both sides, we get $i \leq \log(d/x) - 1$.

Since x is constant, i is in $O(\log d)$. Thus, the number of broadcasts is proportional to the logarithm of the protection zone size.   □

7   Shrinking the Ambiguity Zone

The ambiguity zone is the area where every point is closer to an acceptor than to a rejector but where the difference in the respective distances is less than x. A prover in the ambiguity zone that behaves according to the basic protocol is rejected even though it is inside the protection zone. In this section, we extend the protocol so that a prover in the ambiguity zone is accepted. This, in effect, shrinks the ambiguity zone. The extension is based on the idea of tuning the signal of the prover so that the nearest acceptor hears it while no rejectors do.

The prover in the ambiguity zone behaves according to the communication rules stated in Section 3. If the prover is rejected, it behaves as follows:

If the prover is rejected and the last signal increment is z, the prover decreases the signal strength by $z/2$ and rebroadcasts. Alternatively, if the prover does not hear the decision of the verifiers (the signal does not reach any verifier), the prover increases the signal strength by $z/2$ and rebroadcasts. The prover continues the process until it is accepted.

Recall that no assumptions are placed on the behavior of the malicious provers. Hence, the security of the protocol is not affected by the above modification.

Theorem 6. *Let a (respectively b) be the distance between the prover in the ambiguity zone and the nearest acceptor (rejector). It takes $O(\log(b-a))$ extra broadcast attempts for the prover to be accepted.*

Proof: Observe that the estimate of the number of extra broadcasts does not change if we only consider the case where the prover increases (and never decreases) its signal strength. Suppose it takes $i+1$ iterations before the prover is rejected for the first time, and that the acceptor is reached in j additional iterations. The relation between a and the maximum distance covered by the prover's signal is as follows:

$$a < ix + \frac{x}{2} + \frac{x}{2^2} + \cdots + \frac{x}{2^j} = ix + x\left(1 - \frac{1}{2^j}\right)$$

Since the prover is rejected before it tries to shrink the ambiguity zone, the distance to the prover:

$$b < (i+1)x$$

After subtracting the first inequality from the second, simplifying and taking logarithms of both sides we get:

$$j < \log \frac{x}{b-a}$$

Since x is constant, the number of extra broadcasts is proportional to the logarithm of the difference between b and a.   □

8   Complex Signal Propagation

The discussion thus far has focused on the simple propagation model where we assume that a receiver within a fixed distance from the source definitely hears the broadcast radio signal while any receiver beyond this fixed distance definitely does not.

In this section, we extend the signal propagation model as follows. If the prover sends a signal, then (i) it is definitely received by a verifier if the verifier is no more than some fixed distance r away from the prover; (ii) it may or may not be received by a verifier whose distance to the prover is between r and $r + y$ where y is some constant distance; and (iii) it is not received by a verifier more than $r + y$ away from the prover. As with the original assumption, r depends on the signal strength of the prover. Distance y, however, is constant and independent of the signal strength.

The following two lemmas are equivalent to Lemmas 1 and 2. The proofs are similar.

Lemma 6. *For the complex signal propagation, a certain point on the plane is in the rejection zone if and only if the nearest rejector is at least y closer than the nearest acceptor.*

Lemma 7. *For the complex signal propagation, every point in the acceptance zone is at least $x + y$ closer to the nearest acceptor than to the nearest rejector.*

The results similar to the ones stated in the remainder of the Section 3 and the consequent sections also apply to the complex signal propagation model.

9   Arbitrary Verifier Placement

Consider the following variant of the verification protocol. Rather than being placed at specific, pre-calculated locations, the verifiers are positioned arbitrarily on the plane. We assume that the verifiers have no knowledge of their position or the dimensions of the protection zone. Each verifier is informed as to whether it is inside or outside the protection zone (see Figure 4). We assume the following about the verifier placement: if there is a non-empty intersection between the verifier's Voronoi cell and the area outside the protection zone, then either the verifier itself or one of its Voronoi neighbors is outside the protection zone.

The verifiers are classified as follows:

- each verifier outside the protection zone is a rejector;
- each verifier that has a Voronoi neighbor outside the protection zone is also a rejector;
- the rest of the verifiers are acceptors.

Theorem 7. *The verification protocol with random placement of the verifiers solves the location verification problem.*

Proof: According to classification rules, the outside verifiers are rejectors. By assumption, the verifiers are placed such that a verifier that is inside the protection zone but whose Voronoi cell breaches the protection zone border has a Voronoi neighbor outside the protection zone. Again, by the classification rules, such a verifier is a rejector. Thus, the union of the Voronoi cells of the rejectors covers the area outside the protection zone. According to Theorem 1, the protocol complies with the security property of the location verification problem.   □

In practice the assumptions about the Voronoi neighbors can be fulfilled by distributing the verifiers with appropriate density. For example, there are two sets of verifiers: designated rejectors (labeled "red") and potential acceptors (labeled "blue"). The red verifiers are densely positioned along the border of the protection zone. The blue verifiers are spread throughout the protection zone. However, the density of the blue verifiers is also higher close to the border. To learn about the neighbors, each verifier broadcasts a "hello" message that contains its label. The verifiers approximate the set of Voronoi neighbors by the set of radio neighbors. Due to the high density of the verifiers at the border, the blue verifier whose Voronoi cell intersects the border of the protection zone has a red verifier as a radio neighbor. Hence, this blue verifier becomes a rejector and the above assumptions are satisfied.

10   Practical Implementation Considerations

In the preceding sections, we presented the location verification protocol under some simplifying assumptions for the sake of clarity. In this section, we discuss ways to relax these assumptions so that our protocol can be used in a complete security system.

Secure communication between verifiers is vital to the proper functioning of our protocol. If an acceptor cannot trust its neighboring rejectors, it cannot make an accurate assessment of the veracity of the location claim of a prover. Our assumption of perfectly secure communication between verifiers can be relaxed by employing one of the many protocols available for the same. A good scheme to achieve communication security in wireless sensor networks is described in [11]. TinySec [12] and TinyPK [13] are two practical security systems for wireless sensors.

The reliability of communication is another major assumption in the protocol. We assume that the prover receives all messages sent to it by the acceptor and verifiers receive all messages sent by the prover and among themselves. In the location verification protocol, there are several instances when messages could be lost. First, messages sent between verifiers may be lost. These losses will not affect the security of the protocol because the verifier that expects a message from another verifier will not act until it eventually receives that message. Which means that if the message is not received, the verifiers do not issue a decision, the prover is not accepted and the security of the protocol is not compromised. To guarantee that the prover is eventually accepted, reliable message delivery component needs to be incorporated in our protocol. Second, a message broadcast by a prover could be lost before it gets to verifiers. The only scenario of concern is the case where an acceptor receives the broadcast successfully but a rejector does not. In this case, the prover may be falsely accepted. To counteract this, the rejectors have to be placed within their definite acceptance range as described in Section 8. Another viable solution is to ensure that multiple rejectors cover the rejection zone. For example, there are several independent sets of verifiers covering the whole plane and securing the same protection zone. The prover is rejected when at least one set of verifiers rejects it.

Observe that our protocol does not take into account potential latency in communication between verifiers. This, however, can be handled by introducing appropriate wait-times and timeouts before an acceptor makes the decision. To preserve correctness, if an acceptor does not hear from a rejector, the prover is not accepted.

Another aspect that is not explicitly addressed in the paper is the distributed implementation of the protocol. Notice however, that in our protocol, to issue a decision an acceptor that receives the prover's signal needs to only communicate with its Voronoi neighbors: it needs to communicate with the rejectors to make sure that none of them heard the signal, and with the acceptors to check if they received the signal and if their rejectors heard it. Hence, the implementation of our protocol has to facilitate efficient communication between the acceptors and their Voronoi neighbors. One way to do it is to place the required verifiers in the communication range of each other.

Observe that we assume that the prover has radio range large enough to cover potentially the whole protection zone. However, our protocol can be extended to the case of a limited range prover. For example the acceptors can be placed such that every point in the acceptance zone is no further away from an acceptor than the prover's maximum range.

Acknowledgments

We would like to express our gratitude for helpful discussions to Volodymyr Andriyevskyy of Kent State University, David Wagner of University of California, Berkeley and Ting Yu of North Carolina State University.

References

1. Sastry, N., Shankar, U., Wagner, D.: Secure verification of location claims. In: Proceedings of the ACM workshop on Wireless security, San Diego, CA (2003) 1–10
2. Naik, V., Arora, A., Bapat, S., Gouda, M.: Dependable systems: Whisper: Local secret maintenance in sensor networks. IEEE Distributed Systems Online **4** (2003)
3. Balfanz, D., Smetters, D.K., Stewart, P., Wong, H.C.: Talking to strangers: Authentication in ad-hoc wireless networks. In: Proceedings of the Symposium on Network and Distributed Systems Security (NDSS 2002), San Diego, CA, Internet Society (2002)

4. Denning, D.E., MacDoran, P.F.: Location-based authentication: Grounding cyberspace for better security. In Denning, D.E., Denning, P.J., eds.: Internet Besieged: Countering Cyberspace Scofflaws. ACM Press / Addison-Wesley, New York (1998) 167–174 Reprint from Computer Fraud and Security, Elsevier Science, Ltd, February 1996.
5. Hu, Y.C., Perrig, A., Johnson, D.B.: Packet leashes: A defense against wormhole attacks. In: INFOCOM 2003. (2003)
6. Brands, S., Chaum, D.: Distance-bounding protocols (extended abstract). In Helleseth, T., ed.: Advances in Cryptology—EUROCRYPT 93. Volume 765 of Lecture Notes in Computer Science., Springer-Verlag, 1994 (1993) 344–359
7. Corner, M.D., Noble, B.D.: Zero-interaction authentication. In: Proceedings of the eighth Annual International Conference on Mobile Computing and Networking (MOBICOM-02), New York, ACM Press (2002) 1–11
8. Kindberg, T., Zhang, K.: Context authentication using constrained channels. Technical Report HPL-2001-84, Hewlett Packard Laboratories (2001)
9. Gabber, E., Wool, A.: How to prove where you are: Tracking the location of customer equipment. In: Proceedings of the 5th ACM Conference on Computer and Communications Security, San Francisco, California, ACM Press (1998) 142–149
10. Preparata, F.P., Shamos, M.I.: Computational Geometry: An Introduction. Springer-Verlag, New York (1985)
11. Slijepcevic, S., Potkonjak, M., Tsiatsis, V., Zimbeck, S., Srivastava, M.B.: On communication security in wireless ad-hoc sensor networks. In: 11th IEEE International Workshops on Enabling Technologies: Infrastructure for Collaborative Enterprises. (2002) 139–144
12. : Tinysec: Link layer encryption for tiny devices. (http://www.cs.berkeley.edu/nks/tinysec/)
13. : Tinypk project. (http://www.is.bbn.com/projects/lws-nest/)

Sentries and Sleepers in Sensor Networks

Mohamed G. Gouda[1], Young-ri Choi[1], and Anish Arora[2]

[1] Department of Computer Sciences,
The University of Texas at Austin,
1 University Station C0500, Austin, Texas 78712-0233, USA
{gouda, yrchoi}@cs.utexas.edu
[2] Department of Computer Science and Engineering,
The Ohio State University, 2015 Neil Avenue,
Columbus, Ohio 43210-1277, USA
anish@cse.ohio-state.edu

Abstract. A sensor is a battery-operated small computer with an antenna and a sensing board that can sense magnetism, sound, heat, etc. Sensors in a network can use their antennas to communicate in a wireless fashion by broadcasting messages over radio frequency to neighboring sensors in the same network. In order to lengthen the relatively short lifetime of sensor batteries, each sensor in a network can be replaced by a group of n sensors, for some $n \geq 2$. The group of n sensors act as one sensor, whose lifetime is about n times that of a regular sensor as follows. For a time period, only one sensor in the group, called *sentry*, stays awake and performs all the tasks assigned to the group, while the remaining sensors, called *sleepers*, go to sleep to save their batteries. At the beginning of the next time period, the sleepers wake up, then all the sensors in the group elect a new sentry for the next time period, and the cycle repeats. In this paper, we describe a practical protocol that can be used by a group of sensors to elect a new sentry at the beginning of each time period. Our protocol, unlike earlier protocols, is based on the assumption that the sensors in a group are perfectly identical (e.g. they do not have unique identifiers; rather each of them has the same group identifier). This feature makes our protocol resilient against any attack by an adversary sensor in the group that may lie about its own identity to be elected a sentry over and over, and keep the legitimate sensors in the group asleep for a long time.

Keywords: Energy management, Sentry election, Self-stabilization, Sensor Networks, Sentry-Sleeper protocol.

1 Introduction

A sensor is a battery-operated small computer with an antenna and a sensing board that can sense magnetism, sound, heat, etc. Sensors in a network can use their antennas to communicate in a wireless fashion by broadcasting messages over radio frequency to neighboring sensors in the same network. Due

T. Higashino (Ed.): OPODIS 2004, LNCS 3544, pp. 384–399, 2005.
© Springer-Verlag Berlin Heidelberg 2005

to the limited range of radio transmission, sensor networks are usually multi-hop. Sensor networks can be used for military, environmental or commercial applications such as intrusion detection [1], disaster monitoring [2] and habitat monitoring [3].

One of the challenging problems in designing sensor networks is to lengthen the lifetime of sensor batteries. One approach to solve this problem is to exploit the idea that in some densely deployed networks, a fraction of the sensors can go to sleep for predefined time periods, while the remaining sensors stay awake and perform the assigned tasks in the network. The sleeping sensors save their energy and lengthen the lifetime of their batteries, without significantly degrading the performance of the applications running on the sensor network. Examples of this approach can be found in [4], [5], [6], [7], [8], [9], [10], [11].

In the current paper, we generalize this idea to be applicable to any, possibly sparsely populated, sensor network: replace each sensor in the network by a group of n sensors, for some $n \geq 2$. The group of n sensors are deployed in a location where a single sensor would have been deployed in the sparse network. This group of n sensors act as one sensor as follows. For a time period, only one sensor in the group, called *sentry*, stays awake and performs all the tasks assigned to the group, while the remaining sensors, called *sleepers*, go to sleep to save their batteries. At the beginning of the next time period, the sleepers wake up, and all the sensors in the group elect a new sentry for the next time period, and the cycle repeats.

Note that the sensors in a group are identical in every way so that each of them can behave in exactly the same manner in performing the assigned tasks, when this sensor is elected a sentry of the group. This implies that no sensor has an identifier that distinguishes it from other sensors in its group. Rather, every sensor in a group has the same group identifier.

The identifiers of two sensor groups in the same network, however, are distinguishable so that when a sensor receives a message, the sensor can determine whether this message was sent from a sensor in its own group or it was sent from a sensor in a different nearby group. Note that a sensor in a group needs to exchange messages with other sensors in its group in order to elect a new sentry at the beginning of each time period. A sensor also needs to exchange messages with sensors in adjacent groups in order to perform the assigned tasks, when this sensor is elected a sentry of its group.

An alternative approach to lengthen the lifetime of sensor batteries in a sparsely populated network is to provide each sensor with a large battery whose lifetime is n times the lifetime of a regular battery. However, this alternative approach is less reliable than our approach (where each sensor in the sparsely populated network is replaced by a group of n sensors) as follows. If a sensor fails in a network, then the network can compensate for the failed sensor provided the network is designed using our approach rather than the alternative approach.

The protocol used by a group of n sensors to elect a new sentry at the beginning of each time period is called a *sentry-sleeper protocol*. The goals of a sentry-sleeper protocol are two-fold:

i. Ensure that at each instant not all the sensors in a sensor group are sleeping. Thus, at each instant at least one sensor in the group is awake and so can perform the tasks assigned to the group.

ii. Reduce the time periods where two or more sensors in a sensor group are awake in order to reduce the wasteful use of sensor batteries. (Note that if two or more sensors in a sensor group are awake during a time period, then each of them performs the same tasks assigned to the group during that period.)

Other sentry-sleeper protocols are reported in [5], [11], [4], [8], [7]. The main assumption in these papers is that the sensors in a "sensor group" have distinguishable identities; i.e. they have different physical locations, different connectivity, different message traffic, or different identifiers. Thus, the sensors in the network decide which one stays awake among their neighboring sensors based on these different identities, so that they can not only save their batteries but also provide some level of the performance of the applications running on the network. Unlike these protocols, our protocol for electing a sentry at the beginning of each time period is based on the assumption that the sensors in a group are perfectly identical; i.e. they have identical locations, connectivity, traffic, and identifiers. This feature makes our protocol scalable and resilient against any attack by an adversary sensor in the group that may lie about its own identity (i.e. lie about their locations, connectivity, ...) to be elected a sentry over and over, and keep the legitimate sensors asleep for a long time.

2 Sensor States and Transitions

Before we can explain the main features of our sentry-sleeper protocol, we need to explain, in this section, the different states of a sensor and the transitions between them.

Every sensor in a sensor group can be in any one of two states: an idling state or a sleeping state. In the idling state, the sensor does nothing but wait until either its timeout expires (in which case the sensor executes a timeout action), or it receives a message (in which case the sensor executes a receiving action). An action, whether a timeout action or a receiving action, of a sensor consists of a number of statements that update the local variables of the sensor, send at most a message, or set the timeout of the sensor to expire at a later time.

Also the sensor can execute the special statement "go-to-sleep" at the end of an action. If a sensor executes this statement, the sensor changes its state from idling to sleeping. In the sleeping state, the sensor does nothing but wait until its timeout expires, then it executes a timeout action and changes its state from sleeping to idling. Figure 1 shows the two states of a sensor and the different transitions between them.

There are two main differences between the idling state and the sleeping state of a sensor. First, in the idling state, the sensor can receive messages that are sent by other sensors and execute corresponding receiving actions, whereas in

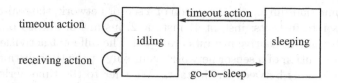

Fig. 1. Two states of a sensor

the sleeping state, the sensor cannot do so since it turns off its radio as well as its processor and sensing devices to save energy during its sleep. Second, the consumed energy when the sensor is in the idling state is much larger than the consumed energy when the sensor is in the sleeping state (as discussed in [12] and [13]). Therefore, for the sensor to save its energy as much as possible, it should stay in its sleeping state as long as possible.

3   Sensor Network Execution

In this section, we present a formal model of the execution of a sensor network. We use this model to specify our sentry-sleeper protocol in the next section. We also use this model to verify and analyze the protocol in Section 5 and 6, and to develop our simulation in Section 7.

The *topology* of a sensor network is a directed graph that satisfies the following two conditions. First, each node in the topology represents a distinct sensor in the sensor network. Second, each directed edge (u, v) from node u to node v in the topology indicates that every message sent by sensor u can be received by sensor v (provided that neither sensor v nor any "neighboring sensor" of v sends a message at the same time when sensor u sends its message).

If the topology of a sensor network has a directed edge from a sensor u to a sensor v, then u is called an *in-neighbor* of v and v is called an *out-neighbor* of u. Note that a sensor can be both an in-neighbor and an out-neighbor of another sensor in the sensor network.

As an example, Figure 2 shows the topology of a sensor network. This network has six sensors, and sensor u in this network has three out-neighbors, namely sensors v, v', and v''. Thus, if sensor u sends a message, then this message can be received simultaneously by the three sensors v, and v', and v''. Note that sensor u is both an in-neighbor and an out-neighbor of sensor v' in this network.

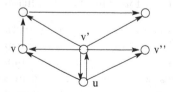

Fig. 2. Topology of a sensor network

We assume that during the execution of a sensor network, the real-time passes through discrete instants: instant 1, instant 2, instant 3, and so on. The time periods between consecutive instants are equal. The different activities that constitute the execution of a sensor network occur only at the time instants, and not in the time periods between the instants. We refer to the time period between two consecutive instants t and $t+1$ as a *time unit* $(t, t+1)$. (The value of a time unit is not critical to our current presentation of a sensor network model, but we estimate that the value of the time unit is around 100 milliseconds.)

At a time instant, the time-out of a sensor u may expire causing u to execute its timeout action. Executing the timeout action of sensor u causes u to update its own local variables and to send at most one message. It may also cause u to execute the statement "timeout-after <expression>" which causes the timeout of u to expire (again) after k time units, where k is the current value of <expression>. It may also cause u to execute the statement "go-to-sleep" which causes u to sleep until the time-out of u expires. The timeout action of sensor u is of the following form:

```
timeout-expires -> <update local variables of u>;
                   <send at most one message>;
                   <may execute timeout-after <expression>>;
                   <may execute go-to-sleep>
```

To keep track of its time-out, each sensor u has an implicit variable named "timer.u". In each time unit between two consecutive instants, the implicit variable timer.u is either "present" or "not-present". Moreover, if variable timer.u is present in a time unit, then it has a positive integer value in that time unit. Otherwise, it is not-present and has no value in the time unit.

If sensor u executes a statement "timeout-after <expression>" at instant t, then timer.u becomes present in the time unit $(t, t+1)$ and its value is the value of <expression> in this time unit.

If timer.u is present and its value is k, where $k > 1$, in the time unit $(t-1, t)$, then timer.u continues to be present and its value is $k-1$ in the time unit $(t, t+1)$.

If timer.u is present and its value is 1 in the time unit $(t-1, t)$, then sensor u executes its timeout action at instant t and timer.u becomes not-present in the time unit $(t, t+1)$, unless u executes "timeout-after <expression>" as part of its timeout action.

If a sensor u executes its timeout action and sends a message at instant t, then any sensor v, that is an out-neighbor of u, receives a copy of the message at instant t, provided that the following two conditions hold.

    i. Sensor v does not send any message at instant t. (This condition indicates that either sensor v does not execute its timeout action at t, or it executes its timeout action at t but this execution of the timeout action does not include sending a message.)

    ii. Sensor v has no in-neighbor, other than sensor u, that sends a message at instant t. (If v sends a message at t or if an in-neighbor of

v, other than u, sends a message at t, then this message is said to *collide* with the message sent by u at t with the net result that v receives no message at t.)

If a sensor u receives a message at instant t, then u executes its receiving action at t. Executing the receiving action of sensor u causes u to update its own local variables. It may also cause u to execute the statement "timeout-after <expression>" which causes the time-out of u to expire after k time units, where k is the value of <expression> in the time unit $(t, t+1)$. It may also cause u to execute the statement "go-to-sleep" which causes u to sleep until the time-out of u expires. The receiving action of sensor u is of the following form:

```
rcv <msg> -> <update local variables of u>;
             <may execute timeout-after <expression>>;
             <may execute go-to-sleep>
```

It follows from the above discussion that at a time instant, a sensor u executes exactly one of the following:

  i. u sends one message, but receives no message.
  ii. u receives one message, but sends no message.
  iii. u sends no message and receives no message.

In the next section, we specify our sentry-sleeper protocol using the formal model of sensor protocols in this section.

4   The Sentry-Sleeper Protocol

The goal of our sentry-sleeper protocol is to make a group of n sensors act as a single sensor whose lifetime is $N * F$ time units, where F is the lifetime of a regular sensor, and $1 < N < n$. The n sensors in the sensor group constitute a sensor network whose topology is fully-connected, i.e. there are two opposite-direction edges between every two nodes in the topology.

During a time period, called a *turn*, $(n-1)$ sensors of the sensor group are in their sleeping states and the remaining sensor is in its idling state. In a turn, each of the sleeping sensors is called a *sleeper*, and the awake sensor is called a *sentry*. At the end of a turn, the sleepers wake up and all sensors in the group elect a new sentry for the next turn. This cycle of a turn followed by an election of a new sentry is repeated over and over until the batteries of all sensors in the group are exhausted.

At the end of a turn, the sleepers wake up, and they along with the sentry collaborate to elect a new sentry for the next turn as follows. Each sensor in the group computes a random period, called a *resolution period*, whose length is chosen uniformly from the range 1 .. 2*$ravg$−1, where $ravg$ is the average length (measured in time units) of the resolution period. Then, each sensor sets its timeout to expire after its resolution period. The sensor that chooses the smallest resolution period in the group times-out first, and this sensor elects itself as the new sentry and starts the new turn by sending a message of the form:

sleep(gid, rt)

where gid is the identifier of the sensor group and rt is the remaining time in the current turn. Initially, the remaining time in the current turn is assigned the length of a turn, which is tl time units.

When a sensor u in the sensor group receives a sleep(gid, rt) message, sensor u recognizes that a new sentry is elected for the current turn and decides to sleep for rt time units. Thus, it sets its timeout to expire after rt time units, then goes to sleep. The range of rt in the received sleep message is 1 .. tl. Thus, the shortest sleeping period is 1 time unit, and the longest sleeping period is tl time units.

After the elected sentry sends the first sleep(gid, rt) message, the sentry computes a random period whose length rp is chosen uniformly from the range 1 .. $2*ravg-1$, and sets its timeout to expire after rp time units. When the sentry times-out, it sends the next sleep(gid, $rt - rp$) message. The sentry keeps on sending sleep messages, until the remaining time in the current turn becomes zero and all the sleepers wake up to elect a new sentry for the next turn.

Notice that the sentry periodically sends a sleep message even when all other sensors in the group are supposedly asleep and cannot receive any messages. This feature is intended to handle the following case. Some sensors in the group may not receive the first sleep(gid, rt) message sent by the sentry at the beginning of a turn. These sensors can receive a later sleep(gid, rt') message, where $rt' < rt$ and go to sleep for a period of rt' time units in this turn.

In this protocol, two (or more) sensors, say u and v, in the group can select identical resolution periods and so they send their sleep messages at the same time. The net effect is that none of the sensors in the group can receive any sleep messages, since the two messages collide with one another. Only sensors u and v consider themselves as sentries, and the other sensors in the group do not recognize that a new sentry has been elected for the current turn. However, our protocol ensures that one, only one, sensor in the group eventually sends a sleep message at some instant t and makes all other sensors go to sleep at t.

A formal specification for a sensor u in the group is as follows.

```
sensor u

const gid    : integer,      {group id of sensor u}
      tl     : integer,      {length of a turn}
      ravg   : integer       {avg length of random period}

var   sentry : boolean,      {Is u sentry?}
      awake  : boolean,      {Is u awake?}
      rp     : 1..2*ravg-1,  {length of random period}
      rt     : 0..tl,        {remaining time in current turn}
      g      : integer,      {group id in received message}
      t      : 1..tl         {remaining time in received message}
```

```
begin
    timeout-expires -> if !awake ->                  awake := true;
                                                     sentry := false;
                                                     rp := random;
                                                     timeout-after rp

                       [] awake and !sentry -> sentry := true;
                                                     rt := tl;
                                                     send sleep(gid, rt);
                                                     rp := random;
                                                     rp := min(rp, rt);
                                                     rt := rt-rp;
                                                     timeout-after rp

                       [] awake and sentry ->
                                       if rt>0 -> send sleep(gid, rt);
                                                     rp := random;
                                                     rp := min(rp, rt);
                                                     rt := rt-rp;
                                                     timeout-after rp
                                       [] rt=0 -> sentry := false;
                                                     rp := random;
                                                     timeout-after rp
                                       fi
                       fi
[]  rcv sleep(g, t) -> if gid=g  -> sentry := false;
                                       awake := false;
                                       timeout-after t;
                                       go-to-sleep
                       [] gid!=g -> skip
                       fi
end
```

It is important to note that in this protocol, the sensors in a group compete to become a sentry purely based on randomization without resorting to any difference in their identities that may give an advantage to some sensors over others in the group. In a turn, each sensor in the group has the same probability to become a sentry. Thus, each sensor can expect to become a sentry once every n turns or so. A sensor u who fails to become a sentry for a relatively long period, say for $3*n$ or $5*n$ turns, should suspect that some sensors in the group are not following the protocol. In this case, sensor u may decide to stay awake (and perform the assigned tasks to the group) and refuse to go to sleep.

5   Stabilization of the Protocol

In this section, we sketch a proof that our sentry-sleeper protocol is self-stabilizing. A *state* of this protocol is defined by a value for each variable and each implicit variable timer.u for each sensor u in the protocol. Note that a state of the protocol corresponds to a time unit between two consecutive instants, since the values of all variables and all implicit variables do not change during any time unit between consecutive instants.

We assume that every state (whether legitimate or illegitimate) of the protocol satisfies the following three conditions.

1. For every sensor u, the implicit variable timer.u is present and its value is at most tl time units. (Note that this assumption is maintained by the execution of the protocol.)
2. For every sleeping sensor u, the value of its *awake* variable is false. (Note that this assumption is maintained by the execution of the protocol.)
3. For every awake sensor u, the value of its timer.u is distinct from the value of timer.v for any other awake sensor v. (Note that this assumption is probabilistically maintained by choosing the value $ravg$ to be large relative to the number of sensors in the group.)

In our sentry-sleeper protocol, a *legitimate* state is defined as a state that satisfies the following *invariant*:

> *At least one sensor in the group is awake, and*
> *at most one sensor in the group is a sentry.*

Therefore, in a legitimate state, the number of sleepers is in the range $0 \,..\, n-1$, and the number of sentries is in the range $0 \,..\, 1$.

The protocol is *self-stabilizing* iff it satisfies the following two conditions [14].

i. *Closure*: Starting from any legitimate state, the execution of any action in any sensor in the protocol yields a legitimate state.
ii. *Convergence*: Starting from any illegitimate state, the protocol is guaranteed to reach a legitimate state.

First, we show that starting from any legitimate state, the execution of any action in any sensor in the protocol yields a legitimate state. The protocol has two cases to consider. In the first case, the executed action is a timeout action in a sensor u in the group. In this case, there are three possibilities to consider when the timeout action is executed.

i. The value of *awake* in u is false: In this case, u concludes that u wakes up from sleeping (by the assumption 2), and makes the value of *awake* true. Thus, u becomes awake, and so the invariant holds.
ii. The value of *awake* in u is true and the value of *sentry* in u is false: In this case, u elects itself as the new sentry and makes other sensors in the group sleep by sending a sleep message. Note that no other awake sensor can execute this timeout action that causes the sensor to send a sleep message at the same time (by the assumption 3). Thus, u is awake and becomes the only sentry in the group, and so the invariant holds.

iii. The value of *awake* in u is true and the value of *sentry* in u is true: In this case, there are two cases to consider depending on the remaining time in the current turn. First, if the remaining time is bigger than zero, u sends another sleep message. Thus, u is still awake and is still the only sentry in the group. Second, if the remaining time is zero, u recognizes that the current turn is finished, and withdraws from a sentry by making its value of *sentry* false. Thus, u is still awake, but is not a sentry any more. In both cases, the invariant holds.

In the second case, the executed action is a receiving action in a sensor u in the group. In this case, there are two possibilities to consider when the receiving action is executed.

i. When u receives a sleep message from another sensor v in the same group: In this case, u recognizes that sensor v is elected a sentry for the current turn, so u goes to sleep for the specified sleeping period in the received message. Thus, sensor v is awake and is the only sentry in the group, and so the invariant holds.

ii. When u receives a sleep message from a sensor in a different group: In this case, u ignores the message and does nothing. Thus, the invariant holds.

Hence, starting from any legitimate state, the execution of a timeout action or a receiving action in any sensor in the group yields to a legitimate state.

Next, we show that starting from any illegitimate state, our protocol is guaranteed to reach a legitimate state within finite executions of actions in the group. There are two states that violate the invariant as follows:

i. A state where all sensors in the group are sleeping: In this case, a sensor u in the group is guaranteed to execute its timeout action within tl time units (by the assumption 1). By executing the timeout action of u, u becomes awake. Thus, at least one sensor in the group will wake up within tl time units, and then only one of the awake sensors will eventually become a sentry.

ii. A state where two or more sentries exist in the group: In this case, only one sentry whose timer value is the smallest, say sensor u, times-out first and then executes its timeout action to send a sleep message at some instant t (by the assumption 3). The other sentries receive the sleep message from u and go to sleep at t. Thus, all the sentries except u go to sleep within finite executions of actions.

Therefore, starting from any illegitimate state, the execution of a timeout action in some sensor makes the protocol reach a legitimate state within finite executions of actions in the group.

6   Protocol Analysis

Our protocol, as described in Section 4, makes a group of n sensors act as one sensor whose lifetime is $N * F$ time units, where F is the lifetime of a regular sensor and N is some quantity, called *the effective number of the sensors* in the group. Clearly, we have $1 < N < n$. In this section, we analyze the protocol and estimate the value of N.

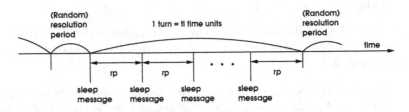

Fig. 3. A time period during protocol execution

Figure 3 shows a time period T, consisting of a resolution period followed by one turn of tl time units. Since the average length of a resolution period is $ravg$ time units, we have $T = tl + ravg$ time units. During a turn, a sentry sends a sleep message every random period rp whose average is $ravg$ time units. Therefore, the average number of sleep messages sent by a sentry per turn is $tl/ravg$.

Let E_{slp} and E_{idl} be the amount of energy consumed by a sensor in the sleeping state and in the idling state per time unit respectively, and E_{snd} and E_{rcv} be the amount of energy consumed by a sensor to send a message and to receive a message respectively. There are two possible cases that can occur during the time period T:

  i. *Case 1*: The sensors in the group do not execute the protocol, and remain in their idling states. The amount of energy consumed by n sensors in this case, E_{nop} is calculated as follows.

$$E_{nop} = E_{idl} * (tl + ravg) * n$$

  ii. *Case 2*: The sensors in the group execute the protocol. The sentry stays in the idling state and sends $tl/ravg$ sleep messages for this time period. Each of the $(n-1)$ sleepers stays in the idling state for a resolution period, receives a sleep message, and sleeps for tl time units. Therefore, the amount of energy consumed by n sensors in this case, E_p is calculated as follows.

$$\begin{aligned} E_p = \quad & E_{idl} * (tl + ravg) + E_{snd} * (tl/ravg) \\ & + (n-1) * (E_{slp} * tl + E_{idl} * ravg + E_{rcv}) \end{aligned}$$

Table 1. Energy consumption of a sensor (in energy units)

E_{slp}	0.003 per time unit
E_{idl}	30 per time unit
E_{snd}	24.3 per message
E_{rcv}	9 per message

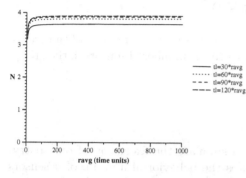

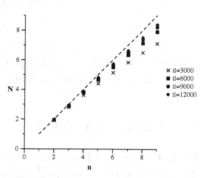

Fig. 4. N vs. $ravg$ when $n=4$ **Fig. 5.** N vs. n when $ravg=100$

From the above analysis, we can estimate the effective number of the sensors N as follows:

$$N = \frac{E_{nop}}{E_p}$$

We present two figures, Figure 4 and 5, from the above formula for the four cases $tl = 30 * ravg$, $60 * ravg$, $90 * ravg$ and $120 * ravg$ in time units. In both of the figures, we use the values in Table 1 for E_{slp}, E_{idl}, E_{snd} and E_{rcv}. These values are computed using the energy consumption model in [12], under the assumption that a time unit is 100 milliseconds, and a time period taken for a sensor to send or receive a message is 30 milliseconds.

Figure 4 shows the relationship between the length of $ravg$ and N when $n=4$ and $5 \leq ravg \leq 1000$ in time units. If $ravg$ is 100 time units or more, then the value of N no longer depends on $ravg$. Similarly, when $n=2$ and 9, if $ravg$ is 100 time units or more, then the value of N no longer depends on $ravg$.

Figure 5 shows the relationship between n and N when $ravg = 100$ time units. From Fig. 5, one can make two observations. First, tl does not have a strong effect on the value of N, especially when n is small. Second, N is closer to n when n is smaller. During a resolution period, all sensors in the group need to stay awake, and so the total amount of energy consumed by the sensors during this period is increased as n is increased. Thus, our protocol becomes more efficient as n is smaller.

In the real execution of the protocol, the current sentry can run out of the battery and die during its turn. Then there exists a time period where no sensor in the group is awake to perform the tasks assigned to the group. We call this time period a *gap*.

We can estimate the total length of gaps over the lifetime of a group of n sensors from a simple formula. When the sentry dies during its turn, the average time period that no sensor in the group is awake is $tl/2$ (because the minimum time period is zero and the maximum time period is tl). Since $(n-1)$ sensors can die during their sentry turns, the total length of gaps over the lifetime is estimated as follows:

$$\frac{tl}{2} * (n-1)$$

The total length of gaps is relatively much smaller than the lifetime of the group. Note that the total length of gaps is related to the number of sensors in the group, not the lifetime of a regular sensor.

7   Simulation Results

We have developed a simulator that can simulate the execution of our sentry-sleeper protocol. This simulator simulates the behavior of a group of n sensors whose topology is fully connected and also allows us to configure the parameters of the protocol such as tl and $ravg$.

For the purpose of simulation, we have adopted the values in Table 1 as well as the following values:

- $tl = 3000$ time units
- $ravg = 100$ time units
- The amount of energy given to each sensor, at the beginning of simulation, is enough to keep that sensor in its idling state for 100000 time units.

We ran simulations of this protocol for the three cases $n = 2$, 4 and 9, and plotted the results in Figure 6 and 7. Figure 6 shows the effective number of the sensors N. Each circle mark represents the average effective number of the

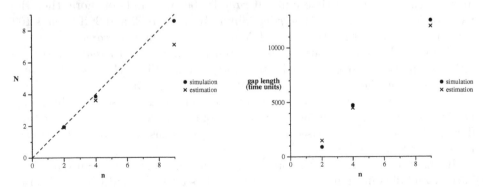

Fig. 6. The effective number of the sensors

Fig. 7. The total length of gaps

sensors over 100 simulations and each X mark represents the estimated effective number of the sensors. The effective number of the sensors in simulation is larger than that in estimation, because in simulation, sensors run out of their batteries and die over time and so the number of sensors in the group decreases over time. As discussed in Section 6, the protocol becomes more efficient as n is smaller.

Figure 7 shows the total length of gaps over the lifetime of a group of n sensors. Each circle mark represents the average total length of gaps over 100 simulations and each X mark represents the estimated total length of gaps.

From the simulation results, we show that the effective number of the sensors N is close to the number of sensors n in the group. That is, the group of n sensors can lengthen its lifetime around n times the lifetime of a regular sensor by adopting our protocol.

8 Related Work

It is suggested in SBPM[7] to divide the sensors in a network into two sets, sentries and sleepers. Sentries stay awake, and provide basic communication services and coarse sensing services, while sleepers go to sleep to save their energy. When the sentries detect events, they can wake up the sleepers for more refined sensing. However, in SBPM, sentries are pre-selected and fixed. Moreover, a central computer decides when sleepers go to sleep. In GAF[8], all sensors that are equivalent in routing are identified using geographical location information. Then, only one sensor in a group of equivalent sensors stays awake and participates in routing, while the other sensors turn off their radios and go to sleep.

In Span[4] and TMPO[11], each sensor exchanges its neighbor information to compute which sensor joins a connected backbone in a network. Only sensors in the backbone participate in routing, while other sensors can go to sleep to save energy. In ASCENT[5], a sensor in a network keeps track of the number of its active neighbors and message loss rate, and joins a network topology only if the sensor becomes helpful. However, once a sensor enters the active state, it continues to be awake until it dies.

Other approaches to save energy in a sensor network have been proposed in [15], [16], [13], [10], [6], [9]. In LEACH[15], to reduce communication cost, each cluster-head collects data messages from the sensors in the cluster, and then compresses and forwards the messages to a base station. In STEM[10], a sensor in a monitoring state turns off the radio. If the sensor detects an event, it turns on the radio and wakes up other sensors if necessary.

Leader election protocols have been studied for single-hop single-channel radio networks in [17], [18], [19] and [20]. However, in general, these protocols assume that a station sending a message can simultaneously listen [17], [18], [20]. These protocols may not be useful in a sensor network, since generally a sensor cannot listen while the sensor is sending a message as in IEEE 802.11.

9   Concluding Remarks

In this paper, we described a sentry-sleeper protocol that can be used by a group of sensors to elect a new sentry at the beginning of each time period. Our protocol is based on the assumption that the sensors in a group have identical identities, and so the sensors compete to become a sentry purely based on randomization. We also showed that our protocol is self-stabilizing. The simulation results showed that a group of n sensors can lengthen its lifetime $1.95 * F$ for $n = 2$, $3.87 * F$ for $n = 4$ and $8.59 * F$ for $n = 9$, where F is the lifetime of a regular sensor.

Our protocol can be applied to a cluster-head election algorithm that balances energy load evenly among the nodes in a cluster. By adopting our protocol, the nodes in the cluster can elect a cluster-head based on randomization without resorting to any identifiers, so some nodes with the highest identifier or the lowest identifier do not have an advantage over others.

Acknowledgment

This work was supported in part by the Defense Advanced Research Projects Agency (DARPA) Contract F33615-01-C-1901, and in part by three IBM Faculty Partnership Awards for the academic years of 2000-2003, and in part by the Texas Advanced Research Program, Texas Higher Education Coordinating Board, under Grant TARP 14-970823.

References

1. Arora, A., Dutta, P., Bapat, S., Kulathumani, V., Zhang, H., Naik, V., Mittal, V., Cao, H., Demirbas, M., Gouda, M., Choi, Y., et al: A Line in the Sand: A Wireless Sensor Network for Target Detection, Classification, and Tracking. Computer Networks (Elsevier), Special Issue on Military Communications Systems and Technologies **46** (2004) 605–634
2. Akyildiz, I.F., Su, W., Sankarasubramaniam, Y., Cayirci, E.: Wireless Sensor Networks: A Survey. Computer Networks, Elsevier Science **38** (2002) 393–422
3. Mainwaring, A., Polastre, J., Szewczyk, R., Culler, D., Anderson., J.: Wireless Sensor Networks for Habitat Monitoring. In: Proceedings of the ACM International Workshop on Wireless Sensor Networks and Applications (WSNA'02), Atlanta, GA (2002)
4. Chen, B., Jamieson, K., Balakrishnan, H., Morris, R.: Span: An Energy-efficient Coordination Algorithm for Topology Maintenance in Ad Hoc Wireless Networks. In: Proceedings of the Seventh Annual ACM/IEEE International Conference on Mobile Computing and Networking (ACM MobiCom), Rome, Italy (2001) 85–96
5. Cerpa, A., Estrin, D.: ASCENT: Adaptive Self-Configuring sEnsor Networks Topologies. In: Proceedings of the Twenty First Annual Joint Conference of the IEEE Computer and Communications Societies (INFOCOM 2002), New York, NY (2002)

6. Xu, Y., Heidemann, J., Estrin, D.: Adaptive Energy-Conserving Routing for Multihop Ad Hoc Networks. Research Report 527, USC/Information Sciences Institute
   (2000)
7. Hui, J., Ren, Z., Krogh, B.: Sentry-Based Power Management in Wireless Sensor Networks. The International Workshop on Information Processing in Sensor
   Networks (IPSN'03) (2003)
8. Xu, Y., Heidemann, J., Estrin, D.: Geography-informed Energy Conservation for
   Ad-hoc Routing. In: Proceedings of the Seventh Annual ACM/IEEE International
   Conference on Mobile Computing and Networking (ACM MobiCom), Rome, Italy
   (2001)
9. Younis, M., Youssef, M., Arisha, K.: Energy-aware Management for Cluster-based
   Sensor Networks. Computer Networks **43** (2003) 649–668
10. Schurgers, C., Tsiatsis, V., Ganeriwal, S., Srivastava, M.: Topology Management
    for Sensor Networks: Exploiting Latency and Density. In: Proceedings of The ACM
    Symposium on Mobile Adhoc Networking and Computing (MOBIHOC 2002), Lau-
    sanne, Switzerland (2002)
11. Bao, L., Garcia-Luna-Aceves, J.: Topology Management in Ad Hoc Networks.
    In: Proceedings of the 4th ACM Symposium on Mobile Ad Hoc Networking and
    Computing (MobiHoc'03), Annapolis, Maryland (2003)
12. Miller, M.J., Vaidya, N.H.: Minimizing Energy Consumption in Sensor Networks
    Using A Wakeup Radio. In: Proceedings of the IEEE Wireless Communications
    and Networking Conference (WCNC'04). (2004)
13. Ye, W., Heidemann, J., Estrin, D.: An Energy-Efficient MAC protocol for Wireless
    Sensor Networks. In: Proceedings of the Twenty First Annual Joint Conference
    of the IEEE Computer and Communications Societies (INFOCOM 2002), (New
    York, NY) 1567–1576
14. Arora, A., Gouda, M.: Closure and Convergence: A Foundation of Fault-Tolerant
    Computing. IEEE Transactions on Software Engineering **19** (1993) 1015–1027
15. Heinzelman, W.R., Chandrakasan, A., Balakrishnan, H.: Energy-Efficient Commu-
    nication Protocol for Wireless Microsensor Networks. In: Proceedings of Hawaiian
    International Conference on Systems Science. (2000)
16. Singh, S., Woo, M., Raghavendra, C.S.: Power-aware Routing in Mobile Ad Hoc
    Networks. In: Proceedings of the 4th Annual ACM/IEEE International Conference
    on Mobile Computing and Networking (ACM MobiCom), Dallas, Texas, United
    States (1998) 181–190
17. Nakano, K., Olariu, S.: Randomized Leader Election Protocols in Radio Networks
    with No Collision Detection. International Symposium on Algorithms and Com-
    putation (2000) 362–373
18. Jurdzinski, T., Kutylowsk, M., Zatopianski, J.: Efficient Algorithms for Leader
    Election in Radio Networks. In: Proceedings of the twenty-first annual symposium
    on Principles of distributed computing, ACM Press (2002) 51–57
19. Jurdzinski, T., Kutylowsk, M., Zatopianski, J.: Weak Communication in Radio
    Networks. Euro-Par2002, Lecture Notes in Computer Science 2400, Springer-Verlag
    (2002) 965–972
20. Hayashi, T., Nakano, K., Olariu, S.: Randomized Initialization Protocols for
    Packet Radio Networks. International Parallel Processing Symposium (IPPS),
    IEEE (1999)

Clock Synchronization for Wireless Networks

Rui Fan, Indraneel Chakraborty, and Nancy Lynch

Massachusetts Institute of Technology, Cambridge MA 02139, USA
rfan@theory.csail.mit.edu, indranil@lcs.mit.edu, lynch@theory.csail.mit.edu

Abstract. Time synchronization is a fundamental service in many wireless applications. While the synchronization problem is well-studied in traditional wired networks, physical constraints of the wireless medium impose a unique set of challenges. We present a novel time synchronization algorithm which is highly energy efficient and failure/recovery-tolerant. Our algorithm allows nodes to synchronize to sources of real time such as GPS when such signals are available, but continues to synchronize nodes to each other, even in the absence of GPS. In addition, the algorithm satisfies a relaxed gradient property, in which the degree of synchronization between nodes varies as a linear function of their distance. Thus, nearby nodes are highly synchronized, which is desirable in many wireless applications.

1 Introduction

Wireless networks are an increasingly important medium for distributed computation. As wireless applications grow more diverse and sophisticated, time synchronization among wireless nodes has emerged as a common requirement of many applications. For example, MAC layer protocols such as TDMA [5] require time synchronization to schedule collision-free broadcast schedules. Time synchronization is essential in sensor networks, which collect data from a physical environment, then tag the data with the time of its occurrence. Time synchronization is also needed in high-level applications to timestamp and order events and signals, and for security purposes. While time synchronization in wired networks is a well-studied problem, the wireless medium presents a unique set of challenges. The primary concern of all wireless applications is energy conservation. A clock synchronization algorithm (*CSA* for short) must carefully regiment its frequency of resynchronization, and avoid flooding. In addition, the algorithm cannot typically rely on a power-hungry source of real time such as GPS. Another characteristic of wireless networks is unexpected and possibly frequent changes in network topology. Thus, a CSA in a wireless medium must continue to function in the face of node failures and recoveries. Lastly, many applications in wireless settings are local in nature. That is, only nearby nodes in the network need to participate in some activity. Thus, a desirable property for a CSA is that it closely synchronizes nodes which are nearby, while possibly allowing faraway nodes to be more loosely synchronized.

T. Higashino (Ed.): OPODIS 2004, LNCS 3544, pp. 400–414, 2005.

In this work, we present a time synchronization algorithm addressing the requirements of a wireless network. Our algorithm is energy-efficient: nodes perform at most one local (1-hop) broadcast per synchronization round. It tolerates dynamic network behavior: the algorithm continues to function when there are arbitrary node failures and joins. A novel feature of our algorithm is that it performs both *internal synchronization*, i.e. synchronizing nodes with each other, and *external synchronization*, i.e. synchronizing nodes with real time. The algorithm allows incorporating a GPS source of real time when such signals are available, but continues to synchronize nodes with each other even in the absence of GPS. Thus, for example, a sensor node can use our algorithm both for timestamping data with real time, and to schedule TDMA broadcasts, which only requires relative time among the nodes. Our algorithm satisfies a relaxed *gradient* property. In particular, the algorithm ensures that the clock skew of two nodes which are distance d apart in the network is bounded by a linear function of d, at almost all times. Finally, our algorithm is practical and easy to implement. It requires little memory and computation, and is suited for resource-bounded wireless nodes.

The remainder of this paper is organized as follows. In Section 2, we describe some related work on clock synchronization. In Sections 3 and 4, we describe our formal model and problem. We present our synchronization algorithm in Section 5, and show that it satisfies the desired properties in Section 6. Finally, we conclude and discuss some future work in Section 7.

2 Related Work

NTP [6] is a widely deployed time synchronization service. NTP relies on a hierarchy of time servers, and assumes that root servers have access to a correct source of real time. In contrast, our algorithm works in a network with no infrastructure support. Access to real time via GPS may exist, but is intermittent. Furthermore, unlike NTP, we tolerate a highly dynamic network, and node failures and joins are accommodated without disturbing the synchronization in the rest of the network. Srikanth and Toueg [7] present an optimal clock synchronization algorithm. However, their algorithm relies on broadcast, and is not suitable for a wireless network. Their algorithm performs only internal synchronization, while we integrate external and internal synchronization. Also, [7] is complicated by the need to tolerate Byzantine failures. Our algorithm only tolerates stopping failures, but is much simpler.

RBS [1] is an efficient CSA designed for wireless networks. RBS performs *post-hoc* synchronization, in which nodes determine the time of an event some time after it has occurred. By contrast, our algorithm performs on-the-fly synchronization, so that we can timestamp an event at the moment it occurs. In addition, RBS performs only internal synchronization.

CesiumSpray [8] is a CSA performing both internal and external synchronization. CesiumSpray achieves high accuracy using the simultaneity of message reception by all nodes in a satellite/wireless network. However, we cannot guarantee simultaneity in the wireless networks we consider because the networks are multihop. In addition, CesiumSpray has lower fault tolerance than our algorithm, and does not achieve the gradient property. Fetzer and Cristian [3] also integrate internal and external synchronization. However, their algorithm is more complex than ours because it deals with faulty GPS information. In practice, we think such failures are unlikely to occur.

Fan and Lynch [2] introduced the gradient property for clock synchronization. They showed that for every CSA, there exist executions in which two nodes distance d apart have clock skew $\Omega(d + \frac{\log D}{\log \log D})$, where D is the diameter of the network. However, their result requires a lower bound on the rate of increase of every node's logical clock. Our algorithm permits logical clocks to be constant for some period of time. Thus, their lower bound does not directly apply.

3   System Model

Our system model consists of three parts: a dynamic set of *nodes*, a *communication network* over which nodes send messages, and a *GPS service* which occasionally informs nodes of the real time. Below, we discuss each part separately.

3.1   Nodes

We wish to model a dynamic system in which nodes can fail or join the system at arbitrary times. To do this, we define N to be the set of *potential nodes*. Each node in N can be in either a *sleeping* or *awake* state, and the state of the node can change at any time. The set of nodes which participate in the clock synchronization algorithm at some time consists of the awake nodes at that time. Failures of nodes are modeled by a node changing from the awake state to the sleeping state. Joins of nodes are modeled by the opposite transition.

Each node is equipped with a hardware clock, which we think of as a variable whose value changes as a differentiable function of time. Denote the value of node i's hardware clock at time t by $H_i(t)$. We assume that the hardware clock of every node has *bounded drift*. More precisely, we assume that there exists $\rho < 1$[1], such that for all nodes i,

$$\forall t : 1 - \rho \leq \frac{dH_i(t)}{dt} \leq 1 + \rho$$

Each node uses its hardware clock and messages it receives from other nodes to compute a logical clock value. Denote the value of node i's logical clock at time t by $L_i(t)$. The clock synchronization algorithm tries to ensure that the logical clock values of the nodes are close to each other, and close to real time.

---

[1] In practice, ρ is very small, on the order of 10^{-5} or 10^{-6}.

3.2   Communication Network

Nodes communicate with each other over a message passing network. In some wireless networks, e.g., ad hoc networks, the network changes depending on the set of awake nodes, because the awake nodes are responsible for routing messages among themselves. Other problems may arise if the network becomes disconnected by too many node failures. However, such network problems are separate from the problem of clock synchronization. Thus, in this paper, we make a simplifying assumption that there exists a virtual communication link between every pair of nodes $i, j \in N$. We assume that each link is reliable, FIFO, and has bounded delay. Regarding the last assumption, we assume that for every i, j, there exists a constant $d_{i,j} < \infty$, called the *distance* between i and j, which upper bounds the amount of time it takes for a message sent by i to be received by j. For simplicity, we assume $d_{i,j} = d_{j,i}$.[2] Finally, we let the *diameter* of the network be $D = \max_{i,j} d_{i,j}$.

3.3   GPS Service

We imagine that all nodes are equipped with GPS receivers[3], and that occasionally, a GPS service transmits a message informing nodes of the correct real time. The times when these transmissions occur are not under the control of the nodes. We model the receipt of a GPS message at a node i by an input action $gps(t)_i$. This message is intended to inform i that the current real time is t. However, the message may not be accurate, in the sense that i may receive the message *after* real time t. This is because it takes some time for the GPS message to propagate to the entire network. However, we bound the inaccuracy of every GPS message, by assuming that all nodes which are awake during the time interval $[t, t + D]$ receive $gps(t)$ no later than time $t + D$, where D is the diameter of the network.

4   The Clock Synchronization Problem

In this section, we define the internal, external and gradient synchronization properties that the clock synchronization algorithm must satisfy. It is not possible to satisfy these properties at all times and at all nodes, when the nodes are allowed to fail and join/recover. Thus, at any time t, the synchronization properties are only required to hold for nodes which are stable at time t. We say a node is *stable* at time t if it has received at least one GPS input before t, and has not failed since receiving that GPS. Let $S(t) \subseteq N$ denote the set of nodes which are stable at time t. We say an execution is *failure free* if $S(t) = N$ for all t. Otherwise, we say the execution is *failure prone*.

---

[2] If $d_{i,j} \neq d_{j,i}$, we can simply redefine $d'_{i,j} = d'_{j,i} = \max(d_{i,j}, d_{j,i})$, then use $d'_{i,j}$ as the distance between i and j.

[3] Actually, it is enough for one node to have a GPS receiver, and for this node to propagate GPS messages to the rest of the network.

The precision requirement deals with internal synchronization of the nodes, i.e., bounding the difference in the logical clock values of any two nodes. Let ϵ be a parameter. Formally, we require the algorithm satisfy

Requirement 1 (ϵ-Precision). $\forall t \forall i, j \in S(t) : |L_i(t) - L_j(t)| \leq \epsilon$

The accuracy requirement deals with external synchronization of the nodes, i.e., bounding the difference between the logical clock value of any node and real time. Let ϵ be a parameter. We require the algorithm satisfy

Requirement 2 (ϵ-Accuracy). $\forall t \forall i \in S(t) : |L_i(t) - t| \leq \epsilon$

The gradient property was introduced in [2]. It requires that at all times, the difference in the logical clock values of any two nodes which are distance d apart in the communication network (i.e, nodes i, j, such that $d_{i,j} = d$) is bounded by $f(d)$, where f is a nondecreasing function of d. The gradient property is desirable in applications where the clocks of nearby nodes must be well synchronized, whereas the clocks of faraway nodes can be more loosely synchronized. An example of such an application is TDMA. In TDMA, only nearby nodes can collide when transmitting, and thus only such nodes need well synchronized clocks for scheduling their transmissions. Please see [2] for additional motivations and discussion of the gradient property. Our synchronization algorithm satisfies a weakened form of the gradient property, where the gradient property holds only *some* of the time. More precisely, let $T \subseteq \mathbb{R}^{\geq 0}$ consisting of the union of nonzero-length intervals. Then we require that the algorithm satisfy the gradient property for all times in T. Of course, our goal is to maximize the size of T, i.e., maximize $\frac{m(T)}{m(\mathbb{R}^{\geq 0})}$, where $m(\cdot)$ denotes the Lebesgue measure on $\mathbb{R}$. Let α, β be parameters. Formally, we require

Requirement 3 ((T, α, β)-Gradient Precision). $\forall t \in T \forall i, j \in S(t) : |L_i(t) - L_j(t)| \leq \alpha d_{i,j} + \beta$

5   Algorithm

In this section, we describe our clock synchronization algorithm. The pseudocode of the algorithm is written in the TIOA language [4], and is presented in Figure 1. Below, we give an overview of how the algorithm operates.

Each node in the algorithm maintains two clocks, a *local* clock and a *global* clock. The local clock of node i represents i's best estimate of the current real time. i's global clock represents i's estimate of the largest local clock of any other node. Roughly speaking, i's logical clock is defined to be the maximum of i's local and global clocks[4]. i's local clock is updated by the occasional GPS inputs which i receives. i's global clock is updated by the periodic internal synchronizations

---

[4] This definition is meant to convey intuition, and is not exactly correct; it is amended in the following paragraphs.

$ClockSync_i, i \in \mathbb{I}$

Constants

$0 \leq \rho < 1$

$0 < \tau$

State

$idle \in$ Boolean, initially $true$
for all $k \in \mathbb{N} : local[k] \in \mathbb{R}$, initially 0
for all $k \in \mathbb{N} : global[k] \in \mathbb{R}$, initially 0
$current \in \mathbb{N}$, initially 0
$next\_sync \in \mathbb{N}$, initially 0

$hardware \in \mathbb{R}$
$max\_gps \in \mathbb{R}$, initially 0
$do\_send \in$ Boolean, initially $false$
$send\_buffer$, a queue of elements of type $\mathbb{R} \times \mathbb{R}$, initially empty

Derived Variables

$mlocal \leftarrow \max_k local[k]$
$mglobal \leftarrow \max_k global[k]$

$logical \leftarrow \max(mlocal, mglobal)$

Transitions

input **wakeup**$_i$
Effect:
  if $idle$ then
    $idle \leftarrow false$
    $current \leftarrow 1$

input **gps**$(t)_i$
Effect:
  if $\neg idle$ then
    if $t > max\_gps$ then
      $max\_gps \leftarrow t$
      $current \leftarrow current + 1$
      $local[current] \leftarrow t$
      $global[current] \leftarrow t$
      $next\_sync \leftarrow \lfloor \frac{t}{\tau} \rfloor + 1$

input **recv**$(t, s)_{j,i}$
Effect:
  if $\neg idle$ then
    if $s \geq max\_gps$ then
      if $t > global[current]$ then
        $global[current] \leftarrow t$
        enqueue (t, s) in $send\_buffer$
        $do\_send \leftarrow true$
        if $\frac{t}{\tau} \geq next\_sync$ then
          $next\_sync \leftarrow \frac{t}{\tau} + 1$

input **crash**$_i$
Effect:
  $idle \leftarrow true$
  for all $k \in \mathbb{N}$ do
    $local[k] \leftarrow 0$
    $global[k] \leftarrow 0$
  $current \leftarrow 0$
  $next\_sync \leftarrow 0$
  $max\_gps \leftarrow 0$
  $do\_send \leftarrow false$
  empty $send\_buffer$

output **sync**$(t, s)_i$
Precondition:
  $\neg idle$
  $t = local[current]$
  $\frac{t}{\tau} = next\_sync$
  $s = max\_gps$
Effect:
  enqueue (t, s) in $send\_buffer$
  $next\_sync \leftarrow next\_sync + 1$
  $do\_send \leftarrow true$

output **send**$(t, s)_i$
Precondition:
  $\neg idle$
  $send\_buffer$ is not empty
  $(t, s) =$ head of $send\_buffer$
Effect:
  remove head of $send\_buffer$
  $do\_send \leftarrow false$

Trajectories

Satisfies
  unchanged:
    $idle, current, next\_sync, max\_gps, do\_send,$
    $send\_buffer$
    $1 - \rho \leq d(hardware) \leq 1 + \rho$

$\forall k \in \mathbb{N} :$
  if $\neg idle \wedge (k = current)$ then
    $d(local[k] - hardware) = 0$
    $d(global[k] - \frac{1-\rho}{1+\rho} hardware) = 0$
  else
    $d(local[k]) = 0$
    $d(global[k]) = 0$

Stops at
  $(\frac{local[current]}{\tau} = next\_send) \vee (do\_send = true)$

Fig. 1. $ClockSync_i$ state and transitions

which the nodes perform. i's local clock increases at the same rate as i's hardware clock. i's global clock increases at a rate $\frac{1-\rho}{1+\rho}$ times i's hardware clock rate. The reason for the rate of increase of i's global clock is so that i does not overestimate the local clocks of other nodes.

When i receives a GPS signal, it updates its local clock to the value of the signal. However, to avoid setting i's logical clock backwards[5], i stores its current local clock value, and allocates a new local clock initialized to the time in the GPS signal. i's *virtual local clock*, *mlocal*, is set to be the larger of i's local clock, and i's stored local clock value. Moreover, i's logical clock value is defined as the larger of i's *mlocal*, and i's *mglobal*, which will be defined shortly.

The way that the transfer of local clock values after receiving a GPS is actually implemented in our algorithm is slightly different from what is stated above, though it amounts to the same idea. In our algorithm, i stores an array *local* of local clock values, and there is an index *current* keeping track of i's currently active local clock. i increases *local*[*current*] at the same rate as its hardware clock, but keeps *local*[*k*] constant, for all $k \neq current$. When i receives a GPS input, i increases *current*. This has the effect of storing i's previous local clock and starting a new one. The new local clock is initialized to the value of the GPS input. *mlocal* is defined as the maximum value in *local*[·]. In addition, i stores an array *global* of global clock values, and updates the array in a similar way to how i updates its *local* clock values after it receives a GPS. *mglobal* is defined as the maximum value in *global*[·].

To maintain internal synchronization, each node executes its *sync* action approximately once every τ time, where τ is a constant. More precisely, each node i stores an index *next_sync*, and when i finds *local*[*current*] $= \tau \cdot next\_sync$, i performs the *sync*$_i$ action. Then, i increments *next_sync*. The *sync* action sends out a message of the form (*local*[*current*], *max_gps*), where *max_gps* is the largest GPS value that i has received. *max_gps* acts as a "certificate" of how accurate i's *local*[*current*] is. That is, the higher i's value of *max_gps*, the more recently that i has received a GPS input, and thus the more accurate is i's value *local*[*current*].

Now, consider when i receives a synchronization message (t, s), where t is the *local*[*current*] of some other node, say j, and s is j's value of *max_gps*. i checks that j has received at least as recent a GPS value as i, and also that j's *local*[*current*] is greater than i's *global*[*current*], which is i's current estimate of the largest *local*[*current*] of any other node. If both conditions are true, then i stores t in *global*[*current*], and propagates the message (t, s) to i's neighbors in the network. Lastly, if $t \geq \tau \cdot next\_sync$, then there is no need for i to do *sync* when i finds its own *local*[*current*] $= \tau \cdot next\_sync$, since j has already done a *sync* with the same timestamp. In this case, i sets *next_sync* to $\lfloor \frac{t}{\tau} \rfloor + 1$.

Lastly, we describe how the algorithm deals with node failures and joins. If a node fails, it does not interfere with synchronization among the remaining

---

[5] Many applications require logical clocks to be monotonic, in addition to being accurate and precise.

nodes. Thus, nothing is needed to deal with node failures. If a node joins, then it initializes its state to some default values, and waits to receive its first GPS input. The GPS input initializes the new node's state to some correct values, after which the node can participate normally in the algorithm.

6   Analysis

In this section, we show that the algorithm described in Section 5 satisfies the requirements described in Section 4. We first describe the notation used in the proofs.

6.1   Notation

Let i be a node, let var be a state variable of i, and let t be a time. Then we let $i.var(t)$ be the value of var at i at time t, *before* any discrete actions have occurred at time t. We let $i.var(t^+)$ be the value of var at i at time t, *after all* discrete actions have occurred at time t. Thus, for example, if $i.current = 1$ at time 5, and i receives a GPS at time 5 which causes i to increment $current$, then we have $i.current(5) = 1$, and $i.current(5^+) = 2$.

As stated in Section 5, nodes perform *sync* actions approximately every τ time. We also assume that the GPS service updates the nodes every T time, for some constant T. That is, suppose $gps(t)$ occurs at some node at time t_1. Then $gps(t')$ must occur at some node at time t_2, where $t' > t$, and $t_1 \leq t_2 \leq t_1 + T$. Given an action $\xi = gps(t)$, we say t is the *timestamp* of ξ. Given an action $\phi = recv(t, s)$, we say t is the *timestamp* of ϕ.

If a node i receives a $gps(t)_i$ input, we say the GPS is *useful* if $t > max\_gps$, so that it causes i to change its state. Similarly, if i receives a $recv(t, s)_{j,i}$ input, we say the $recv$ is *useful* if $s \geq max\_gps$ and $t > global[current]$, so that it causes i to change its state.

6.2   Proof of Correctness

We first prove a lemma which states that in a failure free execution, the *mglobal* of any node is never much more than the maximum *mlocal* of all the nodes. This lemma is used to show that the algorithm satisfies ϵ-accuracy, even in failure prone executions.

Lemma 1. *Consider a failure free execution* α. *Then*

$$\forall t \forall i \in N : \max_i i.mglobal(t) \leq \max_j j.mlocal(t) + (1 - \rho)D$$

Proof.   We begin by proving $\forall t : \max_i i.global[current](t) \leq \max_j j.mlocal(t) + (1 - \rho)D$, then show that this implies the lemma. To prove the former statement, fix an i and a t, and consider the *last* useful message ϕ which i received before time t. Suppose ϕ was received at time t_2. There are 2 cases. Either ϕ is a GPS, or it is a *recv*.

In the first case, we have $i.global[current](t_2^+) \leq i.local[current](t_2^+)$. Also, since i receives no other useful messages during $(t_2, t]$, we have

$$i.local[current](t) \geq i.local[current](t_2^+) + (1 - \rho)(t - t_2)$$

$$i.global[current](t) \leq i.global[current](t_2^+) + \frac{1 - \rho}{1 + \rho}(1 + \rho)(t - t_2)$$

$$\leq i.local[current](t)$$

The second inequality follows because i increases $i.global[current]$ at a rate of $\frac{1-\rho}{1+\rho}$ times its hardware clock rate, which is at most $1 + \rho$.

In the second case, where ϕ is a *recv*, let j be the node which sent ϕ, and suppose ϕ was sent at time t_1. Then we have

$$i.global[current](t_2^+) \leq j.local[current](t_1) \tag{1}$$

Consider the *first* useful GPS ξ that j receives after time t_1, and suppose j received ξ at time t_3. Let the timestamp of ξ be s_1.

Claim. $t - t_3 \leq D$

Proof. Suppose for contradiction that $t - t_3 > D$. Then since ξ takes at most D time to reach i, i must have received ξ by time t, say at time t_4. Consider two cases. Either $t_4 < t_2$, or $t_4 \geq t_2$.

In the first case, let $s_2 = j.max\_gps(t_1)$. Then, since j found ξ useful at time t_3, we have $s_1 > s_2$. Since i receives ξ, which has timestamp s_1, at time $t_4 < t_2$, then $i.max\_gps(t_2) \geq s_1$. But i receives ϕ with timestamp s_2 at time t_2, and i found ϕ useful, and so $s_2 \geq i.max\_gps(t_2) \geq s_1$, which is a contradiction.

In the second case, we also get a contradiction, because when i receives ξ at time t_4, i must either find ξ useful, or i found some other message it received in the time interval $[t_2, t_4]$ useful. In either case, this contradicts the assumption that ϕ was the last useful message i received before time t. Thus, we have $t - t_3 \leq D$. $\square$

Since the first GPS which j received after time t_1 occurs at $t_3 \geq t - D$, then j did not change $j.current$ until at least time t_3, and $j.local[current]$ increased at a rate which is at least $1 - \rho$ in the time interval $[t_1, t_3]$. Thus, we have

$$j.local[current](t) \geq j.local[current](t_1) + (1 - \rho)(t_3 - t_1)$$

Also, since i did not receive any useful messages during time interval $(t_2, t]$, we have

$$i.global[current](t) \leq i.global[current](t_2^+) + \frac{1 - \rho}{1 + \rho}(1 + \rho)(t - t_2)$$

$$\leq j.local[current](t_1) + (1 - \rho)(t - t_1)$$

$$\leq j.local[current](t) + (1 - \rho)(t - t_3)$$

$$\leq j.local[current](t) + (1 - \rho)D$$

Where the second inequality follows from Eqn. 1. Thus, we have shown that in all cases, and for all t, we have $\max_i i.global[current](t) \leq \max_j j.mlocal(t) + (1-\rho)D$. Now, now let t_k^* be the k'th time when i incremented $i.current$. Then, we have

$$i.mglobal(t) = \max_k i.global[k](t_k^*)$$
$$\leq \max_k \max_j j.mlocal(t_k^*)$$
$$\leq \max_j \max_k j.mlocal(t_k^*)$$
$$\leq \max_j j.mlocal(t)$$

Thus, we have shown that $\forall t : \max_i i.mglobal(t) \leq \max_j j.mlocal(t) + (1-\rho)D$.

The next lemma states that in all executions, including failure prone ones, any node's logical clock value is not much greater than real time.

Lemma 2. $\forall t \forall i \in N : \max_i i.logical(t) - t \leq \rho(T+D) + (1-\rho)D$

Proof. Fix an i and a t. Since $i.logical(t) = \max(i.mlocal(t), i.mglobal(t))$, we first show that $i.mlocal(t) - t \leq \rho(T+D)$. Consider the last useful GPS ξ that i received before time t. Suppose ξ occurred at time t_1, and the timestamp for ξ was s. We have $t - t_1 \leq T + D$, because a GPS occurs somewhere in the network every T time, and the GPS takes at most D time to reach i. Now, $i.local[current](t_1^+) = s \leq t_1$, and because i received no other GPS in the time interval $(t_1, t]$, we have $i.local[current](t) \leq i.local[current](t_1^+) + (1+\rho)(t-t_1)$. Thus, we have

$$i.local[current](t) - t \leq t_1 + (1+\rho)(t-t_1) - t$$
$$= \rho(t - t_1)$$
$$\leq \rho(T+D)$$

We have shown that for all i and t, $i.local[current](t) - t \leq \rho(T+D)$. Since $i.mlocal(t) = \max_k i.local[k]$, we have $i.mlocal(t) - t \leq \rho(T+D)$, for all i and t.

By Lemma 1, we have that in failure free executions, $i.mglobal(t) \leq \max_j j.mlocal(t) + (1-\rho)D \leq \rho(T+D) + (1-\rho)D$. Now, we observe that if there are failures in an execution, then the failures cannot cause $i.mglobal(t)$ to increase. Thus, in failure prone executions, we also have $i.mglobal(t) \leq \rho(T+D) + (1-\rho)D$. Finally, since $i.logical(t) = \max(i.mlocal(t), i.mglobal(t))$, we have that $i.logical(t) \leq \rho(T+D) + (1-\rho)D$, for all i and t. $\square$

The next lemma states that any stable node's logical clock value is not much less than real time.

Lemma 3. $\forall t \forall i \in S(t) : t - \min_i i.logical(t) \leq D + \rho(T+D)$

Proof. Fix a t and an $i \in S(t)$. Since i is stable at time t, i has received a GPS before time t, and has not failed since that GPS. Consider the last

GPS ξ that i received before time t, and suppose that ξ occurred at time t_1, and had timestamp s. Then $t_1 - i.local[current](t_1^+) = t_1 - s \leq D$. Also, $i.local[current](t) \geq i.local[current](t_1^+) + (1 - \rho)(t - t_1)$. Since $t - t_1 \leq T + D$, we have $t - i.logical(t) \leq t - i.local(t) \leq D + \rho(T + D)$, for any i and t.   □

Combining Lemmas 2 and 3, we get the following.

Theorem 1 (Accuracy). *In all executions,* $\forall t \forall i \in S(t) : |i.logical(t) - t| \leq D + \rho(T + D)$.

From Theorem 1, we immediately get the following.

Theorem 2 (Precision). *In all executions,* $\forall t \forall i, j \in S(t) : |i.logical(t) - j.logical(t)| \leq 2(D + \rho(T + D))$.

To save energy in practice, the GPS service might update the nodes infrequently, so that T can be quite large. Yet even in periods without GPS, the nodes still perform internal synchronization approximately once every τ time. Since τ may be much smaller than T, we would like a sharper bound on precision, stated in terms of τ instead of T. Unfortunately, there is no such bound which holds at all times. The reason for this is that GPS inputs cause "instability" in the network, as follows. Consider when a node i receives a GPS signal ξ. Since i's logical clock may differ from real time by up to $O(\rho T)$, and since ξ causes i to adjust its logical clock to real time, then $i.logical$ may "jump" by $O(\rho T)$ after i receives ξ. However, since other nodes may not receive ξ at the same time as i, there may be a time period when i's logical clock has jumped forward, but other nodes' logical clocks have not. In this period, the precision is bounded by $O(\rho T)$. On the other hand, we show that if a GPS has *not occurred* within the last D time, then the precision is bounded by $O(\rho \tau)$. To prove this statement, we first show it holds in failure free executions in which *no* GPS inputs occur. Then we show it holds in failure free executions with GPS, and finally, we show it holds in failure prone executions with GPS.

Lemma 4. *Consider a failure free execution in which no GPS inputs occur. Then* $\forall t \forall i, j \in N : |i.logical(t) - j.logical(t)| \leq \frac{4\rho}{(1+\rho)^2}\tau + (1 + \rho)D$.

Proof.   Fix an i and j. Let m be the largest integer such that $i.logical(t) \geq \tau m$. Let t_2 be such that $i.logical(t_2) = \tau m$. Let t_1 be the earliest time such that the *mlocal* of any node equals τm. That is, $t_1 = \min_s \exists k : k.mlocal(s) = \tau m$. Let t_3 be the earliest time such that the *mlocal* of any node equals $\tau(m + 1)$. In the following analysis, it suffices to assume that $t_1 \leq t_2 \leq t_3 \leq t$. Let $d_1 = t_2 - t_1$, $r = t_3 - t_2$, and $d_2 = t - t_3$. We have that $d_1 \leq D$, because the first node to reach τm sends out a *sync* message, which i receives no more than D time later. After i receives the message, we have $i.logical \geq \tau m$. Similarly, $d_2 \leq D$.

We claim that $r \geq \frac{\tau}{1+\rho} - d_1$. Indeed, since there are no GPS inputs, then the maximum rate of increase of the *mlocal* of any node is at most $1 + \rho$. Since $\max_k k.mlocal(t_1) = \tau m$, $\max_k k.mlocal(t_3) = \tau(m + 1)$, and $t_3 - t_1 = r + d_1$, we have $(1 + \rho)(r + d_1) \geq \tau$, from which the claim follows.

Now, again because there are no GPS inputs, the rate of increase of the logical clock of any node is at most $1 + \rho$, and at least $\frac{1-\rho}{1+\rho}(1 - \rho)$. Thus, we have

$$j.logical(t) \leq j.logical(t_3) + (1 + \rho)(t - t_3)$$
$$\leq \tau(m + 1) + (1 + \rho)d_2$$
$$i.logical(t) \geq i.logical(t_2) + \frac{(1 - \rho)^2}{1 + \rho}(t - t_2)$$
$$\geq \tau m + \frac{(1 - \rho)^2}{1 + \rho}(r + d_2)$$
$$\geq \tau m + \frac{(1 - \rho)^2}{1 + \rho}(\frac{\tau}{1 + \rho} + d_2 - d_1)$$

Now, since we have $d_1, d_2 \leq D$, then subtracting the two inequalities above, we get

$$j.logical(t) - i.logical(t) \leq \frac{4\rho}{(1 + \rho)^2}\tau + \left(1 + \rho - \frac{(1 - \rho)^2}{1 + \rho}\right)d_2 + \frac{(1 - \rho)^2}{1 + \rho}d_1$$
$$\leq \frac{4\rho}{(1 + \rho)^2}\tau + (1 + \rho)D. \qquad \square$$

Lemma 5. *Consider a failure free execution, and let t be a time such that no GPS inputs occur in the time period $[t - D, t]$. Then $\forall i, j \in N : |i.logical(t) - j.logical(t)| \leq \frac{4\rho}{(1+\rho)^2}\tau + (1 + \rho)D$.*

Proof.   Fix an i, j and t. Define t_1, t_2, t_3 as in the proof of Lemma 4. Now, since no GPS occurs in the time interval $[t - D, t]$, and $t - t_3 \leq D$, then no GPS occurs in the time interval $[t_3, t]$. Consider two cases. Either no GPS occurs in time interval $[t_1, t_3]$, or some GPS occurs. In the first case, we can prove the lemma using similar ideas as in the proof of Lemma 4. For the second case, we consider a simplified version, in which only one GPS occurs in $[t_1, t_3]$. The general case with multiple GPS signals is similar. Let ξ be the GPS input which occurs, and suppose ξ has timestamp s, and ξ occurs at j at time t_j. Following the proof of Lemma 4, we can show that $|i.logical(t_j) - j.logical(t_j)| \leq \frac{4\rho}{(1+\rho)^2}\tau + (1 + \rho)D$. Also, since $t_3 - t_1 \leq \frac{\tau}{1+\rho}$, we have

$$j.local[current](t) \leq s + \frac{\tau}{1 + \rho}(1 + \rho)$$
$$i.local[current](t) \geq s + (\frac{\tau}{1 + \rho} - D)(1 - \rho)$$

Now, since there is only one GPS in $[t_1, t_3]$, we have

$$j.logical(t) = \max(j.logical(t_j), j.local[current](t))$$

and

$$i.logical(t) = \max(i.logical(t_j), i.local[current](t))$$

Thus, we have

$$|j.logical(t) - i.logical(t)| \leq \max(|j.logical(t_j) - |i.logical(t_j)|,$$
$$|j.local[current](t) - i.local[current](t)|)$$
$$\leq \max(\frac{4\rho}{(1+\rho)^2}\tau + (1+\rho)D, \frac{2\rho}{1+\rho}\tau + (1-\rho)D)$$
$$= \frac{4\rho}{(1+\rho)^2}\tau + (1+\rho)D$$

The last equality follows because $\rho < 1$. Thus, we have proven the lemma in all cases. $\qquad \square$

Theorem 3 (Strong Precision). *Let t be a time such that no GPS inputs occurred in the time interval $[t-D,t]$. Then $\forall i,j \in S(t) : |i.logical(t) - j.logical(t)| \leq \frac{4\rho}{(1+\rho)^2}\tau + (1+\rho)D$.*

Proof. To prove this theorem, notice first that failures have *no effect* on the precision of synchronization. Second, if $i,j \in S(t)$, then they have each received at least one GPS. Using this fact, the lemma follows from very similar ideas as in the proof of Lemma 5. We omit the proof for lack of space. $\qquad \square$

Lastly, we consider the gradient property requirement. Consider two nodes i and j which are distance d apart. Just as GPS inputs caused "instability" which made precision $O(\rho T)$ instead of $O(\rho\tau)$, *sync* messages cause instability which makes the logical clock difference between i and j $O(\rho\tau + D)$, instead of $O(\rho\tau + d)$, as required by the gradient property. However, the gradient property does holds at time t, if there are no GPS and no *sync* inputs in the time interval $[t - D, t]$. More precisely, we have the following.

Theorem 4 (Gradient Precision). *Consider any execution, and let t be a time such that no GPS inputs and no sync inputs occur in the time interval $[t - D, t]$. Let $i,j \in S(t)$ be two nodes which are distance d apart. Then $|i.logical(t) - j.logical(t)| \leq \frac{4\rho}{(1+\rho)^2}\tau + (1+\rho)$.*

Proof. We prove a simpler version of the theorem, when the execution is failure free, and when there are no GPS inputs, but possibly some *sync* inputs. The full theorem can be proved in a similar way, and by following ideas in the proofs of Lemma 5 and Theorem 3. We omit the full proof due to lack of space.

Fix an i,j and t. Let m be the largest integer such that $i.logical(t) \geq \tau m$, and let t_2 be such that $i.logical(t_2) = \tau m$. Let t_1 be such that $j.logical(t_1) = \tau m$, and let t_3 be such that $j.logical(t_3) = \tau(m+1)$. Let $d_1 = t_2 - t_1$, $r = t_3 - t_2$, and $d_2 = t - t_3$. In the following analysis, it will suffice to consider $t_1 \leq t_2 \leq t_3 \leq t$. By the assumptions of the theorem, j does not receive a *sync* in the time interval $[t - d, t] \subseteq [t - D, t]$.

We claim that j does not receive any useful *sync* inputs during $[t_1, t]$. Indeed, suppose j received a useful *sync* ϕ at time $t' < t - d$. Then the timestamp for

ϕ must be at least $\tau(m+1)$, since otherwise j would not find ϕ useful. Since $t' < t - d$ and $d_{i,j} = d$, then i must receive ϕ before time t. But then we would have $i.logical(t) \geq \tau(m+1)$, which is a contradiction. Thus, since j does not receive a useful $sync$ during $[t_1, t]$, j's logical clock increases at a rate at most $1 + \rho$ during $[t_1, t]$, and so we have

$$j.logical(t) \leq j.logical(t_3) + (1+\rho)(t - t_3)$$
$$= \tau(m+1) + (1+\rho)d_2$$

Also, i's logical clock increases at a rate at least $\frac{1-\rho}{1+\rho}(1-\rho)$, so we have

$$i.logical(t) \geq i.logical(t_2) + \frac{(1-\rho)^2}{1+\rho}(t - t_2)$$
$$= \tau m + \frac{(1-\rho)^2}{1+\rho}(r + d_2)$$

Now, since j's logical clock increased by τ from time t_1 to t_3, and j's logical clock rate was at most $1+\rho$ during this time, we have $(1+\rho)(t_3 - t_1) = (1+\rho)(r+d_1) \geq \tau$. Thus, $r \geq \frac{\tau}{1+\rho} - d_1$. Also, we have $d_1, d_2 \leq d$, because $i.logical$ must reach τm (resp., $\tau(m+1)$) within d time that $j.logical$ reaches τm (resp., $\tau(m+1)$). Thus, subtracting the two inequalities from above, we get

$$j.logical(t) - i.logical(t) \leq \frac{4\rho}{(1+\rho)^2}\tau + \left(1+\rho - \frac{(1-\rho)^2}{1+\rho}\right)d_2 + \frac{(1-\rho)^2}{1+\rho}d_1$$
$$\leq \frac{4\rho}{(1+\rho)^2}\tau + (1+\rho)d$$

$\square$

Finally, we consider the communication complexity of the algorithm. We show that each node performs roughly one local (i.e. 1-hop) broadcast per τ time. By comparison, many clock synchronization algorithms require each node to broadcast to the entire network during every synchronization period, which is not feasible for energy-conserving wireless nodes.

Theorem 5 (Communication Complexity). *Let i be any node. Then i performs at most 1 local broadcast every $\frac{\tau}{1+\rho}$ time.*

Proof. By looking at the $sync$ and $recv$ actions in Figure 1, we see that each node performs only one local broadcast for each value of $next\_sync$. The value of $next\_sync$ can only increase when the $local[current]$ of some node increases by τ, and this takes at least $\frac{\tau}{1+\rho}$ time. $\square$

7 Conclusions

We have presented an energy-efficient and fault-tolerant clock synchronization algorithm which integrates internal and external synchronization, and which satisfies a relaxed gradient property. Our algorithm is simple, and easily implementable on resource-bounded wireless nodes.

Our algorithm ensures tight synchronization among nodes when the network is stable, i.e. in periods when a GPS or synchronization operation has not recently occurred. However, when the network is unstable, clock skew may be much larger. Though certain lower bounds exist on the optimal tightness of non-gradient and gradient synchronization, the lower bounds do not immediately apply in our setting, because we do not require a lower bound on the rate of increase of logical clocks. It is an interesting theoretical and practical question whether tight synchronization can be maintained at all times, by allowing logical clocks to remain constant during unstable periods. Another interesting direction of further research is to implement our algorithm on a large scale wireless network, and to compare its average case behavior with the worst case bounds proven in this paper.

References

1. Jeremy Elson, Lewis Girod, and Deborah Estrin. Fine-grained network time synchronization using reference broadcasts. *SIGOPS Operating Systems Review*, 36(SI):147–163, 2002.
2. Rui Fan and Nancy Lynch. Gradient clock syncrhonization, to appear. In *Proceedings of the Twenty-third Annual ACM PODC*. ACM Press, 2004.
3. C. Fetzer and F. Cristian. Integrating external and internal clock synchronization. *Journal of Real-Time Systems*, 12(2):123–172, 1997.
4. Dilsun Kaynar, Nancy Lynch, Roberto Segala, and Frits Vaandrager. Timed i/o automata: A mathematical framework for modeling and analyzing real-time systems. In *Proceedings of the 24th IEEE International Real-Time Systems Symposium*, 2003.
5. Errol L. Lloyd. *Broadcast scheduling for TDMA in wireless multihop networks*. John Wiley & Sons, Inc., 2002.
6. D. L. Mills. Internet time synchronization: The network time protocol. *IEEE Transactions on Computers*, 39(10):1482–1493, 1991.
7. T. K. Srikanth and Sam Toueg. Optimal clock synchronization. *J. ACM*, 34(3):626–645, 1987.
8. P. Verissimo, L. Rodrigues, and A. Casimiro. *Cesiumspray: a precise and accurate global time service for large-scale systems*. Technical Report NAV-TR-97-0001, Universidade de Lisboa, 1997.

Task Assignment Based on Prioritising Traffic Flows*

James Broberg, Zahir Tari, and Panlop Zeephongsekul

RMIT University, GPO Box 2467V, VIC 3001 Australia
{jbroberg, zahirt}@cs.rmit.edu.au, panlopz@rmit.edu.au

Abstract. We consider the issue of task assignment in a distributed system under heavy-tailed (ie. highly variable) workloads. A new adaptable approach called TAPTF (Task Assignment based on Prioritising Traffic Flows) is proposed, which improves performance under heavy-tailed workloads for certain classes of traffic. TAPTF controls the influx of tasks to each host, enables service differentiation through the use of dual queues and prevents large tasks from unduly delaying small tasks via task migration. Analytical results show that TAPTF performs significantly better than existing approaches, where task sizes are unknown and tasks are non-preemptive (run-to-completion). As system load increases, the scope and the magnitude of the performance gain expands, exhibiting improvements of more than six times in some cases.

Keywords: scheduling policies, task assignment, heavy-tailed workloads, load balancing, load sharing, supercomputing.

1 Introduction

The use of a group (or 'cluster') of commodity computers in place of individual and typically expensive servers is becoming more prevalent. Examples include supercomputing clusters (such as the Virginia Tech Terascale Cluster) and high profile websites such as Google and Amazon, among other applications. Such clusters are popular due to their scalable and cost effective nature.

Figure 1 illustrates one common cluster configuration. Tasks, or "jobs" arrive at the central dispatcher, and are dispatched to hosts according to a *task assignment policy*. When a task arrives at the dispatcher, it is placed in a queue, waiting to be serviced in first-come-first-served (FCFS) order. In this paper we assume tasks are not preemptible (that is, they cannot be interrupted), task sizes are not known *a priori* and no load information is available at the dispatcher. This is consistent with many batch and supercomputing facilities (such as those described in [1, 2]) where preemption is not supported due to the enormous memory requirements of tasks.

The choice of task assignment policy used has a significant effect on user perceived performance and server throughput. A poor policy could assign large tasks to overloaded servers, drastically reducing the performance of the distributed system. Therefore, the aim of a task assignment policy is to distributed tasks such that all avail-

---

* This project is fully supported by the ARC Discovery Grant no. DP0346545 awarded by the Australian Research Council (ARC) for 2003-2005 and Sun Microsystems.

T. Higashino (Ed.): OPODIS 2004, LNCS 3544, pp. 415–430, 2005.

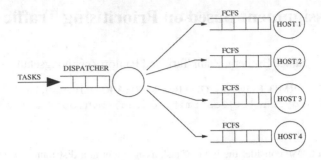

Fig. 1. Distributed Server Model

able system resources are utilised. Obviously it is undesirable to have one server in a distributed system overloaded while another server is sitting idle. However, the question of which assignment policy is the "best" still remains unanswered for many contexts.

Effective load distribution is especially crucial under realistic conditions of extremely heavy traffic demand and highly variable task sizes (i.e. the *workload*) that are commonly experienced in many computing environments [3, 4, 5, 6]. Past research has shown that a heavy-tailed distribution is suitable for modeling these realistic workloads [3, 5].

This paper proposes a new load distribution approach, called TAPTF (Task Assignment based on Prioritising Traffic Flows) which deals with certain inherent limitations of existing approaches in the same domain. TAPTF can improve performance under heavy-tailed workloads for certain classes of traffic by controlling the influx of tasks to each host depending on the variability of the workload. TAPTF also introduces multiple queues with hard processing time limits ('cutoffs') at each host. This enables service differentiation at each host, allowing small tasks to be executed quickly without being delayed by larger tasks. To achieve this, tasks that exceed the cutoff on a given host are migrated to the next host's restart queue (to be restarted from scratch).

TAPTF assumes no knowledge of the service requirements of incoming tasks. We are particularly interested in the areas that TAPTF can improve over TAGS, a policy that performs well when there is no preemption and task sizes are not known *a priori*. TAPTF is supported by a rigorous analytical model, based on fundamentals of queuing theory and priority queues.

The rest of this paper is organised as follows. Section 2 provides some background needed for the understanding of the concepts introduced in later sections. In Section 3 a survey of existing task assignment policies is presented. A detailed description of the TAPTF model is presented in Section 4. Section 5 gives an analytic comparison of TAPTF with existing approaches. Section 6 provides a detailed discussion of the analytical comparisons performed in Section 5. We conclude this paper with some closing thoughts on the usefulness of the TAPTF approach in Section 7.

2   Background

Many distributed computing environments exhibit a wide range of task sizes, typically spanning many orders of magnitude. These 'heavy-tailed' workloads have been found to exist in many computing environments. Crovella et al. observed that a number of file size distributions found on the World Wide Web exhibit heavy tails, including file requests by users, files transmitted via the network, transmission durations of files and files stored on servers [3, 7]. Other examples of heavy-tailed workloads observed include the size of files stored in Unix file systems [4], and the Unix process CPU requirements measured at UC Berkley [6]. Based on these measurements, workload generating tools such as SURGE [8] have been developed to more accurately 'stress-test' servers by generating realistic heavy-tailed traffic. More recently, traffic measurements of the 1998 World Cup [9] and the 1998 Winter Olympics [10] have exhibited heavy-tailed characteristics. The implications of these findings are significant in regards to task assignment policies, given that much of the existing work in the area was formulated under the assumption of an exponentially distributed workload. These so-called 'heavy-tailed' distributions have very high variance, where 10% of tasks can take 80% of the CPU resources.

For the purpose of analysis, we assume that the task sizes show some maximum (but large) value. This is a reasonable assumption in many cases, such as a Unix server which enforces a 'CPU limit' ceiling on how long a process can run. A *Bounded Pareto* distribution is therefore used, which exhibits the requisite heavy-tailed properties, and has a lower and upper limit on the task size distribution. The probability density function for the Bounded Pareto $B(k, p, \alpha)$ is:

$$f(x) = \frac{\alpha k^\alpha}{1 - (k/p)^\alpha} x^{-\alpha-1}, k \leq x \leq p \tag{1}$$

where α represents the task size variation, k is the smallest possible task, and p is the largest possible task. By varying the value of α we can observe distributions that exhibit moderate variability ($\alpha \approx 2$) to high variability ($\alpha \approx 1$). Typical measured values of the α parameter are between 0.9 - 1.3 [3, 5, 7], with an empirically measured mean of $\alpha \approx 1.1$.

In order to compare the relative performance of the various task assignment policies some common metrics are used. We consider the *mean waiting time, mean flow time*, and the *mean slow down* of each task assignment policy. The waiting time refers to the time a task spent waiting in queues to be processed. The flow time is the sum of the waiting time and the service time. Slow down refers to the waiting time divided by its processing time.

Consider for a moment that each host in our basic distributed system (depicted in Figure 1) is a M/G/1 FCFS queue, where the arrival process has rate λ. X represents the service time distribution, and ρ represents the utilisation ($\rho = \lambda E\{X\}$). W denotes a task's expected waiting time in the queue, S its slowdown, and Q is the expected queue length on arrival. Then it follows that,

$$E\{W\} = \frac{\lambda E\{X^2\}}{2(1 - \rho)} (Pollaczek - Khinchin formula)$$

$$E\{S\} = E\{\frac{W}{X}\} = E\{W\} \cdot E\{X^{-1}\}$$
$$E\{Q\} = \lambda E\{W\}$$

3   Related Work

This section focuses on relevant existing approaches to task assignment, focusing on their strengths, limitations and performance characteristics with respect to dealing with conditions of heavy traffic demand and high task size variation. A more extensive review is available in [11].

Traditionally, classical task assignment policies such as *Random* and *Round-Robin* have been used in distributed systems. Under the Random policy, tasks are statically assigned to each member server with equal probability. Using a Round-Robin policy, tasks are assigned to member servers in a cyclical fashion. Both policies aim to equalise the expected number of tasks at each server, and are often used as a base line to compare with other task distribution policies. The performance of both policies are directly related to the variation of the task size distribution, and deteriorates as the task size variability increases, as tasks are assigned with no consideration of each host's load or the distribution of task sizes. Despite this, Random and Round-Robin are still commonly used in many scheduling environments (most likely due to ease of implementation). It has been shown previously [12] that Random and Round-Robin both have similar performance characteristics.

Dynamic policies aim to improve on classical static policies such as Random and Round-Robin by intelligently assigning tasks based on the current load at each host. The LLF (Least-Loaded-First) approach assigns tasks to the server with the least amount of work remaining, attempting to achieve instantaneous load balance. The work remaining can be approximated by the queue length (Shortest-Queue-First), or assuming the tasks service requirement is known *a priori*, the cumulative work remaining in the queue (Least-Work-Remaining). By keeping the load balanced, the waiting time in queue caused by high task size variation can be reduced. It is known that balancing the load minimises the mean response time [13, 14] in the type of distributed system that we consider in this paper. Despite this, the best performance is not always obtained by balancing the load, especially if you are interested in an alternative (and perhaps more important depending on your views) metric such as mean slowdown. Furthermore, truly balancing the load is a problem in itself given that the service requirement is often not known *a priori*. In such a case you are depending on an approximated measure of load (Shortest-Queue-First for example) to balance incoming tasks fairly amongst the backend hosts. Given the highly variable nature of the task size distribution (where the difference between 'small' and 'large' tasks can be enormous) it is easy to imagine how it is a bad policy to depend only on the *number* of tasks in the queue at each backend host, and the effect on performance that can result from using such information to base task assignment choices on.

A Central-Queue policy (where tasks are held at the dispatcher until a host is idle) has proved to be equivalent to a Least-Work-Remaining policy, illustrating that equivalent performance can be obtained without any prior knowledge of a task's size [1, 12].

While exhibiting similarly good performance under an exponential workload, the performance of a Central-Queue policy is equally poor under more realistic conditions of heavy-tailed workloads. Recently, a variation of the Central-Queue policy was considered - Cycle Stealing with Central Queue (CS-CQ) [2].CS-CQ holds tasks in a central queue at the dispatcher until a host is idle. CS-CQ denotes one host to service short tasks and another to server long tasks, but it can steal cycles from an idle host if available (and it is prudent to do so). The application of CS-CQ is limited to domains where *a priori* knowledge of a tasks size is known. Furthermore, Central-Queue policies require constant feedback between the dispatcher and the backend hosts to notify the dispatcher of an idle host.

Many size-based policies have been proposed to counteract the negative effects of heavy-tailed workloads. Approaches such as SITA-E [12], and EQUILOAD [15] partition the workload into size ranges, which are then mapped to backend hosts. These size ranges are be chosen to optimise various metrics, such as waiting time and slowdown. These policies assume that task sizes are known *a priori* (eg. at the dispatcher), which is not consistent with the model we are evaluating in this paper.

Task Assignment based on Guessing Size (TAGS) [1] is an approach that does not assume any prior knowledge of a tasks service requirement. Like SITA-V, TAGS is slightly counterintuitive in that it unbalances the load, and also considers the notion of 'fairness'. This refers to the desirable property that "... all jobs, long or short, should experience the same expected slowdown." [1]. The TAGS approach works by associating a processing time limit ('cutoff') with each host, so a task is run on a host up until the designated time limit associated with that host. If the task has not completed by this point, it is killed and restarted from scratch at the next host. These cutoffs are a function of of the distribution of task sizes and the outside arrival rate, and can be determined by observing the system for a period of time.

Under higher loads and less variable conditions, TAGS does not perform so well. TAGS gains much of its performance by exploiting the heavy-tailed property, by moving the majority of the load onto host 2, allowing the vast majority of small tasks to be processed quickly on host 1. TAGS also suffers under high loads due to excess - the extra work created by restarting many jobs from scratch. As pointed out in [1], "...overall excess increases with load because excess is proportional to λ (task arrival rate), which is in turn proportional the [overall system] load, ρ."

4   The Proposed Model - TAPTF

In this section we propose a new task assignment policy called TAPTF - Task Assignment based on Prioritising Traffic Flows - to address the limitations of existing approaches in dealing with certain classes of traffic.

4.1   Motivation

Harchol-Balter's TAGS approach [1], while seemingly counter-intuitive in many respects, proved to be a very effective task assignment policy for distributed systems. As such, TAGS provides an excellent point of comparison for any new task assignment policy operating under similar constraints. As described in Section 3, the TAGS policy has a number of desirable properties - the most one important being that it does not assume any prior knowledge of the service requirement of incoming tasks, while still maintaining good performance. The TAGS policy performs admirably under realistic highly variable conditions, exploiting the heavy-tailed nature that is consistent with many computing workloads. Despite this, TAGS can produce significant *excess* at the backend hosts - wasted processing that a task incurs (and the corresponding load placed on a host) when it has been placed in the incorrect queue and is subsequently restarted after exceeding the processing limit associated with a host. A task that is assigned incorrectly is penalized by being stopped, placed at the end of the next host's queue and restarted from scratch (upon reaching the front of that queue). These shortcomings are justified by the fact that, by the very nature of the heavy-tailed workload distribution, the tasks that are penalised can amortise the additional waiting and processing time *for the greater good*. Nonetheless, this is wasteful, but how can the efficiency be improved while still maintaining good performance? In response, TAPTF was formulated to address two keys areas:

- Reducing the variance of tasks that share the same queue.
- Reducing the penalty of wasted processing (*excess*) on the backend hosts - caused by tasks that do not complete their processing in time, and are restarted at another host ('handoffs').

4.2   Techniques

In Section 4.1 a number of shortcomings of the TAGS model were identified that needed to be addressed. As such, TAPTF was designed in order to improve on these key areas. The reasoning behind the techniques that TAPTF uses to address the shortcomings of existing approaches are briefly described in this section.

As illustrated by the Pollaczek-Khinchin formula in Section 2, it can be seen that all performance metrics are dependent on $E\{X^2\}$, the second moment of the task size distribution (ie. the variance) in a queue. We can infer that reducing the variance in the service requirements of tasks at each host can improve performance, reducing the chance of a smaller task being stuck behind a significantly longer task. TAPTF reduces the variance in the sizes of tasks that share the same queue by the use of dual queues (an Ordinary (O) queue and a Restart (R) queue) and task migration, in an effort to group like-sized tasks together.

The *excess* - extra work created by restarting many tasks from scratch - needs to be minimised. TAPTF attempts to reduce the amount of 'handoffs' by placing as many tasks in the most appropriate queue (that is, their final destination) in the first instance as possible - reducing the penalty on both hosts and tasks. This is achieved in two interrelated ways. First, by manipulating the fraction of tasks (q_i) that is dispatched to each host we can increase the number of tasks that are correctly assigned to a suitable host - that is, where they can run-to-completion. Secondly, the reason that tasks can enter the system (and potentially finish) at *any* host is due to the lower boundary cutoff of each Ordinary (O) queue being k, the smallest possible task size. Under TAGS, a task that needs to be processed at Host i (e.g. its size is between s_{i-1} and s_i) must migrate from Host 1 to Host i. In TAPTF for the same task, there is a probability q_i that it will be directly dispatched to Host i (an ideal choice), and a probability $q_i + q_{i+1} + \ldots + q_n$ that it be assigned to Host i or higher - where it will not be subjected to any handoffs. This practice becomes crucial as task size variation decreases.

4.3   Conceptual View of the TAPTF Model

As seen in Figure 2, tasks arrive at a central dispatcher, following a Poisson process with rate λ. The dispatcher assigns tasks (in a First-In-First-Out manner) to one of the n hosts (say, Host i, where $1 \leq i \leq n$) at random with probability q_i. Using a well known property of the Poisson process, we can infer that the arrival stream to host Host i is also a Poisson process with rate λq_i.

Due to the heavy-tailed characteristics of the task size distribution (as discussed in Section 2), we assume that the distribution of task sizes (that is, the service distribution) follows a bounded Pareto Distribution $B(k, p, \alpha)$ given by Equation (1). A 'cutoff' (s_i) is assigned to each host in the distributed system. Specifically, tasks are processed on hosts with the following conditions:

- Host i's O queue deals only with tasks whose sizes are in the range $[k, s_i], 1 \leq i \leq n$
- Host i's R queue deals only with tasks whose sizes are in the range $[s_{i-1}, s_i], , 1 < i \leq n$

where $k = s_0 < s_1 < s_2 < s_3 < \ldots < s_n = p$. These cutoffs can be computed in order to minimise certain measurable quantities such as mean waiting time or mean slowdown time. Further information on how the cutoffs are chosen is provided in Section 4.4.

Each host (excluding Host 1) provides two queues, an ordinary queue and a restart queue (denoted by O and R respectively). All tasks in the O and R queues are served on a First-Come-First-Served (FCFS) basis. Tasks sent to a given host from the dispatcher join that host's O queue. After a task has moved to the front of the queue it can begin to be processed. If the processing time of a task on a given host exceeds the assigned cutoff limit, the task is stopped, and moved to the restart (R) queue belonging to the next host. This process is repeated until these tasks run to completion at their final (correct)

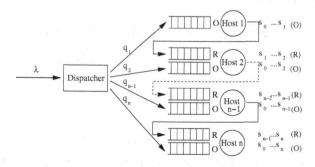

Fig. 2. Illustration of the TAPTF model

destination. Tasks waiting in a O queue have priority of service over those in the R queue at a given host. However, a task which is being served from the R queue will not be pre-empted from service by the arrival of a task into the O queue at a given host. This is the default behavior of the TAPTF (and is denoted as TAPTF-O in the figures in Section 5). It is worth noting that you could also choose to give priority of service to the R queue over the O queue (which we refer to as TAPTF-R).

One way the TAPTF model differs from TAGS is the fixed lower size boundaries at each host ($k = s_0$), so that all tasks with sizes *less than or equal* to a fixed cutoff point can be potentially be processed on a particular host. This means that a task can be dispatched to *any* host initially without being first dispatched to Host 1 (as per the TAGS approach) while preserving the property that a task's service demand is not known *a priori*. In addition, TAPTF uses dual queues at each host in order to speed up the flow of shorter tasks, allowing smaller tasks to be processed quickly in the ordinary queue and migrating larger tasks out of the way, allowing them to group together in the restart queues at subsequent hosts.

4.4 Choosing the Cutoffs

Like most size-based (or similar) policies, the performance of TAPTF is critically dependent on the choice of cutoffs used. From Section 3 we recall that cutoffs refer to the size-range associated with each host. The cutoffs can be chosen to optimise for mean waiting time, or mean slowdown. In order to optimise for mean waiting time, the load must be balanced more evenly amongst the host. To optimise for mean slowdown, load unbalancing techniques are employed, especially under conditions of high task size variation. We have chosen to optimise for both mean waiting time and more importantly, mean slowdown, as it is desirable for a tasks delay to be proportional to its service requirement.

The cutoffs for TAPTF are a function of the task size distribution (in our case defined by the Bounded Pareto $B(k, p, \alpha)$) and the task arrival rate into the distributed system, λ. These parameters can be determined by observing the distributed system for a period of time. Using the mathematical results described in [11], we can work towards obtaining optimal cutoff points (s_i's) for each of our hosts in the TAPTF system. Since our aim is to produce a task assignment policy that minimises the overall expected waiting time or slowdown respectively (depending on our goals), the following optimisation problems need to be addressed:

$$\text{Problem I} \quad \text{Minimize} \sum_{i=1}^{n} E(W_{iO}) + \sum_{i=2}^{n} E(W_{iR})$$
$$\text{Subject to } \rho_{iO} + \rho_{iR} < 1, 1 \leq i \leq n.$$

$$\text{Problem II} \quad \text{Minimize} \sum_{i=1}^{n} E(S_{iO}) + \sum_{i=2}^{n} E(S_{iR})$$
$$\text{Subject to } \rho_{iO} + \rho_{iR} < 1, 1 \leq i \leq n.$$

We can choose to optimise for mean waiting time (described by Problem I) or mean slowdown (described in Problem II).

As described above, the choice of cutoffs depend on the task size variability. From Section 2 we recall that the lower the α parameter, the higher the variability, and the smaller the percentage of tasks is that makes up 50% of the load. TAPTF (which can behave like TAGS by setting $q_1 = 1.0$ when prudent) can exploit this property of the heavy-tailed distribution by running all (or the vast majority) of the (small) tasks on the first host, leaving them under light to moderate load, while the largest tasks filter down to be eventually processed by the latter hosts.

As the variability decreases (α increases) we can no longer exploit the heavy-tailed property so easily. The average size of the tasks we consider 'small' slowly gets bigger as α increases. As such we have to choose our cutoffs accordingly, as well as manipulating the fraction of tasks that are assigned to the latter hosts. We still exploit the heavy-tailed property by processing larger jobs on the latter hosts, but we are not unbalancing the load to the extent we could when variability was higher ($\alpha \leq 1$). As α approaches 2.0, the task size variation is lower, and the other hosts have to start pulling their weight in order to maintain good mean waiting time and slowdown. TAPTF exploits this knowledge to provide better performance in those areas.

5   Analytical Comparison

In order to gauge the usefulness of the TAPTF approach, an analytical comparison with TAGS and Random was performed. Random is included as a baseline, whereas TAGS provides the best point of comparison as it operates under similar constraints (i.e. no *a priori* knowledge of a task's service requirement) to TAPTF. These approaches were evaluated under a variety of conditions and their performance compared using metrics discussed in Section 2 - mean waiting time and mean slowdown.

A range of α values were considered, from 0.5 to 2.0, demonstrating a wide range of task size variation, from extreme task size variation ($\alpha \approx 0.5$) to low task size variation ($\alpha \approx 2.0$), and everything in between. Each α value was evaluated for different system loads (ρ) - 0.3 (low load), 0.5 (moderate load) and 0.7 (high load). For the sake of brevity the results for moderate load have been omitted and are available in the extended paper [11]. These comparisons were performed for two and three host systems, after which we could no longer find optimum s_i's with the computational resources available to us. This is not a big problem in itself as noted in [1], as an n Host distributed system (where $n > 2$) with a system load ρ can always be arranged in such a way to provide performance that is as good or better than the best performance of a two host system (where n is even). This holds true for any task assignment policy.

The analytical comparison was performed in Mathematica 5.0 [16], using the mathematical preliminaries discussed in [11]. The generalised TAPTF mathematical model is also used to model the behavior of TAGS by setting $q_1 = 1.0$ (and subsequently $q_2 \ldots q_n$ to equal 0) - negating the dual queues and multiple entry points and making it behave identically to TAGS. For each scenario, optimum cutoffs are found with respect to mean waiting time and mean slowdown for both TAPTF and TAGS using the NMinimize function in Mathematica to produce the best (and fairest) comparison. This is achieved by finding the s_i's in each instance that produce local minimums for the expected waiting time, $E(W)$ and the expected mean slowdown, $E(S)$.

Task assignment policies that assume *a priori* knowledge of task sizes are not evaluated in this section, as we are motivated by a more pessimistic (and less restrictive) view of the distributed model, where this information is not guaranteed to be available.

In the interests of clear and meaningful results, comparisons of mean waiting time and mean slowdown are performed using the respective TAPTF and TAGS policies optimised for that metric, as described in Section 4.4. The Random policy is included as a baseline for comparative purposes in each instance. Note that the expected waiting time and slowdown graphs are presented on a log scale for the y-axis. Results for TAPTF are only shown where they are better than TAGS, as TAPTF can reduce to TAGS (and achieve identical performance) as described above.

5.1   Two Hosts

Figures 3(a) and 3(b) show the mean waiting time and slowdown respectively under a low system load ($\rho = 0.3$). From our analysis the TAGS policy achieves better mean waiting time and slowdown under conditions ranging from extreme to high variation (where α is between 0.5 and 1.2). The areas where the TAPTF policy improves on TAGS are highlighted on the graphs. It can be observed that in conditions of moderate to low variation (where α is between 1.3 and 2.0), the TAPTF policy can achieve better performance with respect to mean waiting time and slowdown. This performance increase can be attributed to the use of dual queues and by assigning tasks to all servers (or a subset thereof) rather than feeding all tasks into the first host, as per the TAGS approach. Table 1 gives a breakdown of the fraction of tasks dispatched to Host 1 (denoted by q_1) or Host 2 (denoted by q_2). From the table we can see that as variation increases (and α decreases) TAPTF approaches TAGS-like behaviors for optimal performance. We can see where $\alpha = 1.3$, almost all tasks (99%) are dispatched to Host 1. As variation increases further (where α is between 0.5 and 1.2) TAGS-like behavior produces the best results. Conversely, when variation decreases it pays to assign some tasks to the second host. As the variation decreases (and α approaches 2.0) we can afford to assign more tasks to the second host. Figures 3(c) and 3(d) again highlight the effect of decreasing variance on TAGS - as α decreases, the amount of excess load generated by the TAGS policy increases significantly, while the TAPTF maintains consistent load. As the fraction assigned to Host 2 (q_2) increases, so to does the factor of improvement over TAGS, both in expected waiting time and slowdown in addition to system load.

Figures 3(e) and 3(f) show the mean waiting time and slowdown respectively under a high system load ($\rho = 0.7$). The TAPTF policy betters TAGS over a larger range of task variation scenarios than occurred under low load (with TAPTF demonstrating lower mean waiting time and slowdown where α is between 1.1 and 2.0). It can be observed that TAGS suffers significantly under a high system load. As highlighted in Table 1 we are seeing an increased fraction of tasks dispatched to the second host in order to maintain superior performance to the TAGS policy. From Figures 3(g) and 3(h) we can observe a sharp increase in system load (and subsequently excess) where $\alpha > 1.0$. It can be seen that as α approaches 2.0 the factor of improvement over TAGS increases in all metrics.

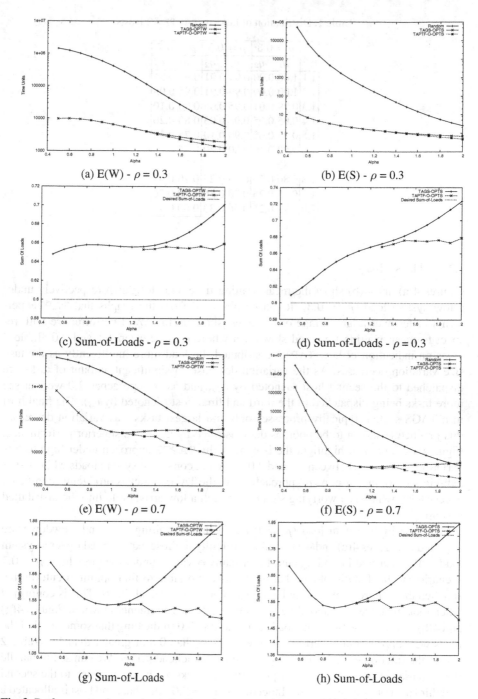

Fig. 3. Performance of a two host distributed system under low and high load. Expected waiting time $E(W)$, slowdown $E(S)$ and corresponding system load comparisons (desired versus actual Sum-Of-Loads) are shown

Table 1. Distribution of tasks in TAPTF - 2 Hosts

α	$\rho = 0.3$		$\rho = 0.5$		$\rho = 0.7$	
	q_1	q_2	q_1	q_2	q_1	q_2
1.1	1.00	0.00	0.99	0.01	0.99	0.01
1.2	1.00	0.00	0.99	0.01	0.95	0.05
1.3	0.99	0.01	0.95	0.05	0.90	0.10
1.4	0.95	0.05	0.95	0.05	0.80	0.20
1.5	0.95	0.05	0.90	0.10	0.75	0.25
1.6	0.90	0.10	0.80	0.20	0.75	0.25
1.7	0.85	0.15	0.80	0.20	0.70	0.30
1.8	0.80	0.20	0.75	0.25	0.70	0.30
1.9	0.75	0.25	0.70	0.30	0.70	0.30
2.0	0.75	0.25	0.66	0.33	0.60	0.40

5.2   Three Hosts

Figures 4(a) and 4(b) show the mean waiting time and slowdown respectively under a low system load ($\rho = 0.3$). It can be observed from the graphs that TAPTF performs better over a large range of α values, showing improved performance with respect to mean waiting time and slowdown where α is between 1.1 and 2.0. Table 2 gives an indication of how TAPTF distributed the load more intelligently as the task size variation decreases. As the variation decreases a significant amount of tasks are dispatched to the second host (denoted by q_2), and as α approaches 2.0 we can see more tasks being dispatched to the third and final host (denoted by q_3). The final host in a TAGS system typically processes only the largest tasks - as variation decreases this practice is shown to be poor, as demonstrated by TAPTF's superior performance. Figures 4(c) and 4(d) highlight the benefit of the TAPTF approach under high to low variation (where α is between 1.1 and 2.0) showing consistent system loads while TAGS exhibits a sharp increase. As α approaches 2.0, the TAGS policy is producing significant excess load, which is a worrying sign under such a low arrival rate into the distributed system.

Under a high system load ($\rho = 0.7$), the mean waiting time and slowdown are depicted in Figures 4(e) and 4(f). Similar difficulty to those experienced under a system load of 0.5 occurred in finding cutoffs for many α values under the three host, $\rho = 0.7$ scenario for the TAGS policy. That is, it was impossible to find optimum cutoffs that satisfied the requirement that the load must be below 1.0 at all hosts. This is confirmed when looking at the corresponding Sum-Of-Loads measurements shown in Figures 4(g) and 4(h), showing the Sum-Of-Loads approaching 3.0 (indicating that some or all of the hosts were approaching overload) where α is less than 0.8 or greater than 1.3. Table 2 shows the fraction of tasks (q_i) allocated to each backend server. We can see to handle the increased system load, a larger proportion of tasks are being assigned to the second and third host on average to cope. Indeed, when α is 2.0, each backend host is allocated a fairly equal share of the incoming tasks (where $q_1 = 0.4$, $q_2 = 0.3$ and $q_3 = 0.3$). Again it can be observed that, as the system load has increased, the range of α values where TAPTF outperforms TAGS is still similarly large - where α is between 0.9 and 2.0.

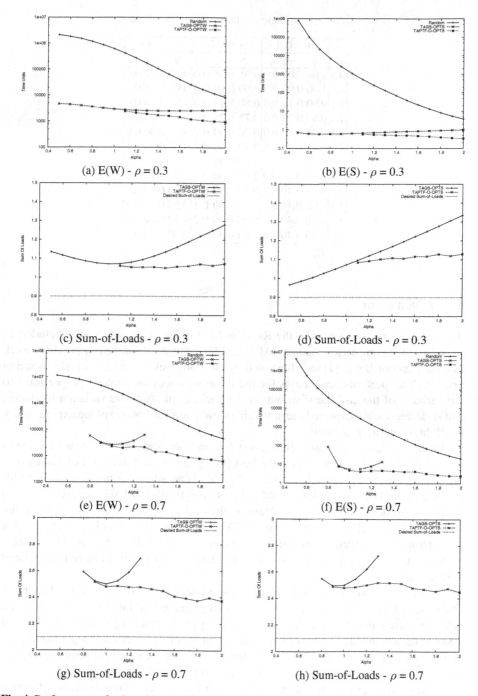

Fig. 4. Performance of a three host distributed system under low and high load. Expected waiting time $E(W)$, slowdown $E(S)$ and corresponding system load comparisons (desired versus actual Sum-Of-Loads) are shown

Table 2. Distribution of tasks in TAPTF - 3 Hosts

α	$\rho = 0.3$			$\rho = 0.5$			$\rho = 0.7$		
	q_1	q_2	q_3	q_1	q_2	q_3	q_1	q_2	q_3
0.9	1.00	0.00	0.0	0.95	0.05	0.0	0.95	0.05	0.0
1.0	1.00	0.00	0.0	0.90	0.10	0.0	0.90	0.10	0.0
1.1	0.90	0.10	0.0	0.80	0.20	0.0	0.80	0.20	0.0
1.2	0.80	0.20	0.0	0.75	0.25	0.0	0.80	0.20	0.0
1.3	0.75	0.25	0.0	0.70	0.30	0.0	0.70	0.30	0.0
1.4	0.70	0.30	0.0	0.70	0.30	0.0	0.60	0.30	0.1
1.5	0.60	0.40	0.0	0.60	0.40	0.0	0.60	0.30	0.1
1.6	0.60	0.40	0.0	0.60	0.30	0.1	0.50	0.30	0.2
1.7	0.60	0.30	0.1	0.50	0.40	0.1	0.50	0.30	0.2
1.8	0.60	0.30	0.1	0.50	0.40	0.1	0.50	0.30	0.2
1.9	0.50	0.40	0.1	0.50	0.30	0.2	0.50	0.30	0.2
2.0	0.50	0.40	0.1	0.50	0.30	0.2	0.40	0.30	0.3

6   Discussion

An analytical representation of the Random load distribution policy was included as a baseline for comparison against TAGS and TAPTF. As discussed in previous work by Mor Harchol-Balter [1] and illustrated by the Pollaczek-Khinchin formula shown in Section 2, all performance metrics for the Random policy are directly proportional to the variance of the task size distribution. As such, as the task size variation increases, and α decreases, the expected mean waiting time and slowdown explode exponentially in all the scenarios examined.

From the figures presented in Section 5.1 and Section 5.2, it is clear that TAGS (or at least TAGS-like behavior) is the best policy under conditions of extreme to very high variation. As mentioned previously, TAPTF is an adaptable task assignment policy, which can behave identically (and reduces analytically) to TAGS (eg. set q_1 to 1.0) when it is prudent with regards to obtaining the best performance for a given scenario. In effect, the TAPTF policy encompasses TAGS ability to exploit a highly variable task size distribution, as well as remaining flexible enough to handle instances of lower variation and higher system loads by virtue of its many parameters that can be manipulated where required.

In areas of lower variation (and even low system load) we can see the benefit of dispatching tasks to hosts other than the first (highlighted by Table 1, Figures 3(a) and 3(b)). It is clear that as variation decreases, it pays to dispatch a growing proportion of tasks to the second host. This is largely due to the fact that we can no longer exploit the heavy-tailed property of the task size distribution, as the variation between the sizes of tasks decreases, and the average size of so-called *small* tasks increases.

TAGS suffers to a greater extent under higher loads, as an increase in excess (wasted processing caused by handoffs) and growing average queue lengths combine to have a detrimental effect on performance under conditions of moderate to low task size variation. It can be observed that as the system load increases, the task variation range where the TAPTF policy betters TAGS becomes larger, and the factor of that improvement (in both mean waiting time and slowdown) increases. For example, consider the two host case. Consider the results shown in Figures 3(a) and 3(e), depicting the mean waiting time under system loads of 0.3 and 0.7 respectively. TAPTF betters TAGS when $\alpha \geq 1.3$ under a low system load of 0.3. When the system load is high (0.7), TAPTF exhibits superior performance than TAGS when $\alpha > 1.0$. Similarly, consider when $\alpha = 2.0$ in each of these scenarios. Under a system load of 0.3, TAPTF exhibits an factor of improvement of approximately 1.5 over TAGS. When the system load is 0.7, TAPTF shows a substantial improvement over TAGS - by a factor of 6.6.

Section 5.2 presents some interesting results for the 3 host scenario. We find that in some cases, as variation increases (and α decreases), the mean slowdown for the TAGS policy actually improves - to a certain point. Consider Figures 4(a) and 4(b), depicting a two host system under a low system load of 0.3. We observe a fairly flat and consistent response from the TAGS policy for the expected mean waiting time and slowdown over the range of α's shown. Slowdown gradually decreases as α approaches 0.7, then increases slightly as α reaches 0.5. This is because as the variation of tasks sizes becomes larger, TAGS can increasingly exploit the heavy-tailed property of such a distribution through choosing effective cutoffs that enable small tasks to be processed quickly, while ensuring large tasks are moved to latter hosts and do not unduly delay smaller tasks. This ensures good results with regards to overall metrics like mean waiting time and slowdown under conditions of extreme to highly variable task size distributions.

Despite the different behavior exhibited for the 3 host scenario, TAGS is still bettered by the TAPTF policy under conditions ranging from high to low task size variation due to the same factors as under the 2 host scenario. Again we see the benefits achieved by dispatching a proportion of tasks to all hosts, not just the first. This is especially true as the system load increases - so to does the factor of improvement of TAPTF over TAGS. The advantages of the generic and flexible TAPTF model are highlighted in Table 2 (and subsequently Figures 4(a) to 4(h)). In several instances (Figures 4(e) to 4(h)) we were unable to find optimum cutoffs for TAGS that satisfied the constraint that the load must remain below 1 at all hosts.

7   Conclusion

In this paper we have presented a new approach to task assignment in a distributed system, TAPTF (Task Assignment based on Prioritising Traffic Flows). TAPTF is a flexible policy that addresses the shortcomings of existing approaches (outlined earlier in this paper) to task assignment. TAPTF demonstrated improved performance (both in mean waiting time and mean slowdown) in key areas where the TAGS and Random policies suffer. Most significantly, TAPTF exhibited improved performance under low to high task size variation and high system load by reducing the excess associated with a large number of restarts and by intelligently controlling the influx of tasks to each back-end host. We found for two and three host scenarios that as system load increases the range of α parameters where an improvement was shown, and the magnitude of improvement increased. Given that TAPTF can encompass the best characteristics of existing approaches, as well as improving on them in what are considered critical scenarios of heavy traffic load and highly variable task sizes, we consider TAPTF to be a worthy policy for load distribution in environments where tasks are not preemptible and task sizes are not known *a priori*.

References

1. Harchol-Balter, M.: Task assignment with unknown duration. Journal of the ACM **49** (2002) 260–288
2. Harchol-Balter, M., Li, C., Osogami, T., Scheller-Wolf, A., Squillante, M.S.: Analysis of task assignment with cycle stealing under central queue. In: Proceedings of 23rd International Conference on Distributed Computing Systems (ICDCS '03). (2003) 628–637
3. Crovella, M., Taqqu, M., Bestavros, A.: Heavy-Tailed Probability Distributions in the World Wide Web. Chapman & Hall (1998)
4. Gordon Irlam: Unix file survey (1993) Available at http://www.base.com/gordoni/ufs93.html.
5. Harchol-Balter, M.: The effect of heavy-tailed job size distributions on computer system design. In: Proceedings of ASA-IMS Conference on Applications of Heavy Tailed Distributions in Economics, Engineering and Statistics. (1999)
6. Harchol-Balter, M., Downey, A.B.: Exploiting process lifetime distributions for dynamic load balancing. ACM Transactions on Computer Systems **15** (1997) 253–285
7. Crovella, M.E., Bestavros, A.: Self-similarity in World Wide Web traffic: evidence and possible causes. IEEE/ACM Transactions on Networking **5** (1997) 835–846
8. Barford, P., Crovella, M.: Generating representative web workloads for network and server performance evaluation. In: Measurement and Modeling of Computer Systems. (1998) 151–160
9. Arlitt, M., Jin, T.: Workload characterization of the 1998 world cup web site. IEEE Network **14** (2000) 30–37
10. Iyengar, A.K., Squillante, M.S., Zhang, L.: Analysis and characterization of large-scale web server access patterns and performance. World Wide Web **2** (1999) 85–100
11. James Broberg, Zahir Tari, Panlop Zeephongsekul: Task assignment based on prioritising traffic flows. Technical Report TR-04-05, Royal Melbourne Institute of Technology (2004)
12. Harchol-Balter, M., Crovella, M.E., Murta, C.D.: On choosing a task assignment policy for a distributed server system. Journal of Parallel and Distributed Computing **59** (1999) 204–228
13. Crovella, M.E., Harchol-Balter, M., Murta, C.D.: Task assignment in a distributed system: Improving performance by unbalancing load. In: Proceedings of ACM SIGMETRICS International Conference on Measurement and Modeling of Computer Systems. (1998) 268–269
14. Schroder, B., Harchol-Balter, M.: Evaluation of task assignment policies for supercomputing servers: The case for load unbalancing and fairness. In: 9th IEEE Symposium on High Performance Distributed Computing. (2000) 211–220
15. Ciardo, G., Riska, A., Smirni, E.: EQUILOAD: a load balancing policy for clustered web servers. Performance Evaluation **46** (2001) 101–124
16. Research, W.: Mathematica version 5.0 (2003)

A Novel Distributed Scheduling Algorithm for Resource Sharing Under Near-Heavy Load[*]

D. Carvalho[1], Fábio Protti[2], Massimo De Gregorio[3], and Felipe M.G. França[2]

[1] COPPE – Engenharia de Sistemas e Computação,
UFRJ, Rio de Janeiro, Brazil
`d.carvalho@ieee.org, felipe@cos.ufrj.br`
[2] NCE/Instituto de Matemática, UFRJ, Rio de Janeiro, Brazil
`fabiop@nce.ufrj.br`
[3] Istituto di Cibernetica – CNR, Pozzuoli (NA), Italy
`m.degregorio@cib.na.cnr.it`

Abstract. This paper introduces SER^H – *Scheduling by Edge Reversal with Hibernation*, a novel distributed algorithm for the scheduling of atomic shared resources in the context of dynamic load reconfiguration. The new algorithm keeps the simplicity and daintiness of the *Scheduling by Edge Reversal* (SER) distributed algorithm, originally conceived to support the *heavy load* condition. Both SER and SER^H distributed algorithms share the same communication and computational complexities and can also be seen as graph dynamics where the messages exchanged between a processing node and its neighbors are represented as "edge reversal" operations upon directed acyclic graphs representing the target distributed system. Nevertheless, SER^H allows such distributed system to deal with the situation of having processing nodes leaving the heavy load behavior and going into a "hibernating" state, and *vice versa*. It is here that SER^H has a communication cost approximately 25% lower than the traditional Chandy and Misra's distributed solution, when operating near to heavy load conditions. In order to illustrate the usefulness of SER^H in this interesting situation, an application in the distributed control of traffic lights of a road junction is also presented here.

Keywords: dining philosophers problem; distributed algorithms; distributed traffic light control; graph dynamics; mutual exclusion; resource-sharing.

1 Introduction

Dijkstra's Dinning Philosophers Problem (DPP) [9] is a simple and remarkable paradigm where important issues associated to distributed systems (DSs), such as concurrency, deadlock avoidance, fairness, liveness, mutual exclusion and starvation avoidance, are exposed. A number of distributed algorithms have been devised to ensure mutual exclusion in the access of *atomic* shared resources, i.e., resources that cannot be accessed by more than one process at a time. In

[*] Supported by CNPq, CAPES (Brazil) and CNR (Italy).

T. Higashino (Ed.): OPODIS 2004, LNCS 3544, pp. 431–442, 2005.
© Springer-Verlag Berlin Heidelberg 2005

particular, Chandy and Misra's distributed algorithm [8] has been considered as a paradigmatic solution for the mutual exclusion problem raised by the DPP. Nevertheless, if in one hand Chandy and Misra's algorithm covers arbitrarily loaded DSs, on the other hand the communication cost observed in particularly interesting situations, such as in the heavy load regime, i.e., when processing nodes are either operating or in constant demand for operating upon atomic shared resources, may be far from ideal.

In this sense, *Scheduling by Edge Reversal* (SER), a simple and powerful distributed algorithm, was originally conceived to support DSs under the *heavy load* condition. SER was firstly applied by Bertsekas and Gafni [10] in the problem of maintaining loop-free routes in computer networks and then as part of Chandy and Misra's DPP solution [8]. Barbosa and Gafni have established important SER properties and the NP-completeness of the problem of finding optimal *concurrency* amounts provided by the SER dynamics over a given distributed system [4, 5]. SER works as follows: (i) the target distributed system is described by an undirected graph $G = (N, E)$, where $N = \{1, ..., n\}$ is the set of processing nodes and E is defined as follows: if R_i is the set of resources used by node i in order to operate, an edge $(i, j) \in E$ exists whenever $R_i \cap R_j \neq \emptyset$, that is, nodes i and j share at least one atomic resource; (ii) an initial acyclic orientation ω is defined over E; (iii) all, and only, *sink* nodes in ω, i.e., nodes having all of its edges oriented to themselves, have the right to operate upon shared resources and then reverse all associated edges, becoming *source* nodes in a new acyclic orientation ω'. This ensures that neighboring nodes in the target DS cannot operate simultaneously upon atomic shared resources. SER is the graph dynamics defined by the endless iteration of (iii) over G. Considering G finite and, consequently, a finite number of possible acyclic orientations over G, eventually a repetition, i.e., a *period* of length t, will occur. An interesting property of SER lies in the fact that, inside any given period, each node operates, i.e., becomes a sink, the same number m of times [4], ensuring "fairness", in the long run operation, among all processing elements of G.

Notice that SER imposes a restless participation of every node in G, a natural requisite of a heavily loaded DS. In the interesting and plausible situation of a subset of G's processing nodes reaching, temporarily or not, the state of having no need for operating over shared resources, such nodes will negatively interfere in the performance of the remaining SER-driven heavily loaded system. This paper introduces SER^H – *Scheduling by Edge Reversal with Hibernation*, a generalization of SER in which processing nodes have the possibility of leaving the heavy load behavior and going into a "hibernating" state, and *vice versa*. In order to illustrate the usefulness of SER^H in this interesting situation, an application in the distributed control of traffic lights of a road junction is introduced here.

SER^H differs from SER in the use of a second oriented edge between two neighboring nodes in G (in this case, a multi-digraph is defined). "Edge reversals" occur exactly as in SER whenever nodes behave as in the heavy load situation; if a node intends to go into a "hibernating" state, just after operating, only edges from the original SER mechanism are reversed; sensing a missing (extra) "edge reversal" by neighboring nodes has the implicit meaning of indicating that such node has just entered into hibernation. Leaving hibernation happens only by request from at least one neighboring node, as to be seen ahead in detail, including a demonstration of the SER^H correctness.

1.1 Mutual Exclusion Algorithms

There is a multitude of mutual exclusion algorithms, as presented in [25]. The taxonomy proposed by Raynal [23] defines three main classes:

Permission-based algorithms – when a process needs access to shared resources, it asks permission to neighboring nodes. Symmetry can be broken through the use of temporal priorities, acyclic graphs and/or majorities. See [1, 2, 7, 11, 13, 18, 20, 24, 22].

Token-based algorithms – the processing node can access shared resources only when it is the owner of a special atomic object associated to such set of resources. See [3, 16, 17, 19, 21].

Centralized coordination algorithms – in this case, the two previous styles may be combined in the final solution. Processing nodes in need for accessing shared resources send messages to a central coordinator, which defines the timing for returning an atomic object defining a unique key to accessing such resources.

Outside this taxonomy, there are distributed mutual exclusion algorithms focusing resources instead of processes in need of access [27]. Mutual exclusion algorithms are fundamental in many areas of Computer Science, such as operating systems, micro-architectures, computer graphics, computer networks, databases, etc., apart from specific multimedia applications such as video conference [14] and mobile computing [26].

SER^H, our contribution, is mainly a permission-based algorithm, in the same spirit of Chandy and Misra's approach to the DPP [8] and Barbosa and Gafni's SER [4]. Moreover, there are still some alternative approaches based on the dynamic modification of the precedence graph (used in Chandy and Misra's approach), usually by means of a process endowed with global knowledge [12, 15].

1.2 Chandy and Misra's DPP Solution

Chandy and Misra's DPP distributed solution uses an undirected graph $G = (N, E)$ in order to represent the neighborhood-constrained system. Whenever two neighboring philosophers are "hungry", the symmetry (the existence of neighbors trying to use a shared resource simultaneously) is broken with the help of a precedence graph $\bar{G}$ containing the same set of nodes and edges of G, but with an acyclic orientation defined over its edges. Each edge e in $\bar{G}$ represents a precedence ("turn"), i.e., the right of a node to use the shared resource before its neighbor. The orientation of the edges is modelled by a function $\omega : E \to N$

such that $\omega((i,j))$ is the node having the turn. When a node i receives a *fork* request from j, i promptly returns the fork if $\omega((i,j)) = j$. If i is "hungry", the fork return is associated to a fork request by message *fork+request*. In the opposite case, when $\omega((i,j)) = i$, i returns the fork only after operating, satisfying j's request.

2   SER^H

Scheduling by Edge Reversal with Hibernation – SER^H combines the behavior of SER for executions under heavy load with the possibility of precluding a node from operation, which remains "hibernating" till the moment it is woke up by a node that is still operating. This new functionality can be achieved without increasing the asymptotic computational and communication complexities of SER.

An informal description of how SER^H works is shown in Figures 1 and 2. The existence of a communication channel between two nodes means that they share at least one atomic resource. The functioning of each communication channel is controlled by a pair of permissions, • and ○. Initially, the pairs are distributed in such a way that an acyclic orientation ω is defined in the graph, as in Figure 1(a).

As in SER, sink nodes have the right of operating by using the shared resources. After that, the edges incident to the sink nodes are reversed, as indicated in Figure 1(b), and the dynamics evolves. Arrows indicate nodes where events

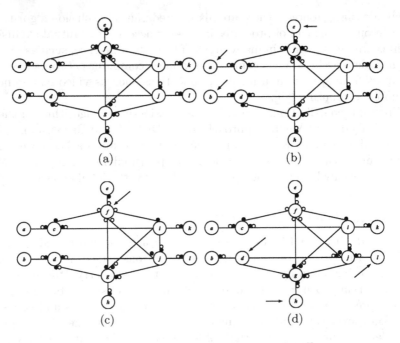

(a)

(b)

(c)

(d)

Fig. 1. An example of execution of SER^H

are occurring. The notion of "sink node" in SER^H is different from that in SER: a sink node has the property of "owning" all the •-permissions (Let us call it a •-*sink node*). Moreover, the reversion of a •-permission along some edge occurs only when the node owns the corresponding ○-permission for that edge. This distinct behavior is introduced in order to implement the new hibernating state. Observe Figure 1(c): node f decides to enter the hibernating state; in this case, it reverses only the •-permissions towards its neighbors, while keeping the ○-permissions. Notice that nodes c, d, e, h, k, and l are •-sink nodes; they are able to operate upon resources. Following the example, nodes d, h and l have operated and reversed their permissions according to the above convention, as in Figure 1(d). The remaining •-sink nodes have not reversed their permissions because they are still operating. Observe now node g: it has just become a •-sink node, and when it finishes its operation it will reverse its •-permissions and enter the hibernating state. We should observe that, in this case, it does not reverse the •-permissions towards f because it does not own the corresponding ○-permission for that edge. At this moment, recall that f is hibernating, and thus it is not requiring resources shared with its neighbors. The final situation is shown in Figure 2(a).

Figure 2(b) shows node c entering the H-state. When some •-sink node decides to wake up a neighbor, it reverses the •-permission towards the hibernating neighbor as shown in Figure 2(c). This is the action performed by node j when waking up f and g, which by their turn reverse all the ○-permissions towards their neighbors, except j, as in Figure 2(d). Upon owning the ○-permissions,

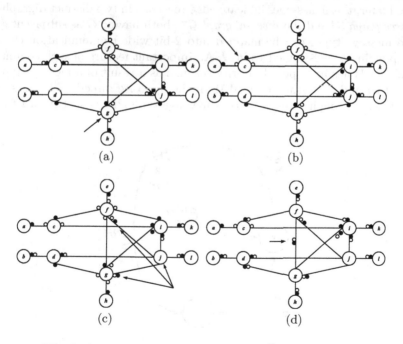

(a)   (b)

(c)   (d)

Fig. 2. An example of execution of SER^H (continuation)

these neighbors must immediately reverse the corresponding •-permissions, as we shall see when formally describing SER^H. Other details will also be discussed, e.g., the situation represented in Figure 2(d), where the permissions move in opposite directions along the channel linking f and g.

2.1   Formal Description of SER^H

Every node in the system may be in one of three mutually exclusive states: *running* (R), *waiting* for edge reversals (W), or *hibernating* (H). We denote by $s(i)$ the current state of node i. *Active nodes* are either running or waiting; *inactive nodes* are hibernating. Also, the following transitions ξ applies:

ξ^{RW} – occurs when a node exits the R-state and enters the W-state;
ξ^{RH} – occurs when a node enters the H-state after accessing resources;
ξ^{WR} – occurs when a node gains the right of accessing all the resources;
ξ^{HW} – occurs when a node is woke up by a neighbor.

Figure 3 shows the state transitions in SER^H. Observe that a node can enter the H-state only after having been in the R-state; in addition, when a node leaves the H-state, it must necessarily enter the W-state. The algorithm assumes that there always exist at least one node in the R-state, since running nodes are necessary to wake up neighboring hibernating nodes. We will return to this issue in Section 3.

SER^H uses three types of messages, namely $\mathbb{PM}$, $\mathbb{PP}$ and $\mathbb{MM}$. As to be explained later, these messages indicate edge reversals in two distinct digraphs, the *resource graph* $\mathcal{G}^+$ and the *reversal graph* $\mathcal{G}^-$, both having G as subjacent graph. These message types can be mapped into 2-bit wide communication channels, corresponding to existing edges in G. An important feature of such communication channels lies in a special priority scheme: as a result of a message type $\mathbb{PP}$ from i to j and a message type $\mathbb{MM}$ in the opposite direction, being simultaneously sent through channel (i, j), a message type $\mathbb{PM}$ is sent from i to j. As

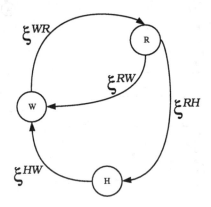

Fig. 3. State transitions

an example, consider nodes f and g in Figure 2(d): this situation often occurs when two neighboring nodes are leaving the H-state simultaneously; in this case a symmetry between these two nodes is created, what could lead to a deadlock. The priority scheme described above avoids such possibility.

Each participating node within SER^H must store two boolean variables associated to each communication channel, i.e., for each neighbor in G. Denote by N_i the set of neighbors of node i. The first variable, P_i^j ($i \in N, j \in N_i$), is true when such node owns the corresponding •-permission, and false otherwise. Message types $\mathbb{PP}$ and $\mathbb{PM}$ are used to inform edge reversals in the resource graph among neighboring nodes.

Message type $\mathbb{PM}$ also indicates edge reversals in the reversal graph $\mathcal{G}^-$, in which an edge orientation has one meaning: if having the same orientation as the corresponding edge in $\mathcal{G}^+$, the right of reversing such edge in $\mathcal{G}^+$. The orientation of $\mathcal{G}^-$is kept at each node by the variable M_i^j ($i \in N, j \in N_i$) and can also be modified by a message type $\mathbb{MM}$. The pseudo-code of SER^H can be accessed at [6].

2.2 SER^H Initialization

The resource graph and the reversal graph can be combined in a single multi-digraph $\mathcal{G} = (N, \mathcal{E})$. Each edge in $\mathcal{E}$ is defined as an ordered triple of the form (i, j, c), where $c \in \{•, ○\}$. Edges belonging to the resource graph are labeled •, and this is indicated in the algorithm by the local variables P_i^j. Edges belonging to the reversal graph are labeled ○, and this is indicated by the local variables M_i^j. We will employ the expression *pair of edges* to refer to the two edges labeled • and ○ linking two neighboring nodes. Then:

$$\forall (i, j, •) \in \mathcal{E} \quad \omega((i, j, •)) = i \longleftrightarrow P_i^j = true \tag{1}$$

$$\forall (i, j, ○) \in \mathcal{E} \quad \omega((i, j, ○)) = i \longleftrightarrow M_i^j = true \tag{2}$$

Four rules determine the orientations of the edges and the possible states for the nodes in the initialization of $\mathcal{G}$.

Rule 1. *Every pair of edges in $\mathcal{E}$ linking active nodes satisfies $\omega((i, j, •)) = \omega((i, j, ○))$.*

Rule 2. *Every pair of edges in $\mathcal{E}$ linking an active node to an inactive one satisfies $\omega((i, j, •)) = i$ and $\omega((i, j, ○)) = j$.*

Rule 3. *Every pair of edges in $\mathcal{E}$ linking inactive nodes satisfies $\omega((i, j, •)) \neq \omega((i, j, ○))$.*

Rules 2 and 3 imply that every inactive node never owns both • and ○ simultaneously.

In order to define Rule 4, we first define formally $\mathcal{G}^+$and $\mathcal{G}^-$. The first one is the oriented graph $\mathcal{G}^+ = (N, \mathcal{E}^+)$ satisfying (3). (Recall that this digraph is the one induced by the edges labeled •.)

$$\forall (i,j,\bullet),(i,j,\circ) \in \mathcal{E} \quad \omega((i,j,\bullet)) = \omega((i,j,\circ)) \rightarrow (i,j) \in \mathcal{E}^+ \qquad (3)$$

The oriented graph $\mathcal{G}^- = (N, \mathcal{E}^-)$ is defined similarly as the spanning subdigraph of $\mathcal{G}$ induced by the edges labeled $\circ$:

$$\forall (i,j,\bullet),(i,j,\circ) \in \mathcal{E} \quad \omega((i,j,\bullet)) \neq \omega((i,j,\circ)) \rightarrow (i,j) \in \mathcal{E}^- \qquad (4)$$

Rule 4. *The orientations of $\mathcal{G}^+$ and $\mathcal{G}^-$ are acyclic.*

2.3   SER^H Correctness

The lemma below show that SER^H preserves Rules 1, 2 and 3. Due to the lack of space, proofs can be found at [6].

Lemma 1.
a. *Edge reversals caused by ξ^{RW}, ξ^{RH} and ξ^{HW} preserve Rules 1 to 3.*
b. *Transitions ξ^{WR} do not cause edge reversals.*
c. *Transitions ξ^{RW}, ξ^{RH}, and ξ^{HW} do not induce cycles in $\mathcal{G}^+$ and $\mathcal{G}^-$.*

The lemma above implies:

Theorem 1. *SER^H preserves the acyclicity of $\mathcal{G}^+$ and $\mathcal{G}^-$.*

3   Simulation Results

The DPP model allows a philosopher to change its state from "thinking" to "hungry" at any point of its execution. In terms of our algorithm, a node can switch from the H-state to the W-state when it needs access to the shared resource set. However, SER^H works with two restrictions: first, a node must be woke up by any running neighboring node in order to leave the H-state; second, a node must decide to stay on the heavy load condition before releasing access to shared resources. Since SER is not designed to deal with arbitrary load conditions, in this section we present the simulation results that show the message costs of SER^H compared with Chandy and Misra's algorithm and how to overcome those restrictions in real life problems. (Recall that SER^H and SER behave exactly the same way under the heavy load condition.)

3.1   Message Costs

In order to compare message costs of SER^H and Chandy and Misra's algorithm, we implemented a synchronous simulation of a graph containing seven nodes totally interconnected (a K_7). The simulation of Chandy and Misra's algorithm was regulated by a given probability p_h of changing the node state from "thinking" to "hungry" at the end of each simulation cycle. On the other hand, the SER^H simulation was governed by probabilities p_r and p_w: p_r is the probability of a node to remain in the heavy load condition after the use of shared

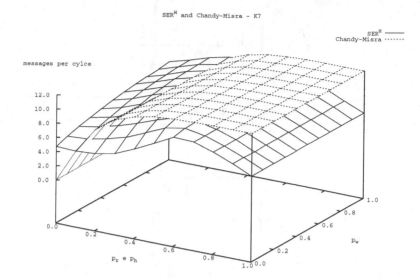

Fig. 4. Number of messages per cycle in SER^H and in Chandy and Misra's algorithm, $0 < p_r, p_h \leq 1$ and $0 < p_w \leq 1$

resources, and p_w is the probability of a running node to decide waking up a hibernating neighboring node. Besides, a node cannot enter the H-state when all its neighbors are in the H-state in order to prevent a global termination of the algorithm.

Figure 4 shows the number of messages per cycle exchanged by the system vs. the probabilities p_h, p_r, and p_w. Observe that SER^H uses less messages than Chandy and Misra's algorithm when the system approaches the heavy load. Moreover, SER^H uses half of the messages used by Chandy and Misra's when it is operating in heavy load. This is mostly due to the fact that Chandy and Misra's algorithm exchanges two messages between neighboring nodes at a time (*request* and *fork*) and SER^H sends both implicitly using only one message.

3.2   Distributed Traffic Light Control of a Road Junction

We modeled the traffic road junction presented in Figure 5(a) using SER^H and Chandy and Misra's algorithm. The model consists of a graph where nodes are traffic lights represented by circles labeled $P_i(i \in N)$, and shared resources are the conflict regions labeled R_j. Edges are defined according to our previous conventions and the resulting graph is depicted in Figure 5(b). The vehicle and pedestrian movement were modeled by distributed asynchronous *cellular automata* with a given vehicle/pedestrian arrival probability (an animation of it can be found at [6]).

In Chandy and Misra's execution, traffic lights with non-empty lane queues change their internal state to "hungry" and then wait for their turn to operate.

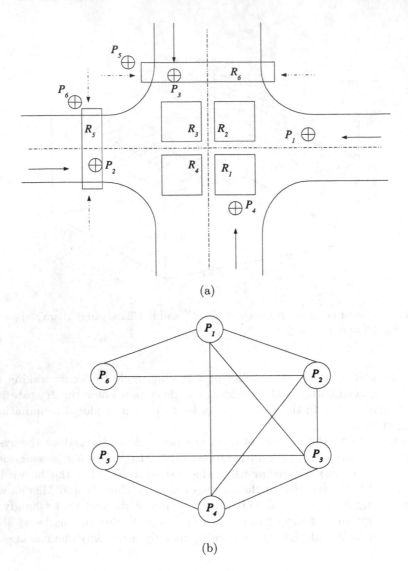

(a)

(b)

Fig. 5. Road junction and the graph model

In order to satisfy the first restriction presented earlier, the SER^H implementation has an additional node, linked to each original processing node. This node works as a "watcher" to wake up the traffic light processing node whose upcoming queue becomes non-empty; otherwise, the traffic light processing node enters the H-state when its queue becomes empty. This behavior overcomes the second restriction presented above. The special priority communication channels are implemented with a simple *3-way hand shake* protocol. The SER^H implementation showed communication costs 17%, 21%, and 28% lower than Chandy and Misra's version when the system was operating with a pedestrian arrival probability of 10%, 50%, and 80%, respectively (vehicle arrival probability of 80% in all cases.)

4   Conclusions

A new distributed scheduling algorithm targeting near-heavily loaded systems was introduced and its correctness demonstrated. Its application on the distributed control of traffic lights revealed its usefulness in this interesting situation. It was shown that a considerably lower communication cost was achieved under the near-heavy load condition, compared with Chandy and Misra's algorithm. Further studies focusing on how qualitative modifications on the topology of active nodes impact the concurrency of the resulting system are of immediate interest. Moreover, the application of SER^H onto problems such as the design of asynchronous timing schemes for low-power digital circuits and systems seems quite natural.

References

1. D. Agrawala and A. El Abbadi. An efficient solution to the distributed mutual exclusion problem. In *Proceedings of the 8th Annual ACM Symposium on Principles of Distributed Computing*, pages 193–200, August 1989.
2. D. Agrawala and A. El Abbadi. Exploiting logical structures in replicated databases. *Inf. Proc. Letters*, 33:255–260, 1990.
3. A. Arnold, M. Naimi, and M. Tréhel. A $\log n$ distributed mutual exclusion algorithm based on the path reversal. *Journal of Parallel and Distributed Computing*, 34:1–13, 1996.
4. Valmir Barbosa and Eli Gafni. Concurrency in heavily loaded neighborhood-constrained systems. *ACM Transactions on Programming Languages and Systems*, 11(4):562–584, October 1989.
5. Valmir Carneiro Barbosa. *Concurrency in Systems with Neighborhood Constraints*. Ph.D. thesis, UCLA Computer Science Department, Los Angeles, 1986.
6. D. Carvalho, F. M. G. França, and F. Protti. Pseudo-code of Scheduling by Edge Reversal with Hibernation. http://www.if.ufrj.br/ ∼ carvalho/serh.html, 2004.
7. O. S. F. Carvalho and G. Roucariol. On mutual exclusion in computer networks. *Communications of ACM*, 26(2):145–147, 1983.
8. K. M. Chandy and Jayadev Misra. The drinking philosopher's problem. *ACM Transactions on Programming Languages and Systems*, 6(4):632–646, October 1984.
9. E. W. Dijkstra. Hierarchical ordering of sequential processes. *Acta Informatica*, 1(2):115–138, 1971.
10. Eli M. Gafni and Dimitri P. Bertsekas. Distributed algorithms for generating loop-free routes in networks with frequently changing topology. *IEEE Transactions on Communications*, 29(1):11–18, 1981.
11. K. D. Gifford. Weighted voting for replicated data. *Proceedings of the 7th Annual ACM Symposium on Principles of Distributed Computing*, pages 150–159, 1989.

12. Kenneth Goldman and Joe Hoffert. A modification to the chandy-misra dining philosophers algorithm to suport dynamic resource conflict graphs. submetido para Information Processing Letters.

13. N. Plouzeau J. M. Helary and M. Raynal. A distributed algorithm for mutual exclusion in an arbritary network. *The Computer Journal*, 31(4):289–295, 1988.

14. Yuh-Jzer Joung. Asynchronous group mutual exclusion. In *Proceedings of the Seventeenth Annual ACM Symposium on Principles of Distributed Computing (PODC '98)*, pages 51–60, New York, June 1998. Association for Computing Machinery.

15. J. Kramer and J. Magee. The Evolving Philosophers Problem: Dynamic Change Management. *IEEE Transactions on Software Engineering*, 16(11):1293–1306, November 1990.

16. G. Le Lann. Distributed systems: towards of formal approach. In *IFIP Congress*, pages 155–160, North-Holland, 1977.

17. N. A. Lynch and M. Tuttle. Hierarchical correctness proofs for distributed algorithms. *Proceedings of 7th ACM Symposium on Operating Systems Principles*, pages 137–151, 1987.

18. M. A. Maekawa. A $\sqrt{n}$ algorithm for mutual exclusion in decentralized systems. *ACM Transactions on Computer Systems*, 3(2):145–159, 1985.

19. J. A. Martin. Distributed mutual exclusion on a ring of processors. *Science of Computer Programming*, 5:256–276, 1985.

20. H. Garcia Molina and D. Barbara. How to assign votes in a distributed system. *Jornal of the ACM*, 32(4):150–159, 1985.

21. K. Raymond. A tree-based algorithm for distributed mutual exclusion. *ACM Transactions on Computer Systems*, 7(1):61–77, 1989.

22. M. Raynal. Prime numbers as a tool to design distributed algorithms. *Inf. Process. Lett.*, 33(1):53–58, 1989.

23. Michel Raynal. A simple taxonomy for distributed mutual exclusion algorithms. *Operation Systems Review*, 25:47–50, 1991.

24. Injong Rhee. A fast distributed modular algorithm for resource allocation. In *Proceedings og the 15th International Conference on distributed Computer Systems (ICDCS '95)*, pages 161–168, 1995.

25. P. C. Saxena and J. Rai. A survey of permission-based distributed mutual exclusion algorithms. *Computer Standards and Interfaces*, 25:159–181, 2003.

26. Walter, Welch, and Vaidya. A mutual exclusion algorithm for ad hoc mobile networks. *Wireless Networks: The Journal of Mobile Communication, Computation and Information, Kluwer*, 7, 2001.

27. J. L. Welch and N. A. Lynch. A modular drinking philosophers algorithm. *Distributed Computing*, 6:233–244, 1993.

Internet Computing of Tasks with Dependencies Using Unreliable Workers⋆

(Extended Abstract)

Li Gao and Grzegorz Malewicz

University of Alabama, Tuscaloosa, AL 35487, USA
{lgao, greg}@cs.ua.edu

Abstract. This paper studies the problem of improving the effectiveness of computing dependent tasks over the Internet. The distributed system is composed of a reliable server that coordinates the computation of a massive number of unreliable workers. It is known that the server cannot always ensure that the result of a task is correct without computing the task itself. This fact has significant impact on computing interdependent tasks. Since the computational capacity of the server may be restricted and so may be the time to complete the computation, the server may be able to compute only selected tasks, without knowing whether the remaining tasks were computed by workers correctly. But an incorrectly computed task may render the results of all dependent tasks incorrect. Thus it may become important for the server to compute judiciously selected tasks, so as to maximize the number of correct results.

In this work we assume that any worker computes correctly with probability $p < 1$. Any incorrectly computed task corrupts all dependent tasks. The goal is to determine which tasks should be computed by the (reliable) server and which by the (unreliable) workers, and when, so as to maximize the expected number of correct results, under a constraint d on the computation time. We show that this optimization problem is NP-hard. Then we study optimal scheduling algorithms for the mesh with the tightest deadline. We present combinatorial arguments that completely describe optimal solutions for two ranges of values of worker reliability p, when p is close to zero and when p is close to one.

1 Introduction

This paper begins developing a scheduling theory for improving the quality of results of tasks executed unreliably over the Internet. We introduce a combinatorial optimization problem, show that the problem is NP-hard, and then study the problem restricted to the mesh where we give optimal polynomial time algorithms.

⋆ Contact author: Grzegorz Malewicz, Department of Computer Science, University of Alabama, 116 Houser Hall, Tuscaloosa, AL 35487-0290, USA, Phone (205) 348-4038, Fax (205) 348-0219.

T. Higashino (Ed.): OPODIS 2004, LNCS 3544, pp. 443–458, 2005.

There is a large number of underutilized computers connected to the Internet. Harnessing their power can enable the creation of a distributed supercomputer that can accomplish sheer volumes of work at a tiny fraction of the cost of a more traditional, more centralized, supercomputer. Several successful implementations of Internet Supercomputers exist today [8, 11, 16, 21]. These enable solving problems composed of a large number of *tasks*. In these implementations, a computer, called a *server*, allows any other computer, called a *worker*, to register and download a piece of software. Then the software requests a task from the server, downloads appropriate data that describe the task, executes the task, and returns the result to the server. This process repeats. When the number of workers is large, the Internet Supercomputer achieves high computing speed. For example, the SETI@home project reported its speed to be 57.29 Teraflops [23]. These Internet Supercomputers are also called Internet or Web Computing platforms, or High-Throughput Computing Grids [4].

SETI@home stated [9] that half of the resources of the project were spent on dealing with security problems. One of them is to ensure the quality of results returned by workers. Some computers, such as the server and perhaps certain workers, are reliable; they will correctly execute the tasks assigned by the server. However, workers are commonly unreliable. That is they may return to the server incorrect results due to unintended failures caused for example by overclocked processors, or they may deceivingly claim to have performed assigned work so as to obtain incentives such as getting higher rank on the SETI@home list of contributed units of work. Several schemes were proposed to improve the quality of results of tasks. The schemes encompass modeling reliability of workers based on the history of interaction with workers [10, 24], keeping track of which task was assigned to which worker [20], sending the same task to multiple workers [11], and verifying results returned by workers [6, 7, 25, 3].

It appears that in general it is fundamentally difficult to develop a method that ascertains that a task was executed correctly, without the task being executed on a reliable computer (cf. [1]). This difficulty has significant consequences on performing a computation described by a directed acyclic graph. Individual tasks of a computation may be quite computationally intensive, and so it may be unrealistic to execute too many of them on reliable computers that may be scarce. Consequently, the server may not always know if a given task was executed correctly or not. When tasks have dependencies, and the result of a task is incorrect, then all descendant tasks, even if executed correctly, may produce incorrect results, simply because their input depends, directly or indirectly, on the result of the one task that was executed incorrectly. It seems plausible that in such setting some tasks may have high impact on the total number of correct results, while other tasks may have low impact. The possible asymmetry means that it may be important to judiciously select which tasks should be executed reliably, and which other tasks can be left to unreliable workers, so as to maximize the total number of correct results.

This paper begins developing a scheduling theory for increasing the number of correct results of tasks executed on unreliable workers, when tasks have dependencies. Let us discuss some tradeoffs. A naive scheduling approach would be to execute all tasks on reliable computers only. Of course, then there is no need for judicious selection at all. However, the number of reliable computers may be quite small compared to the number of unreliable computers. Therefore, when work is assigned to reliable computers only, relatively more time would be needed to complete the entire computation. We could reduce the computation time by including unreliable computers in the computation, at the cost of reducing the number of correct results. Thus we expect that the number of correct results, for a given directed acyclic graph that describes dependencies between tasks, is related to two parameters: the reliability of computers and the deadline to complete the computation. Our ultimate goal is to fully understand this relationship.

One natural way to model unreliability of computers is to assume a probabilistic setting. Each computer will execute correctly with a certain probability. This assumption could be justified, for example, by the fact that one source of computation errors in Internet Supercomputers is overclocked processors [9].

Towards this end we formulate a model of an Internet Supercomputer. Our model extends the Internet pebble game introduced recently by Rosenberg [19]. The computation is modeled by a finite directed acyclic graph. Each node in the dag represents a task. There is an unbounded number of computers in the system. Computer i executes a task *correctly* with probability p_i and *incorrectly* with probability $1-p_i$. This probability is called *reliability* of the computer. There are three types of *pebbles* used to play the game. Initially all sources of the dag are pebbled with an *eligible* pebble. At any discrete time t we select a computer, say i, and a task that has an eligible pebble. Then we replace the eligible pebble with a pebble *executed correctly* with probability p_i, and with a pebble *executed incorrectly* with probability $1 - p_i$. Any task that does not have any pebble but all its parents have executed pebbles is pebbled with an eligible pebble. Any task that is executed incorrectly *corrupts* the results of all descendant tasks; so their results will be incorrect even if executed correctly. There is a *deadline d* by which all tasks of the dag must be executed. The goal is to determine which computer should execute which task and when, so as to maximize the expected number of correct results. Solving this optimization problem is important. One would like to establish theoretical guidelines for how to effectively and quickly execute a computation composed of dependent tasks, using unreliable computers.

The focus of this paper is to study a specific version of the scheduling problem. We consider a dag called a (two dimensional) mesh that is composed of k^2 nodes arranged into k rows and k columns. Each node has an arc to the node in the next column (if it exists) of the same row, and an arc to the node in the next row (if it exists) of the same column. Our choice of a mesh is motivated by the fact that meshes are a convenient way to structure computation and they arise in practice (cf. [19]). We investigate how to compute the mesh as quickly as possible i.e., we fix deadline d to $2k-1$. We assume that there is a single computer whose reliability is 1; this computer is called the server. Any other computer has reliability $0 < p < 1$; this computer is called a worker. Our assumption that there is a single reliable server and each worker has the same reliability p seems to be a natural "first approximation" of an Internet Supercomputer composed of unreliable workers.

We note that even if results of tasks cannot be ascertained to be correct in general without computing the tasks on trusted computers, one could still compute tasks redundantly on unreliable computers and use majority voting hoping to improve the quality of results. Such an approach is orthogonal to the aim of this paper where we want to use as little resources as possible (which is demonstrated by the fact that each task is computed by a single computer), while still obtaining as much quality as possible by judiciously assigning computers to tasks.

Contributions. This paper begins developing a scheduling theory for maximizing the number of correct results of tasks with dependencies executed unreliably over the Internet. Our specific contributions are as follows:

(a) We introduce a probabilistic pebble game that models internet computing with unreliable workers, and a new combinatorial optimization problem.

(b) We show that the optimization problem is NP-hard by a chain of reductions from the Balanced Complete Bipartite Subgraph Problem. In fact the problem is NP-hard even when restricted to bipartite dags computed by a single (reliable) server and (unreliable) workers.

(c) We give polynomial time optimal scheduling algorithms for the mesh under the tightest deadline $d = 2k - 1$, that use a server and workers, where worker reliability p falls into two ranges of values. We show that expectation is maximized when tasks are executed roughly in breadth-first search order, and the server executes exactly one task per "level" of the mesh. We demonstrate that there are two scheduling regimes. These regimes depend on the value of reliability p. The first regime is when reliability is close to 1. We completely characterize maximal schedules in this regime. The server should execute a "central" task at any time. Specifically, at any time, there is some number of "eligible" tasks that can be executed given task precedence constraints and tasks executed so far. These tasks form a diagonal "level" of the mesh. At this time, the server should execute a task that has the most descendants from among these eligible tasks, which turns out to be a central task on the diagonal level (there may be two such tasks, in which case the choice does not matter, as we show), and workers should execute all other eligible tasks. Intuitively, is appears that when p is close to 1, then optimal schedules are "descendant driven". The second regime is when reliability is close to 0. We also completely characterize maximal schedules in this regime. The server should execute an "edge" task at any time. Specifically, the server should either execute tasks in the top row and the rightmost column, or it should execute tasks in the leftmost column and the bottom row. Intuitively, is appears that when p is close to 0, then optimal schedules are "ancestor driven". The demonstration that there are two distinct regimes is, we believe, an important contribution of this paper that indicates that the problem has a non-trivial and interesting structure of optimal solution (that we begin to explore).

Paper organization. The rest of the paper is structured as follows. In Section 2, we present a model of Internet Supercomputing with unreliable workers, and formulate an optimization problem of maximizing the expected number of correct results of tasks. In Section 3, we show that the optimization problem is NP-hard. Then, in Section 4, we give polynomial time optimal scheduling algorithms for a mesh. Next, in Section 5, we discuss related work. Finally, in Section 6, we conclude and discuss future work. Due to space limitations most proofs are omitted from this extended abstract.

2   Definitions and Preliminaries

A directed acyclic graph $G = (V, E)$, or dag for short, on n nodes abstracts *computation* composed of tasks and information flow between tasks (all dags are finite in this paper). We often refer to the nodes as tasks. A *path* is a sequence $u_1, u_2, \ldots, u_k$ of two or more nodes such that there is an arc from u_i to u_{i+1}, for $1 \le i \le k - 1$. In a dag no such path can have $u_1 = u_k$. For a given node u, $P(u)$ is the set of *parents* of u i.e., of all nodes v, such that there is an arc from v to u; $C(u)$ is the set of *children* of u i.e., of all nodes v, such that there is an arc from u to v; $A(u)$ is the set of *ancestors* of u i.e., of all nodes v, such that there is a path from v to u; and $D(u)$ is the set of *descendants* of u i.e., of all nodes v such that there is a path from u to v. Note that $u \notin P(u)$, $u \notin C(u)$, $u \notin D(u)$, and $u \notin A(u)$. A task u such that $P(u) = \emptyset$ is called a *source*, and when $C(u) = \emptyset$ then u is called a *sink*.

A *schedule* describes when tasks are executed and by whom. A schedule has two components. The first component is a function x that takes a natural number $t \ge 1$ and returns the subset of tasks $x(t)$ that are executed at time t. There is a $\mu \ge 1$ such that each set $x(1), \ldots, x(\mu)$ is not empty, and the sets partition the set of all tasks. The number μ is called *makespan* of the schedule. Execution of any task takes one unit of time. A task can only be executed when all its ancestors already have, so for any $1 \le t \le \mu$, $x(t)$ must be a subset of tasks whose ancestors are in $x(1) \cup \ldots \cup x(t - 1)$. The second component is a function c that takes a natural number v and returns a number $c(v)$ denoting the *computer* that executes task v. We assume that there are m computers in the system. It must be the case that any computer executes at most one task per unit of time, so for any $1 \le t \le \mu$, and any i, the number $\left| c^{-1}(\{i\}) \cap x(t) \right|$ of tasks executed by computer i at time t is at most one. For any dag there is at least one schedule (x, c).

Computers are *unreliable*. When a computer i executes a task, then with probability p_i the computer executes u *correctly*, independently from the execution of other tasks. However, with probability $1 - p_i$ the computer executes the task *incorrectly*. We call p_i the *reliability* of the computer. Such incorrect execution affects the results of every task in $D(u)$. Intuitively, an incorrectly executed task u corrupts the results of any descendant task v, because the result of u is used, directly or indirectly, when the task v is executed. We say that the *result of a task is correct*, if the task and all its ancestors are executed correctly. In contrast, the result of a task is incorrect, if either the task or one of its ancestors is executed incorrectly.

We can compute the expected number of correct results for a given schedule (x, c). In order for a task u to be computed correctly, every task in $A(u) \cup \{u\}$ must be computed correctly. The function c defines which computer executes each of these tasks. So by independence, the probability that the result of u is correct is the product $\prod_{v \in A(u) \cup \{u\}} p_{c(v)}$. Let E_u be the indicator random variable equal to 1 if the result of task u is correct, and 0 otherwise. Then the total number of correct results is equal to $E = \sum_{u \in V} E_u$. By linearity of expectation

$$\mathsf{Exp}\,[E] = \sum_{u \in V} \mathsf{Exp}\,[E_u] = \sum_{u \in V} \prod_{v \in A(u) \cup \{u\}} p_{c(v)} \;.$$

Our goal is to find a schedule (x, c) that maximizes this expectation.

Constrained Computing with Unreliable Workers
Instance: A dag G that represents tasks and information flow between them, a deadline d, and m computers with reliabilities $p_1, \ldots, p_m$.
Objective: Find a schedule (x, c) with makespan at most d that maximizes the expected number of correct results.

This paper focuses on the case where there is a single computer, called the server, with reliability 1, and any other computer, called worker, has reliability $0 < p < 1$. In this case our optimization problem has a simpler formulation. Suppose that R is the subset of tasks that the server executes. We call this subset a *server subset*. Let $E(R)$ be the random variable equal to the number of correct results for a schedule with the set R of tasks executed by the server. Then the expected number of correct results is equal to

$$\mathsf{Exp}\,[E(R)] = \sum_{u \in V} p^{|(A(u) \cup \{u\}) \setminus R|} \;.$$

Note that this expectation depends on the graph G and the set R, but does not depend on the sequence x in which tasks have been executed, nor if the deadline constraint has been violated or if the server executed more than one task at a time. Trivially, the expectation is maximized when all tasks are executed by the server, $R = V$. However, then it may happen that either the makespan of the schedule is large, or there is a time when the server is supposed to execute many tasks. We are looking for a server subset R that maximizes the expectation, and a function x, such that at most one task is executed by the server at any point of time in x and makespan of x is at most d. We refer to this restricted version of the problem as Internet Supercomputing with Unreliable Workers (ISUW).

3   Complexity of the Problem

We demonstrate that it is NP-hard to solve the problem of Internet Supercomputing with Unreliable Workers. The proof is composed of two steps. We first reduce a known NP-complete problem called Balanced Complete Bipartite Subgraph Problem (see [5] problem GT24) to an "intermediate" problem of selecting subsets whose union is small. Then we show how to give answer to any instance of the intermediate problem using an algorithm that finds a solution to the problem of Internet Supercomputing with Unreliable Workers. This will immediately imply that Constrained Computing with Unreliable Workers is also NP-hard.

Many Subsets with Small Union (MSSU)

Instance: Nonempty subsets $S_1, \ldots, S_n$ of $[n]$, such that their union is $[n]$, and numbers $a \leq n$ and $b \leq n$.

Question: Can a of these subsets be selected whose union has cardinality at most b?

We give a reduction is from the Balanced Complete Bipartite Subgraph Problem (BCBS) (see [5] problem GT24, and [17] for recent results and references) to MSSU.

Lemma 1. *The Many Subsets with Small Union Problem is NP-complete.*

Proof. The reduction is from the Balanced Complete Bipartite Subgraph Problem (BCBS) (see [5] problem GT24, and [17] for recent results and references). Recall that in the problem we are given a bipartite graph and a number k and we want to know if the graph contains an induced complete bipartite subgraph with k nodes on the left and k on the right.

Let us take any bipartite graph G on $n - 1$ nodes and a k. Consider an expanded graph G' with one extra node n that is isolated. Naturally, G' is also a bipartite graph. Observe that there is a balanced complete bipartite subgraph with k nodes on the left and k on the right in G, if and only if there is such a subgraph in G' (the isolated node in G' cannot belong to the subgraph).

We now define an instance of the Many Subsets with Small Union Problem. Let M be the complement of the adjacency matrix of the graph G'. Note that the bottom row n and the right-most column n are filled with ones, because of the isolated node. We define the set S_i, $1 \leq i \leq n$, so that the characteristic vector of the set is equal to the column i of M. So each S_i is nonempty (because of the bottom row) and their union $S_1 \cup \ldots \cup S_n$ is exactly $[n]$ (because of the right-most column). Let $b = n - k$ and $a = k$.

The graph G' has a balanced complete bipartite subgraph on $2k$ nodes, if and only if we can rearrange rows and columns of M so that the top left k by k square of the rearranged M has zeros only. But this can be done if and only if we can select $a = k$ of the subsets, so that the union of the selected subsets has cardinality at most $b = n - k$. This completes the proof.

We then give a polynomial time Turing transformation from MSSU to ISUW. In our transformation we construct a bipartite dag with sets associated with sinks and elements associated with sources.

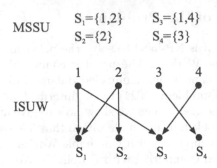

Fig. 1. Reduction

Theorem 1. *The Internet Supercomputing with Unreliable Workers Problem is NP-hard.*

Proof. We take any instance of the MSSU Problem and show how to answer the question posed in the problem, using an algorithm that maximizes expectation for instances of the ISUW Problem.

Let $S_1, \ldots, S_n$ be any nonempty subsets such that $S_1 \cup \ldots \cup S_n = [n]$ and a and b be numbers at most n. We construct an instance of the ISUW Problem. The dag describes subset membership. It has two "levels": the "bottom" tasks correspond to sets, while the "top" tasks correspond to elements of $[n]$. So each level has n tasks, and the total number of tasks in the dag is $2n$. We place an arc from a top task i to a bottom task j, if element i is in subset S_j. See Figure 1 for an example of the dag constructed for given subsets. We notice that each top task is linked to at least one bottom task, because the union of the subsets is $[n]$. Moreover, each bottom task is linked to a top task, because each subset is nonempty. We define the deadline to be $d = b + 1 \leq 2n$, and reliability of a worker to be $p = 1/n^2$. Let R be a server subset that maximizes the expected number of correct results under the constraints.

We argue that any maximum solution, including R, must have a special structure. First, $|R| = d$. Indeed, the cardinality of R cannot be larger, because then the deadline constraint would be violated, and it cannot be smaller, because then expectation could be strictly increased by executing one more task on the server without violating constraints. Second, at least one task of R belongs to the bottom level. Indeed, if R had d tasks on the top level, then one of them would be executed at time d or later. But this task has a child, and so this child could only be executed at time $d + 1$ or later, thus violating the deadline constraint. Third, for similar reasons, at least one task from R must be on the top level. These three observations imply that any server subset that maximizes expectation has cardinality d and has at least one task on the top and at least one on the bottom level. Note that for any server subset with these properties, there is a trivial way to execute the $2n$ tasks under the constraints. The server subsets constructed in the remainder of the proof will have these properties, and so we do not explicitly construct functions x in the remainder of the proof.

There must be a server subset R' with the same expectation as R, such that exactly $d-1$ of the tasks from R' belong to the top level. Indeed, we demonstrate that as long as there are two tasks in R that belong to the bottom level, we can remove a bottom task from R and add a new top task to R without decreasing expectation. Thus we can keep on removing and adding tasks until exactly one task from R belongs to the bottom level, never reducing expectation. Suppose that there are two distinct tasks v and w from R that belong to the bottom level. Since $d \leq n+1$ and two tasks from R are at the bottom level, then there is a task u at the top level that is not in R. Let R' be a server subset equal to R except that v is excluded but u is included instead. Clearly, R' has cardinality d and has at least one task at the bottom and at least one task at the top level. It remains to be seen that R' has no smaller expectation. In R, u contributed p to the expectation and v contributed p^h, for some $h \geq 0$ (when v has parents only among R then $h = 0$). In R', however, u contributes 1 and v contributes at least $p^h \cdot p$. In addition, the contribution of any task other than v that has u as a parent will increase as well. No other task will change its contribution. So the difference in expectation is at least $(1 + p^h \cdot p) - (p + p^h) = (1 - p) - p^h(1 - p) \geq 0$. In fact this difference must be exactly 0, because R is maximal. Thus expectation for R' is the same as expectation for R.

Suppose that maximum expectation is z. We shall see that by inspecting z, we can answer whether there are a subsets in the instance of the MSSU Problem, such that the union of these subsets has cardinality at most b.

We have seen that there is a server subset R', such that the expectation for R' is the same as for R, and that $b = d - 1$ of the tasks from R' are on the top level and one is on the bottom level. Let us find out how much each task contributes to z. The remaining $n - b$ top tasks are not executed by the server. Thus the contribution of the top tasks to the expectation is $b+(n-b)/n^2$. We now study the contribution of the bottom tasks. Let us assume for a moment that no bottom task is executed by the server. If all parents of a bottom task are among the b top tasks executed by the server, then the bottom task will contribute exactly $1/n^2$; let k be the number of bottom tasks u such that the parents of u are among the b tasks, $0 \leq k \leq n$. Recall that each bottom task has a parent. So each of the remaining $n - k$ bottom tasks has a parent that is *not* among the top b tasks executed by the server. Hence such bottom task will contribute at most $1/n^4$ to the expectation. Let us now account for this one bottom task executed by the server. If $k \geq 1$, then the bottom task must be among the k tasks, because otherwise expectation could be increased by executing at the server any of k tasks instead. Thus, when $k \geq 1$, the expectation z is in the interval $[y, y + 1/n^3]$, where $y = b + (n - b)/n^2 + 1 + (k - 1)/n^2$. If $k = 0$, then each bottom task has at least one parent that is not executed by the server, and so expectation z is in the interval $[y', y' + 1/n^2 + 1/n^3]$, where $y' = b+(n-b)/n^2$. Consequently, these $n + 1$ intervals, for $k = 0, 1, 2, \ldots, n$, do not overlap. Thus there exist k bottom tasks whose parents form a set of at most b tasks. Since b is known, the value of k can be determined by inspecting z. Observe also that it is not possible that there are strictly more than k bottom tasks whose parents comprise a set of at most b top tasks, because then maximum expectation would be strictly larger than z.

Corollary 1. *The Constrained Computing with Unreliable Workers Problem is NP-hard.*

4   Optimal Algorithms for the Mesh

In this section we present optimal solutions to the scheduling problem of Internet Supercomputing with Unreliable Workers on a mesh. We fix deadline to the tightest one possible on the given mesh. Under this constraint, we completely describe the optimal solutions for two ranges of values of reliability p of workers. When the reliability is close to zero, then a server subset maximizes expectation if and only if it contains only a continuous sequence of "edge" tasks. There are two such subsets in a mesh. When the reliability is close to one, then a server subset maximizes expectation if and only if it contains only "central" tasks. There are exponentially many such subsets. The remainder of the section defines the mesh and demonstrates a basic structure of any optimal server subset. Then optimal scheduling algorithms are given for the two ranges of worker reliability. In particular, edge and central server subsets are defined, and combinatorial arguments that ascertain optimality of the subsets are presented.

4.1   Preliminaries

A *mesh* M_k, for any given $k \geq 1$, is a dag with nodes $V = \{(i,j) \mid 1 \leq i, j \leq k\}$. There is an arc from any node (i,j) to node $(i+1,j)$, as long as both nodes belong to the mesh. Similarly, there is an arc from (i,j) to $(i,j+1)$. We introduce orientation of the mesh. Specifically, the node $(1,1)$ is the North-West node, and the node (k,k) is the South-East node. See Figure 2 for an example of a mesh and its orientation. A formal definition of orientation should be clear to the reader. We use Figure 2 to refer to "left", "right" etc. A *level* ℓ is the set of nodes (i,j) of mesh M_k such that $i+j = \ell+1$. There are exactly $2k-1$ non-empty levels of M_k. The levels partition the nodes of the mesh. For any node on level ℓ, if the node has a parent, then the parent is on level $\ell-1$, if the node has a child, then the child is on level $\ell+1$. Column j is the set of nodes that have the second coordinate equal to j. Row i is the set of nodes that have the first coordinate equal to i.

We begin with a lemma that exposes a structure of an optimal solution to our restricted problem. The subsequent lemma states that any server subset that maximizes expectation must have exactly one task on each level, no more and no fewer.

Lemma 2. *For any $k \geq 1$, and the mesh M_k, let R be a server subset that maximizes the expected number of correct results and x the corresponding function such that x has makespan at most $2k-1$. Then any level ℓ, $1 \leq \ell \leq 2k-1$, shares exactly one task with R.*

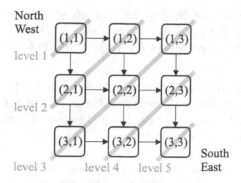

Fig. 2. Mesh M_3

This lemma considerably simplifies scheduling. Since any server subset R that maximizes expectation has exactly one task per level, we can trivially generate the function x that dictates when tasks are executed such that the deadline constraint is met. We simply schedule task execution level by level (breadth-first search order). Thus we do not explicitly construct any function x for any such server subset, keeping in mind that an appropriate x can be trivially generated.

The next question that we need to answer is: Which task should be selected on each level? We note that for any reliability p of worker, $0 < p < 1$, it is always better to execute on the server a parent of a task, instead of the task because then expectation will be strictly increased. Unfortunately, tasks on any given level are not comparable (no task is a parent of any other on the same level). Therefore, this simple observation does not help us decide which task of a given level should be executed by the server. We need a different decision algorithm instead. In the remainder of the section we present two optimal algorithms, one when p is close to 1 and the other when p is close to 0.

4.2 Optimal Algorithm for Workers with High Reliability

This section completely characterizes optimal server subsets when the reliability of worker p is close to one. We observe that then it is better when the server executes a task with more descendants. This determines which task of any odd level the server should execute. For even levels, selection is ambiguous, but we show that it does not matter, as expectation will be the same no matter how we choose.

The next lemma explains that as long as p is close enough to 1, it is better that the server executes a task with strictly more descendants. The proof observes that a task with more descendant adds strictly more to the expectation than any task with fewer descendants no matter which the other tasks are in the server subset.

Lemma 3. *Let G be a dag on n nodes, reliability p of worker be $(1 - 1/n)^{1/n} <$ $p < 1$, u and w be two nodes such the set $D(w)$ of descendents of w has at least* *one more node than the set $D(u)$ of descendents of u, $|D(w)| \geq 1 + |D(u)|$, and R be a server subset that contains neither u nor w. Then the expected number of correct results for the server subset $R \cup \{w\}$ is strictly larger than for the server subset $R \cup \{u\}$.*

Note that $(1 - 1/n)^{1/n}$ is asymptotically close to $1 - 1/n^2$.

The lemma almost settles the question for p close to 1. One can see that for any level of mesh M_k, tasks that occupy a "central" location of the level have most descendants across tasks on the level. Thus each level will have a single "central" task in an optimal R. The main issue, however, is that any even level has two "central" tasks that have the same number of descendants. The existence of these tasks makes room for ambiguity. Our next goal is to demonstrate that this ambiguity has no effect on the expected number of correct results.

For a given mesh M_k, we call a server subset R a *central server subset* if it is composed of specific tasks. It contains tasks (i, i), for any $1 \leq i \leq k$, and, in addition, for any $1 \leq i < k$, either task $(i, i + 1)$ or $(i + 1, i)$, but not both. Note that for any central server subset, each level of M_k contains exactly one task from the subset. We prove that expectations for central server subsets are the same by noticing that if task $(i, i + 1)$ belongs to R, then we can replace the task with task $(i + 1, i)$ without changing expectation.

Lemma 4. *Let R and R' be any central server subsets. Then the expected number of correct results for R is the same as it is for R'.*

We gather the observations developed so far to prove a theorem on the structure of optimal solution when p is close to 1.

Theorem 2. *Let $k \geq 1$, worker reliability $\left(1 - 1/k^2\right)^{1/k^2} < p < 1$, and deadline $d = 2k - 1$. Then a server subset S for mesh M_k maximizes the expected number of correct results if and only if S is a central server subset.*

4.3   Optimal Algorithm for Workers with Low Reliability

This section completely characterizes optimal server subsets when the reliability of worker p is close to zero. The argument has two parts. We begin by showing that any server subset that maximizes expectation must contain either all tasks of the top row or all tasks of the leftmost column. This is shown by observing that there is a tradeoff: it the first row contributes much to the expectation, then the rest of the mesh contributes little, and vice versa. A symmetric argument is applied to the leftmost column.

Lemma 5. *Let $k \geq 3$ and $0 < p \leq 1/6$. Let S be any server subset of M_k that has exactly one task per level. If S does not contain all tasks from the top row nor does it contain all tasks from the leftmost column, then S does not maximize the expected number of correct results.*

The lemma immediately implies that any optimal server subset must contain either all tasks from the top row or all tasks from the leftmost column, whenever

$0 < p \leq 1/6$ and $k \geq 3$. This settles the question which tasks from levels 1 to k must belong to an optimal server subset. What about tasks from level $k+1$ and higher? The subsequent lemma provides an inductive argument that settles this question as long as p is small. The key observation that gives rise to the proof is that the tasks on level $b + k - 1$ and higher contribute little compared to the contribution that task (b, k) would make when included in a server subset.

Lemma 6. *Let $k \geq 3$, $0 < p \leq 1/(2k)$ and $2 \leq b \leq k - 1$. Let S be any server subset of M_k that has exactly one task per level. If*

(i) *S contains all tasks of the top row and the $b - 1$ top tasks of the rightmost column, but not task (b, k), or*

(ii) *S contains all tasks of the leftmost column and the $b - 1$ leftmost tasks of the bottom row, but not task (k, b)*

then S does not maximize the expected number of correct results.

Given a mesh M_k, we call a server subset R an *edge server subset* if it is composed of specific tasks. Such subset must either contain only tasks of the top row and the rightmost column, or only tasks of the leftmost column and the bottom row. The following theorem completely characterizes the structure of optimal server subsets S for small enough worker reliability. We can prove the theorem using observations developed so far.

Theorem 3. *Let $k \geq 3$, worker reliability $0 < p \leq 1/(2k)$, and deadline $d = 2k - 1$. Then a server subset S for mesh M_k maximizes the expected number of correct results if and only if S is an edge server subset.*

5   Related Work

The combinatorial optimization problem introduced in this paper is related to two known hard problems. In the Network Reliability Problem (see [5] problem ND20) we are given a graph where each edge e has a failure probability $p(e)$, a subset V' of vertices, and a number q. The goal is to decide if the probability is at least q, that for each pair of vertices in V' there is a path connecting the vertices, such that the path has no failed edges. Our problem is similar, because we check if all ancestors have been executed correctly (which resembles checking for the existence of paths with no failed edges from the node to all ancestors). However, our optimization goal is different, as we count the number of nodes for which all ancestors have not failed. In a different problem, called the Network Survivability Problem (see [5] problem ND21), we are given a graph where each edge and each node has a failure probability, and a number q. The goal is to find out if the probability is at least q that for all edges $\{u, v\}$, either the edge or one of its endpoint nodes u or v has failed. The problem is similar because we also consider probabilistic failures in the graph, however in our case we consider more global dependencies, as we look at all ancestors of a node. There are many other hard sequencing and scheduling problems [2], but their objective is different as they typically aim at minimizing makespan and do not model computer failures.

A probabilistic model similar to our model is studied by Sarmenta [22] but for independent tasks. Tasks are generated in batches. A batch consists of n tasks. There are p workers. Once a batch is generated, its tasks are assigned to workers; recomputation is allowed, and redundant assignment is allowed, too. At most a fraction f of workers is faulty. A faulty worker returns incorrect results with probability s, independently of other results. The goal is to compute results of each task so that each result is "credible" enough (several measures of credibility are proposed). Author considers two basic mechanisms: (1) spot check a worker by verifying if the result computed is correct—this helps estimate worker reliability and exclude faulty workers from computation, thus reducing the fraction of faulty workers over time, (2) redundantly compute a task until a certain number of results agree—this helps increase confidence in a result despite possibility of workers being faulty. Author shows that the combination of the two techniques is advantageous. Results are validated using a simulation.

There are scheduling problems that arise in Internet Supercomputing, other than the problem studied in this paper. The papers of Rosenberg [19] and Rosenberg and Yurkewych [18] introduce a formalism for studying the problem of scheduling tasks so as to render tasks eligible for allocation to workers (hence for execution) at the maximum possible rate. This allows one to utilize workers well, and also lessen the likelihood of the "gridlock" that ensues when a computation stalls for lack of eligible tasks. The papers identify optimal schedules for several significant families of structurally uniform dags. The paper of Malewicz et al. [13] extends this work via a methodology for devising optimal schedules for a much broader class of complex dags. These dags are obtained via composition from a prespecified collection of simple building-block dags. The paper introduces a suite of algorithms that decompose a given dag to expose its building-blocks, and a priority relation on building-blocks. When the building-blocks are appropriately interrelated, the dag can be scheduled optimally. Motivated by the demonstration in [13] that certain dags cannot be scheduled optimally, Malewicz and Rosenberg [14] formulate a scheduling paradigm in which tasks are allocated to workers in *batches* periodically. Optimality is always possible within this new framework, but achieving it may entail a prohibitively complex computation. However, restricted versions can be solved optimally in polynomial time. Malewicz et al. [15] show how to increase the speed of computation in the presence of network failures, by appropriately sequencing computation of disconnected workers.

Malewicz [12] introduces a parallel scheduling problem where a directed acyclic graph modeling t tasks and their dependencies needs to be executed on n unreliable workers. Worker i executes task j correctly with probability $p_{i,j}$. The goal is to find a regimen Σ, that dictates how workers get assigned to tasks (possibly in parallel and redundantly) throughout execution, so as to minimize the expected completion time. This fundamental parallel scheduling problem is shown to be NP-hard when restricted to constant dag width and also NP-hard when restricted to a constant number of workers. These complexity results are contrasted with a polynomial time algorithm for the problem when both dag width and the number of workers are at most a constant.

6 Conclusions and Future Work

This paper began developing a scheduling theory for maximizing the expected number of correct results of tasks executed on unreliable computers, when tasks have dependencies. We introduced a combinatorial optimization problem, showed that the problem is NP-hard, and gave optimal polynomial time algorithms for restricted versions of the problem.

Our study opens several avenues for follow-up research. Which dags admit polynomial time optimal scheduling algorithms? Is there a constant factor approximation algorithm for the general problem? How to effectively schedule when each computer i has its own reliability p_i? How does possible asynchrony, or partial synchrony, (when tasks may take various amount of time to compute) affect scheduling decisions? One could consider a different optimization goal of maximizing the expected number of correctly computed sinks (in the case of one sink, we are then maximizing the likelihood that the sink will be correctly computed). Unreliability of computers could be modeled in a different way than probabilistically. We could assume that at most a certain number f of tasks will be incorrectly executed. We decide which tasks should be executed on a reliable computer, while an adversary decides which other at most f tasks will be executed incorrectly. Which tasks should be executed on a reliable computer, so as to maximize the worst-case (i.e., the lowest) number of correct results of tasks?

References

1. Barak, B., Goldreich, O., Impagliazzo, R., Rudich, S., Sahai, A., Vadhan, S., Yang, K.: On the (Im)possibility of Obfuscating Programs. (CRYPTO) (2001) 1–18
2. Crescenzi, P., Kann, V. (eds.): A compendium of NP optimization problems. http://www.nada.kth.se/~viggo/wwwcompendium/node173.html
3. Du, W., Jia, J., Mangal, M., Murugesan, M.: Uncheatable Grid Computing. 24th International Conference on Distributed Computing Systems (ICDCS) (2004)
4. Foster, I., Kesselman, C.: The Grid: Blueprint for a New Computing Infrastructure, 2nd Edition. Morgan Kaufmann (2004)
5. Garey, M.R., Johnson, D.S.: Computers and Intractability. Freeman, New York (1979)
6. Golle, P., Mironov, I.: Uncheatable Distributed Computations. RSA Conference – topics in Cryptography (2001) 425–440
7. Golle, P., Stubblebine, S.: Secure Distributed Computing in a Commercial Environment. 5th International Conference Financial Cryptography (FC) (2001) 289–304
8. The Intel Philanthropic Peer-to-Peer program. http://www.intel.com/cure
9. Kahney, L.: Cheaters Bow to Peer Pressure. Wired News, February 15 (2001) http://www.wired.com/news/technology/0,1282,41838,00.html

10. Kondo, D., Casanova, H., Wing, E., Berman, F.: Models and Scheduling Mechanisms for Global Computing Applications. 16th IEEE International Parallel & Distributed Processing Symposium (2002)
11. Korpela, E., Werthimer, D., Anderson, D., Cobb, J., Lebofsky, M.: SETI@home - massively distributed computing for seti. Computing in Science & Enginering, Vol. 3(1) (2001) 78–83
12. Malewicz, G.: Parallel Scheduling of Complex Dags under Uncertainty. (2005) submitted for publication
13. Malewicz, G., Rosenberg, A.L., Yurkewych, M.: On Scheduling Complex Dags for Internet-Based Computing. 19th IEEE International Parallel & Distributed Processing Symposium (IPDPS) (2005) to appear
14. Malewicz, G., Rosenberg, A.L.: On batch-scheduling dags for Internet-based computing. Typescript, University of Massachusetts (2004) submitted for publication
15. Malewicz, G., Russell, A., Shvartsman, A.: Distributed Cooperation During the Absence of Communication. 14th International Symposium on Distributed Computing (DISC) (2000) 119–133
16. The Olson Laboratory Fight AIDS@Home project. http://www.fightaidsat home.org
17. Peeters, R.: The maximum edge biclique problem is NP-complete. Discrete Applied Mathematics, Vol. 131(3) (2003) 651–654
18. Rosenberg, A.L., Yurkewych, M.: Optimal Schedules for Some Common Computation-Dags on the Internet. IEEE Transactions on Computers (2005) to appear
19. Rosenberg, A.L.: On Scheduling Mesh-Structured Computations on the Internet. IEEE Transactions on Computers, Vol. 53(9) (2004)
20. Rosenberg, A.L.: Accountable Web-computing. IEEE Transactions on Parallel and Distributed Systems, Vol. 14(2) (2003) 97–106
21. The RSA Factoring By Web project. http://www.npac.syr.edu/factoring
22. Sarmenta, L.F.G.: Sabotage-tolerance mechanisms for volunteer computing systems. Future Generation Computer Systems, Vol. 18(4) (2002) 561–572
23. SETI@home: Current Total Statistics. http://setiathome.ssl.berkeley.edu/totals.html, May 9 (2004)
24. Sun, X.H., Wu, M.: GHS: A performance Prediction and Task Scheduling System for Grid Computing. 17th IEEE International Parallel & Distributed Processing Symposium (2003)
25. Szajda, D., Lawson, B., Owen, J.: Hardening Functions for Large Scale Distributed Computations. IEEE Symposium on Security and Privacy, (2003) 216–224

Author Index

Lecture Notes in Computer Science

For information about Vols. 1–3499

please contact your bookseller or Springer